An American in Europe at War and Peace

An American in Europe at War and Peace

Hugh S. Gibson's Chronicles, 1918–1919

Edited by Vivian Hux Reed

together with Jochen Böhler

DE GRUYTER
OLDENBOURG

ISBN 978-3-11-099248-9
e-ISBN (PDF) 978-3-11-067227-5
e-ISBN (EPUB) 978-3-11-067238-1

Library of Congress Control Number: 2020937584

Bibliographic information published by the Deutsche Nationalbibliothek
The Deutsche Nationalbibliothek lists this publication in the Deutsche Nationalbibliografie;
detailed bibliographic data are available on the Internet at http://dnb.dnb.de.

© 2022 Walter de Gruyter GmbH, Berlin/Boston
This volume is text- and page-identical with the hardback published in 2021.
Cover image: Hugh S. Gibson. Courtesy of the Gibson Family.
Typesetting: jürgen ullrich typosatz, Nördlingen
Printing and binding: CPI books GmbH, Leck

www.degruyter.com

An American in Europe at War and Peace

Hugh S. Gibson's Chronicles, 1918–1919

Edited by Vivian Hux Reed

together with Jochen Böhler

DE GRUYTER
OLDENBOURG

ISBN 978-3-11-099248-9
e-ISBN (PDF) 978-3-11-067227-5
e-ISBN (EPUB) 978-3-11-067238-1

Library of Congress Control Number: 2020937584

Bibliographic information published by the Deutsche Nationalbibliothek
The Deutsche Nationalbibliothek lists this publication in the Deutsche Nationalbibliografie; detailed bibliographic data are available on the Internet at http://dnb.dnb.de.

© 2022 Walter de Gruyter GmbH, Berlin/Boston
This volume is text- and page-identical with the hardback published in 2021.
Cover image: Hugh S. Gibson. Courtesy of the Gibson Family.
Typesetting: jürgen ullrich typosatz, Nördlingen
Printing and binding: CPI books GmbH, Leck

www.degruyter.com

"It's a great life if you don't weaken."
Hugh S. Gibson, Paris, August 14, 1918

Hugh Gibson

Biographical Note

1883 August 16	Born, Los Angeles, California
	Attended Los Angeles Military Academy
	Attended Pomona College
1907	Graduated, Ecole Libre des Sciences Politiques, Paris
1908	Took the Diplomatic Service Examination
1908–1909	Secretary, American Legation, Tegucigalpa, Honduras
1909–1910	Second Secretary, American Embassy, London
1910	Private secretary to the Assistant Secretary of State, Washington
1911	Clerk, Department of State, Washington
1911–1913	Secretary, American Legation, Havana, Cuba
1913	Observer, elections for Constituent Assembly of Santo Domingo
1914–1916	Secretary, American Legation, Brussels
	Liaison between Herbert Hoover and the Belgian Government for the Commission for Relief in Belgium
1916	First Secretary, American Embassy, London
1917	Assigned to State Department-War Missions
	Author, *A Journal from Our Legation in Belgium*
	Aide to Lord Balfour, British Minister of Foreign Affairs, during visit to the U.S.
	Attached to Belgian War Mission during visit to the U.S.
1918	First Secretary, American Embassy, Paris
	Advisor to General Pershing
1918–1919	Member, Interallied Mission to Countries of former Austro-Hungarian Empire
1919–1924	Envoy Extraordinary and Minister Plenipotentiary to Poland (Warsaw)
1922	Married Ynes Reyntiens, Brussels
1924	Attended Temporary Mixed Commission for the Reduction of Armaments, League of Nations, Geneva
	Maintained as Ambassador-at-Large, League of Nations
1924–1927	Envoy Extraordinary and Minister Plenipotentiary to Switzerland (Bern)
1925	Vice-Chairman, American Delegation, Arms Traffic Conference, Geneva
1926–1930	Chairman, American Delegation, Preparatory Commission for the Disarmament Conference, Geneva
1927	Delegate, Conference on Private Manufacture of Arms, Geneva
	Chairman of American delegation and conference, Conference for the Further Limitation of Naval Armaments (also called Tripartite Naval Conference or the Three Power Conference), Geneva
1927–1933	Ambassador Extraordinary and Plenipotentiary to Belgium and Envoy Extraordinary Minister Plenipotentiary to Luxemburg (Brussels)
1928	Doctor of Diplomacy and Political Science, Universite Catholique de Louvain
1929	Birth of son Michael Francis, Brussels
1930	Delegate, London Naval Conference
	Doctor of Law, Universite Libre de Bruxelles

1931	Doctor of Law, Yale University
	Observer, Conference of Experts for a Moratorium on Intergovernmental Debts (also called the London Conference or the International Conference of Ministers), London
1932–1933	Acting Chairman, American Delegation, General Disarmament Conference, Geneva
1933–1937	Ambassador Extraordinary and Plenipotentiary to Brazil (Rio de Janeiro)
1935	American Representative, Mediatory Group to end the Chaco War between Bolivia and Paraguay Delegate, Chaco Peace Conference, Buenos Aires
1937	Author, Rio
1937–1938	Ambassador Extraordinary and Plenipotentiary to Belgium and Envoy Extraordinary and Minister Plenipotentiary to Luxemburg (Brussels)
1938	Retired from foreign service
1939	Author, Belgium: The Country and Its People
	Vice-President, Belgian American Educational Foundation
	Chairman, A.R.A. Association
1940	Escaped from France during German occupation
	European representative for the National Committee on Food for Small Democracies
1940–1941	Director General for Europe of the Commission for Polish Relief and the Commission for Relief in Belgium
1942	Author, The Problems of Lasting Peace (with Herbert Hoover)
1944	Author, The Road to Foreign Policy
1945	Author, The Basis of Lasting Peace (with Herbert Hoover)
1946–1947	Member, Herbert Hoover Food Mission (Herbert Hoover, Chairman)
1947	Member, Investigatory Committee for postwar German economic policies
1950	Death of Ynes R. Gibson
1952	Director, Provisional Intergovernmental Commission on Movements of Migrants from Europe (ICEM)
1954 December 12	Death of Hugh Simons Gibson, Geneva

From Hoover Institution HG Papers

Table of Contents

Acknowledgements —— XI

Abbreviations —— XIII

List of Images —— XV

Introduction —— 1

Source Editions —— 11

Biographical Index —— 655

Place Index —— 743

Acknowledgements

A project of this magnitude takes a village to produce. The editors would like to thank all those who provided insight, guided us to correct context, and introduced us to a large, star-studded cast. Foremost among these is Michael Francis Gibson (1929–2017), Hugh Gibson's son. It was Michael who first told us of the existence of the incredible Log his father had kept during the last six months of the Great War and the first six months of the uncertain peace that followed. It was also Michael who made many of the personal identifications and explained the intricate relationships Hugh had with many of the characters. Thank you, Michael!

We would also like to thank the archivists at Hoover Institution Library and Archives in Palo Alto, California, especially Linda Bernard, Irena Czernichowska, and Carol Leadenham. Their assistance in finding supporting documents and identifications was indispensable. We are also grateful to student assistants Anna Bundt and Barbora Fischerová at Friedrich Schiller University in Jena, Germany, who went to enormous lengths to investigate historical contexts and Gibson's favorite meeting places in Paris, London, and Rome, and to check the biographical index. And we were lucky enough to have such great colleagues as Prof. Ota Konrád and PD Dr. Rudolf Kučera in Prague, Dr. Danilo Sarenac in Belgrade, and Dr. Ljiljana Dobrovšak in Zagreb (in Gibson's times called Agram) who found for us political and public figures in the 1919 European newcomer states Czechoslovakia and Yugoslavia and their short biographies which were mentioned by Gibson, but which we would never have found ourselves.

A very special thanks goes to Dr. John Rector (professor of history emeritus, Western Oregon University) for his generous donation of time, insightful reading and careful checking of the manuscript. Thank you for your endless support!

Thank you, Dr. Elise Wintz of DeGruyter, who has believed in this project from the start. She has provided guidance and encouragement throughout the process.

Lastly, we thank our spouses and families for their unstinting support.

Vivian Reed
Jochen Böhler

Abbreviations

AEF	American Expeditionary Force
ARA	American Relief Administration
CN or CNSA	Comité National de Secours de d'Alimentation
ComPub	Committee on Public Information
CRB	Commission for Relief in Belgium
G2	Intelligence Headquarters
GQH	General Headquarters
K of C	Knights of Columbus
SOS	Service of Supply
YMCA	Young Men's Christian Association

List of Images

Image 1:   Sketch of Hugh S. Gibson —— V
Image 2:   Map of Paris —— 9
Image 3:   Map of Europe —— 10
Image 4:   Signed Portrait of General Joffre —— 35
Image 5:   Chaumont —— 58
Image 6:   View from Chaumont —— 58
Image 7:   Signed Portrait of Villalobar, Spanish Ambassador to Belgium —— 64
Image 8:   Henri Lambert —— 81
Image 9:   Frederic Dolbeare —— 95
Image 10: Map of battle lines in France, June 1918 —— 192
Image 11: Guy d'Oultremont —— 243
Image 12 Signed menu from August 5, 1918 —— 284
Image 13: Projectile plan, August 1918 —— 294
Image 14: Edith Cavell's Prayer Book —— 342
Image 15: Polish National Committee —— 348
Image 16: Reginald Foster —— 399
Image 17: Bebeth de Lynden and Ynes Reyntiens —— 415
Image 18: Leysin —— 455
Image 19: Ramon and Jack Reyntiens —— 456
Image 20: Mihaly Karolyi —— 519
Image 21: Clary Family —— 528
Image 22: Ynès Reyntiens —— 585

Introduction

Paris in spring-time has a reputation – light and romantic. Spring 1918, however, was different. It was cold, often dark; shells fell and cannon boomed. Europe was convulsed in war. Although the United States declared war on Germany the previous spring and Austro-Hungary in December, American troops only arrived in large numbers starting in early 1918. Before their arrival, diplomats, propagandists and intelligence officers buoyed the Allied cause. It was now one year after US President Wilson's famous promise to promote self-determination and worldwide democracy.

The first months of American participation in the war made little impact on the military situation. However, the psychological impact was widely felt. As the military branches prepared, the intelligence sources (both American and Allied) indicated several sources of potential dissention among the new Allies. The US State Department was concerned about Allied fears of American domination, partly due to the wild claims made by American propagandists that all would be well in Europe as soon as the Americans arrived to straighten things out. Strange as this sounds to modern ears, one can imagine how the proud and war-exhausted Allies as well as to the determined Central Powers heard these exaggerated promises.

Into this wartime scene of tension and uncertainty a young American diplomat arrived in Paris on March 25, 1918. With the unassuming title of Secretary of the Embassy, Hugh S. Gibson in fact was entrusted with much broader powers. Basically, in his own words, he was "running the whole show in Europe" on issues involved with propaganda. (May 14, 1918) By the end of the summer 1918, when an Allied victory appeared likely, he had reigned in the worst propaganda excesses. When President Wilson's January statement of the principles for peace, his famous 14 Points, sparked national movements among many nations within the disintegrating empires, Gibson was assigned as the official US liaison to both the Czech and Polish National Committees forming in Paris to negotiate independence for their countries. Upon the Armistice of November 11, Gibson's focus shifted from the military aspects of diplomacy to the humanitarian. While retaining his responsibilities with the Czechs and Poles, Gibson was now assigned as diplomatic liaison to Herbert Hoover's nascent American Relief Administration and ventured to the little known reaches of Eastern Europe.

Hugh Gibson's Background

Hugh Gibson's background was quite different from the most turn of the century American diplomats. Far from being the scion of a wealthy family, Gibson's parents were social activists of modest means. When Hugh was born in 1883, Frank Gibson was a local bank manager and his wife, Mary, a teacher. They had suffered the loss of three of their four children to various childhood diseases. At age 4, Hugh survived a bout of polio that left him in frail health. Mary educated Hugh herself, for the most part, preparing him to attend Los Angeles Military Academy and Pomona College – all before he turned 18.

Sadly, at that point, Frank died. Mary sold their home to finance the completion of Hugh's education in Europe for the next five years. As they traveled, Hugh became fluent in both French and German – and developed a love for diplomacy. He was one of the first Americans to graduate from Paris' prestigious Science Po in 1907. From the day he passed the Foreign Service exams with flying colors in 1908, Gibson's career was on an adventurous path. For starters, he was promptly sent mule-packing to the remote Legation in Tegucigalpa. On his next assignment, he was mugged in a Havana restaurant by a Cuban journalist protesting US policy in 1912. Two years later, he was posted to Belgium "for a rest," just as the German armies marched into Brussels in August 1914.

The suffering of the Belgians led Gibson into a life-long friendship and humanitarian work with Herbert Hoover. At the same time, it introduced him to the top crust of Belgian society – and to his future wife, Ynès Reyntiens, whose family was among the Belgian aristocracy. Their paths often crossed as they dashed about Belgium, helping people in whatever capacity possible.

Feeding the bourgeoning ranks of Belgians facing a critical food shortage quickly became an issue of central importance. In the fall of 1914, having made his way across enemy lines to London with Belgian representatives Henri Lambert and Émile Francqui, Gibson attended a life-altering meeting on October 20. Other attendees were US Ambassador Walter Page, Spanish Ambassador Alfonso Merry del Val, British Foreign Minister Edward Grey – and Herbert Hoover, an American mining engineer.

With much thought but little hesitation, Hoover took a hiatus from his mining business and accepted the task of feeding the Belgians. The Commission for the Relief of Belgium (CRB) was up and running within a short time. Hoover's magnificent handling of this overwhelming task launched Hoover's public service career of astonishing longevity, variety, and productivity.

After serving as diplomatic liaison between Hoover and the Belgians for over a year, Gibson was transferred to London, and then to the War Missions section of the State Department in Washington. As 1917 began, Russia was convulsed with revolution and the Germans increased the sinking of American merchant ships. The United States declared war on Germany on April 6, 1917. President Wilson sounded the note that carried around the world – American would fight to "make the world safe for democracy." War was declared on Austria-Hungary on December 7, and American troops began arriving in France *en masse* in early 1918. By this time, Hoover's responsibility had grown to overseeing food issues for all the Allies.

Gibson's work during the transition from war to peace in Europe
After Gibson's work with the War Missions in Washington, he was ideally suited for a special assignment. Officially, he was assigned as Secretary of the US Embassy in Paris under Ambassador William Sharp in April 1918. Although this title was a standard one and in line with Gibson's career path, it was actually a cover for his real assignment. The State Department proposed a title along the lines of Assistant Secretary of State, but given the wide range and sensitive nature of his assignments, Gibson himself requested the standard designation. He preferred the ability to work quietly behind the scenes to a prestigious title. Six weeks later, he doubted the wisdom of this. On May 14, 1918 Gibson wrote: "I fear I made a mistake not to accept a handsome title conveying the idea that I was running the whole show in Europe." This sentence is indicative of both the sweeping powers entrusted to Gibson and to his own unassuming character.

Gibson's assignments from his base in Paris were far-flung. Military, intelligence, propaganda, and diplomatic agencies often worked at odds with each other, sometimes within the same agencies. Gibson's job was to coordinate activities between and within these groups to conform with military and diplomatic realities. These individuals and organizations had been relatively free to act independently while the US was neutral. Part of Gibson's complex task was to reign in and coordinate various American agencies which received information and disseminated it. With the declaration of war, it became critical for the diverse American institutions to speak with a united voice and in support of their Allies.

One of Gibson's most important roles was that of diplomatic advisor to General John Pershing, Commander of the American Expeditionary Forces on the Western Front, 1917–1918. As might be expected, Gibson was privy to Pershing's plans and offered diplomatic and political advice to the General. He also served to relay Pershing's concerns to the State Department. Several visits to the front to hold private meetings with Pershing and his General Staff at Headquarters, all highly confidential, provided Gibson with a unique and intimate acquaintance with conditions on there. His records of these meetings comprise some of the most valuable material in this volume.

Coordinating with Pershing meant Gibson needed solid control on incoming intelligence. Therefore, his assignment also included working with the Chief of Military Intelligence in Europe, General Dennis Nolan. Here again, Gibson's secret notes tells this complex story. As Gibson travelled to and from the front and all across Europe, he was often the recipient of pertinent information, all of which he handled discretely. Every evening he recorded these conversations with diverse leaders and reflected on their contributions to the war effort, making detailed analysis of the issues, conflicts, and political situations he encountered. All of this is spiced with all sorts of entertaining gossip and poignant insights.

Military intelligence also fell under Gibson's mandate. As with General Pershing, he worked closely with General Nolan, which offered him an unparalleled and sweeping understanding of what was going on behind the scenes on all fronts. In addition, Gibson was tasked with the delicate mission of correcting the missteps of the US Committee on Public Information (ComPub). Under the direction of George Creel, ComPub was responsible for filtering the information the American public received as well as the propaganda the American government presented in Europe. From the State Department's point of view as well as Gibson's own, ComPub overstepped its bounds and created several public relations problems. Gibson was sent to reign ComPub in and defuse these problems.

Very quickly upon Gibson's arrival in Paris, he ran into Jan Horodyski, a Pole from the Austrian crownland Galicia who worked behind the scenes in Britain and the United States in order to promote the Polish cause. Gibson had met him in Chicago during his work with the State Department's War Mission. Although Gibson approached Horodyski with a healthy skepticism, he also gleaned much valuable information from him about issues involving Poland, American diplomacy and propaganda, and much more. Most notably, it was Horodyski who introduced Gibson to Roman Dmowski, the leader of the Polish National Democrats, one of the influential political movements with ambitions to rule the country after gaining independence. These contacts would prove vital during Gibson's assignment as first US Minister to Poland, a position he gained at the very end of the period covered by this edition.

Upon the official US recognition of the Polish National Committee in September 1918, Gibson was promptly charged with acting as the liaison between the Poles and the US Embassy. He was simultaneously charged with the same role for the Czechoslovak National Council, represented by Tomáš Masaryk and Edvard Beneš. They were organized, and communicated their needs and desires clearly and in a timely manner. Gibson appreciated their forthrightness, and at some points believed he might be appointed as the first US Minister to the new Czechoslovakia. Although he did his best to balance his attention between the two groups, several factors kept him from being closer to the Polish inner circle. These included the perception that the Czechs were more immediately forthcoming with information and that Gibson himself hoped to be assigned to work with Herbert Hoover.

On the other hand, the Poles presented a more troublesome picture. Led by Roman Dmowski, Polish Ambassador to France Maurycy Zamoyski, and world-renown pianist Ignacy Paderewski, the Polish National Council was perceived as disorganized and un-united in regards to their expectations. Gibson eventually received the information he requested, and became aware of the enormity of the challenges facing the proposed new nation. Upon the Armistice of November 11, 1918, both Czechoslovakia and Poland came into being. Until such a time as proper representation was arranged in the spring of 1919, Gibson remained the primary liaison with both nations.

As the end of the war approached and the humanitarian problems became a terrible reality, Gibson became more and more involved with Hoover's plans for the American Relief Administration in Europe. This was where his real interest lay and he approached the task with dedication. Eventually, after the November 11 Armistice, he was assigned to Hoover as the diplomatic liaison for the American Relief Administration (ARA).

New Year's Eve 1918 found Gibson newly arrived in Vienna as the diplomatic representative with a small team of ARA experts sent to take initial stock of what had been enemy territory in Central and Eastern Europe. From Vienna, they embarked on an amazing journey which took them from Prague to Belgrade and from Trieste to Budapest. Much of this journey was by train. In an unexpected twist, the new Austrian government put the railway car formerly belonging to Emperor Franz Joseph at Gibson's group's disposal. Gibson found the tassels on the cushions in stark contrast to the views of devastation from the gilded windows. There are very few American witnesses to these early national days in Eastern Europe, and Gibson's account is as fascinating as it is valuable.

Ironically, although Gibson always intended to include Warsaw on this trip, it was not to be. Several times a planned foray into Poland was disrupted at the very last moment by some unforeseen disaster. Various members of the ARA team went on to Poland while Gibson was called elsewhere. As it turned out, Gibson was not posted to Prague in the spring of 1919 as he suspected he might be. Rather, President Wilson appointed him as the first US Minister to Poland. After so many false starts, his journey to Warsaw was completed by the end of April 1919.

The story presented here is Gibson's diary entries offered from a unique and in-depth vantage point. This record differs the average diary commonly kept by diplomats of the time, and from the normal method Gibson used to keep his daily diary in a specific way, for a specific reason. Generally, Gibson's diary took the form of a daily letter to his mother. This habit started in 1908 in the mountains of Honduras, and continued until Mary Gibson's death in 1930. However, when Gibson arrived in Paris in April 1918, the US was at war and all Americans fell under the rule of military censorship. Therefore Gibson was particularly careful in his writing, given his access to sensitive information. From March through November 1918, his letters were transformed into a "secret log" which he kept in his immediate possession until his death. These were bound by month, and later deposited at the Hoover Institution Archives by his son, Michael Francis Gibson. On December 1, 1918, Gibson resumed the letters to his mother. Where the information was not sensitive, Gibson bound copies of the letters into the Log between December 1918 and April 1919. To a casual researcher, these look identical to the letters in the files with all the rest of the twenty-two years of letters to his mother. However, a postscript is attached to many of the letters, recording the sensitive information Gibson preferred not to send in the open mail. These are not found in the record of Gibson's regular correspondence with this mother, but only in the copies of the letters filed with the Log.

Of course, not everything that Gibson witnessed and noted down was top secret. On the pages of this edition, we encounter him as a keen observer and witty commentator of his times and peers, of Europe's population and landscapes which he tirelessly travelled in overcrowded night trains, military jeeps and diplomatic limousines. He empathizes with the suffering of the people and is outspoken in his aversion against the Germans with whom he became acquainted during his tenure at the American Legation in Brussels (1914) where they were the brutal invaders and occupants of Belgium. The Spanish flu added to the misery with almost 8,000 people succumbing in Paris alone by the end of 1918. We witness Gibson nursing and worrying over friends who were affected. Not surprisingly, given the intensity of his schedule and the many dangers, he also struggled with illness. As we accompany Gibson on his trips all over the continent, we learn about the ongoing hardships, armed conflicts and revolutions that shook the continent months and years after the armistice, the very scenery that Hoover's administration at that very moment entered in order to bring relief. Wherever he is, on the road or on the rail, in a luxurious hotel or Spartan quarters, Gibson hammers everything that comes to his mind into the keys of his stalwart Corona travel typewriter. And thus we learn in passing of the everyday work of a diplomatic spy – such as the burning of classified maps and documents or inventing a new cipher key – as well as of the vagaries of funny pen wars of diplomatic writers, obviously a popular trend in these days (Gibson himself had just published a book on his deployment to Belgium). And then there's also a world beyond the hectic days and nights of a travelling envoy of the State Department. Rarely enough, but still, Gibson manages to break free and to visit his future fiancé (a fact which he is not yet aware) in the Swiss winter resort Leysin. When we read his breathtaking reports on racing sleigh rides with his friends down the Alpine mountain slopes, we grasp something of this man's vitality and love for people, for life, and for its adventures. As the hundreds of pages of his personal notes prove without the shadow of a doubt, Hugh S. Gibson was not only a humanitarian, he was not only a gifted writer and a brilliant diplomat with an extraordinary insight in characters, politics and history – he was also a very likable person. A combination rare to find.

Gibson's Post-Paris Life
Gibson was appointed as the first US Minister to Poland on April 15, 1919. He settled his affairs in Paris and headed east on the 24th. Gibson arrived in Warsaw

just in time to witness the first Polish National Day on May 3. It was a solemn, festive and wondrous occasion – the first in over a century! This day is described in detail, as are Gibson's next five years in Poland, in *An American in Warsaw: Selected Writings of Hugh S. Gibson, US Minister to Poland 1919–1924* (edited Vivian Reed, et. al. University of Rochester Press, 2018)

In May of 1924, Gibson was transferred to Bern as US Minister to Switzerland 1924–1927. This was followed by his first Ambassadorship to Belgium 1927–1930. From there, he was named Ambassador to Brazil, where he served from 1930–1933, before returning to his post in Brussels in 1937. President Roosevelt hoped to utilize Gibson's diplomatic skills in Germany in 1938, but by then Gibson and many others knew the situation was too far gone in the direction of war for any kind of diplomatic success. Therefore, Gibson chose to retire rather than accept the post of Ambassador to Berlin in 1938.

The Gibsons traveled to Spain in 1939 and joined the world in dismay when Poland was once again dismembered in September. Immediately, the Poles approached Hoover to coordinate aid once more, and many of the old team stepped back into humanitarian service for the second time in their lives. By early 1940, Gibson accepted the role of Director General for Europe of both the Commission for Polish Relief and for Belgian Relief. His adventures in that capacity included racing around France trying to connect with the fleeing Polish Government in May and June 1940 during the onslaught of the German invasion. He escaped through Spain and arrived in London just in time for the Blitz to begin. In London, Gibson reconnected with many of the Polish leaders and friends whom he knew from his Warsaw years.

True to the writing habits formed during his early years, Gibson wrote copiously about his work during the Second World War. When he was not negotiating for relief measures for Poland and other endangered populations, he addressed the Allied nations regularly as a NBC political commentator. He was frequently aired opposite Edward R. Murrow of CBS. All this is another story, to be explored in a separate volume.

Shortly after the Germans invaded Soviet Russia in the summer of 1941 and the United States entered the war in December 1941, the Gibsons returned to New York. Gibson teamed up with Hoover to write *The Problems of Lasting Peace* (Garden City: Doubleday, Doran and Com., 1942). While Hoover turned his attention to national politics, Gibson continued to speak and write in support of peace.

When the Allies prevailed and the miseries of war ceased, new dangers rapidly replaced them for Poland and the world at large. The Cold War pitting the pro-democratic west against the pro-communist east began almost immediately. Poland found itself, due to the Yalta Conference, squarely in the Soviet sphere. As physical rebuilding began in Poland, a massive political restructuring was also in the air. Gibson and several of his fellow American humanitarians had a unique view into this new beginning.

Following WWII, Hoover recruited Gibson and Maurice Pate, as well as other former colleagues, to active duty once more. The veteran humanitarians undertook a whirlwind famine relief survey of the world in the spring of 1946 at the request of President Truman. Thirty-two years had elapsed since they had taken up the task of feeding Europe in 1914, and they were still working together for the good of all.

After Ynès Gibson's death in 1950, Hugh continued to utilize his diplomatic skills for the good of humanity. In 1952, he took on the task of helping the war's displaced persons re-settle overseas as the Director of the Provisional Intergovernmental Commission on Movements of Migrants from Europe. Illness plagued him, but his sense of humor remained. Gibson was preparing for another hearing the morning of his death on December 12, 1954.

Throughout Gibson's eventful diplomatic career, two precepts ran steadily. Gibson lived out his unflagging commitment to democratic ideals and worked out his unfaltering conviction that humanitarian care was the obligation of those with power and resources. His closest and most long-standing associates were of the highest caliber, and together this group of exceptional humanitarians created and sustained a stunning variety of long-standing service foundations world-wide. Gibson argued consistently and passionately that only supporting a strong democratic governments would maintain peace, protect citizens, and allow nations to flourish. At this moment in history, Gibson's precepts are as apt as they were when penned one hundred years ago.

About this edition

Hugh Gibson's original copies of this log are housed in Boxes 68–69 of the Hugh Gibson Papers at the Hoover Institution Archives at Stanford University in Palo Alto, California. The letters to Mary Gibson are located in Box 35. Letters to other people were included by Gibson in his Log, and are found within it. The one exception is the April 18, 1918 letter to William Castle, which is found in Box 17. Copies of many of the telegrams Gibson mentions are found in Box 99. All are open to the public. Hugh's son, Michael Francis Gibson (1929–2017) made many of the personal identifications and set the context of the story. The editors have elected to make the entire document more readable by correcting Gibson's shorthand or any clear mistakes. We have added complete names where Gibson abbreviated with simple initials when we are certain of his meaning. In addition, we removed simple chitchat from this edition for the sake of relative brevity. Most importantly, we have added contextual footnotes and a Biographical Index to help the reader get the most out of Gibson's record.

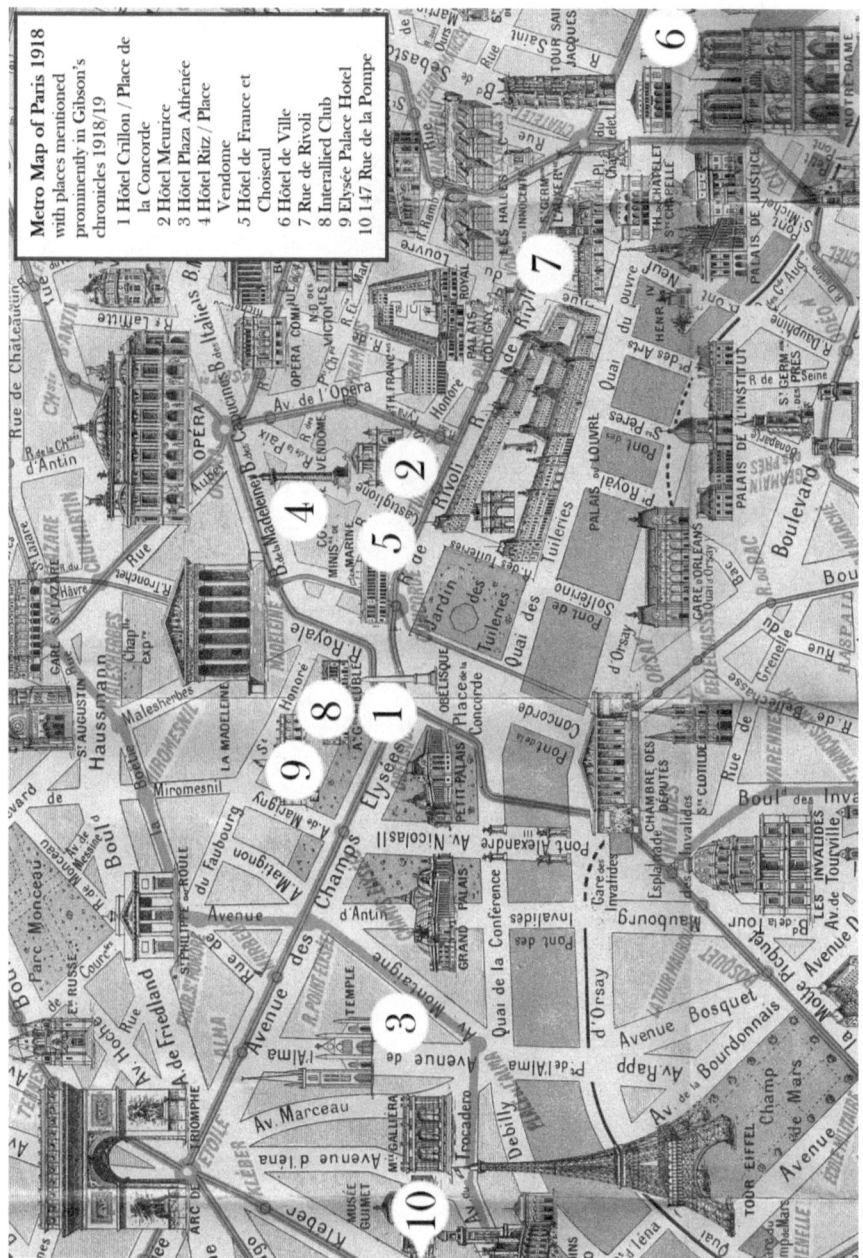

Image 2: Map of Paris © cheltenhamroad.wpcomstaging.com (courtesy of David Cheaney)

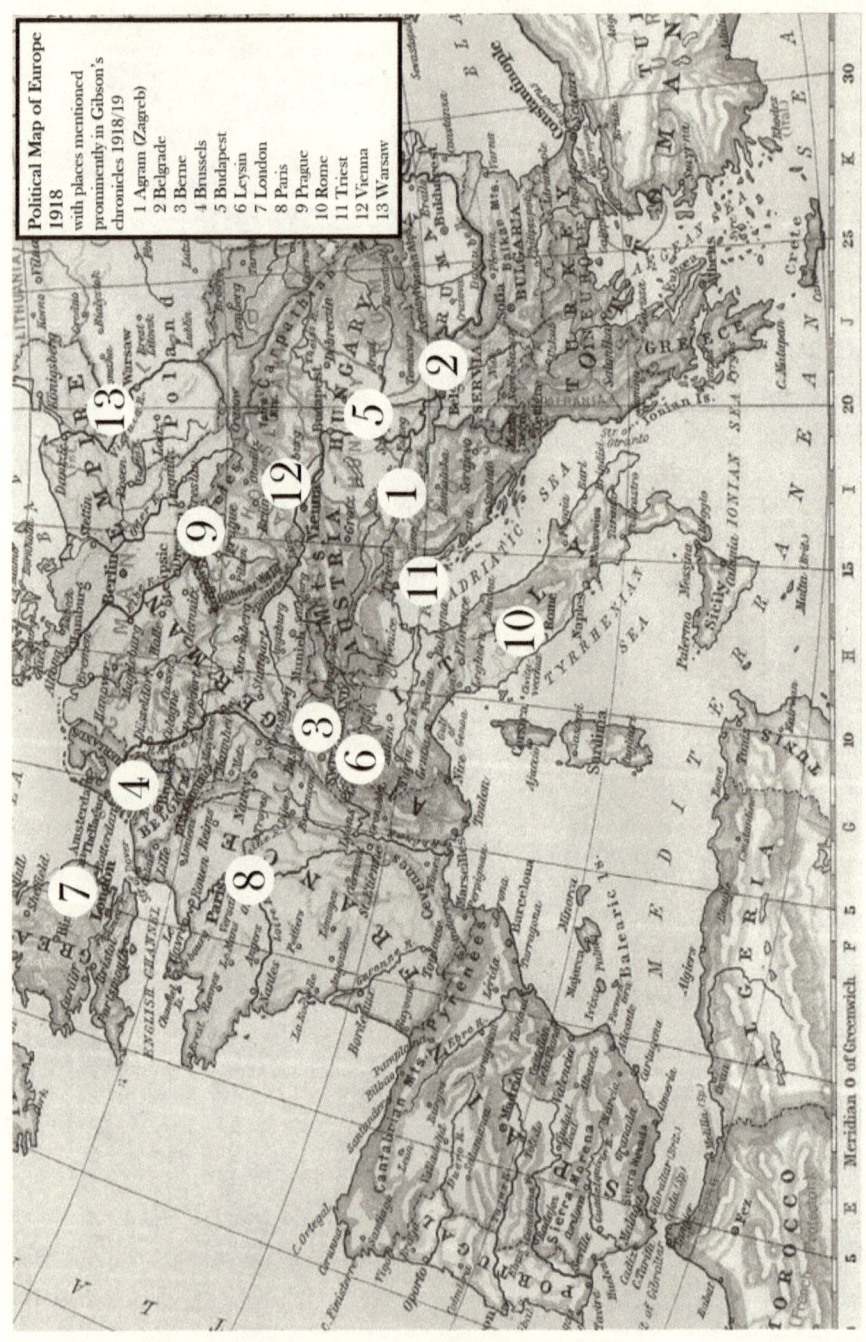

Image 3: Map of Europe © WikiCommons

Source Editions

Letter to Mary Gibson   Washington, D.C. February 13, 1918

Today has brought the long-deferred decision[1] as to my fate and I was able to send you a telegram a few minutes ago to tell you that I was starting for home to see you before leaving for Paris. There have been so many ifs and ands that I have not been able to tell whether there was really any probability of my going and this morning brought me the first really definite decision.

For your information I may say that the job is most interesting. Since the war began – or rather since we got into it – there has been such a multiplication of official activities and agencies that confusion and discord have inevitably resulted. Our people are all over the place on the battle front in France, in Switzerland and Italy and Spain and Portugal, etc. and none of them are footloose to move about and find out about the activities and viewpoint of the others. That of course does not make for harmony or understanding. Creel has his people in every country and they have no central shop where they can focus their views. Palmer is at headquarters trying to do a big job all alone and doing it blind. And there are a lot of other elements. So far as I can see I am to be the coordinating element. To make my situation regular as it should be I am to be assigned to the Embassy at Paris but am not to be loaded with office work and am to be free to use my judgement about traveling over Europe. I am to keep my eyes open and iron out any troubles that present themselves to me or that may be indicated by the Department. It will be a whale of a job but mighty interesting. There are other activities that will develop but in the main it will consist chiefly if keeping posted and in smoothing out difficulties.

I have to go over matters with a lot of people here before I can sail but they will not be able to talk things over in a final way for a couple of weeks yet so I promptly put in for permission to run out to California to see you. I thought of telegraphing to ask whether you could come on here but every one of the individuals I have dealings with would want to see me every day if I stayed and it would merely mean that I would spend most of my time in offices without really accomplishing much. Therefore it seemed better to cut loose completely and have what little time I can have absolutely free. Then when I come back they will be ready for

---

[1] Gibson was assigned to Paris on February 13, 1918. Previous assignments included Havana, Brussels, London and Washington. In Washington, he was attached to the person of British Foreign Minister, Lord Balfour, in April 1917 and to the Belgian Mission in June 1917.

me and I can sit with them in their offices day and night for the few days that I shall be here after my return. I prefer to compress it this way than to dawdle off the time.

I telegraphed you not to make any unnecessary engagements because I shall not have time to prepare any speeches before I leave. I had meant to take a few days off and prepare several lines of talk so as to have them ready for every possible occasion when I got back. But as it is I shall be running day and night until I leave and I shall have nothing really worthwhile except the old story about life in Belgium during the occupation – and of course that cannot be give over and over in one place. And besides I want to be as free as possible from dates so as to have the maximum of visit with you.

I don't know how long this job will last but that will depend largely on my own views. If I can comb out the situation and report that it is ready to turn over to somebody else I may be heading home very soon. On the other hand, it may develop into something that will keep me busy indefinitely. As a roving commission, I shall probably spend only a small part of my time in Paris and there is a lot of interest to be found in other places. A good deal of time will probably be spent at General Pershing's headquarters. However, I can tell you more about the job when I get back.

I am going up to dine with Edgar Rickard and talk over some business things with him. There is very little else that I am required to do and if I can get them out of the way I shall try to clear out of here on Friday night so as to have that much time with you at home.

Letter to Mary Gibson   Washington, D.C., February 14, 1918

I have had a busy day trying to get as many things settled as can be attended to now so that I need have as little as possible to look after when I come back.

I have made tentative reservations for the steamer and have cleared my desk so that I can put in all my time getting ready for my new job when I make my flying visit here.

Had dinner with Phil [Patchin] and Polly this evening and afterward went down to the river to watch the ice jam which is the greatest in years and is doing all sorts of damage, carrying away boat houses, motor boats and all sorts of other things. It was pretty dark and there was a heavy mist so we could not see as much as if we had been enterprising enough to go down to see by daylight.

Letter to Mary Gibson   En route through Arizona. February 25, 1918
 (I'm not sure about that date but anyway it's Monday) [Correct date]

Just from force of habit I start my letters again even if there is nothing to report.

It's a darned shame to have so little time for a visit but I am mighty glad I took what I could get. It was such a lot better than heading off across the water again without a sight of you...

I have spent the morning trying to write some letters and get a little forrader with the matters of business that have been lying in my portfolio. I wrote Arthur Page at some length and advanced various good and sufficient reasons for getting out a cheap edition of the book[2]... Apparently a deadly dull crowd on the train – but 'twas ever thus. At any rate they don't use up any of my valuable time and I got to bed last night at eight. It's hotter than Tophet and there is no sign of the snow that was everywhere when we came through a few days ago

Letter to Mary Gibson   En route through Kansas. February 25, 1918
 [Incorrect date, actually February 26]

Still plowing along on time with every prospect of keeping it up as far as Chicago.

Nothing thrilling going on aboard and I have had plenty of time to think how glad I was to get home and how sorry I was to have to go. Three flying visits ought to break the charm and next time I ought to be able to stay a respectable time. Anyway here's hoping.

Young Blankenhorn of Pasadena, a friend of Donald Dickey, introduced himself yesterday at dinner time and I dined with him and some friends of his – a man named Washburn and his sister whose name I do not remember. They are an agreeable trio and helped to break the monotony.

There is not a trace of the snow that was so thick when I came this way before and it looks as though there had been no rain for a year.

---

2 The year before, Hugh Gibson had published his book on his WWI experience under the title *A Journal from Our Legation in Belgium* (Doubleday Page, 1917).

Letter to Mary Gibson   Chicago. February 27, 1918

When I stepped off the train this morning Howard Linn handed me your telegram so I feel I have reestablished communication.

Howard is going down to Washington tomorrow but could not get ready in time to go with me. He is going to find about his own work.

Mrs. Linn may go over on the same ship with me but is not yet sure.

I had lunch with Howard [Linn] and his wife and Alice[3] at the Blackstone. Alice charged me to send you her love – which I do herewith. They are all busy as bees so I forbade them to look after me and came back here to put in the time until 5:30 when I set out on the last stage of my journey. I shall profit by the occasion to be barbered and have a swim in the pool.

I see by the morning paper that Frank Gunther is engaged. It has been in the cards for a long time. ...

Letter to Mary Gibson   Washington, D.C., March 1, 1918

Back again and deep into the swirl of things.

Phil [Patchin] was waiting for me when I got in yesterday and we had enough to talk about to last us until midnight.

This morning I had talks with Polk and George Creel and Arthur Woods and got a lot of things attended to. Creel is going away tonight but will be back Sunday night and we are to have another session on Monday. I am just as glad to have a respite for I have a thousand and one things to settle with people inside the Department before I can get under way. It will be a close thing to make the ship.

Lunched with Hoover and Edgar Rickard and had a good talk with them. H. was a good deal disturbed by my story of the lady [Mary Hunter Austin] who is delivering his message to the nation. So far as I can make out she has no commission to do anything of the sort but received mild approval for her statement that she was going to preach the true gospel of conservation whenever the occasion offered. The plan for the democratization of the world was viewed with horror, chiefly because the Food Administration was mentioned in it. A telegram was to be written and dispatched to the lady this afternoon telling her to keep off the scheme and to pipe down on the personal representation of the chief. ...

---

3 Probably Alice Roosevelt Longworth, the daughter of former US President Theodore Roosevelt.

Letter to Mary Gibson   Washington, D.C., March 2, 1918

Last night Arthur Woods was called away just before dinner and my evening pow-wow with him went by the board. At dinner time, Mrs. Hoover called up to say that Hoover had gone out to make a speech at a dinner and that she wanted to talk to me about something important. She had some people to dinner and was taking them afterwards to see the Spanish dancers – and would I come along and join them. I could not get away for dinner but joined them afterwards for the show which was very interesting – even if all the dancers were ugly as sin – and in the words of the little German lady *ETWAS MONOTONE* [somewhat monotonous].

After the show I took the lady home and heard what she had to say. Some of the Black Hand are evidently after the scalp of the gentleman so that he shall not loom too large later on and the plans are being laid deep and dirty. He doesn't know anything about it yet and she wanted to talk it over first and get some side lights on it. I don't know whether there is anything I can do to help but I have been turning it over and over in my mind and hope that something will come of it. I may have more to say on this subject later on.[4]

Today has been one long talkfest and I was glad that there was no evening session arranged. I am going to dine with the Hoovers and try to forget about the sort of shop I have been talking all day. I shall have to talk another kind as Edgar Rickard will probably be there to go over some of the things they want me to do for them when I get across. ...

I had a shock yesterday. Went around to the General Staff to see Phil Sheridan about some matters we had not finished when I started for California and found everybody rather puzzled when I asked for him. He died rather suddenly just after I left from an infected finger and was buried ten days ago.

Tomorrow I am to lunch with the Belgian Minister [Emile de Cartier] and Casenave, the French Financial Commissioner, who is an old friend. They want to talk over what I am to do and arrange to give me letters and other help.

I found a pile of dinner invitations but have sent out a sort of circular to say that I am leaving and that I shall not have a chance to dine anywhere.

I don't know whether I told you that d'Ursel is probably going on the same ship with me – also Mrs. Howard Linn. Howard has been here all day and has just left on his way back to Chicago.

Have been trying to get news all day about the ship and just when it is to sail. There is a great deal of uncertainty about that sort of thing these days but so far as

---

4 It is not clear what Gibson is referring to here. The issue is mentioned as well on July 23 and 26, 1918.

I can make out she will be a day or two late – which suits my purpose very well for I shall have a lot of talking to do beyond the amount I had counted on. It is terrible that amount of gabbling that is necessary to put things over when there are a lot of people involved.

Letter to Mary Gibson   Washington, D.C., March 3, 1918

I have spent most of the day tearing up papers and packing books and documents and odds and ends that I shall have to leave here. There is always a lot of this sort of thing to do and I am glad to have some time to do it right.

I went out to lunch with Cartier and Casenave who brought with them André Tardieu and Coujet [Couget], the French Minister to Mexico, who is going over on my ship. He is off to New York tomorrow to stand by for the départ. It has turned cold again but was fair and there was a big crowd at the Montgommery Country Club where we went. They were still gathering when we left to shoot clay pigeons but we all had work to do and left the sunshine to the idle rich.

I was to have dined again with the Hoovers tonight but have so much to do that I have just telephoned that I cannot go. They are having all the CRB [Commission for Relief in Belgium][5] people that are in the neighborhood and I should have enjoyed seeing them.

I dined there last night. The others were Lord and Lady Reading and the Rickards. Reading is a tremendous sort of person with the amount of brains and charm that would be necessary to pull the son of a Jew[ish] merchant up to the position of Lord Chief Justice. There was good talk and we did not leave until after eleven.

Tomorrow I am supposed to spend in session with George Creel. I shall report in due course as to what happens.

Letter to Mary Gibson   Washington, D.C., March 4, 1918

Have spent this whole blessed day pow-wowing with various people and am to have a still more strenuous time tomorrow. Ira Patchin has come down from New York and we are to have a set-to this evening at Phil's. Tomorrow I spend the

---

5 The Commission for Relief in Belgium was developed and run by Herbert Hoover at the request of the Belgium government in the face of the German invasion of Belgium in August 1914. Gibson, then posted as Secretary of the Embassy in Brussels, accompanied members of the Belgian government to London to seek assistance. Hoover agreed, and within weeks supplies were arriving in Antwerp and continued feeding Belgians throughout the war.

morning on my own job cleaning up the last odds and ends. Then I lunch with Creel and spend as much of the day as may be necessary getting thru with him. If I get thru in time there is to be a session with the War College people. Otherwise it will go over until the next day.

My old tub has not yet got in from the other side, so it will be several days before she can even hope to pull out. I am very glad of it for there are a thousand things that ought to be done that could not possible be attended to if I got off on time. I could fill two or three weeks here to great advantage. One things that complicate my affairs is that Arthur Woods lasted just three days on his job with Creel and has now gone to the Signal Corps where he is to take a commission. I don't know yet who is to replace him, but I hope that the replacing will be done in time for me to have a yarn with the new man before I get away.

Letter to Mary Gibson　　　　　　　　　Washington, D.C., March 5, 1918

Just thru another strenuous day – and glad it is over.

A morning session with Capt. Blankenhorn of the War College, lunch with George Creel at which we talked over a lot of things, a short yarn with Joe Tumulty afterward, some talk with Polk and then some preparation of letters and telegrams to be sent. Later I am to go up and have further talk with Frank Roosevelt at his house. That is about enough for one day.

Will Irwin has accepted the job of replacing Arthur Woods and will be down in the course of a day or two to go to work. I am delighted for he is a good friend of mine and I have hopes of being able to work in harmony with him.

Warren [Wood] has returned to our midst and came to see me this morning. He would have had a commission weeks ago but for a most unfortunate slip. He was told that if he would present a memo of his qualifications it would be acted upon at once. He wrote it but by some unaccountable way filed it in his letter file with the carbon copy and it never went to the Navy Dept. When he made inquiry they said they had never heard from him and had made their full choice of Rear Admirals without him, – assuming from his silence that he had changed his mind. The story is much longer than that with a wealth of detail to lend an air of verisimilitude to an otherwise bald and unconvincing narrative. It took a good hour in the telling. He went off to see Jack Towers and said he would come to see me immediately afterward as he thought it would be useful for me to take him around and introduce him to Mr. Daniels or Frank Roosevelt. I believe it is considered helpful to know what you want and go after it.

Letter to Mary Gibson   Washington, D.C., Wednesday, March 6, 1918

French Strother called me up this morning and came to breakfast with me to talk about shoes and ships and sealing wax, etc.

At the office I found a message that Warren [Wood] wanted to speak to me at once. He had found the Navy Dept. unappreciative of his qualities and standing pat on their statement that there were no vacancies he could fill. It was therefore up to me to find some way of getting him a commission or failing that, I should take him along with me as he would be very useful. I promised to inquire as to the situation while saying that I was in no position to accomplish anything. I made the inquiries but they were fruitless and I shall doubtless have a session with the young man tomorrow.

Walter Rogers came down from New York and I had a nearly all day session with him filling the intervals by talking with Bullitt and Coffin. I am amassing a load of documents to take with me and enough plans to keep me busy for a long time to come.

This evening I went home to dine with Creel and had over two hours of talk without interruption. Now if I can have a good quite time with Will Irwin I shall be ready for the plunge.

D'Ursel is not going with me. He came in to say good-bye as he is off at once.

A letter this morning from Cruger in our Legation at Havre. He remarks among other things: "His Excellency [Ambassador Sharp] will never forgive you for getting ahead of him but it is *sua culpa* [his own fault]." H.E. evidently so far forgot himself as to speak out loud.

Letter to Mary Gibson   Washington, D.C., March 7, 1918

Have had another day filled with talk and have had two yarns with Warren over the telephone. I have not been able to land anything for him although I have tried all I can for Aunt Leona's sake. There is not so much I can say on his behalf as I should like but perhaps he will fit in somewhere.

I lunched at the French Embassy and had a most interesting talk. Nobody there but the Ambassador and Madame Jusserand and the de Laboulayes. The Ambassador has sent a telegram to the Foreign Office announcing my arrival in such terms as to make me hesitate to go for fear I cannot hope to live up to the reputation that he has given me. He is also outfitting me with letters to various high officials and to other people who will be useful. Altogether it was a very profitable couple of hours.

Huntington Wilson has also arrived and came in for a talk after lunch. After I had cleaned up the things that were on my desk I went out with him for a walk as I felt the need of letting the cobwebs be blown out of my head.

This evening I am to dine with the Hoovers. I had hoped to dine and talk with Will Irwin but he has not yet arrived in our midst so that has to go over until he is ready to come.

Letter to Mary Gibson   Washington, D.C., March 8, 1919

You may observe that I have another typewriter. I traded in the other one and paid a little extra so as to have one with the accents for writing in Spanish and French as I shall have to do from now on. I also like this smaller type as so much more goes on a page and my letters don't look as long as they otherwise would.

No sign of Will Irwin so far but I have had plenty to do. This has been another day chiefly filled with talk but I feel that we are getting somewhere and that I am better off than I should have been had I sailed as originally planned. My old tub, by the way, has just pushed her silly nose into the dock and will not be ready to sail for several days more.

I have just come back from the country where I went to see Phillips who has just come back from the hospital. He had a rather severe operation and is looking far from well. There were a lot of things that had to be talked over with him but I felt rather ashamed to talk shop with him when he was in this condition.

Dr. [James] McBride called me on the telephone this morning but I could hardly hear him and only gathered that he was casting about for the best way of getting some good out of your plan for Americanization. He seemed to think that the most that could be hoped for would be to let some of the people who are already boosting plans of their own takes such of your ideas as they would use. He said he would write to you at once.

Several telephone calls from Warren [Wood] who says he has great ideas and must have converse with me. I was tied up both times and could not see him but shall have to do so tomorrow. From experience I know about what his fine ideas are in advance.

Lunched with French Strother and talked over some things that are to be done on the other side.

Have not had a chance to talk to Phil today so shall probably dine with him and get things talked out once more. He is probably going up to New York tomorrow for a day or two.

Letter to Mary Gibson Washington, D.C., March 9, 1918

A hectic day with a lot of stuff from outside sources to help fill to the point of discomfort. Among other things I had two visits from Warren [Wood] who comes to stay each time and has to be derricked out. Also a couple of telephone conversations with him which are of the same enduring order. Also a visit from Mr. Dockweiler, one from Major Osterrieth, one from Whiteley and several others from people you don't know but who take up just as much time as though you did.

I have a clipping from the *SPECTATOR* (the London one) with more than a page review of the great book. Usually the *SPECTATOR* takes special pride in poking new books full of holes but this time they were lavish in praise – in fact I could not have written it better myself. I hope it does some good to the sales for I am of a mercenary turn of mind. Nasmith sent me a page from the *TELEGRAF* of Amsterdam with more than a column of review. I waded laboriously thru that amount of Dutch and was rewarded by finding that the constant readers were ordered to invest at once. I hope they do as they are told.

The French Ambassador [Jusserand] has outfitted me with some splendid letters to those in high places in Paris. They are given to understand that I am the great white hope[6] and that they can tell me their real names without danger of being betrayed. I was really surprised and touched at the character of these letters.

The present plan is that as soon as I get to Paris I shall set out for the Headquarters and stay there for a few days for talks, etc. Then to Bern for more talk, then on to Rome for ditto and finally to Madrid. I may go on to Lisbon but think I can leave that out of the first round. Also from Rome I may take it into my capricious mind to run over to Corfu and see how the Serbian Govt. likes living in the Kaiser's villa[7] and then on to Athens to see how they are getting on. All that will depend on what happens when I get on the ground and find the needs to be. At any rate, it looks as though there would be plenty of movement for some time to come.

---

6 In 1910–1911, a black American boxer, Jack Johnson, enjoyed sustained success in both beating white boxers and flaunting relationships with white women. The "great white hope" was the white boxer who could beat Johnson. A movie was produced about the battle between Johnson and the great white hope in 1970. Gibson often used the term to refer to President Wilson in the sense that Europe was looking to him to bring peace in 1917. Here, the term is applied to Gibson himself as an indication of Jusserand's regard for Gibson.

7 In 1917/18, Serbian, Croat and Slovene representatives met on the Greek island of Corfu to advance the creation of a 'South Slave State' (*Yugoslavia*), which was finally proclaimed on 31 October 1918.

At lunch time Homer [Earle] asked me to pick him up so that we could have a yarn. When I got over to his office I found a table spread with eats and all the staff of the Division gathered for wine and wassail – or at least the latter. It was a nice party and a nice thought and I enjoyed it immensely. Just like Homer to have thought of it.

Late in the afternoon I had a long yarn with Huntington Wilson. He is very low in his mind and needs a lot of comforting. It is very distressing but I don't see much that I can do for him.

I think I have perhaps landed a job for Warren [Wood]. At any rate, he got another installment of cash for him today and arrived with pockets bulging.

Phil and Polly [Patchin] are giving me a farewell party tomorrow night – just their family, Homer [Earle], and a few of their family friends. Phil goes up to New York on the midnight train. I was going up with him but Will Irwin has sent word that he will be here on Monday morning so that settles that. I have a load of things to talk over with him and hopes that the whistle will not blow before I have them talked out.

I am still in the dark as to when we shall shove off but am promised definite information in time to enable me to get to that ATLANTIC PORT we read so much about.

Letter to Mary Gibson   The Albany, Washington D.C., March 10, 1918

This is a Sunday and we are in the midst of a raging gale which is blowing over trees and smashing windows at a great rate. There has been a tornado in Ohio and we are seemingly getting part of the edge of it here.

I had counted on getting thru with a lot of work todays but have had to put in most of the time doing some drafting of letters for the Food Administration. That is to say Edgar Rickard impressed me to help him write an important letter and I have spent nearly the entire day writing and rewriting it. I have not seen a soul all day but am going up to dine with Phil [Patchin] and Polly and Homer [Earle] and the rest of the part in the course of an hour or so.

In the intervals I packed a little more and am just about as ready as I can be. It is getting tiresome sitting about waiting for the whistle to blow and I shall be glad when the call comes.

Letter to Mary Gibson   The Albany, Washington D.C., March 12, 1918

Word came yesterday afternoon that I should have to go up to New York today at noon and there was a wild scurrying about to get ready that lasted until well after midnight. The scurrying is about to begin again and will last until train time.

In the intervals I went up and said good-bye to the Rickards, the Masons and Patchins and Hoovers. Mr. Hoover was just back from New York and I stayed on longer than I should yarning with him. ... Good talks yesterday with Creel and Will Irwin and some more due this morning.

Letter to Mary Gibson   Aboard *de Touraine*. Thursday, March 14, 1918.

As we set off down the harbor I take my Corona[8] upon my knee to render an account of my doings, to be posted from the other side of the water.

There is no telling these days when ships will sail and although it was definitely announced that we should push off this afternoon I was not at all sure. Nonetheless I came down early with Arthur Page and Ira Patchin thinking that we would find out and if there was a further delay we would all go back up town together. But when we got to the barbed wire fence fifty yards or so from the pier the sentry stopped the cab and said that none but the passengers could go any further. No arguments availed and I had to get out and leave the others in the cab. A smart hail storm had set in so I bade them a hasty farewell and ran for my life with armfuls of sticks and umbrellas and bundles and passports and steamer tickets and other odds and ends. I had expected to discuss in dignified and measured terms the chances of our sailing and telegraphing you in the light of the latest news. However the sentry told me that we were going so I tore a sheet out of a notebook and standing there in the shelter of the cab scratched off a message which Arthur Page took back up town to send to you. It was just as well I did for once on the steamer we were under absolute news quarantine and I could not have sent you a word.

I got away from Washington Tuesday [March 12] at noon and had a hectic day and a half in New York. Phil [Patchin] was waiting for me when I got to New York and stayed on till the midnight trains so I had another chance to see him. He had talked things out pretty thoroughly with Rogers etc. so we had little shop to talk. He had got tickets for *SEVEN DAYS LEAVE*[9] and we went with Ira and Mary

---

8 Gibson carried a Corona typewriter everywhere and used it constantly to produce his letters and journal. He named his "Cora."

9 A Broadway play written be Walter Howard which was performed between January and June 1918 in the Park Theatre.

Patchin. It was a fine melodrama – very mellow – with spies and submarines and all that goes with that sort of mixture. The audience was just the sort to attend the show and hissed the villain with real enthusiasm. After it was over went to see Phil off at the train station and then home to bed.

Wednesday morning I went down town and attended to a number of errands and talked to some people over the telephone winding up at the cable censors for a yarn with Rogers. We went over to India House at lunch time and foregathered with Arthur Page and Bertm [Robert Patchin] and Ira Patchin. Then back to the censor's office and had a lot more conversation. I gathered up a lot more loose ends and was glad I had the time to talk.

In the evening we – Ira and Mary and Arthur Page and his wife – went to see *POLLY WITH A PAST*.[10] I wish you could have been there for it was delicious. We laughed ourselves sick over it.

This morning [March 14] we made straight for Rogers' office and had another talk with him and with George Barr Baker, an old friend of mine who is now a Naval Censor in New York. Before lunch we got through with our talk and I was loaded to the guards with the information I needed for my trip. We all went back uptown to the Vanderbilt where I met Ira [Patchin] and Arthur [Page] and Captain Merriam for lunch. Then straight here.

I am rather beat and looking forward to a good rest on board. More anon.

Log   On Board *S.S. Touraine*. Off New York. March 14, 1918

The old tub pulled out this afternoon only about two hours late in a sloppy rain and a cold wind. Most of the delay was due to the embarkation of 650 troops, mostly casuals with some engineers. They are a rough looking lot. The Naval Intelligence bund on the dock were very busy, running after the people who were all right including myself and letting the suspicious characters go thru unmolested. After one days experience on that dock I could write a most helpful handbook for spies on how to carry bales of despatches aboard. But perhaps the spies themselves get out a monthly handbook of their own.

About the time we pulled out I found Mrs. Howard Linn who was distressed at not having seen Howard to say goodbye. She had come aboard thinking to settle herself and then go back with an easy mind to visit with him. Once she got on the authorities would not let her go ashore again so there was no goodbye for the Linn family.

Miss Larner was also on board and appeared about the time we pulled out.

---

10 A 1917 Broadway play, made into a silent movie of the same name in 1921.

I found Brigadier General D.L. Brainard who is going to Lisbon as Military Attaché with his wife and an officer and temporary gentleman named Captain de Masi (also accompanied by his wife). Masi has for years been a Hearst newspaper man and began by assuring me that there could be no higher recommendation for a newspaper man than to have a long record of service under that sterling patriot. I didn't argue the question with him but held my own views. There were other people in plenty – Shaun Kelly who is the son of the Paris lawyer who used to be counsel of the Embassy, Townsend of Doubleday Page who is coming over to work for the Red Cross Magazine and has been put into khaki for the purpose, much to his disgust. Morris is with us, on his way to Paris to represent Brown Bros. the well-known money owners. On the dock I was hailed by a man in uniform who proclaimed himself as Luther Bradford and said that he used to be secretary of the California Club. With him was George Gordon, brother of Mrs. Roland Leigh.

Those were about the only people I knew. The chorus was made up of YMCA workers – the thin-lipped, sharp featured type who call each other BROTHER and make me want to tell improper stories on all occasions – Knights of Columbus and Red Cross workers, a stenographic unit that is going over to work for anybody the R.C. can wish them on and a miscellaneous lot of nondescripts who are accepted by all on board as secret service agent and spies – although there is a good deal of disagreement as to which are the spies. The man [George Peed] at the head of K. of C. is in civilian clothes. I remarked upon this to him and he replied that there was more distinction in this, adding:

> "Anybody can be a Lieutenant-Colonel these days if he can get his mother's consent".

Also two women doctors got up like Field Marshals. They made a brave start but there is hope that with a little rough weather they will be asking for beef-tea and allowing us to tuck them in.

Letter to Mary Gibson   March 20, 1918

Each day since we sailed out of New York harbor I have cherished the most honorable intentions about ticking off the rest of this letter to be posted on arrival in France, but so far it has been so beastly rough as to preclude any sort of activity in the letter-writing line. But I have at last solved the problem my locking my cabin door, wedging all the packages into a compact mass so that they cannot pursue each other about the place. I have set up the tripod of little CORA and sit with my back against one wall of my cabin, my feet firmly planted against my bunk and the tripod gracefully grasped between my knees. And now the ship, in impotent rage at being fooled this way, is lashing about and causing a tremendous clatter in neighboring cabins. It is a real feat to keep seated.

We got off within a few hours of scheduled time, the delay being caused by taking on several hundred troops, mostly casuals and detached units. ... There are a number of Red Cross workers of various sorts, most of them seemingly rather uncomfortable in khaki. The YMCA crowd seems to revel in the military flavor and salute each other and everybody else with great fervor.[11] There are also a lot of assorted women and girls, some in uniform and some not who are going over on various sorts of relief work. Two women doctors, got up like field marshals made a brave start parading the deck and looking earnest but they soon succumbed and have become very meek and grateful to anybody who will tuck them in or get them some beef tea. Seasickness is the one sure-cure for vanity – for the time being at any rate.

There are more people on board but they are sort of chorus for those I have described and are roughly grouped as contractors and spies. Everybody I know on board has picked on one of these nondescripts as a spy and keeps him under careful observation. If a real spy got through the examination at the dock, he has earned the chance to ply his trade. ...

Log   March 20, 1918

On the morning after sailing we woke up to find the old tub rolling heavily and few of the passengers about. The air in the staterooms was like that in the snake house at the zoo and it was surprising that any of them live thru the confinement. The TOURAINE has always been noted for rolling but now that they have loaded her with one big gun forward and two aft all on high platforms, she is outdoing herself. The consequence is that there is little or no sleep to be had no matter how tightly you wedge yourself in with pillows and suitcases. Fortunately Arthur Page provided me with a liberal assortment of trashy detective and mystery stories and I pass most of my night following Lone Wolf thru his adventures and helping

---

11 The Young Men's Christian Associate (YMCA) was active throughout allied terriotries during WWI, and in some cases, far beyond. By the Armistice of November 1918, YMCA workers were active across Europe from France to Russia. They were dedicated to offering good food, clean recreation, and various other supports for the young men in the stressful circumstances of war. See Kenneth Andrew Steuer. *Pursuit of an Unparalleled Opportunity: The American YMCA and Prisoner-of-war Diplomacy Among the Central Power Nations During World War I, 1914–1923* (Columbian University Press, 2009). For Poland, see Paul Super, *Twenty Years with the Poles* (White Eagle Printing, 1947).

Fibsy trail down murderers. Horror stories are not the sort of diet to feed to some of the people on the boat who are already sufficiently stirred up by the thought of submarines. The sea has got rougher each day but we have about reached the limit of the acrobatic ability of the ship so I hope it will stop now.

We have passed very few ships and have not been told of any converse with them. All of them have been extensively camouflaged and we have worked hard on them thru our field glasses. This afternoon a comic looking steamer of the tramp type passed across our bows within a few hundred seemingly on a voyage from the North to the South Pole. She was camouflaged in most weird and fantastic ways with splotches and spirals and sunbursts of white and black and different shades of gray. Several we have passed in the dusk and very like phantom ships they looked, their camouflage making them appear to sail through the air and with never a light showing anywhere.

We have a lot of sailors aboard travelling 2nd Class, a clean looking lot, and a lot of soldiers going steerage. They were pushed on board at the last moment under temporary command of a young Capt. Clarke, just out of a training camp. Some of the men are old hands and they are making his life wretched. Of course they began to complain without loss of time and were aided and abetted by the dear brethren of the YMCA and other idiots who sympathized with them and took up collections to buy them chocolate creams. FACT! The result was that we soon had complaints and General Brainard and I were asked to come into council in the Captain's cabin to talk things over. The men were claiming the rations and treatment that they thought coming to them under army regulations and the captain, after business of shrugging shoulders and raising eyebrows, said the transport officer in New York had not made any contract and had merely told him that the men were to be accommodated as steerage passengers. In accordance with this the purser had laid in supplies for so many steerage passengers and he admitted that this was not what he would have chosen for soldiers. However that was not a matter for him to decide and there was just so much on board in the way of stores. And he intimated that he could not stop at the corner grocery and stock up. And then in the good old French way after reserving all rights he began to tell what he would do – and the outcome on the whole was very satisfactory. The fault clearly lies with the transport officers in New York who passed on conditions. The company notified them in writing that the TOURAINE was not fitted for the transport of troops but they had her looked over and decided differently without asking for any changes in her equipment. However the men will get a sufficient ration for the rest of the trip – but it will be another story to see whether the complaints stop.

Last night one of the men died of pneumonia. It was a happy release for he had been suffering dreadfully and there was no hope beyond landing him to die in a hospital.

The second day out we had lifeboat drill and were made to assemble on deck and put on our belts. The whole proceeding was a farce as it was left in the hands of stewards who were considerably bored and in any event had no authority to make seasick or lazy passengers attend. A good many people came on board with those comic life suits which are fitted with everything but the kitchen stove and electric light. They were somewhat upset when told that as the suits were heavy they would not be allowed in the boats.

Log   March 21, 1918

Our soldier was buried this morning at four. Only a few people, most of them in khaki, turned out for the burial. The little group gathered on the forward deck where a wooden chute had been rigged ready to be lowered. Two of the Catholic priests read the prayers. One of them gave a little talk which was really splendid and should have been made before all the men on board. It was the sort for soldiers to hear and did good to those who did hear it. When he had finished the bosson [boatswain] blew his whistle as a signal to the bridge and the big ship without a light showing, slowed down and came to a complete stop. The wind died down and though the sea was heavy the sky cleared. The chute was lowered until it just touched the water and the body, done up in canvas and weighted, was let down to the surface and then released. It disappeared without a sound while the priest murmured his last prayers. Taps was sounded but with a muffled bugle as we are in the danger zone and no chances were taken. And then everybody stumbled back to bed over the sleeping soldiers on the decks.

Every porthole is shut tight and covered with black cloths to keep in every ray of light. The ventilators seem to have been banished and the atmosphere in our cabins is like that of the snake house at the zoo. Everybody complains of headaches and there is a general plan to sleep on deck tonight.

Log   March 22, 1918

After being rough all the way across it has suddenly become fine and the sea is smooth as silk which is all wrong in the eyes of those who don't like submarines. And worst of all although the weather has turned fine we can't have a port open and even the ventilators are battened down tight. The air was bad when we started and has been getting worse day by day and is now poison. So last night we decided to sleep on deck. That is to say Mrs. Linn and Miss Larner decided and I went along to shoo off trespassers. Just to furnish entertainment a detachment of the gun crew who was off duty settled down besides us and began to warble. One of the huskies climbed into the chair next to mine and beat time to his song upon my arms and ribs with his solid elbow. I finally got him rolled over without giving offence and without discouraging the flow of song. Knowing the taste of the sailor man in song I was somewhat anxious as to what would be forthcoming but all the output was of a strictly Kindergarten variety. In particular they warbled over and over the old ditty

> *"Dans des terres étrangères*
> *Des familles entières*
> *Sont mortes du choléra!*
> *Ha! Ha!*
> *Le papa*
> *La maman.*
> *Tous les enfants sont morts.*
> *Le chien*
> *Le chat*
> *Le singe*
> *Vivent encore."* [12]

They also had a ditty to the effect that:

> *"La lavature à l'huile*
> *Est bien moins difficile*
> *Que la lavature à l'eau*
> *Mais c'est beaucoup moins beau"*[13]

With all the versions and repetitions that suggest themselves.

They had run out of French songs and were starting on the rendition of some American anthems when a bosuns mate came along and "invited" them as they say in their lovely language to go back to work. The soldiers and sailors began pouring up from below and settling themselves for rest wherever they liked. Far be it from our boys to pay any attention to the distinctions between first, second and third classes. An old Belgian priest chose a chair near us and all thru the night gave us the most wonderful selections of grunts and groans and snorts and snores I ever heard in my life. And every now and then he broke the silence with a loud and plaintive note like the whistles of a ferry boat – TOOO-OOOO-OOOT!

---

[12] *"In the foreign countries, whole families died of cholera! Ha! Ha! The daddy, the mum, all the children are dead. The dog, the cat, the monkey are still alive."*
[13] *"The painting on oil is much less difficult than the painting on water. But it's much more beautiful."* Gibson erroneously writes *"lavature"* (the word doesn't exist in French) instead of – as in the original of the song – *"peinture"*.

And about dawn he rose up coughing and sputtering and stamped loudly upon the floor to start his circulation. Miss Larner in a thin thread of voice and about the fierce temper of a strawberry said: "Please don't make so much noise!" But it never got to him and he went his noisy way.

Below decks things were less peaceful than where we were – although I am free to admit that I did not sleep a wink and felt like a pretzel from trying to wrap myself around one chair in such a way as not to fall off.

During the night some of the bad eggs among our men broke into the galleys and set guards with fixed bayonets to stand off the upholders of law and order while they broke down doors and plundered the refrigerators and wine cellars. They got away with all the fruit on the ship, a lot of the meat that had been cooked for today and six kegs of beer. Then when they got somewhat illuminated they walked about the ship seeking whom they might devoir and one ugly little sweep who seems to have been responsible for most of the trouble decided that he would like to bayonet the Second Officer of the ship. There was considerable outcry as the S.O. was touchy about it, and all hands and the chorus came charging onto the scene. The lawbreaker defied his Captain when ordered to give up his gun and behave so he was overpowered by some Bluejackets and put in the brig. I hope the uplifters on board are pleased with the fruits of their meddling.

I stood by for the dining saloon to open so that I could get in and have some coffee to wake me up. Just as the door opened a steward came running down shouting that the maître *charpentier* [chief carpenter] had fallen overboard. The screws were grinding hard to stop the ship and she backed as fast as she could to the place where he had gone over, a boat being lowered as we went. When it was launched they picked up his hat but though we all searched the surface of the sea for over an hour with glasses we never saw a sign of the man himself. Probably he hit the side of the ship in falling or was hurt on hitting the water so that he never came to the surface. It is a case of particular hard luck. He was a retired employee of the line who had served for many years and had come back to work so as to release a younger man for the war. At the end of this voyage he was to have gone on a pension.

Log   March 23, 1918

A quiet day with nobody fallen overboard – but worse things moving. Yesterday evening General Brainard sent word to me that he wanted to see me in his cabin – which is the biggest on the ship and the only place people can meet to talk. He told me that he had received word from a woman on board to the effect that we were carrying along two officers who were trying to establish communications with Germany. She said she wanted to give us the details but was observed by the officers in question all the time and left the problem to us. There was a sing-song in progress in the Second class saloon next to the General's cabin so Mrs. Brainard went out and spotted the woman and after chatting with her as though she had known her before, asked her into the cabin. She is a Mrs. Jeanne Carpenter who says she has done some confidential investigations for the Dept. of State. She said that Dr. Charles Hutter and Capt. J.O. Kutz had approached her and a young woman who is travelling with her asking them to undertake to write letters for them to relatives in Switzerland. They claimed that officer's mail was carefully censored but that women working for the Red Cross would be more free to communicate. The story, told in great detail and with a good deal of digression, is an ugly one. After we had heard it thru and asked a number of questions we asked them to put their statement in writing which they agreed to do. The other young woman is a Miss McGovern. General Brainard will turn matter over to the General commanding at Bordeaux when we get in.

Log   On the Train Bordeaux-Paris, March 24, 1918

To the great surprise of all hands we eased into Bordeaux this afternoon after having disappointed all the pessimists as to our ability to make it.

About twelve o'clock three dirigibles came out to meet us and convoy us in to shore. The day was perfect and the sunlight, smooth water and pretty peaceful villages at the mouth of the Gironde brought quick forgetfulness of the miserable days on board.

Soon we began to pass signs of war, shipyards, warehouses, docks lined with transports and supply ships, mile after mile of them – and above them all the American flag. They were all humming with industry and American soldiers and sailors were everywhere cheering the men on our boat.

The customs and passport people came on board as we reached the bar and their work was done before we ever reached Bordeaux so that we could go ashore without loss of time. Mrs. Linn, Miss Larner, Shaun Kelly, and I piled into a one-horse cab with thousands of pieces of baggage and made for the CHAPON FIN. Little Alexander Hamilton, the witless Vice Consul at Havre tried to charge into our midst but we all urged him to go to the Consulate and announce his arrival and he set off with a suitcase in his hand to do our bidding. But as we came by the YMCA headquarters Alexander looms up out of the pavement in the dusk and springs upon the step, hurling his suitcase into Kelly's lap and announcing joyously that there was nobody at the Consulate. So he joined forces with us and stayed to dine. We had a bang-up dinner, the first since leaving New York, and although the restaurant rolled somewhat when we came in it was steady enough when we left, a reversal of the usual procedure.

Soon after we got seated Mr. Bucklin, the Consul, came in and joined us for a little while. He had spent hours on the dock waiting for the ship and had missed us when we came ashore. He is a very presentable citizen and seemed to show real interest in his job. When he went out I accompanied him to the door and he besought me to come back and have a yarn with him about intelligence, propaganda and other matters of pressing importance.

Letter to Mary Gibson   March 25, 1918

... It seems to me that I have learned more about the real state of things in this one day that I have been in Paris than I had learned in three months that went before. I am sorry that I can't sit down and write it all to you but it can't be done. As being next best, I have invested in a big loose leaf notebook and shall try to keep a log from day to day. ...

Log   Hotel Meurice,[14] Paris, March 25, 1918:

Our train eased into the station this morning a little before eight, a quarter of an hour ahead of time and we were dumped out in the Gare d'Orléans into an empty station that did not expect us and showed no joy over our coming. After struggling with our baggage with the aid of a she-field-marshal who was a specialist in window washing and did not care to become a porter we found some sleepy men who got us as far as the cab rank. But there were no cabs and no immediate prospect of any.

The new German guns had been firing since seven o'clock, plumping in a shell every fifteen minutes or so and the cabbies had betaken themselves and their nags into the cellars. However that was the last shell fired during the day – but the Germans alone knew of this fact and cabs were scarce for some time. After seeking them for a quarter of an hour we went into the estaminet [café] of the station and coffee and a sticky red mess which the tieless waiter described as "jemb". We were Mrs. Linn, Miss Larner and I. Alexander Hamilton the worthy but painful

---

[14] One of the oldest luxury hotels in Paris at 228 rue de Rivoli, home (until June 28, 1918) and frequent meeting point of Gibson and his associates.

V.C. trailed us for a little time but tactful shoo-ing did its work and he made for the [Hôtel de] Crillon[15] with other less lucky or more polite people.

After we had consumed coffee without sugar and mulatto rolls without butter (waiter registered indignation when they were asked for) I went forth and summoned cabs. Placing the two ladies in the first one I went back into the café to get their luggage. Then when I came out they were nowhere to be found. I staggered up and down the street with the two bags, peeking into every cab and finally decided after invoking the aid of the YMCA, Knights of Columbus,[16] cops, flower girls, soldiers, villagers, etc. that they had fled leaving me to attend the luggage. First I when to the Crillon where I thought I could dig myself in and telephone to find the missing ones. The clerk threw me out on the plea that there were no more rooms. Thence to the Meurice where I was more fortunate and established myself in luxury. Baths, hot <u>and</u> cold, shampoos, fresh clothes and all the comforts for man and beast.

Telephones declined to afford any clue to the vanished ladies so I decided to get under way for the Embassy with my precious bundle of ciphers. As we rolled off the Élysée I spotted Miss Larner and Mrs. Linn convoyed by a handsome young man, heading in the same general direction. Hailed them with courteous toot-toot learned from BRAVE BELGE on board TOURAINE and got them into the cab. It seems they had waited for me uncounted hours before the station, hidden under a newspaper or something of the sort and finally left only when convinced that my throat had been cut out and that I was being chucked in the river by the Huns. They had about made up their minds to spread the alarm and have the river dragged for me. Effects exchanges, peace made, CURTAIN.

The Ambassador had left town for a few days but I found [Robert] Bliss, [Arthur Hugh] Frazier, Fred Sterling, [Jefferson] Caffery, [William] Andrews and other worthy citizens who made me feel welcome and as though for the first time they were convinced that with my arrival there was some hope of our winning the war.

Incidentally they seemed thoroughly down in the mouth about the news from the front. The Boches[17] seem to have pushed back the British lines most successfully, to have occupied Péronne and crossed the Somme in several places. On the

---

15 Former palace of the Paris nobility, the Hotel de Crillon at the corner of Place de la Concorde and rue Royale served as one of the most luxurious and exclusive Parisian hotels of Paris since March 11, 1909. I was a frequent meeting point of Gibson and his associates as well.

16 Catholic fraternity that evolved in the late 19th Century in the United States and was engaged in charity work.

17 "Boche" was a slang term used by the Allies during WWI to denote Germans. It derives from the French word "caboche" or head of cabbage.

whole the news looks pretty sick. I heard from unauthorized sources stories of 25,000 British prisoners, 300 guns captured and other equally cheering news.

It looks as though they were making a formidable drive to pinch the British army and put it out of business. If the move is at all successful the fate of the war may be decided in the course of the next week or ten days. I had planned to go down to G.H.Q. in the course of two or three days and thence to Switzerland, but so long as things remain in this troubled state I shall try to stay here. It looks as though the stormy petrel [bird] had got plump into the thick of it again.[18]

Sent my passport to the F.O. to be viséd.

Telephoned Arthur Orr and arranged to lunch with him at the [Hotel] Plaza [Athénée][19] at one o'clock. Frazier was going down town and as I am still a free man I walked with him although it was a little early. Found Arthur waiting for General Foulois, his Chief, head of the Air Service on this side, and after careful consideration it was decided to be kind and let him lunch with us. He is the youngest General in the army, a self-made Connecticut boy with perfectly direct manner and a clean eye. He is not afraid to speak his mind when there is occasion for it. While we were at lunch Cabot Ward, now a Major in the counter-espionage service came up to the table with some fawning words about not being able to resist the temptation to salute a former chief. The former chief rounded on him with a grunt and waded into him about trying to steal men from the air service without referring matters to him. His conversation bristled with such phrases as I WON'T STAND FOR IT. I'LL TAKE THE MATTER TO HEADQUARTERS. THAT SORT OF THING CAN'T BE PUT OVER ON ME. Ward almost groveled and intimated that he'd sooner choke his grandmother than think of such a thing but his protestations only brought forth fresh blasts from the general and C.W. finally beat a disorderly retreat. Whereupon the General calmly resumed his lunch, remarking with satisfaction that SOME GUYS WERE LOOKING FOR TROUBLE AND THAT THIS ONE CAME AND HUNTED FOR IT – AND GOT IT.

After lunch Arthur excused himself with a deal of tact and skill and we set out to do errands. First we came here and gathered up packages belonging to Mrs. Linn. Thence to her abode, 1 Impasse Conti, where Arthur practiced a perquisition [sic] and came out with two letters from Alice. Mrs. L. not on the premises but

---

18 The German Spring Offensive had started near St. Quentin on March 21, 1918 with 'Operation Michael'. Within a few days, the German Army was able to conquer large terrains and to take significant numbers of prisoners-of-war and guns. The offensive was halted after a week by the bringing up of French reinforcemnts and bad weather conditions.

19 Close to Champs-Élysées, at 25 Avenue de Montaigne, the Hôtel Plaza Athénée was one of the leading hotels in Paris. Constructed in 1911 and opened in 1913, it was frequent meeting point of Gibson and his associates.

A. left a note saying that we would come for her at 7 ½ to dine. Thence to Brentanos where a genial clerk assured me that he could not keep any of my book in stock although orders clogged the London mails. He fished out one however and asked me to autograph it for him. Here I ran into Mrs. Meert and her two daughters. Meert is at La Rochelle where he is in uniform.

More errands and then to Arthur's hotel when I ran into Townsend who had crossed on the boat with me. As we left we espied Perry Osborne who is sporting the leaves of a Lieut.-Colonel. He has just reached Paris today but managed in some way to get down to Chaumont[20] first and see all the crowd. He was down in the mouth as he could be about the offensive and seemed to be quite prepared for a trip to the Pyrenees. It is his sister, Mrs. Sanger, who occupies Mrs. Wm Astor Chanler's flat where Mrs. Linn is staying.

Arthur dropped me at the Embassy while he went about his business. I got off some telegrams to Washington including one for Leland [Harrison] about the case of the two officers on board the TOURAINE, one announcing my arrival, and another to Creel suggesting that some good man should be sent to float up the Gironde to Bordeaux and write the story of what is to be seen there. It is a fine way to convince people at home that the money from the Liberty Loans[21] is being quickly and effectively translated into punch and out to help loosen the purse strings of some people when the next loan comes along. I should like nothing better than to do it myself if I were only triplets or did not have so many odd jobs that require immediate attention.

Had a most satisfactory talk with Dawson who is charged with compiling intelligence on political matters for the Ambassador. He got out a few exhibits which were most interesting to me, though it is evident that His Excellency [Ambassador Sharp] puts them carefully away in the safe as rapidly as they are handed to him. D. had a remarkable number of sources of information and lists them under symbols, – Joffre, Fabry, etc. This sort of thing is a fine beginning for what I want to get started and I only hope that there will be nothing to stand in the way of developing the system.

---

20 From September 1917 to July 1919, this town in the Département Haute-Marne (Region Grand Est) was the location of the General Headquarters (GHQ) of the American Expeditionary Force (AEF) in World War I, established by General John Pershing. At one point, over one million soldiers stationed here. It features prominently in Gibson's descriptions, and he would often pay it a visit.

21 Between June 1917 and May 1920, the US Treasury in total issued five war loans (four Liberty Loans and one Victory Loan) in order to finance Allied and US troops, calling on the patriotic duty of US citizens.

Image 4: Joseph Jacques Joffre, Commander in Chief of the French Army, inscribed by hand for Hugh Gibson. (Courtesy of the Gibson Family)

While we were talking Kerney came in and I was very agreeably disappointed. He is a clean-looking citizen who realized that he has had a very big job entrusted to him and that he doesn't know anything about it. His lack of assurance is encouraging. He has been the editor of a Trenton newspaper, is a friend of Joe Tumulty, and does not speak a word of French. He has now been here about three weeks and not a dish washed yet. He talked good sense about the difficulties of getting propaganda when the French already had more of their own intensely interesting news than they could hope to print in their one page papers, about the need for planting only stories that would command attention, and of studying a whole lot before loosing off any fireworks just to give the impression in Washington that things were being accomplished. After an hour or two of talk I walked home with him to the Crillon and then alone to the Meurice. The beady-eyed Alexander Hamilton spied me as I parted from Kerney at the door and bore down upon me with gentle hints that he was open to suggestions for the evening. I was sufficiently obtuse to meet the situation and got away.

Arthur came for me on time with his Rolls-Royce, some swank in belonging to the brutal and licentious soldiery, and we went on for Mrs. Linn and thence to

Voisin.[22] A. had qualms on the way because he had neglected to order a table but when we got our first peek through the door he yelled to the chauffeur to wait under the impression that the place was closed. There was not a soul there. We were reassured however by the head waiter who sadly explained that all the world had cleared out for the south and east because they were annoyed by the big guns and the few people who remained in town were not venturing forth because they feared a raid or a renewal of the bombardment. In the afternoon as A. and I passed the Gare d'Orléans the whole sidewalk was packed with people fighting their way in to the outbound trains. They were not in lines as in ordinarily crowded times but in packed masses with policemen herding them like sheep. Luggage was piled in the street ten feet high and I began to have misgivings about my things arriving from Bordeaux. How are they ever to get thru this mess?

Despite the Boches and other troubles we managed to get a good dinner, though it seemed a bit weird to have no butter and only a sort of inferior hair tonic in a bottle in place of sugar for our coffee. Arthur, the perfect a.d.c. had a little package of loaf sugar in his pocket and we were spared this terrible suffering.

Arthur announces that invitations these days bear the inscription RAID or SHINE.

A little before half past nine the bill was presented with a gentle reminder MONSIEUR, C'EST L'HEURE. For at half past nine all these restaurants must close their doors. We were courteously but firmly planted on the street as the clock [struck] and groped our way along a street of inky blackness made worse by silly blue lights, to the waiting motor. The streets seemed deserted after what one remembers of Paris in old days so there was no delay because of traffic and in no time we were delivered to our various places of abode.

I have not had time to look for a place to live but all hands at the Embassy discourage the idea of a flat because of the impossibility of getting and keeping servants. Servant rooms are at the top of the house and these ignorant and superstitious people are prejudiced against the idea of having bombs dropped on them as they sleep. Hotels are extortionate – they probably have to be to keep from starving so I suppose I shall have to eat hearty while my fortune holds out and then throw myself in the river. Eggs, according to Arthur, have reached the price of one

---

22 Voisin's was the renowned Parisian restaurant in the rue St. Honoré, famous for its exotic Christmas menu of 1870 (during the Prussian occupation) by the chef Alexandre Étienne Choron. One of the favorite meeting places in Paris of Gibson and his colleagues in 1918/19. After a long successful run, Voisin closed in the late 1960's

franc each. If I were not tied to my present post by the war, I should become a hen and get rich.

Frederick Palmer has gone to London with Secretary Baker and General Bliss and may not be back for several days, although nobody ever knows. If he comes here I may manage to postpone my visit to G.H.Q. for the present. Oscar Crosby is here in the hotel but I have not seen him yet. I see in the paper that Carl Ackerman is also here but he has not appeared so far. I shall look him up tomorrow and try to talk some propaganda in Switzerland.

A few letters waiting for me when I arrived including one from Frank Gunther insisting that I attend his wedding on April 27th. One from Galpin who seems to be in the thick of things.

A telegram from [George] Creel as follows:

> "Understand Rickey resigning. Urging him remain until successor is chosen. Please write estimate of general situation and recommendations. Considering CHURCHILL WILLIAMS, Assistant Editor, Saturday Evening Post, for London position. Italian situation according reliable advices again extremely critical."

Creel evidently somewhat disingenuous about the [Vira] Whitehouse matter. Kerney has a telegram from him sent thru Naval Intelligence instead of State. In the course of it he says:

> "If you desire to return to Switzerland I will have to force Legation to change its attitude. If you think Legation will persist in secret to antagonize however or if its attitude has destroyed your usefulness in Switzerland, then stay in Paris with Kerney."

Some ten days ago there was a conference here of the Allied propaganda agents. Crosby, Kerney, Dawson and [Frank] Marion attended for us. Nothing done save to bewail the defects of our various systems. Agreed that Italy and Spain presented the most pressing problems, and that so far as the United States was concerned Spain was clamoring most loudly. Accordingly Marion is to get to work there at once despite his recent rows with [Ambassador to Spain, Joseph E.] Willard.

One of the shells from the German guns fell across the street from the hotel just inside the railings of the Tuilleries Gardens. A crowd was standing about it all day. I suppose I shall have to go over and look at it myself although I have seen holes in the ground before and can find no logical excuse for yielding to the curiosity.

Arthur [Orr] is a good deal disturbed about the friction between Americans and French. A number of other people have shown anxiety on the same subject. It seems that our military and some civilians have assumed a very managerial attitude and have antagonized the French officials. On the other hand the French Govt. seems to have seized the opportunity to get a little of that well-known Yankee money. When we detail an officer to serve with the French we continue his pay and allowances and the French have no expense. When they assign an officer to serve with us we are expected to pay him in good American terms. There seems to be a disposition to turn an honest penny whenever possible. If the British or French in America want land for flying or other similar purposes we hand it to them with a sweet kiss. Not long ago our people looked about for a place to try machine gun work from the air. They finally picked out an utterly useless swamp near Bordeaux because nobody would under any conceivable circumstances set foot upon it. The French Govt. smiled and said they would be delighted to hand it over to us – in consideration of a payment of twenty millions of francs! When we complained at this they immediately brought the price down to twelve million. But the point was that they should have been glad to give it for nothing in view of the purpose for which it was required.

It seems that the dictatorial and antagonistic manner of some of our people – an alarmingly large number of them – is resulting in weakening our hold upon the feelings of the French and is throwing them back into the arms of the British whence they had scrambled with a good deal of satisfaction when we came along, the assumption being that we were their great white hope and more likely to be sympathetic than the English.

Log   Paris. March 26, 1918

Very little news of what is going on at the front although on the whole people seem to be more optimistic. The papers speak of forty German divisions being engaged in the drive. As a matter of fact, there are an even hundred of them which is an entirely different matter. At one point the Germans seem to have advanced twenty kilometers into the English lines; that was day before yesterday however and they may not have held it. They have taken the village of Ham which is serious as there are no organized defenses between Ham and Noyon and a rapid advance at this point would render possible a threat against Paris. The Germans were fighting yesterday in the outskirts of Noyon. Opinion in some well-informed quarters seems to be that the German plan is to reach Compiègne and then propose peace, having previously terrorized Paris by the rapid advance, the way for which has been paved by recent air-raids and the long-distance guns. However the French have retaken Tergnier, near La Fère and the junction between the French and British armies is complete. Furthermore the Germans have advanced into a sort of pocket so that the Allied tactics will probably be an attempt to cut them off. The Germans have sacrificed their men ruthlessly in the attack and if the Allies could transform this partial German victory into a defeat the effect in Germany should be far-reaching.

Saw a lot of people today but gathered little news of importance. Dropped in to see Major Mahan, the Military Attaché, and in his waiting room found McNally, the Consul General from Zurich who is here on leave after a trip that causes some uneasiness. His son-in-law is in the German Navy and comes now and then to see him at Zurich. The Allied Ministers at Bern have protested against his retention of that post and the closing of the frontier fortunately keeps him here until Washington can be heard from. He accompanied Mrs. Adolphus Busch and her party from Switzerland and took them to Spain and now he is showing an undue anxiety about getting back to Switzerland. The suspiciously inclined look knowing when they speak of this anxiety.

Also ran into Carl Ackerman who is filled with dope about the publicity situation in Bern. I am to lunch with him tomorrow and hear what he has to say. McFadden, War Trade Board representative, came along and bade us both to dine with him at the Bristol tomorrow night saying that he would also ask Kerney.

Ran into Pink Simpson in the hall and had a little chat with him. He is with McFadden who also represents the Food Administration.

Joe Green called on the telephone and I had a little yarn with him.

Frazier went with Col. House to London and is filled with disgust over conditions in the Embassy. He was not responsive to my remarks about the staff and crabbed them pretty thoroughly. He said the Ambassador had acted childishly and had had a diplomatic illness while the Mission was in town. That Ned [Bell] was very aggressive. That Frank [Gunther] was a complete ass. That Laughlin seemed to have lost his grip, etc., etc. I hope the minds of other members of the Mission were not similarly poisoned.

The Ambassador [Sharp] came in while we were talking and I met him for the first time. He asked me to go to see him at three.

Lunched with [Robert] Bliss alone at his flat. He is much perturbed by the messages Fred [Palmer] and I have brought about the Dept.'s discontent with the way things are going here. He realized things are not altogether what they should be and says that steps have been taken to remedy some of the superficial defects, but that the more important and vital things are almost hopeless as they rest entirely with the Chief [Ambassador Sharp] who shows no inclination to accept suggestions or even give him opportunities to talk things over.

I think I relieved his mind by saying that I was not coming over with the idea of setting up an independent Embassy and that on the contrary all my efforts inside and out would be to make things easier.

We talked about the question of propaganda and he agreed with me pretty well on the points I have allowed myself to have preconceived notions about.

As to sources of information, he said he had kept on the string for me a Frenchman who had lived long in America and felt that he could help both countries by keeping us in touch with the labor movement here. He is to trot him out and let me have a look before long.

On the way back to the chancery we met William Martin, the Chef of Protocol. He must have run like a lamplighter all the way back to the Foreign Office for we had hardly got back to the chancery when a boy came in with his card and my coupe-files [card allowing first passage].

His Excellency [Sharp] had not come in at three and it was nearly six when I got word that he would see me. He was agreeable but not particularly responsive and certainly not genial. He evidently had some sort of feeling that I was coming over to do second story work and that there might be trouble. He began by saying that he had letters from the Dept. telling him to "cooperate" with me: that he "guessed we wouldn't have any trouble getting on" etc. He said he had a bad time getting thru his work as most of his day was taken up with seeing people. In order to say something I remarked that the free-born American considered it his prerogative to deal with the chief but he replied that that was not the trouble: that these were all IMPORTANT people and that they could not be referred to Secretaries of the Embassy. "For instance you come along and I have to see you. You wouldn't understand it if I referred you to one of secretaries without seeing you myself. And there are equally important people coming along all the time." Also he complained that he had to draft important correspondence. I put in a feeler by remarking that fortunately letters did not know whether they were done by the chief or referred to somebody else to be drafted for signature. Whereat he said that the less important stuff of course he allowed the staff to do for him, – as he could not be a clerk.

He said he could not understand the attitude of the Department as to matters of political intelligence. That they seemed to expect him to send news of what was going on in Germany whereas the only way of getting such news was thru Switzerland – and that the French Government had instructed its Embassy there to keep our Legation informed. He did not seem to have grasped the point of the Department's letters on the subject and they had "got under his hide".

I said that we could get all the newspaper comment from the press but that the Department looked to him for balanced and considered views. That the mass of telegrams coming into the Department each day was so great that nobody could hope to read them all and that the most valuable of them were not those that merely dumped in raw material but those that boiled down the news to the minimum and gave predigested conclusions. I went over this with appropriate gestures in several different ways but fear it did not get much effect.

After tomorrow's pouch goes off we are to have another and fuller conversation and perhaps we will get somewhere.

At 7:30 General Foulois and Arthur [Page] came for me. We then picked up Mrs. Linn and went on to Foyots to dine. As we entered I ran into Farrar-Smith with whom I promised to foregather.

An extremely good dinner and a good deal of gloom about the war. On our way home we stopped at Mrs. Linn's so that Arthur could get some things she had brought over for him. We found that Mrs. Sanger was having a party and stopped on until after eleven. Perry Osborne came in and after the others had gone we settled down and gloomed some more. Foulois said that it looked to him as though the Germans would get near enough to hold Paris under bombardment and would then offer peace with Alsace-Lorraine, the occupied provinces and Belgium held out as bait – and all hands agreed that if this were done the jig was up. Mrs. Sanger had lunched with a member of the Govt. who told her that the civil population had been evacuated from Compiègne and that the General Staff had also moved out. Foulois has ordered in a lot of motor trucks to get things out of Paris for him as a matter of precaution, – but even the remote need for that sort of precaution is not very comforting.[23]

Secretary [Newton] Baker is back from the front this afternoon and will probably leave tomorrow. [General] Pershing is with him.

This afternoon Topping came in to see me and we had a little chat. He is very happy in his new job with the Associated Press and did not show any enthusiasm over my suggestion that he come with me. I am to have him for lunch in a day or two and talk over things in general. He says that Brand Whitlock gets two hundred thousand dollars out of his book on the war.

Log   Paris. March 27, 1918

Another strenuous day without much accomplished.

Found Frederick Palmer waiting for me at the chancery and as we could not find a quiet place to talk we arranged to have lunch together at the Savoia and he went his way. I had to stop by the Meurice and break my engagement with Ackerman. At the Savoia ran into Goedeke and Davis Wills who is now a Major. Albert Byran came in with some ladies so it seemed quite an old Washington crowd.

Palmer is in his usual gloom. He is fed up with having a lot of regular officers over him and is hoping to be transferred to other duty. He thinks Pershing would do anything to make the situation tenable for him if he were to put it on personal grounds but he is unwilling to do thing and prefers to ask for other duty. He wants

---

23 The Ministerial Council discussed the evacuation of Paris on March 24, 1918.

me to go down to H.Q. with him day after tomorrow and I shall go whenever he is ready. He wants me to talk with Pershing and Col. Nolan (in charge of intelligence) and others. His idea then coincides with mine as he wants me to go to Switzerland, Italy, Spain and Portugal and try to get a general idea of what is going on, what we can hope to do to influence opinion, and above all how we are going to do it. I tried to get some specific needs but he did not have any in mind and threw me back on the same generalities that have been given me by everybody else, namely that when I am on the ground I can tell better than anybody else.

He says that everybody here is getting sick and tired of our boasting and press-agent publicity and that something must be done to choke it off. When Mr. Baker came along he had the idea that he could do good by giving out statements, but after he had seen something of the offensive and its effect he decided that a blank page was the best contribution he could make. He has telegraphed to Washington to stop the flow of such news. Mr. Page had sent a similar recommendation from London. General Foulois told me last night that he had got Pershing to send a blast to stop Coffin's outpourings about what we are going to do in the air in the indefinite future. That ought to have some cumulative effect. After returning to the chancery I sent a telegram to Polk to the following effect:

> "Public attention completely absorbed by offensive, with no present interest in American news, and particularly sensitive to publicity telling of our achievements or what we are going to do. Important that no such news be sent during present crisis. Palmer asks me to say for him that he emphatically approves of the foregoing and that he can authorize me to say that Mr. [Newton] Baker is of the same opinion. Mr. Baker has refrained from issuing statements which he had prepared as he deemed it wiser for us to keep silent at this juncture."

Palmer is convinced as many other seem to be that peace is very near and will be forthcoming at the end of this offensive. It is self-evident that a failure of this much advertised offensive to get thru would be disastrous to opinion in Germany but it remains to be seen whether it would smash the hold of the war party upon the people. Undoubtedly it would have an enormously depressing effect – but we have still to stop the offensive.

After lunch we went around to 10 rue Ste. Anne and saw Joe Green and Wickes who are both Lieutenants in the press division of the Intelligence Section. They are also depressed by the discouragements of their jobs and Green has asked for a transfer although he has not yet allowed it to be known.

He told me something of the Inter-Allied Propaganda Conference which was held here several weeks ago. Pichon headed the French Delegation and other big men were representing the other countries. We were represented by a group of men who had not met together to discuss their course and only one of whom spoke French. Kerney, a Trenton newspaper man, just landed, headed the delegation: [Frank] Marion, a movie operator from Creel's bureau, seconded him. The others were Robinette, an Assistant Naval Attaché from Stockholm, Joe Green, a Second Lieutenant of Reserve and a Capt. Smith. Brrrrr!!!! Kerney made a little speech in which he said we had no plans and knew nothing about anything. Then to make matters thoroughly pleasant Marion got up and said Kerney had no right to include him in that or speak for the moving picture business: that he had been a movie man for years and knew all about it and that he would tell them a few things for the good of their souls, which he straightway did. Then Robinette arose and laid down the law at length in regard to the Scandinavian countries. He talked more than any other man at the conference and the American delegation talked more than any other delegation, – so we seem to have won on points. Altogether it must have been a disheartening affair in which these fellows made monkeys of the United States.

The army is apparently of the opinion that the entire press ought to be abolished and they are not going to spend any money on that sort of propaganda. Joe Green has spent a lot of time and effort building up relationships that would be useful for propaganda work, but he says that it has all been thrown away, and he is through.

Just to give a pleasant end to the party and show what the army things of our work he called in Captain Smith who has been assigned to help Kerney. He is a frightful little critter, sloppily dressed, slouchy and chewing gum. And his way of talking is quite in character. He will be a whale of a lot of help in doing anything.

Here is a verbatim transcript of a statement made by Marshal Joffre in strict confidence on the 27th of December, predicting a good deal of what has been come to pass. It is pathetic.

> "The German attack upon our front may not come within a week and may not come within a month but it is bound to come and will find us unprepared – because we are not preparing a counter-attack. There is only one means for resisting such an attack, and that is attacking at another point while organizing resistance at the point threatened. Now, a modern battle takes several months to prepare and to plan. We are not preparing one, nor or the English, and so our position will be week when we are attacked, whatever the number of trenches that we have dug and the earthworms have thrown up.
>
> An entirely new development in methods of attack is to be foreseen from the Germans. We have no definite information on the subject of the form it will take, but it is certain that there will be something new, if only a new and more formidable use of gasses or other existing weapons. The effect which this may produce upon soldiers, added to the possible effect of local success of the Germans, are among the dangers which may be considered as serious in the present condition of the country generally.
>
> Our partial and uncoordinated methods of offensive can hardly be expected to bring success. The English offensive at Cambrai failed, among other reasons, partly because of lack of coordination between Allies and partly because the English did not know how to profit by their victory. Making a new use of their tanks, they made a fine advance, as they

have done before, profiting by the surprise of the Germans. But once they had reached their new positions, the English did not know what to do next. They have so specialized upon trench warfare that they no longer know how to make open warfare. They stopped long enough to allow the Germans to reform and attack: they had made a "hernia" in the German line which they were not able to hold and which was pushed back: we had not been warned in advance so that we had not been able to organize to support them; and so victory was changed into a defeat."

Another interesting bit I picked up in the course of the day was a rumor that is circulating thru the Bourse to the effect that a movement is on foot at the Senate to replace the present Govt. by a Triumverate composed of Clemenceau, Foch, and a Deputy named Peytral, – to be conducted on the lines of Napoleon's Consulate. It seems that Poincaré and Caillaux were intimate in past years and it is reported that Caillaux intends to drag Peytral into the trial. This might readily force Peytral to resign, which would supply the opportunity for the change in the form of Government.

Late this afternoon I came in and found the Secretary of War [Baker] wandering about the waiting room. It seems that he had an appointment with the Ambassador at four but that His Excellency had not turned up or sent any word, a little habit he has. The Secretary did not seem over pleased with it but was amiable and we had a little talk before I left him to wade thru an extra which was brought in. He is off this evening for Italy but will return to our midst before going home. I hope then to have a yarn with him so that he can tell some of our troubles to those that need to hear them.

It comes to me confidentially from Palmer that Col. House will be over in April for another visit.

Topping called up this afternoon and said that the Associated Press had despatches saying that the German advance about Albert and toward Amiens was being held.

On my way home called on Edith Wills but she was not at home.

At 7:30 dropped in on McFadden at the Bristol where he revels in King Edward's old suite for the sum of sixty francs a day. Kerney and Ackerman and Kerney's daughter were there and we all went over to the Ritz[24] to dine. In the dining room found Colonel Grant who is now at Versailles and asked me out to lunch with him.

---

[24] One of the most luxurious and exclusive hotels in Paris (and even the world), the Ritz at 15 Place Vendôme looks back at more than three centuries of service. The English term 'ritzy' – as symbol for highest quality – is derived from its name. It was one of the most frequent meeting points of Gibson and his associates.

After dinner went back to the Bristol and sat about settling the affairs of nations until an advanced hour of the night. McFadden had no idea of the gravity of the military situation and bundled us out of the house when we told him about it. We had a long talk about the economic situation in Switzerland – some of which I understood – and also about the possibilities in the propaganda line. All agreed that we could do better propaganda now with troops and food than with the press.

Walked back to the Crillon with Kerney and when we came back to the Meurice, Ackerman told me what he had had on his mind for hours. He had it most confidentially from Pomeroy Burton that the British Govt. suspects the French of having decided to give up the struggle and of having opened discussions with Germany. A British representative has been sent here to investigate and exercise necessary pressure. From other indications I cannot believe that the French have yet weakened to the point of negotiations but the British suspicion is genuine enough.

Log   Paris. March 28, 1918

I get word from several sources that Joffre, Lt. Gen. Phillips and [James] Thomas, the English Labor leader all say (independently and unconscious of each other's views) that the Bolshevik movement in England has become serious and that an organized peace movement is in full swing, exploiting the gravity of the food situation and the real suffering of the people. It is considered by some that this movement might result in separate peace negotiations.

Joffre says that for some weeks past it has been known that the morale of the English soldiers, as well as civilians, has gone down considerably, and it has been expected that if the Germans chose for their attacks the point they have chosen, the British would fall back and their line might even be broken.

In France there has been a growing suspicion against the English for some time. The fact that Haig kept his Cambrai offensive a secret until two days before it started has been extremely resented. As a matter of fact he told both Joffre and Pétain three weeks before, but under oath of secrecy, pledging them to conceal it even from their staffs for fear of indiscretions. This detail is not yet known. But an atmosphere of distrust was created which may explain the reports now current. France suspecting England of plans for a separate peace, and England suspecting France.

In France it would seem that pretty well everything hinges on the Labor movement. If this battle turns out badly the socialist and labor men will demand peace and attempt to force a revolution if the Government resists. Joffre recognizes the danger. If the rear crumples up the armies will have to yield also.

Smith, our old London – Berlin courier, came in this morning from London, via Havre, where he heard from the Minister that I was here. He had not come through Amiens as is usual and does not expect to go back that way.

Ackerman in this morning after a scouting expedition and says that the British are opening a formidable counter-attack which is equipped for two days. If it succeeds well and good – if it doesn't then good night.

Confidential news from Italy to the effect that an Austrian offensive is expected on the Piave.[25]

The press has received orders not to send any more paper into Amiens for the present.

Lunched with Joe Green. Palmer had telephoned to ask that I go down to GHQ tomorrow morning and my passes were ready for me. I signed away all my rights and property in order to get them.

Went to Cercle Volnay[26] for lunch and had a good talk with Joe who is rather discouraged and sore. He is stagnating here and tried to be sent as Liaison officer with the Belgian army, but he was passed by and Bill Cresson made a Captain and sent to the job. He is sore on Col. Nolan who seems to have been pretty rough with him and according to his story has no conception of his job. Pershing has treated him very handsomely and has earned his devotion.

On the way back ran into Horodyski who was in America in connection with the recruiting of the Polish Legion. He rode into the chancery with me and said he was most anxious for a good long talk.

Log   Headquarters. Chaumont. March 29, 1918

I got away from the Meurice this morning at a little after seven and got to the Gare de l'Est without any amount of time to spare for the train. Fortunately I had taken the precaution of reserving a seat for the train was crowded. I was in a compartment with three French Majors and a girl worker of the YMCA She displayed curiosity about me and when I told her what I did for a living she remarked in an understanding way: "Oh, yes, SECRET SERVICE." I tried to disabuse her mind of this but she knew better and I was marked down as a gumshoe man. The Majors discussed everything on earth but kept mostly within screaming distance of the

---

25 An Austrian offensive at the Piave was prepared from end of March 1918 onwards and was launched in mid-June, but soon proved abortive.
26 Cercle Artistique et Littéraire de la rue Volney, rendez-vouz of artists where Gibson and his associates often went.

war. One of them had been with the Rainbow Division[27] and was filled with admiration for the men and particularly for the way they are fed and provisioned. They also discussed America for two of them had been there some time. They evidently did not know we were Americans, the Y.M.C.A younger person did not matter as much as she spoke no known language, – and they discussed American women in great detail and with a favorable decision as to their charm and virtue.

As our train dawdled into Troyes sometime after it was due in Chaumont I was constrained to get a sandwich and smoke an after luncheon cigar in the corridor. While I was doing it I got into a conversation with Major Walker who was going to GHQ for his first tour of duty there. He was interesting about things in general and a little fed up by our constant chatter about what we are going to do. While we were talking Col. T.B. Mott came along with a few French officers in tow and stopped to speak.

We rolled into Chaumont at about three o'clock and I was met in a pouring rain by Lt. [Edwin] Watson of the Press Division, G.S. He dropped my bag at the Hôtel de France and then took me straight up to GHQ. Found Palmer in action with Major McCabe and Col. Sweeney. Bentley Mott also came in and aired some views as to how the world should be run. Went down to see McCoy who is secretary of the General Staff. He looks well and flourishing and asked me to move right up and stay with him. He has the house next to General Pershing where he and Logan have established a sort of branch of 1718.[28] Logan is away for some days and I shall not see him this time. Norman Whitehouse was sitting outside the door acting as a bellhop for McCoy. Dropped in to see Capt. Griffith and he took me across the hall to see Seymour Blair who is a flossy private engaged on translating the Hun press. He had no idea his sister was on this side of the water and nearly blew up with joy. He is doing extremely well and his superior officers told me he would soon be promoted to 2nd Lt. He will come up to Paris in the course of a week or so when he can get a uniform that is up to his idea of what self-respecting private can wear. He is an attractive boy and seems to have made good. When I got downstairs from seeing him, Barnes was waiting for me. He seems more cheerful and content than he used

---

27 The Rainbow Division refers to the 42nd Infantry Division of the US National Guard was formed when the US declared war on Germany in 1917. Douglas MacArthur was credited with its nickname. The Rainbow Division remains in action, headquartered in New York.

28 1718 refers to the residence of a group of bachelors beginning diplomatic, political or military careers in Washington, DC, located at 1718 H. Street between 1907 and 1922. They jokingly referred to themselves as "the Family," and formed close bonds. Key members included William Phillips, James Logan, Willard Straight, Hugh Gibson, Basil Miles, Frank McCoy, Charles Evans Hughes, Leland Harrison, Joseph Grew, James Dunn, Francis White and Norman Armour. This group continued to meet for annual "Homecoming Dinners" until the 1950's.

to be in old Department days but even at that he would be gloomy for anybody else. There was another boy from the Department cipher room who was playing about as a Lt. But I can't for the life me recall his name.

On the whole it seemed like Old Home Week with familiar faces in every room.

McCoy told me he wanted to have Basil Miles and Henry James brought over to help him out and had prepared a telegram for General Pershing's signature asking that they be commissioned Majors and sent along. He had the telegram in his desk with the notation "WILL NOT SEND. JJP." So that's that, and he had sent a telegram to Basil suggesting that he try to get his commission on the other side.

Palmer and I went down to the Guest House where he lives, to talk about things in General; from there to Gen. Pershing's where he had a little yarn with Secretary Baker and the General. The big news will come out in the course of a day or two, but I was let in on it tonight. General P. went this afternoon to see Gen. Foch and placed all our forces at his disposal for use in the present offensive. It was done without conditions and in a simple way that could not but be touching to the French. No answer was given but there is little doubt that they will be used. The announcement will be made when the French have definitely declared their readiness to avail of the offer. That will be the finest piece of propaganda that could be put over and should go a long way toward correcting the unfavorable impression made by the flow of boasting news from the U.S.

I talked to Palmer about having Joe Green assigned from the Press Division to my work and having Capt. Smith taken out and lost. He promised to attend to the matter.

Palmer is anxious to have me go to London and get all possible lines on conditions in Spain and Switzerland. I may find time to do it before starting the grand tour.

Paul Cravath came in while we were coming out and I had a little talk with him. He seems to be just playing about getting a look-see.

Palmer walked over with me to Colonel Nolan's mess and I found quite a troop, Major MacGruder, Major McCabe, Major Camoneli, Captain Hubbard and a few others. Nolan was late so we went ahead and he joined us when he got ready. He is a keen regular officer who was jumped from Captain to Colonel to take over the Intelligence Division. He was very pleasant and I think we shall get on. He suffers somewhat from the feeling that he knows all about the French although he does not speak a word of the tongue. He knows the Cubans, Filipinos, Panamans, and thinks he has discovered another form of wop.[29] Perhaps time will remedy a

---

[29] In the now politically incorrect jargon of the time, "wop" is a derogatory term applied to Italian immigrants to the US. Sometimes it was used for other groups of immigrants as well, as it is here.

good deal of that including the idea that everybody is trying to put something over on him. I stayed on and talked with him after dinner until he had to go back to the office. We yarned at some length about the handling of newspaper men on the front, the need of getting a higher type of correspondents, the desirability of getting some writers out that were not newspaper people but could give the American people a picture of life at the front; I suggested some people like Margaret Deland, Mary Johnston, and Mrs. Norman [Vira] Whitehouse, who though different in type command good audiences. Also the need of getting the right sort of French men of letters and artists down and treating them as they should be treated. Nolan agreed and had notes taken on a number of subjects. He has been impressed by the good accomplished by Baker's visit and is now keen to get a number of others over from the Cabinet.

The STARS AND STRIPES people have asked me to write an article for them about the Belgian army. They say that nobody seems to remember that the Belgians have done anything since their first stand and they think it would have a good effect on our troops to know that the Belgians have kept it up all this time and are still going strong. If I get a chance to visit the Belgian front and see something of what they are really doing I shall not fail to write them something.

Talk of having Ian Hay come over as the great WHITE HOPE and write about our army. I agree with Palmer in thinking that it would be better to have that job done by an American and leave Hay in his own field which is nothing but the British army. I imagine they will tell him frankly that they think this but that if he comes he will be received with open arms and shown everything that can be shown.

I wish I had more prospect of having time to prowl about Chaumont for it is a charming old town and must have some history which I have not been able to unearth. It abounds in little towers and doorways which come down from other days and have not been altogether spoiled. GHQ is quite on the edge of town in a cavalry barracks which give lots of room and though not luxurious with its white-washed walls and little rooms affords a room to pretty well every officer who requires one. The General [Pershing] has taken over a rather pretentious house which seems not to have made up its mind as to whether it is a château or a villa and sports a lot of conservatories and other fixings of the high life. It is about half a mile away from GHQ on the main road back to town. McCoy's pleasure palace which is far less impressive is across the street on the fork of the cross-roads.

Log   Grand Hôtel de France. Chaumont. March 30, 1918

I was wakened this morning at seven and looked out of my little box of a room to find that it was still raining cats and dogs outside. The night had been made unsleepable by chatty neighbors, village drunks and American soldiers who seemed to be strolling about the streets in the most casual way and indulging in song on no provocation at all, – not even that of being drunk. It was cold and clammy and I got up grumpy and remained so until after I had shaved and sponged in cold water which was brought in a hot water can as a matter of flattery. There is not a cab in the blessed town and I had neglected to tell the brutal soldiery to send a car for me so I set out on foot for McCoy's for breakfast. I found McCoy just in from an early morning ride with Major Harjes, Mott and Count [Pierre] de Chambrun, younger brother of my friend the Marquis [Charles de Chambrun]. He is a genial soul who is said to be a splendid officer and is attached to the French Military Mission at GHQ We all had breakfast off a little table about as big as my hand before an open fire and settled many of the most pressing problems of the human race. Nobody had seen the communiqués and all were anxious to get over to the shop and see them. There was a lot of talk about the High Command and various candidates were advanced, most of the votes going to Foch and Pétain. I held my own counsel but they would have been somewhat interested in my news that Foch has already held the place in fact for some time and that it will soon be announced.

After breakfast we rode over to GHQ in a military car and I foregathered with Palmer. At ten I met Colonel Conger and he took me thru Intelligence A. I was much interested in the maps showing the order of battle of the enemy and in seeing where our information on the subject comes from. As a matter of fact the work is really done by the British and French and most of our work consists in copying their data onto our own maps. There is some local intelligence work done by the units on the front who gather their material from trench raids, facts pumped from prisoners, captured letters, talk overheard by listening posts, etc. This is well pieced together so far as I can judge and we keep a pretty good idea of what we have before our men. Also the charts showing the history of various enemy divisions during the past few months, how much they have fought, how much and when they have rested and where they are at the present time. This information requires a tremendous amount of detail work and checking and seems to be accurate.

Those I pitied most are the poor souls who have to comb out the German newspapers from small towns, reading the death notices, lists of decorations and items of local gossip to spot the whereabouts of units on various dates. The big papers are either discreet or are held under more rigorous censorship, but the little papers are still spilling the beans in the good old way. I remember that early in the war the German General Staff used to find great help in the little English church papers which told about the losses with a thoughtful mention of units and places. The British Govt. shut these leaflets up but this time Brother Boche has evidently not been as thorough as the Briton and the news still reaches us.

After getting thru a lot of this stuff I went up to the economics Division and had a little talk with Major Morris. He was discursive and did not offer much of value but when he had talked himself out he took me across the hall to Ogden Mills who is a Captain and a disgruntled one at that. He clamors for intelligence on economic matters and is filled with ideas as to just what he needs. It is a pleasure to find somebody who knows just what he wants. I got a general idea of his work and read some of his memoranda recommending changes in the way of doing it. He is to send me copies of these after submitting them to Colonel Nolan.

I had declined to go back to lunch with McCoy because Conger had asked me, but he disappeared and so I went off with Norman Whitehouse and his crowd who have named themselves modestly the INTELLIGENT MESS. They have a place next to Nolan, far more swanky and comfortable. Ogden Mills had just had a run-in with the GHQ printer who can't understand why he should be required to spend his time setting up a long dissertation on economics. After some discussion he held up a bundle of galley-proofs disdainfully and remarked: "Hell, this aint war! It's BULLFIGHTING."

On going back to GHQ I dropped in at McCoys to see Mrs. Larz [Isabel] Anderson who was there for lunch. She has just come down from the Belgian front and brought me messages from a lot of people. She had seen Aunt Leona and was able to tell me about her. General Alvord was also at lunch and as we found out they yesterday had been Mrs. Anderson's birthday there was a gay drinking of health in RUM, the only drink to be found on the premises.

On going in to see Griffiths I ran into Exton (once upon a time Eckstein) who used to be in the CRB He has acquired a game leg somewhere and is now working in the library, considerably to his disgust, – but then most of our civilians have acquired enough soldier traits to growl all the time. Had a yarn with Sweeney and saw Blair again and got messages for his sister. Cravath was about the place arranging to go up to the front and it was suggested that I stay over until tomorrow and go up with him, to which I gladly assented.

At about five Palmer and I shoved off in a car which we had requisitioned. We stopped at General Pershing's house and had a talk with Secretary Baker. He grows more affectionate and now calls me by my first name though I continue to be respectful and call him Mr. Secretary. He is off for the Italian front tonight, accompanied by General Black, Mott, [Ralph] Hayes, etc. I filled him up with ideas on propaganda and how it should not be done so that he could retail some of it to the President and some to Creel when he gets home. He seemed in a receptive mood and I gave him all he would take, – until General Pershing came in and I had to let him go. He and the General were slated for a final round so we cleared out and left them alone after a few words of politeness. The General seems to be flourishing and strong and his face has grown in character under the responsibility he has had. He has everybody here on their toes and it is really comic to see him move with his satellites all scurrying around and saluting and worrying for fear something may not go just the way HE likes best. And apparently there is some reason for their anxiety for HIMSELF does not hesitate to wade into his subordinates when displeased. OFF WITH HIS HEAD, says the Duchess of the GENERAL. Baker was quite anxious to know how people at home looked upon his trip, seemed to fear they would look upon it as a junket and feel that he should have stayed at home. I was able to reassure him on that point and also tell him some of the feeling of our people over here about the value of the visit to their work, especially as it affected their work after he got home. He seemed pleased and relieved. He also inquired seriously about Senator Chamberlain's condition and whether he was recovering from his operation as fast as could be desired.

From there we went back to Palmer's to draft some telegrams and incidentally to have some tea. General Black was there and we renewed old Cuban days and the great day when we took the MAINE out to sea and sunk her. I asked for the first time whether the work that Harley Ferguson did in the course of raising her resulted in any new light as to the cause of the sinking. He said that it was established beyond any doubt that she was sunk by a slow explosive from the outside but they had never been able to get any further than that.[30] Palmer has today determined to give up his present job as the Press Censor and accept the place of official historian of the war. That means he will have a car and be allowed to wander about all over the place and keep posted on what our troops are doing. He will probably also have charge of the preparation of the War Diary although that is not definitely settled. He is much relieved to get out of the censor job which is about the worst on earth. That will now devolve upon Colonel Sweeny for who my prayers are lifted up.

While we were at tea Lt. Hunt came in and presented himself as the officer who had been designated to accompanied Mr. Cravath and me to the front tomorrow.

The afternoon papers say that the Huns turned their big guns on Paris yesterday afternoon and landed one on a church where a big congregation was gath-

---

30 On February 15, 1898, the USS Maine exploded and sank in Havana Harbor, an incident contributing to the ourbreak of the Spanish-American War. The reasons for the catastrophe have never been fully established.

ered for a Good Friday service, killing 75 and injuring 90: The church as a matter of fact was Saint Gervais. The Cardinal Archbishop of Paris pertinently remarked: "They have chosen the hour of the death of Christ to commit this new barbarity."[31]

Palmer dined with me at the hotel and then we groped our way up to Colonel Nolan's to say good-bye. The streets were as dark as the inside of a fish and it was fortunate that we had some sense of direction as we would otherwise have wandered off to the Boch lines. Nolan was not there but I left a note for him and rambled back to get early to bed.

Log   Chaumont. March 31, 1918

A long and weary day, thank you, and no telling when it will end.

I was called at six and told that there was no way of getting any breakfast before seven. As that was our time for starting I scuttled along to the Guest House and clamored for coffee which was forthcoming, – with real sugar. Cravath was poking about and Hunt joined us on the dot, closely pursued by Major McCabe who had been specially detailed to accompany us for some mysterious reason at which he hinted in the afternoon.

Fortunately we had an open car and made good time to Neufchâteau where we stopped at the censorship and I had a few minutes talk with Gerald Morgan who is in charge of the office. He is a Lt. now and seems to have a remarkable hold upon the newspaper men. These latter have their headquarters at Neufchâteau and scatter from there for their sightseeing.

The only one about was a comic cut named Ferguson although we have a number of correspondents out of all proportion to the size of our army. If the British accepted correspondents as we have they would have something like thirty-five hundred with their army according to figures that were given me yesterday.

It is a long pull to get to the front from GHQ and the trip is farther than it would be from Paris to the front. The country gives no hint of war and we might have been back in the old days before 1914 for all the sights of war outside the towns. There was not a sound of guns which seemed rather strange after the way we used to hear them pounding in Belgium. In all the villages there were quantities of American soldiers billeted and some of them so far forgot themselves as to salute the officers in our car. Each house bears a placard showing exactly what it

---

31 On March 29, 1918, a German shell struck the church Saint-Gervais-et-Saint-Protais during a concert that was attended by many members of the Parisian high society. 75 persons were killed, 90 injured.

offers in the way of billets for officers, men and horses. In some of the towns there were large numbers of Indo-Chinese militarized laborer whom the French seem to find very useful for work behind the lines.

From Neufchâteau we made thru the edge of Toul past some of the fortifications which seem to be supplied by a well-designed vicinal, and thence on to Mesnil [Le Mesnil] where is the headquarters of the First Artillery Brigade. We stopped first and exchanged a few words with Colonel King and then went in to see General Summerall who was expecting us. He took us thru his headquarter and showed us his map making, intelligence and other matters of interest. His brigade is extended on a front of about four miles extending from the point of the Saint Mihiel [Mt. Saint Michel][32] salient eastward. His guns, some of which date back to 1870, are disposed in depth in a rather complicated manner but the map helps to understand.

While we were yarning, Dorsey Stephens barged out of a cubbyhole in the wall and ran into me. I had inquired about him but nobody knew where he was. He looked as well as a horse and as happy as a clam and I was delighted to have a first hand sight of him so that I can let his mother know about him. We were just setting off to lunch with the General [Summerall] so I could not stop to talk with him but promised to look in again after lunch.

The General's mess was in a vile dump across the street from the wooden hut that serves as headquarters but the food tasted good after all our hours of fasting. I mentioned Dorsey and the General quite sat up. He allowed that Dorsey was one of the brightest and most useful officers at headquarters: that his colonel spoke of him most highly and that he was one of the first men that he (the General) had recommended for promotion. That ought to please his mother.

As we were coming out from lunch we ran into General Lassiter who was military attaché in London in my time. He had come to relieve the First Brigade with his own. The First Division is to go into action under Foch before any of the others and then are getting under way now. Lassiter took one look at headquarters and all the little shacks crowded around it and remarked: "Good Lord, man, I'm going move all that the first things I do. It's a wonder you have not been bombed off the face of the earth with everything bunched together like that." General Summerall took it calmly and was apparently quite willing to let Lassiter do all the hard work he liked.

Gas masks and shrapnel helmets were brought out for all of us and we were shown how to put on the masks. They were of the English model with a pair of

---

32 Site of a famous medieval monastery, built on a rock ashore which with high tide is embraced by the sea.

tongs which grasped me by the nose and almost refused to let go. I could stand the gas better than the mask. The new tin hats are far more comfortable that anything of the sort I have seen before and we all wore them from the time we set out until we got back to Mesnil. The General took Mr. [Oscar] Crosby who was an old friend in the first car with him and the rest of us went in our own car. We were told to run a hundred yards or more apart as a good part of our way lay in plain view of the Boche observers and it was thought useless to have more than one car of us bagged in case they loosed off anything at us. There was a lot of camouflage along the road, most in the nature of very transparent fences thru which we must have been quite satisfactorily evident. Now and then there were signs, evidently for those who had no imaginations to the effect that this was no place for loitering and that we were in view of the enemy. We finally stopped the cars rather far apart in the shelter of a rise of ground and clambered over some camouflage made of colored burlap rags fastened on wire netting laid on the ground. An unexpected opening led us down some steps to a roomy, stuffy dugout where eight men are accommodated for sleeping purposes when things are quiet. I judge however that it is more healthy there than sleeping out of doors at any time for the fields on either side of the road were pretty badly torn up with shells and the road was evidently under constant repair. After the sleeping dugout we messed about in another where there was telephone connection with headquarters to be used only in emergency for demanding barrage protection or some other urgent work. Across the street there was a very extensive camouflage of wire netting raised several feet above the ground. It must have covered an acre or so and had everything on it but the kitchen stove. After crawling along under it for some distance we descended a couple of steps and got to two 75, one of which was the first gun fired by American troops in the war. It was just an ordinary 75 without any self-consciousness and had a bad dent in its nose which had been put there yesterday by a shell which burst just outside the emplacement. The gun was roofed over with a single layer of rails and some sandbags over which very convincing camouflaged had been erected. This affords no real protection save against shell splinters. A direct hit wouldn't leave enough of the shelter to fill a teaspoon. The gunner on duty was snappy in his manner and knew what he was about. The General snapped out questions at him like a rapid fire gun about his range, the time it would take to place a barrage, the time it would take to shift to the alternative and place a shell on the Boche parapet, and other similar practical questions. The gunner was as quick as his General and knew just what he was talking about. It showed the good effect of the constant hammering to which Summerall subjects his men. We went on to another gun alongside and the gunner was put thru his paces in the same way. S. is a merciless taskmaster and is the slackers dread. It gives all the more point to what he said about Dorsey.

After floundering out from under the wire we got back into the motor and went on toward the lines to what was once the village of Mondres. The fields on either side of the road were nothing but shell holes and the road had a few fresh dents on it. It runs along in the shadow of a hill several hundred yards away but the Boche has the exact range of course and keeps the entire district covered with shells so as to make life as uncomfortable as possible. There are very few people in sight, one or two soldiers who had definite business somewhere and were moving as though in a hurry. We passed some old guns placed under cover near the road but it was too hot to get out and look at them. McCabe announced as we drew near the cross roads at the entrance to the village that it was known as DEAD MANS CORNER for obvious reasons. McCabe was getting nervous as he had orders to "bring Mr. Crosby back". There seemed to be no such order about me but I moved along with the crowd. We had to draw past an open space in view of the enemy in front of what had once been a house in order to get to the artillery observation post on the edge of the slope which led down to the trenches. The house where it was established was a sad mess but held together enough in some mysterious way to permit the construction of rickety wooden steps leading to a ledge just under the roof. Here we found two observers with the periscope glasses which they adjusted so that we could have a look at the trenches and no-man's land. Things were perfectly quiet and it merely looked like some complicated sewers during the lunch hour. After we had stared our eyes out our empresarios got us started and took us back to Mesnil where we left the General and got under way for our return trip to Paris.

Stopped for a few minutes at Neufchâteau for gasoline and had another little yarn with Morgan. While we were there Draper of the A.P. came in and tactfully failed to remember me. After being led up and introduced he vaguely remembered having seen me somewhere, – all to the enjoyment of the officers present who knew something about him.

We made splendid time back to Chaumont, stopping once or twice in passing detachments of troops. Talked with some of them and found them enthusiastic over the idea of getting into the big fight. Those who were going in to hold the present line expressed disgust that they could not be in the big show.

We made the station at Chaumont in ample time only to find that the train was two hours or more late and that we should not get to Paris much before midnight. At the guichet [window] I ran into Robert Jackson who is a Lt. at Artillery H.Q. and seems to be making good. We rambled about the old town and had a good talk about old times in Belgium and elsewhere. Wherever we went about the town the children came out and followed us bombarding us with scraps of English they have learned, but specializing on demands for chewing gum. To think that we have come over with protestations of friendship and are debauching the coming generation with gum!

Log   Paris. April 1, 1918

Our train did not roll into Chaumont until nearly half past eight last night and we came into the Gare de l'Est at a little before four this morning. We were pretty near dead but a short sleep and a cold tub put me into shape for the day.

At dinner on the train last night Cravath was full of conversation about Crosby. He wanted to know why Crosby was so vindictive against Herbert Clark Hoover. Said he had lied to the American people about conditions in Belgium and seemed to be down on him generally. His own diagnosis was about right, – that Crosby was not a good subordinate and that his vanity was hurt by having to serve under anybody. I let it go at that.

I was wakened early by a telephone message from Horodyski asking me to dine with him today or tomorrow but had to put him off until I could find out about my plans. Shortly after the Crosbys called me on the phone and asked me to lunch. Shall have to see them later.

To lunch with Mrs. Sanger. Those present: Mrs. Linn, Mlle Thompson, Monsieur [Paul] Painlevé, Grasty and Perry Osborne. Just before we went in to lunch the big German gun – which by the way Painlevé says is planted at St. Gobain – dropped a shell not far away and people swarmed off the trams and looked about to see where it had lighted. Nobody seemed in the least excited – only mildly curious about it – and we all went in to lunch as though everything were peaceful as could be.

Painlevé spoke of 70,000 British prisoners and 1100 guns lost to the Germans – one fifth of the whole British artillery on this front.

Mrs. Sanger tactfully inquired whether there was any truth in the report that the French guns were charging the British rent for the trenches occupied by them. Painlevé replied:

> "Pourquoi pas? Ce sont de très bonnes tranchées. Il y a de l'eau à tous les étages." [Why not? These are very good trenches. There is water on every floor.]

Soon after returning to the Embassy another of the big shells was plumped near the chancery but I don't know just where it landed. In all the Boches dropped twelve shells upon us during the day.

Dined with Dawson at his hotel. He is very much down in the mouth about the situation at the Embassy. He is very loyal to His Excellency [Sharp] but is quite discouraged by the knowledge that most of his work never gets any results. He brings in his political information and hands it to the Ambassador – who then usually files it in the files. It seems that little Bryan who was one of the most incompetent clerks I ever had, has acquired a considerable ascendency over the Chief by flattery and by open hostility to any member of the regular staff who

Image 5 and Image 6: Chaumont, 1918, as Gibson saw it, and the view from General Headquarters over the French countryside. (Public Domain)

ventures to make suggestions or differ with His Excellency [Sharp] in matters of opinion. He plays upon his suspicions and altogether keeps the old gentleman worked up against everybody. He will not allow Dawson to be made a Special Assistant because he says that it is his policy to keep anybody about him from having authority or position. According to what he told Fred [Sterling] he attributes his success to the fact that in politics he never allowed any of his supporters to have his full confidence; he held separate and secret meetings with each of them in turn and gave each one his particular piece of work. That is his idea in the Embassy. He tries to keep all the threads in his own hands and to keep the various members in the dark save as to the part of their own work they are allowed to see. Altogether it is about as baffling a situation as I have ever seen. The members of the staff as loyal to the Ambassador and are anxious to help him, but his suspicions make it utterly out of the question for them to do so effectively. Dawson will probably resign soon unless he gets some sort of assurance that his work is not being completely wasted. He also wants some sort of rank other than that of clerk in order to add to his efficiency in getting information, – a perfectly reasonable desire on his part.

Log   Paris. April 2, 1918

At a little after three this morning I was wakened by the tooting of the siren warning of an air raid. I don't think people mind the raids very much but the siren sounds like the screams of a soul in terror of hell and is enough to give people hysterics. At first I thought I would stay in bed but after a bit it got monotonous as there was no sleeping because of the scurrying of the guests and the firing of barrage, so I put on a dressing gown and fur coat and walked down the darkened stairs to the cellar. I found a lot of people gathered there, all of them more pretentiously dressed than I, with a couple of Americans who had come in off the streets on their way home from the Gare de l'Est, – the same old train I had taken the night before. Presently Carl Ackerman came in and we had some chat. Then one of the hotel people arrived in some excitement to chase us out of the bar where we were sitting because it was the one part of the cellar that had nothing in particular over it, being under the court. There upon we moved uncomplainingly into the next room which would have been just as bad in case a bomb burst in the bar, for there were no walls to speak of between the two rooms. [Sheldon] Crosby came floating down in a sketching toilet and cigarette and joined us with a large amount of conversation. He had recently come back from the Italian front where the King had pointed out to him the place where the Italians expected the German drive. There is evidently a well-founded belief that the drive is coming there before very long perhaps even before the end of the present offensive on Amiens.[33] The Italians have sent a certain number of troops to France to help out and the British and French have withdrawn a good part of the troops they had sent to help out in Italy so that this would seem a good time for the Boches to get to work there.

Crosby also said that he had talked with Winston Churchill yesterday and that he admitted the heavy losses of British guns but said that that did not matter as there were plenty more near at hand to replace them as fast as necessary. What did worry him was the shortage of trained gunners, but he said that was giving just as much concern to the Germans as to our people.

We heard plenty of barrage but very few bombs and after a time I got bored and sleepy and moved upstairs to bed. On the first floor, which is also a refuge, was the old King of Montenegro [Nikola I] surrounded by his staff and looking highly indignant. I scuttled by lest he should absent-mindedly decorate me as seems to be his wont when bored.

Having promised Horodyski to go and seen him at the Ritz at three for a real talk I dropped in on Frazier to learn what I could about his present status. It seems that he stands rather high with the Foreign Office in London, has a good deal of standing at the Vatican, is a close friend of Sir William Wiseman and has some other good connections. Although it is not supposed to be known the British Government and our divide of his expenses and he is supposed to keep us informed as to anything he picks up in the way of news. He has sent in a good deal since coming over this time but has received no acknowledgement from Polk of any of his recommendations, which seems to make him a little sore. Frazier mentioned this in one of his recent telegrams to Col. House but has heard nothing yet in rely. But being that sort of sleuth is not what it might be for it seems that some of the British are not altogether sure about the gentleman and have dispatched Rakes (the King's Messenger) to keep an eye on him. Not that Rakes would ever discover anything if it were there.

I lunched at the Embassy and sat next to Madame Waddington who is a most interesting old lady, still full of interest in life and snapping comment on everything and everybody. I got her started on de Blowitz and she snapped out "Wretched little imposter. Name wasn't even his own. He was a dirty little German Jew – but a successful charlatan." Waddington was French Foreign Minister at the time of the Congress of Berlin and she told of some of Bolwitz' tricks to get there.

---

33 On the situation at the Italian front, see annotation 25. At the end of March 1918, Amiens was threatened by Operation Michael as part of the German Spring Offensive.

There was a Mrs. [Violet] Gray at the Embassy, Mr. and Mrs. Crosby, Cravath, Fred Sterling and I. We stayed afterward until I had just time to get to the Ritz for my appointment.

Horodyski had a number of things on his mind and took them up one at a time and talked them out.

First he was much distressed because Stovall had been allowed to return to Switzerland. Said that Hugh Wilson had bucked up the whole place during the absence of the Minister but that as soon as he came back the Legation had lapsed into the old rut. He says that the Minister has no connections, no views on big matters and that generally everything is going to pieces. Horodyski says there must be a change and that we should either leave Hugh there as Chargé with an adequate staff to handle the situation, or appoint Vernon Kellogg as Minister. That K. has a great deal of prestige from his work in Belgium, he knows the German minds and the German official from dealing with them and that he could do a great work; he made the reservation that while this was the thing to do now it might no longer be the right solution six months from now.

Having disposed of this he [Horodyski] went on to the case of Professor Herron who lives in Geneva and gives out the impression that he is the personal representative of the President. He apparently seeks no camouflage but on the contrary advertises extensively and has everybody watching him. H. thinks he is a bad lot and ought to be suppressed. Thinks he has been in conversation with the Austrians and Bulgarians with a view to finding out their peace terms. (Frazier told me in the morning that Horodyski had favored having Col. House go to Switzerland and enter into conversations with Czernin; that he, Frazier, had also favored it for a time but had come to the conclusion which seems rather obvious, that a thing of that sort could not be kept secret and that there would be a bad mess if it were discovered; that if there were to be discussions looking to dislocating the alliance of the Central Powers it must be done thru somebody less en vue than the Colonel)

Horodyski said he was going to Switzerland to try to meet Pacelli, the Papal Nuncio at Munich who has just been to Rome and is not on his way back. Horodyski wanted to go to Rome to see him there and endeavor to find what he was driving at. He fears that it will be next to impossible in Switzerland as there will be too many spies about to make conversation very safe.

That brought him to the question of getting propaganda done for us by the Vatican. The German and Austrian representatives at the Vatican are sitting up in Switzerland and communicating thru their diplomatic bags which pass uncensored. The Vatican, according to this good Catholic, is merely a big business concern and the Boches have played the game according to the rules, spending huge sums in masses and generally making themselves good customers. Each of the

Cardinals has the distribution of certain funds, foundations, incomes, etc., and in this way the money gets percolated down thru a large body of Chanoines,[34] and other clergy who naturally have an interest in seeing the good work keep on. So far the Boches have had the monopoly of this sort of thing and H. thinks we ought to get to work and try to corner a little business for ourselves. If this were done for a little time and it was made clear that the United States was important to the Church he believes it might be possible to stir the Pope out of his neutrality (for he believes that he is not pro-Boche) and get him to send a few blasts into Germany. It would undoubtedly have an enormous effect if he could be prevailed upon to do this but whether it could be arranged in this way remains to be seen.

It seems the Allied cause is very poorly represented at the Vatican. De Salis, who is the British representative, is stupid and without influence. Carton de Wiart is the Belgian and has apparently harped so much upon the sorrows of his unhappy country that everyone flees when they see him coming, – so he is less than no help at all. None of the other allies is represented at this time. The Boches have their men in Switzerland, very active and with freedom of communication. The late Spanish representative was intensely pro-Boche, but H. did not know about the new man. Being something of a misanthrope he was inclined to believe on general principles that this one is also a bad egg.

This all led down to the idea that the United States should be represented in some form at the Vatican. That we should pick out some impressive gentleman, preferably not a Catholic, who would give an idea of culture and friendliness but at the same time have a lot of force, – an easy man to find. He need not be regularly accredited but could be sent to settle some pending matter and allowed to remain for an indefinite time.

He [Horodyski] says it would take someone that can be persevering without irritation for the Pope is somewhat slow and stupid and yet wants to keep things in his own hands and is ambitious to do big things; that it is this quality that the Germans have played upon. He was Under-Secretary of State under Rampolla when Leo XIII was on the throne. When Pius IX succeeded him the Under-Secretary remained in office for a short time and was then removed from office by his chief [Rafael] Merry del Val, who rather bluntly told him that he was too stupid to keep the place. That of course has not endeared Merry del Val to the Pope and he is now much out of things. As he holds to many of his old perquisites and is still Director of the Church of St. Peter, he wields a good deal of influence with a part

---

34 During the First World War, Germany and the Central Powers gave significant financial assistance to the nearly bankrupt Vatican state, securing them a certain amount of influence. Chanoines are catholic clergymen sudued to ecclesiastical rule.

of the clergy and is well-informed as to what is going on, so that he is a valuable man to cultivate, – and he may someday come back to power.

After exhausting himself on that subject Horodyski turned to the best and biggest suggestion, not new but vital, – that we establish somewhere on this side of the water a Supreme War Council[35] for Diplomatic and Political questions. Now all matters have to be referred to London, Paris, Rome, Washington, Tokyo, Havre, Corfu, Lisbon and the Lord knows where else and the interchanges of views waste a shameful amount of time, so that when a decision that would have been right is eventually taken it is no longer suited to changed conditions. Horodyski is for having each of the nations concerned, at least the more important of them, establish a representative at Versailles just as has been done for the Supreme War Council, a man with nothing to do but decide questions in constant discussion with the people on the ground. Each should have subordinates who could take care of the paper work and relieve them of all but the job of <u>thinking</u>: His first choice would be Hoover; his second Polk, and this third Hoover [sic]. He wanted to sit right down and begin cabling about it. He thinks that the British would be opposed to it at first. I am sure that everybody would be opposed to it at first and from that time on until after some years more of war we are driven into it as we were driven into the Supreme War Council.

Horodyski feels that our representative on such a board should spend a great part of his time on flying visits to the United States so as to keep in touch and keep the Government posted as to changing conditions. It is doubtless the way to do it but again there would seem to be little chance of getting it done that way. Horodyski says that during the next four to six weeks he thinks I will have great influence on Washington, that after eight weeks they will pay little to no attention to me and that at the end of three months he will not want to bother with me unless I have proved my intelligence by starting for home. He evidently exaggerates the importance of my mission but no words of mine can convince him that I am not the GREAT WHITE HOPE.

From seeing him I went to the Vendôme[36] to call on Mrs. Whitehouse. On the way [I] ran into Mrs. John Ridgely [Alice] Carter who promptly asked me to lunch tomorrow. Mrs. Whitehouse was busy "conferring with Kerney" as per George's [Creel] instructions but turned her guns on me. She is very intelligent but not in a big way and is chiefly interested in the minutiae of her job. She has evidently had her head somewhat turned by her success in the suffrage campaign and is

---

35 The Supreme War Council was the central command of the Allied forces, founded 1917.
36 Place de Vendôme is one of five royal squares in the heart of Paris. Several of the hotels and boulevards that feature prominently in Gibson's narrative are located nearby.

inclined to be intolerant and overbearing. She had evidently decided in advance to see whether she could put me in my place and set me to work under her orders. As soon as we got settled she told me that COMPUB [Committee on Public Information] had sent her a tremendous number of films for exhibition over here and that the titles were in very poor French; that somebody had to sit down and go thru them on the screen, cutting out the films that were not suitable and write fresh titles for those that were chosen. I did not grasp the point until she turned a beady eye on me and announced that would be my job. I laughed in her face whereupon she grew slightly snippy and inquired in a peremptory way what I was going to do. I declined to get excited and went on laughing at her and refusing to take her seriously until she abandoned the matter. It was a raw play but doesn't matter. We are to lunch with Kerney on Thursday and talk over things in general with a view to seeing whether we can prepare some telegrams to put Creel on the right track.

While I was there Joe Green telephoned that Teddy Curtis had arrived for a few hours and would be at his office at six. I went over and had a few minutes talk with him. He is looking fit as a fiddle and seems to be happy. He is doing intelligence work at Évian-les-Bains and I may manage to see him when I go to Switzerland.

Image 7: Rodrigo de Saavedra y Vincent Villalobar, as Spanish Ambassador to Belgium, joined Gibson on many missions for the neutral countries during the early war years (1914–1916), inscribed by hand for Hugh Gibson. (Courtesy of the Gibson Family)

He says that Villalobar is on the British suspect list as "*tout-ce-qu'il-y-a-de-plus-Boche*" [all there is of more German] and that there are serious reflections upon his morality.

Green walked home with me to the hotel and after I had dressed for dinner went with me as far as the Hôtel de France et Choiseul[37] where I went to gather up Mrs. Linn. He is going to be transferred to intelligence work with Major Harjes and expects to be happier there than he has been under Nolan.

Took Mrs. Linn to Mlle Thompson's at 134 rue de Grenelle. There were just the three of us for dinner in what is really a beautiful flat. There was a good deal of talk about œuvres of various sorts and the jealousies that they all suffer from. The Red Cross is evidently on a monopolistic rampage trying to standardize all charitable effort in France as though they were building Ford cars. They have notified Mlle T. that her work will be taken over and that all matters affecting children will be handled by them. She is up in arms and unless I miss my guess she will not come out second best.

She was also interesting about the first days of the war and the flight of the Govt. to Bordeaux. Told of going to lunch with Viviani one of the days that things looked rather bad and having him maunder tearfully: "Après une guerre affreuse nous aurons une paix boiteuse" and a lot more of the same sort of cheering stuff. After lunch he hastened off and made a splendid speech beginning: "Mes chers concitoyens, jamais notre situation n'a été meilleure, etc."

No cabs to be had so we walked home thru the pitch black streets. I am for an electric torch if I have to do much of this sort of thing.

As Joe Green and I were walking back to the Meurice the last shell of the day from the big gun fell not very far away and exploded with a considerable bang. Nobody seemed particularly interested although a number of people came to the doors of their shops to see whether it had landed anywhere near enough for them to have a look.

Log   Paris. April 3, 1918

Spent a good part of this morning about town with Warrington Dawson burning maps and other necessaries for our work.

Lunched with the d'Ursels, Avenue Élisée Reclus e. Lambert, Military Attaché of the Belgian Legation and one of the Secretaries were also there as well as Mme d'Ursel and two daughters. After lunch two more came in.

---

37 Luxury hotel (formerly known as Hôtel de Crozat) built in in 1704 at 241 rue de St. Honoré. Frequent meeting point of Gibson and his associates.

They were all a good deal upset by the death in the Saint Gervais disaster of the 16 year old daughter of the Belgian Consul-General. After a long search he found her body in the Morgue and was able to identify it was only by her teeth, – she was so frightfully mutilated. All the Legation was going this afternoon to the funeral of the Counselor of the Swiss Legation and his wife.[38]

A telegram from Irwin yesterday to say that while the United States does not wish to be represented on the Inter-Allied Propaganda Council, it is desired that I sit on the body "informally", – meaning I supposed that I shall cross my legs and smoke a pipe. I am holding it up and debating whether it will be worthwhile to try to explain the situation to them and make it clear that we should either be fully represented or keep out. Most of the work will be done in committees, the chief object is an exchange of ideas and there is no earthly reason why we should not be represented, – aside from our unfailing timidity about getting mixed up in things. I am not at all keen about being the representative but should prefer to have Dawson designation for that honorable position.

It looks very much as though the German idea was to make alternate thrusts at Amiens and Paris (thru Compiègne) which they can do very easily on their interior lines. At each of these changes of objective the Allies would have to move troops and lose some of their force. They may not be more than a coincidence but it certain has seemed to be the idea so far.

There seems to be a good deal of apprehension about the attitude of labor just now. A lot of the workmen who are being combed out of the munitions factories are displaying a strong resentment against being sent into action, and this taken with the labor demonstrations which are scheduled for the first of May, may bring us some excitement. Fabry remarks, apparently as a result of what he has heard in the inner circle, that the revolutions is coming but will not be, probably, until after the war. If the French win it will be in a row among the leaders over the spoils. If the French lose it will be in a bicker about who is to blame. This is an easy and free-hand way of diagnosing a complicated situation but there may be something in it. There is no doubt that a lot of people who have been very guerriers [sic] until this time are now anxiously looking for a termination of the present battle which would give France an honorable opportunity for peace.

Topping came in to see me at 6:30 and told me some items of interest. Czernin announced before the Austrian parliament in the most solemn manner that before this offensive Clemenceau had made him offers of peace. In answer to questions from the press C. said that this was a complete lie. But when the press tried to send this out in cable despatches the censorship killed them. Apparently it is felt that it

---

38 See annotation 31.

will take more than this denial to kill the story. What it all means is hard to tell from this.

Topping said that Whitlock was furious about my book; that he read every installment of it in LAND AND WATER[39] and spoke his mind freely about it. He also spoke his rage that his name did not figure more prominently. But Topping remarked that if I had gone ahead and told his part of the story he would have been still more enraged, – the very consideration that kept me from doing it. When the manuscript of Whitlock's book was sent to Polk, Whitlock wrote him that he did not care who passed on it but that under no consideration did he wish me to see it. Quite like him.

It also seems that after I left Whitlock, not content with the dirty trick he put over on me, wrote at length to the Department trying to do me as much harm as possible. It seems that although Mrs. [Ella] Whitlock was for some reason quite as bitter against me as he was she prevailed upon him to tone down some of the more vicious statements, probably because she saw that they would defeat his ends. Although I have never been able to understand why he felt any resentment against me his efforts to get me out of Belgium are comprehensible, though not on any ground creditable to him. But after I got out he had no reason for wishing to harm me and his effort to do so shows a streak of meanness which I did not think he had. I always thought that he was actuated merely by weakness and a desire to follow the line of least resistance. I did not think he was that vindictive.

Dined with Mrs. Linn at the France et Choiseul. The other guests were M. and Mme Leverier, Mme. Vermeren, Mr. and Mrs. Roy McWilliams, Pierce of the Red Cross and Danielson and Mlle. Thompson.

McWilliams said he had met the Ambassador [Sharp] today for the first time. After learning that he had not been long in the service he remarked in a kindly and helpful way: "It isn't hard. All you have to do is remember to be polite."

Log   Paris, April 4, 1918

A quiet day at the chancery enjoying rain.

Lunched with Caffery at the Cercle de l'Union. He had also Mme. Andrews, Dawson and Frazier. The Norweb's were slated to come but evidently got lost on the way and did not put in an appearance.

---

39 *Land and Water* was a British magazine known for its commentary on the war and its aftermath, edited by Hilarie Belloc.

Had a talk with Frazier about a lot of things and among others learned that Herron had some sort of mandate to converse with the Austrians. Frazier was inclined to believe that it was a mistake to have commissioned him to do things. I know it was.

A letter from Menocal to say that he had fixed Warren Wood with a commission as ensign. I got off a note to Aunt Leona to tell her so.

Dined with Eliot Wadsworth at the Castiglione. He left for Italy on the eight o'clock train so we had a hasty meal together and a little conversation. Preston was also there and was frank enough about our diplomatic representatives. Cussed the chief here and Minister in Bern.

James Hazen Hyde sent me one of those invitations that scatter like shot from a gun, would I dine on Thursday, Friday, Saturday or Sunday or lunch on one of the last two days? Result I have accepted for Saturday night. Fred [Palmer] says he wants to give me an earful about the situation and plead to have Col. House come over. He wants him to come to stay and settle things here in conference with representatives of other countries. It is the obvious thing to do but I don't see any great prospect of its being done.

A letter from Frank Gunther asking me to go over and be his best man at the wedding. I would give a lot to stand up with him thru the ordeal but fear it can't be arranged and have written to tell him so.

Had planned to get off long letters to Creel, Irwin, Polk, Phillips and Phil but the matters about which I must write require too much consideration for slap dash treatment. I don't want to risk doing anybody an injustice thru hasty work and yet I don't want to lean too much the other way and whitewash where it should not be done. All this stuff will have to go by the next bag.

A telegram from Hugh Wilson asking me to go and stop him at Territet where he is having ten days leave.

Mrs. Whitehouse is going home. She wavered about whether she should go or return to Switzerland but apparently she wants to go home and tear a few people to tatters. She is fiercely vindictive about Hugh Wilson and I should not be surprised if she tried to make trouble for him on general principles.

Log   Paris. April 5, 1918

Several callers this morning including Edith Wills and Wellington. Edith is going to the hospital on Tuesday for an operation and I am to dine with them on Monday. She has become so accustomed to being operated on that doesn't seem to bother her in the least.

Wellington has been engaged for the past six months on reconstruction work and the offensive has wiped out everything he has done and left him up a tree. He is casting about for some sort of job in the army and came for advice as to whether he should go with Major Harjes where he had a chance or with Major Campanole who had made overtures to him. I suggested that he look over what C. had to offer before making up his mind.

Frazier was to have lunched with me but telephoned that he wanted me to lunch with him and ask no questions. As I found out at lunch time the reason was that Arthur Orr had turned up and was coming with us. We had a chatty lunch at Voisin's and then I dropped Frazier at General Pershing's H.Q. where there was a big pow-wow going on with the Secretary.

Frazier is enthusiastic about [Tasker] Bliss. Says that he has the scientific mind to a very high degree and is able to eliminate every consideration save those that should be included and that when he has focused his mind the view is accurate. Also he said that Pershing was largely responsible for the choice of Foch as Commander-in-Chief. Bliss he says is a pessimist – in the right sense – but that he has estimated that we can land 1,800,000 men in France during the year 1918: That of course means cutting down our efforts in the air and concentrating on men.

Dawson had a long talk with Joffre this morning. Here is a résumé of it:

"Our counter-intelligence is beginning today, with General Demeny's Army. We have between 25 and 30 reserve divisions still on their way to support the movement. But we are compelled to support the English to an extent which weakens our own position for a counter-offensive. We have already replaced the English Fifth Army, which was the one to yield before the German attack, and which is the one referred to in the German communiqués about disorder and disorganization in the British troops.

The situation is certainly serious, while perhaps not being grave. If the battle ends quickly, it will be because we lose it. If we are to win it must last two or three months at least. We have done something by stopping the Germans: but they advanced to a depth of 60 kilometers; and to weaken their positions and strengthen our own, we must win a positive victory. Otherwise the moral balance will remain in Germany's favor, even though she goes no further.

Germany's effort is now concentrated upon Amiens. Her plan is plain. She means to destroy the British army. She will not succeed in doing that, though she may take Amiens and do much damage.

The French communiqués are absolutely deceitful. The German communiqués are telling more truth. At the moment when Clemenceau was expressing his complete confidence at the Chamber, he was staggered by the news which had reached him and the gravity of the situation of which he was well aware. If our civilian moral is as good as it is today, the fact must be attributed to ignorance of the true state of affairs. We hear today of partial successes or the holding of our lines yesterday. The truth is that the Germans advanced yesterday three kilometers nearer to Amiens. They have now attained the outskirts of the village of Villers-Bretonneux, though the English, at last reports, still held within the village. The Germans also being northwest of Moreuil, they are now within 15 K. of Amiens, and occupying heights which allow them to see perfectly the town, the Cathedral, and all the positions around. We are cut off from the main RR [railroad] line to Amiens via Breteiul and St. Just. To reach Abbeville we must go round by Beauvais, which means serious loss of time and complications in our transport.[40]

Clemenceau's responsibilities in this entire situation are very heavy.

The Versailles Conference had decided upon the principle of mobile reserve divisions to remain at the disposal of the Allies in the event of a German attack. Its opinion was also converging towards an inter-allied Commander-in-Chief. But Clemenceau wants to manage the war himself; he wants no rival authority either among the allies or in the army itself.

He went to England at the same time as Foch and Weygand and the Italians for the conference about the interallied commander and the mobile reserves. Clemenceau resolutely fought both principles in the name of France. General Foch protested against his attitude, but Clemenceau over-rode his objections. Foch then demanded that his protest be put on record in the minutes of the meeting. The conference broke up without any measures being taken for either the command or the reserves, and it was by Clemenceau's personal fault.

They came back to France. A few days later the Germans attacked and found us unprepared without a command and without mobile reserves. We came within a hairsbreadth of utter ruin. All that more or less saved us was Clemenceau's sudden reversal of his policy, and his sudden assent to a species of interallied command and the hasty improvisation of a mobile reserve army.

Done some days ago this helped to save us from ruin. Done some weeks ago it might have brought us to victory, and certainly would have rendered it impossible for the Germans to have advanced over sixty kilometers of our ground and hold it. But even now the solution reached is only a patched-up solutions: FOCH HAS NO REAL AUTHORITY. HE IS MERELY A COORDINATING OFFICER SINCE PÉTAIN REMAINS GENERALISSIMO OF THE FRENCH AND HAIG OF THE ENGLISH.

Clemenceau is trying to cast blame on the English, alleging that they opposed the inter-allied command and the organization of mobile reserve divisions. This is absolutely false. I know the entire story from several officers who were present at the meeting in London and have given me full details. I have told the truth to President Poincaré, who had been informed by Clemenceau that it was the fault of

---

40 On April 5, 1918, the Germans had occupied Le Hamel (about 15 miles east of Amiens) and even tried to launch an attack to the line of the Avre River in the city's vicinity.

the English. I don't know whether the President has got the truth from anyone else, but he got it from me. However, the President is not a man of much courage or initiative, he is entirely under the influence of Clemenceau, who is a strong man – indeed the only strong man in the government.

There is much talk of Austria going to pieces and being tired of the war. But the fact remains that she is still fighting, and there are at the present moment 113 Austrian batteries cooperating in the battle. I do not, however, consider them capable of attempting a big offensive against Italy without the assistance of Germany.

The hope for the future continues to rest exclusively with America. France, England, Germany are all exhausted while able to still fight on and hold on. American alone is fresh and able to make a gigantic new effort. General Pershing's action in putting his army at the disposal of the Allies was very fine. Those two divisions – for he has only two divisions ready for actual fighting – may not accomplish much militarily, but the encouragement for us and the stimulation for America are of the utmost importance.

There are only two things America can do for the present – hurry on the sending of troops and intensify their training. She is doing both, so we have every reason to be content. At the start much valuable time was lost because there was not a sufficient proportion of French instructors for the American army. It was largely our own fault; the attitude of many of the officers was to wish to absorb the American army into the French army, and so French officers, instead of seeking to help on the American army, tried to substitute themselves for American officers. The United States had the feeling that their army must remain the American army, and this was a very popular feeling. Now there is a better understanding and I personally am glad that the American divisions at the front are under the command of American generals keeping in close contact with the French and profiting by any teachings which experience allows the French to give.

A telephone message from GHQ this morning says that Bolling, Bill Phillips' brother-in-law, is missing. He disappeared last Friday in Amiens while the town was being bombed and has not since been seen.

Dined alone at the Meurice after a visit from Joe Green and am ready for an early to bed so that, as Ned Bell says, I shall be strong and can get up and go to work for my country in the morning.

Log   Paris. April 6, 1918

Mrs. Whitehouse got off this morning for Bordeaux en route to the U.S. As soon as she had shoved off along came a telegram from Creel asking her to stay here and do special work with Kerney. We have telephoned and telegraphed to Bordeaux to try to head her off and bring her back but I fear she is set on going home and getting the scalps of some of our friends in Bern.

Kerney came in with Merriam who is going to Rome for Creel. He has no interest in getting material for his work but has set his teeth and thinks of nothing but getting down to Rome. Just as we had about got him convinced that he ought to stay a few days and learn his business along came a telegram from Mr. Page in Rome asking when Gibson and Merriam could be expected – and adding that they were both needed urgently. So now the gentleman plans to get off on Monday.

George Rothwell Brown turned up this morning to my disgust but I cannot say to my surprise. He should never have been allowed to cross the ocean but COMPUB apparently is unable to refuse the people who should be refused.

Lunched with the [Robert] Blisses. They had M. de Crozier, former French Ambassador in Vienna and several other people who were not particularly thrilling.

From there went back to the hotel, put on my wedding garments and was picked up by Bliss and Frazier to go to the Hôtel de Ville [town hall][41] for the ceremony of our first anniversary in the war. The Ambassador [Sharp], Secretary Baker, General Bliss and all others in authority were there for us. Pichon, a few Generals and the municipal authorities represented the French. We select souls were ushered into a small room where we looked each other over for some twenty minutes before being turned in with the proletariat. The Ambassador presented me to Pichon thus: "Mr. Minister this is Mr. Gibson connected with my Embassy." And then turning to me "Mr. Pichon, you know, is the French Minister for Foreign Affairs."

Then we were formed in procession, I with Gen. Bliss, and ambled out into one of the state apartments where the crowd was gathered. Each of the councilmen in turn delivered himself of a speech and then the Ambassador read a few words in English. Then much champagne and some toasts which I could not hear. I was impressed to serve the Secretary as interpreter as Mott had run away and got lost at the critical moment. And then Bliss, Frazier and I ran off and left them to the mercy of the mob.

There was only a small crowd outside the Hôtel de Ville for there was some fear lest a large crowd gather and then the Hun chucked in a shell from the big gum.

Kerney is responsible for a few good ones in course of the past day or two. Yesterday he remarked: "There's a lot of difference between Trenton and Paris – and you notice it here more than you do in Trenton."

---

41 Located at Rue de Rivoli, site of several receptions and meetings described by Gibson.

In talking of the President and the chances of reconciling him with Col. George Harvey, he said: "The President is warm-hearted. That is he's steam heated, but warm-hearted."

Dined with James Hazen Hyde at his house in the rue Barbet de Jouy, a splendid old place which was built when they weren't worrying about the price per front foot. Mrs. Hyde's father, Mr. Leishman, was there and also a young British Lt., formerly Hyde's private secretary – sporting the name of Broderick. After dinner we sat around the fire and drank coffee with real sugar in it and discussed all sorts of things.

Hyde is deeply interested in propaganda matters and has some good ideas. He has of course valuable connections in France and can be of great help. On Wednesday he is giving a big luncheon for a sort of convention of high-school teachers and I am bid to go and tell them all about our plans for keeping our cause before France. That may be difficult inasmuch as I have not yet been able to discover any plans.

Log   Paris. April 7, 1918

About fairly early this morning and took the 10:30 train from the Invalides for Versailles in company of Dawson.

We ran into Col. Picard as we got out of the train and stopped to talk with him until the guards began slamming the doors of his train. He is much interested in getting a lot of American officers to go to St. Cyr (of which he is Commandant) not for the ordinary course of instruction but to browse around and pick up what may seem of most interest to them. He thinks we are spending too much time and effort trying to teach the officer the work of the common soldier. While the officer should know about everything his soldiers have to do there is no need for him to excel in each and every one of them. If an officer could do everything, such as trench digging, grenade throwing, bayonet work, etc., better than his men, he would no longer be an officer – "*ce serait un ange*" [he would be an angel]. He wants to devote greater attention to intelligence, initiative, ability to think and lead under stress of danger and difficulty. He says that knowledge of the detail work of soldiering will not help an officer in battle but that all the men instinctively turn to him for guidance and gauge the posture of affairs and their own action by what they can read in the face of their immediate superior, – and this is more true today than it has ever been before. All this seems pretty clear but nobody else seems to be working along those lines.

We stopped at the Prefecture and had a talk with the Prefect. Picard seemed frankly worried about the turn of affairs in the region of Compiègne, as the Boches seem to be making a push in that direction. He said that large number of troop trains had been pouring thru toward the front, British and French troops coming back from Italy and a large number of American troops "from an unknown point". He took courage in the thought that these were from one of our bases, thus adding to the total number of fighting troops in France. I thought it more likely that they were our troops from the front being brought around this way in order to avoid congesting the lines nearer the front, but refrained from saying so in order that he might keep the small comfort he had gleaned from his imaginings. He had the lists of trains on his desk and shuffled them about as though movement would help win the battle.

From there to Mrs. Huntington's where we stayed to lunch. She has a charming old flat over-looking the Neptune Fountain. She is now 78 but quick and responsive as 30. The Baron de Menenval, who was French Minister to Belgrade in the time of Milan, the Countess de Saint Cermen and her mother were there for lunch and conversation never slackened.

Came back to town on the 4:50 and I had time to digest the papers before Clarence Gagnon came along to dine with me. He is bitter against England about the way Canada has been treated and has developed into a regular Sinn Feiner[42]. The best thing he said was about the retreat of the Fifth Army: "Only the Irish were killed, only the Scotch were wounded and only the English were missing."

Paris. April 8, 1918:

Lunched today with Kerney at his flat in the rue La Pérouse. He had Joe Green and Pierce of the Red Cross. We talked propaganda in various forms but did not get anywhere in particular. While we were at lunch James Hazen Hyde called me up to say that George Leygues, Minister of the Marine and former Chairman of the Committee on Foreign Affairs of the Chamber, was anxious to see me and would telephone me. He wanted to urge me to accede to the request – as though I would refuse a properly humble cabinet Minister.

It was settled that on Wed. I am to speak on behalf of our propaganda effort to the Rectors of the French Universities who are to gather at lunch as guests of Hyde. I prepared some brief remarks which Dawson is putting into French for me so that I may be more sure of myself.

---

42 Member of the Irish republican party, Sinn Fein, which demanded independence for the British part of Northern Ireland and its reunion with the Republic of Ireland in the South.

Dined with Davis and Edith Wills at the Hôtel Vernet. Also saw Mrs. Wellington and Mrs. McDougall who are staying there. Major Moreno came in after dinner and I walked down town with him. He was interested in the affair of Mrs. Carpenter and asked for information. I told him that it had all been in the hands of Military Attaché but he snorted. He complained mildly that there was not the cooperation that there should be between Embassy and the Gen. Staff – the fault lying with the Embassy.

Paris. April 9, 1918:

Nothing very astonishing going on but had an interesting day. The Germans seem to have made some advances which do not seem to have occasioned much alarm but which help to widen their salient in a most useful way.

Dined at the Castiglione with Preston and Major Perkins who is in charge of the Red Cross. We got together in our feeling about the need for shutting down on propaganda, particularly on rubbing in on the French all that has been done for them. He is having a rather bad time with [Henry] Davison and Poison Ivy Lee who want to make publicity material out of every little service we render. His idea is quite properly that the service itself does the propaganda and doesn't need any pointing out. In deference to Lee's desire to get publicity material he was taken up to Compiègne the other day while the stragglers and refugees were pouring through the town. Just as they arrived, some Hun planes began dropping bombs and Ivy disappeared. He was found after a time in the cellar and when he was dragged out he announced that he was off for Paris as there was no STORY to be found there. Perkins was overwhelmed with the STORY to be seen on every side but Ivy couldn't see it while the bombs were falling.

Perkins is anxious to meet Irwin Cobb and I have promised to round them up for dinner together.

Mabel Boardman is coming over for a visit and all the R.C.s are cussing.

Lunched with Kerney, Franck (the tramp) and Dawson at K's flat. Lots of talk but we didn't get anywhere.

Log   Paris. WEDNESDAY, APRIL 10, 1918: MOTHER'S BIRTHDAY

Got up this morning feeling like the end of a misspent life and found little to do at the Embassy.

Lunched at the American University Union as the guest of Hyde who had all the Rectors of the French universities and a few American guests. Hyde spoke briefly and introduced Stokes of Yale who made a rather lengthy speech in comic French which was well received because he had something to say. Then Lucien Poincaré, Rector of the University of Paris, made a few remarks in a very gracious way and then I was offered as a sacrifice. The idea was cordially received and all hands promised to do their best to help. The first party will start sometime next week.

Found Bliss as we came out and we took a taxi back to the Embassy together to talk over odds and ends.

When I got back to the chancery I was called on telephone by Capt. Watson who said Major McCabe was on his way up to talk to me and that in the meantime they wanted me to be thinking over the question of accepting a commission in the army to do intelligence work. I said I would think in over but I doubt whether it will go any further than that.

Mrs. Whitehouse came back to town last night and left again for Bordeaux this morning. She sent a hot telegram to Creel laying down the law about the conditions under which she would consent to return to Switzerland, namely that the Legation should be made to behave itself, should rent offices for her and that she should have a diplomatic passport. She plans to return the first of May if Creel capitulates on all points.

Dined at Voisin's with Frazier, Hyde and the Counselor of the Italian Embassy. He is a creature of Orlando, not much fancied by Sonnino, but full of ideas and gossip. It made interesting talk and I found that Count Cigogna was a great friend of his: he was immediately pleased by my story of how Cigogna behaved about the passport. Also knows Heineman very well and trusts him.

Log   Paris. Thursday, April 11, 1918

A day of strenuous work, so strenuous that I clean forgot about lunch and did not budge out of the chancery until after three in the afternoon.

Spent most of the day writing a long letter to Phil [Patchin] telling him all about everything that has happened or is likely to happen during the rest of the war. I thought this was easier than writing a lot of separate letters to Polk and Phillips and Creel and Will Irwin; for in this way I could write in a more free and easy way and let Phil do the diplomatic part of the work by imparting the information.

A most interesting letter from Norval Richardson about the work they are doing at the Embassy in Rome to make our point of view clear to the Italians. They seem to have got good results with the funds at their disposal and want me to go down and give them more money. I haven't any money to give them but can make generous representations in Washington which may be as good as money.

Went down to the Press Division at the Hôtel Ste. Anne a little after three and had a short yarn with Major McCabe. He broached the subject of my giving up the diplomatic service and accepting a commission in the army to do intelligence work. I told him that if I could render more service in that way I would do anything that seemed best but that so far as I could see I would be of greater use to the army if I remained a civilian, footloose and able to do things that could not be done by a soldier. I said I would work just as enthusiastically for them as if I were in uniform and that seemed to reassure him somewhat. He said he would bring the question up again later. I did not raise the question of the rank they were prepared to give me.

I did some errands after leaving there and then dropped in at the Café de la Paix and absent-mindedly asked for a sandwich. At first the waiter seemed disposed to throw me out be evidently decided that I was only an ignorant foreigner and not to be done violence. He told me gently that ONE did not eat at that hour of the day and that the only place food could be served was in the railway station. S. I lunched on a glass of beer and a cigarette.

Thence back to the hotel after a stroll up and down the rue de Rivoli.[43] I stopped in a Galignani's and found a handsome pile of the greatest work on the war, both American and English editions. The clerk told me that they had just sent down to Chaumont 55 copies that had been ordered for the library of the General Staff. I should like to think that it was considered necessary to the winning of the war to have every officer read it but fear it was no more closely traceable to the fact that Exton has something to do with the ordering and let his enthusiasm boost the size of the order.

Soon after I got back to the hotel one of the shells from the big gun burst near enough to make the windows rattle and the echoes rolled along for an astonishing time. I sat tight as I did not suppose it was near enough to be seen but when Joe Green came along to take me out for dinner he told me that the row had taken place just across the street in the Tuillerier [Tuillerie] Gardens. Old Brother Boche is getting near enough to be uncomfortable.

We went to the Escargot where we had a good dinner despite the fact that the place was filled with foreigners like ourselves. Then on to the Casino de Paris where we saw a rotten show, leaving before it was finished.

And so, as Mr. Pepys[44] used to say, so home to bed.

---

43 One of the main streets in Paris with the townhall, the Hôtel Meurice, the Louvre, some churches and exclusive restaurants nearby. Gibson and his associates would therefore pass it almost daily.
44 Samuel Pepys (1633–1703) was a British administrator most famous for the diary he kept.

Log   Paris. Friday, April 12, 1918

At a little after eight the Boche began chucking shells into the neighborhood but I had a fit of laziness and did not budge from my bed until after nine.

Before I had finished reading my morning mail at the Embassy Kerney came in with Frederick Palmer for a yarn and they were shortly followed by Majors McCabe and MacGruder and Lt. Franck. We had a long talk about how the army and the COMPUB crowd could be of service to each other but did not get very far. We did agree that there should be some speeding up of the taking of movies of fighting and horrors to be fed to European countries and that there should be another sort of pictures to be sent to America.

Kerney is a good citizen but he is not a self-starter and does not like to get down to brass tacks. That is going to be the greatest trouble about getting things done here. I shall simply have to keep after him until we do get things started, but he is more inclined to go about on joy rides than to stay here and get his office organized.

At one I went down to General Foulois' office and took him and Arthur [Page] out to lunch at the Plaza Athénée. They left immediately afterward for Tours. While we were at lunch Mr. Thackara, the Consul-General, came along and I met him for the first time.

Kerney and Palmer came to my office at three and we set out to find Lt. Tonnelat who has charge of airplane propaganda in enemy countries. He was not known at the Maison de la Presse or at the Foreign Office so we dumped Kerney overboard in the rue Ste. Anne and came back to the chancery where Palmer and I had another TALK. He is strong for limiting our activities in the way of propaganda to Germany to sending the right sort of people to camp in Switzerland as businessmen or in any other capacity save that of correspondents and get in touch with German liberal elements. He is going to suggest that Gen. Pershing send in a recommendation along that line.

He [Palmer] told me that when Pershing went to see Foch to offer our troops he had made his little statement in French which was quite an achievement for him – and doubtless added a lot to its effect. He also said that the British are still giving ground and that the situation looks sick.

C. Lyon Chandler turned up here yesterday on his way to Bern as Vice Consul. Wot next [sic]?

Sent a telegram to Rome to say that I had no money for them but would make appropriate recommendations to Washington – and wished them well. Also a telegram to Will Irwin to say that Rome should have an adequate sum to spend at this critical time and that I would make a full report after my visit there next week.

Bliss knew where Tonnelat was to be found and made an engagement for Kerney and me to see him tomorrow morning.

Dined at Hyde's where there was a real party – Kerney and Mary, Mordecai, Father Hemmick (in Red Cross uniform), Mlle. Thompson, Mrs. Lathrop and Mr. and Mrs. [James] Scott. Mlle Thompson was much intrigued by the idea that Father Hemmick was really a priest as he seemed too gay and human, – *et puis il avait deux jambes* [and on top of that, he had two legs].

At a little after ten the windows were rattled by some guns placed nearby and soon afterwards we heard the siren announcing the raid. Nobody seemed to be in the least interested in the idea of going into the cellar but Scott went out and brought in a taxi-driver who was waiting in the street. And then all hands settled down and went on visiting and playing the piano and otherwise acting in a way that would have been most discouraging and puzzling to the Hun.

Somebody sprung a good story about Gen. Summerall. It seems that he was wandering near the front lines and passed a sentry who failed to salute. Summerall went back and laid down the law to him about saluting all officers who pass, and wound up: "Of course I'm only a general and I don't care a hang, but someday a 2nd Lt. will come along and raise h— with you."

I also heard that I am credited with the remark to Pierce – who was also present – that I understood he was the trellis for Poison Ivy Lee. I didn't say it but I should like to have done so.

About eleven we decided that we could go out without being chased back in by the police so all of us set off on foot. People were peeking out of their windows all along our line of march and seemed more interested than frightened. When we got in front of the Chamber of Deputies we saw a big fire on the other side of the Louvre, flames that raged high in the air and then died down suddenly. I set out to see the show but found that it was quite a distance down the rue de Rivoli beyond the Meurice and yielded to sleepiness. For some hours there was row of fire engines and Red Cross Ambulances and the hotel porter said that a number of people had been killed and wounded.

It was not much of a raid but for some hours the search lights were hard at work trying to pick up any stray boches that might be lurking about.

Log   Paris. Saturday, April 13, 1918

The big gun served as an alarm clock this morning and I really got up. The shells fell for a little while at 20 minute intervals but I don't know where any of them fell.

At eleven Kerney and I went to a branch office of the Ministry of War (30 Ave. Marceau) to see Lt. Tonnelat who has charge of preparing material for trench propaganda. To my great delight I found that his assistant is Hansi [Waltz], the author of *Professor Knatschké*. He is a big solemn looking man of about forty two and gets a lot of quiet fun out of his job. Most of his work is quite serious but now and then he draws a cartoon to be chucked over into the Boche trenches and he has also got out one or two fake German newspapers filled with all sorts of jokes which do not seem to be properly appreciated on the other side of the lines. His fake ads seem to be most resented. One of them recommends the use of STINKO, the best substitute for butter, stove polish, shoe polish, soap and axle-grease. Another recommends a fine assortment of belts as the best substitute for bread, eggs, meat and milk. Still another offers the best SUBSITUTE FOR COFFEE SUBSTITUTE. There is also an ad asking for news of Prince Henry of Prussia who has not been heard from since August 4, 1914, – news to be sent to the Admiralty, Whitehall where a handsome reward will be paid.

We talked for an hour or two about the mechanical side of getting material across. Tonnelat says that he is opposed to the use of the trench mortars because the enemy immediately sets about reprisals on the particular sector of trench from which papers are thrown. He says that the very best means is the airplane but that so far he has been unable to get any machines assigned exclusively to this work. Aviators who go on bomb dropping expeditions are sometimes made to carry packages of literature but have little enthusiasm in the work and generally rid themselves of the whole supply as soon as they are out of sight, not caring much whether it falls on our side or in no man's land. There is not much enthusiasm over the use of balloons because it is hard to control them and when the wind is in the wrong direction there are sometimes weeks together when they are of no use. Some French machines have been picked up in Italy and any quantity of them have landed in Switzerland where they are worse than wasted. However they were interested in knowing that Major Lahm of our Signal Corps has a scheme that may be workable. Tonnelat is all for trying out all possible systems. He says the French balloons are really no good as the device for dropping the packages does not work well. He says the British device is better and may be adopted here. Another thing they are getting ready to try is a special shell to be fired from the 75s to a distance of two or three kilometers. The forward part of the shell is filled with tracts which are scattered by the explosion. The good point of this scheme is that an arrangement can be made to shoot off a large supply of material all along the front at the same time so that it will be out of the question for the enemy to undertake reprisals. Tonnelat has sent me a line of samples of what they send over and I shall send them to Washington for the information of Will Irwin. The French started out with reasoned articles telling all about the war from the French point of view but they soon came to the conclusion that this had little or no effect and now they concentrate largely on reprints of speeches and

Image 8: Henri Lambert was a friend of the Reyntiens family, and became also a friend of Gibson's. (Courtesy of the Gibson Family)

articles from German papers that are not allowed to reach the troops from the other side. There is a considerable mass of this material for some of the socialists are speaking freely and the [here a page appears to be missing from Gibson's original]

I also asked about the chances of getting material smuggled across the border into Germany from Switzerland. Tonnelat says they have a flock of Alsatians who do this as volunteers and that there is very little expense connected with the work. He thought we might be allowed to use their machinery for this.

He also brought up the subject of [Frank] Bohn and asks that he be warned not to put any letters in the Swiss post. Lt. Schule said Bohn had stayed at his hotel here and was very indiscreet. I shall sent a message to Bern asking them to warn him. Government is afraid to forbid publication in certain socialist papers. However they are able to prevent the papers getting to the front and the soldiers are kept in ignorance of some of the things the socialists are trying to get to them. If the troops can be convinced that these are authentic reprints they should have something to think about. Lunched with McFadden at Voisin's and settled some of the problems of the human race that we left the other night for lack of time.

At 3:30 the Ambassador [Sharp] summoned all the Secretaries to his office and had a mothers meeting. He held forth at length on the sloppy way people are failing to keep office hours and said that he would hereafter insist that all hands be in the chancery at 9:30 and remain there until six. The idea is O.K. but it was put in a very ominous way and His Excellency remarked to Fred [Sterling] alone that if any secretary failed to keep the hours he (H.E.) would ask for his recall. I suppose that inasmuch as I have a roving job and no chancery duties I am not included in this arrangement.

At four I had a conversation with Bliss and a Frenchman named Lambert who advances a proposal to set up a system of political information for us. It is the sort of information we need but I fear he has too complicated an idea of the sort of scheme that we are in a position to undertake. He wants to have six or seven people under his general direction to cover every field of activity and thought in France, not letting them know they are working for the Embassy and making himself the filter for their reports. I am not very much inclined to trust the whole show to any one individual for fear he would not give us the uncolored facts we want to get at. However Bliss and I are going to send a telegram to Polk asking for an appropriation to start some sort of system and once we get some money in our hands we can begin to worry about the details.

Kerney got into the hands of some enthusiasts who told him that the way to save France and make them love the United States was to distribute leaflets in the schools. He has some written and pictures made for them and has taken to call on Cardinal Amette and others high in authority who agreed to permit their distribution in various sorts of schools. It would require about six millions of them and the cost would be approximately thirty-seven thousand dollars. Irwin telegraphed me this morning to say that they would approve the scheme if I recommended it. I think it is piffle but don't like to begin turning down Kerney's ideas and have talked it over with him frankly. Shall try to send some telegrams on Monday that will let him out gracefully.

Also a telegram to say that Creel agrees that if I sit on the Inter-Allied Propaganda Conference it should be as a regular representative of the U.S. However the matter is being taken up with the President and we shall have a decision soon.

Clamor from Rome for moving pictures and we got some off to them this afternoon by courier.

The situation of the British army looks pretty bad to my expert eye. The Germans are advancing and the British seem to be giving ground without any particularly long stand anywhere. The French are throwing in so many troops to stiffen the British lines that there seems to be no hope of a counter-offensive on a large scale.

Dined with Mrs. Linn who had also invited Swan and Miss [Dorothy] Cane. After dinner we went to the Athenée where we saw a most amazing play LA DAME DE CHAMBRE which left nothing to the imagination and went full tilt into everything. I think all hands were a good deal embarrassed but there was nothing to do but see it thru and we stuck.

At dinner I ventured a prediction that the big gun would soon set to work bombarding us at night but it was not taken very seriously as a prophecy. But as I was climbing into bed one of the shell burst not very far away and four more came along at twenty minute intervals. Charming!

Last night's raid killed 26 and wounded something over 75.

Letter to Mary Gibson   April 14, 1918

... Thursday afternoon I stopped into a park you know on my way home and sat me down to read my papers. I had not got far when one of the big shells burst between four and five inches behind my right ear. As a matter of fact, it was several hundred yards away but it made enough row to seem nearer. Fortunately nobody was hurt and the police had a rather hard time keeping the crowd away from the hole in the ground. People have a mania for souvenirs and as the Govt. wants to examine the shells there is a scramble between the people and the police as to who shall have the pieces. Old Brother Boche keeps chucking in his shells with the greatest regularity but people don't seem much concerned and are amused at the accounts published in the German press of panic-stricken mobs fighting their way out of town and riots in the Place de l'Opéra to bully the Govt. into making peace and ending this reign of terror. I think it might be a different story if these big shells were dropping in German towns. Last night they began firing them after dark and we had five big fellow not far from my neighborhood. If the Boche had twenty of these guns, he might make life uncomfortable but with only one old blunderbuss, people don't bother much. ...

Friday night I dined at Hyde's and while we were there the alert was sounded. Not a soul budged from the drawing room except to make sure that the servants were not playing about in the streets. After we paid tribute to the Boche by waiting half an hour, we all walked home and got to the Seine in time to hear the church bells sound the all-clear. The siren that sounds the alarm is far worse than the raids but the ringing of the church bells brings joy to the heart. And as the bells began to ring we came in sight of a tremendous fire in the quarter you know well. Two of the bombs had fallen near together and one of them had broken through a big gas main and set it on fire. The flames raged high one minute and then died away almost altogether. The streets were filled with ambulances and fire engines and military cars and crowds stood watching the show. Twenty-six people were killed and seventy odd injured – and the bird man got away. It is a rotten business and I wish we could go in for in on a big scale and give them a taste of it so that they would scream for an end. It doesn't do any good here for the people to refuse to be impressed or terrorized – but people are killed just the same, a few every day either by the big gun or by the aviators, and practically none of them are of any military value. The German doesn't have much luck in the way his shells fall. One of the early ones fell on a Church we know on Good Friday afternoon – and that enraged everybody. Day before yesterday another fell on a crèche and killed a number of young mothers and new born babies. That was another bad piece of work for the Hun. If they could hit a massed formation of troops or a munition dump some day they might be able to brag, but they have made a sorry record so far.

Log   Paris. Sunday, April 14, 1918

Stayed abed late this morning for the first time since I left home and got some real rest.

When I started I went over to the Press Division and had a little yarn with McCabe, MacGruder, Col. Heintzelman and one or two others. Then went to lunch with Joe Green and Wickes at the Royale.

Spent the afternoon going over an accumulation of papers and telegrams and got some stuff ready to go off tomorrow.

At seven Joe Green came along for me and we went up to the Hôtel Vernet where we picked up the Wellingtons and Wickes. Saw Davis Wills and learned that Edith, after a hard week, was coming along much better. He has been badly worried. We went to Laperouse and had a bang-up dinner which was Joe's celebration of being transferred from the Press Division to Major Harjes' place for intelligence work.

And so home to my downy.

Log   Paris. Monday, April 15, 1918

A pouch in from Washington but nothing in it for me aside from a lot of information points.

Spent the morning getting off a lot of cables about propaganda with a few ideas for them to think over in Washington. Turned down the idea of distributing leaflets in the schools as being little calculated to get us a return on our money.

Lunched with Dawson and Fred Sterling at a low dive on the Place de l'Alma, where we met M. Jessé-Curélly of the Maison de la Presse.

After lunch Frazier wished upon me a visit from Madame Kening-Kenynsch, Fondée de pouvoirs de la Société des Gens de Lettres Lettons, Attaché à la Maison de la Presse Française, who wanted to start the U.S. on a career of propaganda in the Baltic Provinces. Her idea is all right but we have more than a handful trying to attend to the pressing jobs in Western Europe, so I fear Lithuania will have to wait.

A professor Rudolph Altrocchi, turned up this morning with a diplomatic passport and letters from George Creel, on his way to Italy to help out Capt. Merriam. I filled him up with all the good doctrine I had ready and turned him over to Caffery to have his passport attended to. These diplomatic passports have become a joke to the Foreign Office.

Started out late in the afternoon to make some calls but found nobody in. Went first to the passport office, 11 rue St. Guillaume, where I tried to get a diplomatic permit de circulation, but could find nobody who knew anything about it, and went my way. Thence to Hachette's where I did not find Mr. Bréton and left my card and Jusserand's letter. From there back to the rue St. Guillaume where I made another unsuccessful try and finally to Chevrillon's office in the Avenue de l'Opéra. He is away until Wednesday so I left a card and made my way back to the Hotel.

At 8 dined at the France et Choiseul with Mrs. Linn who had asked General and Mrs. Speares, Danielson, Mrs. [Anne O'Hare] McCormick, Mlle. Thompson and Mordecai. After dinner Miss McCook and Miss Crane came in and we spent an abandoned evening rolling craps – with the result that Mlle. T. cleaned us all out. Speares is the youngest general in the British army – 31: He has had unholy luck, according to his own story but seems to be withdrawn from active service and stuck on staff work here.

Log   Paris. Tuesday, April 16, 1918

The big gun chucked in some shells during the night and one of them about two o'clock made enough row to create the impression that it was rather near.

Frazier brought me another of his pet bores this morning, a man named McCarthy, who spent a good deal of time and money translating the President's speeches into French and distributing them. He seemed more bent on finding out who in blazes I was and just what I was doing than to tell me about his business and generally was insufferable. As he was evidently a crank I took pains to be patient with him but breathed a sigh of relief when he went.

Frazier has good information tending to show that the submarine is on the downgrade. In the first half of April they got only 75,000 tons which would make a monthly total of only 150,000, a low record. He says Sims has some good men in London who have been devoting themselves to the problem with some effect. Our destroyer program has been set back two months by the severe winter but by June we shall have 25 new destroyers over here which will make a very decided difference in what can be accomplished.[45]

Frazier had a message from Sir Horace Rumbold, British Minister in Bern, who is most anxious that I should hurry on there. Horodysky is there and wants to go on to Rome with me. In the course of the morning the following telegram came from the American Minister at Bern:

> "I have an important and urgent matter to discuss with you and hope you are planning to come to Bern soon. Please advise me relative thereto."

I shall try to go down in the course of the week.

Bréton called up this morning and asked me to go to see him any morning before twelve. Shall have to defer it until after my return.

Lunched with Bliss at his flat. We went down with Colonel [William] Mitchell of the Aviation Section who is a plain spoken fellow and devoted most of the ride to roasting Coffin and others for the failure to get airplanes over. He said in a grand manner that he had everything ready and that if they would just give him enough machines he would clean up the American front in no time. Later he remarked in reply to something I said that Foulois hadn't been over here any time and didn't know anything. Mitchell may be a good officer but he talks too much.

There was quite a crowd to lunch, all men, including the Minister of Public Instruction, Dr. Mott of the YMCA, Dr. Carrell, Capt. Tyler, the Rector of the Institut

---

[45] After the American entry into the war, the massive deployment of US destroyers aimed at securing Allied cargo transports and passenger ships against attacks by German submarines

de Grenoble and Wm Martin, Chef du Protocol. A lot of talk after lunch and we did not get back to the chancery until a scandalous hour.

Col. Fabry came in this afternoon to see Dawson and I saw him just to speak to him. He is quite cheerful about the situation on the front so far as the French are concerned and even thinks the English are stronger than they are given credit for being. He announces that Bolo [Pasha] will be shot tomorrow morning or the next day.

Dined with Randolph Mordecai in his charming flat, 5 Square du Roule. He also had Mlle. Thompson and her pretty sister, Mrs. McCormick, Lucy Linn, Father Hemmick, Danielson, Capt. McCormick.

Log   Paris. Wednesday, April 17, 1918

A telegram from John Garrett this morning that a Dutch newspaper wants to translate and publish my book in feuilleton if they can do so without remuneration. He thinks it would be very helpful to American interests if I would accede to the request. I answered that I had no right under my contract to dispose of foreign rights but suggested that he communicate with Curtis Brown who would doubtless be sympathetic.

The Germans have taken Bailleul and Wytschaete and do not seem to have stopped. It doesn't look good to me.

The big gun yesterday killed fourteen people and injured a number.

The Meurice has closed the top floor and I was moved down to the fourth. Lots of people are clearing out.

Lunched with Goedeke at the Plaza and had a good talk. He says that Mrs. J. [Lucy James] has sold her Newport house and has given nearly all her fortune to a work to take care of the children of Scotch officers killed in the war. After twenty-five years the foundation is to be devoted to some other good purpose. She is almost morbid about spending money on herself which is all wrong as she needs to treat herself kindly.

Goedeke is enthusiastic about Cabot Ward and the work he is doing but says that there is a lot of fighting against him on the part of Naval Intelligence and that he is having trouble with the Embassy to get information that he should have.

Lucy Linn says that she hears there is a cabal against Foulois and that he is slated to be shipped home. Perhaps Mitchell *y est pour quelque chose* [did his bit].

Joe Green telephoned after lunch that there has been another change in the High Command. He had no idea as to what it meant.

Dined with McFadden at the Bristol. He had asked Drs. Mott and Harte of the YMCA and we had a quiet dinner in McFadden's rooms. I was shocked at the tone

Mott took about the war. He says that unless the Allies are able to gain a decisive victory this year it will not be worthwhile to go on for although we may win in the end it would be at the cost of too great sacrifice. That we might beat the Germans in a military way but at the cost of destroying our own races. That we might defeat them commercially after the war but at the cost of being ruined ourselves, and that if there is not a decisive victory in the field this year – which he says he does not expect – we had best make any arrangements we can get. It sounds dangerous to me to let a man of those ideas go wandering about through the army.

Log   Paris. Thursday, April 18, 1918

Nothing startling today at the chancery but I had a quiet lunch with Dawson at the Plaza Athénée.

At 6 we went to the Maison de la Presse where we had a good talk with Jessé-Curélly who handles the foreign end of things. He said they were anxious to cooperate with us but had a hard time keeping in touch with Kerney.

After discussing a lot of ways of getting a maximum of American news into the French papers [Jessé-Curélly] made the suggestion that we assign a man to the Maison de la Presse to be present at the daily conferences with the newspaper men, tell them the news from America, sound them out on what is and is not of interest, keep Washington advised as to dropping certain lines and stressing others, and generally get things on an understanding basis at the other end of the wire.

It is evident that we cannot expect to get the press to make daily visits to Kerney's office or to the Embassy. The only place they go regularly is to the Maison de la Presse and therefore it seems axiomatic for us to meet them half way. But we don't always act on axioms and I shall have to put it up to Washington. They apparently think that American news is in some demand but the fact is that with papers reduced to one sheet there is hardly room to publish the communiqués, leading articles and ads. The small amount of space that is left after these have been provided for must be divided carefully so as to get the greatest possible amount of interest. If we are to get any considerable share of that space we must keep posted scientifically as to what is interesting and keep after the newspaper men thru personal contact to get them to print what we provide. If we set up our own show we cannot expect to see any French newspaper men except on the occasions when they want something specific, but that will not get any day to day news into print.

Tramped through a drizzle to Dawson's hotel where we had dinner and then went over his memoranda of political information as far back as last August.

Some of the material he gathered is of the greatest interest and would have been most valuable if it had been sent to the Dept. at the time it was turned in to the Ambassador.

A telegram from Hugh Wilson that he will meet me in Geneva on Saturday morning.

During the afternoon Topping came in to see me in great distress. His wife has sued him for divorce and the A.P. have as he thinks treated him very badly. He is going to leave them on the first of May and will perhaps come to me. He plans to fight his wife's divorce suite as he says she is all wrong and unreasonable and that he can't let it go. He seemed desperate and talked of enlisting but I urged him to do nothing until I came back from my trip. I loaned him a hundred dollars to tide him over. I was mighty sorry for him but there is nothing you say in such circumstances.

Letter to William Castle   Paris, April 18, 1918

... As this is not a wheeze of complaint I now come to the remedy which has caused me some sleepless nights. If you go after him [Kerney] he will sit down and send you a telegram of generalities about the great things to be done in the near future. We are full of such plans and have unbounded faith in them. So a direct frontal attack is not advisable.

But if you were to jump on me for my failure to get things started I think we could take a mean advantage of his kind heart and might get him started rather than see me hurt. Why not send him a telegram saying that you had expected me to organize an adequate office in a proper location and get things started. That so far you had received no report that things were moving as they should and that you want something started without more ado. You might add some rough stuff about the fact that the critical situation makes it imperative that our organization get down to effective work without loss of time and that you must insist that there be no further delay. A little more-in-sorrow-than-in-anger talk from me after getting such a cable might get things started.

I feel pretty mean to sit down and write a letter like this for the man has been extremely nice to get along with, but I am forced to the conclusion that unless you know what the real situation is and can take some intelligent action we are not going to get anywhere over here for an indefinite time.[46]

---

46 See the State Department action below, May 9, 1918.

Log   Paris. Friday, April 19, 1918

Spent the morning at the chancery cleaning things up for my get-away.

Had lunch with Major Ward at the Inter-Allied Club[47] in the Rothschild house, Faubourg St. Honoré. Saw Perry Osborne, Dr. Carrell, Campbell-Turner and several other people I knew. Ward is having his sorrows with the Embassy which refuses to let him see their lists of Americans in France. The Consul General [Thackara] does the same and the intelligence people have to gather their material in the most laborious way from local French records. Perhaps it has been worthwhile however because although the Consul General reported that there were something over five thousand Americans in France the searches so far made by the army have located a little less than fifteen thousand. Ward is anxious to have somebody in the Embassy to whom he can occasionally confide. He has on several occasions given His Excellency [Sharp] very confidential information concerning people under suspicion or worse only to have the document itself turned over to the party in interest. One of these people came in to Ward's office the other day brandishing a revolver and threatening him with death. Ward is a touchy fellow and did not like this.

Had a short talk with the Ambassador [Sharp] who was just getting under way with Mrs. Sharp who is starting for America. His Excellency accompanies her as far as Bordeaux. He was considerably exercised by the fact that Kerney had recommended Gibbons as Chief of the Speaker's Bureau in France. It seems that Gibbons has been running amuck and recently made a speck here before a large audience of Frenchmen in which he severely criticized our Govt. for not having sooner got into the war. Paul van Dyke and George Sharp were present and came away indignant.

Broached to His Excellency [Sharp] the idea of getting an extra man to come in and read the papers under Dawson's direction so as to leave him free to go about and gather information. It was accepted if I could find a man who would do.

Most of the time this afternoon it was alternately snowing and raining.

Judge Ben Lindsey and his wife came in late in the afternoon in quest of Kerney and their letters which had been sent in his care. I was unable to unearth their letters but assured them we wanted to do anything they wanted and sent them away happy. They bear letters from George Creel introducing the Judge as the

---

47 Also known as Cercle de l'Union interalliée, the Interallied Club was established in 1917 in the course of America's official entry into the war. Supported by various statesmen, ambassadors and other important societal figures, its purpose was to offer moral and material resources to officers and personalities of the Allied nations.

best-beloved man in America and urging that the whole force of the Government machinery be put behind him. George neglected to say how far behind him.

I had a telephone message from Lt. Tonnelat asking that I urge Bohn to refrain from mentioning anybody's names. French agents report from Bern that he has talked too much and that he is too free with names. I assured Tonnelat that I would lose no time in communicating with Bohn on arrival at Bern and that all would be well.

Had dinner alone at the Hotel and got down to the Gare de Lyon where I was to be met by Dangaix at 7:40. I stood about and waited for him until the last minute and then got on the train to find him comfortably installed. The French Govt. had undertaken to make reservations for us and see us thru to the frontier. Late in the afternoon however they telephoned around that they had not been able to do anything toward getting us a special car and that we would have to make our own reservations. I sent Bobbie [Robert Bliss] down to the station and he had *toutes les peines du monde* [all the trouble in the world] to get any ticket – and could not get any sleeper. Result, all the members sat up as best they could. Several of us contrived to get couchettes which were only one shade worse than sitting up.

Received a telegram today from Will Irwin with much enthusiasm about a new balloon device for dropping literature on the poor Hun. He described all the mechanism in the comic blue code, a copy of which is in the possession of every station master in Europe. If the dear Hun is interested he has some interesting suggestions as to how to improve his own balloons. He evidently wanted me to go straight to Italy without bothering about Switzerland. The telegram ended:

> "While Italy is important things are at a standstill in Bern. Mrs. Whitehouse returning to fight it out with State Department. In meantime Ackerman has applied for the job. Within ten days can if necessary send Swing who looks to me like ablest candidate. Merriam and Embassy seem to be taking hold well in Italy."

I shall now spend my spare time praying that they won't send Swing who is under suspicion of the French secret service. WHY, WHY do we always have to pick out agents who are under suspicion? Swing wouldn't do for five minutes no matter how able he is. Aside from praying I am going to send a telegram tomorrow to head him off if possible. Ackerman is certainly more available and is not under the disadvantage of being suspect.

In the course of my talk with the Ambassador he told me he had been around to see Lord Bertie whose recall was announced in yesterday morning's papers. He has been ill in bed for ten days and in that time has not had a bite to eat. He told the Ambassador with a wry smile that the first he knew of his recall was yesterday morning. Why in blazes do the British do such brutal things. They killed poor Spring-Rice by just that heartless and devilish way of kicking him out after years of hard and able service. Republics may not be grateful but... Lord [Edward] Derby is coming over as British Ambassador but if he doesn't curb that free and easy tongue he won't last long or be popular.

Log   Bellevue Palace Hotel. Bern. Saturday, April 20, 1918

We were called at the crack of dawn this morning and pulled off the train at Bellagarde. There our passports were carefully scanned for the frontier is closed to all but those bearing the highest credentials from the Foreign Office. Each of us in turn was taken into a little wooden coop and prayerfully questioned as to how much good money we were taking out of France. The *poor douanier* [customs officer] who had me did not press the matter or ask to see but contented himself with asking me over and over to assure him that I was not taking out more than the law allowed. Our bags were marked without examination and loaded back into the train by an ancient porter who stood guard over them while we went back to the station and had breakfast. Sebastian used his *beaux yeux* [beautiful eyes] to such good effect that the waitress brought us a big plate of butter.

At Geneva the Vice-Consul Edelman was waiting for me and led me straightway to the Consulate where he wanted to talk over propaganda and intelligence work. He is doing the political intelligence relating to the Near East and seems to get some good material although he does not think it worthwhile to ask for the allowances that have been granted to his French and British colleagues.

He has gone at the propaganda in the right way and has kept it under Swiss cover. He showed me a pamphlet of the President's speeches which he had got a Professor of the University of Geneva to get out and distribute under his own name, we paying the bills for printing and distribution. He printed and mailed five thousand pamphlets for a total cost of 1,000 francs, which is dirt cheap.

Of course this French portion of Switzerland is the least urgent so far as our efforts are concerned but there is nonetheless plenty for us to do. Edelman thinks that this can best be done thru straight news, reprints from American periodicals and pictures which could be displayed in shop windows. I shall recommend that a lot of magazines be sent him as raw material. He is to make me a memorandum on his ideas of the sort of educational work we should undertake.

Had a chat with Haskell, the Consul, who seems an intelligent sort and who is much interested. He had an interesting despatch for me in regard to the formation of a pro-ally moving picture company which has a plan for freezing out the German companies and thus stopping their propaganda which covers every corner of the country. At present they get films from allied countries thru neutral agents, the sort of thing that will draw a crowd. They run 2,000 meters of Charlie Chaplin or Douglas Fairbanks and in between 500 of their own propaganda. If we can create a monopoly for the use of allied films in Switzerland so that the Hun can no longer get hold of them we can pretty effectively cook his goose, – for nobody will go to see nothing but Boche propaganda and he can't hope to get much worthwhile made in his own country or from neutral countries. Of course it would be pretty soft for the monopoly but they are not doing altogether from love of the Allies.

Hugh Wilson came in about half past ten, having come down last night to ride back and have a good yarn. We pushed off in his car at about eleven and drove to Lausanne for lunch. It was bitter cold and dismal but offered a chance for an uninterrupted talk.

It seems that [Ambassador] Stovall came back in a much more amenable state of mind and has not interfered with the running of the shop. Anything that is done and submitted to him he approves. If it lasts the place can run this way indefinitely, though of course it is not the ideal way.

Herron seems to have got the bit in his teeth and developed as a full-fledged representative of the President. His conversations with Lammasch have unfortunately been talked about by Lammasch himself so that a lot of people, including our allies, have heard about it. Herron plans to send a telegram to Washington saying that he seems to be in some error as to his exact functions, that in any event there is nothing for him to do at present and that it might be a good plan for the Department to ask him to go and talk things over, so as to put him on the right track and get the benefit of the information and ability he undoubtedly possesses.

He is also somewhat concerned about Horodyski who is waiting for me here in the hope that I will go down to Rome with him. Has some information he has promised to show me tomorrow.

There is also some material to be looked into about McNally who seems to have got in bad with everybody. His son-in-law,[48] who is a German naval officer on active service has been allowed to visit him in Zurich three times since last August, for several weeks at a time. Despite warnings from the Legation that it would be wiser to see him quietly somewhere he has had him come to stop with him at his hotel and has introduced him generally. He went to Spain after one visit from son-in-law without telling the Legation the purpose of his trip and was

---

48 McNally's daughter, Madeleine McNally (1894–1960), was married to German Lieutenant Fritz Menzing, according to Alfred W. McCoy in *Beer of Broadway Fame: The Piel Family and Their Brooklyn Brewery* (Excelsior Editions/State University of New York Press, 2016). However, Madeleine's grave indicates she was the wife of US Marine Major Andrew L.W. Gordon (1897–1973), making it likely that she had a first and second marriage.

most anxious to get back to Zurich where his son-in-law had come to wait for him – and waited for several weeks in some impatience, finally returning to Berlin a few days ago. It seems rather unlikely that the German Govt. would be letting one of its officers play about this way with an enemy Consul unless they were getting something out of it. The information he has secured from son-in-law seems to the Legation to consist chiefly of unsupported statements and generalizations such as could be written out here by the yard. He has bragged to his colleagues of having a private cipher with the Dept. of which the Legation was ignorant. He is violently anti-English, talks against the French and preaches the doctrine that Germany cannot be beaten. He seems to have done a lot of harm by spreading the idea that the U.S. is not in the war in earnest and that we do not intend to do anything in the way of fighting. He associates chiefly with Germans and Americans of doubtful loyalty.[49] Haskell sent the vice consul [Edelman] away on a "mission" and went thru the offices. There was a lot of confidential material lying about loose, which proved carelessness but nothing more. However there were several drawers which were locked and these may yet have to be looked into. Full telegraphic reports of his activities have been sent to the Dept. which does not seem to attach much importance to them and telegraphs back that it knew of McNally's connections when it sent him to Zurich. The French have reached the point of intimating that they would detain him at the frontier if he endeavored to return though they would deplore the necessity for interfering with an American official.

Bohn seems to be active but Herron thinks he is doing good work. He may be thrown out of Switzerland at any time but if he gets something done first he is apparently quite prepared to be chucked out cheerfully. Herron reports him as an attractive fellow who will be all right if he can be made a little more discreet. I shall see him tomorrow and labor with him along that line.

Lunched at the Lausanne Palace with Ackerman who was awaiting us. Also saw our Consular Agent [Dexter] and King, an American Intelligence Officer who knows Ed Curtis. As we sat down at table I observed the Chevalier de Waepenaert with his wife at an adjoining table. I had not seen him since old days in Cuba and had a few minutes talk with him.

Ackerman has telegraphed Creel suggesting himself to run COMPUB business in Switzerland in case Mrs. Whitehouse does not come back. I think he might do as he knows the country pretty well and has sane ideas about the sort of work that could be done.

---

49 For more on McNally's actions, see Robert Murphy, *Diplomat Among Warrior: The Unique World of a Foreign Service Expert* (Doubleday & Company, 1964).

Image 9: Frederic Dolbeare was a Secretary at the US Embassy in Bern, Switzerland, in 1918. Later he accompanied Gibson to Warsaw as First Secretary of the American Legation there. (Courtesy of the Gibson Family)

Started out right away after lunch and had a dreary ride with one blow-out, reaching the Legation at 5:30. Saw the Minister [Stovall], Dresel, Dolbeare, Dulles and several others and waited while the pouches were opened and everybody got their share. Had a short talk with the Minister about things in general and then back here where we found Mrs. Wilson [Katherine] and talked until dinner time.

At dinner we were joined by Sawyer, representative in Switzerland of the British Ministry of Munitions and by several other people who sat around and talked until after eleven when I was glad to get into my little bed.

Found a note from Dresel asking me to lunch on Monday with Davison and Eliot Wadsworth who are due then from Italy. He later announced that they could not get across the frontier from Italy and would not visit us but that the lunch would go ahead anyway.

Ackerman toady advanced an idea that may be well worth considering. He says that our supplemental news service is just about no good because every time there is anything of importance we send a long story which gets here after Havas or Reuter has come thru with a few lines which get published and spike all chance of a full showing later. His idea is that during the war the Govt. get up an official news service under some business name and furnish it at a rate that will assure its being taken generally. It would not cost so very much and would give better results so far as this particular country is concerned than any other idea I have come across.

Log   Bern. Sunday, April 21, 1918

Got up late and had breakfast alone in the big dining room.

Thumped on my typewriter until half past eleven when Hugh Wilson came along and carried me off to the Legation.

There I was shown the dossier on McNally which I must say looks very suspicious although of course there is no definite proof of any improper activity. Although the people who went thru his office the other day found a lot of papers lying about they got nothing in the way of evidence about his relations with the enemy. There were three drawers of his desk locked and if there is anything wrong that is where it probably is. There may have to be another expedition to take a look.

There was also a dossier on Horodyski which was really nothing beyond some charges made by a Pole who is travelling over here on an American passport "on Polish matters". Horodyski says he was involved in the wrecking of a bank in America but was not punished because he was engaged to the daughter of the President of the bank and that the latter made good his defalcations. It may all be true but there was nothing to it beyond a lot of unsupported statements.

Moore came to lunch with us at the hotel.

Harold McCormick came up after lunch and had coffee with us.

At 2:30 I went around to the KREUZ HOTEL by previous gumshoe arrangement to have a yarn with Frank Bohn. He was not in at the time but soon came dashing up the stairs out of breath after running madly from a lunch with a lot of German revolutionary pals. He wanted me to go right around and mix it up with them but I tried to convince him that it was better for him if I kept away and say as little of him as possible. I cautioned him about talking so much and he promised to be careful but seemed rather distrait and I am not at all sure it sank in deep. However I shall keep after him and hope to have him impressed before I get away.

He [Bohn] is a most attractive fellow, full of enthusiasm over his work and convinced that success is coming. He said" "We'd have won out before this if it hadn't been for the Russian collapse. But we'll get 'em next winter as sure as can be. There's nothing to it. They've got 3,000 German socialists in prison and the Austrians have been sending them to the front and letting the Germans open up on them from behind with machine guns. This may work for the moment but the time is coming when it will be too big for them. And we can hasten the day. We'll get 'em next winter SURE":

He says his French and Italian colleagues are trumps, full of intelligence and enthusiasm and that they will supply a great part of what is needed for the work if we will furnish some money. They have next to nothing now and are having a hard time of it against the German who has spent 25,000,000 marks in the past year.

In yesterday's FREIE ZEITUNG, Bohn had a very well-written article telling of what the German-American have done for freedom in America and how they are now pouring money into the army because they feel that they are fighting as well for the United States. It is just the right line to take. Today the GAZETTE DE LAUSANNE reprints the article with approving comment. I complimented Bohn on this and he seemed very much pleased. He said he had another coming out in the course of a day or two. He does not seem to feel that he will be run out of the country but is quite prepared to go if he can accomplish something first.

He [Bohn] wants to go to Holland soon and get to work with some of the German socialists and for the purpose is anxious to have some funds so that they can be helped out as much as may be necessary. He wants me to telegraph Washington recommending that he be given 5,000 per month and allowed to see what he can do with it. He is to draw me up a memorandum of his ideas as to what can be accomplished here and I shall try to frame some sort of telegram tomorrow. His work is the right sort and it remains to be seen whether he is the right man to run it. Whoever does run it must be a wild radical and they are not apt to be over well balanced.

Bohn says that a lot of the radicals in Germany are holding out because they are not content with the idea of a republic. They want to go all the way of the Bolsheviki. His job at present is to pray with some of the people and convince them that they had better try for a "limited objective" as they say in trench warfare, and be patient about going the rest of the way.

After seeing him we went back to the Legation and I went over some more matters with Hugh Wilson. He had a very interesting letter on American propaganda on Switzerland from the Geneva Professor who translated the President's speeches. He has some sane ideas on the subject and I am going to send his letter home for them to ponder – and also with the suggestion that the President write him a little note of appreciation of what he has done, for the gentleman appear to be a little vain and would probably be more pleased by such a letter than by a decoration.

Also some memoranda as to conversations about Mrs. Whitehouse, showing what impression she had made here. On the whole it was not very flattering. Her good looks and charm were dwelt on by all hands but the general impression was that she depended too much on them to get her thru; that she was not particularly intelligent and that she resented having anybody, no matter how qualified, try to teach her anything. They bore out about what I had thought from my short experience with the lady.

[Nesta] Sawyer last night brought up a story that I have heard several times to the effect that she was pro-German. I have had it with many variations but they usually dwell upon the fact that before the war her husband was supposed to be very hard up, that he was a friend of Bernstorff and lunched with him often after the outbreak of the way,- and that he LATER BEGAN TO BUY HOUSES. So there you are. I think I convinced Sawyer that he had hold of the wrong end of things and he has gone buzzing off to spread the true story.

Invited to dine with the Schellings at eight and went down with my pockets stuffed with cigars not knowing that it was to be anything more than a little family party. Found a large assemblage gathered to do honor to the great Red Cross mission which has failed to show up. I sat next to Madame Paravincini, the wife of the Chief of the Diplomatic Section of the Political Department, or the nearest thing they have to a Minister for Foreign Affairs. I knew him when he was Counselor of the Swiss Legation in London. She told me how hard poor "Para" had to work – and that things were far harder than in the good old days before they came back to Switzerland. She said it was dreadful no longer being able to speak her views out loud, having to associate not only with allies but also with the dear Boches and having to keep her eye on herself all the time.

Among the other guests were our Minister and Mrs. Stovall and Miss Sawyer, Sir Horace and Lady Rumbold, Lord and Lady St. Cyres, Professor Rappard, Major Iselin (a cousin on my friends to whom I detailed a story of the arrival of the Laughlin heir), Major and Madame Favre, the Belgian Minister and Madame Peltzer, Colonel Godson, our military attaché, Capt. Davis, Dresel, etc, etc, etc.

After dinner I had quite a yarn with Sir Horace. He did not seem much concerned about the question of McNally and said that he did not suppose the question had been taken up by Lord Reading in Washington. That he had said to the Foreign Office that the matter was in the hands of the Legation here and that he supposed they had let it go at that. Hugh [Wilson] and I intimated that perhaps somebody on the ground would have greater effect than a paper telegram sent in by us. Perhaps he will take the hint.

He remarked that the labor situation in England was much better than it has been in the past few months. That the next two months will be uneasy but that after that he thinks there will be a distinct improvement.

He seems to be of the opinion that Horodyski is of considerable value. Says he headed off the "Papal Nuncio at Munich and tapped him". I don't know what he got out of him but Sir Horace says he is coming up here to see me and that I can find out then.

There are some members of the German Reichstag down here to talk to anybody that will listen to them and they have been telephoning around to all hands and the cook trying to get a hearing. Herron wrote to Hugh Wilson that they were after him but that he did not propose to see them and that moreover during the present posture of affairs he intended to make himself rather inaccessible to anybody coming from Germany. They will probably get after me.

The dear Huns seem to have this place well policed and Sir Horace comforted me with the statement that in view of my own bad record in Germany they had undoubtedly assigned somebody to keep an eye on me. I wish him well for he must have had a dull time of it so far.

He said that he had received from several sources news that things were rather wobbly in Austria and that we might expect trouble there about the first of May. That coincides with the news we have but I will believe bad news about the Central Powers when it really comes off.

Professor Rappard has been doing good work for us and I must send a word to Hoover to write him in a genial vein. He was on the Swiss mission that went to the U.S. on the food question and says that he has been writing to the Swiss press staking his reputation on our coming through with food as per agreement. He is a keenly intelligent man who speaks perfect English and has done a lot for us. He seems to be ready to help lay our case before the Swiss and we must not waste him.

He says he told Mrs. Whitehouse that she must bear in mind that the Swiss press takes an unusually high plane and is for the intellectual classes who dominate the rest of the country. That the papers here resent any stuff prepared on the lines that the Hearst papers would print but that they will use good stuff even if it does not altogether agree with their ideas.

We must get out in pamphlet form or otherwise under the aegis of some prominent Swiss the [Karl] LUXBURG stuff, Andrews revelations as to German deviltry in Romania, the President's speeches, Muelhon's articles, Prince Lichnowsky's revelations and other material of that sort. In this way we could undoubtedly do a lot of good.

I am to lunch on Tuesday at the British Legation and get what Sir Horace has to say.

On Wednesday we lunch at the Stovall's.

Tomorrow night the Wilson's are giving a dinner for me – though I did not know it until one of the guests told me.

Log   Bern. Monday, April 22, 1918

Got started early this morning at the chancery and wrote several telegrams that required some writing. There are a number more that must be done before I leave here but it is hard to talk to so many people and comb out the ideas and draft the telegrams all in the same 24 hour day.

Took a look through the chancery with Hugh [Wilson] and visited the outlying buildings where the staff is housed. They occupy three buildings now but have a new place where they can all be under roof if the Minister does not take it as a home.

At one o'clock Dresel gave a big luncheon at the Bellevue – another of the parties for the Red Cross Mission which has not arrived. It was a bang up meal with far too much to eat and drink. I met all the guests of whom there must have been thirty five and among them remember the British, Serbian, Italian and American Ministers, Onou, the Russian Chargé d'Affairs, Paravincini, d'Hauteville, Whitehouse, Col. Godson, Davis, de la Croix, Rappard, the French Military Attaché and some of the Legation people. We ate heavily and then conversed lightly until three when Hugh Wilson came and rescued me to start on a career of crime.

After starting some people to work ciphering my telegrams we went down to the French Press Bureau to call on Heguenin and Poncet, two keenly intelligent Frenchmen who know what they are about and seem to be achieving results. I feel a good deal of hesitancy in talking with them for we have sent over so many cranks and have talked so big about what we were going to do – and altogether we have done just exactly nothing.

Heguenin is for our spending some money buying or helping Swiss papers but I did not lead him to expect much help in that direction as I do not think we will come thru. Heguenin spend a lot of time trying to show the light to Mrs. Whitehouse but is not very confident of having achieved success. He says she came over with the idea that she was going to sweep Switzerland off its feet by organizing great public meetings and preaching American doctrine broadcast, whereas he says that nothing can be accomplished until you have spent time cultivating some important Swiss people and gaining their confidence; that with their support and influence a great deal can be done but that the rough neck method will not go. He felt that Mrs. Whitehouse resented being told these things but toward the end of her stay her protests became less vigorous. I judge that he did not consider her intelligence very high.

He brought up the questions of a German professor close to the Berlin Foreign Office who has come down and wants to see some Americans to whom he can talk peace. He called on Heguenin and talked to him at length, evidently to his embarrassment. Hugh suggested that the learned man see Field in Zurich rather than Herron. H. agreed to this and said that he feared Herron was not discreet and that he might talk too much whereas the problem was to make the Boche do the talking. There seems to be a general agreement that Herron does not keep his own counsel.

Heguenin has established a book shop in Zurich and others in other towns. Hearing that we were going to Zurich he gave us a note to the people who are running it and asked us to go and see it. It is apparently a good center of propaganda and incidentally pays good profit. The shop at Basel he says is a failure because the Alsatian lady who runs it is so filled with enthusiasm about helping France that she has no thought for the shop.

After finishing with him and promising to eat food with him on my next visit we went up to the NEUE KORRESPONDENZ BÜRO where we saw Lévy, the little French Jew who runs it. He made improper advances to Mrs. Whitehouse so her situation would not be altogether happy in case she came back and had to work with him. He told us something of his news services which seems to consist chiefly of *deux coups de téléphone par jour* [two phone calls a day] from the Ministry in Paris with the news of what is going on, plus a careful reading of the Hun press. He in his turn calls up the big Swiss papers and tells them the news and mails it to the others. His chief pride which he showed us was two whole telegrams which enable him to receiveand send at the same time, thus providing that he has a system that is equal to any emergency. He says our news service which comes from America is rotten although it occasionally had an item or so of interest. He is strong for special articles on the economic side of the war – wherein he agrees with pretty well everybody I have talked with. They all say the Swiss eat up figures and prefer them to any other form of mental diet.

From his people I went to the Kreuz Hotel for another yarn with Bohn who annoyed me by dropping in at the hotel just as we were going to lunch. He ought to know better but I fear that no amount of talking to will teach him that sort of thing. He had a stone deaf Swiss with him when I arrived. He left in the course of a few minutes and then we got down to real shop. Bohn says that his French and Italian colleagues are filled with ideas as to how they can bring off the revolution in Germany but that they are hampered for lack of money. That they will furnish brains and connections if only we can dig up the money – in fact a repetition of what we went over at our last pow-wow. He said that he had it in mind to stage a comic international socialist conference here in a few months. That the Boches would send a flood of people and that the other belligerents would do so except England who would probably worry a lot about it in the House and end by sending nobody, refusing passports, etc. That this would be best and most convincing camouflage. A few of the Boches he expected to be sincere and they would go back and talk the sort of thing that they would hear, that the allies were just coming into the war and that they were determined to keep it up indefinitely no matter what reverses they suffered.

Bohn has some more articles coming out in the FREIE ZEITUNG and is making preparations to have it got into Germany by all the existing smuggling systems so that it can be brought up and read in the Reichstag by some of the socialists.

His great job just now is to make the radical socialists content themselves with the idea of bringing about some reasonable measure of reform in Germany and not trying to carry it to the full Bolshevik limit.

He needs fifty tons of paper for the FREIE ZEITUNG as they have been threatened with a stoppage of their paper supply if they persisted in their ways.

I have promised to telegraph George Creel and ask whether there is any chance of their being given decent financial support. If the thing is worth doing at all it is worth doing well.

Before leaving I again warned Bohn about the need for discretion in talk and writing so as to keep himself and his friends out of trouble. He was so enthusiastically understanding that I began to be encouraged until he volunteered – among his reasons for discretions – the fact that he had helped organize the I.W.W. [Industrial Workers of the World] Just why that should be considered a claim to consideration for conservatism I don't quite make out.

From there I went back to the Legation where I found McFadden looking very weary, just in from Paris to attend the Wood Conference[50] with my fellow travelers.

A telegram from the Department to say that McNally is coming back to his post but that the British and French have been told that his return does not necessarily mean that he will remain there indefinitely. Blah!

At eight we rounded up for dinner, a dinner that the Wilsons were giving for me. The guests were Lord and Lady St. Cyres, Count, Countess and Mlle. Ehrensvärd (Swedish Minister and pro-Boche enrage), the Schellings, Professor Rappard and McFadden. I sat next to Lady St. Cyres and found her most amusing and intelligent. After dinner we all went to the Legation where there was another of the famous parties for the Red Cross Mission. I met Lady Acton who told me that her husband had read my book with great interest. After expressing the opinion that

---

50 In the second half of April 1918, a conference was held in Bern to negotiate the supply of the AEF, including wood for barracks, food and technical equipment under the conditions of the blockade.

he must be a man of excellent literary taste I was presented to him. He [Richard Lyon-Dalberg Acton] was Chargé in Darmstatdt before the war at the same time with Lancken and joined heartily in the cheering when I expressed my unvarnished views about the gentleman.

Also saw and talked to Craigie of the British Legation, Sir Horace and Lady Rumbold, the Romanian colleague, name unknown, the Sawyers [Ernest, Ethel and Nesta], Charlie Russell, Dulles, Col. Godson and a few more odds and ends.

The hotel here is filled with both Boches and those that don't like them. We get mixed constantly in the corridors and the lift and they all seem to derive a lot of pleasure from glaring at each other. Rode down in the lift this evening with two couples that seemed about as congenial as a pair of Seidlitz powders. It must be rather humorous to live in that atmosphere if you have not the Boche mentality to cramp your style.

Sir Horace gives me thrilling accounts of the way the Hun polices this place and genially remarks that there is undoubtedly some cut-throat who has the job of keeping an eye on me. I wish him well for he must find it a painfully boring job.[51]

Charlie Russell told me today at lunch that the Legation at The Hague is a complete mess. That John Garrett is one cold foot and will not leave anything to anybody; that if the simplest telegram is to be written it must be submitted first to His Excellency with the suggestion that he write it; he then sits down unless it frightens him and pops out something to the Department – but that none of the staff are allowed to do <u>anything</u>. He says that Marshall Langhorne is *non compus mentis* [not in his right mind]. Kirk seems to be the only member of the family who has any brains.

Log   Bern. Tuesday, April 23, 1918

Got up fairly early and had breakfast with McFadden, Sebastian and Harry Maude.

Spend the morning at the chancery talking with all hands and writing some telegrams – attached in paraphrase. Decided to leave tomorrow afternoon with Hugh Wilson for Zurich and leave there for Rome Friday. As nearly as I can make out there are to be at least four changes of train which is a bore.

---

51 Although Gibson is repeating here what he has stated above, the duplication offers an insight into how he jotted down his notes. His remarkable recall allows him to record an incident days later almost verbatim, which only increases his veracity.

Lv Zurich	1:30 pm
Arr. Chaisso	10:37 pm
Lv "	6:09 am
Arr Como	6:20 am
Lv "	6:50 am
Arr Milan	8:13 am
Lv Milan	1:30 pm
Arr Rome	7:50 am

Have been combing out some ideas about our work here and sent Ackerman to work to draw up a definite plan. Also drafted a telegram to try to draw some indication from the President as to the tone to be adopted toward Austria when she becomes articulate and gets ready to talk peace as the Boches are beginning to do. ...

Horodyski came in at three and yarned about all sorts of things. He is convinced that a revolution is coming in Austria in the course of the next ten days or two weeks and is already rubbing his hands in anticipation. We scoffed at his prophecies but he smiled benignly and let it ride.

His great plan for saving the human race now rests upon having some Americans go to Rome to talk with the Vatican. He has a whiff of some sort of negotiations looking toward peace that are under way between the Pope and the King of Spain and wants us to find out more about it. The Papal Nuncio [Pacelli] at Munich has come out for a short visit and has now returned to his post but is due to get back to Rome shortly so there is evidently something stirring. Other Papal representatives from the Central Powers are shortly expected in Rome so things may begin to buzz there. Horodyski got off a telegram to Polk urging that some steps be taken to get in touch with the Vatican and suggesting that I be used for the purpose. When the telegram was shown me I asked that the mention of my name be stricken out and this was done. The Minister [Stovall] added a little comment of his own however in which he said that he had supposed the suggestion at my request but that the matter was worth careful consideration; that I felt some doubt as to whether I was suited for the work on account of bearing an official label. He added however that my work in cooperation with Merriam would entail seeing a lot of people and would offer a reasonable explanation of any visits to the Vatican. It was suggested that thru Craige it would be probably possible to arrange for the initiative to come from the Vatican. The Department was asked to telegraph me instructions to Rome where I shall be on Sunday morning – D.V. [Lord willing] and the criks [creeks] don't rise.

Also did a long telegram to Frank Lyon Polk concerning the symptoms of an approaching German peace drive. Said that if the present offensive is stopped without any definite achievement that the Boches can point to the Austrians will soon renew their efforts to get in touch with the Allies. That it is essential that our people be given a line on the President's wishes so that they may know how to govern themselves. The allies have seemingly abandoned all idea of detaching Austria and our representatives ought to know whether we are going to fall in with them or continue to frown less fiercely upon the Austrians in the hope of driving in a wedge there. I suggested that the President might take occasion to elucidate this point in one of his public utterances.

Stayed at the chancery until seven o'clock and on getting back to the hotel made little visits to Mrs. Wilson and Mrs. Schelling.

Dined with the Wilsons and Dolbeare and spent the evening yarning.

Log Bern. Wednesday, April 24, 1918

Got started early this morning and sent off a whale of a telegram to Will Irwin telling rather fully of the situation here as regards our work and setting forth a rather elaborate tentative plan for his discussion with Mrs. Whitehouse. I also wrote him a long letter along the same lines with variations and elaborations. It will get there a good deal later but may cause him to go over the matter a second time to our advantage.

Also wrote Ned Bell at some length in regard to John W. De Kay.

Prepared a new method of cipher to use between our various missions. They have heretofore been without anything of the sort.

Bern – Zurich
At one we went to the Minister's [Stovall] house to lunch. Found Mrs. Wilson, Dulles, McFadden and a young Englishman with one who had been shot down on the western front and spent eight months as a prisoner in Germany. I did not get his name. There never was such a meal; it went on course after course, each better and more deadly than the one before until I showed symptoms of bursting and slowed up.

Just to keep our hand in we got off a few more telegrams after lunch and got back to the hotel in time to pack and catch a five o'clock train, but when we had been comfortably installed we learned to our disgust that it did not pull out until 5:30, the hotel porter not having got things straight.

Nearly expired from apoplexy on the train because a swinish Swiss officer stamped into the compartment and not finding a place to his liking to hand his overcoat, pulled my biggest bag out of the rack and threw it on the floor in the middle of the compartment. I maintained a dignified and haughty silence, merely because I could think of nothing at the moment sufficiently scorching to say to him. Hugh [Wilson] and I rearranged the bags and treated the gent to large quantities of silence all the way to Zurich.

At the station we were met by Wirth the Vice-Consul, and taken to the Hotel National where he had engaged rooms for us. There Dr. H.H. Field was waiting to have dinner with us and chat about things in general. He is a splendid old chap with a head like Michael Angelo, a Quaker of Quakers with a serene gray eye that is a comfort. He has been here long enough to be known and trusted by everybody and hears a great deal that is of interest. Even Germans and Austrians come to him frequently to get his views as to our state of mind and what terms they would likely to get. He fills them up with the right doctrine and what he tells them has been proven right so often that a lot of them are beginning to believe we are perhaps in earnest after all.

We dined at an excellent restaurant "Muegenin's and did not get up from table until after eleven – which was not so startling as we did not sit down until after nine.

Log   Hotel National, Zurich. Thursday, April 25, 1918

We got started fairly early as we had a lot to do. Dr. Field had booked us up for a lot of visits so that I could get some line on what people here were thinking. After a visit at the Consulate we set out on a tram for our first visit.

It was to Professor [Leonhard] Ragaz, one of the most extreme radicals in Switzerland, socialist, anti-militarist, etc. He has like Gustave Hervé, evoluted [sic] with the war and has been an excellent influence. When the Bolsheviki began to wobble he telegraphed them to refuse peace terms to the Germans and said that they were endangering the whole future of human development. Of course the radicals in this part of the world jumped on him and said that he had not stood the test of his theories but he stood pat and is beginning to swing some of this sort around to his way of thinking. His wife [Clara Ragaz], whom we did not see, is quite as radical as he and writes and speaks a good deal. She went to the Ford Peace Conference, worse luck. They live in a musty old-new building on top of the hill; the little sitting room into which we were shown was about as echt-Deutsch as anything could well be. Photographs of sentimental young people and a plaster cast of a very fat lady draped over a tomb.

Ragaz came bustling in and welcomed us in German which is the only language he speaks. As our German was not up to the subjects we wanted to talk about we agreed to talk in English which he understands and let him reply in German – and the arrangement worked well.

He is a man who makes an instant impression of sincerity and who is deeply saturated in the things he talked about – chiefly the human side of the war and the effect that it was going to have upon the development of liberal movements. He is an ardent admirer of the President and talked at some length about the need of having his messages and speeches translated by somebody who knows the languages as they should. He feels that the President is doing a great deal to clarify the thinking of all sorts of people who have not taken the trouble to think right before and he is anxious that the effect shall not be lost thru mishandling of what he has to say. Ragaz made more of an impression on me than any man I have met in a long time and I should have enjoyed talking to him for several hours, even with the handicap of the two languages. He made one observation which impressed me. That a lot of radicals were just as much opposed to the President as they were to the Kaiser – they felt that the Kaiser was labelled as an autocrat and nobody expected anything of him. Whatever he did or said was explained, but the President was supposed to be an innocuous ruler over a democracy and it hurt them that he did not wave the red shirt with the best of them.

Hugh had his eye on the clock and when he saw that we were due for our next visit he remarked diplomatically that we could not take any more of Ragaz's time – and so we went on our way, I reserving my right to come back and see him and his wife when I came back to Zurich.

From his house we went down the hill to the University of Zurich where we called on Prof. Seippel who is by birth and tradition of Geneva. He was a distinct contrast to Ragaz with the *air pondéré* [steady mindedness] of the Genevois. He too talked of the work that we should do to make Switzerland and the U.S. understand each other better. He leaned to the good old academic formula of exchanging professors and students between the two countries and told of one of his Swiss friends who had gone to America to erect and run a big chemical works in connection with the war. He has written back with much enthusiasm of the way he has been allowed a free hand in his work and the friendly treatment he has received from the native of our young country. He seems to have been a good propaganda agent. Seippel also spoke of the need of arranging to have the President's speeches properly translated and distributed in Switzerland. Both he and Ragaz emphasized the need of having as much of this sort of thing as possible done by Swiss and of avoiding the use of any sort of official propaganda.

He said that although German Switzerland had at one time been distinctly pro-German, the tide had turned at last and that the feeling was increasing in our favor. He said that this had been particularly marked since the beginning of the offensive. As he put it, *l'offensive donne à réfléchir* [the offensive gives pause]. He spoke with a good deal of feeling of the fact that there was every reason for understanding between the Swiss and the U.S. and added that the conviction was growing that the United States are their best friends, that the food question will be well arranged. Rappard has given several lectures in this part of Switzerland and has apparently convinced a lot of people of the true fact which the Boches were trying hard to conceal or obscure.

We went back to the Consulate and gathered in Wirth who asked us to lunch at the same old restaurant where we had a disgustingly good lunch.

At a little before two we climbed into a taxi which we annexed for the afternoon and set about cleaning up the rest of our visits.

First to the top of the hill again to see Prof. Bovet who is the most charming man we met in the course of the day. He plied us with coffee and conversation until after the hour when we should have been at our next call. He runs WISSEN UND LEBEN, an intellectual sheet which has a relatively small circulation but a good deal of influence. He had printed an article by John W. De Kay and wanted to know about him as he had received certain warnings and WANTED TO KNOW.

Hugh [Wilson] told him as much as was necessary for him to know and he seemed grateful. He seemed to have it in for Mrs. Whitehouse as she had done here and got him all stirred up about doing something for us and had gone away after promising to come back soon – and had faded away to America. He remarked dryly when a woman claimed the rights of man he expected her to keep her word as a man would be expected to do. I tried to save her by saying that she had been called home for consultation and appeased him somewhat.

He [Bovet] told us something of a new paper they are planning to start here, to present public question in a purely Swiss way without the limitations that would be imposed on them by the papers that have been bought by the Germans or by the timidity of the purely Swiss press. He, like all the other men we talked to, was very critical of the timidity of the of the political crowd and said that they hoped to hound them into having some convictions if they wanted to keep their places, adding that when a man got an elective place in Switzerland he seemed to acquire life tenure although people might criticize him as long as he lived. He thought that a new influence in the newspaper world might put some life into politics. After getting him to promise to dine with us we went our way to the NEUE ZURICHER ZEITUNG.

First we saw M. Fueter who is acting as chief editorial writer on foreign politics. He is a stiff citizen who had no ideas on any subject that we could find and assured us that the Swiss press was not interested in anything that we could give them in the way of news. It was a painful interview as he was such a complete bonehead but he was equally bored and passed us on to the military critic, Lt. Colonel Habicht, a little bullet headed man like von Jarotsky, who had a life sized portrait of Hindenburg over his desk and German maps and pictures on the other walls. He spoke a painful German French but was scrupulously polite. I asked him whether the Swiss military writers would take any interest in visiting our front and sizing things up for themselves – and he immediately took notice. He put himself forward as the first visitor and allowed that he would be glad to honor General Pershing whenever the occasion offered. At my suggestion he also gave me the names of Col. Feyler and Capt. De Traz of the JOURNAL DE GENÈVE and Lt. Col. Riggenbach of Bâle. We'll see.

After showing us a new map with the news that the Germans had renewed the offensive and were advancing in the direction of Amiens he led us to the office of the acting editor-in-chief, M. Rietmann. He was more genial than Fueter but nothing to write home about. He said that he was interested in news from America but that it generally came along so late as to be of no value; that the handling of our news by foreign agencies was a great mistake and that the question of bad translation did us a lot of harm. He had been over the matter with Mrs. Whitehouse but she had done nothing about it and he had not heard from her.

At just the right moment Dr. Field charged in upon us and bore us off to our next call, upon Ecker [Egger] of the University. He was a solid little man with an intelligent eye and a genius for talking comic French. In the hall downstairs he had an old stained glass window with a porky lady balanced on a ribbon with the name of one of his ancestors, which led us to remarks about the portrait of Whistler's Mother, and thence to the story of the old English lady who went to see Anthony and Cleopatra and commented afterward that it was "so unlike the home life of our own dear Queen" which brought down the house.

Ecker [Egger] told us more about the new paper they were planning to get out and some details of how they expect to get an allowance of paper and smoke some of the politicians out of their holes. He is one of the strong men in this part of the country and that he may play a big part politically later on. From there we went to a house of quite another sort, that of a rich businessman, M. Hürlimann. His wife is English and had already gathered in Mrs. Field for tea. It turned out to be the birthday of both Mrs. Hürlimann and Dr. Field and the wedding anniversary of Hugh Wilson, so there was quite a celebration.

Hürlimann had definite ideas about the new paper to which he was strongly opposed. He said that a twice a week paper without any news would command very little attention and that if they bought some broken down daily and gave it a tonic they would do much better both as regards circulation and the securing of financial support from people like himself.

There was a painful moment when they brought up the question of the return of McNally à propos of expressing their regret over the departure of Keene who is now our Consul in Rome. There was nothing to do but maintain an absent-minded silence but it was anything but pleasant.

After dropping Dr. and Mrs. Field at the Consulate we went up to the tip-top of the hill again to call on Dr. Fleiner who is the most famous of all those we saw during the day. Before the war he was professor of Constitutional Law at Heidelberg, but he did not seem to acquire the true doctrine for he has been shooting his classes full of pro-Ally talk to such an extent as to cause general comment and some bitterness.

He is evidently a Jew and his French family was funny even to an American but his ideas were on the right road – although I fear he might be somewhat timid about letting Switzerland get too much committed to our side even in thought. He assured us that German-Switzerland was growing more and more pro-Entente every day and told us some more about the success of Rappard's lectures.

We left him in time to stop in at the Consulate, gather up our belongings, brush up at the hotel and go on to our favorite restaurant in time to receive Prof. Bovet with a cocktail, which he had never met before. He allowed us to gather that his favorite tipple was Bourgogne and we governed ourselves accordingly. He gathered a genial bun and was most entertaining.

I got him [Bovet] started on Italy where he lived for years and learned to speak the language like a native. He gave me letters to two of his friends there and regaled us with yarns of his *jeunnesse* [sic, youth] which must have been some *jeunnesse*.

For one thing he told us that when he was young and had not the sous he became engaged in secret to a young lady of the riche bourgeoisie whose family was thoroughly disgusted. Finally his belle-mère said that if he could be sure of an official position in Italy she would consent. He went to his friend Martini – not the inventor of the cocktail and told him of this promise. Martini promised to arrange the matter. Bovet returned to Switzerland, told his family-in-law that everything was arranged. The marriage took place and they made for Italy only to find that the ministry had been overthrown. Martini got in well with the new crowd and again promised to arrange the matter and at the last minute the Ministry was again overthrown. Bovet, *ayant une âme comme la franchise même* [being an honest man], decided to blow out his brains because he had deceived his mother-in-law. Martini produced a new Ministry at the critical minute and again promised that all should go well – and again the darn thing was overturned. Martini was appointed governor of some place [Eritrea] or other and was on the point of leaving so Bovet saw no alternative save to shoot himself. He decided to do the decent thing, however, and go to say good-bye to his good friends the day of his departure and then go home and make for the other world. As he came into the room Martini held out a little paper and said simply that the last thing he had done was to get the decree signed giving Bovet a chair in the University. Bovet learned afterward that Martini had made the signature of the decree one of the conditions of his acceptance of the post of governor – AND, he wound up, *NE ME PARLEZ PAS DE LA FAUSSETE DES ITALIEN JE LES CONNAIS AU FOND* [don't talk to me about the Italians – I know them by heart/I know their inner selves]. As he told it, it was a touching story and at the same time kept us in gales of laughter.

He [Bovet] also told us of his son who had been a good deal of concern to him as he was anti-militarist from conviction and refused to do his military service, but after refusing as a matter of principle to serve with the Swiss colors he went and enlisted in the French Foreign Legion. That is the sort of anti-militarist one can respect and the old gentlemen was immensely proud.

He also told us of the last visit of the German Emperor here to see the Swiss maneuvers. When his suite was absent for a few minutes he spoke frankly of the burdens of his position and one helpful conversationalist remarked that the socialists must be very troublesome, to which Hugh Wilson remarked:

"The socialists, BAH! Whenever the time comes I can twist them around my finger, but the people who worry me are the Junkers, and I shall have a lot of trouble with them."

And Wilhelm does not seem to have been so stupid about that.

And so we broke up at half past eleven and started back for our hotel for a real night's sleep before my start for Italy.

Insert 252
Bovet spoke of the freedom of the Italians from class distinctions so far as living relations went and contrasted it with Switzerland. He said he was of the petite bourgeoisie, the bourgeoisie being composed of
   La Ville [Urban] Bourgeoisie
   La Riche [Rich] Bourgeoisie
   La Grande [Grand] Bourgeoisie
   LA BOURGEOISIE and
   La Petite [Petty] Bourgeoisie

He said that the feeling between these various subdivisions are very definite and that they did not mix in any degree – that he was always putting his foot in it when in Geneva because he failed to remember who was in each class and because he referred to them all indifferently as though they were all human beings.

Insert 253
Professor Ragaz is a Theologian from the Canton of Graubunden. He has been very active as a popular preacher in his home Canton. His tendencies are distinctly socialistic, he being a member of the Socialist party. His views in advocating pacifism and non-resistance are well known. For some years he has been a Professor of Theology in the University of Zurich. Prior to the war he created

rather a stir by supporting a strike movement, which found little support amongst the general public. At the beginning of the war he published an article under the name of "Helveticus" which was the first pronounced stand taken in the public press of East Switzerland against the tendency of following the footsteps of Germany. This article was published in separate form and created a very deep impression. He is the editor of a religious Monthly, which is pledged to the cause of democracy in religious and political affairs. The act, however, which caused possibly the greatest sensation since the war was the protestation of Professor Ragaz in an appeal to the Russian Maximalists, calling upon them not to conclude a premature peace with the German Government and proclaiming that such an act, though possibly bearing the name of a step towards peace, really meant the harming of the cause of permanent peace, in giving the autocratic Imperials the chance to turn all their forces against the West. Report has it, that numerous anonymous letters have gone forth, warning Professor Ragaz that his life would be in danger if he continued in his present course. He has today quite broken with the socialist organization, charging it with absolute one-sidedness in its relations with the present world problems.

Insert 255
Professor Seippel has been in Zurich for about twenty years. He came here while yet maintaining his connection as editor on the staff of the Journal de Genève. His duties are those of teaching French literature and thought in the Federal Polytechnical School. He has failed to be transformed into a cosmopolitan representative of the Union between German and French culture, but at the same time has shown a very clear understanding of German thought and has been an exponent of the best that there is in French Culture. He is politically very moderate in his views, having been a warm friend of Professor Foerster and of Romain Rolland.

Insert 256
Professor Bovet has likewise been long in Zurich. He comes from the Canton de Vaud. In contrast to Prof. Seippel he has assimilated completely the German Culture and in his use of the two languages knows today no different whatsoever. He has been from the first politically extremely active, representing the cause of decentralization and also the endeavor to avoid German bondage from Switzerland. As editor of "Wissen und Leben" he has played a very important part in molding the views of Swiss intellectuals.

Insert 257
Professor Fleiner began his career as professor of ecclesiastical history in the University of Basel. He had a call to Heidelberg, where he reached great fame as one

of the leading teachers of political history of German tongue. As a staunch democrat he felt it his duty to sacrifice all his personal interests and returned to Zurich when the Imperialistic fever spread over Germany. His position is unique in that no German has ever ventured to attack him – on the contrary, his lecture-room is crowded with German students and Germans in mature life. He is perhaps today the leading Professor in the Zurich University.

Insert 258
Dr. Fueter comes from Basel. His brother is Professor in the University and he himself gives courses in journalism. On the staff of the *Neue Zuricher Zeitung* he has charge of the comments on foreign affairs but it is to be noted that conflicts or interests between Switzerland and various countries are regarded as in the field of the editors for internal affairs. The most noteworthy work of Dr. Fueter can be found in his weekly review, published in the Friday morning edition of the *Neue Zuricher Zeitung*.

Insert 259
Mr. Reitmann is the right-hand man of Dr. Meyer, editor in chief of the *Neue Zuricher Zeitung*, and one of the heads of the liberal party in the Canton of Zurich. Like the editor in chief, he is well disposed towards the Entente and especially towards America, but timid in his acts, and tries to maintain a careful equilibrium.

Insert 260
Colonel Habicht is the military expert on the staff of the *Neue Zuricher Zeitung*. His articles seem to me extremely uninteresting and without decided character. He tries to maintain a precarious equilibrium, he has been several times on the French front and maintained after these visits an enthusiasm for French military action, continuing for a period of six to eight weeks.

Insert 261
Professor Egger is professor of political economy and was Rector of the University at the beginning of the war. He is very active in reacting against the danger of the Swiss standpoint being submerged by the wave of Germanism coming from the North. He has also been active in Red Cross work. His lectures in Basel and elsewhere seem to have produced a considerable impression.

Insert 262
Mr. Hürlimann is Vice-Director of the Ruchversicherungsgesellschaft [Rückversicherungsanstalt], one of the strongest financial institutions in the country, and which is now seeking to establish a sister concern in America. The Director is

Alsacian. The field of activity of the company extends far beyond the limits of Switzerland, but the Entente interests predominate to a very high degree. Mr. Hürlimann, who is married to an English lady has been since before the war the constant adviser of British authorities particularly in regard to financial matters in Switzerland. He is one of the staunchest friends of our cause I know.

Log   On the train en route Zurich-Chiasso. Friday, April 26, 1918

Hugh [Wilson] came to the station this morning and saw me off on the 8:50 for Chiasso. By rare good luck I got a compartment to myself and kept it all the way except for some Huns, three of them, who got in and rode for a few miles before we got to Lugano.

About one o'clock I got out at a little station and got some sandwiches and a bottle of beer which I consumed in the compartment while a trainload of Boches ate at table d'hôte.

The afternoon I spent alternatively reading and looking at the mountains and trying to keep awake. Through the St. Gothard for the second time – and I can't say I enjoy the scenery inside the tunnel for it seems much like other tunnels.

At Lugano all the bullet heads got off the train. It must be some sort of German colony. Blah!

It began to rain gently as we pulled out of the station and kept up the rest of the way.

Hotel Metropole. Como
We drifted into Chiasso at about half past five and tramped, – three or four of us – down to the frontier with a genial porter pushing all the bags on a little truck. Traffic is not what it is when the frontier is open. The Swiss passport office put me through in short order and the customs refused to take any interest in my bags, so I went on thru the gates to the Italian side and engaged the Italian forces. The passport people called me in and put me in a chair – evidence that they had received a telegram about me from the Legation at Bern and perhaps from other sources – and began firing questions at me. I told them everything about myself that I know and hope I made them happy. Then they went out with me into the tiny custom house and swept all my things out with a *beau geste* [nice gesture] so that I could stand outside and wait for the tram to come to take me to Como. There was a lady with her son, the only other thru passengers, and they were both hard at work going through their trunks with the aid of about four or five functionaries. It is war time and they are taking no chances – as is right. Nonetheless the lady was not ready for the tram and I was the only one that got away.

I was dumped off in the Piazza with the information that there would not be another train for Milan until morning. A drunken porter came along and volunteered to take me to a hotel. He headed for one that a one hundred paces my nose told me was not what I was looking for, and after trying him with general instructions to take me to the best hotel in town I picked out one by sight from a distance – and came here. It is nothing to brag about but is clean.

And anyway it is a relief to get away from those damned Boches.

Log   On the train en route from Milan to Rome. Saturday, April 27, 1918

A drizzly day which seems to please the native as it does his counterpart at home – and to annoy the foreigner to the same extent. I got up at seven and had a shivery breakfast in an open window overlooking the lake. The drunken porter who landed me in this place must have been far drunker than I thought at the time – for he assured me that this was the best hotel in Como.

After getting ready to leave by an 8:30 train I was told that it did not go until 9:10 so I put in the time walking up and down stairs and looking out of the window. The chambermaid called upon me for expert opinion as to how long the war was going to last. She has a husband and four brothers at the front and is not unwilling to have the Boche finished any time America gets ready to administer the coup de grâce. The head waiter was also conversational and said that Italy was a cockawhoop [sic] and sure to hold out longer than the Hun. The piccolo also had some ideas on the subject but as he had a hairlip and spoke some comic dialect into the bargain I did not get the value of his views.

At Milan I piled all my belongings into a taxi and drove to the Consulate where I saw the vice-consul, a Mr. Funk, a very amiable young gentleman who told me that the wagon lit [sleeping car] conductor would be able to give me my reservations, and then wanted to bow me out. I stood tight however until he had inquired as to the hour of my train and after a vain hint that he might send a messenger to see me through the difficulties of the crowded station I took my leave, which was about all I could take. The Consul [North Winship] is in Rome for a few days.

At the station I found most of the population of northern Italy gathered in front of the ticket window. I sized up an intelligent looking employee and tried French on him with some success. I gave him much treasure and bade him get me my ticket, see plunder aboard the train, fetch the wagon-lits man to be in the café, and settled down to lunch. He did the first and third and started off with the porters to do the second but evidently abandoned them on the way for they soon came staggering into café under the burden of my bags and started a race riot intended to tell me that they could not get through without me. I compromised by entrusting them with my tickets – and it worked.

I found myself in a compartment with a garlic smelling son of the country who treated me to much conversation to which I could but poorly respond. However I gave him some papers to read and that quieted him for a time.

At Bologna we stopped for dinner in the station. Bologna is the headquarters of the Italian General Staff and consequently there was a great deal of movement and any number of soldiers in the station. I found a place in the crowded restaurant at a table with an American YMCA man and a one-armed Italian Lieutenant. The YMCA man was preening himself over his wobbly Italian and was very conversational – the Italian being dutifully polite. After the YMCA man left after telling me the story of his life and how he was off to meet Dr. Mott and show him how to win the war, the young Italian opened up in French and was worth talking to. He was an engineer before the war and was working in Hungary when hostilities broke out. He seems confident as to the final outcome but said the people were getting very tired and that they must have some hope.

Log   Hotel Excelsior. Rome. Sunday, April 28, 1918

To my considerable surprise I had a good night's sleep on the train but under a misapprehension got up at seven thinking that we were soon due in Rome. Instead we did not roll in until nearly ten.

There was nobody to meet me at the station, not even porter from the hotel, and I had a beast of a time getting a porter and landing my luggage in a cab and getting to this hotel where I have a nice enough room on the top floor as far as possible from the lift. If I stay on here I shall have to buy a bicycle to get to and from the lift. Also no telephones in the room which makes it convenient when people leave messages for you to call them up right away. Horodyski has rooms engaged for us at the GRAND[52] and I think I shall move over there as soon as they are ready.

I was dead for food and managed to get some breakfast in my room about eleven and while waiting for it got a much-needed bath and shave. With my breakfast came a note from Richardson saying that he would be at the chancery all morning but that if I was tired not to trouble to go in and pay my respects to him.

---

[52] The Grand Hotel Plaza is the most antique and prestigious hotel in the center of Rome, very close to Vatican, Roman squares and monuments. Frequent meeting point of Gibson and his associates.

That he had some people going to his house to talk business and counted on me to be there. I let it go at that.

Before I had finished dressing Peter Jay came in and chatted for a little while. He said he had planned to meet me and bring me to the hotel but that Richardson had assured him I was HIS and that he had made all arrangements for me and would have charge of me while I was here. Peter is expecting an infant next month and is proud and happy. I am to lunch with them as soon as I can get permission from my empressario.

At a little before noon I went over the then chancery which is still in the same place it was when I went there in 1904. Richardson was there and received me graciously, introduced me to Consul Wilber who came in to see the Ambassador [Thomas Nelson Page], and then took me upstairs and left me with Merriam whom he describes as very good.

Merriam was about as chatty as usual which is to say he was completely dumb, but he did pull out a three page memorandum in which he had somewhat abstrusely diagnosed the whole Italian problem and figured out how we were to solve it in the next three months. I read it over twice but don't quite remember what it was all about.

We went up to Richardson's house with [William] Hurley, a U.P. man who is working with the Embassy for the time being. At Richardson's we found John Bass and Winship, the Consul from Milan who is down here for a few days.

During lunch we talked ways and means and after lunch went on with it but I have not gathered many definite ideas beyond the fact that they all considered the situation here acute and feel that we should do something in a big way at once. They all got after [Secretary of War] Baker when he was here – for a three hour visit – to send some American soldiers to Italy as the thing best calculated to make the people realize that we are really with them in the fight. But he turned it down with the typical statement that "even if we lose Italy that doesn't mean that we have lost the war". ...

Irwin has telephoned that I am in entire charge of all propaganda in enemy countries and the General Staff and pretty much everybody else has been informed accordingly. Washington has never informed me of this and I think I shall send them a little reminder of the fact tomorrow, not because I am peeved at the neglect but because it is an active way of explaining that I have not done anything definite along those lines. I have been gathering the dope for Kerney who at last account was going to handle the question.

Winship says that the socialists and the pacifists are active in his district and that we must get to work on them. He is getting a good deal of stuff into press and is accomplishing some other things at his own expense – his request for three hundred dollars monthly have gone unanswered for some months. He is strong for movies for the ignorant people who will not read or listen to lectures and all others present jumped in and agreed.

Winship says his vice consul [Funk] is a mess and on the blacklist, that he has had to put him on purely routine work and keep from him anything of a confidential nature as he is not to be trusted. But his repeated wails to the Department and to Carr personally have been without avail and he is a good deal discouraged.

Merriam seems to be more articulate on paper than in speech and had been after the Consuls to get them stirred up to help. Three of them have not answered him and the Consul at Florence [Frederick Dumont] wrote back an offensive letter in which he said that there was no need of Merriam's work there and that he had better keep away and not spoil a good situation. Florence being notoriously one of the most critical points in Italy that does not speak very well for his knowledge of what is going on in his own district and Carr may have to be informed.

We are to have a meeting tomorrow at five to thrash things out and try to frame up a telegram to Washington setting forth the needs of the situation here in money and otherwise. They seem to have offered no definite plan of operations but to have confined themselves to asking for separate things as the need arose, which does not give Irwin any picture of what is going on. Unless they are able to come through with generous quantities of money I fear there is not much to be accomplished but we shall have to make a stagger towards it and abide by the result.

On the way home Bass told me that he had had a long talk with Cardinal Gasparri who cursed out the Entente very thoroughly, saying that they were rotten with secret treaties and that altogether he could not see that there was much to choose between them and the Germans. I asked Bass whether he had asked the Cardinal why, in that case, he leaned to the Boches, but he seems to have been too tactful for that and says the whole crowd at the Vatican claimed to be strictly neutral

According to the stories told at lunch the Red Cross must be no particular credit to us. They are said to be tooting their horn every time they give a nickel and clamoring for gratitude all the time – and incidentally they seem to be gathering all the suspects together and giving them jobs. One particular woman who had been mistress of one of the members of the German Embassy and was still dining regularly with the Boche left to take care of the archives, was denounced as unfit to hold a position in the Red Cross. Perkins who is in charge here sent for the woman and told her all that was said about her so that she was put fully on her guard and – and she still keeps her place with the Red Cross <u>because she denied that there was anything wrong with her</u>.

I spoke to Bass about Cortesi and was told that while he is very valuable and knows a lot one must always remember that anything said to him will go straight to the Vatican. Sounds to me like rather a useful man to have around the house.

Log   Hotel Excelsior. Rome. Monday, April 29, 1918

This morning I got to the Embassy at a little after ten and found all hands on the job. Jay had polished off his desk and was ready to talk so I settled down and spent half an hour with him. I was then taken in to see the Ambassador [Page] who put me in a big chair and then proceeded to inform himself as to the purpose of my mission. He was very vague about it having seen nothing but a telegram from the Department saying that I was to help out the COMPUB people and work with the Military Censor, and also a telegram from Irwin which told Merriam that I knew all about propaganda in enemy countries and was in charge of it. His Excellency had some sort of idea that Creel was a member of the Department of State and that I was a member of his bureau, and I don't think I succeeded in disabusing him entirely of the idea. I talked at some length on the subject but he seemed to reserve all rights. He was greatly worked up about the case of Newcome who was a clerk here and after being relieved of his charges and dropped from the service has now cropped up as Chief of the Passport Bureau in New York. The Ambassador told me that the Italian secret service picked up a letter from an Irish girl in Germany addressed to a friend in American under cover to Newcome, asking for information as to ports and other military works in the country and saying that the information should be sent to her through Newcome in a registered letter which would reach her without fail. The Ambassador finally made such a row about Newcome's general behavior and unreliability that he was withdrawn. His new assignment has caused a great deal of concern to everybody and the old gentleman is going after it again with a hot telegram. If the man is wrong it is certainly a dangerous place to put him.

Lunched with Capt. Merriam at the Hotel Royal[53] where Altrocchi joined us. We got some talking done but not as much as I should have liked for as soon as we really got into things Mr. Keene, the Consul, came along and sat into the game. He is a pleasant only chap who is filled to the muzzle with stories and shoots them off at the slightest provocation. He was Consul in Florence when Mark Twain was there and told of some of his doings. Mark had a row with his landlady and both sides kept at the Consul to draw him to their side. Finally Mark came in one day with a face like a thunder cloud and with the veins standing out on his temples, announced: "I have seen the last of Signora …. that I intend to see until I meet her in hell!" And then he sat down and spoke his mind in a way that made Keene shudder although he had been an engineer in his time and was used to pretty good cussing. I had seen some

---

53 The Hotel Splendide Royale was a luxury hotel located at Via Veneto, close to Villa Borghese. Frequent meeting point of Gibson and his associates.

of the Keene's friends in Bern and Zurich and was able to give him news of them to such effect that he booked me up for a meal at an uncertain future date.

Dropping back to the hotel after lunch to change for the afternoon I ran into Mabel Boardman who is dressed like a Field Marshal and covered with service medals representing who knows what. She is setting sail for Paris in the course of a day or so, so Eliot [Wadsworth] will probably have his hands full again.

At 4:30 we had another meeting at the Embassy, Merriam, Richardson, Bass, Winship, Altrocchi and Hurley. Tried to get them to come down to the brass tacks and tell what they wanted to accomplish and how they proposed to go about it if the wherewithal was furnished. It is always easy to get people to talk about their plans but hard to get them to come down to something definite. The meeting finally broke up because Merriam had to go off to see somebody and I shall have to draw up the plan tomorrow on the basis of what we talked about.

Merriam had made an engagement for me to go and see some Italian official but had not said anything to me about it so I went ahead to the Embassy although it seemed to afford him a certain amount of pain.

The Ambassador [Page] lives on the top floor of a great building down the street a couple of blocks from the chancery. We went up in an asthmatic lift and landed in a wonderful apartment of the sort you always come upon unexpectedly in Rome. Room after room of vast proportions with all the furniture and decorations that are suitable for rooms of sixty by seventy. There were a number of people there and I met enough of them to keep me busy for some time.

First Mrs. Train, wife of the Naval Attaché [Harold Train], whom I had met in the morning, Mrs. [Lucy] Becket (a former sister-in-law of Czernin, now divorced from her Austrian husband and apparently bearing it very well), Dr. Mott of the YMCA who was running for a train, General Scriven whom I had wished on me in the morning at the chancery, Miss Boardman, M. Besnard, the French Directeur des Beaux Arts who looks as though he would grace his residence in the Villa Medici.[54] We had quite a chat and I parted from him after accepting eagerly his invitation to go down and see his *jardins fleuris* [flower garden]. The Consul [Joseph Haven] from Turin was there and refused to get enthusiastic over the interest of his post, said they had had some riots there a few months ago but had not attached any significance to them until the Embassy had started a riot at not being informed. He seemed genuinely distressed at a mere riot in the town with machine guns on the corners and five hundred people killed was nothing.

---

[54] The French Academy in Rome was created in 1666 and since 1803 was located in the Villa Medici. In 1913, Paul-Albert Besnard had become the director of the Villa Mecici, and only 1922 of the École des Beaux-Arts in Paris.

Aldrich of the Red Cross (Major) told me something of Davison's trip. Said the Mayors of the various town they visited in the north of Italy were all afraid of the pacifists and did not dare received them publicly because even the Red Cross had a taint of the war. That all of them came around secretly and expressed their appreciation of what the Red Cross had done but that the pacifist sentiment was too strong for [something appears to be missing here from Gibson's original] Aldrich expressed his opinion that the sentiment was so strong as these politicians believed and that they would not now be reelected in spite of all their precautions.

Met a Mrs. Lowry, sister of Norman Armour who is now living in a train at Vologda. Also Miss Stanton whom I knew is Washington and who used to dine with the Farrar-Smiths. Likewise Mlle. Robilant, known to the Embassy crowd as "Gaby," daughter of the Italian representative on the Supreme War Council at Versailles [Mario Robilant]. She is engaged to one of his aids and charged me with all sorts of messages for him without bothering to tell me his name.

Cortesi, the A.P. man, came in and was agreeable but did not fall over himself as I had been led to believe he would. Shall have to see him later.

An amiable old English lady who gushed properly over my book, as most of the people did, said that Arthur Asquith was being married today to Betty Manners, Angela's sister.

Gaby and some of the younger Embassy crowd played the piano and sang after the crowd left and I did not get away from the Embassy until nearly eight. That meant a quick change to get to Jay's by half past to have dinner with them and the Train's. We had a most interesting evening with a lot of talk on the subjects that most interest me.

Train got up the plan for an American offensive in the Adriatic. Simms approved it and sent it on to Washington where it was again approved. But when it got to the Inter-Allied conference it was killed because the Italians objected "for political reasons." I think the Italian reasons would have held only in the event of success. It would have hurt their national pride to have had the Yankees come in and do anything big in the Adriatic.

The Italians have organized five thousand Bohemians into regiments and have planted them on the front where they talk across to the Austrian trenches, sing their little songs and generally try to get over some effect. And when they have done their best they are moved to some other sector of the front. That is the sort of propaganda.

Julia Brambilla, Julia Meyer as was, has expressed a desire to look into my bright young face and the Jay's have asked her and her husband to come to lunch on Thursday. In the evening I am dining at the Embassy although they are not supposed to be entertaining and I was asked to say nothing about it. Why the reason for the secrecy, I don't know.

Tomorrow I lunch with Lane.

I expect that Horodyski will turn up tomorrow and I may have to move over to the Grand to join him.

I was carefully warned by all hands not to leave anything lying about at this hotel as it is supposed to be carefully gone through for the benefit of the enemy. I leave nothing about anywhere so I can feel easy in my mind.

Mrs. Jay said all the news she was getting recently from England was to the effect that Mr. Asquith was gaining strength steadily.

There is a certain amount of amusement as to the military rank of the Red Cross. The other day one of them, enjoying the rank of Major, got after Mrs. Jay with the statement that Mrs. Page evidently did not concern herself with the seating of her tables as she should. It developed that he had been seated below another Red Cross Major to whom he was senior in point of service with the institution!!!!! The poor diplomats have not got one more thing to worry about.

Log American Embassy. Rome. April 30, 1918

A conference this morning at nine with Merriam, Richardson, Winship, Bass, Hurley, and Altrocchi to talk over plans. Merriam was inclined to spin a web of psychological theories about things that did not lead anywhere so I finally suggested in despair that we adjourn and that I try to frame up a plan based on what I had heard and that we then get to work and see whether we agreed about it.

At twelve I went with Merriam and Bass to the Ministry of the Interior to see Gallenga, the Sub-Secretary in charge of Propaganda. He is a charming big chap with the open face of Winston Churchill without the smugness. His mother was English which was considerate of her as it made it far easier for me to talk with her son.

Gallenga first went at me hard to know why we did not join the Allies in the propaganda business and help them present a united front to the enemy. I had to stall on that question and say that I was still awaiting a decision from Washington although I am pretty well convinced that there will be no real joint effort.

Then to my great surprise he opened up in regard to the internal situation in Italy and said that it was desperate. That war-weariness and German propaganda together had produced a most dangerous state of feeling. That not only the ignorant people and soldiers in the trenches but also the intelligent classes and officers at the front were gradually coming to feel that the advantage was with the enemy and that it was hardly worth while going on. He said that within a few months the Government expected to have machine guns in the streets to repress disorders but that he did not know how long such repressive measures would be effective. He said the Govt. would not give in but that the problem was whether they could keep the people going. He then came to the purpose of this rather startling conversation by saying that we could do more to steady this situation than anybody else by flooding the country with propaganda to impress upon the people that America was in the war with all her resources and that it was therefore in the interest of Italy to keep on fighting. He said they would be glad to work with our people but that the situation was most alarming and that if we wanted to accomplish anything we must get to work at once.

Strangely enough his suggestion was along the lines I had already drafted before going to see him but I had not dared to make it appear that the need for our work was so urgent. After talking with the Ambassador [Page] about it I sent a telegram to Polk telling him of the conversation and asking that it be considered in connection with my long telegram to Irwin suggesting a plan of campaign. In the letter I asked that at least ten thousand dollars per month be allotted to Italy. Paraphrase attached.

Lunched with Lane, McMillan and Hinckley at Lane's flat, the one that Sargent used to have, looking out over the whole of Rome. Nothing startling developed from the conversation except that the Pope is a naughty old gentleman who had more to do with some of the ladies than is usual considered comme il faut [proper] in his profession.

Loaded up the telegraph room with so many messages that the poor boys did not get away until after nine. I shall try to give them a respite for a few days.

I picked up Riggs in the street and had him pilot me to a poor Italian restaurant where we dined on poor food and poorer wine. And then home to bed.

Log   Rome. Wednesday. May 1, 1918

Got up at a leisurely hour and strolled over to the Embassy where I found no immediate demands upon my time. Had a long chat with Richardson about all sorts of things and a little talk with the Ambassador which is to be resumed later.

At twelve found Horodyski at the Grand and learned that he has not got any more line on the situation. He plans to put in the next two days nosing about and we are to lunch together on Friday. He now has it lined up that the next coup is to get the Pope to settle the Irish and Canadian questions right and get some credit as well as rendering a service to the Allies.

Had lunch with Gallenga who had also asked Merriam and John Bass. He has a fine big library with a ten acre table to work at which quite took me.

One amusing yarn he [Gallenga] had was about a trick they turned in Switzerland some months ago. They learned that in the American Consulate at Zurich there were a lot of papers bearing on the Austrian spy system in this country. After studying the situation they turned the problem over to one of their best police officials who chose five or six of the most desperate criminals in Italy to do the job. There was an expert safe blower, and expert second story man, etc. They got in the windows on the ground floor of the building and dug a hole in the ceiling thru which they climbed into the office of a bank which was just under the consulate. When they got this far and the thugs got the smell of money they went off their heads and said they would not go any further. That this was too soft. Finally the detective promised them that if they would only go on and get the papers for him he would let them rob the bank on their way back. So they went thru the next floor, got the papers and eight thousand francs belonging to the consulate, but on their way back they were disturbed and the bank was not robbed. And as the thugs were returned to prison they could not even keep what they had got. The Govt. could not take it. They could not return it to the Austrians and altogether it was a bad problem for the red tape experts. Finally it was turned over thru unofficial channels to some charity and all is well.

Gallenga was quite frank about the bad behavior of the troops in the big retreat. He told of one of his friends, a General, who patrolled the roads with a motor lorry loaded with soldiers. Whenever he came on any retreating troops he hauled them up before him, took their names, carried out a drum head court martial and had them shot. That sort of thing on a considerable scale served to steady the army when it reached the Piave.

At half past five Richardson took me to call on Speranza, who draws up the daily political reports of the Embassy on which the weekly telegrams are based. He is a delicate man, looking a good deal like Robert Louis Stevenson and seems to have a way of worming out news that is needed. We drank tea in the presence of a suffocating fire which really warmed me for the first time since I reached Rome. Not much shop talked but I am going back for another round with him more at our leisure.

From there to the Countess Manzoni whose husband is in the Foreign Office. She was born a Cuban, married one of the Terry's and INHERITED. Found languages flying thick and fast with no notice of changes of cars. Miss Stanton was there, also the Marquise de St. Paul [Marie C.D. Feydeau de Brou, then St. Paul], a dominating old French lady who put her foot into it with everybody and did not seem to care a hang. Also a Russian officer who has gone into the Serbian uniform so that he can keep fighting[55], the representative at Rome of the Polish National

---

55 Whereas Bolshevik Russia had made peace with the Central Powers in the Treaty of Brest-Litovsk in early March 1918, Russian soldiers, the Serbia Army was still fighting them.

Committee[56], a Mrs. [Eustace] Percy of the British Embassy, a young Italian named d'Addoni, who was at Prague when the war broke out as correspondent of Italian papers. The Count de San Martino, former Spanish Ambassador at Petrograd, etc. etc. First there would be a spurt in good English and then without any warning everybody would flop over into French. Thence to Italian which was needed for the more violent talk, etc. My brain was in a whirl when we left.

Dined with the Richardson's who had Miss Stanton, Signora Coletti, whose husband is a prisoner in Austria, and McClure, the TIMES correspondent. I was interested in what they had to say but they pumped me instead about the eternal question of Belgium.

After dinner we went to the opera and saw TOSCA, not because we wanted to but because there was to be a manifestation in honor of the U.S. and somebody had to go to represent the Embassy. The opera was poor and the house was not over full. Between the second and third acts an old party named Casano who is one of the most famous bores in Rome came out and made a long speech about America with a lot of the poorest lantern slides I ever saw. Most of them seemed to be nothing but pictures clipped from newspapers. The audience being frankly bored tried to applaud and cheer him off the stage but he declined to be discouraged and stuck it thru. We wound up with the portrait of the President which really did bring forth a tremendous amount of enthusiasm – and so it ended well. [added below in pencil] At one of the most painful moments a man leaned out of the gallery and boomed: "Viva ma basta!" [Lively but enough]

I came back to the hotel with the idea of writing a few letters before going to bed but to my surprise found that it was almost one o'clock and no time left for such amusements.

Log   Rome. Thursday, May 2, 1918

Got started late after writing some private letters which have been on my conscience for some time. Nothing startling for me at the chancery but I managed to put in the morning comfortably. Went home to lunch with Peter Jay and found the Brambilla's and Mrs. Burnaby, the Ambassador's daughter (who used to be Mrs. Preston Gibson).

---

56 The Polish National Committee had been formed in 1917 in Lauzanne and then moved to Paris. It saw itself as the legal representation of Polish statehood, although in 1917/18, there was the puppet government called 'Regency Council' in German occupied Poland, followed in November 1918 by the new government of indepenedent Poland under Józef Piłsudski. Konstanty Skirmunt represented the Polish National Committee in Rome.

Peter [Jay] and Keene, the Consul General, went out to play golf and I went back and labored until a little after five when Richardson took me in tow with Mrs. Richardson and let me to the home of Miss Kemp around the corner from Lane's apartment. It is a dingy little street but off the street (no sidewalk) you step into paradise, lovely rooms wandering down a hillside, with little courts and gardens and marble pavilions and glass rooms, all living together in a way they could not anywhere else.

There were a number of people already gathered including the Erskine's of the British Embassy, Mrs. Berdan, who insisted in considering me a Frenchman and speaking in French to me, McClure of the TIMES, Skirmunt, the Polish representative and a few others.

There was a girl who sang and everybody enjoyed their own ecstasies over the music and then Miss Kemp got up and warbled a little and everybody was polite and all the time I wished I could go out into the splendid little garden and enjoy the sun and the dull brown wall of the palace next door. When they were both sung out we were allowed to scatter and I made off for a little talk with McClure.

Walked home with the Erskine's and made myself beautiful for dinner at the Page's. The Ambassador has recently lost his brother and they are not entertaining but had a family dinner for Mrs. Burnaby who is going back to England with her husband in the course of a few days. There were Capt. and Mrs. [Harold] Train, the [T. Hart] Anderson's, the Burnaby's and Mrs. Burnaby's Gibson son [James McMillan Gibson], Mme. Colletti, Lane, McMillan and the Richardson's. After dinner the rug was rolled up in the big sala and McMillan entertained us all with complete foolishness until a scandalous hour of the night.

Log   Rome. Friday, May 3, 1918

As we were coming away last night Richardson told me that Merriam had been to see the Ambassador [Page] to complain about the way I had treated him in sending off a telegraphic report to Irwin. It made me rather peevish as I had put the whole matter up to him as to whether I should telegraph or not, or whether the plan I had drawn should go as his or mine or the result of joint conference, or whether we should add to it or subtract from it or change it in any way. And after he had sulked and acted most ridiculously he finally said to let it go. However anything for a quiet life and I promised to go to work this morning to butter him up. I asked Richardson to feel him out however and see if he could learn whether there was any earthly thing I could do or refrain from doing to please the gentleman. I told him the other night when the telegram was under discussion that my one and only object in coming here was to help him and make his work as easy as possible, but that he would have to tell me what he thought would be most helpful to him. I tried every angle I could think of to get him to tell me whether he wanted me to mix in or keep out and apparently all I succeeded in doing was to give him a grievance. It is hard to help some people.

I went up and had a long yarn with him and John Bass but we did not talk any real business. It was all spinning of theories and though agreeable did not help to smash the power of the Kaiser.

Had lunch with Horodyski who has been feeling out the situation and now wants to embark upon a series of calls with me. I am standing him off until I hear something from Washington.

After going over the weekly political telegram with Jay I set out for a tramp around town and found my way down to the Corso for a stroll. It was blazing hot and the shops were uninteresting and the populace was keeping off the streets so I wandered back.

Log   Rome. Saturday, May 4, 1918

Got up with the idea that I would put in the morning writing quietly at the hotel but about eleven remembered I had promised to meet Horodyski at 10:30 to introduce him to Jay. Scurried over to the chancery in time to find Horodyski coming out. Led him back and started him in the right way. He is to come back and see the Ambassador [Page] on Monday.

Lunched with Hinckley out of doors on the Pincian Hill. The food was rotten and we had to send everything back but at any rate it was out of doors and we had no overcoats on and I was content.

Hinckley is a good deal distressed about the lack of system in the chancery and is anxious to get something started. He spoke very nicely about the different members of the staff but said that that did not make things run smoothly.

Stayed in the chancery and yarned with Merriam until 4 and got off a telegram to Carr asking that he send a circular telegram to Consul in Italy instructing them to cooperate with Merriam. Hope it will have some effect.

Dined with Merriam and Altrocchi at the Royal and went afterwards to see la Galli in a 15th Century Florentine play which was most amusing. It enrages me to be able to understand so much and yet to be able to say so little when it comes my turn to talk.

In the theatre saw Prince Skirmunt and Mme. Colletti and began to feel that I was acquainted with Rome.

Log   Rome. Sunday, May 5, 1918

Horodyski called for me this morning at half past ten and we went down together to the Palazzo Borghese[57] to see Count de Salis, British Minister to the Vatican. It was a treat to drive in off the dirty street into the great double courtyard with fountains and statues and an air of space and wealth and grandeur that suits my simple tastes. We climbed up a lordly spiral staircase to the second floor where a French speaking servant let us into a room that any of the Popes could have been proud of. The decorations were of the period and the furniture was evidently original, for it would be impossible to furnish any such place with modern things and keep the air of this.

De Salis is a quiet little grey haired man who seems very timid and speaks in the almost whispering voice of the very deaf. He was glad to see me but spoke with great caution, urging me at each new word to consider what he told me as confidential. He is quite wrought up over the idea of our sending a representative to the Vatican, preferably openly and accredited, but otherwise he thinks we should get somebody on the ground. I held out no hopes on the subject and limited myself to expressing interest in his views.

He then raised the question of the Papal representative in Washington and asked about his influence. I told him I knew nothing about it but that so far as I had been able to observe he did not have much of a position and that he certainly had not built up anything in the nature of an unofficial Legation of any power. He said he thought the Vatican should send over somebody who would play a bigger role and really stand for something in Washington. But he remarked with extra soft pedal that the Pope [Benedict XV] was VERY STUBBORN and that he was unlikely to make any change. Then he repented of the harsh word STUBBORN and appealed to me for another. I gravely suggested that in speaking of one so far above us we might perhaps better use the expression LOYAL which de Salis accepted with equal gravity.

He spoke of having me meet Cerretti and talk with him but said that it might be suggestive of a drive upon me if he were to ask me during this week as he had another dinner for him on Saturday. After much backing and filling he finally confided in me that he was having the prelate to meet Mr. Page, – the which was something of a shock as he has been so violently anti-church. It seems that each of them expressed the wish to meet the other and that de Salis is acting as the proprietor of neutral ground where they can properly meet.

---

57 Famous palace in Rome near the river Tiber.

I let the matter ride as I am not at all anxious to mix in these matters but Horodyski insisted on his trying to fix some sort of date for us to meet before I left Rome.

It looks to me as though my telegrams from Switzerland might at least have had enough effect to cause the Department to instruct the Ambassador [Page] to sound the situation and see whether there is anything to be learned from the Vatican. That may be only my mean and suspicious nature but it seems strange for him to start off on the quest of the church after raging at them from his home on the Quirinal all these years.

From there we went to the British Military Mission which is in reality their intelligence service and met Major Lygon who was interested in trying to put over a special piece of propaganda which had fallen into his hands and which he had already sent me thru Horodyski several days ago. I told him I would look into it and see whether I could do it. He had been forbidden to touch it with tongs by his superiors but was still anxious to get somebody to start it off.

From there back to the chancery where I found Richardson with a telegram from Creel to tell me that Mrs. Whitehouse would probably return to Switzerland, that Swing would not be sent if the French objected and that Ackerman would probably not be used in Switzerland. He told of several people who were to be sent over to Italy to get to work and of some of the equipment that might be expected soon. He asked that we try to get something started on propaganda in enemy countries. We can get things started whenever they answer my telegrams and tell me what we can have in the way of money, staff, and participation in the various inter-allied boards.

Also a telegram from Hugh Wilson to say that unless something was soon forthcoming Ackerman was starting for home.

Richardson and I walked around to the Hotel Royal and left copies of the telegram for Merriam.

At 12:45 [Guiseppe] Brambilla came for me but not in his car as he had planned. It was in the garage for repairs but had been held up by the arrival of lots military cars which needed immediate attention. We therefore got into a low-necked cab and drove down to the place the tram starts from only to find that there was no tram. Brambilla then ordered the cabby to drive out to his house and friend cabby refused flatly. An altercation ensued which resulted in Brambilla getting out and taking the number of the cab. Cabby then decided that we were a mean pair and that it would be the part of wisdom to take us, but Brambilla had got his back up and refused in his turn. Another cabby who came along refused to play with us and had his number taken after a violent argument which would have started a popular uprising at home. Finally a round faced cabby came along grinning as though he rather preferred driving us to any other form of amusement and we got under way. We drifted along through clouds of dust and reached the bottom of the long hill which leads up to the Brambilla's home. Here the horse lay down with the remark that he was all in and could not think of hauling us up that long hill. As the horse spoke only Italian the driver interpreted for us and we got out and walked. It was a long pull and when we arrived we were not only late for lunch but covered with dust an inch deep.

An Italian lady had been asked to lunch but had sent word that she would not be there so we sat down without loss of time and inhaled spaghetti and other native dishes with some wine grown on the place.

Brambilla has an old farm house which he has fixed up to a certain extent. He has a sweep of hills and fields and plans to build some day on top of the highest hill where there is a view as good as any near Rome. In the meantime he is having some fun doing over the house where they now live. From the terrace in front of the house there is a fine view of St. Peter's and a lot of things of interest which make you extra glad you are living in the country and not in the middle of town.

After lunch we sat down indoors and played with the dogs and tore people's characters to shreds and generally had a pleasant time until four 'clock when we set out down the hill to call on the Abbott's whose villa is next door. On the way down we ran into Sir Henry Howard and his daughter coming up in their [Cadillac] Victoria to call. They turned back with us to kill two birds at the Abbott's. Sir Howard fell upon me on the war, which in my eyes is highly commendable.

At the Abbott's we found the Iddings, Mrs. Berdan and several others and were fed with large amounts of tea and cakes. The villa is lovely in itself and has a splendid garden. On either side of the house are two great stone pines which are said to be among the largest in Italy. Mrs. Abbott spends most of her spare time praying that they may not be struck by lightning.

Mr. Iddings and his daughter brought me back to town in their Victoria and dropped me at the foot of the hill.

After writing some letters I dressed and went down to the Circolo della Caccia[58] to dine with Horodyski, Skirmunt and McClure. We had a bang-up dinner and then locked ourselves up in a little two-by-four room and talked until nearly midnight.

Horodyski evidently has a drive under way against Steed of the TIMES and attacked him from every angle. Said he was weak, narrow, vain, over-ambitious, etc. That he had gone crazy over the Jugo-Slav and wound up by saying that he was filled with the idea of being Foreign Secretary. McClure began trying to

---

[58] The Circolo de la Caccia (Italian: Hunting Circle) is an exclusive mens' club in Rome mainly visited by the city's aristocracy.

defend him but under the onslaughts of Horodyski finally had to drop out and keep quiet. We came back to the subject we had discussed with de Salis in the morning and agreed that if we were going in for nationalities we had the Belgians and the Poles already to our hands without erecting with the MORNING POST calls "fancy" nationalities like the Jugo-Slavs.[59]

As there were no cabs to be had we walked up the hill together and Horodyski stood on the corner and talked to me for a long time about the need for us to be represented at the Vatican. That is evidently his main idea in having me so much in sight these days. I am willing to hear what he has to say and let it sink in but I shall be very much surprised if we ever send a regular accredited man to the Pope.

Horodyski is to have an audience of the old gentleman in the course of the week and may have something of interest to say. He plans to go back to Paris with me a week from Tuesday.

Log   Rome. Monday, May 6, 1918

Horodyski's big cigars were too much for me and I woke up with a head. Fortunately there was nothing much waiting for me at the Embassy. I got off a couple of telegrams and tried to get Merriam keyed up to sending something to COMPUB about propaganda in enemy countries but he set his teeth in his comic way and went back over and over to his idea that this is my job and that he would have nothing to do with it. There is something the matter with the man's mind.

Had a talk with Horodyski after he had seen the Ambassador [Page]. He professed to be charmed but evidently had not got far with his representation at the Vatican.

Spent an hour or so with the Ambassador talking about the improvement of the information service which seems to be a matter of getting people to do it as nobody now in the Embassy makes any pretense at be able to do that sort of work and consequently it is not being done. Speranza is already on the ground and is well suited for certain phases of it. John Bass might also be prevailed upon to remain and divide his time between Merriam and the Embassy but I don't know just how much use he would be on this sort of thing. His Excellency thinks he would be perfect "because he is a famous war correspondent".

---

[59] The term Yugo-Slavs means "South Slavic people" and would soon serve as a common denominator of the population of the "Kingdom of Serbs, Croats and Solvenes", founded in November 1918.

Went home to lunch with the Ambassador and had another good talk. Most of it was about the various bickers in the staff at one time or another. His Excellency swears by Richardson and merely tolerates Jay. They have evidently rubbed each other the wrong way – that is Richardson and Jay have – and in every instance His Excellency takes the side of Richardson.

The King of Montenegro [Nikola I] came to call at the Embassy and left a card with a mourning border just like any ordinary citizen. The Ambassador incautiously asked when the King would receive him and was snapped up for half past four this afternoon. This looks as though he were going to try down here the game he has endeavored to get under way with the Ambassador in Paris. He is after CASH.

John Simpson came it to say good bye as he is going back to Paris this evening. He said a telegram had been received just as he was leaving announcing that somebody else had been appointed to represent the Food Administration, that if McFadden was out, he Simpson might be also out of a job when he got back to Paris.

Went to the Embassy at five and talked to a swarm of people, most of whom I had already met one place or another. There were Mrs. Woodward and Mrs. Berdan and the Misses Howard and the Countess Robilant and Gaby, and the Lowry's and White and Hubbard and the usual tea party crowd.

And then back to the hotel to dine alone in my room and write a load of letters in an endeavor to clean up my correspondence. The courier came in this morning from Paris but brought no letters for anybody. They have probably gone to Madrid or some such place as the mail service in the Paris Embassy seems to be a complete mess.

Log   Rome. Tuesday, May 7, 1918

Had a quiet morning's work at the hotel and took over an imposing assortment of letters to put in the bag.

Found Merriam with a telegram saying that the Liberty Loan had been oversubscribed by fifty percent, having produced four and one half billions instead of three billions hoped for. There were twelve million subscribers which was twice as many as there were to the First Loan. Inasmuch as the last Italian Loan produced three hundred millions that should give them a jolt. No wonder they think we are a lot of money bags.

Tried to get Merriam to talk about the subject of propaganda in enemy countries as he had been instructed to do, but he has gone on some sort of hunger strike and says that he has made his recommendations to Washington and has nothing further to say. He gave me a copy of Bass' report to him but I have not seen the telegram he sent and do not propose to ask for it. Altrocchi is going off on a tour of speech-making and Merriam is left alone to run his ship. I shall be curious to see how he makes out.

Lunched with Riggs at the Royal.

Spent most of the afternoon taking a nap after having come back for the purpose of doing some quiet work.

Richardson produced before lunch Commendatore Apolloni, President of the Circulo Roma-Parigi[60] before which I am elated to talk about Belgium next Tuesday afternoon. As I am leaving for Paris that same evening I tried to get them to set is ahead a little but for various reasons it could not be done and I am to do as I am bid.

At a little after five went down to tea with Mrs. Berdan and found there the Gaisfords, British Secretary to the Vatican, Mrs. Rock, daughter of Iddings, and an Italian lady whose name I did not catch. Riggs and Hinckley came in late.

Dined with the [Peter] Jay's who had also asked young White, who is in the Naval Aviation Service. He is a fine looking youngster, son of Sanford White, which must be a dreadful thing to have hanging over him all the time. We sat up after dinner and destroyed the characters of various people we disliked and altogether A PLEASANT TIME WAS HAD BY ALL.

Log   Rome. Wednesday, May 8, 1918

Life was not strenuous this day so something must be brewing.

I spent the morning in leisurely fashion framing a telegram to Irwin about propaganda in enemy countries. After showing it to Merriam let it go after lunch. This was the first time that I have been able to get him to talk about business. I pray that this may be some evidence that the hunger strike has been broken, but I knock on wood.

Took Merriam to lunch at the Grand and for once he got almost articulate. He told me something of his reform efforts in Chicago when he had drafted some legislation to forbid the sale of spirituous liquors and had limited the content of wines and beers to 7 %. The wets[61] came to him and complained and he told them that intelligence on their part would dictate immediate acceptance of what he had planned. They said that within a very short time they would undoubtedly be forced out of business anyway and that the best thing they could do would be to

---

60 A contact circle for artists from Rome and Paris.
61 "Wets" refers to those who wished to be allowed to purchase and consume alcohol during Prohibition, as opposed to the "drys" who would have neither.

fight step by step until they were driven out. He must have been an uncomfortable antagonist if he tackled them the way he tackled me. My experience of reformers does not incline me to reform.

Took Peter Jay for a walk through the Villa Borghese[62] and listened to some of the local squabbles such as the row between General Scriven, who appears to be an old ass, and Colonel Buckey, who seems to take himself too seriously. It is a problem to dispose of the old mutts of generals who have accumulated on the shelves of our shop – and the way we seem to have adopted is to wish them on the Foreign Service in one way or another.

Came back to the hotel and tried to write out something to say to the Roma-Parigi crowd, but did not get very far.

Dined at the Circulo della Caccia with Horodyski who had spent the day at the Vatican. On Sunday or Monday he wants to get Monseigneur Ratti to dine with me. Ratti is going to Poland as the first Nuncia the Vatican has sent in the past 150 years and the occasion is useful as affording an opportunity to fill him up to the neck with propaganda. I am supposed to load him up with large quantities of talk about the interest of America in the future freedom of Poland. It is really a great chance and I am sorry we have not some more people here to get hold of him and train him in the way he should go.

After dinner Horodyski sat down and wrote a telegram to Sir Wm. Wiseman telling him that the only thing the United States can do to win the war at present is to send a representative to the Vatican. He wanted to mention me in it but I declined absolutely to be boosted for the job. I don't care to have them thinking in Washington that I am touting myself for any sort of job, – which I am not.

Word has come from Pershing on the quiet that troops are coming to Italy. They are troops coming direct from America to complete their training but the effect will be good in Italy. It is rather surprising that the Ambassador should not have been told.

His Excellency left today at lunch time for a week at Sorrento and looked as happy as a school boy at the prospect of a rest.

Learned today that Article XV which so enraged the Vatican in the Secret Treaties[63] was to the effect that if Italy so desired the Vatican should be excluded not only from the peace negotiation but from the questions leading up to peace. If that is correct the Allies certainly laid themselves open to charges of idiocy first for having put such a thing on paper and second for having allowed it to become public.

---

62 One of the largest parks in Rome.
63 In paragraph XV of the Treaty of London (1915), France, Great Britain and Russia had committed themselves to assist Italy in any opposition to Vatican attempts to join future peace negotiations.

Telegram from Irwin   May 9, 1918
1261 GOLLY

For Gibson from Irwin:
The trouble about our European work is that we do not seem to be getting things done. Weeks ago I was prepared to have an officers commissioned to go to the front to arrange the troublesome matter of getting information into Germany but was stopped by information from you and Kerney that you could get all the people you wanted there and that it was unnecessary. We are preparing our distributing balloon here and taking other measures to ensure preparation and distribution of matter in Germany and Austria but this is of no use unless you or someone makes arrangements over there. Had expected you to organize adequate office for Kerney in proper location and that has not been done. Must insist there be no further delay. Am willing to greatly increase Paris office with assistants and all necessary help as soon as I see any symptoms that anyone is doing anything. Both Creel and I greatly dissatisfied.[64]

Log   Thursday, May 9, 1918

On coming to the chancery in the morning found a telegram from Will Irwin giving me blazes – the one I had asked for in order to get Kerney stirred up to doing some work. Not much use to send it here as it should have come through Paris where Kerney could have had a look at it. However I shall take it back with me and reproach him with it. Copy attached.

Lunched with the newly-married Andersons in their nest in an old palazzo in the lower part of town. Went up three flights of stone stairs like those leading to a light and airy sewer and came out into a room that might have been a little small for a Republican National Convention but was big enough in all conscience for anything else. They were fortunate enough to get it furnished for it was too hopelessly big to furnish unless one expected to settle down permanently in Rome. The Richardsons also came to lunch and we had a nice quiet time with good simple Italian cooking and much talk which went on until nearly three. I have not yet got used to the leisurely way of dawdling about after lunch here and begin covertly looking at my watch immediately after getting up from table. But so far as I can

---

64 This telegram from the State Department responds to Gibson's request of April 18, 1918. Progress can be seen developing below.

see they get through a good deal anyway and as they work late hours they are entitled to something in the middle of the day.

Spent most of the afternoon puttering about at the chancery and then brought Anderson and Lane to the Excelsior for tea.

Dined at McClure's with Horodyski and Lt. Hazen who is one of [Reginald] Hall's men here. Hall came down here not long ago but I missed him. He is now Admiral Sir Reginald Hall, if you please, and very glad I am of it.

McClure was full of the crisis in London and ventured the prediction that Lloyd George would talk them around. He usually does and seems to be a sort of political cat with that animal's capacity for landing on its feet. This time he has several elements in his favor. Nobody wants to throw out the Government at a time like this. Then there is the question of Ireland and he can always trade off a postponement of the Home Rule Bill against Unionist support. He can pretty well be depended on to stave off trouble for a few weeks but I am inclined to think that his name is on the gate and that his days are numbered.

Horodyski told us after dinner about his going back to Austria after the war broke out. He scouted about to find out whether there was any danger for his class being called and was told that there were still some months leeway. The day after he got to Vienna he learned that he would have to go up before a board within a month. Off he went for a maaskur [masker] as he was told that the only men who were sure to be exempted were those who were too fat to be of any use. He gained forty kilos in one month and got thrown out by the board as unfit. Just as he was congratulating himself Bobrinsky broke loose with his fool speech at Lemberg and the Poles were in such bad odor that he saw little chance of being allowed to leave the country.[65] One morning as he was walking along the street cursing his fate a man came up very deferentially and took off his hat and addressed him. Horodyski did not know him but the man said that he came from Galicia where Horodyski's father was Marshal of the nobility. The man bootlicked and dawned and showed anxiety to be bien vu and Horodyski, not knowing what else to ask him inquired what he was doing in Vienna. He said he had been driven out of his home town ahead of the Russian advance and that he was now handling the question of passports for Switzerland at police headquarters. Horodyski's heart nearly stopped beating but he showed very little interest beyond saying casually that his sister was ill at Davos – which was quite true – and that he might have to go there

---

65 In September 1914, Russian troops had occupied the Austrian part of Galicia. On September 26, the newly appointed Russian governor of Galicia, Lieutenant General Count Georgiy Bobrinsky, had called in its cultural capital Lemberg (Polish: Lwów, Ukrainian: L'viv) on all residents – including millions of Poles – to stay calm and cooperate. Thus, Austrian Poles came under suspicion of sympathizing with the enemy.

to see her; that if he did he would count upon his new found friend to get him there. Friend said he would be delighted to serve in any way one so highly placed and when in due course Horodyski went to him, he fixed things in no time and in January 1915, Horodyski got back into Switzerland.

McClure ragged Horodyski somewhat about the Polish question and said that there was a scientific expedition to Africa to study the habits of the elephant. The German professor wrote a solid four volume work with a long title which showed everything that was in the book. The Englishman wrote a fat volume with plenty of photographs of himself in shooting clothes and called it THE ELEPHANT AND HOW TO KILL IT. The Pole wrote a thick pamphlet and called it THE ELEPHANT AND THE POLISH QUESTION.

There also cropped up a yarn of correspondence with Beatrice Fairfax.[66] A girl wrote her and said: "I went out with my young man last evening and before dinner I drank seven cocktails. With dinner I drank a quart of champagne. Did I do wrong?" The answer was PROBABLY.

TELEGRAM sent by HORODYSKI to Sir Eric DRUMMOND to be forwarded to Sir Wm. WISEMAN and Lord READING
Rome. May 10, 1918:

After full consultations with various elements I am convinced that the United States could serve not only her own interests but the interests of the Allied cause by taking any of the three following steps, stated in order of preference:
1. To send a regularly accredited mission to the Vatican,
2. To send a special and temporary mission to the Vatican,
3. To send a confidential representative to the Vatican.

In view of my knowledge of conditions in America I believe the second could and should have the maximum chances of success. The advantage of this plan lies not only in the fact that it would consolidate the Catholics of the Entente Powers and have a helpful influence in Ireland, Canada and Australia and would have a good effect on the Catholic Party in Italy, but also it would deprive

---

66 "Dear Beatrice Fairfax" was an advice column in the New York Evening Journal, starting in July 1898. It was the original first "Miss Lonely Hearts" column to offer advice to the anxious – on all kinds of topics, especialy love.

the Central Powers of the pretext for saying that they are the only united block showing due reverence and respect for the Church. Such a representation could exert a powerful influence in drawing still nearer to us the Poles, Czechs, Jugo-Slavs and other similar elements in the Central Powers and could be easily an established channel for propaganda to the National Bishops who can be reached in no other way. The United States representative would be in a specifically favorable position to deal with the Vatican since his Government are not parties to Clause XV.[67] Its influence could therefore hope to bring the Vatican somewhat nearer to our side, and in my opinion much nearer to our side. This change, no matter how slight, would be of inestimable value to the Allied propaganda. I consider this to be the most important single achievement open to us from the selfish point of view of the Allies.

The choice of the individual is of vital importance in this matter. Above all he should not be a Catholic as this would work against him at home. 2: He should be a man of distinction and not a professional political boss. 3: He should speak either French or Italian. 4: He should have a first class Secretary who I think should be a Catholic.

From my knowledge of affairs in the Vatican I would suggest someone of the type of President Wilber of Stanford University or Dr. Vernon Kellogg.

The time is the important element and decision should be taken without loss of time. If Colonel House and the State Department so desire I will be glad to put myself at the disposal of the new representative during the beginning of his mission.

Kindly inform me at your earliest convenience of the chances of success of this plan.

HORODYSKI

---

[67] The then neutral United States were not signatories of the Treaty of London in 1915 (see annotation 61).

Log   Rome. Friday, May 10, 1918

Found several telegrams at the chancery this morning. One from Hugh Wilson with some interesting information as to the shortage of food in Austria. Another from Irwin saying, among other things, that I would do well to stay on here for the present. I shall gladly do so although I think I might do well to go up to headquarters for a few days. Also I want to try to get Kerney started to work. There is evidently a need of it as I have not been able to get a line out of him since I left Paris three weeks ago.

Lloyd George wriggled out of if for the moment all right by the use of some of the expedients we had foreseen but I am not betting on his being able to keep his seat very long.

In parting last night, Horodyski gave me a copy of the telegram he was sending Eric Drummond as to our being represented at the Vatican. I spent a good deal of time trying to decide how best to post Washington about it and had a long talk with Jay about it. Shall let the actual drafting of the message go over till tomorrow so as to simmer.

Lunched with Jay's and talked some more about the same subject.

Got off a message to Paris asking them to send my letters down here as I was going to stay on for the present.

Went for a walk with Jay and stopped in at a bookshop in the Piazza d'Espagna where a girl showed me a copy of my book and recommended it as worth reading – much to Jay's delight.

From there to the Gaisford's to tea and had a good talk with Gaisford. He is quite of the opinion that the Vatican is inclining more and more to our side and that if we play the game right we can do good work there. We did not discuss the subject of American representation other but he said that Father Fay of the Red Cross who has left for home gave them some straight talk and accomplished a good deal. He says that he Pope is getting more and more disgusted with the behavior of the Germans toward him and the rest of the world and that before long we shall come into our own.

He also said that there was a regular channel of communication between the Foreign Office and the Vatican. There is an official in the Ministry of Public Worship who is theoretically in charge of the buildings belonging to the Ministry, who is used as a messenger. That they at time communicate in writing by means of memoranda carefully avoiding salutations, etc.

Log   Rome. Saturday, May 11, 1918

Spent the morning drafting several telegrams to Washington and Paris and got them off before lunch. Sent FLP [Polk] the substance of Horodyski's telegram but added that during the absence of the Ambassador I hesitated to offer my own views. I did this because Jay was evidently somewhat worried for fear His Excellency [Page] would feel that something had been put over on him during his absence. However FLP will doubtless be able to do a reasonable amount of thinking himself and I can send my comment along after His Excellency's return to Rome.

At one Brambilla came for me with Aldrovandi, the Capo de Gabinetto of Sonnino. He is supposed to be a crabbed and rather unrepaying person but I took something of a liking to him and found him reasonably responsive, although he was not overwhelmingly effusive. There was no one else at lunch and we had a good chance to talk. I did not press the opportunity by going into important matters as I thot [sic] it better to put in the first talk getting acquainted so that I could tackle bigger matters with more assurance afterwards. Aldrovandi said he was present at the conference when Pershing made the offer of our troops and described it much as Palmer had. The Italian are most anxious to get some American troops into Italy for the effect both on the army and on the civil population. As a matter of fact there are some troops coming but I could not tell them so. They are not coming to fight but to complete their training – and they are coming straight to Italian ports from America. The fact that they are in Italy will in itself do a lot of good.

Soon after lunch Aldovrandi hurried back to town and the rest of us stayed on to tramp to the top of the hill and see the view from the old tower where the Brambilla's hope someday to build. Mme. Brambilla and I whooped it up with sneezes in honor of the glare and the dust and I came back almost blind. The view is the best I have seen anywhere near Rome and commands everything as far as one can see. Parts of the tower date back to B.C. [Before Christ] and there are layers accounting for pretty well every subsequent period. It is a shame not to use it in the new house but there seems to be a good deal of doubt as to the solidity of the foundations and the possibility of shoring them up to stand the strain of a new house. Underneath there are some Etruscan remains but the Government has put up iron grills to bar access to them. Brambilla hopes someday to get an expert and start in to uncover whatever is there. It is hard to understand how he can have patience to leave such things undiscovered.

We came to town in a tram as Aldovrandi had taken the motor and when I rolled up to the Embassy it was five o'clock. Jay was about to set off and we took a tramp together. He led me to a secluded nook near the Coliseum and showed me an imposing portal with the inscription still clear: *EMPIRE FRANÇAIS. DÉPÔT DES POUDRES ET SALPÊTRES.*

It was a dependence of the Prefecture of Rome and has evidently escaped the hand of the reformer.

We tramped for about an hour and talked about pretty well everything including Jay's dislike of Richardson who apparently does just about nothing at the Embassy and resents any orders from Jay. He has sensibly refrained from going to the Ambassador [Page] about his bickerings as he knows it would do no good but he evidently felt this would be a good chance to tell somebody – and he let me have it with both barrels.

Stopped in at Jay's on the way back and borrowed some things to read – including Richardson's book to which his name is not signed THE AMERICAN AMBASSADOR. He asked me the other day whether this had got him in bad in Washington and I did not quite understand what he meant. But after reading at it for a time I understood the reason for his anxiety. It is a rotten book in that it makes the diplomatic service look rotten and depraved – It made me mad but I could not stop and am going through it.[68]

At eight I dined with the Speranza's at the Palace. On the way in ran into Sir Henry Howard and his daughters and had a little talk. Miss Howard is leaving for America tomorrow and I envy her. The rest of the family announced that they would be on hand to hear me at the [Circulo] ROMA-PARIGI when I speak on Tuesday.

The Richardsons also dined with us and Colonel Buckey came in afterwards and put jazz into the conversations. It was agreeable but I had hoped to have a real talk with Speranza which will have to be deferred to another time. As I was leaving he led me aside and said the word had gone on through Rome that I was here on a secret mission to the Vatican. I wonder who started that little tidbit. Perhaps it is just as well I have carefully refrained from seeing any of the Vatican crowd.

Log   Rome. Sunday, May 12, 1918

By way of change saw hardly anybody and spent most of the day in my rooms thumping on the typewriter and reading and writing. Waded thru Noval Richardson's book THE AMERICAN AMBASSADOR which made me distinctly peevish because of the contemptible way it paints the diplomatic service. Also read a thriller by John Buchan called THE POWER HOUSE.

---

68 The book which depicts the US diplomatic service in a quite bad light was published in 1917 by Scribner & Sons under the pseudonym Lawrence Byrne.

Forgot to eat lunch and at half past four had some tea in my room.

At a little after eight went over to the Royal and prevailed upon Riggs to eat some dinner with me. It ended up in my dining with him and getting home early to bed.

Log   Rome. Monday, May 13, 1918

Tomorrow it will be two weeks since we got off our telegram 1559 to COMPUB as to activities to be undertaken here and still no reply.[69] Richardson and I made frequent forays to find Merriam and confer with him as to the blast to be sent about it – as Merriam himself had suggested. Late in the afternoon we prepared a draft to submit to him, thinking in our childish fancy it would save time and please the gent we were trying to help. He came in about six and I showed him the results of our labors. The only effect was that he was peevish because it was done in his absence and went off with his hair all ruffled up. He is getting too dam temperamental for me. He goes entirely on the comic theory now that I came over here as an assistant to Kerney and that I am "in training" to succeed to his throne when he goes home to America. In the meantime he is convinced thru some kink in his own mind that I am supposed to handle trench propaganda. He seems to resent any attempt to help him or any desire to discuss matters of business which he now seems to think are his own private property. I think my real mistake was that I adopted too meek and lowly an attitude in dealing with him when I came, disclaiming any authority or desire to boss the show and playing up as my one and only aim in life the desire to HELP him. That evidently was not the way to do it and now I may have to try the other way, which will not be pleasant.

During the morning a telegram came in from the Department to say that they were very much interested in the reports of the CONGRESS OF OPPRESSED NATIONALITIES held at Rome last month.[70] That the "proper authorities" whoever they might be, should be told that the U.S. sympathizes with the aspirations of the nationalities of the Austrian-Hungarian Empire to have a voice in their own development. That the matter should be brought to the attention of the Minister of Foreign Affairs with the statement that we wish to be of service in the matter – and asking for his counsel.

---

69 Telegram 1558 [not 1559] from the Embassy in Italy to the Department of State, https://history.state.gov/historicaldocuments/frus1917-72PubDip/d22 (last access February 27, 2020)

70 In April 1918, a group of Italian journalists had organized the Congress of Rome, which addressed nationality issues concerning the populations of the Habsburg Monarchy.

Horodyski came in to see me in the course of the morning with an account of his visit to the Pope on Saturday. He had an hour and evidently said his little say at his ease. He gathered the impression that the Pope was a good deal irritated by the attitude of the military party in Germany and by the overbearing manner of the Governments of the Central Empires. He seemed to lean a good deal more to the side of the Allies than he had when last Horodyski saw him, though of course he does not expect to see him come out in the open as a supporter of the allied cause. He seemed to have a good deal more friendly feeling for us than for any of the others, probably largely on account of the fact that we were not parties to clause XV. H. gathered the idea that the Pope would welcome some means of direct communication with the President thru a representative here. Of course Horodyski probably gave him a good opportunity to voice such an intimation as it is part of his present scheme that we should be represented at the Holy See.

I was to have lunched with the Brambillas at their place in the country and after waiting in vain for Brambilla to turn up and get me I took a low-necked cab and set forth thru the dust and wind. As I drew up to the foot of the last hill I met Brambilla's butler on his bicycle coming down to tell me that the Marconi's could not come and that the Brambilla's were waiting for me at the Circulo della Caccia. So round we turned and went back for lunch at the club.

A pouch in during the day with a wagonload of letters which I have not yet had an opportunity to read carefully. Several from Will Irwin showing that he has gone off entirely on the propaganda in enemy countries as <u>the</u> important thing we have to do – which is bunk. One from Bell saying that he has an important and confidential matter which it is necessary to communicate to me and that he wants to write me when I get back to Paris and he knows he can send me a letter in the bag so that it will reach me. Wonder what it is.

Wanger came in to see me during the afternoon to talk about the flying camp at FOGGIA. For some silly reason they have picked out one of the most unhealthy places in Italy, saturated with malaria, because Wanger says, Colonel Bolling said he did not want the men to be near a big city where they would have temptations. That was not the subject of his complaint however. He said that he and a great many of the others had enlisted before the draft was put thru so as to get into the thick of it. That they have been over practically a year now and have not seen a bit of service. They have learned to fly Coprone's and are ready to go into action. BUT we have no such machines and the training they have received does not fit them to fly French or British machines. We are sending some Caprones to the U.S. to be copied so that it can be hoped that in the course of some months we shall have some of our own on the western front. But in the meantime these hundreds of men are utterly idle. For the Italians have neither the machines nor the gasoline to keep them up in the air just for practice. However at the Italian front there is a clamor for additional pilots and Wanger suggests that our men could be put on as alternate pilots on the new machines which are to be put into commission very soon – they require two pilots and our boys could be put on as the additional men. That would get them into active service where they are really needed, would be a starter towards having some troops on the Italian front and as these machines are the pride and joy of Italy, every time one of them with an American on board, accomplished anything we would get it heralded far and wide that Americans were really doing something on the Italian front. I don't see how we could in any other way get so much effect out of the use of so few men. The next thing is to figure out how it can be arranged.

At eight went to the Palazzo Borghese to dine with de Salis. To my surprise I found Monseigneur Cerretti, the Papal Under-Secretary of State. No other guests but Horodyski and Gaisford.

Found that His Excellency [Cerretti] is a friend of Archbishop Hanna and that gave me a start. After dinner we got off in a corner thanks to careful maneuvering by de Salis and had a good talk.

I had a good chance and filled His Excellency [Cerretti] with talk about the determination of the United States, our resources and the fact that with the whole Anglo-Saxon race involved were not coming out second best. I did not spare the bragging tone and told him about the number of troops in France (the statement of Mr. [Newton] Baker that we had exceeded our hope of having 500,000), the over-subscription to the Liberty Loan, the number of subscribers, etc. He himself had spent several years in America and seemed to have some comprehension of the meaning of it all.

He spoke of the desirability of thorough understanding between the President and the Vatican and I told him there was no difficulty about that. That the President's game was open and above board and that understanding of it was not dependent on any subtle explanation. Then we went on to the general attitude of the people to the Church and I told him frankly that I thought the people in America were disappointed in the failure of the Holy Father to come out and express himself about grave moral wrongs. That this was a state of affairs that could be remedied at any time but the sooner the better. I said that people looked upon the Pope as claiming the spiritual leadership of the human race, and that he was therefore supposed to be concerned solely with the triumph of good and the defeat of evil. That we knew we were fighting the battle of right and justice and that people generally could not understand why the Pope was not more frankly beside us. His Excellency [Cerretti] brought up the old remark that the Pope is the father of all his people, German and Austrian as well as the Allie, but I came back with the equally old remark that a good father does not hesitate to correct and reprove his children when they do wrong and point out the right path to them. His

Excellency came finally to the point which had evidently been in mind when I was asked to dine. He said it would be a good thing for the President to be represented at the Vatican, he realized that we could not appoint a regular mission but suggested that someone might come over informally as Mr. Taft did and talk things over now and then. I expressed interest but said that I knew nothing about that sort of thing but that doubtless the Holy See could have its views conveyed to the President thru its own people in America.

Then we dropped the serious side of things and talked about his travels in America and Australia. He did come back long enough to say that the present Papal Delegate in Washington [Giovanni Bonzano] is not up to what they expect of him. That he was sent there before the war when it was purely an ecclesiastical mission but now there are greater demands than he can meet.

I had the chance to tell him something of Cardinal Mercier and hope some of it went home.

Came home with Gaisford and Horodyski and chatted until midnight.

At one state of the proceedings Cerretti and I got to talking about the American newspapers and to my surprise he announced casually that what he enjoyed most in the was MUTT and JEFF[71] !!!!!!!!!!!!!!!!!

Log   Rome. Tuesday, May 14, 1918

It rained the whole blessed day and made everything too dreary for words.

In the morning I found Jay much excited because he had had something of a scene with Sonnino. He had gone to the Consulta [Consulate] to tell Aldrovandi about the telegram about our attitude toward the Oppressed Nationalities Congress. Sonnino was by chance in the room when he arrived and he seized the occasion to tell him instead of Aldrovandi. He read the telegram and watched both men stiffen. Jay then said: "I believe the Ambassador has already had the pleasure of discussing this matter with Your Excellency [Sonnino]. He will again talk the matter over with you on his return and in the meantime I am merely bringing the views of my Government to your attention." Sonnino was quite angry and emphatically denied having ever discussed the matter with Mr. Page. Jay then insisted to Aldrovandi that the Ambassador had discussed the matter and Aldrovandi seemed quite upset but did not venture anything beyond the fact that the "whole matter was

---

[71] *Mutt and Jeff* is to a comic strip popular in the early 1900's about a miss-matched pair of friends.

much exaggerated in importance and that the Italian Government had not given the Congress the measure of approval that people had attributed to it." He suggested that Jay get information about it from the Ministry of War, – intimating that they were trying to run the whole business and showing some temper about it. Apparently the War Office has put something over on the Consulta.

Lunched with Skirmunt at the Excelsior. He was filled as usual with the Polish question and was quite interesting. He said recent letters received from Poland revealed some anxiety as to just what the President [Wilson] meant by referring to territories that were "indisputably" Polish. He also said they planned to send a sort of special Ambassador to the U.S. in the hope that he would be able to get the real facts about Poland before the President. Probably they will send one of their men now in Paris and he said he wanted to introduce me to him when I got back to Paris.[72]

Richardson and I had a talk with Merriam before lunch about sending a reminder to Irwin. Merriam still quite touchy and intimated to us rather clearly that we were interfering. He said he alone was responsible and that he should send any telegram concerning conditions here. We wished it onto him and he doped up a bone-headed message and got it off over his own pretty signature. I am afraid it is going to be utterly out of the question to do anything with him as he is so confoundedly suspicious and jealous of the little privileges.

I tried to get him to take me around to see the man in charge of propaganda for the interior but he persistently sidestepped it and Richardson had no better luck. I finally abandoned it but shall have shall have to send some sort of message home to get things put right. I fear I made a mistake not to accept a handsome title conveying the idea that I was running the whole show in Europe. That sort of thing undoubtedly has its effect on a certain type of mind. My idea was that I could render all possible service to these people without assuming an office that would put them relatively lower in rank. Blah.

At six went to the Roma-Parigi and gave a talk on the Germans in Belgium to a crowd of 150 or more. There were a lot of them I did not meet but among those who were there were Sir Rennel Rodd, the British Ambassador, the Belgian and Swiss Ministers, the Belgian Secretary, General Morel, Countess Manzoni, Mrs. Berdan, Sir Henry Howard and Miss Howard, Mrs Speranza, the Keenes from the cradle to the grave, all our Embassy, Major Byrne, Larry White, and a flock of others – enough to make sure that some of the things get across.

---

[72] In his famous '14 Points', Wilson had put the resurrection of the Polish state – which had been dismantled by the German, the Austrian and the Russian Empire at the end of the 19th century – on the political agenda in January 1918.

Dined with [Stuart] Farrar-Smith and Capt. Yarnell at the Excelsior. After dinner went off to the Grand to see Horodyski and took him to the station and put him on the train for Paris with Farrar-Smith.

He had a lot of things to talk about but it was mostly a rehash of the things we had already been over.

Log   Rome. Wednesday, May 15, 1918

Spent morning talking with Merriam and drafting a telegram to COMPUB about impossible situation that has grown up here. ...

Lunched with Merriam and Altrocchi and an Italian prof. of psychology who has donned the uniform of a Lt. and is charged with handling the packages for the soldiers at the front.

Dined with Lane and Larry White and a young flying cadet named McLane who has been disqualified because he cannot stand the high altitudes. He has tried every imaginable way of getting into active service even enlisting in the infantry but red tape gets in the way and he is flat up against it. He was in the ambulance corps before we came into the war and got the Croix de Guerre but our people seem to have no place for him. It seems rotten waste and somebody must have work for him to do. He says that Foulois is going to be canned.

Log   Rome. Thursday, May 16, 1918

Put in a morning at the chancery but did not get very much done. Richardson had another session with Merriam with a view to getting him keyed up to letting me play some part in the propaganda game but completely without success, – so I abandoned all hope of getting him around without a bump from home and sent off my telegram to IRWIN. It is a painful thing to have to send in another row to put on the record but it is a choice between the risk of being considered temperamental and the certainty of having work held up.

At noon we had a pow-wow in Col. Buckey's room. He has been making up his mouth for a confab for several days and this morning rounded up Richardson, Merriam and me to talk over a number of things. He began by telling us the news he had which was chiefly that there was no truth that the Austrians were bombarding Venice with long range guns. They could do it if they wanted with 15 in. naval guns but evidently have not thought it worthwhile. There was a report that the offensive had opened on the Italian front yesterday but he had not been able to get any news on that point and would get none until later in the day.

We brought up the question as to whether our man – if we decided to have one – on board at Padua, should be a civilian or an officer. Buckey was emphatically of the opinion that he should be in uniform as otherwise he would not be able to get anywhere or have anything done. He was all for asking one of the officers on the American Military Mission at Padua be asked to take on this work in addition to his regular duties. We thought very little of that but suggested that he write up and ask the officer to come down and talk things over, which may bring him here Saturday morning. I don't for a minute believe that this work can be done by any man in his spare time but it would doubtless be useful to have an officer who knows the ropes when a new man comes and who can start him on the right path. After Merriam had refused to discuss propaganda and he wouldn't touch it he suddenly veered around and took a violent interest in the subject to the extent of saying that he would telegraph Washington his views on the subject. I was glad enough to have him show some interest and gave it cordial approval. Far be it from me to notice inconsistency if he will only play with us.

At one "Major" Byrne of the Red Cross came for me in one of their cars and drove me out to the beautiful VILLA AURELIA[73] which has been taken by "Col." Perkins as Red Cross headquarters. They do themselves with much pomp and comfort which should fill them with benevolence.

Col. Perkins was there as was also Major Fuller and they were soon followed by Sir Henry and Miss Jesse Howard. I was a good deal shocked at the way these men sized up the situation. Byrne told me that morale in Italy was better than it had ever been and that the pessimistic talk of officials was not to be listened to. I supposed he had some good information from people in the field and inquired about it. It developed that he got most of it from his servant and a waiter at the hotel. The waiter, he said seriously, was a man of the sort who should be Prime Minister of Italy for "he is a man of fine feeling, he makes a beautiful speech and he believes wholeheartedly in the high aims of the war." Apparently nobody else had given him anything. I found Col. Perkins about as sound. He seemed GAGA and I kept looking at him intently for he did not seem old enough for the simple things he said.

After lunch I had a cigar and a good talk with Fuller and felt a little cheered about the Red Cross for he seems a two-fisted citizen with his feet on the ground. Major (Dr.) Collins, who is also of the troop, was there but did not add much to the hilarity of the occasion.

The Red Crosser's brought me back to the chancery where I pottered about and watched my wheeze to IRWIN being got into cipher. I hated to see it go but steeled myself and bade it good-bye.

---

73 Since 1909 seat of the American Academy in Rome.

Rambled about town for a time aimlessly, bought some light literature and then read and wrote until time to dress and go to McClures to dine.

It had turned quite warm and was still light so the big dining room windows were open and I watched the birds swooping about over the black trees of the Pincian Hill as though in a stage picture.

We thrashed out pretty well every pending questions, including whether we should send flour or grain to Italy to get the best use of tonnage and dock facilities, the personal habits of the Prime Minister, our airplane production, the desirability of our sending troops to this country, the morale of soldiers and civilians, the sympathies of the Vatican, etc.

Log Rome. Friday, May 17, 1918

As I knew the Ambassador was due back last night I went over fairly early to the chancery to see him but had to wait until noon before I could get in as there were swarms of people and constant interruptions. Jay had undertaken to tell him about my telegram transmitting Horodyski's message and had apparently given him an entirely false impression of it – although he doubtless did his best to do it with entire accuracy. His Exellency was very wroth and when I went in with the message to show it to him he began to tremble with rage and talk about it. I finally managed to insinuate that he would perhaps understand better if he read the message itself. He did so and it was rather amusing to watch his anger shift from me to Horodyski. He did not say anything definite but before he had read very far his comment had ceased to be levelled at me and he began to cuss Horodyski and Eric Drummond and everybody else concerned in what he considers a plot against the independence of these United States. He allowed that Eric was a pervert and when I ran to the rescue he explained that he meant he was a protestant who had become a convert to Catholicism. He damned Horodyski as an adventurer and crook and said he would have him kicked out of Rome, that he would find out what the British Ambassador had to say about this sort of thing, etc. He seized a block and said he would now write a telegram to Washington and tell them wots wot ... but just then Richardson came in with word that General Scriven was outside with a telegram recalling him to America and he should be received at once.

So the meeting adjourned for the moment and I was told to stand by to finish this matter before lunch. When we resumed the Ambassador wrote page after page and handed them over to me to read as he finished. He said that Horodyski was an adventurer who was seeking to make a position for himself through his ability to insinuate himself into the good graces of people of influence or influential connections. He had accompanied Eric Drummond, a convert to Catholicism, to call upon Cardinal Gibbons in Baltimore, and had done several equally wicked things which were also detailed in this simple way. I should have liked to advise against sending anything of the sort bur feared my advice on the subject might be regarded as a defense and less than no good. After hammering Horodyski to a pulp he then went on to say that the Pope was filled with hate for the President and our ideals and that it would be a surrender of our best traditions for us to have anything to do with him; that it would be a step toward the regaining of temporal power by internationalizing the Papacy and would be a slap at Sonnino whom the Pope was also bent on destroying. Altogether it sounded as though we should lose the war if anybody came over to talk to the Pope. And when it was all over he folded it up and put it in his pocket and we went to the Embassy to lunch accompanied by Lane. Mrs. Page had a long letter from her daughter Mrs. Burnaby saying that PERSHING was going to be recalled – but with no news as to who should succeed him.

After lunch the Ambassador put me in a chair and gave me an hour or more on the villainous behavior of the Vatican, its designs upon us, and this experiences with Father Heeth, Father Fay, Marquis Something-or-other Turner and other Catholics who had done shifty things. I could hardly get the point of most of the stories except that the people were not trustworthy but I think they were aimed at me to convince me of the danger of dealing with the Vatican.

On returning to the chancery Peter [Jay] told me that his sister-in-law Martha McCook, who arrived this morning from Paris, also brought news that PERSHING was to be withdrawn. It seems, according to her story, that there was a big row at the Abbeville Conference[74]; that Pershing announced that he could no longer consent to brigading his troops with the British and French and that they must have their own Divisional formations, that the French and British thereupon waxed very wroth and the meeting broke up after almost reaching the state of blows; that P. slept over it and then sent round word next morning that he had changed his mind again and that things could go on as before. It sounds very fishy to me. 1st because John Joseph Pershing is not the sort to change his mind in that wishy-washy way and 2nd because he could hardly have decided a matter of that great importance without agreement from home. I shall be very much surprised to find any truth in the story.

A telegram came from Washington to say that we could have ten thousand dollars a month to spend in Italy and that we were to fly at it. The War Department

---

74 At the meeting of the Supreme War Council in Abbeville on May 1 and 2, General Pershing had advocated the independence of American troops in Europe, meeting the resistance of Foch, Clemenceau and Lloyd George who argued that they still lacked the necessary experience. Pershing did not withdraw, but the discussion on the topic went on for months.

is asking Pershing to send us some soldiers to make speeches through Italy. Heaven be praised they are apparently getting up some steam. Also stated that my name has been sent in as American member of the "General Propaganda Board" whatever that may mean. I imagine it is the "Inter-Allied Conference Information and Action Abroad" which sits in Paris and not the other Board over which Northcliffe presides in London.

A distressing letter from Warrington Dawson to say that he hopes I will hurry back as he has about come to the end of his rope and wants to get out. His doctors say he has a chance of getting a great deal better if he will lead a life of complete idleness but he hates to get out and carry away the impression that his work at the Embassy has been a failure, which it has been through no fault of his own. He got Sterling to take up with the Ambassador the question of giving him some sort of official status so that he could hope to get more effective work done. His Excellency promised to take the matter up with the Department and push it, – but LA NUIT PORTE CONSEIL [sleep on it] and as he says:

> "I was sent for the next afternoon, and was very gently and kindly admonished for not understanding the situation at all and seeing matters in the wrong light; and not appreciating all the kindness shown me and the privileges granted me; and making the mistake of having social ambitions whereas my independent position ought to be enough to satisfy any reasonable man, etc."

It is a crying shame for he is a priceless member of the staff and His Excellency seems to begrudge him any standing at all. He had standing before as an author and a newspaper man but the minute he came into the Embassy people began to ask when they dealt with him just what his rank was, – and as he is merely listed as a clerk they began to wonder whether he was very much of a fellow after all. He says now he is willing to risk his health if he feels he can really get something done that is worthwhile but that if the game is to go on as at present he had better get out and go back to writing novels at Versailles. He urges me to hurry back – for he says:

> "I am going to try to postpone a definite decision until you return for I believe you can get to the bottom of hidden complications so subtle that they are baffling to all of us who have hitherto tried to understand them."

Because of Merriam's susceptibilities I had the Embassy doctor the telegram to me in such a way that he might think it was addressed to him. I suppose he feels that I have been snubbed for he showed it to me only after it had been pointed hinted by Richardson that I ought to see it, and then in a rather *haut-en-bas* [condescending] manner that was rather amusing to those who were behind the scenes. But I had foreseen that and did not cry.

Log   Rome. Saturday, May 18, 1918

This morning found Paul van Dyke and Prof. Nettleton at the chancery to talk with the Ambassador about founding a University Union in Rome similar to the one in Paris. His Excellency had to go out and left them to talk with Richardson and me. We got them convinced that there was a great work to be done by them when Col. Buckey came along and threw cold water on the whole scheme. However they are going ahead far enough to see whether anybody agrees with us and perhaps they well end by doing something.

Lunched with Henry Lygon at the Grand. He said the Italian Secret Service had told him that there were big strikes on in France and that yesterday there were 90,000 men out in Paris alone. It sounds as though it were pretty bad and the censorship has not let a line of it into the papers. It needs only a little start of that sort to set off a big Bolshevik movement here.

After lunch I went over to see Speranza and talked with him for nearly three hours. He knows conditions here extraordinarily well and feels quite at a loss as to the future. I gave him the best hints I could as to how to improve the weekly telegrams being sent in and he quite grasped the reason for what I said. The prevalent idea here seems to be to compress the messages into such small space that it is out of the question to tell any real story of conditions.

Had asked Merriam to dine with me but he had something else to do and agreed to do so tomorrow. I accordingly gathered in Hinckley and took him to a restaurant he picked out in the Via Nazionale where we had a bang-up dinner and ran into Larry White, McMillan and a number of aviation officers we knew. After dinner all hands adjourned to McMillan's flat and amused themselves with poker or talk. I slipped away early – at half past eleven.

Log   Rome. Sunday, May 19, 1918

Got over to the chancery a little before noon but found only [Peter] Jay on the premises. Sat around and read the papers until it was time to walk home with Jay for lunch. The only telegram for me was one from Hugh Wilson saying that I could be useful if I would go to Bern on the way back to Paris.

Nobody at the Jay's for lunch except Mrs. J's sister Martha McCook who is doing all sorts of things for the YMCA – according to the Y.M.C.A's I have seen, doing it well.

At 3:30 we went out to the Villa Borghese to see the ball game between the Army and Navy Aviator teams. There was a crowd of a couple of thousand people draped round the walls of the stadium and a goodly sprinkling of American boys from Foggia and other camps, but there was little jazz and nobody mobbed the Umpire, Anderson.⁷⁵ The game was poor but the Navy had the best of it and trimmed the Army badly.

I walked back with Capt. Yarnell, Sim's chief of staff and Lt. Col. Dunlap. We dropped in at the bar of the EXCELSIOR and found our friend Greppi, nearly one hundred gayly chatting to a beautiful lady in pink. The old gentleman was born in Parma in 1819 and started the Austrian diplomatic service under Metternich. I have not had a chance to talk with him at any length but should like to start him to work telling of his experiences. He fought under Napoleon III in 1859 and when Garibaldi came along he was still fighting but getting rather elderly. His memory is good and his interest keen. He eats a whopping great dinner every night and goes to the opera or the theatre every time there is anything worth seeing.

At eight I gathered up Merriam and Altrocchi and took them out to dine at the same place I went last night with Hinckley. We ate on the sidewalk whenever food was brought us until about half past ten. Then M. and I went down to the Sala Umberto and saw a poor variety show while A. went to work.

And so after a few chapters of VANITY FAIR – to bed.

Log   Rome. Monday, May 20, 1918

A dull morning waiting on the Ambassador [Page] who said he wanted to talk with me but finally went off to see the Prime Minister without my having had a chance to see him.

Could get no sleeper on the train for Bern until next Sunday so decided to go straight back to Paris and thence to Bern if necessary.

A pouch in from Paris with one letter from Mother and various screeds from other people. One from Ned Bell in regard to the important and confidential matter concerning which he wrote me some time ago. It was to the effect that Horodyski was a person who was already being paid for his work and the British secret service were afraid he might try to hold me up for money in return for information. I sent him a telegram to say that I was wise to the gentleman and that he need have no fears. The good old feller was afraid I might get stung.

Took Wanger off to lunch at the Grand and talked about propaganda in general and the movie end of things in particular. We also swapped reminiscences as to our experiences when the Governor [Whitman] of New York and [John P.]

---

75 Probably reference to umpire Frank Anderson, who was the dean of the Southern College Baseball Coaches 1916–1944.

Mitchel had their spat over Joffre. I had to have Wanger chucked out of a luncheon at Philadelphia where he was sent to pry Joffre loose from the Mayor for a party with the Governor at the Metropolitan Opera. W. was thrown out then but the Governor won out eventually and got Joffre.

I woke up with a bad knee and by lunch time could hardly walk, so I did not wait to see the Ambassador and retired to the hotel to rest it up in preparation for a sortie at the time of Mrs. Page's reception.

Dined at the Jays. There were Miss McCook, bright as a dollar, Col. Buckey and Major Lygon. We paired off after dinner and I had a long talk with Jay, chiefly about the service and its future and the usual gossip that people like to go in for whenever two members of the comic service get together. My game knee was hurting like blazes but I stuck it out until the others got under way and then clamored for a cab and made for home, dropping the Col. on the way. He is much overworked and suggested that I might be able to do something for him at GHQ. I am to have a yarn with him before I get away and see whether Nolan cannot be prevailed upon to lend a hand.

Log   Rome. Tuesday, May 21, 1918

Got up with a bad knee and took a cab around the corner where I found the Ambassador waiting to see me. He took me into his room and closed the door and gave me the third degree about Horodyski for whom he has developed the most intense dislike. He said he was writing a long letter to the President to go by this bag and that he wanted me to tell him all I knew. He wanted to know how long I had been acquainted with Horodyski, how much I had seen of him while here, what I know about his background, etc... He did not seem so anxious to know what I could tell him as he was to explode against Horodyski which he did in the midst of everything I tried to say. I did not go into any joint debate on the subject as His Excellency was in no state of mind to listen to it, but tried to convey to him that Horodyski was well known to the Department, that they had had a long time to size him up, that they were not letting themselves in for anything with their eyes closed, and that he could be sure that Horodyski was not going to run the foreign policy of the U.S. His Excellency was not to be mollified with words however and locked himself up for a couple of hours to dictate the letter to the President. He gave me a very pointed lecture about "mixing up in Vatican politics", saying to would ruin me and end my career. I tried to interrupt long enough to say that I knew the game well enough to be more afraid of it for myself than he could ever be for me, but he paid no heed. He informed me that it was believed that I was here on some sort of special mission. I replied that in the sense that people use the expression here I was on a special mission and that no secret had been made of it. That he himself had been told by the Department just what jobs I would have to attend to, and that if people persisted in thinking that was merely a cover for something else I did not see what we could do about it. That perhaps their interest would fade away when nothing startling happened during my visit. The old gentleman evidently has it in his head that there is more to all this Horodyski business than he has been told, but I have told him all I know and have not tried to put over any of my own ideas. I don't see how I could have been fairer or more loyal.

When the letter writing was over the Ambassador led me home to lunch. There were no other guests but just as we were finishing Mr. George Page came in and afterward Lane arrived from his trip to Florence to pay his respect to Mrs. Page.

In the afternoon I wrote a short letter to FLP [Polk] to tell him something about the Horodyski business so that he might be posted in case the matter was raised as a result of the Amb's letter.

At 5:30 I went to the Gaisford's for a cup of tea and found a selection of Italian beauties who helped pass an hour. Donna Maria Somebody came in and claimed me because I was a friend of her first cousin Princess [Charlotte] Charles de Ligne. I promised to take back tender messages to the old lady and must now scurry round and learn Donna Maria's name.

Lane came for me at seven and we went down to dine at the Restaurant Umberto where we were presently joined by Larry White and a young flying Lt. of the Navy. Lane was near dead of rose cold [allergies] so we broke up early.

I went to the Royal to see Merriam who is off tomorrow morning. He had Altrocchi, Hearley, the little psychologist, Lt. and Dr. McKenzie, a British subject who speaks broken English and good Italian. He is handling the gifts to soldiers at the front and was talking about the propaganda value of his own job. Bade McKenzie goodbye after some talk and then Hearley dropped me at the hotel.

Log   Rome. Wednesday, May 22, 1918

Got up feeling like the end of a misspent day and made my way over to the chancery a little before twelve to find a line from Julia Brambilla asking me to join her and Miss McCook for tea at the British Embassy; they run the terrace there as a sort of public tea room for the benefit of the mutilati [sic].

Went down to Piale's with Wanger to find something to read on the train tomorrow but had no luck there and little better at Wilson's across the Piazza d'Espagna. Picked up some trash and got back to the chancery in time to gather in Col. Buckey and lead him off to lunch at the Grand. The poor little man is all in and although not squalling he will not be able to keep up his present pace very long – and if he gets sick the whole machine stops. In addition to all his ordinary work he has had to take over passport control and has been given no further staff to take care of it. He has an average 3000 visas a month and under present conditions has to see any number of people himself and listen to their cases. It is utterly ridiculous. The British have twelve officers and twenty clerks to take care of the passport control alone and they seem to be fairly busy. What he needs more than anything else is clerical help and I am going to see Nolan and ask if he can't do something to relieve the situation.

When I got back to the chancery I found two telegrams. One from Phil [Patchin] to say that he had shown my long telegram to Irwin who was going to take appropriate action and would telegraph again.

The other was from Irwin to say that I was to spend the funds at my disposal for entertaining and other purposes in my discretion.

Went to Jay's at a little before five and at the hour my ladies appeared. We waited until half past so as to go over to the Consulta for Brambilla and thence to the British Embassy. The gates were open and in Peter's smart Victoria we drove in state only to be told when we came to the tea house that there was nothing doing on Wednesdays. Just as we were going away we were swooped down upon by a commanding Mrs. Barton who took us in to see some rather good pastels portraits that were on exhibition. In talking of the money they were making for the mutilati [ones mutilated by war], she remarked that the American Red Cross gave them 100,000 lire for every 100,000 they raised themselves, – dismissing this as nothing by the casual remark: "Of course they are so much richer than we are" which I supposed was meant to be flattering to our sordid souls. Miss McCook averted an explosion by a hasty retreat from the room and soon after we took our leave. But the lady did not intend to let us get away with any more money than she could help and reminded us in so many words that we were expected to pay for having seen the pictures. We paid and escaped.

At the foot of the steps we met Lady Rodd whom I was anxious to see because of the curious descriptions I had heard of her and of her manners, if any. If I had not been coached about her in advance I should have thought she was being most pointedly rude to Miss McCook and me, but nobody seemed to notice it. She was fearfully and wonderfully arrayed in a gown that would have done splendidly for a fancy dress Arabian Nights affair but was not just the thing for wandering about the garden in the middle of the afternoon.

Leaving Brambilla to do some business at the chancery the rest of us shook the dust of the Embassy from our shoes and hied us in a cab to the Villa Borghese to take tea out of doors. It rained and we took refuge in the covered porch for half an hour and ate some discouraged ices and thence to our various places of abode.

Dined with the Jay's who had nobody but Miss McCook and the [Harold] Train's. After dinner much talk including some from Train about our Navy's activities in European waters that were surprising to me. I got somewhat roused because this sort of thing was not being properly played up instead of spending time and money spreading boob stories like the one John McKenzie telegraphed from London. It seems that we have laid about two thirds of the barrage in the North Sea which the British have been advertising so extensively. Also that we have gone in for a more liberal expenditure of depth charges than anybody else has thought of so far. One of our younger men got out not long ago on the trail of a submarine and dropped twenty-four charges as compared with two or three as is customary – and his action was approved.

Another bit was to the effect that not long ago there was a gas attack on a section of the front held by our Marines. After a time a man in Marine uniform came up from the rear, removed his mask and called out that the gas was gone. Our men took off their masks and 260 of them were gassed. It turned out that the kind gent was a Hun who had some sort of antidote in his nose and mouth – and the right thing was done by him.

Log   Rome. Thursday, May 23, 1918

Got over to the chancery at a little after ten and presently found myself in the midst of a party, the Brambilla's, Mme Colletti, and some of the staff gathered to watch the arrival of the Prince of Wales [Edward Albert] to celebrate the 3rd anniversary of Italy's entrance into the war.

When I got there the preparations were under way. The streets were filled with police in their comic opera costumes, secret service men who were almost as easily recognizable, troops of school children with banners and all sorts of societies, etc. Court carriages with footmen fore and aft in bright red coats with the tailes [sic] neatly hanging down full length instead of being sat upon ... Celebrities passed by on their way to the station, the British Ambassador and Erskine, the Syndic, Prince Colonna, the Primier, Orlando, etc. etc..

Then the procession came up the street and turned our corner. There was practically no cheering but there was a great waving of hands and handkerchiefs and hats and umbrellas and in no time at all the whole thing was over. All we saw was a flash of a little red face under a huge pith helmet, seated next to the Duke of Genoa. He looked somewhat bored and would have looked more so if he had known of the dreary round of entertainment that has been prepared for him while he is here.

Lady Rodd is keeping up her reputation by asking families to separate in the most unusual way. She has taken Mrs. Erskine without her husband which would be quite all right if necessary but on the other hand she has asked Mr. Page without Mrs. P which is unheard of. Mrs. P is to come in after dinner. Other people are asked in most casual ways or left out if they really should be there, and all Rome is seething and having one of its best hates.

Lunched with Wanger who has a plan for the moving picture business in Italy – but has been unable to get Merriam to touch it or consider it. It is based chiefly on the sane idea of helping private enterprise to do our work by showing our films in the regular commercial way. But Merriam says that we are not over here to advance American commerce and that he will have nothing to do with anything of the sort. I asked Wanger to make me a memo of the plan and will see if the idea cannot originate in Washington.

At four went to the Embassy and had a little talk with the Ambassador. From something I picked up casually I judged that he might have been alarmed by the idea of my telegram about the Vatican and wanted me done away with. I inferred that he had written or telegraphed to ask that I should not return to Rome. If this is so, it is filthy for I have told him of every step I took, most of them in advance, that is all of them where there was any initiative on my part and he cannot complain of any lack of frankness on my part. I could not very well go and ask him whether this was so without involving the innocent person who spilled the beans, but I put out feelers and he expressed himself as glad I had come and anxious I should return from time to time. It may have been merely camouflage to cover his tracks but it seems he is given to playing close to his vest and I was not altogether easy in my mind.

When I was there he [Page] was just signing a letter to the Secretary about Newcome, whose scalp he is determined to have. I have never heard anything from him on the subject of Newcome that was at all convincing and the Department evidently feels that there may be something to say on the other side, otherwise they would hardly be keeping him on now. He cussed Newcome up and down to me and asked if I had any opportunity to put in a word against him. It is not pretty to see a man of his age so vindictive against anybody. I only hope he has no axe out for me.

He [Page] also opened up about the need for Americans in Italy and begged me to see General Pershing and show him where his duty lay in that matter. There is no doubt that American troops would have been an excellent propaganda but I can't quite see myself telling the General how to run his army.

However, we parted with urging on His Excellency's part that I should return and promises on my part to do so any time he should telegraph that it was desirable. Now we shall see.

From there on foot to Jay's where he and his sister were waiting to take me out to the Villa Aurelia where I understood there was to be a garden party. We had a pleasant drive and talk out and back but the party itself was one of those that are the most painful I know, a gathering to tell Americans what fine people they are. When we arrived a large company was gathered in the salons and Col. Perkins was reading a telegram addressed to him by the King of Italy to say how much he thought of the Red Cross and of Perkins, etc. Then Apolloni got up and made a long speech in Italian and English to the same effect. While this was going on Miss McCook and I escaped to the garden to hide our blushes. We gossiped while the Ambassador and other spoke and returned only when we heard an unusually long and hearty burst of applause and judged that the speaking was over. When we got back into the house we found the hungry animals fighting around the big table in the dining room for tea and ices and sandwiches, too earnest to talk until they had filled themselves up. There were swarms of people there and by the time I had shaken hands round and talked for a few minutes with Barry formerly of the CRB now doing publicity for the Red Cross it was nearly seven and time to start for home.

Peter sent me home in his Victoria and I found Lane waiting for me at the front door of the hotel. The Andersons were coming to dine with us and we were to go ahead and order – so off we went to an out of door joint where we had been once before with Larry White and McLane. The Andersons never appeared although we stayed on till nearly ten. Col. Buckey followed me to the hotel and besought me to see Col. Nolan and try to get him some extra help to relieve the situation. He is worried about the machine breaking down when our troops get here and there is nobody to handle them. Apparently the Military Mission under General Swift is a sad bird affair and he gets little help from them.

After telling me all the troubles he could he gave me his car and sent me to the station in time to catch my train.

Log   Enroute Rome to Paris. Friday, May 24, 1918

Got away last night with a flat wheel which bumped and bumped so persistently that sleep was out of the question.

The porter said that we should have breakfast at Spezzia [La Spezia] and I was up and about a little after seven so as to be ready. We were an hour or more late in getting in and when we did we stopped just long enough for a glance at the crowd in front of the station buffet – and then under way again without any breakfast. Several times we stopped in stations where sandwiches were sold up at the front end of the train but our stops were always so short that we never got any. We pulled in to Milan at a normal lunch time and found some filthy food in the station restaurant, – some cold omelet laid out on the buffet and some evil smelling codfish. I laid in a little chocolate and got back onto the train to make up in cigars what I missed in food.

I shared a cabin with a wearisomely conversational Englishman who told me with minute detail all his deadly dull adventures about losing his railway ticket and finding it again, etc. He is lower middle class with the painful twang that I always long to produce when twitted about American twang but such people are not easily to be found when wanted. I took refuge in VANITY FAIR and finished it down to the end – and it was a treat after not having looked inside its covers for six or seven years at least.

It was hot and dusty and dirty all day and I sneezed and enjoyed hay fever to the full.

Somewhat after five we pulled into Turin where we stayed for twenty minutes and where my companion and I laid in a supply of sandwiches, boiled eggs and wine which we consumed on our way to Modane, not liking the idea of going hungry any further. And it was just as well we did.

At Modane where we had to change trains we were herded like cattle into one end of the custom house while the soldiers from the train were put through. Then we were chased to the other end of the room and let into a shed one at a time to have our passports gone through. I managed to get my baggage passed on the strength of my diplomatic passport but could not get near enough to the door to have my passport put through in the same way. I then bethought me of the letter given me by Major Lygon in Rome and hailed an R.T.O. [US army Radio Telephone Operator] who was passing by and presented it with a request that he smooth the way. He looked rather bored and blandly replied that all I had to do was to stand in line until my turn came and that afterward I would have time to dine in the buffet. I was so peevish at this that I did not bother him and waited my turn in the smelly crowd, being near the end of the line. As a result we got through about five minutes before the train pulled out and had to run for it. My friendly officer was standing by the train talking to some nurses as I passed and genially asked if everything was all right. I turned on an idiot smile and snapped out YES as I legged it dinnerless for the train. I hope he'll come to me for help someday – but then I'd probably be ass enough to help him.

And so away for Paris on a train without a flat wheel, and with prospects of being in Paris in the morning.

Log   Paris. Saturday, May 25, 1918

Our train pulled into a junction this morning about eight and we had ten minutes to swallow a cup of coffee and get some papers which was just that much better than yesterday's experience. And at 10:30 we came into the Gare de Lyon and actually got a cab which shows that Paris is improving. I shared mine with Wills, the chatty Englishman, that is to say I shared it and he took it alone and paid for it. He dropped me at the MEURICE where I found a room waiting and hot water running in the tub. I landed *à propos* [at the right time] for nowadays there is hot water only two days a week as in Switzerland. The rest of the time a pitcher of hot water is all that is to be had and cold baths are the order of the day.

At the chancery I found that there had been a complete move yesterday and that my room was waiting for me – and furniture. I shall have to go forth on Monday and get a supply.

There was a bundle of letters for me but nothing of much interest, thank heaven. Everybody seemed busy and I did not take up much of their time. I knew Dawson had troubles to tell me so I bade him down to VOISIN'S where we had the first real meal I had looked upon since leaving Rome. Dawson's situation is not as bad as I feared – it got bad but he left it for me to straighten out with the Ambassador [Sharp] which I shall have to do in the course of the next few days. I wanted to know a lot about what was going on here in the way of war news but he was so full of his own troubles that I had not the heart to press him for what would keep.

A telegram for Kerney to say that I am the representative on the Inter-Allied Propaganda Council, whatever that may be, and that I am supposed to move about from one place to another overlooking the work and coordinating, etc. It is supposed to put him and others on the right track about my position and while it is a feeble document it will have to do.

Left the Embassy at four and walked down town to do some shopping. Met Ogden Mills who has been attached to the Second Division as interpreter instead of working on economic intelligence as he was when I last visited Chaumont. He likes being at the front but is to be here only until tomorrow morning and I therefore had no time for a real talk with him. Went to Brentano's[76] and got some books wanted by the people in Rome and then home to the hotel where I messed about with my papers and read until dinner time, dined alone and got to bed early.

Log   Paris. Sunday, May 26, 1918

Got up late and put in the morning arranging tons of papers and reading some of the stuff that has been sent me for use in the French press together with the questionnaire sent out to Creel's people, than which... [sic]

---

[76] Brentano's. Annotation: A bookstore north of the Tuileries Garden, specialized in American literature. Opened in 1895, it was frequented by customers such as Mark Twain or Scott Fitzgerald.

Lucy Linn telephoned and asked me to lunch with her at the Ritz. She also rounded up Arthur [Page] who is in town for a few hours and left immediately after coffee to get back to Tours where he is taking his course in flying. Foulois has been made air commander of the First Army – *qui n'existe pas encore* [which does not exist yet] – and has gone to Chaumont. There is a long story or intrigue and worse but among other things Foulois gets an active command which he has really hankered for in his heart ever since the show began. I did not get a chance to hear very much of it from Arthur but we are to have a session when he gets back the end of the week.

From there went up to see Kerney and spent the afternoon with him until nearly seven. We yarned about things in general and about his trials and tribulations in particular. When I arrived I found Monsieur _____ [sic] who had been sent by Clemenceau to tell Kerney that the entire French propaganda service was at his disposal. Hyde took Kerney to see Clemenceau and he has now grown into quite a statesman with ideas of running the war in general. He has also been down to Chaumont and dined with the General [Pershing] and talked with him a number of times and on the whole he has decided to drop ordinary work and handle only the larger phases of the war. He has got a number of people engaged on various activities but did not seem to know how much good they were. Has acquired a large suite of offices in the Élysée Palace Hotel[77] and moves in tomorrow. The caller spoke no English and Kerney no French, so I had to act as interpreter. It seemed to be a little embarrassing to Kerney as he had evidently talked to Clemenceau about things that were not strictly in his province and he was afraid the Frenchman would spill the beans. However by careful jockeying dangerous subject were avoided and the caller sent on his way rejoicing.

The latest news Kerney had was that Mrs. Whitehouse would not return to Switzerland. I am a pessimist and think she will come back. There still seemed to be some idea of sending Swing.

Creel has made a couple of bad gaffes lately and the national sport seems to be baiting him. However he will probably weather the storm as he stands high with the Great White Chief who does not desert his friends. Mrs. Whitehouse said she had not the heart to disturb him because he was being bedeviled by so many other people. She also remarked that anarchy reigned in COMPUB and that there was much disorder under the "untidy curls of Will Irwin".

At seven Travis Coxe came to see me, looking brown as a berry and in his corporal's stripes which he has won since I saw him last. He is an automatic telegra-

---

[77] First traveler grand hotel at the Champs Élysées, frequent meeting point of Gibson and his associates.

pher and was sent over in some haste so as to get to work – but when he got here he learned that there was no automatic telegraph on this side of the water. So he is in the Élysée Palace doing errands and acting as interpreter to some officers, though without either the rank or emoluments of an interpreter. He looked rather lean and I thought he needed a good feed so took him to Voisin's and did him as well as I could. It was worth it for he waded into the good things as though he had not had anything to eat for months. We talked over old times in Cuba and Tegucigalpa until the restaurant closed at 9:30 and then separated at the Place de la Concorde.[78]

Log   Paris. Monday, May 27, 1918

Got up to the chancery this morning at a little after half past nine and by dint of much pushing and pulling managed to get myself installed in my new office, the one evacuated by the Ambassador. It is large enough for me to work in attended by a regiment of cavalry and I don't know whether I shall have the nerve to keep it if the rush of work keeps up for other people. Several of them could be put in there and I could take a smaller room that would be big enough for me and my stenographer.

The big gun began firing between seven and eight dropped a shell at ten minute intervals for a good part of the morning. I should like to risk a little money that this means the beginning of the offensive at the same time. It would be their way to kick off.

Took Frazier to lunch at Voisin's and got some talking done. He has again taken up the question of a change in Switzerland although he has no particular hope that anything will come of it. I know McFadden has done the same thing and perhaps if enough people keep hammering at it there may be some result. Frazier is pushing [Robert] Bliss for the job with the proviso that he should have somebody assigned to him as advisor in financial matters. McFadden is rather in favor of Cassatt because of the fact that he is a business man who would get things done.

I told Frazier of my telegram suggesting that the President come out with a statement about our attitude toward Austria and he enthused as he has been driving at the same point and mine went in quite independently.

Tardieu came in and talked with us for a time and then lunched at the next table. He expresses much enthusiasm over our war preparations and says that

---

[78] One of five royal squares in the heart of Paris. Several of the hotels and boulevards that feature prominently in Gibson's narrative are located nearby.

people are really accomplishing wonders and that we need not worry. He has turned in a long report part of which has been printed and it is said his private conversation is more enthusiastic than the glowing report. He left Casenave behind "as he is too much of an American". [Sheldon] Crosby, he says, is probably on the ocean now, which rather surprised me as I thought he would remain once he got home. Frazier says McAdoo sent him telegrams that would have made any man with any sort of feelings get out long ago and that he doesn't see how he can continue to hold onto his post.

Had a long talk with Lambert, the man who wants to organize an information service for us. There has been no reply from Polk and I learned from [Robert] Bliss that Polk has been very ill, seems to have had some sort of nervous breakdown. Put Lambert off for the time being by explaining about Polk's illness and promising that I would make another inquiry from somebody else.

Lambert chattered about all sorts of things ranging from propaganda to secret service and ordinary politics. Among other things he took a crack at my old dancing teacher George Washington Lopp, who he says is a crook of the first water. The Red Cross got hold of him and after they had been put onto him, he was taken on by the President of the American Chamber of Commerce. Shall ask Cabot Ward to look into him.

McFadden came in with Dr. Durand who is in Europe on a special mission for Hoover and brought a letter from Edgar Rickard. He wanted to know about the food situation and I gave him the next best thing to definite information, – an idea of the absolute lack of knowledge on the subject by everybody in Rome. He knew something of the seriousness of the situation and I told him some more. I urged him to go down or send somebody to make up an opinion as to the real food situation which is essential to an understanding of the political and military situation. He decided to leave for Rome this week and said that he might think it best to make that the center of his activities, coming back here when it seemed necessary. He spoke nicely of the way Simpson is doing the work and said there was no reason he could not be left in charge. At his request I drafted a telegram to go to Hoover from all three of us telling our views and announcing his departure for Rome.

Walked down town with [Herbert] Williams, the Commercial Attaché, and dropped a card on Davis and Edith Wills. Passing the Crillon, I ran into Caspar Whitney who was just getting out of a cab. He held me up to show me letters from his wife and tell me what a wonder she is; he also announced that we should dine together some evening this week.

Lucy Linn told me yesterday that she had been told by the Dr. that she had appendicitis and must not undertake anything serious for some time in the way of work. She is signed up with Lafayette Fund and also promised to go travelling around for the YMCA helping organize plays in the camps among the soldiers. For some reason I did not get wrought up about it at the time but since then have come to, and this evening telephoned and booked her for lunch tomorrow so that I can tell her how to manage her affairs. It's none of my business but she has nobody to boss her over here and I should hate to look Howard in the face if I stood by and let her work herself into the hospital.

[Penciled in by hand] Dined alone in the hotel and wrote a letter home. Just as I was getting into bed to read the end of *La Tulipe Noire* when the siren began tooting and guns loosing off all over the neighborhood. They were so peppery about it that I decided upon the better part of valor and took my book and cigar down to the bar. There was a 3rd rate crowd there so I finished my book and cigar in comfort while the guns roared and snapped and barked and then went up to bed.

Log   Paris. Tuesday, May 28, 1918

Dawson had a talk with the Marshal [Joffre] this morning in regard to the newly resumed offensive—memorandum attached hereto [See below]. The old gentleman appeared very much depressed at the lack of preparation to meet the offensive which has been expected for some time and which could be met only with a strong counter offensive. The French reserves apparently are used up in trying to stiffen the British lines to such an extent that there is little hope of offering sufficient numbers of them for an offensive at another point.[79]

I lunched at the Laurent[80] with Major Cabot Ward who said that the English divisions referred to were part of General Gough's Fifth Army which caved in earlier in the offensive. They were placed at Berry au Bac which is a well defended position, easy to hold. It was thought that they could get back their morale in holding such a strong position. The Germans apparently made them the object of special attack and have crumpled them up a second time. Feeling among the French troops is very strong about the former British fiasco and it is doubtful whether anything about this one will be made public.

Ward promised to make a special effort to send trained intelligence officers to help out Buckey at Rome. He took the name of Travis Coxe and has promised to ask for him, presumably with a commission.

---

79 On May 27, 1918, the Third Battle of the Aisne started, when the Germans tried to push through the British and French positions and almost reached Reims. The Allies, though, were largely able to hold their lines.
80 Very famous and exclusive restaurant, prominently placed in the heart of Paris.

Ward's service has now been extended to Great Britain which is known as Base three. There was a good deal of trouble putting it over on General Biddle and Colonel Slocum as each of them wished to have the intelligence work under his orders, which was manifestly impossible. MI5 took Ward's view of the case and supported him so strongly that his view prevailed.

Went into Kerney's new offices at the Élysée Palace Hotel but he was away in the country and is leaving tonight for Lyons and Marseille where he will be gone for some days.

Frazier got off a telegram concerning the attitude of the subject races in Austria-Hungary scouting the idea of an immediate up-rising but reporting the belief that a revolt might be expected by next March. There is little probability of a Bolshevik influence in Bohemia on account of the large proportion of educated people, there being practically no illiterates. He urged, as I had done from Switzerland, that the President make some public utterance as to his attitude toward Austria and the question of the opposed nationalities. There will be a good opportunity at the congress of these nationalities to be held in Paris very soon.[81]

Mrs. Jeanne Carpenter came over on the Touraine – came here to say that she was in some trouble as a result of having made charges against two officers on board. The signed statement which she gave General Brainard and me to be sent by General Scott through proper channels to the intelligence was handed to the two officers in questions when they came ashore and they were ordered to tell whether or not they were guilty. She has had various other unfortunate adventures largely, it seems, as the result of talking too much.

Cabot Ward said that some days ago the Minister for Foreign Affairs [Pichon] sent for him and asked him to take a look into the activities of Kerney and James Hazen Hyde. He said that Kerney was very indiscreet, was talking about things which had nothing to do with his work and were too delicate for him to talk about; that he seemed to be in communication with the government at home and might give false impressions. He inquired as to the status of Hyde, saying he represented himself as Kerney's "deputy". Ward gave a very sensible answer to the effect that no undue importance should be attached to Kerney's talk as he was not doing anything underhanded, but was perhaps somewhat expansive in his talk and lacked definite knowledge as to where his functions ended. As to Hyde, he said that the Minister doubtless knew his record, that he was perhaps more bent on pushing Hyde than on any other part of the game; that he had no

---

81 After the Congress of Rome which addressed nationality issues (see annotation 67), a couple of similar – but smaller – meetings and congresses took place in Rome and – apparently – Paris.

official status but that he was rendering real service in helping Kerney' that his wide acquaintance and his willingness to spend money were a distinct help in the work and that perhaps the two of them would get their real position straightened out.

Ward told the substance of the foregoing to the Ambassador.

At eight I went to the Ritz to take Lucy Linn out to dine. After sending my card I waited for some time and watched people come and go. After a time a fearfully and wonderfully decorated lady came down and looked over the few people in the hall. After a time, she came back with the porter who pointed me out and I was greeted with a welcome-to-our-city smile by the lady who held my card in her hand. She turned out to be Elinor Glyn!!!! Wot next.

While I was waiting for a second try I ran into Major Fuller, the bright light in the Red Cross at Rome. He is up for a few days. After a few minutes Grant Forbes came along fresh from home and English, and then McFadden. Finally the right lady was produced and we went off to dine at Voisin's. I preached to her about not undertaking to work for the YMCA which seems to be a job that would entail a great deal of travel and hard work for which she is not fit. She promised to undertake nothing of the sort and I promised if necessary to get her some sort of job that would justify her staying on this side of the water until Howard [Linn] came along. Landed her back at her hotel a little after half past nine and had a good long evening to write letters and read.

MEMORANDUM of Conversation with Marshal Joffre, May 28, 1918.

On the nights, Sunday and Monday, the German began their attack with exceedingly heavy bombardment extending from Rheims almost to Soissons. Shells were used in unprecedented quantities and the gasses were in greater volume and more deadly than in any previous attack. At the same time attacks were made to the north between Locre and Vormezeele and against the American Army between Moreuil and Montdidier. In the north the Germans advanced a little toward Ypres but in the course of the afternoon this ground was retaken by the allied armies. In the Montdidier region the Americans lost their first positions but recaptured them in violent counter attacks, conducted with such fury that one American battalion broke through the German lines and got as far as the second German positions and had to be recalled so as to escape capture. This is considered a very glorious feat of arms for the Americans.

The main battle has not developed favorably for the allies. Three English divisions approximately in the center, crumpled up completely and withdrew in disorder, offering practically no resistance. This threw the brunt of resistance upon what is known as the Lenoir division situated on their left which held as best it could at price of terrible sacrifices. The allies were gradually beaten back losing first the entire Chemin des Dames, and then losing the river Aisne from the region of Cormicy to Celles. The French and British armies now occupy a line on the left bank of the Aisne on a plateau of slight elevation, which allows for slight resistance. The attack is on a line traced from Cauroy some 10 kilometers northwest of Rheims, through Blanzy, Vauxcere, Vauxtin and Celles, on the right bank of the Aisne. From this last point the line extends toward Foembray and the edge of the forest Coucy, but definite information is lacking as to the positions of the two armies in this region.

When this battle began, the attack between Rheims and Soissons appears to have had the nature of a decoy. But it now seems more and more likely that owing to the importance of the ground captured, ten kilometers in depth, including points of great strategic value like the observations of Chemin des Dames and the Aisne River and canal, the Germans have brought up divisions from other points and are making their main attack. It is difficult to judge at present what their objective may be.[82] The French and English stand a chance of being able to organize their new positions but the situation is undeniable a very serious one. Such divisions as we dispose of are needed in order to resist this attack which is by far the heaviest which has yet been seen and consequently we can spare no divisions for organizing a counter attack of a large scale which offers the best means of resistance under such circumstances. Furthermore, the Germans may not yet have abandoned their plan for a mass attack in the region of Ameins [Amiens], probably between Arras and Albert, for which they are positively known to have been preparing for several weeks past.

---

82 This attack was no decoy, but part of the German Spring Offensive, a desperate attempt to force a victory at the Western Front.

Log   Paris. Wednesday, May 29, 1918

Big guns began at 6:30 shells flying in the neighborhood of Gare d'Orléans. It is said that since the gun recently began firing, the shells have been of 240 caliber which evidently shows that they are making changes and improvements.

Dr. H.H. Field came in to see me on his way from Zurich to England where his father-in-law is very ill. He goes on this afternoon but plans to be in Paris for some time on his return. He reports that feeling toward the allies and particularly toward the United States is becoming more and more favorable in German-Switzerland. The tide was turning in our direction when I was last in Zurich but he says the situation has improved to such an extent that it can safely be said that more than half of the people in German-Switzerland are on our side. He accounts for this partly by the brutal tone of German demands and partly by the action of the French Government in arranging matters favorably to Switzerland. Apparently the trade conference at Bern settled a number of matters and did it in a way to earn good feeling from the Swiss. McFadden took it upon himself to dominate the situation and apparently did so with a good deal of tact and to excellent effect. Dr. Field says that Fray, who has charge of the trade negotiations and who was formerly actively pro-German is now expressing himself in quite different terms.

He says that the newspapers which Egger, Fleiner, and Bovet and others were organizing when I was in Zurich has made considerable progress. They have very sensibly purchased an existing daily paper in order to insure a supply of paper and are going to run it as a daily rather than a weekly as they has originally planned.

I asked him whether the peace feelers from Germany were continuing and he said that there had been an unfortunate incident which had frightened the Germans and it was doubtful whether they would put out experimental feelers unless there was something very definite to be gained. It seems that a rather important German came to Geneva to see Herron and talk with him very frankly. Herron, who appears to be anything but discreet apparently talked and within a few days there was a very sensational article purporting to give the substance of the discussion in the DAILY MAIL. The German indignantly denied the truth of the story and went back to Germany. Apparently the DAILY MAIL story was accurate but it should not have been published and Herron's usefulness is this regard seems to have ended.

I asked Dr. Field about the man who claimed to represent Ballin, etc., whom we had asked him to see at Bern. He said on discussion this man proved not to represent any commercial interests but to be merely a university man with general ideas which he thought it desirable to get before the American people. He disclaimed any official status and said that the legation must not know of his conversation. However, at the conclusion of the conversation, Dr. Field had made it very plain that we were not interested in talking terms of peace until the Germans modified their dictionary, he said that they talked about "no annexations" while gobbling up parts of Russia and were guilty of other similar inconsistencies; that until they were ready to do as they talked there could be no common ground for discussion. At the conclusion of the talk the German asked him to draw up and sign with him a protocol of the conversation, – which seems rather peculiar if he had no official sanction. Dr. Field declined to do this and the German then said that he himself would draw up a memorandum of the conversation as he remembered it and send a copy to Dr. Field from Germany, that he could do so through the legation pouch.

After he returned to Germany the DAILY MAIL story broke and Dr. Field does not expect anything more on the subject.

Lunched with Caffery and Andrews and heard something about the Conference on Mutilés de la Guerre which Caffery has been attending in London. Also something more from Andrews about life in Romania during the bad days.

The offensive seems to be going badly. The papers have begun to make admissions as to places that have been lost without saying anything as to the state of affairs. However the Germans have advanced across the Vesle at Fismes and Bazoches and reached Bruys and Arcis-le-Ponsart. These two places are almost on a direct line from Rheims to Paris and bring the Germans that much nearer to us. It looks as though they might be driving toward Château-Thierry which would be a name to conjure with. They are advancing down a gently sloping table land and as the French say *ON SE CRAMPONNE OÙ ON PEUT* [WE HOLD ON WHERE WE CAN]. It is not cheerful.

The big gun kept up firing all day and planted several shells in the neighborhood of the Invalides. Hyde, who telephoned me yesterday said that a number of shells had fallen within a few hundred yards of his house and that he had sent his wife to Versailles. I am to lunch there tomorrow.

A letter from Dresel who is worried for fear people have not proper understanding and appreciation of Hugh Wilson and what he has done. McFadden evidently talked to him about the need of improvement there and suggested that it might be well to send a man of the rank of Counsellor as well as a new Minister. I shall have to write him and try to calm him. I believe the Department has a full appreciation of the really splendid work Hugh has done and that he will not suffer even if they are a little slow in recognizing him. I learn that McFadden has been boosting [Robert] Bliss and me for the job of Minister there, which must cause some amusement in Washington. I should like to see Bliss get it but should be very much surprised if he did. Frazier is pushing the matter as well as he can but is not at all confident of success.

Travis Coxe came in to see me this evening to say that he had been ordered up to the Somme front as a telephone switchboard operator. He knows nothing about the job but they told him that all he had to do was "to push plugs in and pull them out" so he is off for a try at that. He is keen to be in the thick of things and will probably see something of the big show.

Going out to dinner I ran into a man in correspondent's uniform who hailed me by name and turned out to be Hazen, a Portland newspaper man whom I met when I was there with the Belgian Mission last year. He is over here following the Oregon troops but is not trying to get up to the front as the brave fighters he is attached to have never got any further than Blois.

Dined alone at the UNIVERSELLE and enjoyed a quiet time. Tomorrow being a holiday we are going to keep the Embassy open only half the day, – in the afternoon.

I find that there is a good deal of resentment here at our opposition to the Japanese intervention in Siberia. It is said that the President's support to the Bolcheviki is in a measure responsible for the hopeless conditions existing in Russia and that he risks making these conditions still worse by opposing Japanese intervention. The whole subject of assistance to Russia has been hanging fire for weeks and grows every day more urgent. Baron Giers, the Russian Ambassador in Rome, gave Mr. Page a memorandum on the subject while I was there and I know there has been a general appeal for the Allies to do something to help Russia get on her feet and resist the German advance which grows more overwhelming everyday.[83]

I learn that Orlando and Lloyd George are coming to Paris for a conference to be held on Saturday on the attitude which the Allies are to adopt toward Russia. Among the subjects discussed will of course be that of Japanese intervention.

The Japanese Government has telegraphed asking the French Government whether its active support can be counted upon at once to back up Seminoff [Semyonov] in Siberia while waiting for the military action which Japan is preparing in view of an understanding with the Allies. France has not felt able to reply as anything she might say now would appear to commit her. As a matter of fact her only effective forces in Siberia at the present moment are some 400 to 500 marines.

It is reported in French Military circles that a French military mission is very shortly to be sent to Washington to discuss Japanese intervention.

---

[83] At first, American politicians were not totally opposed to the revolutionary changes in Russia in 1917, which did away with one of the most oppressive regimes in Europe: Tsarist Russia. In the summer of 1918, Britain, France and the United States launched armed interventions in Northern Russia and Siberia which soon turned disastrous.

About half past eleven the sirens began screaming and I went down stairs to see what was up. It was beautifully clear but there was nothing to be seen. The barrage was very faint at first but soon began rattling away briskly to the south and east, the flashes of the bursting shells making a very pretty sight. There were some faint sounds of bombs but they must have been very far away and I doubt whether any of the machines got over Paris itself. After watching the fireworks for a time I went back to bed and did not hear the berloque [trinket].

Log   Paris. Thursday, May 30, 1918. Decoration Day[84]

Did not leave my room until after noon as the chancery was closed to the public and I felt that I could do with a little rest.

I set out for Hyde's a little before one and walking down the rue de Rivoli ran into Miss Stanton who had just come from the American Church.

As my car drew up at Hyde's the driver nearly fell off his seat as he saw a crowd drawn up in front of the next house which had been hit fair and square by one of the big shells. It is a handsome place built around three sides of a court. The two story lodge on the side adjoining Hyde's place had been knocked into a cocked hat and there was enough masonry piled up in the courtyard to build a palace three times the size of the one that had been destroyed.

Found Judge and Mrs. Lindsey already there and we went into the garden for lunch, which is better than the dining room because you do not risk having the house come down on top of you.

The Judge was full of interesting talk about his trips to the front and some of the Americans he had been travelling with. Among others he had done some trips with Hamilton Holt who had shamed him by his mania for collecting loot and by rowing with the French conducting officers as to whether he could carry the stuff away. Before he left here I know that Holt violated the confidence of Marshal Joffre by telling his remarks to everybody he met.

There was also a Reverend Mr. Cannon who came over on the same boat with the Judge and represented the Anti-Saloon League.[85] He had the warmest letters from Mr. Daniels and felt he was on a high and beautiful mission. On the boat he was nosing about and inquiring about as to the contents of the teacups before the officers at lunch. When he got here he went off the trail of the Demon Rum and

---

[84] Deoration Day was the precursor to the current US holiday of Memorial Day, celebrated on the last Monday of May.
[85] The Anti-Saloon League was the primary organization leading the movement toward prohibition in the US during the early 20th Century.

was delighted when he found a lot of correspondents taking a drink in the evening at the officer's club because he was then able to satisfy himself with his own eyes of the fact that the press was corrupted with drink and was (therefore) concealing from the American people the true state of affairs as to the immorality in the American army.

Mr. Cannon asked if he could go into the trenches and talk to the men about their spiritual needs. The officer to whom he applied said that he might do so if he so desired but painted a rather terrifying picture of DEAD MAN'S CURVE and other places he would have to pass while the Hun chucked shells onto them. Under those conditions Mr. Cannon decided that he would hardly be warranted in going but he suggested as a compromise that he should go part way to the front and talk to the troops "when they come out of the trenches in the evening".

Why DO we have to send such people abroad?

We talked of all sorts of things until nearly four. Both the Judge and his wife have made such a point of talking with frankness about subjects that are usually taboo, that they have come to the point of not wanting to talk about anything else. It is of course a virtue to be frank but I can't get up much enthusiasm about filling the lunch time conversation with nothing but venereal disease and immorality.

The news from the front this afternoon was not of a particularly encouraging nature. The advance continues pretty steadily and I don't see where we can make any stand this side of the Marne.[86]

Dined alone at the hotel and got early to bed. At a little after 11 the sirens sounded off again and hot barrage made sleep out of the question so I got up and took a look, going back to bed a little before midnight. None of the bombs dropped in our neighborhood although there were a number of them sprinkled over the city.

The big guns began firing again during dinner and one of the shells fell on the Madeleine[87] where the service had been held in the morning. This was the day the Allies had agreed not to bombard Cologne because of the religious festivals that were being held there.[88] That is just the sort of appreciation the filthy swine would show for such treatment.

---

[86] At that point, Gibson could not know that within a few days, French counter attacks would bring the offensive to a halt and to push the Germans back.
[87] The head of the statue of St. Lucas of the Madeleine Church in Paris was cut off by a German bomb shell on May 30, 1918. It is still missing.
[88] The festival commemorated Corpus Christi, proclaiming the body of Christ in the Eucharist, is celebrated by Catholics around the world.

Log   Paris. Friday, May 31, 1918

A quiet morning at the chancery writing odds and ends of letters.

The news from the Front was bad. Dawson saw Joffre who told him that the Germans had pushed on to the Marne and were going strong. Later I heard from other sources that matters had taken a turn for the better and that the Boches were driven back 4 K. from Château-Thierry where they entered last night. Lambert came in to see me during the morning and said that a lot of *nous-sommes-trahis* [we are betrayed] talk was going about; that the refugees from Château-Thierry said that the Germans "*sont entrés comme chez eux* [as if they were at home here]", etc. There is bound to be a lot of such talk when things are going badly and it does no good when morale is doubtful. In the afternoon I heard that the socialists had agreed to make a drive on Clemenceau and try to force him out by Tuesday unless things had straightened out by that time. That would probably mean that he would be replaced by Briand and that a peace drive would result.

Lunched at the [Robert] Bliss's with a lot of people who looked rather like a Congress of Oppressed Nationalities. There were Poles, Tchechs [Czechs], Yougo-Slavs, Dalmatians, etc. as well as Jack Carter, Fred Coudert, Gallavresi and one or two others. I had some talk after lunch with the Pole who is anxious to have the non-English speaking Poles in the American army turned over to the Polish Legion. I tried to turn him over to Frazier but he is determined to do things his own way and we finally compromised on his giving me a memorandum.

A filthy cold drove me home to bed late in the afternoon but I got up in time to dine with McFadden at the Ritz. He had Lucy Linn, Mrs. Sanger and her brother Perry Osborne.

Before I could get back to bed again we had the sirens screaming again and the electric buzzers in the hotel made such a row that sleep was out of the question. However I did manage to rest. After half an hour or so the bells began to ring and then ten minutes more the sirens sounded off again. However, the barrage was very far away and I got to sleep before the clear signal was given.

Log   Paris. Saturday, June 1, 1918

A long day of conflicting news.

Lambert came in to see me in the course of the morning to say that the Germans had advanced as far as Villers. He seemed surprised that the Government had not given us warning to get ready to start for points west. He said there was to be a counter-attack in the course of the day.

Later Dawson went to the IIIème Section[89] and learned that the situation seemed to be somewhat stabilized. The Germans had made an attempt to pass to the south of Rheims but had been driven back which saved the town for the time being at any rate. The wind is said to be right for French gas today. ...

After lunch a YMCA man named Harold Ickes of Chicago came in with a letter of introduction from George Creel saying that "he is willing to establish relations with you [Gibson] that will put some of his time at your disposal." I don't know what I am going to do with a tame YMCA man. He is off for several weeks to various camps and is then coming back to see me. ...

The Lansing girls are at Épernay and we have not been able to get in touch with them. The War Ministry got after them this afternoon and is going let us have news of them later.

At 5:30 Dawson and I went to Neuilly to see Marshal Joffre. The old gentleman has aged five years since I last saw him and is much depressed as to general conditions. Memorandum attached as to what he had to say. After talking himself out on the military aspects of the situation he talked a little about politics; said there was a drive on to overthrow Clemenceau and that during the week he had been approached by supporters of Barthou and Briand who wanted his help. He has consistently refused to get mixed up in politics or do anything against the Government at the moment. He says that the morale of the army has been sapped by a reversal of his determined tactics and the adoption of a policy of yielding always in the face of attack. That the soldiers have come to feel that they must be spared as Pétain has spared them and that it would be hard to change their state of mind on short notice as might be necessary in an emergency. He [Joffre] decried the Clemenceau policy as one of opportunism and said that such a policy of drift obtained that no preparations had been made against the possibility of evacuating Paris. This seems to be accurate for the Embassy has received no hint that we are expected to get out or get ready.[90]

Turning to lighter things the old gentleman talked about his trip to America, of Warren Robbins and Long and Bill Nye and the railroad accident and a lot of other incidents. He seems to remember the trip as a happy dream, despite Viviani and other features.

Stopped at the chancery with Dawson and prepared a memo of the conversation for the Amb. Then back to the hotel where I dined alone in state, being too far gone with cold and hay fever to ask anybody to dine. After dinner sat around and

---

89 Probably the 3rd office (operation and instruction) of the French command of the North-Eastern theatre of operations.
90 At the end of May 1918, Pétain was considering retreat. In this crucial moment, Clemenceau kept his nerves and did not evacuate Paris.

talked with Mrs. Crosby and her two daughters and the Andrews. Presently Orlando and Sonnino came along with their staffs which included Aldovrandi, and we had half an hour or so of talk. The Italian Ambassador [Longare] came along and joined in and before we got thru we had a young mob chattering. After a time we went out into the rue de Rivoli for a breath of air and an estimate as to whether we might expect a raid.

The others scattered to work or poker and I took to my bed. At about midnight there was an alerte but I did not go down until the barrage got pretty hot. It was a great sight to see, – the most intense I have yet seen. There were some bombs dropped but they were not very near us although at one time the planes were right overhead and we could hear them plainly. When the fire died down I went back to bed and before I got to sleep heard the bells ringing.

Log   Paris. Sunday, June 2, 1918

Got up with a beast of a cold and not feeling like a day's work but the call was strong to find out what the news was and I made my way to the chancery about eleven. There was nobody about the place except the Ambassador [Sharp] who was reading the telegrams and enjoying his cold. He evidently wanted to talk and showed me a telegram that Kerney has left to be forwarded to Washington dealing with a lot of things that had nothing to do with propaganda matters. The Ambassador said he would probably have to send it but it would be accompanied by some remarks of his own. Just as he was getting down to discussing some of the defects of the Kerney situation when Meriwether came in and put an end to it.

At one I met Major James, successor to Frederick Palmer in the Censor's job at the Interallied Club, and had lunch with him. I was too groggy to be much use as company, but we had a lot of things to talk about an-1d kept at it for a long time. James seems to be a regular citizen with real ideas and a desire to do his job right although he is a cavalryman and naturally would prefer to be with the troops. We got in his car and rode out as far as Versailles where we took a walk and got some more talking done. James is anxious as I have been ever since I got over to draw up some sort of policy with some general guidelines of endeavor which we can undertake and which the people in Washington can guide themselves by. We are going to try to force Kerney to adopt some such scheme and let him take the credit if he so desires. James is a good deal disturbed by Kerney's unwillingness to work and his tendency to turn the men with him into personal attendants. Orders have been prepared relieving Franck because he was being made a sort of valet. I am just as glad I have not burst forth on the subject as I would merely risk getting a reputation as a sorehead, – and this way other people can try to home some idea of the mess that prevails here.

I dined alone at the hotel and afterward sat down and talked for some time with Mrs. Kohl of San Francisco who has a hospital at Passy for babies. She told me last night about a couple of houses near the hospital where the most remarkable signaling goes on every night: She had told me that the nurses after watching this for some weeks had got so that they could tell in advance whether there was to be a raid or not. I rather laughed at the idea but while we were talking a telephone message came from the hospital to say that the lights were very active but that there would be no raid. After we had talked about it for some time Mrs. Kohl suggested that we get in a taxi and go out to see.

It was a long drive out but we did get there in time and climbed to the top floor where we watched from a dark room what was certainly a suspicious performance. There was a five story building, an apartment house some two hundred yards away. It was built, so they say, by Germans before the war and has been unoccupied until the last couple of months. Even now there is no sign of life by day, but in the evening there are all sorts of activities. There were several windows showing lights that would have had any ordinary person arrested. They all seemed to be covered with a translucent curtain. In one window there was a faint light evidently in the back of the room which moved slowly to the front and then went back again several times. In one of the others a heavy curtain was drawn and withdrawn several times by a man whose figure was clearly to be seen. Then both of these windows were darkened and two or three others appeared with various sorts of lights. The house next door also got busy and there was a great business of turning lights on and off, drawing curtains slowly and quickly, lights that turned around and went up and down. There must have been a lot of people busy at it, but there was nothing to show what purpose such a performance could serve. If it was the work of Huns, they were taking a curious and seemingly needless risk. In showing such lights when they could supposedly get word from one place to another without any such elaborate procedure. And the French certainly needed nothing of the sort to get word from one place to another for they have every known sort of communication at their disposal. However people are not staying up all night for months together doing that sort of thing for fun and it may be some fun trying to find out what is back of it. It is too much like Nick Carter[91] stuff to take very seriously but I shall try to get somebody to look into it.

---

91 "Nick Carter" is a fictional private detective who made his first appearance in 1886. He was the brain-child of Ormond G. Smith, and actualized by John R. Coryell. Nick Carter adventures were printed in various magazines and popular until the 1930's.

Log   Paris. Monday, June 3, 1918

This morning I rode over to the Ecole Militaire with Dawson who was going to see the Marshal [Joffre]. I did not go in as I thought they might be able to talk more freely *à deux*. The old gentleman seemed somewhat reassured for the moment, saying that the Germans seemed to be stayed temporarily. They had advanced down the north bank of the Marne as far as Nogent in a narrow shoestring which was extremely vulnerable and would be easy to cut off if desired. They had made a big drive at Soissons but had been held fast. His idea seems to be that they will slacken their attack as they have done on other occasions, bring up fresh supplies of guns, munitions and men and make another attempt several weeks hence. He believes that they have the strength for another such effort. The situation according to his way of looking at it is still very grave but not necessarily lost for the moment.[92]

Lunched with Frazier at Voisin's. He has been having a most interesting time at Versailles where the critical situation has evidently got on the nerves of some of our brave allies. Sonnino apparently lost his temper completely yesterday and broke out with the statement that they did not need to come in the war and that in fact they had been offered a great deal more to stay out. Lloyd George, Mr. Balfour and Clemenceau showed the greatest patience and good humor and kept things going although they did not yield to the prima donna.

Dawson suggested that we take the story of the signals at the hospital to Autrand, Prefect of the Seine and accordingly we are going to see him tomorrow morning at 10:30.

Dexter, the Consular Agent at Lausanne and Edelmann, the Vice Consul at Geneva, came in this morning on their way to GHQ for a talk with Nolan. I had only a few minutes to see them but they are filled with despair at the idea that Mrs. Whitehouse may go back to Switzerland. They say she has done a lot of harm and what we need is somebody to go up and clean up the mess she has made.

Dined with Major Perkins at his new house, 26bis rue de Lubeck. He was to have had Otto Kahn also but the old gentleman has gone down to Chaumont and we had the place to ourselves. Preston had been taken ill and was in bed. After dinner we talked until Batty [Lord Mountbatten] came in with an account of a talk he had just had with Bourgeois, Pétain's aide. His theory which he does not advance as a governmental decision but merely as something that may happen, is

---

[92] By that time, the situation at the Western Front looked better than Giobson thought, since on June 3, 1918, the Allied troops counterattacked, inflicted severe losses on the Germans, and the recovered terrain.

that Paris will be evacuated in the course of the next few weeks; that with the big front and narrow neck of the present salient the Germans are able to move their men about as they like to meet attacks and that little can be accomplished there; that the allies are only getting their troops down from the Amiens front at the rate of about two divisions a day which is not fast enough; that our men have to be taken on long detours in order to get them anywhere and that Paris is an obstacle rather than an asset in the defense; that he thinks the plan will be to let the Germans fight their way forward at as heavy a cost as possible and then abandon the place to them. That then it will be easier to maneuver the armies and that everything will depend upon one throw of the dice. He wants the Red Cross to get ready for the end by beginning immediately the evacuation of all their supplies. That will be the subject of a pow-wow tomorrow morning after which I am going to see Perkins for news.

Some official called Perkin's office on the telephone this afternoon and asked that the American Red Cross undertake to evacuate the Louvre. Perkin's representative asked: "Have you a sense of humor?" and when the Frenchman said he had, replied: "Well, if you'll give me the Venus de Milo and the Winged Victory, I'll do the job for you."

On the way home as I was passing the chancery the alert sounded – but it was a false alarms and the clear signal sounded soon after. I could see shrapnel bursting to the north but could not hear a sound even before the sirens began.

Log   Paris. Tuesday, June 4, 1918

At 10:30 I went to the Hôtel de Ville with Dawson to see the Prefect [Aurand]. He was very circumspect in what he said about the situation but gave us to understand without saying much that the situation was very grave and that he would prefer not to go into details. I told him a little about my trip to Rome and something of public feeling in Italy which is of interest to him. As he is an enthusiastic amateur detective I told him of the signals which we had seen in Passy and he evidently got to work for later in the day I got a message from the hospital to say that the police had suggested that they repeat their statements to me.

From there I went to the Red Cross and had a yarn with Major Perkins. He had just come from a conference with the Provost Marshal and other authorities in regard to the possible evacuation of Paris. He seemed to feel that it was more or less imminent and that he had better get to work and clear out the supplies now in Paris. He counts on very little sleep for the next few weeks.

Lunched with McFadden at the Ritz where we saw a lot of people, Frank Page, now a Major, on his way from the front to an unknown job in London – which distresses him deeply, Grasty, the Carter's, Mrs. [Robert] Bliss, Warburton, Tony Drexel [Biddle], and a flock of others.

I put in part of the afternoon dictating stupid letters and memoranda and then went home and to bed as I was all in. At seven roused myself sufficiently to dress and go to the Bliss's to dine. We had a real yarn that lasted until a little after ten, – and so home to bed.

Log   Paris. Wednesday, June 5, 1918

No particular news this morning although the Germans seem to be limiting themselves to little thrusts here and there. The big offensive seems to have slowed up for the moment at any rate, and we may not know any more for some days or weeks, according to the amount of recuperation the Huns need before they are able to drive again.

Went to see Kerney and had a little talk with him before lunch. He is puffed up with the trips he has taken and the amount of space he has had in the newspapers. He has now given himself out as Director in Europe of the Committee for Public Information and has the Military crowd believing him. I was obliged to puncture that little bubble because they were submitting for his approval various things that I had asked for in Italy.

Kerney had a letter from Creel assigning to his staff the Marquise de Polignac and another American lady married to a Frenchman. Each of these ladies – the latter at any rate – draw $250 per month – and the good Lord only knows what they can do. Neither of them seems to have any very definite idea. The second lady was there after lunch when I went back, evidently a stage friend of Blanche Bates, *un peu sur le retours* [worn out].

Lunched with James who is trying to bring some order out of chaos and has made a little progress. He is a good deal afraid that there will be a Congressional investigation of the conduct of the C.P.I. work abroad and a scandal over the expenditures. He wants to get the army out of it altogether and for that purpose is relieving the army men who had been assigned to help.

A letter from Hugh Wilson says that Frank Bohn has gone back to the United States.

James came back to the chancery with me and met Frazier. Then back to see Kerney again but found him deep in converse with his new lady and did not stay long. She was off to evacuate a home she has in Meaux and seemed to be more interested in that for the moment than anything else.

Fabry came in to see Dawson in the course of the afternoon and said that the French were having all they could do to hold the Germans even now that the main drive had stopped and there was nothing to meet but local thrusts. There are not enough reserve divisions to defend an extended front if the Germans are able to extend their front of attack. The only action left to the French is to withdraw everything north of Amiens back as far as the Somme. This would shorten the line considerably and would release some forty three divisions. Of course it would also release German divisions which are needed to hold the longer line as at present constituted.

Lucy Linn telephoned me this morning and said that she had made up her mind to go back home as she felt she was no longer justified in staying on and eating food without doing any more work than had been provided for her thus far. In the evening I went in to see her and found her looking very tired and ill; she has not been at all well; she is lonesome and has no news as to when Howard is coming and altogether she seems to have about given up the sponge and WANTS TO GO HOME. I had not the heart to argue with her but contented myself with reminding her that she would feel pretty badly if she got him and found Howard on the point of sailing for this side of the water. However she feels she wants to be off and I am to find out about ships for her and let her know tomorrow.

Had a quiet dinner alone at the hotel and got a night's sleep without a raid.

Log   Paris. Thursday, June 6, 1918

Another busy day without getting much of anywhere.

Lunched with McFadden who had rounded up Mr. Grobet, a Swiss Federal Counselor, and Pierce to go to Laurent's. Grobet told me some encouraging facts about McFadden's trip to Bern and the way he had got things straightened out. After lunch I wrote a little note to Edgar Rickard and told him about it for the information of Hoover. It is a comfort now and then to be able to say something nice about somebody.

James came for me at four and took me down to the Base Censor's office which is under his orders. This gave us a chance to talk about a number of things.

Frazier got off a telegram to the Colonel saying that he had observed that our propaganda which was a valuable instrument was not getting any effect because of the fact that the agents sent over to do the work were almost without exception utterly unfitted for it. I was given a clean bill of health as being alive to this condition but it was added that in my position I was unable to speak with the same frankness, and that if the right sort of man were sent over with full power to run the thing I would be the first to put myself under his orders.

Had another quiet dinner with Andrews whose wife was ill and who was consequently dining alone.

Sat and talked with the [Oscar] Crosbys and Mrs. Kohl until eleven or so and then went upstairs to read. Some little time after the sirens began to toot and we began one of the liveliest raids since I have been here. A large number of machines were involved and we frequently heard them over the hotel. I went down into the rue de Rivoli and watched the barrage for an hour and then went to bed without waiting for the *berloque* [fire fighters' bell]. Some bombs were dropped but they were far away and we could not tell what damage they had done.

Log   Paris. Friday, June 7, 1918

This morning the big gun began hammering us with more than usual enthusiasm. The shells have been falling in the outlying districts for some days but today two of them fell down town, near the opera we are told.

Seymour Blair came in to see me this morning and thanked me for looking out for Lucy as though I had saved her life once or twice a day. He wants to get into Intelligence work if he can and I made an appointment for him with Cabot Ward. If he can't get into that it may be possible to fix him with Major Harjes.

Lunched with Hyde who had rounded up several of the French propaganda people including Major Schaix, Kerney, Lewis, Roberts, Major Johnson, Major Pierce, etc. Frazier and I went over together.

After lunch ran into Col. Fabry who had come in to see Dawson about a newspaper OUI which he is evidently running and which he wants to get to the American troops. He is coming back tomorrow to see if Bliss and I am to have James here if I can so that they can talk about it.

Fabry seems to feel that the Germans are strong for another powerful drive between Montdidier and Lasigny, but that if that fails they will have to rest a couple of months before undertaking anything big. And that any new drive after such a preparation would no longer be as advantageous to them as what they have already done.

State Senator Cotillo of New York came in on his way to Rome. He is a cocky little Italian politician who has a chip on his shoulder and proposes to put Merriam right by pushing his face in. It will be curious to see how they get along together.

Dined with Bliss at the Interallied Club which is a delight in this weather. We dined in the garden with a crowd and had a long talk afterward. Bliss is beginning to realize something of the folly of trying to do all the detail work of the chancery and perhaps there is hope that he will reform his evil ways. *Ojalá* [God willing].

Log   Paris. Saturday, June 8, 1918

Another strenuous day. Senator Cotillo came in before lunch and began to blow off steam about the outrage to which he was subjected in not having a diplomatic passport. He is a rough neck of the worst sort and I am wondering how long he will be able to get on with Merriam.

A telegram after lunch to say that Hugh Wilson will get here on Monday morning.

One from Will Irwin to say that Will Sperry wants a job, and suggesting that he be made liaison officer at the MAISON DE LA PRESSE.

Lunched with McFadden and talked shop.

Tracy Lay came in and exuded pessimism about the socialist and labor situation which he considered very dangerous. He predicts that if we have to evacuate Paris there will immediately be a revolution and Caillaux will make a try for power.

Dined alone at the hotel and got early to bed.

Log   Paris. Sunday, June 9, 1918

Took advantage of the Sabbath day to stay in bed until all sorts of hours.

Arthur Orr called up early and asked me to lunch with him at the Ritz. He was a good deal upset by Lucy's troubles and was insistent that she should go home at once. She has evidently decided to go and plans to make for Bordeaux to stay there until her ship is ready to sail. She is in a really dangerous nervous state and is ready to go to pieces at any moment. We had lunch in her drawing room but there was not a smile in her.

After lunch I picked up Major Pierce of the Red Cross and went with him to the Bliss' to see Colonel Godson who had come in from Chaumont during the night. We talked about some matters of shop including how to take Fife out of the Red Cross and let him do propaganda work. It was agreed that the best thing would be to have him assigned as an intelligence officer under Godson to handle his press work. This will do the trick if they don't run foul of the lady [Vira Whitehouse] and cause her to believe that this is a dirty plot to take over her work while she was away. It will be up to Godson to keep his peace with the lady.

Godson left GHQ last night and at the last minute Mr. Otto Kahn asked if he could give him a lift. When they were about 25 kilometers out of Paris the essence ran out and the car stalled. Godson tramped five kilometers to a garage and went back with relief. When he had rounded out his 10 K. there was no car to be found, so he turned round once more and tramped to a town where he learned that a car answering to the description had gone through some time ago. He bullied them into giving him a car and rolled up to the Ritz at 4:30 to find that Mr. Kahn had arrived and gone peacefully to bed. Some soldiers had come and pushed the car to the top of a hill whence they had coasted to a place where they got just enough essence to get them back to Paris. AND MR. KAHN DID NOT CONSIDER IT WELL TO RISK GOING BACK FOR THE COLONEL. The Col. was one peevish man when he told about it.

One interesting but almost unbelievable thing he had to tell was that the Germans[93]

Log   Paris. Monday, June 10, 1918

Hugh Wilson got in this morning from Bern at 10:30, but by a series of accidents I missed him at the station and did not find him until middle of the afternoon.

Lunched at a little restaurant near the Embassy with Hansi [Waltz]. He gloomed over some German Swiss newspapers through the meal. If he had not been in a French officer's uniform he probably would not have had a pleasant time.

Jessé-Curélly was also lunching there and I had a few minutes talk with him.

Went from there to see Dawson who was laid up in bed but will be about in a day or two.

Hugh Wilson came in shortly after my return. He had come to Paris because of certain matters he did not consider it safe to write or telegraph. There are evidences of a new German peace drive which he thought we should know about. It seems they plan to push their lines at least far enough to get Paris within range of their guns and then offer terms which will be irresistibly tempting to the French and will let England out with a certain amount of face. I rounded up Frazier for dinner and we talked things out at length.

Topping came in to see me just before dinner with better news as to his personal affairs but very gloomy about the political situation. He says that the Barthou-Briand tribe are maneuvering to oust Clemenceau so as to constitute a view to concluding immediate peace. Caillaux seems to be exerting a powerful influence from behind the bars and a strong effort is being made to get Thomas to join the gang. Topping says that when the last drive was made on Clemenceau the old gentleman was nearly down and out and unless the vote had been favorable he would have gone without a whimper. Topping seemed to fear that there is a good deal of chance for a Coup d'État in case it becomes necessary to evacuate Paris.

---

93 Follows blank page.

Paris. Tuesday, June 11, 1918

Spent the morning at the Chancery thrashing out some things with Hugh Wilson and others.

Lunched at the Interallied Club with Kerney, James, Hyde, Millais of the Ministry of Marine. Viviani was there but I did not fall on his neck.

After lunch James and I took Hugh Wilson to the Press Division and got the passes for our trip to Chaumont, from Wickes who has just got his promotion to Captain. Dropped in to see Kerney on the way back.

Dined with Hugh Wilson at Miss Armsby's who has Miss Tower living with her, Caffery was there and to my great surprise Lucy Linn, who had resurrected herself and announced that she was not going home after all.

Log   Chaumont. Wednesday, June 12, 1918

Took the eight o'clock train from the Gare de L'Est with Hugh Wilson and reached Chaumont a little before two.

We had a compartment filled with young American officers including Lieutenant Atkinson of the Marine Corps, the only one I knew. They seemed to be afraid of no censor under the seats and spoke their minds pretty freely, devoting great energy and enthusiasm to cussing out the YMCA. They objected particularly to having men of military age engaged on this work and say that the ranks are filled up with huskies who would do perfectly well in the trenches if it were not for their liking for soft billets. They say the YMCA is in bad with the whole Army and that it will take very radical changes to create a better feeling. Some kind friend has got to repeat this to Dr. Mott.

On the other hand they are all enthused about the work of the Salvation Army which seems to have cut out all pious activities and to be devoting itself to making pies and doughnuts in dug outs just behind the front where they are most appreciated by the boys. One of the officers said he was going up to the front with a Major General the other day and that the General dispatched him to buy a pie when they drew near the dugout, but the square-faced old dame who ran the show sent back word that there were no pies for generals and that every one she could make that day was going right into the trenches where the fighting was hot and where the boys "needed the pie".

We were met at the station by a Lieutenant Bristol who had known Hugh Wilson as a kid.

Lunched at the Hôtel de France and went over to GHQ where Colonel Nolan was waiting for us.

I first disposed of the troubles of Colonel Buckey at Rome, describing the situation as well as I could and urging Nolan to send him a few officers and a lot of field clerks. Nolan said he would try to produce a few officers but that it would be very difficult to get any clerks. I was rather insistent on this point, however, laying stress upon the difficulties of the situation and Nolan finally promised to do his level best toward making that situation workable. He took notes as to Buckey's needs and said he would follow the matter up.

Next we (Gibson, with Col. Nolan and Hugh Wilson) went into the developments which might be expected in the eventuality that is became necessary to evacuate Paris, or in the other possible eventuality that the Germans established their line near enough to bombard Paris. The three of us agreed that in either case, it was probably that Germany would offer terms of peace which would be tempting to France, and would offer England such terms as would save her face. In either case it seems that the situation would be filled with difficulties for us. Problems which would then confront us are:

1) If France and England having concluded an armistice, what would be our position? If we went on fighting, Germany could bring pressure to bear on France and England to make us conclude an armistice, or, what seems more probable, she could turn her entire force against the American Army, which would undoubtedly be surrounded and crushed.

2) If we desired to continue the war, it would have to be on sea and commercially. In that event how could we disengage our Army now in France. It would be manifestly impossible to get it embarked for home before it could be disposed of by the Germans. There is little likelihood that it could be transferred to Italy as it is to be presumed that when the peace drive came Austria would eliminate Italy by a tempting offer which would at least bring about an armistice and make it impossible for her to receive our troops. The only alternative that I could say would be to conclude a definite armistice or march our Army into Spain for internment, provided, of course, they could make an expeditious get away.

Nolan's reports agree with those I had received as to the dangerous state of moral in England, France and Italy, the peril of a strong defaitiste [defeatist] movement particularly in France. We talked over possible means of preventing any of those countries from lying down on us. The only one that seemed at all practicable was to get the President to give out a solemn warning calculated to stiffen the determination of the belligerent peoples. It would not do to let the crash come before delivering the message, for in that case those in power would see that it did not reach the people and in any event it could not have the same effect. With the governments in France, England and Italy strongly committed to a vigorous prosecution of the war, it would be to their selfish interests to circulate such a message, and see that it reaches all classes of the people and was favorably considered by them. Such a message could not, of course, be addressed directly to those peoples, as it would then look like scolding, or a threat. What seems most desirable would be to have the President make a speech on some special occasion and address some remarks of pitying rebuke to any misguided American elements that can be found for the occasion, who have visage the possibility of seeing any of our allies quit the struggle. He could point out in a magnificent way the French and English have fought for four years without abatement of courage or determination; the vital end for victory that will be guarantee of liberty for the future; he could tell of the fresh courage brought them by the rapidly increasing American Armies who have gone to fight so brilliantly and have given high hopes for the vastly larger forces that will soon be engaged. He could then go on to say that America has gone into the war on this unprecedented scale because it is realized that here is a great undecisive struggle to determine whether we are to go ahead or to go back; that if we all keep on victory will be sure and Germany will not be able to impose her will of reaction upon the world; that on the other hand, it is evident that the withdrawal of our European allies would mean a German victory or an indecisive peace; that Germany would be without doubt under the terms of peace she would be able to enforce the dominant power in Europe; our knowledge of her policies and her past acts are enough to prove that she would so crush other countries and so keep them down that they would not be able to resist her will for a long time to come and that, therefore, it could not be expected that America would ever again be in the future after a disastrous departure from its stay at home policy be tempted to throw its young manhood into another European struggle.

This would of course have to be wrapped up in very nice English, but it should carry a warning which would be considered here and would doubtless have a far greater effect than if we were to wait until after the crash to begin our plea.

I promised to talk the matter over with Frazier and draw up something to be considered by all those interested, in the course of the next few days.

After leaving Nolan we went to see several people and found that Colonel Sweeney was in bed with the grippe and that Major MacGruder was in the hospital having his tonsils taken out; Frank McCoy gone to command the old 69th New York, now knowns as the 165th; Norman Whitehouse nowhere to be found, etc. Saw Jim Logan for a minute as he was very busy, we could not dine or lunch with him but agreed to drop in on him for breakfast. Stopped at his house on the way back to the Guest House to see Martin Egan, but found that he had just left for Paris. Ran into Commander Williams, whom I had known in Washington, and who has nowcome to serve as Naval Liaison with General Pershing.

At 7 we messed with Nolan. There were very few others there, only Lieut. Col. Howe who has taken over the mail service for the Army, Major Moreno and Captain Hubbard. He talked with Nolan and Moreno until quite late. Nolan says that the Commander in Chief does not endeavor to follow the details of the diplomatic situation but that he had orders from Washington to keep a general line on the situation in all allied and neutral countries so that we would not be taken by surprise by any movement and would understand any situation that was brought before him. He said that they had had no assistance from the diplomatic or consular services and had had to depend upon the work of their own men who were not trained in diplomatic or political questions. He inquired whether I could undertake to give a good deal of time to acting as diplomatic liaison for the commander in chief, keeping him informed as to general situations and developments. I said that I should like the work very much, but I should prefer to take the matter up with Frazier and make sure that this would not conflict with or duplicate work he was now doing with General [Tasker] Bliss, and that it would be agreeable with him. I agreed to come down again next week and talk the matter over and bring McFadden for a talk. Nolan said that if agreeable to me the Commander in Chief would telegraph to ask that I be relieved of certain other responsibilities so that I could be foot loose and free to follow out this particular work.

In the course of a talk with Col. Nolan he said that the Germans had at first put third class troops against those we had in the Château-Thierry region but after a few days fighting had removed two divisions of these and had replaced them with their best qualified shock troops. He had the histories of these divisions which showed that they had fought brilliantly in several big offensives and were the best that Germany could command. This may mean merely that they take our troops more seriously than they did at first and that they feel the need of better troops to deal with them. On the other hand, it may mean that they propose to direct a crushing blow at them with the view of disposing of them and delivering a blow at our morale.

Log   Chaumont. Thursday, June 13, 1918

Had breakfast with Jim Logan who had several guests and therefore did not develop much conversation.

On going to G.H.Q I tried to see George Quekemeyer, who has come to Chaumont as Aide De Camp to the Commander in Chief [Pershing]. He is away for the day but I left a note for him. Howard Barnes was also missing.

At 11 we started a two hours' talk with Col. Nolan going into a number of other questions. Among other things I mentioned the difficulties of transportation and he promised to see if he could not provide me a car. Hugh Wilson brought up a number of questions affecting the situation in Switzerland and got an undertaking that improvement would be made.

Colonel Van Deman is on his way over and will look into a number of these matters.

We lunched at Nolan's mess and got the 2:30 train back to Paris, getting in about half past seven.

Paris.
Dined with Hugh Wilson at the Meurice.

Log   Paris. Friday, June 14, 1918

Got to the Chancery to find a lot of unimportant letters, including one from the Club to say I was canned for not having paid a bill I did not receive. Telegraphed Joe Grew to save my life. McFadden came in to say that Lucy Linn had changed her mind again and is starting for home tomorrow. There was a telegram to me from Howard asking for full details but I contented myself by telling him when to meet her, that she was very homesick and that it was well for her to return.

Talked with Frazier about the idea of my undertaking to be liaison for the General [Pershing] and learned that he heartily approved. He is going to talk with General Bliss about it at my request in order to make sure there is no misunderstanding.

Talked to him about the possibility of having the President giving the message of warning which we discussed with Nolan. It appealed to him and he is going to turn it over in his mind so we can discuss it again later and get off some sort of telegram.

Had lunch at the Ritz with McFadden and Mrs. Linn, who goes home tomorrow. After lunch ran into Lord Murray of Elibank and his brother Colonel Murray is now in the political intelligence department of the foreign office and had come over to look into the general situation here with a view to determining:
1) The security of the Clemenceau ministry;
2) The likelihood of any move that would bring about the making of a separate peace by France. He had not had time or opportunity to see many people but his impression was not at all encouraging. He gathered that the Clemenceau Ministry was likely to fall at any time and if it did the group would probably replace it with only one idea, that of concluding a separate peace.

Apparently the British Government is much more concerned as to the state of public opinion, and it follows that if Germany offers any sort of terms to France, the result may be disastrous to us.

Lord Murray had today arrived from Algiers. He said that there were a number of American ships there trying to deal with the submarine menace but that it was not under control like in northern waters. The Mediterranean being rather thick with submarines. Eight British ships have been sunk only in the last few days, one with about 4,600,000 lobs of supplies for Saloniki. He said the Germans evidently had excellent intelligence as this ship was singled out from a large convoy of relatively unimportant ships.

I talked with the Murrays so long that I was late for my appointment with Martin Egan who said he wanted to go into executive session with me. I promised to go down to Chaumont on Tuesday and have a good talk with him there.

Took Hugh Wilson down to the press division and got our passes to go tomorrow to the front with James.

Yesterday's papers have for the first time made open mention of the possibility of evacuating Paris, it being announced that those who desire to get away for the summer or take their children to the country, would be given special facilities and that measures are being taken to remove art treasures. Today's papers had further mention of the possibility of evacuation.

Log   Paris. Saturday, June 15, 1918

A long day and a lively one.

At 9:30 Major James came for me at the chancery and we went off to pick up Hugh Wilson at the MEURICE. Thence away to Meaux where we stopped and got our travelling directions. The roads were almost empty and we had no trouble in making time.

Just out of Meaux we came upon marching troops of the 4th Division who have just come down from the British front and looked hard as nails.

A little after noon we came upon a detachment of military police lunching under some trees and discovered among them Col. Langdon and Major Broadhurst who bade us in to lunch with them. We had the luxuries we could not get in Paris, including butter, milk and honey, together with some scrambled meat – there was a debate as to whether it was mule or alligator but everybody seemed to eat their share.

The camp kitchens were surrounded by ducks, chickens and rabbits to say nothing of casual furniture and china that had been removed from neighboring houses. Broadhurst said that the French soldiers were the best little looters he has ever seen and that the example was not good for our men. The peasants who had left their homes would find very little when they got back for the houses had been stripped and most of the vegetables and fruits carried off for the armies.

They were all quite cheerful about the lively time we would have if we went to the front as the Hun was throwing over a lot of gas and High Explosives shells. However we got some masks from the office and found our way to the H.Q. of the Second Div. which was near Bezu, – pronounced by the military police BAYZOO. H.Q was established in a farm house and the outbuildings around a courtyard. From the air the whole thing would look perfectly natural for the center of the court was filled with the regulation manure heap, there was an old cart tilted back with its shafts in the air, and poultry and cows wandered about at will. Under one of the barns were the motors belonging to the staff. Ours we had been obliged to leave under a tree a kilometer away, coming the rest of the way on foot so as not to give any ideas to scouting airmen. The arrival of civilians caused quite a little flutter and we had to do some quick explaining. General Bundy came out and talked to us and there was a brigadier general who came along and got conversational but did not disclose his identity. Col. Conger was not to be seen as he was in bed with a touch of gas acquired yesterday. Saw de Chambrun and listened with pleasure to his tribute to the American troops. He was with the first Division and is now having a go with the Second. Undertook to let his wife know that he was well but too busy to write although he warned me that that excuse was nearly threadbare.

After looking at the maps being made up in G.2 and seeing something of the areas where gas and High Explosives shells had been dumped in during the night and the disposition of our own forces we walked back to our car past a truck which was mothering a sausage. In the car we set out obliquely toward the front and eventually reached a little farmhouse with the inevitable court where Gen. Harbord had set up his H.Q. as Commander of the Marine Corps. There we found Major Lay, weary after fifteen days and nights with little sleep, the Gen. himself, Col. MacCloskey and a group of young officers who were keeping track of the effects of our fire on the boche line. They told us how to get over to the battalion H.Q. of Maj. Watson and sent us on our way. Lay told me that they had had seven hundred casualties in the previous 24 hours and that most of corps was all in. The sacrifices of the Marine Corps is dreadful to think of especially as they are such highly trained men and so hard to replace. Their morale is still one hundred percent and they don't think of getting relief.

At Division H.Q. they told me that during the night they had sent over 9,000 shells on the Boche from that divisions alone.

We found Major Watson about two kilometers near the lines in a small farm house busily engaged trying to keep his men under cover so they would not be spotted by the Boche airmen. It required a pretty good flow of language to keep them under cover, but Pa Watson has it. There was a battery of 155's in a clump of woods thirty yards from the house and when they loosed off about once in

Image 10: This map France and the current battle lines in June 1918 was attached to Gibson's Log on June 15, 1918. (Courtesy of the Gibson Family)

ten seconds, the house all but fell down. There were several batteries of 75's shooting over the house from across the road and all the woods around about were filled up with guns of various calibers.

The brigade under Colonel MacCloskey comprises 165 guns which are on a very small front and apparently have a very unpleasant effect on the Huns. Some idea of the fire maintained was gleaned from Watson's statement that his battalion averages about two thousand rounds every day.

Watson took us to a wood about a kilometer closer to the lines where there was a battery of 75's well concealed. The wood was filled with men and with horses used to haul the ammunition from the main road near brigade H.Q. These guns were not fired as their flash is clearly discernable by day and there was nothing to be gained in inviting trouble. The 155's just behind us evidently attracted unfavorable attention and High Explosive shells were bursting about half minute intervals in the neighborhood. The men of the battery have dug themselves in very comfortably in nice wet earth where any ordinary human being would die of rheumatism in a week. However, they are all as hard as nails and seem to thrive on it. While we were there the report came in the Germans were shelling Lucy, a small village just over the Bois de Belleau, and our hospitable hosts asked us to go up and take a look. Pa Watson was rather against it as he said the whole road was being shelled but that *if* we got through we could get a relatively safe outlook from a clump of trees on the side of the hill about Lucy. It seemed too bad to miss, so we set out for the main road again to Maison Blanche where we found the H.Q. of the 6th Infantry. We were made to put our car under a tree so as not to afford too much notice to the prying Hun, and then asked inside where there was almost standing room. Found Major Evans whom I had known in Washington and Lieutenant Wood and others. A receiving station underground about 100 yards down the road had just been hit by a H.E. and all hands were buried. A digging party was out rescuing them and we learned afterwards that they escaped with no killed and only four wounded. Another report came that very near our destination an officer had just been killed and four men badly wounded. We sat out along the Château-Thierry road, the evening hate was evidently beginning, and the big shells began to stream overhead. Wood wanted us to watch him and throw ourselves upon our faces if he did, which seemed a rather superfluous warning. Some shells broke but none nearer than a hundred yards and we gained the edge of a small wood just above Lucy and watched a halfhearted bombardment of the town through Wood's glasses. We saw about all we needed for our own satisfaction, but he thought we really needed to see the Bois de Belleau and Bouresches, which have figured so largely in the recent fighting.

In order to do this we had to skirt the wood in the open on the side toward the German line in view of the Hun snipers, going one at a time, and we did not loiter by the wayside. We reached a slight clearing and went up one at a time for a look at the Bois de Belleau and other points of interest, then back along the same path to the main road to H.Q. French planes were spotting battery hits and the German shrapnel was bursting around them, but to very little effect. Wood, who is an inquisitive fellow, stopped in the middle of the road and wanted to watch the show with his glasses, but as there was no cover anywhere in sight and German shrapnel is distinctly hard, we edged him along toward H.Q. Thence back to brigade H.Q. where we took some letters for MacCloskey and on back to Paris.

Log   Paris. Sunday, June 16, 1918

Got up fairly late and got a thrill from the news that the Austrian offensive had at last begun and that the Italians seem to be holding them.[94]

Hugh Wilson came in and stood by while I tried to hammer out a telegram suggesting that the President make a speech to keep France and Italy keyed up to continuing the struggle.

We set out on foot for our lunch at Miss Armsby's and stopped in at the chancery to see whether there were any developments. We showed up Avenue Jules Janin a little after one but were ahead of all the other guests who were slow coming. There was Mrs. Parish who has been nursing at the front with the French army for the past two years, Miss Tower, Miss Withers, who has just come from doing canteen work at Château-Thierry whence she was moved just one lap ahead of the Hun; an American named Curley in a blue French uniform and a game leg. Also Southgate of the Embassy. Other people seemed to be expected but none came and finally we sat down and waded into a barbaric spread. After lunch Mrs. Bigelow came in and told her nursing troubles.

Mrs. Parish told one amusing yarn of her experiences. She was working one evening when the Médecin Chef [doctor] came in with a weary looking man and said something to her. But she disliked the Médecin Chef and "so she paid no attention to him." They weary man sat down on the edge of the bed and drooped; presently he said mildly: "I'm very tired." Mrs. Parish snapped out at him ""Well, you've got nothing on me" and went on with her work. After a time the weary man again remarked patiently: "I'm _very_ tired". Mrs. Parish was getting annoyed by this time so she turned around and looked him over, and not finding anything more the matter with him she said: "Your face is very dirty." He meekly admitted that might be so when the Médecin Chef returned and announced: "*Votre lit est prêt, mon Général.*" [Your bed is ready, my General] It was the French general in command of the Third Army. Mrs. Parish then showed signs of activity, got him a cake of soap, a pillow slip for a towel and a pair of pajamas, – and thereby made her peace. The next day when the General left he asked particularly to see her and in saying good bye apologized for his dirty face. She tells it as the story of how she did not get the Croix de Guerre.

I came back after lunch and finished writing my telegram before Hugh Wilson came in from seeing Schaumex. Schaumex is quite optimistic about the futility of

---

94 Austria had prepared an offensive since the end of March 1918, which finally started on June 15. However, for the Austrian troops, it ended with the disaster of the Second Battle of the Piave River.

the Boche attempts to reach Paris, – and after seeing the country they have to cover I am inclined to side with him. He also feels that there would be no change in policy if Clemenceau were to be overthrown especially as regards peace offers.

The bombs last night fell in the Place de la Nation but did not do much damage.

McFadden came to dine but Hugh [Wilson] was obliged to go away and listen to the troubles of a friend and McF. and I dined alone. He has evidently been sat on by Vance McCormick and Gordon Auchincloss for meddling in matters that they did not consider any of his business. It is the usual thing. They asked him to write them confidentially about anything that they ought to know about – and when he does do they get up on their ear and scold him for it. He says he is through writing them privately.

After dinner we sat down and talked for a little time with Mrs. and Miss Crosby who are trying to decide what to do. After some talk Mrs. Crosby decided that they would clear out at once for London, much to the disgust of Miss Crosby. They seem to expect Mr. Crosby the latter part of the month.

We walked over to the Vendome together to call on Mrs. Whitehouse who has just come in via London. She reports American very warlike. Says George Creel was getting himself hammered no end but that he could not learn to stop making speeches. Said Will Irwin was not the man for his place. She is to dine with me tomorrow evening so that we can talk shop. She wants to leave for Switzerland on Wednesday.

Coming back to the hotel I found Hugh with Gallavresi and Barzini whom I knew in Belgium early in the war. We talked about Japan and Mexico and forgot about the war for a time.

Memorandum by Joffre.   June 15, 1918

For the present, at all events, Paris may be considered as safe. The Château-Thierry, Villers-Cotterêts, Compiègne front is stable, there may be slight local engagements, but the Germans plan no further attack there just now. They realize that they cannot take Paris in this manner. And they are not going to run the risks of a big failure at a juncture when they must succeed if they are ever to succeed. They have done a great deal of thinking in the last month, largely owing to the American Troops. They fully realize, now, what American intervention means, for they have felt the American soldier at work. They would have taken Paris if they could, but their real objective was and is to destroy the French and British Armies before America can put a big army in the field.

Now they recognize the necessity for haste, especially since one month from now we may expect to see an entire American Army Corps fighting with its individuality as an army corps, and this will continue.

According to such information as we can get, the Germans now dispose of between thirty and forty entirely fresh divisions in the North. I believe they are going to try their supreme effort of the 1918 campaign against the English, planning to turn again towards Paris after smashing the British Army. Such preparations might require some weeks; but these new divisions may already be in position, for all we know, and in that case the attack might be imminent. I myself incline to think it will come within the next two weeks, and probably within a few days. They have everything to gain by promptness, especially in view of the rapidity with which American troops are arriving.

The attack may come anywhere between Amiens and Arras, but I foresee it will be to the South and West of Albert, where there are only British troops. The reports we receive of the spirit and the condition of the British troops are not at all encouraging. Should the Germans succeed in their attack, it would mean a separation of the French and British Armies, with very serious consequences. Then, of course, the way would be opened for a further drive towards the Channel; after which another attempt towards Paris might be undertaken.

General Dubail's removal was entirely political; the friends of Sarrail have never forgiven Dubail for writing the report declaring Sarrail unfit to command an army corps, on the strength of which I had him removed from the French front. A year ago, when those mutinies occurred in the army and it was believed that discipline had weakened seriously, I was offered the position of Military Governor of Paris, but I declined, partly because I considered that my place was at the front, but also because I would not sanction the removal of Dubail from a post which he was well qualified to fill. There were no reproaches against him as an officer then, as there are none now, and I am glad of the distinguished position given him as Grand Chancellor of the Legion of Honor. Having said this in justice to Dubail, I may add that General Guillaumat is a very capable officer in whom I have very great confidence, and I am sure he will do well as Military Governor of Paris.

Franchet d'Esperey's appointment to Salonika is a form of banishment because of his share of responsibilities in the Chemin des Dames affair. He is a good officer without being at all brilliant, but he is scarcely enough of a diplomat to fill the Salonika post with any high degree of success. Militarily, the Salonika front will have less and less importance from the French and English standpoint, progressively as the Greek Army increases, because we need keep less men there. The importance of that front is as a barrier against the use of Greek ports as bases for submarines to interrupt Mediterranean traffic and cut off Suez. Since the Venizelos Government has come into power, that situation has been made safe. Nor is much to be feared from a Bulgarian attack on the front there. Bulgaria is saving her strength for a war with Turkey.

General Duchêne has been disgraced for his share of responsibility at the Chemin des Dames, and is replaced by General Degoutte, a better man, though Duchêne himself is of no mean ability. It is said that General Anthoine also is about to be removed, because of this same affair. The "responsibilities" of all three, d'Esperney, Duchêne and Anthoine, are exaggerated. The true cause lies higher. Notably Duchêne asked in advance for reinforcements which were not allowed him, and so the line could not be properly held when the attack came. The Germans themselves had expected to reach only the Aisne, and were greatly surprised to find they could reach the Marne.

Log   Paris. Monday, June 17, 1918

After a quiet morning at the Embassy, had a call from de Garmendia. Lunched at Interallied Club with McFadden and Hugh Wilson. Spent more of the afternoon getting passes to go down to Chaumont. Colonel Dawes sent word in the afternoon that he hoped we would come down the first thing in the morning, and as he had not been able to get hold of us he set out at 3 o'clock. We were told that Captain Ballard at the Élysée Palace would attend to our passes so I took McFadden's car and went to see him with the letters saying that General Pershing wanted to talk with us. After waiting sometime Captain Ballard came out and said that it was none of his business but that the best thing was for me to go down to the Hôtel Ste. Anne and see Captain Dunlap. I got Wickes to take me up to see Dunlap who said that such passes were not his jurisdiction but that I could see Major Sombodyorother. Major Barker was a Marine who seemed surprised and annoyed that anybody should think he had anything to do with getting passes for civilian motorists and said they had to be got through the French. Being insistent I got him to telephone Captain Charpentier who said that I should see Lieutenant Witterspach at 194 bis rue de Rivoli. After much wrangling with policemen, etc., I managed to reach this personage who looked over the papers I had showing that we were wanted at Chaumont and then called up Captain Charpentier to inquire whether he should telephone Chaumont to find whether there [were] any objection to a pass being given us. After satisfying himself on this point he said very suavely that the matter was perfectly all right and that I should come back day after tomorrow. It was only by dint of much perseverance that I convinced him that there was any reason for our going down as requested, and he agreed to have the passes ready by nine o'clock in the morning. This little matter took up about two hours.

Upon returning to the Embassy I found Hugh Wilson ready to set out and accompanied him back to the hotel to see him off.

At eight o'clock I called for Mrs. Whitehouse and took her to dine at Voisin's. She had a copy of the telegram I had sent Creel outlining the work to be done in Switzerland and seemed to be quite in accord with the suggestions that had been made. We went back to her hotel after dinner and talked things out for about an hour. I think she may get on better this time.

Log   Paris. Tuesday, June 18, 1918

Went for the motor pass at nine o'clock and asked the orderly to take my card into Lieutenant Witterspach, but he knew better and said that the pass was to be found on the fourth floor and that he could get it, so he made three fruitless trips to the top floor, taking about fifteen minutes on each journey and finally found the pass exactly where I told him it was to be found, so that we got away from the Passport Bureau at 10 o'clock, and, after a visit to the Embassy, set out at eleven.

We got to Provins at one and had lunch. Reached Troyes about five, laid in a supply of gasoline and rolled up to GHQ at eight o'clock. The chauffeur was a cautious soul and had taken about eight hours of actual running time.

CHAUMONT
There was nobody at GHQ who knew anything about our business so we stopped at Logan's where he, Martin Egan, George Quekemeyer and Major Bowditch, were emerging from dinner. They said that General Pershing was expecting us to dine at his Chateau in the country and that it was up to us to hurry as we were about

half an hour late. The Chateau is about six kilometers out and we reached it at about a quarter past eight. The General was dining alone with his staff, consisting of General McAndrew, Col. Boyd, Col. Dawes, Major Collins, Captain [DeLancy] Jay and Lieutenant Hughes. He has taken over a handsome modernized Chateau with large rooms down stairs and a comfortable number of bedrooms. As we were so late he had given up hope of us and had put Dawes and Jay into the rooms that we were to have had and we were relegated to the Guest House. After dinner we yarned for about half an hour when it was announced that this was to be a wild night, a YMCA man was going to sing. A flat chested bird named Stanley, who looked like a hot water bottle and had a deep bass voice came in and warbled to us about Danny Deever[95] and other cheering things. Telling us between songs that he just loved to sing to men and liked nothing better than to appear at the Lambs Club or at Sing Sing. General Pershing has good control over his muscles and did not let his face slip once.

Quek [Quekemeyer] told me about Tom Bridges losing his leg. Said that when he came out from under the ether he asked what they had done with his leg. They asked if he had any wishes in the matter. He replied "Yes, give it to the Lion cub, he hasn't had a square meal for a month."

As we were leaving General Pershing said he wanted to see me and talk with me more at length about the work I was doing and the possibilities for the future.

Log   Chaumont. Wednesday, June 19, 1918

After breakfast went up to Logan's house for a long talk with Martin Egan. He had been looking into the propaganda situation and had reached the same views I have been firing into Washington, namely, that we are trying to do it in a halfhearted and frivolous way with people who are not of sufficient caliber and that we either should do it right or drop it. He also talked about the lack of information at GHQ concerning political movements and asked whether I was able to undertake the work. After we had thrashed things out he said he would telegraph or get the General to telegraph suggesting that we both take a transport home stayfour or five days to talk things over and come back by the same boat.

Went up to GHQ at eleven and saw McCabe who has been made a Lieutenant Colonel. He came back to the subject of my taking a commission and said the idea would be to give me field rank and make me chief of the section. I held out on the

---

[95] "Danny Deever" is the title of a 1890 poem by Rudyard Kipling. It is a ballad that describes a crime and its punishment in India.

ground that I could be more useful as a civilian but he was not at all convinced and urged me to reconsider.

Saw Howard Barnes and had a little talk with him, also Exton.

Lunched with Logan, Martin Egan, and Sherman where the talk was mostly about Washington. After lunch McFadden had an hour with General Pershing while I went through the political situation with Nolan. He is a good deal disturbed by the character of propaganda we are doing and his ideas seem to be those held by Egan and me.

He showed me a rather interesting memorandum on the Bulgarian situation from Tyler, concluding from the Cabinet crisis that Ferdinand is getting ready to protect himself by trimming his sails to whatever situation may develop.[96] He says there is a great field for allied activity in Bulgaria but that he fears Pichon may be inclined to spike it because of his known hobby for Japanese participation in the war. We got away from Chaumont at six o'clock and had a blow out just as we reached Troyes. We tried all the hotels but could not get any rooms so had a hasty dinner and pushed on to Nogent, which was reported less crowded. It soon got dark and we learned that the angel chauffeur had disconnected his lamps because there was no use for them in Paris. We barged along in the dark at a snail's pace reaching Nogent about midnight. We waked up the people in the two hotels but were firmly turned away as there was not a bed to be had, so we decided to push on to Provins. About this time it began to rain and a few kilometers out of town we ran into a wooden barrier which had been put across the road to prevent traffic. The chauffeur must have been asleep as he never slowed up as we went through a group of sentries and sped on our way. At 1:15 we reached Provins and found a disreputable looking hotel where they allowed us to have a room with two beds. We laid down with our clothes on and passed away.

While talking with Nolan, the French and Italian communiqués were brought in and he and Eltinge went over them on the maps. The French seemed to have been successful in repulsing the attack at Rheims and as only three German divisions were involved, it seems probably that if they care to make a great effort, they can take the place, which is not a little more than a heap of ruins, but which has great moral value. The Italian front seems from a surface reading of the communiqué to be holding, but there was something very doubtful to be read between the lines.

---

96 The Treaty of Bucharest between the Central Powers and Romania, signed on May 7, 1918, did not secure Bulgaria full control of the province of Northern Dobruja. This triggered a government crisis in Sofia, and on June 20, Prime Minister Vasil Radoslavov resigned.

Log   Provins. Thursday, June 20, 1918

After breakfast we found that the car had enjoyed another blow out during the night and it was ten o'clock before we got away. About half way to Paris we had still another puncture and rolled up to the hotel at one o'clock very much bored.

Paris.
After letting the threatening situation develop without making any preparations for the evacuation of the city, a burst of speed seems to have come within the last few days. Every allied officer in Paris has been required to fill out a form showing how many people he has working under him and what archives and supplies he would have to move in case of an evacuation. Officers are to be allowed to take out their families on the official trucks or trains, but this does not apply to civilian employees or private soldiers which is probably largely a matter of academic interest as very few soldiers have their families over here. Full provision has been made for the Embassy staff through the Provost Marshal. The plan is being made with a view of clearing the town upon an hour's notice, if necessary. Each person is to be allowed 100 lbs. of baggage.

Went home at 6 o'clock and passed away until dinner time when I took Mrs. and Miss Crosby over to the Ritz to dine with McFadden. The Ambassador [Sharp] was also there and we sat around and talked until half past ten. McFadden now proposes to marry off his brother to Miss Crosby and the Ambassador entered a nephew in competition.

I took Mrs. and Miss Crosby back to the Meurice and then McFadden led me aside and showed me a letter that had been left for him by Mrs. Whitehouse who left this evening for Switzerland. She said she had learned with deep sorrow that McFadden had been spreading malicious stories about her to the effect that she and her husband were agents in the pay of the German Government and a great deal more to the same effect. She elaborated on this at great length and told about what they had done with the money derived from the sale of their Long Island house; how much they had paid for their house at Newport and a lot of bunk of the same sort. She added that she regretted this particularly because she had considered McFadden her best friend on this side of the water and who would help her, rather than hurt her, and it pained her deeply to find this was not so. She added also that Hugh Gibson was also circulating the same stories but that she could not complain about that as she had no reason to expect any friendliness from him. We yarned about this some time and decided to write her demanding the name of the trouble maker who told her the lie.

Log   Paris. Friday, June 21, 1918

A nice quiet day. Fortunately there was nobody in their offices during the morning so I could not see several people with whom I had a solemn obligation to talk.

Bill Cresson came in for a little talk. He is now chief of the military mission with the Belgian Army. He says that the Germans are making a certain amount of headway in their work among the Flemish; that all the patriotic Flemings are in jail in Germany and that the Swine are being bribed and bought and cajoled into working with the Germans. He says that the Belgian Cabinet which used to have ten members in times of peace has gradually expanded to twenty one members and that their main occupation is raising their own salaries; that the socialists are beginning to get after the Government vigorously because of this and that there are evidences that the allied governments who are putting up the money are not altogether pleased. It appears that de Broqueville got out because of the fact that some of these members objected to having him go ahead without consulting them. Inasmuch as he is the whole government himself it seems ridiculous that these purely decorative dodos should be considered in any way. Bill wanted me to go back with him to the front tomorrow and as I pleaded inability to do so, he made the invitation available any time. I shall try to go down later on.

Frazier brought in Whitney Warren who had some great thoughts on how to win the war through having French newspaper correspondents live at GHQ I undertook to lay the matter before James and wrote him on the subject.

Lunched with McFadden at the Interallied Club where I ran into Chauncey Hackett, who is now a lieutenant in the Signal Corps. We sat next to him at a long table as all the little ones were filled. Opposite him was a grouchy Brigadier General who had merely snorted when Chauncey and a friend saluted him. He turned out to be General Allaire, the Provost Marshal, who has been sent here as a step on the way to being canned. If Chauncey had had any say, he would have been canned before leaving the table.

On returning to the Embassy, Edith Wills came in for a minute and then Madame Baguès who announced in anguished tones that her little sister, aged eighteen and a friend, had been pinched by the intelligence officers at Bordeaux. She was all het up [sic, upset] and I promised to get on the job and straighten it out. After a time a telephone message came back from Ward's office saying the young ladies had been arrested because the intelligence officers were suspicious and had taken offense because the young ladies had made a false statement in their declaration by saying they had come over to work for Kerney, whereas they had merely a letter from Creel suggesting that perhaps Kerney would give them a job.

However, they are now on their way from Bordeaux. Lambert came in to say that the great danger was now the commune and that the government was settling it by sending large numbers of working people away and reestablishing factories in different parts of the country.[97] The word seems to have gone out from the government to get valuables away against a possible day of roughhouse.

A pouch from Washington with bundles of letters. One from Phil [Patchin], telling something of Mrs. Whitehouse's visit to America. He has the following to say on the subject:

"I understand that Vira has departed for Switzerland. There is likely to be a pretty serious situation and I want to tell you the whole thing, but with the warning that it is really a delicate matter. I took your confidential telegram, sent from Rome, to Irwin, over to him and Bill unbosomed [sic] himself. He said that Vera had come back with murder in her heart as you said she had, and proceeded to raise the devil around here. She dominated George [Creel] and had things her own way. She saw the Secretary [Lansing] and Mr. Phillips but not me, which is only another example of many where people don't consult anybody who knows anything about a subject. Unluckily Mr. Polk was away. I do not k now what she said to the Secretary but she had nothing but kind words for Hugh Wilson and everyone else connected with us when she spoke to Phillips. I know this was not her attitude when she talked with a number of other people. She still holds the State Department responsible, as near as I can get to the facts, for her being scruppered [sic]. And, also as near as I can fathom the situation, without having been in on any of these multitudinous conversations and conferences that have been going on, there has been somewhere some dirty work at the cross roads. You will recall that when it first became public that Norman Whitehouse was going to Switzerland, the Legation telegraphed the Department advising against this step. At that time the Legation did not even know that it was a lady coming. The matter was taken up with George and George framed the telegram to the Legation which stated that if desirable the Legation could make a public statement that Mrs. Whitehouse was over there for a study of conditions, particularly with reference to women and children. As we know, Mrs. Whitehouse refused to operate under this statement, in which, possibly she was not far from right. I have always thought that very likely her indignation was largely due to the fact that she did not know that Creel was the author of the telegram, that is, her indignation against the Department. From what I have now heard, however, she does now know that Creel wrote the telegram but says that Creel receded from the position he took in that telegram and that the Department failed to inform the Legation in Switzerland that he had so receded. I heard this only yesterday and it was all news to me. Mr. Polk, I think, kept me

---

97 In 1917 and especially 1918, strikes and protests shook the war-ridden country, kindling the French government's fear of the spread of revolutionary fever.

advised of the developments in the case. That George ever made a request that we inform the Legation that he had changed his view, I do not recall, and, further, I know that if he had changed his mind and did want new instruction to go, the Department would never have refused to send them. We were very careful, I distinctly recall, to let George send precisely what he wanted to send and to let him handle the matter. It is just as well that you should know these things.

"Bill does not believe that the thing will work well. However, Mrs. Whitehouse is going back under the best possible auspices. She bears a letter from the Swiss Minister here to the President of the Federal Council and also a letter from President to the Minister. She is to have full and free opportunity to carry on her work in the way that she deems fit. I hope that she will succeed, for failure will most probably will result in blame attaching to the Department, although Heaven knows we are only too anxious that the trick be successfully done. At this end we are going to give every bit of cooperation possible and you should do the same over there. Incidentally, I hear that she rather has it in for you, which should worry you a lot, and is possibly due, in fact probably due, in fact wholly due to the fact that you know something about it and also that you were in the Department during the late unpleasantness. But don't let this friendly tip interfere with amicable relations, but be very careful about getting on the grass.

"Apparently one thing must be kept in mind. It is that Mrs. Whitehouse in her own field must be a complete boss. As I understand it, Switzerland is her field, but the first thing you know she will try to collar the rest of Europe. She is intolerant of the suggestion that there is a division between propaganda in a given country and propaganda in an enemy country. She wants it all. Let her have it her own way. It is much the best thing to do at this juncture. I think it unlikely that Bill Irwin will remain where he is very long. He did not plan to stay on indefinitely and I do not think that he will be there more than a few weeks more. He is not having a happy time.

"Don't let these things I tell you put you in a belligerent mood because the better thing, by far, is to do what we all can do to help this thing out and to put it through to success. Lord knows the work has to be done and that it is very badly needed. We must do what we can in the circumstances.

Phil also gives an amusing account of the visit of Prince Arthur of Connaught [on 5/25/1918]:

"Yesterday and the day before we had with us His Royal Highness Prince Arthur. He came unofficially and informally. The informality was the best of all. We had a troop of cavalry at the station consisting of what are called "Military Police," from Camp Meade. It was the rottenest looking troop of cavalry you ever saw, consisting of a lot of very shaggy and un-manicured horses or ponies, mounted by what seemed to me to be a group of Pennsylvania's leading coal miners. Captain

Kelley was in command. As the Prince, in a White House car, passes the escort they all saluted and looked very stern. They remained at attention until all the automobiles passed them on the plaza. Then they began to wheel around the escort the ten or fifteen automobiles. Unluckily the Prince's car started off down Massachusetts Avenue, headed by an enthusiastic motor cop on a motor cycle. Without much ceremony the procession worked up a speed of twenty five miles an hour, and the cavalry behind set into a brisk trot to keep up. It was soon to be seen that the cavalry was falling behind, so Captain Kelly issued an order and put his troop to a gallop. Whereupon soldiers of the Army began to be spilled from North Capitol street to about tenth street when the gallant captain decided to abandon the chase and let the Prince shift for himself which the Prince did exceptionally well. We went up Massachusetts Avenue to Dupont Circle, turning the corners at 30 miles an hour with a wild gang of bicycle police racing around all sides. The motorcycle cop managed to stay with us, but the boys in blue who had to use their legs were obliged to drop behind with the one exception of a fellow who hung on to our automobile and was towed to the Embassy, with our taxi driver muttering and murmuring that under any other circumstances he would be sent to jail for life for speeding. At the Embassy I more or less took command of the troop of cavalry. The Captain seemed to have no notion of what he was to do and a long legged and big nosed British Colonel nearly put him out of business when he told him that His Royal Highness wished to review his escort. We had several conference as to just how to carry out this remarkable request, an unusual procedure, but finally managed to give His Royal Highness a close up of real American cavalry. Then we had to decide whether the cavalry should escort the Prince to the White House. Captain Kelly said that he had been ordered to do so. We fixed it with the chauffeur not to run away again. Then Captain Kelly asked me how one got from the British Embassy to the White House, as he was unfamiliar with the city. As soon as they had called the Emergency Ambulance and revived me I got hold of a bicycle cop who promised to lead the captain, followed by his troop of cavalry and the Prince, and his Aides and everyone and everything to the Executive Mansion. I did not wait to see the thing through but I understand that it went off alright. I had to give the Captain detailed instructions as to how he should carry his troop down the Avenue beyond the west entrance of the White House and himself return and salute as the Prince's car passed in, etcetera, and then to turn his bloody horses around and have them ready to shove off up Connecticut Avenue, still guided by the policemen, when he returned to the Embassy. I told him that after that he could go home with his horses if he wanted to. He seemed to be quite satisfied and frequently during our confat [sic] said "Yes, sir," to me. Had on a new straw hat.

"In addition to all the above, it appears that the station the British Ambassador butted in and so far as we are aware Aides to the President who went to the station haven't been introduced to the Prince yet. But there was no question about the battalion of British officers being present nor the squadron of Embassy attaches. Every silk hat, and brass hat, from Connecticut Avenue and N Street was present. It was a lovely day. Now Bill Nye has taken the crowd to the Coast. I wish him the best of luck."

Log   Paris. Saturday, June 22, 1918

The morning passed away so fast that I got little done besides dictating some letters although I had sworn an oath that I would go out and make some calls on various people that I ought to see. Prof. Archibald Cary Coolidge came in on his way to Stockholm as a Special Assistant of the Dept. to study the Russian situation. We were getting down to brass tacks when Bill Cresson came barging in and took charge. Bill spend some months in the south of Russia and announced himself the authority on that phase of the matter, – not but that he knew pretty well all there was to know about other parts too. He was quite insistent that Coolidge should leave with him after lunch for the Belgian front where Bill has his notes which he will give the only existing true impression of what is going on. Coolidge declined gently but firmly but Bill led him off to pay some visits about the Embassy and we shall have to get together again later on.

Lambert came in to see me during the morning and said that there was a good deal of feeling through governmental circles that the evacuation was only deferred and that it was wise to move out valuables while the moving is good. The timid politicians seem to be very apprehensive of a commune and are moving a great many workmen away from Paris. Five thousand are being sent away each day and they are being carefully chosen among the roughest elements. They are scattered through the country to various points where factories are being set up so as to break the cohesion of the Paris organization. It is a sensible thing to do even if there is only an off chance of trouble.

Lunched with Dawson and heard of his talks this morning with Joffre, Fabry and George [McFadden?]. They are all rather pessimistic as to the eventual turn of the offensive.

Worked until late at the chancery trying to clear away the accumulation of papers and write some letters.

Dined with Fred Sterling in his new flat, 7 rue Talleyrand. His sister, Mrs. Porter, her daughter and Mrs. McCombs, formerly Dorothy Willliams were the others. We sat round and gossiped until ten and then scattered for home in the expectation of a raid which did not materialize.

Memo from Dawson's interview with Joffre.   June 22, 1918

We lack definite information about the movements of German troops preparing the new offensive, but no one can doubt that this offensive is imminent. The very gravity of the internal condition of the Central Empires makes it all the more necessary for them,[98] and makes it all the more imminent while promising to be of desperate severity.

The reports current of a drive to be attempted in the direction of Nancy appear to me as doubtful. No movements of German troops have been reported by our observers there, and until now we have always had at least some information. If Germany were to attempt this, she might take the place, which it would be difficult for us to defend, owing to the concentrations we have had to make at other points notably along the Château-Thierry Villers-Cotterêts Compiègne line. But Germany could not accomplish enough to justify her in making proportionate sacrifices of lives at a moment like this. If Nancy were to fall and our line there driven back, it would be a blow to French morale, but nothing more; it would not influence the French army as a whole or the English Army and the war would go on. At another time, such a blow might be worth dealing, from Germany's standpoint. Now, she must do more if she is to win victory before America has enough forces over here to be our savior.

On the other hand, we do not know about the divisions Germany has gathered in the north, and there is every reason to believe that the next blow will be dealt there against the English Armies. There are two possible points of attack, one between Arras and Amiens, near Albert, the other between Arras and Lens. I myself am inclined to believe Albert is threatened. By striking a smashing blow at the English Army there, the Germans may hope to cut them off from the French and drive them back towards Flanders and Belgium. This cutting of connections between the two armies could be very grave. The English would certainly be demoralized, and we should be badly shaken. Then the Germans could turn back towards Paris.

---

98 In 1918, Germany and Austria-Hungary were facing severe food and supply shortages, and revolutionary fever was on the rise.

However, another strategy would be open to them if they considered the former too difficult to accomplish because of the precautions we have taken. If they attack between Arras and Lens, it would mean that temporarily they have given up thoughts of Paris, and seek to take Calais, Dunkirk, perhaps, Boulogne and other ports in order to control the Channel. But they would not necessarily smash the British Army, which might retreat in good order west and south, retaining contact with our troops. The Germans might then try for Paris again, after recovering from their effort; but they would find the way batted by the two Allied armies, acting in harmony.

Should the Germans reach the Channel, it would be deplorable, because then submarines would infest those waters and render traffic impossible. But this would be preferable to the loss of Paris.

The morale of Paris has been affected by the conditions under which the partial evacuation has been announced to the public, by apprehensions about the military situation, and by the very calmness of these last days and the absence of long distance shells and air raids, considered rather ominous since this has always been noticed for the few days preceding the drives. While the spirit of the Army is as magnificent as ever, the morale of the interior is certainly less good than it was. For this reason, and from the fact that our principal war manufactories are now grouped around Paris, I think that if Paris were to fall, the war would be ended.

Owing to the change in the morale, a slight German success might have far reaching consequences. An advance in this next push though far smaller than the advance made in the first days of the former pushes, might even produce a panic in Paris.

Politicians have, unfortunately, made use of this situation in party interests. There has been talk of agitation for peace in labor circles, and it is said that the General Labor Confederation is actively working for peace. Precise and detailed facts would have to be put before me to make me believe this. I think that such grounds as may exist for this talk are based not so much on the actions of labor men as those of politicians who are enemies of Clemenceau and are making unfair use of the preparations for evacuating Paris. They say: "Clemenceau is giving up half of France, to continue the war between Central France and the Pyrenees." That is not true, Clemenceau is doing nothing of the kind, he is merely taking very necessary precautions, and will continue to war wherever he can for as long as he can. Such distortions of the truth are on a par with his political enemies, who allege that he will sign and immediate peace if he comes to power. I have had three conversations with Briand since the beginning of the year, and I am convinced that he would sign a premature and unfair peace.

There is, however, an awkward situation arising, partly among politicians in France and partly in our relations with England. At a recent sitting of the Parliamentary Army Commission, Clemenceau went very far in discussing our shortness of men, he said that we suffered from a veritable "crisis in our effectiveness," to use his words, and that the fault was England's. This alarmed certain Members of Parliament who did not understand military affairs particularly, so that it contributed towards shaking confidence in our defense, and reflected on the morale of the country; and, being whispered about, it reached the ears of the English. Now relations are somewhat strained, in consequence, between the entourage of Mr. Lloyd George and that of Clemenceau. England was angered and discouragement was sown in France, at the very moment when we ought to have faced the situation with the utmost resolution and we needed the greatest cordiality and confidence in our relations with our Ally.

General Micheler has been appointed to succeed General Berthelot, recalled from America. Berthelot's mission was to inspect French officers in American training camps. Micheler will also do this, but he will have other work which has not yet been specified in writing."

Memo from Dawson, June 22, 1918

News coming from different sources, both official and unofficial, and from various countries, agree in representing the international situation of Austria as being very serious, and that of Germany as being bad, while not so bad as that of Austria.

The Third Bureau of the Staff, founded by General Foch, received on June 21st from both Bern and Stockholm telegrams giving details of this situation which agreed entirely, although these two points do not communicate with each other. Austria is stated as being on the very verge of starvation, to the extent that numerous babies and children are dying. There is great discouragement over the failure of the offensive against Italy, and not much more would be needed to bring Austria to the point of suing for peace.

The Germans are also disappointed at not attaining more important results from their offensive on the western front, and are alarmed by their high losses. Germany now admits having lost an average of 8,000 men per day since March 21st, making some 720,000 men. French estimates of German losses during this period had been between 800,000 and 900,000, so that that the figure tally fairly well.

In the Ukraine, the Germans have seized the lands and divided them into large estates with a few owners who want to make the peasants work on them like serfs in old times. Under the Russian regime, many peasants had been small land holders. In the present indignation at being robbed of their lands and their rights, they are refusing to work and are rebelling. Far from being able to recall divisions from the Ukraine, it is likely that not only the Austrians, but the Germans will have to send fresh divisions there to prevent a revolution.[99]

From totally different sources, Marshal Joffre learns that Germany and Austria are in a very bad way, especially Austria. Although this has often been stated before, there are now many details and all reports agree. If the Italians were to organize now for a big counter offensive, it is probable that they would reduce Austria to making peace. Unfortunately, the Italians are just as tired of fighting as the Austrians.

Colonel Fabry, confirming the above, adds today that he learns on trustworthy authority that serious internal disorders of a revolutionary character, have occurred in Austria.

---

[99] Rural unrest was rising in Ukraine in 1918, and peasant armies under the command of warlords – so-called 'Atamans' mushroomed almost everywhere.

Log   Paris. Sunday, June 23, 1918

Loafed until noon and read trash and otherwise sought to forget that anything serious was going on.

Started up the street toward Kerney's for lunch and ran into Mordecai who tramped with me. Also met McCabe who held me up and said that Col. Nolan had turned down the idea of my taking a commission on the ground that I was too valuable. I told him that conditions had changed somewhat recently and that I might be inclined to reconsider the matter. He said he would get back to GHQ, take the matter up with the General [Pershing] and let me know the result. He said he would telegraph me and wanted me to come down without fail if an S.O.S. were sent out. I gave my word.

Kerney had a young Lt. Rose from New Jersey for lunch, nice clean chap who is bored by not being in a fighting job.

After lunch Mary and Rose went off together and Kerney and I talked some shop. I asked him point blank whether he had repeated to Mrs. Whitehouse the gossip she charged me with spreading. He said she had asked him whether he had heard the yarn and he had answered in the affirmative. She asked him for and he gave her my name and that of the Marquise de Polignac. He did not tell her that I had spread the story but merely that we had talked it over. Mrs. Whitehouse wrote a blast to the Marquise and threatened her with a libel suit. It looks to me as though she had had a tantrum without waiting to find out what it was all about. It may be that she wants just this sort of thing to account for any failure that may come in Switzerland that that she is content to have us furnish her with the excuse. Kerney admitted that he had been very indiscreet in the way he spread the yarn, rather than letting me tell the lady myself which I was quite prepared to do. He is going to write her a letter straightening things out so far as he can, though it is always difficult to do after the fat is in the fire. He could not account for McFadden being mixed up in this story although he remembered that Vira had been rather peevish about him and said he had gossiped about her. Blah!

Log   Paris. Monday, June 24, 1918

Alfred Gilbert Smith, brother of Ward Line Harry Smith, came in this morning on his way to Madrid where is to handle tonnage questions for the War Trade Board. He was closely followed Dr. Alonzo Taylor who came in this morning as full of conversation and information as ever. The Doc announced that Hoover will sail from the United States between the 7th and 15th of July, and plans to clean up his business in London and go straight back home. Taylor agrees with me that he should come to France and if possible make a short trip to Italy. We are going to telegraph him to that effect tomorrow and shall follow this up by direct action when he gets on this side.

The Doctor [Taylor] came over on the Leviathan eight days from Washington to Paris. There were thirteen thousand troops on the ship, which constitutes a record.

Lunched at the Meurice with the Andrews who had invited Mrs. Maxwell, Juliette Crosby and Captain Stickney. Flavor was given to the meal by a pleasant spat. Mrs. Maxwell who is a large with large pearls and a great contempt and boredom for almost everything dropped as a casual remark to the effect that she was no longer quite so much ashamed of our native country as she had been for many years. Thereupon Juliet waded into her like a thought bricks and I settled down in my chair and grinned, while she said all the things I wanted to, but couldn't.

After lunch Dr. Morton Prince of Boston came in. I had had a good deal of correspondence with him last year over his desire to copy portions of my book in pamphlets he was preparing, but I had never seen him before.

Gallavresi had asked me to lunch to meet Perilli who is here on his way to London and as I could not lunch, I stopped to talk to them for a little while. He had half a dozen Italians and they were all drunk with joy over the news of what is going on on the Piave.

Dined at the Ritz with McFadden, Taylor and [H. Alexander] Smith of the Food Administration. When the Doc got slightly jazzed up he began to tell yarns about the Irish legion raised by Sir Roger Casement. Roger got forty seven Irishmen all of whom were renegades and had lived in New York and Boston, and most all of whom had been policemen at one time or another. They received generous promises as to money, easy living, handsome uniforms, etc., and out of forty seven hundred Irishmen, he got just one percent. However, they were brought to Berlin a few days before. There was extensive advertising of the triumphant march of the Irish legion, no mention being made of the number involved. When they arrived they were marched down the Leipzigerstrasse. Here all went well as there were no saloons. However, as they turned to the left on the Friederickstrasse the first thing they saw was a bar and with one accord the entire army marched in, and cheering thousands who had gathered to watch them, considered it perfectly natural that they should want a drink and patiently waited for them to come out. They had one on the house, reformed in line and marched about twenty feet to the next bar where they got another. After that they no longer went to the trouble of reforming their ranks but straggled along the street from one bar to another while the crowd grew peevish and then to make a perfectly good Irish story of it, when they reached the Unter den Linden, they gathered defiantly together and sang God Save the King. There was a moment of horrible consternation and then the whole crowd was wiped out of sight. There were ominous reports of what happened to them and our Embassy made inquiries. They were met with the statement that these people had become German subjects of their own volition and that it was none of our business what happened to them, and so far we have never found out.[100]

A less cheering thing is the Doc's statement that we are in for a very bad coal situation next winter. He says the whole matter has been frightfully mismanaged and that Garfield does not learn anything. He will, however, probably get out before the end of summer. The doctor expects a shortage of about one hundred million tons.

Taylor had a good yarn about the sinking of the Tuscania. It appears that one bunch of survivors were picked up on a raft where they were joyfully singing "Oh Boy! Where do we go from here." Somebody sent Taylor a newspaper clipping of a sermon delivered by an English Clergyman on the value of religious conviction in war time. In support of his argument he told some splendid American men who, when facing death in the icy waters of the sea, were picked up singing that fine old American hymn, "Where do we go from here."

Log   Paris. Tuesday, June 25, 1918

Spent the morning at the Chancery waiting for Lewis to take me to the cable office to fight about a bill for Walter Rogers. He did not come, however, and the call was put off until the afternoon. Just before lunch the Ambassador sent for me and wished upon me the visit of Madame Anna Kemin, the Lithuanian propagandist. She used to be one of Frazier's customers and was wished on to me by him. Finally took to the Ambassador whence she is handed back to me. I saw her after lunch and explained that there was nothing doing in the way of spending large sums for propaganda in Lithuania. What she wanted was to be sent to Stockholm to carry on the propaganda from there at our expense.

After she had left the Ambassador stuffed the keyhole and asked me whether I know of anybody in the government service or out of it who had been writing to Washington that visiting Americans were associating with the enemies of the Clemenceau Government. He said he had a message from home but that it was of a purely personal character and that he could not tell me any more without giving

---

[100] The Irish Brigade was built out of Irish soldiers captured by the Germans. They fought on the German side since 1915, hoping thus for independence for their country after the War with Germany victorious, or for material gain. Their maximum strength was 55 men. In 1918, the unit featured grave disciplinary problems.

away his informant. I told him I know nothing of any such communications but that the clue he gave us was not sufficiently definite to identify anything.

Took Major James to lunch at the Meurice where we thrashed out a lot of odds and ends of business. He is quite keen for me to take the commission and go to work on the General Staff.

Charley Carstairs came in after lunch and bad me to dine on Thursday as Hélène is leaving for the south of France at the end of the week.

Charles Campbell, Jr., came in, dressed as a first lieutenant. He has laid down to the State Department just what its duty is toward him. He says that inasmuch as his wife married him knowing him to be a diplomatic officer and considering herself entitled to the treatment accorded to the wives of such exalted public servants, he feels that when he resigns to put on a uniform, his wife should still be entitled to a diplomatic passport. Rather subtle reasoning. He clinched the matter by saying that the Department of State could not be less decent than a wholesale grocery.

Captain Cutcheon dropped in before leaving Tours to suggest we get some speed about finding a flat so that he would have a place to lay his head when he came back to town.

At five o'clock went with Lewis to the French cable company where we have a half hour with Mr. Focqué, a dapper, dry-as-dust, little French functionary, who thinks only in terms of charts and tariffs and regulations. He was ready to make an equitable arrangement of the matter submitted to him, but felt it necessary to explain to us in words of one syllable over and over just what mental processes led him to the decision he had taken. Each time he went through with the story we assured him that we quite understood and were entirely satisfied, whereupon he would launch out upon a fresh explanation and we got away just at six o'clock.

Going back to the Élysée Palace found Suydam, who has just finished his trip as bear leader to some Dutch correspondents and is about to leave for London. He walked back with me to the hotel to talk over all sorts of odd matters.

At eight I picked up Professor Coolidge at the University Union and took him over to dine at Hydes. Kerney being the other guest.

A little before one o'clock Doc Taylor burst into my room with the news that Stettinius and Barney Baruch sailed for France last Thursday and would be in our midst early next week. He said that there were no two ways about it I could not go home, but must stay here to educate Baruch as to the needs of centralizing all munition activities on this side of the water.

The President of the Republic [Poincaré] today signed a decree placing Paris within the zone of the armies. It was purely a military measure and will be helpful in handling foreigners and other undesirables.

Log   Paris. Wednesday, June 26, 1918

Spent a lazy morning at the Chancery and went down early to meet Louis Chevrillon with whom I went to lunch at the Cercle Volnay. Eddie Hunt also joined us, he being about to go home after a break down. Also Doleant and St. Paul.

Chevrillon is very anxious to get Hoover to France and is going to London to meet him and coax him over.

He [Chevrillon] was recently at Verdun and told an amusing yarn about the way everybody gauges the progress of the way by their own particular jobs. He was talking with a friend there who has charge of the carrier pigeons on a short front and asked him how the campaign was going. His friend replied: "Splendidly. In the last ten days the Germans have lost forty pigeons and we have only lost two."

After lunch went up to the Gaumont Palace to see Kerney's film, but got grumpy because I could find no seat and came away early in the game. Blount was there in his lieutenant's uniform and told me his wife was in from the country for the day, so I went with him to find her and have tea.

His young brother [Richard Blount] was also there in his uniform as an orderly with his croix de guerre and the red Foragère of the Foreign Legion. The youngster was first decorated for having captured thirty-one Germans single handed and bringing them in at Verdun. He was later cited in the order of the day for having brought in his officer who was mortally wounded when he himself was badly hurt by a big shell. He is now repining at his peaceful job and wants to go back to the trenches.

Dined alone at the Meurice where I was joined by Major Slade whom, when I last knew him, was vice president of the Northern Pacific Railroad. He is now working in the transportation service here and unlike most people with desk is very happy with his work. He is very much wrought up by the lack of centralization of authority on this side of the water, wherein we agree. He says that in the British service the director of transportation is a major general on the staff of Marshal Haig; that in our service he is a brigadier general who cannot approach the Commander in chief except through S.O.S. in Paris. Inasmuch as transportation is one of the vital phases of fighting, it is hard to understand why this should be so.

About eleven o'clock Doc Taylor dropped in filled with rage and humor. It seems that some months ago the Allies told us that we must get all the nitrates in the world for the manufacture of explosives. In order to accomplish this we apparently committed highway robbery, murder, bigamy and arson, refused to let nitrate to go to Italy and France for the farmers and generally got ourselves thoroughly disliked. And then when things were going with some speed, Loucheur calmly walks in and wants to know why in blazes we are making so much fuss over nitrates inasmuch as we are now manufacturing more munitions than can be shipped or used. At this stage of the game the Doctor simply gagged as words failed him.

It seems that the coming of Stettinius and Baruch was merely a figment of the Ambassador's imagination. They are coming but apparently there is no reason to believe them now on the water. Taylor seems to think that Crosby is on his way, however. Says that he had his wings clipped while in Washington, and that he had got a dressing down from the President, McAdoo and pretty well everybody else. They expected him to return in a much chastened mood.

While we were talking the alert sounded and Smith of the Food Administration said he wanted to see the show so we all went down into the rue de Rivoli and smoked a cigar. At least one bomb was dropped across the River and made a very pretty little fire. We got to bed a little after twelve.

Coolidge tells me that when in Washington, Polk was out and that while he derived a little amusement from the seriousness with which both Phillips and Auchincloss assured him that the whole burden fell upon them.

Log   Paris. Thursday, June 27, 1918

Was to have gone to see the Prefect this morning but got word putting it off until tomorrow as today is his public reception day and he had more to say than he could in the short time at his disposal.

A letter from Peter Jay announcing the arrival of a daughter last Wednesday.

A very friendly note from Mrs. Whitehouse for all the world as though she preferred me to her own family, urging me to come down to Switzerland as soon as possible.

Lunched at Randolph Mordecai's with Kerney, Hyde, Jack Carter, Harris of the Red Cross and Fred Sterling.

Harris said that Perkins is supposed to be like Caeser's wife, all things to all men, and know all about the affairs of all the Red Cross people. The other day he received quite a delegation of them and his helpful private secretary whispered in his ear that the man with "the whiskers" had just lost his son. When the old boy with the bush came up Perkins asked him to sit down and said very sympathetically: "You have had a hard time." The old chap replied rather cheerfully: "Yes, it has been very hard, but I am much better right now." And at the same time Perkins observed his private secretary flying signals of distress in the corner so he judged he had got the wrong man. As the old fellow went out he stopped and said to the private secretary: "That Commissioner is a fine fellow." And then after pause: "But how in the hell did he know my feet hurt me."

There is also told about visiting a hospital the other day and having one of the Red Cross uplifters try to cheer up a wounded man. The uplifter beamed upon this poor fellow in bed and said quite cheerfully: "Well, everything is all right isn't it, old man." To which the soldier replied indignantly: "Jesus Christ, no. It maybe for you but you ain't lost both your legs." After that the uplifter thought he would try a different tact so he got on very well with a burst of speed and said to him: "Well you Marines got hell from the Germans didn't you?" The marine pulled himself up and answered: "Well Mister, I ain't no bookkeeper, but if them Germans don't owe us a lot of hell, I'll eat the ledger."

That was about it for the uplifter.

From lunch I went to the automobile club with Kerney and Hyde to see Major Chaix who is the real head of foreign propaganda. We had a very profitable talk with him and left with a feeling that things were moving.

Suydam told me the other day that he took his Dutchmen to call on Marshal Joffre. The old gentleman talked to them at some length about the Americans and spared no efforts to make them out fine soldiers. He did not actually say they were better than the English, but arrived at it by indirection. He said the best soldiers England had were the Canadians and Australians and that the Americans are quite as good as they.

Went to the Traveler's Club[101] at seven and found Charley Carstairs, Geoffrey Dodge, Preston, Eustis and several others wrapping themselves around cocktails. Went home with Charley to dinner; saw Hélène for the first time since Pachy, and dutifully admired the baby. Charley manufactured a cocktail composed of one part gin, and nine parts dynamite and there was plentiful conversation. Came home in time to be greeted by a perfectly good raid. The Belgian girl who comes out and stands in the street every night with her mouth open watching the show disregarded the injunctions of the manager of the hotel and set off down the rue de Castiglione. After she had been gone about five minutes we were all standing on the curb watching the show when three bombs went off almost near enough to make all the brave spectators trample each other to get through the first door. I went through the hotel on my way to see where the show was, when I met the Belgian maid reeling in with a first class case of hysterics. She wept and screamed and paused only long enough to ask for cognac and then went off into another spasm. All hand gathered around to feed her drinks. After she had absorbed several, she stopped crying, beamed on all hands and said: "Ah, quelle belle émotion." Two of the bombs had fallen in the Place Vendôme and one on the Ministry

---

101 The gentlemen's Traveller's Club has been using the rooms of the Hôtel de la Païva at the Avenue des Champs Élysées in Paris since 1904.

of Justice next to the Ritz. Went over to the Place Vendôme with Andrews before the police arrived and found every pane of glass in splinters. The bombs in the Place Vendôme had done practically no harm aside from dragging out two or three hundred wooden blocks of the pavement. The one that struck the Ministry of Justice evidently hurt a number of people as they brought out a number on stretchers and took them away in ambulances.

McFadden was in his birthday clothes brushing his teeth when all the windows in his apartment blew in. He broke all records in dressing and we found him in the street with his neck tie over one ear very much pleased with himself and convinced that he ought to be decorated.

Martin Egan was tempted to get up and watch the show but was too lazy but when he heard the bomb whistling, had the presence of mind to pull the bedclothes over his head. All the windows and part of the wall blew in and bounced back off the inner wall on to his bed. If he had not been careful he would have been cut into ribbons, and with his figure that would look very silly. After a vain hunt for relics we all went back and treated ourselves to a drink before going to bed.

Log   Paris. Friday, June 28, 1918

This morning Baron Fritz de Menton came in to see me. I had not seen him since the Germans gave him his liberty in 1914. He says he was arrested on his arrival in Antwerp, kept in prison sixteen days and given the third degree. The Belgian authorities could not understand why the Germans should have given him his liberty but he finally satisfied them on that point and they returned him to his regiment, subsequently promoting him twice. He is now a major.

Lunched at the Volnay with Chevrillon, Coolidge, Lewis, Doleant, Berthot, Major Jacquemin, Lichtenberger, and Caspar Whitney.

At 4 Col. Nolan came in to meet Coolidge in my office and had a good talk with him. Martin Egan came along and we had a good yarn together about various matters while Coolidge and Nolan were having their confab. After Coolidge had gone we had another round up with Nolan and put to him the desirability of our going home to talk things over and get the propaganda work put on the right basis. He is rather opposed to the idea of our getting away for fear we may not bet back. However he and Martin are to talk it over some more and see whether the General will stand for it.

Nolan said that he was afraid it would not be possible to let me have a care for the present because of the fact that with the great shipments of men it had not been possible to get over enough transport. Later he will try to do so.

He was good enough to say that he found my memoranda very valuable and that the long one I sent him a few days ago of Dawson's talk with the Marshal [Joffre] he had sent to General Pershing for his information [see Dawson's Memo, June 22, 1918].

[Donald] Stone came in for a minute to ask for a little service and told me that the Germans had dropped 12 bombs in the last night raid. He also said that the transport AMERICA had been torpedoed.

Went house hunting with James and found a delightful apartment 147 rue de la Pompe.[102] Four bedrooms, two salons and a big studio on the roof comfortably furnished as a living room. The occupant does not wish to get out but we put it up to the agent to get him out at once and let us have possession as soon as possible.

After that we went to the Parc de Montsouris and dined out of doors at the Pavillon du Lac where we were surprised with butter and sugar. Got back in time for a flivver of a raid that did not bother us.

Log Paris. Saturday, June 29, 1918

Had a fairly busy morning without getting very much done and then took Caffery home to lunch with me.

Will Sperry came in to see me late in the afternoon with news that his mother had died a couple of weeks ago. He seemed very much depressed. He is coming back to take another examination to see whether he can get a commission. Had been turned down twice on account of his hearing but does not despair.

Met Ben Thaw and Caffery and went to the Travellers Club for a libation. Thence to the Bécasse a new restaurant off the boulevards where there is a scandalous disregard for food regulations and consequently a generous amount of custom. Home thence to the Théâtre de l'Abri where we inhaled foul air, saw a fair show and watched the antics of that rare bird – a drunken French officer. All hands tried to quiet him but he was not taking any advice and added greatly to the piquancy of the show by his running comment.

Home at eleven and to bed with the customary raid.

---

[102] In contrast to the Hôtel Meurice, Gibson's new location is roughly an hour's walk away from the very center of Paris.

Log   Paris. Sunday, June 30, 1918

Had planned to put in this day in bed but at a little after nine Frazier telephoned to say that he had given me the wrong information in regard to the landing of American troops in Italy, – so there was nothing for it but to go up to the Embassy and send a telegram to Hugh Wilson explaining the situation.

Just as I was getting ready to start James came along in his car and wanted me to go with him for a spin in the country. After getting off the message to Hugh Wilson we went out to Versailles and lunched at the Reservoirs;[103] thence to Saint Germaine n Laye where we walked about in the park. Then back to tea at Clarence's [Gagnon] studio. He had some crumby people looking at his pictures but we stayed bravely with him for over an hour.

Dined alone at the hotel and talked afterward for a time with Mrs. Crosby. There were two raids soon after I got to bed but the barrage was at some distance and I went to sleep before the berloque sounded. This is getting to be a bore.

In the evening before coming up I ran into Major Watson who has come into town to be operated for appendicitis.

Log   Paris. Monday, July 1, 1918

Dave Wills came in this morning with Colonel Wise of the Marine Corps and the announcement that they had a loving pair they were determined to marry off before the sun went down. A Red Cross nurse and an Army officer. After explaining to them that it was probably out of the question to get through all the red tape in that time. I gathered the necessary information as to procedure and sent them off to see if they could race through it all before the public offices closed. The betting is heavily against them.

Colonel Wise tells me that his regiment lost eighty percent in the fighting at Château-Thierry and that he lost nineteen out of twenty six officers.

The day I was on the front the Germans had pretty well plastered the place with gas shells. Watson tells me that the night I was there we tossed over some 7,000 shells of our own new gas and that the Hun had kept very quiet ever since. Our new gas is evidently unpleasant stuff and Watson says it is the best means he knows of making Christians out of Germans.

---

103 Luxury hotel and most famous restaurant in Versailles visited by the Parisian high society. Frequent meeting point of Gibson and his associates.

Went home to lunch with Frazier in his new flat and destroyed a few characters. Lloyd George and Orlando are expected tomorrow, very secretly, to attend another session at Versailles. Apparently the subjects to be considered are American man power, intervention in Siberia and various Balkan problems. They will have plenty to do.

Dined at Laurent's with McFadden, Mrs. Elkins, Lord Tweedmouth, and a friend of Mrs. Elkins, whose name we never learned aside from the fact that is called Ruth.

Log   Paris. Tuesday, July 2, 1918

Morning of sorrow and tribulation.

Took McFadden to the hotel for lunch and talked large amounts of shop.

Went home in the middle of the afternoon and took to my bed with the Spanish grippe.[104]

Amen.

Log   Paris. Wednesday, July 3, 1918

Lunched with James at the Interallied Club where we sat out of doors and froze. Met Hyde with his neck wrapped up in a mattress feeling very content at looking like a *blessé* [injured person].

Knocked off early and loafed until dinner with Andrews and Major Slade.

Log   Paris. Thursday, July 4, 1918

Got an early start in a frock coat of the vintage of 1905 and a top hat holding two and a quarter gallons, and come to the Chancery with Andrews. Went over with a number of staff to the Tribune in the Place d'Iena [Iéna] for the dedication of the Avenue de Trocadéro as the Avenue President Wilson. The President's tribune was very well got up in red velvet with trimmings and flags. Poincaré arrived as we reached our seats, and was surrounded by the allied ambassadors, the French

---

[104] In spring 1918, Europe was afflicted by a pandemic wave of the "Spanish flu" (or French: "La Grippe"), which peaked in Paris in autumn and cost the life of near to 8,000 people in the French capital alone.

Cabinet, Orlando, Sonnino, Lloyd George, and some of the dominion Prime Ministers and other dignitaries. Madame Poincaré was in a tribune across the way and we all put in about fifteen minutes watching the antics of a comic opera policeman who furiously protested against everybody's movements and then let them do exactly as they liked.

When Lloyd George came in he shook hands with Lord Derby and in a voice that was not to be heard said: "Rather amusing our celebrating the anniversary of the worst licking we ever got."

After they had played the Star Spangled Banner and the Marseilles, M. Adolphe Chéroux made a speech and was followed by Dubost and Déschanel. The Ambassador [Sharp] followed with a very good speech, but that made very little difference as none of the speeches could be heard farther away from where we were. The Ambassador was followed by Pichon who read a rather lengthy manuscript.

As soon as the speech making was over the military band struck up a review march and some French troops appeared convoying two American military bands, one in brass hats. There were a number of regiments of infantry and Marines, some of whom had been two days before in the fighting line at Château-Thierry. Their reception was all that could be asked. They were followed by two regiments of French troops with wicked looking bayonets and their tin hats. They too got their full share of applause. One of these regiments was the 53rd Colonial Infantry with its flag decorated with the Croix de Guerre and the troops wearing the foragère.

At 12:30 all hands repaired to the d'Orsay Palace for the Chamber of Commerce lunch. We had a lengthy wait as usual before going into the tables and I had a chance to talk to a lot of people among them Blount, Topping, Kelly and Rafael Ortiz.

I had a comfortable place, seated just in front of the speaker's table, next to Captain Henry Klotz and opposite Reinach Klobukowski and the Duc de Guiche.

When the clash of plates had died down Walter Berry made an extraordinary good speech in French, the only fault being that it was much too long. Among other things he absolved the allies from ever paying back any of the money we had loaned them and gave them a full outfit of ships to win back their trade after the war. He was followed by André Tardieu, who replaced Clemenceau, detained at Versailles. After he had told us what fine fellows we were, General Bliss made a mournful speech mostly about the Elesian field and the slowly rolling Styx. The Ambassador spoke for a few minutes, addressing all his remarks to Lord Derby in a very happy way. Derby had not expected to speak, but there was a loud clamor for him and he made a very neat little speech which finished off the occasion very well.

It was quite a zoo. In my neighborhood I noticed Marshal Joffre, Viviani, General Bliss, Autrand, Prefect of the Seine, Maurice Barrès, Cambon, Francis de Croisset, Deschanel, Fabry, Franklin-Bouillon, and a flock of others.

Had a few minutes talk with Joffre and some others on the way out but everybody was groggy and anxious to get away.

At 5:30 went to the Ambassador's reception and yarned with a number of people. Among others there were Madame Poincaré, the Cardinal Archbishop of Paris [Amette], and General Pau, who got quite an ovation from the crowds gathered in the street.

Dined with McFadden, Bliss and Sterling at the Ritz and then went to the Gaumont Palace where a much beribboned captain told us very positively that we could not come in even if we were the American Ambassador; but by being very persistent we attracted attention of people that recognized us and finally did get in to some rather poor boxing and a half-hearted battle royal in which six coons pummeled each other for about five minutes, and then home to bed.

A letter from Mrs. Whitehouse in the afternoon mail saying that all is well, – in fact something of a crawl.

Also a letter from Richardson in which he suggests, evidently at the behest of the Ambassador that I come to Rome for the next year. I don't see it.

The French translation of my book turned up this afternoon, minus about forty pages which are promised at an early date. I fear the delay in finishing this will make it impossible to publish it until the autumn.

The Ambassador woke me up on the telephone and asked me to lunch tomorrow with the Prince [Albert] of Monaco, Melville Stone, Webb Hayes and Elmer Roberts.

Miss McCook, back from Rome, also telephoned and offered to punch my meal ticket, but it could not be done.

McFadden was a source of much joy to me in his frock coat and topper and I gleefully called everybody's attention to the Get-Rich-Quick Wallingford. In the course of the afternoon Mrs. Norweb tells me she had met a lady who was much amused at having seen together in the morning Wallingford and Blackie Daw. As I was undoubtedly Blackie Daw I lost all interest in the joke.[105]

Log   Paris. Friday, July 5, 1918

Went down this morning to see Bréton, the manager of Hachette, and give him the translation [of my book on Belgium]. He was in a most amiable mood and said he would put somebody to work on the manuscript at once with a view to getting it out immediately, although he feared that unless d'Ursel came through with the

---

[105] Refers to George Randolph Chester, *Wallingford and Blackie Daw*, Indianapolis 1913.

missing parts within a few days, we would miss the crest of the wave and would have to let it go over until October.

Went home with the Ambassador [Sharp] to lunch. The party was made up of the Prince of Monaco, Melville Stone, Elmer Roberts and Colonel Webb Hayes, the same old Webb. He has not been on speaking terms with me since I refused to help him through the lines from Antwerp to Brussels without a passport, but I am mean enough to ignore the fact and greeted him conspictiously [sic], I made him shake hands, which must have hurt his puny soul, if any. George [Barr Baker] tells me that one day the Ambassador was going on a trip to our front and Webb with his usual brazen nerve said he would go along. George telephoned to GHQ [that Hayes] was coming and in about an hour a message came back from General Pershing that Colonel Webb Hayes was not wanted. The Ambassador tried to explain it to Webb on the ground that all preparations had been completed on the basis of two people, himself and George. Running true to form, Webb then suggested he would take George's place, and the Ambassador had to tell him the whole truth. So Webb has been sore at the Ambassador for some months and relations have just been renewed. The old Prince was very chatty on his hobby of oceanography. He also got wound up about the Kaiser and said that in July 1914, they were walking on the deck of the Hohenzollern at Kiel; that the Kaiser stopped and pointed out three British dreadnaughts in the harbor and said: "Just remember that those are built to fight me and it they ever turn them loose the world will get a surprise such as it has not had for a long time." The Prince said that during this the Kaiser got very much excited, shook his fist and his eyes took on a *regard d'acier*. Then remembering himself he broke into a laugh and said: "You can also remember that those silly fools will spend all day and night dancing on board their ships with young women who come off to visit them."

He [Webb Hayes] told also of King Edward VII's visit to Kiel in 1906 or 1907. He said he went out with the Kaiser to meet him on the Hohenzollern, and as they came in the whole German fleet filed past in review, but that King Edward never gave them a look but poked about with his glasses on the other side of the ship evidently doing it to bedevil the Kaiser, and finally the Kaiser somewhat impatiently called his attention to the fact that the review was being held in his honor, whereupon Edward replied: "Go along, I didn't come over here to see that sort of thing. I came for the races. Where is Lord Brassy's yacht?" The Kaiser nearly had apoplexy, and the King kidded him along until the end of the review when he stood up like a little man and took the salute.

He also told of a conversation had at the table with the Greek royal family just after the beginning of the war and said the Queen laid the whole blame for everything upon King Edward; said he had always hated Germany and had done everything to ruin her and that the war was the direct and logical outcome of his wicked policy.

Another charming little thing he told, was that during the Boer war, the Assiette au Beurre[106], published a very vulgar picture of Queen Victoria in kilts and that he had it on his yacht when he went to Kiel. The Emperor came on board to lunch with his suite and spied this paper on a table. He laughed himself sick with it and carried it all over the ship showing it to every member of the party commenting in a gratifying way on the way the French had "made a monkey of Grandma".

We burbled on until after three, when Stone without any strict regard for Princely rights, got up and left. The Prince [Albert I of Monaco] then took the hint and we were able to get back to work.

Memo dated July 5th, 1918 [unsigned]

In preparation for their new offensive, the Germans have withdrawn some forty divisions from the fighting line on this front, and are training them while resting them at the read. Added to the forty fresh divisions which we previously knew they were holding in readiness near St. Quentin, this makes about eighty divisions at their disposal for launching their attack, which they are compelled to venture not only for the sake of their prestige but because they are fully aware that America's help means time is not working for us.

According to the reports of our observers, they are considering three points as objectives. One is Champagne, between Chalons and Rheims; another between the Oise and Arras, in the direction of Amiens; and the third is in the region of Mount Kemmel.

The first of these three, in Champagne, will probably mark the beginning of the operation, but it will be of secondary importance. Its objective is to attract our troops there, but the Germans will of course profit by any local advantage they may gain.

The attack on the British front will be the main operation, since the enemy's idea is still to separate the French and British armies, and smash the British once and for all, if possible.

---

[106] French satirical weekly magazine mainly published between 1901 and 1912.

It is not certain whether they will attack both towards Amiens and at Mount Kemmel. Perhaps they are only organizing to as to try one or the other, as circumstances may dictate. They cannot attack at both this points, in addition to Rheims, if they mean to use large bodies of troops. Very possibly the movement towards Kemmel is only a feint; their policy would suggest the Amiens line, to separate our armies. Then, if that operation succeeded, a swift blow might be dealt to the north to finish demoralizing the British.

Nothing definite is yet known from any reliable source about possible plans to bombard Paris from a distance. This idea has created more of an impression on the minds of the public than anything else, but whatever one hears of it is only irresponsible rumor. Plans for the partial evacuation of Paris, and a general evacuation if necessary, are continuing, very wisely. Comparatively few civilians are leaving at present; the activity in railroad stations has dropped almost too normal, and a certain number of people are even returning. But many would leave again quickly enough if the long-distance cannon were to begin firing again.

What is more important, is that work for removing war-manufactories from the Paris region continues. Such enterprises were causing very prejudicial congestion. Problems of transportation, feed, and supplies will be facilitated by having these plants transferred elsewhere, so that everybody will be better off, whatever the result of the German offensive. Also, for political reasons, it will be better to get thousands of workmen away from the immediate neighborhood of the capital.

I doubt whether the Government will now leave Paris, whatever may happen. No definite decision about leaving has yet been taken, and there appears to be less and less prospect of such a decision. What is being done, and rightly, is to remove to towns in the center, and in the Loire valley, various services dependent upon the Ministries, whose work can continue just as well there, whether Paris is threatened or not. But the responsible heads of the Ministries, what might be called the directing powers, will remain at their posts.

Log   Paris. Saturday, July 6, 1918

Topping came in during the morning with a new scheme to get rich with the publication of a weekly paper to be called LE COURIER FRANCO-AMÉRICAIN. I suggested that he see Lewis for news and get the Red Cross, Knights of Columbus, YMCA etc to subscribe for large numbers. He went off full of optimism.

He wanted to know all about my French edition so that he could get advance publicity.

Took Capt. Taylor out to lunch and had a good talk with him. He gets a good deal from the Inter-Allied Mission but feels rather badly that he is seldom in a position to reciprocate with news. It will be up to me to furnish him with some now and then.

Letters from home. Phil [Patchin] and Julia write that Josephine has been hovering on the brink of death for many weeks and has just been declared out of danger. They have had an anxious time and are all exhausted. The child was still born but they are all so thankful that Josephine was spared that they think of nothing else.

Phil has a good suggestion which I shall try to put over at GHQ. He says:

> "Speaking of news from the front I have a great and noble idea. Why can't you suggest to somebody that sometime when there is a small raid in which we get the worst of it that they frankly say so in the communique? For instance instead of saying that the Germans lost 7 killed and 8 wounded and that our losses were "slight" let them say what the German losses were, and if ours are bigger, frankly say that 10 of our men were killed and 15 captured, or whatever the case may be. Just one line of frankness of this character would ring around the world. It would be the first time in this war that it was done and would, I know, attract a great deal of attention. This would serve a rather theoretical purpose in one way, but it has its practical side – sometime when we wanted to get away with a whopper, people would be more inclined to believe us."

Went in and had a talk with Kerney but did not get anywhere as he was tugging at the leash to get away somewhere and could not fix his mind on anything. I am going to dine with him on Tuesday and see if he can do any better.

Pennoyer came in with his wife and we had a little visit while I tried to find out about his visiting his brothers who are in the armed forces of Uncle Sam.

When I got back to the hotel I found Joseph Scott waiting for me and bade him to lunch tomorrow. He is over for the Knights of Columbus but it is largely a matter of camouflage as his main idea seems to be to get his boys and take them home.

Just as I was getting ready to go out to dinner Arnold Brown and his wife Ida came along to ask me out to dine with them. Arnold who is now a Capt. is on his way back to the western front from the show in Italy and is in Paris only for the evening. It was hard luck I could not dine with them but we had a little visit with them before going on. A. looks splendidly but says he is bored and dreads the idea of another winter in the mud. He has not had a scratch so far.

Found quite a crowd at the Volnay and as usual I might have come a good deal later for we did not sit down until after eight. I was placed next to Kerensky with his doctor to the other side. Others at our table were Simpson, Hunt, Dolléans, Besnard and a fox-faced Russian. Kerensky began by refusing to take the chair that was indicated for him saying he never liked to sit between people and wanted to sit at the end of the table. Everything was then rearranged to suit him and he sat down and stared moodily at his plate. I waded into him, determined to make the lion roar and soon had him going on food conditions in Russia, etc. He decided just as he was getting interesting, that he had a bad headache and from that time on threw out only occasional crumbs. He has an evil face, the face of some prehistoric beast, a dirty eye and a degenerate mouth and chin. Looks as though he lived on drugs.[107]

I tried to get him started on how he escaped from Russia and he set off as though to tell us, saying that he had 2000 kilometers to do and that it had taken him fifteen days to go that far. Then he suddenly announced that his headache was too bad and that he was going home. He and his friend doctor thereupon left their places and fled while all the room looked on amazed. I fear me there may have been some grumpiness in his going because of the fact that he was not put at the table with the Ambassador or the one with the Minister of Blockade [Worthington-Evans]. As a matter of fact, for all his crudeness, he was the one man in the room who stood head and shoulders above all the rest as a world figure and it was pretty bad to put him at a table with his underlings.

The President of the Club made a happy little speech in which he paid tribute to America and after him can the Under Secretary of Blockade, who in turn was followed by his Chief, Lebrun, the Minister. He spoke well, partly about America and partly about the need of an economic blockade of Germany. He tried to launch into English for a peroration but got tangled in an ambitious sentence and had to shrug his shoulders and sit down amid the cheers of the crowd.

The Ambassador did not speak.

Walked up and down the boulevards with Pink Simpson and Eddie Hunt for half an hour or so and then turned in. Hunt has had a breakdown and is now going home for a rest.

---

107 Kerensky had headed the Russian provisional government after the February Revolution 1917 and fled Russia after the Boplshevik Revolution in October, desperately seeking support for his lost cause in Paris. According to his grandson, Kerensky used morphine since he had a kidney removed in 1916.

Log   Paris. Sunday, July 7, 1918

Went over to the École Militaire at 10:30 and waited half an hour to see the Marshal [Foch]. When I got in the old gentleman was charming as always and I explained to him just what the STARS AND STRIPES wanted from him in the nature of a message on the 14th of July. When he had agreed to attend to that we had some little chat about things in general, mostly about Bulgaria and the chances of a good revolution being pulled off soon. The prospects seem to be pretty good.

Back to the chancery for a little work, then to the Wills to tell Edith about the news from the Masons, then to the Élysée Palace to pick up James for lunch and finally to the hotel where [James] Scott joined us. We had an interesting time and fixed it up for James to send S. on a trip to the front so that he would have some ammunition to use in waking up peoples when he went home.

As we were finishing van den Branden came along fresh from Rotterdam and we sat and talked with him for some time. He said the food situation was getting worse in Belgium and that unless something was done soon there would be difficult in maintaining the good morals that we have had so far. The Germans have taken all the wool from mattresses in private houses, copper and all sorts of things that they had not touched when I was still there. Severin now charges 800 francs for simple suit of clothes, and it is not always able to get the material. Shoes cost 300 fr a pair. People of means are having sheets dyed to make dresses and blankets to make overcoats. Soap costs five francs a cake when it can be had. Bronze and copper is being taken wherever it is to be found. Count Jean de Mérode had some fun when they came to his house. He had a big bust of the Kaiser which the latter had given him before the war. It was stuck away in the garret but when he heard of the search for bronze he had it brought downstairs and put in the salon. When the Germans came he pointed that out as the biggest piece of bronze he had but they recoiled in horror and said they could not touch it. But he was firm and insisted that bronze was bronze. So finally they put the Kaiser in a cart and hauled him away to the vast amusement of all the neighbors who had been put *au courant* [well informed].

A month or so ago an officer stopped at Braconnier's place and asked if he could see the chateau. There was of course nothing to do but let him have his way and when he had admired everything he asked whether he might return and bring some friends with him. Braconnier was obliged to agree and in the course of a few days twelve motors drew up and disgorged the Kaiser and his staff. He was introduced merely as a friend of the officer who had come the first time. The whole crowd spoke nothing but French. One officer broke into German in calling the Kaiser's attentions to something and was sharply told to speak French.

Braconnier kept up the pretense of not knowing who his visitor was and had some fun. The Kaiser finally told him it was a shame Belgium had not let the Germans go through. Braconnier said they had no choice but to do as they had.

> "Why not?"
> "Question d'honneur!"

That was about all for that.

Then the Kaiser turned his attention to the beautiful park and admired the fine old walnut trees. B. said in a matter of fact way:

> "Its just as well you came now for next week you can no longer admire them."
> "Why not?"
> "Because German soldiers are coming to cut them all down."

The Emperor exploded and ordered that no such thing be done.

Braconnier was asked to accompany the party to the gate where orderlies had opened large hampers for a picnic lunch. They offered him a sandwich but he declined and on being pressed for a reason said that he never ate between meals. The Kaiser then offered him a glass of port but he went through the *même jeu* [same game] and said that he never drank between meals. So the Kaiser went away with only the consolation of knowing he had saved the trees.

Took to my bed for the afternoon and got up only in time to go to the Ritz to dine with McFadden who had rounded up Frazier, Mrs. Sanger, Miss Biddle and Countess Somebody who felt that the war was awfully stupid and uninteresting.

Log   Paris. Monday, July 8, 1918

A rare day with not a single visitor from outside the Embassy. I had plenty to do in the way of writing letters and dictating so kept at it hard until six o'clock.

Had lunch with McFadden and Andrews at the Meurice.

Dined with Martha McCook and Mrs. Whitridge who had also asked Miss McCane and Major Ward. We talked everything but shops until half past ten and enjoyed a really good time.

Log   Paris. Tuesday, July 9, 1918

Spent a lazy morning at the chancery with an opportunity to clean up a lot of odds and ends.

Lunched with Stetson at the Meurice and had a good talk.

Late in the afternoon went with James to look at another flat but it was not tempting and we came away still clinging to the hope that we should be able to get the one we want.

Dined alone at the Meurice and got some letters written before to bed.

Log   Paris. Wednesday, July 10, 1918

Kerney is going down to Lyons for the festivities of the 14th [of July][108] and from there to Aix for a talk with Mrs. Whitehouse. He suggested that I go along and share the general discussion. I cannot go to Lyon but thought it might be well to go to Evian for a look at Teddy Curtis, joining them later at Aix and returning with James by motor to GHQ. Telegraphed Teddy to say that I could come if he was to be there, and to Hugh Wilson to suggest that he join me and come back with James and me to GHQ. Shall probably go down by train on Friday night so as to have Saturday with Teddy.

Wanger came in from Rome with stories of what is being done there. He reports that Merriam is taking hold very well and is getting himself liked. Richardson is writing a movie drama for a beautiful Italian actress to perform for American propaganda and generally the proper-gander hangs high.

He says that the Italian success on the Piave might have been far greater but for the fact that one of the generals who is several hundred years old failed to seize his opportunities and let one hundred thousand easy prisoners escape out of his clutches in a way to make you weep. The General has been retired but that does not capture a hundred thousand Austrians.

Sent Wanger over to the Élysée Palace to have a talk with Hoagland, the movie distributor sent over by Creel. Wanger is convoying six Italian newspaper men on their way to the United States for a visit.

Lunched with Dawson and [William] Huntington at a nearby restaurant and got back early to what I had hoped would be a quiet afternoon.

First came Campanole with a message from Col. Nolan. Kerensky has asked to see General Pershing and failing that somebody of authority at the General Staff. He claims to have some documents of the greatest importance and of a confidential character. It seems that Kerensky saw Trotsky before he left and had quite a talk with him and it is inferred that this may be some sort of game put up by Trotsky. They had also inferred that Kerensky is really out on a mission to get

---

108 July 14 is the national holiday in France.

funds for the Bolchevikoi, – and that fitted in with the line of talk he gave me about the need for money.

I told Campanole that I thought it was rather a dangerous game for me to get mixed up in and that in any event I should not care to have anything to do with it without first consulting the Ambassador [Sharp]. I thought Dawson might with the Amb's consent be used to greater advantage than I. A little jockey, named Mitchell, is in touch with Kerensky and they are going to send him to see me.

After him came Cal O'Laughlin who is now a Major and is doing some odds and ends of things for the staff. He is working for Nolan at this time and is trying his turn at digging into the propaganda situation. They all do it at one time or another when they first turn up – and drop it in disgust before long.

He has the usual sorrow that the whole thing is such a mess and is stirred up as people always are when they get over by the need for serious work. However if he keeps up his interest and gets something done he will be a new species.

While he was with me Miss Lansing came in for a few minutes and passed the time of day. She was looking splendidly and seems to enjoy her work. She and her sister were at Épernay but were evacuated from there during the June drive. I don't know where they are now.

Had an hour or more with Cal. He is going back to GHQ and the present plan is for us to have a big pow-wow when I get back there from my trip.

Col. Van Deman came in for just a minute and passed the time of day – which seems to be the custom. We are to get together for a real talk later, but just when I can't make out for he is to have only a few days more and so am I.

Wanger came back with some telegrams he wanted to send and we had a few minutes talk about various things. He is to come back tomorrow for a longer talk.

Bucklin, the Consul at Bordeaux came in for a few minutes. There were so many interruptions over the telephone and otherwise that I did not get much out of him beyond the fact that it would be good to plan for me to go down to Bordeaux for a look.

Carrigan, the Consul at Lyon also came in and went through the same performance.

Capt Emanuel Victor Voska, General Staff Corps N.A. came in to see me after lunch, saluting very punctiliously when he entered and left. He is a comic little Czech who speaks Webber and Field English and has gestures to match. He seems to be very intelligent, however and is bent on creating all sorts of trouble where trouble out to be created. He knows Beneš and a lot of the other leaders of the Yougo-Slavs and Czecko-Slovaks and has been engaged in their propaganda for years. He is off to GHQ with the intention of coming back next week and we are to go into things more thoroughly. I seem to have spent the day storing up odd jobs for the future.

Davis Wills telephoned in the afternoon to say that he had some troubles he wanted to talk over and wanted me to dine.

Log   Paris. Thursday, July 11, 1918

Joseph Scott came in this morning accompanied by Timmins of Los Angeles. Scott spent yesterday at the front and was given a taste of shell fire which pleased him very much in retrospect. He is leaving Saturday morning for England to get his three boys and wants to come back this way so as to have a more prolonged trip to the front. As he is a good propaganda agent, I wrote Ned Bell urging that an effort be made to let the boys come back by France so that their father could be filled up with information.

Smith the courier came in and I sent him off with a tin hat for Ned Bell. He brought no news.

Carroll came in with the news that he has been transferred to Bern to do passport work. He leaves on Saturday.

Wanger came in for a few minutes but had to leave to take care of his wops. He had a good talk with Hoagland and feels that the moving picture situation is getting along very well.

Colonel Van Deman is to be here only until Monday, so I decided to abandon the trip to the south of France, and try to settle some more important matters with him. Telephoned Nolan that I was moving in on Saturday and would be glad to put him up whenever he could come to town, particularly if he could come while Van Deman was here.

Lunched at one with Louis Hauzeur, a Belgian who has large interests in Spain, and a friend of de Broqueville. Tyler and Morton Fullerton, the *Times* correspondent, were also there.

Hauzeur talked very interestingly of the political situation in Spain and the stupidity of the allied attitude toward that country. Before I left he gave me a voluminous memorandum with four annexes which he had prepared from time to time as to various phases of the Spanish situation.

Went from his place to rue de la Pompe where I saw Captain Zeigler and made final arrangements to take over the flat on Saturday. On returning to the Embassy found Roy Wheeler of the *New York Tribune* who had been in Belgium early in the war. Fixed him up with a letter for the Minister of Foreign Affairs and sent him on his way.

At 5 o'clock went down to Davis Wills' who had had a long talk with Kerensky in the morning. Made a memorandum of his conversation and sent it to Nolan by the afternoon courier, copy attached.

Colonel Harry Maude came in and gave me a choice of invitations which I could not accept. Kerney, his daughter and Major James came to dine with me at the Meurice. We were joined after dinner by Colonel MacKloskie, Captain ____ [sic] and Juliette Crosby. Clare Torrey came in later and joined us and we made quite a party.

CONFIDENTIAL
Mr. Kerensky said that he has tried without success to get in touch with the American Ambassador [Sharp]. He was most anxious to see the Ambassador and talk about the situation in Russia as it affects the allied cause and the remedies to be applied.

Mr. Kerensky says that he represents a coalition of parties, but he did not say which elements comprised his coalition.

He says that intervention offers the only possible solution of the present situation. The Russian people, he says, would welcome a purely <u>American</u> intervention. He understands, however, that a general <u>allied</u> intervention is more feasible and believes it would be accepted in the right spirit by the Russian people. Any form of intervention is preferable to one of a purely Japanese character. He did not commit himself for or against Japanese intervention.

Mr. Kerensky emphasizes his belief in the essential similarity in the ideals and aims of the Russian and American people. This he felt should command a friendly hearing for representatives of the Russian people from American representatives. He added with some amusement, but apparently without bitterness that he had expected a cordial reception, but had found "that Americans are greater diplomats than Europeans," whatever he meant by that.

Mr. Kerensky said that unless we were prepared to see Russia dominated by Germany we must take immediate steps to organize and control her actions. He got somewhat excited about the element of time, that action must be taken at once, that if put off until September, it would be too late. He concluded by writing down in Russian a statement which follows in translation:

> "I see that not only in Europe but in America one does not understand the whole seriousness of the situation and the grave importance in view of attaining the aims of the war to decide practically all questions with the representatives of the Russian nation. We do not ask anything. We want to clear up the situation and the responsibility much be taken off our shoulders. During the past three months we have been trying by all means to get a decision and we can't get it."

Log   Paris. Friday, July 12, 1918

This morning Major Warburton got a telegram from the Military Attaché at Madrid asking: "When and in what capacity Hugh Gibson was coming to Madrid?" I referred Warburton to the Department's Circular telegram concerning my duties and he sent off a reply. I told Major Lang who was here some time ago that I was going to Madrid and he probably repeated it on arrival. It may have frightened Charley Wilson less I was coming to take his job away from him. I wrote Wilson and the Ambassador that I had to go to Madrid about various pending matters and was anxious to see them both and wished to time my visit so as to have the benefit of their advice.

A note from Colonel Nolan to say that evidently the First Division is scheduled to participate in the ceremonies on July 14th, but that it is to be kept confidential until announcement is to be made by the French. The Boche not yet aware that the whole Division has been withdrawn. The First has been relieved by a French Division and it is therefore up to the French to make the announcement.

Had lunch with Frazier at his flat. He hears from William Wiseman that Colonel House may be over here any time.

On his way over [Sheldon] Crosby said that his difficulty with Ned Bell had been thrashed out and that their relations are on an entirely agreeable basis, the which afforded me a great deal of comfort.

Dined with McFadden at the Ritz and afterward foregathered in his rooms with old Charles Carroll of Carrollton, a nameless French officer, Mrs. Wellman and Mrs. Owen Johnson [Esther Cobb].

Ran into Harold Fowler who is still a major in our aviation service and is now stationed near Dunkirk.

Log   Paris. Saturday, July 13, 1918

Hugh Wilson telephoned this morning from Evian, having failed to receive my second telegram. Inasmuch as he had got that far he decided to come up by the night train as there were several things he wanted to talk about.

Lunched at the Ritz with McFadden and Mrs. Johnson.

After lunch gathered up my belongings and moved from the Meurice to 147 rue de la Pompe, and got settled by dinner time.

Stetson came in to dine and after dinner people began straggling in. Torrey, Wickes, the Duke of Wellington, Mrs. Elkins, Mrs. Johnson, Mimi Scott, Elliott Cowden, Charles Mendl and several others whose names I never got. So the whole place was christened with cigarette smoke and I got to bed about one o'clock.

Log   Paris. Sunday, July 14, 1918

As I was lazy and it was raining, I let the parade go unnoticed. At 11 o'clock Hugh Wilson arrived with plenty to talk about. Memoranda on these subjects attached.

He said that the moral in Germany is going down rapidly and that there has been a great slump in the last two months despite the advances made in the various offenses. This tallys very well with information given my by van den Branden.

He says that he is on friendly official relations with Mrs. Whitehouse, but that she will not speak to either the Minister or his wife, even in public. It seems that the Minister wrote a private and confidential letter to the President about her in which he expressed himself rather frankly. This letter was shown to Mrs. Whitehouse while she was in America and consequently she is furious. She did not see the President and it must have been shown her by Joe Tumulty or George Creel.

Frazier came in to lunch but had to leave soon afterward as he was getting off to England by the morning train and had a lot of preparation to make.

After Frazier had gone Colonel Van Deman came in accompanied by Cal O'Laughlin. We talked about the NcNally case and the situation in the office of the Military Attaché at Bern. He got some frank information on the subject and he appears to be in a reasonable and sensible state of mind. He will go down to Bern the latter part of this week and says that he will reserve his recommendations on both matters until after he has looked them over on the ground. He seems convinced that McNally should be taken out without loss of time.

Van Deman wants me to go with him to Spain and defer my trip until after his return from Switzerland.

Later in the afternoon we went out to call on Miss Armsby. Finding her away went down on the Boulevard to see the crowd. Although it was trying to rain there was a mob on the streets and they seemed very cheerful. Quantities of the soldiers from the review in the morning were still wandering about. Every imaginable kind of uniform including Poles and Czecho-Slovaks. A down-pour drove us home. Colonel Maude came in to dine and brought with him Captain Farrah-Smith who has just got back from Italy and had some interesting talk as to the improved situation there.

About half past twelve I heard a rumbling like the purr of a motor that was missing occasionally and thought somebody had left a car nearby with the engine running, but after some time Hugh Wilson came in and said he thought there must be a raid on the outskirts as he could hear the barrage. We went out on the balcony where we could hear very clearly the rumble of heavy fire with an occasional louder report from a big gun. The sky in the direction of Château-Thierry was lighted by constant flashes almost like an aurora borealis. Having satisfied ourselves that the old Hun had set to work again we went peaceably back to bed.

Log   Paris. Monday, July 15, 1918

Offensive or no offensive Paris took a holiday to make up for the fact that the 14th came on Sunday. Hugh and I came down to the Embassy to see if we could get his passport visaed for immediate return, but there was not a soul on the premises. The Ambassador was at Lyon with Sterling, Dawson, George Sharp and the Military and Naval aides. Frazier was on his way to England. Caffery and Southgate away on leave. Bliss nowhere to be found and Cabot without a telephone. We decided that we had better make a virtue of necessity and defer his departure for a day.

We went down town to see Major Perkins, but the Red Cross was closed so we went to the Café de la Paix where we watched the crowd for half an hour.

Glenn got up out of a crowd of officers and came over to hail me. He was in the fight at Cantigny and had a slight scratch in the back of the neck, but seemed to be all right. He was due to start back for the front in the afternoon.

Stetson came to lunch with us and while we were having a peaceful yarn afterwards the first shot of the big gun exploded not very far away. It was followed by intermittent firing until dark. In different parts of town I heard twelve or fifteen shots, but saw no damage.

At two thirty I took Juliette Crosby over to Red Cross Hospital Number 3, to see Pa Dawson who is coming along very well. While we were there Colonel Neville came in with some yarns about the Marines he commanded in the Bois de Belleu.

He told one story about a private named Leonard from Chicago who went out on a small operation, strayed from his playmates and lost his rifle. The Germans picked him up armed with nothing but his entrenching tool. The Captain commanding the German detachment said to him:

"You are our prisoner." To which Leonard replied with much conviction: "Your prisoner, hell. There are Marines over there, and over there and over there, and you got just about so long to make peace with your Maker." He was so convincing in his bluff about the swarms of Marines about to attack that the officers took counsel together and after a few minutes four officers and 78 men surrendered to one private armed with a shovel.

He lined up his crowd up and marched them back to regimental headquarters where Colonel Neville, after recovering from his surprise, ordered out some guards to take the crowd back to brigade head-quarters. Leonard, however, said that he guessed that inasmuch as they had followed him for three kilometers and a half they would not try very hard to get away, and he took them all the way back without any help.

He was yesterday decorated with the Distinguished Service Cross by General Pershing himself.

After taking Juliette home I ran into Cravath and had some talk with him about the news from England, whence he has just come.

He says that a week from tomorrow the Lord Mayor [Horace Marshall] is to give a banquet to Hoover at which he will be given the freedom of the city, the only American so far as I know except Colonel [Theodore] Roosevelt to ever receive it.

On my way home ran into Louis Lehr who is with the First Division and was on his way to join them as they were to move up in the course of an hour or two in support of the troops at Château-Thierry. The First has been made into a division of shock troops and will probably take a lot of hammering from now on.

Talked with the Censorship from time to time during the day. They were suppressing all the rest of the news which on the whole seemed to be very good. The Germans have taken the village of Prunay on the other side of Rheims, and to the west of Rheims have advanced in the direction of Chatillon. They are bombarding with what are called demi-Berthas the towns of La Ferte, Meaux, Chalons-sur-Marne and Monmirail. Apparently this bombardment was quite steady and from a number of guns. The Germans advanced across the Marne on about fifty pontoon bridges in the vicinity of Jaulgonne, and advanced to a depth of about three and a half kilometers. The American troops attacked and drove them back to the river, thus enabling our forces to withdraw all their artillery without loss. After this had been accomplished they fell back.

As a whole the offensive has been a failure in that there has been no advance to compare with the first day of any other offensive. The dispatchers from French and American Headquarters are very satisfactory in tone.

The German wireless does not even mention the launching of an offensive which evidently shows that they do not feel they have been repaid for the effort and losses which they have sustained.

Dined with McFadden at the Ritz. We were joined by Colonel Dawes and Colonel ____[sic]. Harry Maude came in as we were finishing and we talked for an hour or so.

Log   Paris. Tuesday, July 16, 1918

Got Hugh Wilson's passport under way this morning and sent him on his way to attend to errands and find his cousin Paul Wilson whom he brought home to lunch.

Joe Green showed up just before lunch and I brought him home with me also. He is just out of the hospital where he has been carved into slices and is just able to navigate. He has a month's sick leave and is about to clear out for the south of France to get rested up. Harjes has been very kind to him and tells him that he can either go back to his previous job or have a fresh job with a Corps when he is ready.

Put in very little time at the Embassy in the afternoon and went down town with H.W. to watch the passing crowds at the Café de la Paix. Telephoned Nolan through Wickes to ask whether I could go down to see him on Thursday morning with various matters that I wanted to talk over with him.

Had dinner at 6:30 and started Hugh [Wilson] off to catch his train.

McFall of the Associated Press turned up from Washington to take over Draper's job. We talked from 8 until 11 and promise to talk more. He has very little news from home as he has been in London for several months.

Log Paris. July 16, 1918

Di Fiori, a confidential agent of Ludendorff, came to Switzerland a few weeks ago to see Professor Herron.

He [de Fiori] broached the subject of peace terms in the usual way with a lot of customary talk about the spread of liberal ideas in Germany. Herron is rather impatient with such talk and decided it was time for a little plain speaking. He painted a very good picture of American preparation, efforts and determination and said that there was no occasion for discussing abstract liberal ideas; that we would talk to Germany when we had her beaten. He took the precaution of having a stenographic record made of the conversation and gave a copy of it to De Fiori who immediately returned to Germany.

De Fiori and Professor Foerster, Professor of History at the University of Munich, laid the matter before the Crown Prince Rupprecht of Bavaria, who is something of a liberal. Herron's very able statement of America's military effort impressed the Crown Prince, who said that if these things were true as they seemed to be, there was not a chance of Germany winning the war, and every probability that she would be beaten.

At his instance a meeting of the Bavarian Cabinet was held with the King as presiding officer. The transcript of the conversation was read and discussed at length. It was agreed that the time had come to make offers of peace which could be discussed, and a memorandum was drawn up embodying terms to be offered. Within ten days after his return to Munich, De Fiori was sent back to Geneva to acquaint Herron with these terms and ask him whether in his opinion they would form an acceptable basis for discussion. The Bavarians said they did not wish to run the risk of being snubbed and put in a difficult position with the rest of Germany; that of course they did not expect Herron to give them a definite statement as he had made it very clear he had no means of knowing the President's mind, but that they would like for him to give them his honest personal opinion as to whether the terms submitted could form the basis of discussion. They said that these were what they considered "middle terms" and that any points were open to discussion and concession; if his opinion was favorable they would endeavor to gather together the small states of Germany and bring pressure to bear upon Prussia with a view to forcing a serious peace offer.

The terms included the restoration of Belgium, but not restitution, Germany guarding certain indefinite rights of navigation on the Escaut [Schedt River] and the mouths of the Rhine.

The evacuation of northern France.

The granting of autonomy to Alsace-Lorraine, with allegiance to the Empire.

Free trade to be established so that these colonies could turn to either France or Germany as their economical or commercial interests may dictate.

Poland to be established as an independent state, not embracing Galicia or the Province of Kulm. Poland to have access to the sea through Danzig through special arrangements to be made with a view to facilitating her commerce.

The treating of Brest-Litovsk and Bucharest to be open to reconsideration.

Strangely enough nothing was said about the freedom of the seas; and nothing about Italy.

De Fiori was told that any conditions which did not consider the vital subjects of Russia and the east would be unthinkable.

De Fiori returned to Munich about ten days ago [July 6] and has not been heard from.[109]

Additional Note, July 16, 1918

A reliable Belgian named van den Branden, who has recently come from Rotterdam, says that he has talked with a number of Dutchmen and others recently returned from Germany. They all report, even those who are pro-German, that morale is visibly growing worse in the course of the last two months, and there is more open talk of the necessity for an early peace. Some of van den Branden's informants were in German towns while they were being bombed by allied aviators. They said that the effect was startling. The civil population and even some of the troops being panic stricken, running about and screaming somewhat as the German papers picture the population of Paris.

---

[109] After 1916, certain political circles in Austria and Bavaria occasionally tested the ground for separate peace negotioations with the Allied, but to no avail.

Van den Branden, who I have known for some years, is very conservative and has from the beginning of the war, been rather incredulous as concerned stories of discouragement in Germany.

Hugh Wilson tells me that the news received recently in Bern quite bears out the statements of van den Branden's informants, both as to the increasing discouragement of the last two months and the effect of allied air raids.

Additional Note, July 16, 1918
A Bulgarian revolutionary committee has been formed in Switzerland for the purpose of attempting a coup d'état in October. The plan is to overthrow the Tsar and turn against Turkey in conjunction with the army of Saloniki [Thessalonica]. The committee claims to have one important general in the Bulgarian Army and a certain number of officers, by no means a majority, and a great part of the rank and file in their organization. They ask only for a message of sympathy with their aims, for the purpose of improving their moral situation, and the promise of a loan to enable them to constitute their new government and undertake their military enterprise, – The lone of course to be made only after the successful accomplishment of the coup d'état.

An effort is now being made to find out how serious the committee is and how able to carry out its plans.[110]

Log   Paris. Wednesday, July 17, 1918

The Ambassador and his family entire came back from the Lyons trip this morning. I rescued Dawson from his desk and claimed him for lunch.

[John] Stuart of the International News Service[111] appeared from Washington to open up the Paris office of that concern which has been closed for some time. We had a yarn and I promised to give him various steers.

Lewis telephoned me about various matters and I had him to lunch and talk things over. It is a comfort to have a place to talk to people in comfort.

After lunch Brantingham came in and talked for a little time. He is mighty anxious to get into some sort of active service despite his years and I think he would be very useful. Shall take the questions up with Nolan.

---

110 In the end, Bulgarian revolutionaries were not successful, to the contrary: At war's end, they were suppressed by a democratic government under a new Tsar.
111 The International News Service was founded by Randolph Hearts in 1909. In 1918, they were sued by the Associated Press for copyright infringement. The US Supreme Court ruled in favor of the Associated Press, with Louis Brandeis writing the minority objections.

Blount came for me at 4:15 and we went around the corner and had tea with Infanta Eulalia. Mrs. Blount and her daughter were also there and we had a most amusing time, – changing from French to English and from English to Spanish without warning.

The old lady wanted to know what I was going to Spain for and I told her to talk to people. She said: "Well, you won't learn anything. Alfonso will talk to you at length and he will say a lot of nice things about the Allies. And the next day he will see the German Amb and he will say a lot of nice things to him about the Central Empires. That is all right for he is a King and neutral and he must do that sort of thing." "You will talk to a lot of other people and most of them will tell you what they think you want to hear. You won't learn anything that you could not learn here without the trip. I can tell you one thing, though, right now and that is that no matter what happens Spain will never enter the war. They have just one thought and that is to go on being comfortable and making money and you can't wheedle or drive them into hostilities." And there is a good deal of truth in what the old lady says.

She said she was furious about the duration of the war as she was a prisoner. She had left Spain because she could not stand the heat and the etiquette and she would not go back there no matter what happened. And there was no other place that she could go now. She scoffed at the idea of beating Germany in the field and after setting forth the weaknesses of the Allies with a good deal of frankness allowed that she might be wrong to express herself so frankly as people called her pro-German.

I was told to hook up with Dato. Romanones she said was not altogether clean and there was some suspicious against him. Maura was too "*cassant*" [brittle] and would probably hurt my feelings. Etc. Etc.

She said the Germans kept it clearly before the Spaniards that they could not think of fighting on the side of the Allies. They could not help England which had robbed them of Gibraltar. They could not go with France which had barred their way in Morocco. They could not line up with the United States which had robbed them of Cuba and the Philippines. Also the Germans made the most of the allied efforts to bring Spanish exchange down to normal.

Mrs. Blount tactfully looked at her wrist watch when my time began to run short and Her Highness [Infanta Eulalia] kindly said *VAYASE, VAYASE* [leave]. Which we did. As we went out she asked me to come back and said that if I went to Spain she charged me with a message for the King. There was a wicked glint in her eye so I knew something was brewing and was not surprised when she said grimly: "Give him the benediction of his doting Aunt." I see my picture giving him the message.

From there we went to [Gommar] Neefs. Blount had asked to say a word on behalf of their son [Cyriel Neefs] who is now a terrassier [excavation worker] with

Image 11: Guy d'Oultremont was a friend of the Reyntiens family, and became also a friend of Gibson's. (Courtesy of the Gibson Family)

the Belgian army and wants to go with [Guy] d'Oultremont on the mission to our GHQ

Thence back to the Embassy where I found Stanley Washburn waiting for me to talk about propaganda over the enemy lines. He has had a lot of experience with the work in the Russian and British armies and has constructive ideas about how to go about what we have to do. He is nervously in a very bad state however and is ready to blow up with rage because the AEF does not act at once on his ideas. He evidently insulted Nolan when he was in GHQ and rowed with Conger. He said: "I shall go on fighting him probably for I don't like him." He had a long memorandum which he read to me; it gave a lot of good ideas as to how to do the work and some thorough data on the mechanical side of the situation. I shall see Nolan about him and see whether some of the row cannot be straightened out so that he can be used. He is too good a man to go to waste.

Gallavresi came in and wanted me to go with to see Nitti. Frazier said he wanted to see Nitti when he came to town and G. wanted me to take his place as Frazier had referred him to me when he was not here. I did not know what was to be discussed with Nitti however and begged off. I telegraphed Frazier however and asked him when he was coming back and whether there was anything I could do for him.

Dr. Morton Prince asked me to dine on Friday but I could not do it.

James got back before dinner. They had a good trip but stormy sessions with Mrs. Whitehouse who refused to talk business because Kerney had not met her at the station with a car, – he not even knowing when she was coming. She finally left the party in a tantrum and refused to play ball until she had been cajoled for some time. They took her to Bellegarde yesterday morning and saw her off across the frontier.

Log   Paris, July 18, 1918

Spent the morning in the office.

Davis Wills sent me up a memorandum in regard to Kerensky's talk with Mitchell, the substance of which is embodied in the attached copy of letter to Colonel Nolan.

Dr. Gibbons came to lunch and told some of the sorrows of the trip to Aix.

Kerney had no news when Mrs. Whitehouse was due to arrive in Aix and waited for her at the Horel Mirabeau. It seems Gibbons had taken it upon himself to write her that the party would stop at the Splendide. She came spitting fire because Kerney had not met her at the station or even sent a car for her and he made the mistake of being humorous about it. She then waded into him saying that his life was just one long joy ride; that work was being done in France and that she would have nothing to do with him. Dr. Gibbons thought to do the tactfuly thing by saying: "There, there you must not speak that way to Mr. Kerney. You must remember his position. He is not the same man he was three months ago." Which infuriated the lady more than ever. Finally she got up from the table and left the crowd saying she would have nothing more to do with them. James followed her up and made an ineffectual effort to act as mediator. Kerney got plainly worried and was up the next morning at the crack of dawn to wake James and Gibbons and get them started on the work of conciliation. They finally, after several hours talk, got the lady on talking terms with them and escorted her back to Bellegrade where they arranged the formalities and put her across the frontier, without having discussed any business.

Kerney was all for continuing the trip to Monte Carlo, but James had some sense of responsibility and refused to go, so the party returned to Paris by way of Beame.

At three o'clock there was a meeting at the Élysée Palace Hotel in regard to propaganda in enemy countries. Major Chaix, represented France, Colonel Lord Osborne, Colonel Fisher and Captain Kenny, England, three fierce looking barbers attended for Belgium, and the distinguished citizens on foot were Colonel Nolan,

James, Watson, Kerney and myself. There was a lot of general talk, but Chaix tried to keep to the point with a certain amount of success. It was finally agreed that we would discourage the formation of an interallied council on the subject of enemy country propaganda and would recommend instead the establishment of constant liaison, each of us appointing one representative to confer with Chaix. Col. Nolan asked me to represent the Army and I agreed pending the arrival of the firemen who are said to be on the road. Nolan had a telegram saying that several people were on their way over to take up this question.

The first meeting is to be at three o'clock the first of August.

After the conference broke up Nolan brought me back to the Embassy and I had a few minutes talk, but no time to go in to the various matters on my list, which consisted of just eighteen items.

Before leaving the Élysée Palace I called the Censorship on the telephone and learned from Blount that our advance had brought us to heights dominating Soissons and that we had taken fifteen thousand prisoners. The news was so unexpectedly good that I thought he was pulling my leg and had to be assured that he was telling the truth by calling up the Associated Press.

Blount and Lieutenant Smith, who is James' new side kick, came to dinner, but left early. James told him with a solemn face that the office opened at seven o'clock, but on the first morning he need not come until half past. The poor fellow swallowed hard and said that he would be on time if he could get an alarm clock. Whereupon James blew up and said that he need not come around until noon.

About midnight the sirens began, but I went to sleep and did not hear the clear signal.

Log Paris. Friday, July 19, 1918

This morning the cook came in at breakfast and said there was a soldier who wanted to see me. Finding nobody in the hall I looked in the kitchen and found Travis Coxe. He had started up in the elevator, but he was chased out by the concierge who told him to go to the kitchen where he would find somebody. To the manifest alarm of the cook I brought him in and had him have some breakfast with me.

Stanley Washburn came in during the morning and I made an appointment to take him to see Tardieu at three o'clock.

Saw Kermit Roosevelt who is just back from Mesopotamia and very much worried about the lack of news from Quentin [Roosevelt]. Richard Derby was with him. He says things are at a deadlock in Mesopotamia, as rolling stock on both sides has played out. The British dismantled all the double tracks in India and reduced that country to a single track system. The tracks they have used in Mesopotamia, but they are exhausted. England is bringing back more and more men from Mesopotamia to this front, but can do so safely as the Germans are not likely to undertake much. He says the situation is pretty bad between the Turks and Germans as the Turks hate them like poison. It seems that the situation of Bulgaria and Turkey is likewise full dynamite.

Captain Waldo came in to lunch and fetched me back to the shop.

At three o'clock had a talk with Tardieu at his new office, No. 4 bis Boulevard des Invalides. I had nothing particular to talk to him about, but told him something of my functions and said that I stood by to cooperate in any way I could. I also urged him to put in a word to avoid too much entertaining for Hoover as he wanted to have the time free for other things. I told him that in England the entertaining was limited to the one function of the Lord Mayor, and told him that it would be well if something of the same sort was had here.

After hearing Washburn's little song he suggested that we pick up Pionan. He sent us over to see Chaix where we had a long and interesting discussion. Washburn is now going to try to get some means of distribution for our front and Chaix agrees to prepare him the material to distribute.

Dined with Colonel Maude in his apartment in the rue de Rivoli. He had Major Davison D.S.O., George McFadden and Captain [DeLancy] Jay. By going out I missed Arthur Ruhl who came in to dine. I shall hope, however, to see him later.

Memo to Nolan, July 19, 1918

CONFIDENTIAL
Kerensky is still in town endeavoring to get in touch with American officials. He began by being very secretive, keeping his information as a bait. As time goes on, however, he is letting out a little more information.

From what he has said to various people and from the conversations of Dr. Gavronsky with Mitchell, whom Major Campanole knows, it is possible to form an idea of his mission.

He says that Count Mirbach, the German Ambassador to Russia, told Lenin and Trotsky about two months or more ago, that Germany was prepared to revise the treaty of Brest Litovsk if Russia would conclude a military alliance with Germany and permit the use on the Western Front of the Russian prisoners of war now in

Germany, about 1,600,000 in number. Trotsky and Lenin agreed to these conditions.

The agreement came to the knowledge of the Russian Patriotic Party, a consolidation of the Social Democrat, Jewish and Revolutionary parties, and in order to retard the conclusion of the alliance, the Party ordered the assassination of the German Ambassador [Mirbach] on May 31.

The Russian Patriotic Party then decided to send Kerensky to ask the Allies to help Russia. If the answer is favorable the Party will start an anti-German propaganda with a view to bringing Russia back into the war in an active role. If the decision is unfavorable they would be disposed to make a military and economic alliance with Germany as the only recourse open to them to retrieve the country from anarchy. Kerensky claims to have documents to support all his statements and it is believed we shall have these in the course of a few days.

Dr. Gavronsky states that if the American Government refuses to receive the emissaries of the Russian Patriotic Party, and if the Allies refuse to aid Russia, it is likely to bring about the assassination of the Allied Ambassadors. This has already been proposed by German propagandists.

Kerensky has already had interviews with Lloyd George and Clemenceau, and neither has given him a definite reply. Both said that the decision rested with America. Clemenceau was apparently rather forcible and said that France had had enough of Russia as an ally and preferred to have her remain neutral.

Kerensky, with whom I had some talk at dinner some days ago, seems to lack sound data or views as to the international conditions and problems of the country. He talked freely enough but vaguely, and a good part of what he said on matters of fact was rubbish. This may be accounted for by the fact that he is taking drugs, according to the statement of his friends, and is going in for other forms of dissipation. He gives the impression of a man whose mind fails to focus.

I am giving the substance of this to the Ambassador for repetition to the Department of State.

Log   Paris. Saturday, July 20, 1918

A hectically busy morning in the office. Just before lunch Norman Davis came in on his way to Spain where he is to act as representative of the Treasury. He had with him Senator Hollis of New Hampshire.

He says that Stettinius is on his was over to remain here as representative for the War Department.

Franklin Roosevelt is also on the way and will be here in a few days.

He says that Frank Polk is far from well and merely goes through the forms, coming down to the Department to sign correspondence.

Stetson came to lunch.

Worked at home until four. Went down to the Meurice to see Nitti. Had about an hour with him which is described in the attached memorandum. Nitti seemed to be a great deal more sure of himself than he did when he was in America and talked very convincingly. The Italian Ambassador [Longare] came in while we were talking and remained for the last half hour or so adding his arguments to those of Nitti.

Dined at the [Robert] Bliss'. General Bliss was to have been there but sent word that he was detained at the front and would not be back until Sunday or Monday. Cravath was there and Father Hemmick, and George McFadden and Cabot Ward.

Ward told me after dinner that the beauteous Russian lady I had signaled to him as suspicious had developed into a most interesting case and that there were wide spread developments.

Ward is off to act as intelligence officer of a division for a week or so.

Additional Note July 20, 1918

At 4:30 I called upon Signor Nitti at his request. He talked for about an hour about the necessity of sending American troops to Italy and asked that the matter be brought once more to the attention of the American Government. He says that Italy is now obliged to face the entire Austrian Army, which has a superiority of some 22 divisions and 3500 guns. Before the collapse of Russia two thirds of the Austrian Army was on the Russian front and only one third on the Italian front, so that the burden of the Italian Army has been greatly increased. Italy has called ruthlessly upon her population until she has a class composed largely of boys of 16 and 16 ½ years in the Army, which he described as "immoral". It is true that there are some allied troops in Italy, but there are more Italian troops (including labor battalions) in France than there are Allies in Italy. These labor troops are building roads, diggings trenches and stringing wire in France, while the same vitally important work is being neglected in Italy. Signor Nitti said: "Nous ne voulons pas faire de concurrence à la France. [We do not want to compete with France] We feel that everything America does for France is a contribution to the general cause. But we do feel that the Italian front now constitutes a point of weakness which should be strengthened in the common interest. We cannot afford to face an avoidable disaster."

Before the sending of American troops in large numbers the Germans had a decided superiority on the Western Front, but the rapid increase in our forces has at least reestablished the balance. The Italian Government, therefore, feels that it is of vital importance that either some of the troops now in France, or those soon to be sent, be despatched to Italy to reduce the Italian inferiority in numbers.

He says there is no place where American participation could have so great an effect; that the war is fought in Italy chiefly by the peasant class which is the one best acquainted with the United States and most sincerely devoted to that country; that the sending of American troops to Italy would be welcomed by these people and would fill them with fresh courage for continued resistance in a way we cannot realize.

He said that with their superiority of men and artillery, it is quite possible for the Austrians to overwhelm the Italians, particularly if support is given by Germany. He said that Italy would doubtless have been badly defeated in the last offensive but for the gross stupidity of the Austrian commanders who were so avid for glory that they undertook an offensive on the entire front, which was more than they could handle.

Log   Paris. Sunday, July 21, 1918

Spent the morning cleaning up papers at home. Horodyski came in to lunch. He had just come from Switzerland and is on his way to England. He has seen a number of people recently fresh from Austria, and says that the situation there is ripe; that by the expenditure of a little money and some skillful propaganda they could be thrown into dissolution. He does not take much stock in the revolutionary committee that is planning to disrupt Bulgaria, but says all that will come with trouble in Austria.

He says that the Italian morale is not so actively bad as it was but that the soldiers fought very badly. He had it from a number of Austrians that if the Italians had fought reasonably well there would have been a really great Austrian defeat.

Soon after Horodyski had gone Wanger arrived and renewed attack he had already made upon James. Everything wrong about the way the Army handled things. The only way of winning the war was to give practically supreme authority to what he called the Ministry of Information, which, according to his conception was to coordinate the work of the diplomatic and consular services, Army and Navy; put an end to secret diplomacy by pityless publicity and thereby render impossible future wars. He proposed that we should have monthly meetings in Paris of all the representatives of the "Ministry", and examine representatives of the Army, Navy and other services to learn what they were expected to do.

He also announced that Merriam planned to invite Orlando, Gallenga and others on frequent trips to the American front and accompany them himself as they would be flattered by being accompanied by "the Commissioner himself". I tried to put in a word to let General Pershing have some share in inviting guests to the American front and who should act as accompanying officer, but this was not well received.

He was very insistent on something being done at once and left in some disgust at my lack of responsiveness, although he gave me some comfort in the statement that James did not give him any satisfaction either.

Went for a drive with James to the Buttes de Chaumont. At 8 o'clock Mrs. Whitridge and Martha McCook came to dine. They cheered me by the statement that Wanger was an Austrian Jew known at Follgia as the Austrian Ace because he had smashed so many machines.

Log   Paris. Monday, July 22, 1918

Quiet morning at the Chancery.

News from the Censorship that the Germans have begun destroying their ammunition dumps, burning property and crops in the rear of their lines with a view to withdrawal. Our people seem generally pleased with this. It would seem to give no ground for cheerfulness as it evidently means that the Germans are preparing for a strategic withdrawal in order to gather forces for an attack upon the English or elsewhere. Of course, the immediate drive upon Paris is forestalled, but the allied success is not so great as though the Germans were being fought back.

Joseph Scott, Stetson and Major Cabot Ward came to lunch. Scott feels he must sail at once so as to reach the United States in time for the convention of the Knights of Columbus on August 8. Ward offered to give him a man to put him through the formalities and I delivered him at Ward's office.

Ward telephoned that he was in a bad fix. The English had already signaled Scott as a dangerous character, now the French have made him the subject of a first class signal and to add fuel to the flame, he has just received a report from the United States saying that Scott has done pretty well everything possible to make him undesirable; that he has been preaching against enlistment in the Army on the ground that that would mean fighting under English officers; that he had Mrs. Sheehy-Skeffington stay with him while she was in the West and presided at ten of her meetings. This all the most part balderdash as Scott has been one of the leaders in various sorts of war work and either somebody is trying to black hand him, or they have confused him with some other Joseph Scott. Through the routine of the system, Ward's people had already signaled Scott to both the British and the French. And from the strength of this report he said it would be pretty hard for him to ask them to disregard the signal, and it will be impossible for Scott to catch his ship Tuesday night; that he (Ward) would, however, arrange for Scott and his boys to go home of a transport from Brest. He telephoned me two or three times in the course of the afternoon about progress and seemed a good deal upset about it.

Frazier came back from London with messages from old Sir William Tyrrell, who is now at the head of the political intelligence division of the Foreign Office.

Wrote to Frank Polk urging him to come over here for a rest and change. Also wrote Mrs. Polk urging her to get him started.

Goedeke came to talk over various intelligence matters and stayed to dinner. He is the prize case of conscientiousness that I have discovered so far. He says that every time there is an air raid, he puts on his tin hat and runs down to the office so as to be there in case the place gets hit and the confidential records scattered over the neighborhood.

Berthot telephoned in regard to the possibility of getting up a CRB dinner for Hoover when he comes to Paris. He also wants to arrange to take him to the front and has asked me to go along. I promised to talk to the authorities at GHQ about some general provision to release the CRB boys for the occasion of Hoover's visit.

Goedeke passed on to me for the information of qui de droit [whomever it may concern] the fact that GHQ ought to take a long look at G-2, SOS. He says that the Chief [Harbord] is the most arrant liar and four flusher and that there is very nearly a mutiny there. I shall suggest to Nolan that he send up somebody in whom he has confidence to talk to the men in office. If he does I think he will learn some things of interest.

Log   Paris. Tuesday, July 23, 1918

Berthot came in this morning with plans for a CRB dinner for Hoover. He wants to ring in a lot of refugees from the invaded districts, take Hoover to the front and show him some of the farming and manufacturing districts so that he can form an idea of the food shortage. His scheme is too darned ambitious but there is no holding him down until we get some news from Hoover. He brought a list of CRB members in France and I intend to ask GHQ to grant as many as possible leave to come up for the CRB reunion.

Scott came in much upset at the delay in getting his ship. Cabot Ward has fixed it up for him to sail on a transport and he is to leave Paris tonight in spite of all the gum-shoe men.[112]

Blount came in with his younger brother and I sent them off with a letter to Cabot Ward.

Fred Sterling came home to lunch; also had James' younger brother who is in the transport service and another young officer rejoicing in the name of Smith. They are ashore for forty-eight hours and glad of the change.

Quekemeyer came in during the afternoon a good deal perturbed about the Black Hand work against General Pershing. There is apparently the beginning of a drive to oust him, and Quek feels that it would be a calamity, in which I concur. There are indications that March is at the bottom of it.[113]

Stettinius has arrived in Paris and is at the Ritz. Quek has to stay here for a day or two to look after him.

Colonel Maude telephoned that Sanborn had arrived from Madrid and asked me to dine with them on Thursday, but I did not feel safe in accepting as I am still waiting for a chance to go to Chaumont.

Dawson had a talk with the Marshal [Joffre]; memorandum attached.

Boyd telephoned me late in the afternoon that General Pershing would see the Italian Amb. At 6. The General is in no mood to send troops to Italy until the Govt there can provide rolling stock to keep them supplied. He says he is not going to send troops down there just to please the Italians and then leave them to starve. Gen. Bliss evidently feels strongly that the war must be won on the West front – but I can't help feeling that there is danger in letting Italy go downhill if it can be helped.

---

[112] The term "gum show men" was used to describe persons planted in factories during labor disputes to inform management of troublemakers – basically, a spy.

[113] It is not clear what Gibson is referring to here. The issue is metioned as well on March 2 and July 26, 1918.

Memorandum of Dawson's meeting with Joffre.   July 23, 1918

The offensive has come to a stop on both sides and this battle may be considered as ended, although there may be further scattered engagements and raids along the line.[114]

For instance, General Débeney is beginning today a small attack on a front of seven or eight kilometers near Montdidier, but no great importance can be attached to it.

The results of our counter offensive on the general situation can only be viewed with satisfaction. We succeeded in doing what we started out to do, we established the important principle of counter attacking on a large scale to defeat the enemy's plans, and the morale of both the army and the interior has been greatly improved in consequence.

If the Germans had attempted to fight this battle out, as at one moment there appeared to be a prospect of their doing, they would have exhausted their resources for this year. However, they have now ceased to attack or even to resist. They appear to be retreating in good order to the prearranged line. In point of fact, their retreat from the southern bank of the Marne was also voluntary and done in good order, whatever may be alleged to the contrary. They were surprised by the attack General Mangin started on them from Château-Thierry; this attack was eminently successful, for the General Mangin knows how to conduct an operation admirably; but being surprised, the Germans decided not run risks, and so recrossed the Marne. They had furthermore made the mistake, in this offensive, of attacking quickly after a short artillery preparation of a few hours. This principle had been successful for them during the spring and early summer campaign when attacking positions on which we had had only a very few weeks to establish ourselves. They evidently overlooked the fact that we had had many weeks to consolidate our line from Soissons to Château-Thierry, and along the Marne, and so we started out with an advantage over them.

---

114 In mid-July, the German offensive had run out itself. In the course of the Second Battle of the Marne which lasted until early August, the Allied – facing severe losses – drove the German troops back into their spring positions.

General Foch and his staff, including General Buat, imposed our counter offensive upon Pétain, who was opposed to the principle, as always. I know from General Weygand himself that the very day before our counter offensive was launched, Pétain resolutely opposed it; General Foch sent a staff officer to him, not only to impose it upon him, but to remain with him and to see that he did nothing at the last moment to create complications.

By their present policy of abstaining from a continuation of the battle, while we on our side are not continuing the offensive, the Germans remain free to prepare a further offensive this year. We know that at the present moment they have fifty entirely fresh divisions, ready to be used wherever they please. Of these fifty divisions, twenty-nine have remained throughout in positions opposite to the English, ready to attack; and they are there at the present moment. The other are at points unknown to us, although we know they have not yet been used. In all likelihood, another offensive will come in consequence, either immediately, or after a short breathing space, probably against the British front.

Log   Paris. Wednesday, July 24, 1918

Travis Coxe came in to see me the first thing this morning at the chancery. He has heard nothing from Cabot Ward but I feel fairly sure that his affair will go through.

Bill Cresson came in for a few minutes to say that he had instructed all the Gendarmerie to look after Aunt Leona and would do anything for her that he could. He was sure she would have no trouble about her papers. He said there was a very interesting situation developing between the Belgians and the English and that he wanted to talk to me about it. He is off for GHQ tomorrow and asked me to go down with him.

Lunched with Colonel Harry Maude at his apartment to meet Sanborn who is here for a few days from Barcelona. He looks like a race horse and is interested in his work. He besought me to go down to Spain as soon as possible and look into what he considered a very serious situation. The Spanish Government has embargoed the horses purchased for our army and there is no way of getting them to France. We have to get together with our allies and decide on some common procedure in dealing with the Spaniards. The German propaganda according to Sandy [Sanborn] is gaining ground and while nobody thinks seriously now that Spain will come in on the side of Germany there is good reason to believe that Germany can induce to Spaniards to put all sorts of obstacles in our way. Among other things there is a crying need of a very vigorous and intelligent propaganda.

A letter from Willard to ask me to stop off and see him at San Sebastian on my way to Madrid.

On getting back to the Embassy I found Capt. Antonelli, French Military Attaché at Petrograd, recently returned from that post. He talked very well and I shall seek another opportunity to talk with him. For one thing he says it is folly to think of ever getting the Russians organized and fighting on our side. He says that the best we can ever hope to do is to improve their low state of morale to a point where they can reconstitute a law-abiding society and pull themselves together. He says that we cannot understand how completely even substantial people are demoralized; they weep openly and say that they have abandoned all hope and are unable to do anything for themselves; that the allies must come and protect them from the Germans and from the Bolcheviki. They will never he says be able to do anything for themselves and that if we don't put them on their feet the Germans will. He feels sure that the Bolcheviki have little real following and that the only reason that they stay in such power as they exercise is because there is no organization to the important elements that are opposed to them. They are not strong and could not resist but unless something radical is undertaken against them there is no reason why they cannot drift along for an indefinite time without being suppressed. He gets little satisfaction out of the fact that the Murman Coast people have proclaimed themselves in our favor; he has just come through that country and says that it is utterly worthless so far as effective military support is concerned; there are a few people scattered far and wide over the bleak country and there is no cohesion among them. Our expedition he does not feel can be of any real use as it is too small and far away. If they really move forward the Germans will press forward and occupy Moscow and Petrograd, – and we are cooked. He thinks that the real solution is a big allied intervention through Siberia with adequate and convincing assurances to the Russia people that the movement is undertaken entirely in their interest to help them reestablish themselves in peaceful life and with no idea of fitting them for a renewal of the war. So far as I can make up we are to undertake a large work of reconstruction and rehabilitation with only so much military force as is required to protect our workers.[115]

The Ambassador [Sharp] is furious with Kerney because of the way he is playing himself up as personal representative of the President, etc. The other day Kerney attended a meeting of a radical socialist group known as the Ligue des Droits de l'Homme. Notes appeared in several papers to the effect that he had discussed

---

115 See annotation 80.

social questions and the matter of peace terms. Some of the papers called attention to the importance that must be attached to his words as the close friend and personal representative of the President of France [Poincaré]. The talk itself was bad enough but the press agenting of it was a good deal worse and has succeeded in stirring the Amb to the depths. There have been a large number of newspaper mentions of the gentleman as the President's personal advisor in France. He seems to have developed a mania for that and his henchmen, Hyde and Gibbons, feed him on talk about the great position that he has built up for himself in France and what a figure he is. He is quite carried away with it and is no longer able to play with the meek and lowly. The Amb stopped me in the hall and told me he was telegraphing and writing in the hope of "finding out who is who over here."

The German wireless today reports the sinking of the Leviathan. This afternoon the censorship said there was not a word of truth in it.

We are advancing on La Fère-en-Tardenois and have it under bombardment from a distance. At any rate that means that we have got artillery across the Soissons-Château-Thierry road.

Additional Note July 24, 1918
Lieutenant Étienne Antonelli, French Assistant Military Attaché in Russia, called on me today, introduced by Captain Henri Lorin, Head of the Bureau of Economic Studies founded by the French President of the Council. Captain Lorin told me about Russian and Siberian conditions which might be of interest to the Ambassador.

Lieutenant Antonelli said in substance:

"Allied intervention in Russia is wanted, and even prayed for, by all classes save the Bolsheviks. But they want a peaceful intervention, and not a military movement in which they might be caught; they want to be protected against Germany's military enterprises and also to have what is strictly needed for a life in the way of food and clothing. To give an idea of the suffering there: a tablet of chocolate now costs eighty or ninety roubles; a suit of clothes, some two thousand.[116]

"There is fighting, bickering, and oppression in all parts of Russia where the Germans have already penetrated, so the Russians know the Germans do not stand for peace, whatever the treaties they may sign. And the absorbing desire of the Russians is for peace. Therefore the Allies seem to bring the only hope.

---

116 Russia was utterly devastated after years of war and the following experience of revolution and civil war. People were starving to death, the famine reaching its peak in 1921/22, with an estimated death toll of at least two million people, despite efforts of the American Relief Administration to ease the Russian population's suffering.

"But it must be a strictly Interallied intervention. To allow the intervention of Japan alone would be a grave mistake. The Russians mistrust the Japanese, and would mistrust any nation acting alone. The Japanese, who are admirably informed as to all which is occurring in Russia, know this, and that is why they do not insist upon independent intervention. I think an intervention by Japan and the United States together would also be a mistake. Although France and England could not spare much in the way of troops, they would have to be represented so as to allow no misstatements.

"The way for this would have to be prepared by a clear and simple statement addressed to the Russian people, proving that the Allies are coming only to help them, with entirely peaceful intentions, and are coming as an armed force only so as to protect themselves and the Russians against the Germans, but the intervention properly speaking has a disinterested and economical character. Little need be done in advance; in fact, the Bolsheviks ought not be given too long a warning and allowed time to attempt their usual counter-propaganda by alleging that is an attempt to draw Russiainto war again, the surest way to arouse Russian suspicions and to prevent effective action.

"The Bolsheviks cannot be trusted as a government. But at the present time, no other form of government is conceivable in Russia. They cannot be dealt with, because they are so completely in the hands of the Germans that they cannot call their souls their own. The Germans, or German agents, do exactly what they please. Germany holds the knife on Russia's throat by saying: "If you don't do thus and so, I shall immediately come in with my soldiers." Nor can the accredited Ambassadors and Ministers take action, bound as they are to the Bolshevik Government. The way must be prepared by the foreign military and economic missions themselves when they get there, and immediately before they begin to act. There can be no doubt as to the readiness of the welcome which they will receive.

"Intervention through Archangel would probably be better and more direct. Some well-informed people I know in Russia estimate that it would take two years for intervention through Siberia to be thorough enough to makes its influence felt in European Russia; and by that time, if nothing is done directly, European Russia will have become a German Colony"

Log					Paris. Thursday, July 25, 1918

The first thing this morning James left for Toul with Kerney to visit Foulois, expecting to be back on Saturday night.

Soon after I reached the chancery Simons and Spargo of the Socialist mission rolled in for a few minutes talk. I telephoned Maverick and he came down and took them away. They said that Frank Bohn had not come with them as it was not thought necessary to have him along unless there was to be some very important international meeting of the party, – whatever they may mean by that.

Van Rensselaer came along late in the morning with wails about the way he was being treated. He said that he had been recalled after having been in Madrid for only six months and that he considered that equivalent to an expression of dissatisfaction with his work. He had telegraphed Phillips offering his resignation and if it was accepted he proposed to apply for a commission. He thought I could arrange the matter for him but in a cowardly way I referred him to Warburton.

Word came from GHQ that Nolan would like to have me go down tomorrow so I got my pass before lunch and laid my plans to go down first thing in the morning with Davis Wills who will provide the car.

Dawson and Huntington came home to lunch with me and we talked a number of things, among other the possibility of getting some hard workers in to relieve Dawson of the routine of his office so that he would be free to circulate and talk to people.

Clark, formerly of the CRB came in after lunch. He is now with the Red Cross and expects to be stationed at Châlons-sur-Marne.

Davis Wills came in with Mitchell, the jockey, who used to be in the Russian secret service and manages to pick up a number of useful items. He had it from Trubnikoff, formerly chief of the Secret Service here in France that the Germans were sending two millions of dollars in the form of French twenty franc pieces to New York from Stockholm to pay off German spies and for similar purposes. He did not know just how it was being transported aside from the fact that it had left Sweden eight or ten days ago and was thought to be in the Swedish official mail. T. had it from Kauffman of the German Secret Service in Zurich. That will be worth looking into.

Mitchell is an amusing character. He was born in France and his English is very elementary except that he has great fluency in cuss words. Otherwise he has the greatest difficulty in making himself understood. He has laid aside money from his makings and is on easy street. He has only one ambition and that is to round out his career by becoming a commissioned officer. He is not what would be chosen for an officer under ordinary circumstances but he certainly does collect news and it might well be worthwhile to consider it.

Lambert came in to see me and I had to put him off again with the promise that I would take the matter up tomorrow and give him a definite answer when I returned to Paris on Saturday.

Late in the afternoon Walter Lippmann came in with Capt. Blankenhorn and Lt. Merz and we had a very satisfactory talk. They have come over with instructions from the Secretary of War to go into the question of propaganda in enemy countries. They pussy-footed carefully to see whether they would be treading on my toes but I whooped with joy at the prospect of having somebody to play with and we got down to brass tacks. I got off a message to Nolan to say that they would come down on Saturday and report if that was agreeable to him and added that I would stay down to confer with them. They are going at the matter sensible and without previously conceived ideas. They plan to spend several weeks talking with everybody they can find who knows anything about the matter and then GET TO WORK. Apparently this matter is to be taken out of the hands of G. Creel. [Newton] Baker and Col. House are both interested in the work and so we ought to have no difficulty in getting funds and personnel. The boys bring satisfactory letters from Baker to the General and I begin for the first time to have some hope that we can accomplish something. I have promised to take them around to call on the people that are handling the work as soon as they come back from GHQ.

Davis and Edith Wills came to dine and visited on the old home way.

The Ambassador [Sharp] sent for me in the afternoon and summoned me to tell him what I really thought of Kerney and his work and the harm he was likely to do. I did not get a chance to tell him for he told me instead what he himself thought and what he intended to do about it, – what he intended to do but that he intended to get some decision as to who was Ambassador over here. He warmed up to his work and said that he would not stand for this sort of thing continuing and that if he could not accomplish his purpose any other way he would resign and go home and talk, – that he would not have his freedom of speech curtailed if he felt that he could be of more service to his country and the Administration by telling the truth from the housetops. He asked me for some exhibits of foolish propaganda and named the ones he wanted. There is evidently a fierce letter brewing.

Log   GHQ, AEF. Friday, July 26, 1918

Got under way this morning at a little after eight with Davis Wills in his Winton[117] with an army driver who will come to some bad end unless he is lucky enough to get killed in an accident. He nearly put us out of the game by driving at high speed across a ditch, throwing us up against the top of the car, cutting a slice out of the top of Davis' head and mashing my hat into its component straw.

---

[117] Founded in 1896, Winton Motor Carriage Company was one of the first American automobile manufacturer. It supplied the US military during the First World War and was sold to General Motors in 1930.

We stopped at Provins (French GHQ) long enough for a cup of coffee and then shoved on beyond Troyes (where Davis demanded and got more coffee) before we pulled up by the side of the road and ate the lunch which had been prepared for us.

Reached here a little before four and found rooms ready for us at the Hôtel de France.

Nolan was waiting for me and had set his afternoon aside that we might have a good talk. I kept him going until dinner time when we repaired to his mess and had a recess with the usual crowd plus Marquesson and Bill Cresson.

Thence back to GHQ where there was more talk until a late hour of the night.

I poured out information I had been accumulating since my last visit, including some news about Kerensky, the Bavarian peace move, the Bulgarian situation, the Spanish situation, Briand and his trip to Switzerland, Mitchell's story of the gold on its way to America for the German spies and propaganda.

I told him that Frazier had spoken to the General [Pershing] about Warburton's indiscretion and that he had suggested that Nolan should give a fatherly talk to Warburton. Nolan said he was much flattered by the General's assumption that he could do anything but that he had no such illusions. Warburton, he said, was constitutionally indiscreet and that there was no way of reforming him in this regard; that he would not willingly give away anything and would be sorry each time he did, – but that he would not be able to avoid doing it again next time. He had already had one such talk with him but that the result was just exactly nothing.

I suggested that it might be a good plan to ask the Marshal [Joffre] down to review the First Division now that they were tried veterans. He did so when they were in training here and another visit now would have an excellent effect. Nolan thought the idea good and said that he would take it up with the General.

I also made the suggestion that he have somebody take a look into the situation at G-2, S.O.S. I did not offer any details but said that I preferred to let him find out the situation for himself. He evidently understood that there was something afoot and said that he would have it looked into at once. He added that C.W.[118] was a sick man and that he feared that he had over-worked.

I brought up the Lambert matter and he authorized me to go ahead and make arrangements to begin on the first of August. He wants it confined chiefly to Socialist and Labor matters. I said it would require fifteen to twenty thousand dollars a year and he said that he could arrange for the former amount which will, I believe, be adequate for what we have in mind.

---

118 Perhaps Cabot Ward.

I spoke of the importance of having Hoover talk to the General [Pershing] at some length and see some of the men about him so as to form some firsthand impressions as to what is going on. I said that any number of cranks were coming over and taking home unbalanced ideas and that we could not do better for the General than build up some fund of accurate information about him and his work where it could be applied if necessary. He admitted that the Black Hand was getting to work and that it was time to form some intelligent opinion.[119] I also suggested making some fuss over Franklin Roosevelt and Arthur Page, both of whom are due before long. He asked me to write to Arthur and say that they would be glad to see him at GHQ and show him anything they could that would be of interest to him. He said that the General was leaving GHQ soon to take command of the army in the field and that he might be back for some time to come but that he would doubtless arrange to see Hoover either in Paris or somewhere else.

I spoke of the possibility of having the King of Italy visit the front and he said that he thought it would be better to defer it for the time being. There was some uneasiness about the fact that the General was being played up in the press too much for his own good and that too much KING BUSINESS would not help the situation. The King and Queen of the Belgians are coming down some time in the fall and that is about all that can be undertaken for the time being.

I made a plea for Brantingham and left a memorandum suggesting him as a useful man for intelligence work. He said he would have inquiries made as to whether he could be used but feared that he was too old for a commission. It would do the old chap a world of good if he could put on the uniform and I don't see why he could not have that satisfaction if he does the work. It will have to be followed up later.

I also spoke of the inadvisability of having too much talking done about our ability to continue transporting troops at the present rate. Chiozza Money made a speech in the House of Commons the other day in which he said that we had managed to bring over men at the rate of 300,000 a month without reducing the flow of necessary supplies, – the inference being that we would continue at the present rate indefinitely. I thought it would be better to prepare the public mind for a reduction by talking now about the need for increased supplies and munitions. Nolan said that for some time we would continue to send over untrained troops to finish their training in France and that the number would really be kept up for some time, but that the idea was good in itself and that he would tip off the

---

119 It is not clear what Gibson is referring to here. The issue is mentioned already on March 2 and July 23, 1918.

British Mission to tone down that sort of talk so that people would not be led to expect the impossible.

Left memoranda with him in regard to a number of small matters that he promised to have attended to.

He had not heard anything about the mission of Walter Lippmann and his little playmates but I told him what I knew, including the impression that they would play the game and not try to run amuck. They are due to be down tomorrow on the noon train and Nolan asked me to stay over to have a talk with him after he had seen them and knew more of what they planned to do. He said that he very much wanted me to take charge of the entire question of propaganda in enemy countries with full authority over this crowd and such others that might be assigned to it. He mentioned Cal O'Laughlin and Stanley Washburn, both of them Majors. He said that he thought it would be better for me to be in uniform and suggested that I be a Major. I said that if it could be done it would be better for me to be a Lt. Col. as in that way I would not be under the disadvantage of trying to boss men who were my senior in point of service, and it would also give me added prestige in dealing with my colleagues from the other allied armies. He said that it would be difficult and that he doubted whether he could put over any more Lt. Col. commissions with the War Department.

He says he has not the time to keep full control over propaganda and that he wants it to be run sanely. Both he and the General say that their minds would be easy about it if I assumed charge and that they would leave me a free field. It is a flattering proposal but I am inclined to think that unless I can be a Lt. Col. at least I had better remain a civilian and put on all the side that may seem desirable. Nolan said that the General would telegraph the Secretary of State to release me for a year at least to handle this question with the assurance that I could be of just as much use to the Dept. of State as I am now. Martin Egan had told him that he was sure the Secretary of State would not release me but I believe that on such a request he would do so.

Nolan wanted to get things settled at once but I suggested that he wait until he had seen the orders of the new crowd and decide then what it was best to do. He agreed and the matter remains in abeyance.

Nolan said he was somewhat surprised to note in a recent memorandum I sent him that Joffre was under the impression that Pétain had opposed the offensive and had to be driven into in. On the contrary it was planned by Pétain and carried out by him. JJP [Pershing] proposed it and when told that the allies had not enough troops to carry out the operations offered enough Americans to turn the trick. I judge from the way it was told that JJP practically was the inspiration of the whole movement. He felt the time had come to crack the Boche and put enough pressure to bear to make his view prevail.

All the information at GHQ is to the effect that the morale of the French army has improved immensely as a result of the offensive and that further offensive action can be taken without fear that the men will not stand up under it.

Log   GHQ, A.E.F. Saturday, July 27, 1918

Got up at the crack of dawn and walked through the rain to Logan's where I joined the crew for breakfast. Those present: Logan, Martin Egan, Morrow and Roger Williams.

After breakfast Martin and I had a long talk.

He is a good deal worried about the amount of prominence being given to the General in the papers as he feels that is constitutes a distinct element of danger. He has prevailed upon him to permit the mention of other general officers which has been forbidden since the beginning of our operations. I applied all my pet theories about how to save the situation. He fell in with them and some of them he was already trying to carry out. He agreed with me on so many points that I feel he is a man of great brain power.

At GHQ found a telegram to say that Hoover would arrive here on the night of the 30th and that the CRB dinner had best be arranged the first of August. Telegraphed back to Wickes to suggest that he telegraph all member in such a way that they could show the message to their commanding officer and ask for leave. It should be possible to get together a considerable number of those who are not in the actual fighting.

Gathered up Frederick Palmer and Davis Wills and took them down town to a restaurant to lunch. Palmer's book comes out in the fall.

When I got back to the shop found that Lippmann and Co. did not catch the train and will not be back until tomorrow. I thereupon decided that the best thing was for me to get back to Paris and return whenever Nolan wanted me. He agreed and I set off.

TONNERRE

Not a cuss word. Just the name of the town we have stopped in for the night. I went back from GHQ to the hotel expecting to find Davis waiting for me to push off. Did not find him until well after five as he had been sitting in the stuffy little salon looking up the street waiting for me to put in an appearance. We had been within a few feet of each other for a couple of hours. Bowden came along and we had a little talk before starting off in a driving rain.

As we got out of town the chauffeur took the wrong turn and we decided to keep on and stop either at Châtillon or some other town along the road. We picked up at a little station a French officer who was disconsolate because he could not get a train back to his home in Châtillon. We whisked him down there in no time and deposited him at his front door to his considerable relief. Then on to a busy hotel for some dinner. A new American regiment had just been dumped into the town and officer and men were swarming around getting their bearings and sizing the place up. Lots of them had on the green ribbon of the Mexican border expedition which is quite startling.

We pushed on after dinner in the dark and made this place a little before ten. Tomorrow being a Sunday we shall stop off at Fontainebleau to let Davis see the Chateau which he has never seen.[120]

This morning while I was in seeing Boyd I ran into Bonham-Carter and had a little talk with him. He was over with his Chief, Lord Weir, the Air Minister, seeing Stettinius. I got called into the inner office and while I was there Bongy [Bonham-Carter] had to go and left a message to say he was sorry. I too was sorry as I wanted to talk to him at some length.

Log   Paris. Sunday, July 28, 1918

Got up this morning at a little after seven and shoved off an hour later.

We had a beautiful morning and good roads with no hurry in our minds about reaching town so we lolled back and took things easy.

Went through Moret where our charming little villa has been replaced by a pretentious three story building which has no charm at all.[121] The little town itself was just the same except for the fact that it was filled with American soldiers who looked quite out of place in the narrow old streets and dangling their legs over the old walls.

Trotted through the Chateau at Fontainbleau with a small crowd mostly composed of wounded niggers.[122] Nearly all the furniture and all the good pictures have been carried away so that only the empty shell remains. There was a fussy old boy in frock coat and straw hat who clung to the guide, repeated everything he said in an awe-struck voice and then turned around and imparted it to all hands as though they had not heard or grasped it. He was a nuisance to the guide but the best part of the show to me.

---

120 Prominent daytrip destination in the south of Paris.
121 Gibson had passed the town before on his way from the front back to Paris.
122 Rather untypical for him, Gibson unreflectingly uses here this racist term which – sad to say – was the parlance of his time.

Wandered out into the park and took a look at the carp who seem depressed by the war and did not appear in any considerable number.

Took to the car again and found our way to the HÔTEL DE LA VANNE ROUGE at Montigny sur Loing where Arthur Orr and I used to go. It has lost its charm of many years ago and was filled with undesirables, – that is people who were undesirable to us. However we had a good lunch by the river and then started off for Paris where after many adventures by land and sea we arrived before five o'clock.

James was here along and we had a peaceful dinner.

I had talked over his affairs with McCabe and Nolan and found that they thought he would make a mistake if he did not go to GHQ and take over G-2-D. He does not want to do it but they feel that he stands a better chance of getting in line for action if he goes there and lets people have a look at him. He will probably do it although with great reluctance. I shall be mighty sorry to see him go from here but am afraid it is the best thing for his future, – if the best thing is considered edging ones way into the fighting line.

Memo from Joffre.   July 27th, 1918. SECRET

The Germans are still holding their fresh reserve divisions massed in the North, and they would be able to attempt an offensive against the English at any time. Probably south of Arras and at Kemmel. Nevertheless, I have heard nothing definite to show that this offensive is imminent. It is probably that difficulties in means of communication are hampering the Germans. I should not be surprised if this same reason prevented them from following up their advantages in their earlier offences this year.

The English have completely reorganized and reformed their forces, they have done fine work in this respect, and they appear to be in good condition to resist a shock.

I very much doubt whether any conclusive military result can now be obtained by either ourselves or our enemies this year. It looks as though we would both continue until the end of the season scrapping at various points along the line and reverting to a war of exhaustion carried on more or less in the open, after the war of exhaustion waged in the trenches.

Our losses on the Soisson-Château-Thierry front, and along the Marne, have been exceedingly heavy for the past five or six days. On the first day of Mangin's offensive, we advanced eight or nine kilometers, losing scarcely a man. But the price must be paid afterwards in such affairs, and the Germans now have their batteries in position against us, and have brought up the reserves they need.

Log   Paris. Monday, July 29, 1918

A busy day at the office without accomplishing very much.

This morning I learned from James that Creel had telegraphed Kerney that Keeley, now in London, would soon come to Paris to attend the conference on enemy country propaganda on August first. That he would be the American representative on this conference and would have charge of all enemy country propaganda in England, France and Italy. The telegram added that Engell, whoever he may be, would "head the American propaganda unit in Italy." I telephoned this to Nolan that he would perhaps do well to defer any decision in my case until he had straightened this matter out to his own satisfaction.

[Louis] Brown, Burton Holmes manager, came in during the morning to get help in his trip to Italy. He says Burton Holmes will be in to see me when he comes back from his present trip.

Fred Sterling and Dan Pierce came in to lunch. Pierce said that several days ago he got into Soissons, although the papers have not yet given us to understand that we had access to the place. He says that the French guns are on the heights to this side, throwing shells over the town onto the Germans and that the Germans are not bombarding the town itself as the French are not occupying it and there is no temptation to waste the ammunition. Several other people he says have been some distance to the east of S. without running into any Germans.

After Coxe came in with news to the effect that he had lunch with Cecil Carter and Maude. Sanborn was also there so they had an old home week.

Topping come in looking for news. His new paper is coming out tomorrow and he is considerably excited about it.

Lt. Griscom, a nephew of Lloyd, came in with a letter of introduction from Blankenhorn. He came over with Lippmann, Blankenhorn troup and is intent on finding all about propaganda in enemy countries. He suggested that they would be very glad if I would consent to work in liaison with them and eliminate the delays that would result from having to send everything home for a visa. I said I should be glad to work with them but did not tell him that I was asked by the army to boss the troup. The more I think about the matter the more I am inclined to believe that it would be better for me to do the work as a civilian.

Griscom says that Will Irwin got out because Creel crowded him out so as to make room for Sisson. Will is coming over to join the troup and is to take a commission. Creel is supposed to have given Mr. Baker a waiver in writing of all hold on propaganda in enemy countries and nobody seem to be able to understand the word that Kelley is coming.

Hoagland, Van Arsdale and Wheeler came in with word that they had had a great success on their trip to London. They needed to be fixed up with some letters to GHQ and I came through as was evidently expected of me.

Whipple, who was in Antwerp with Clayton, came in to see about getting his fiancée out of Rotterdam. I told him to write a letter about it and that I would be glad to see what could be done at the Embassy.

Seel got word that he had been drafted and should start for home as soon as possible. He is trying to find some formula under which he can remain over here but it would perhaps be just as well for him to go along home for he does not seem to get hold very quickly and I fear he will never make much progress in his present work. And he is a type that needs a little soldiering.

James got a hurry call to GHQ and went down on the evening train after an early dinner. He is probably to be fitted into McCabe's job and they want to give him a little preliminary canter. I charged him to talk over my affairs with Nolan and see whether it would not be better to put me in charge of the work as a civilian or appoint somebody else with enough military rank to be unquestioned boss of the crowd and let me help him. I am unwilling to raise with Nolan the question of giving me a higher rank as I do not care to be in the position of worry about my own personal standing at a time like this when there is work to be done. James promised to talk it all over and let me know if there were any developments.

A flock of letters from home including five from mother. Hays has asked her to be one of the five women to form an advisory board to the National Committee on the resurrected Republican Party. She wrote him back a Sockdollager in which she said that the women has no interest in partisan politics and that it would be just as well to "show them" before launching anything new; that they had not been taken in by being allowed to sit on committee with no authority. That no women had been given authority over the work that women were doing in the war, either in labor or food control or anything else. That the Republican Party had ignored all the suggestions that women had made in California as to the conduct of the last political campaign and that the election had been lost because of that. Altogether she told him that it was time for the parties to wake up. She said she could not go to Chicago to his meeting but gave him this advice with her best wishes.

A long letter from Stockton with oodles of gossip. He said an old gentleman had been in at the Food Administration lately and in praising Hoover, had said: "Hoover comes from fine stock. His Mother was a Quaker and his father a self-made blacksmith" SOME BLACKSMITH

Log   Paris. Tuesday, July 30, 1918

Nothing very startling during the morning.

Just before lunch Bill Cresson came in and said that Nolan had spoken to him "hypothetically" of taking on the political intelligence work. Bill says he told Nolan that he would do better to get me and that Nolan agreed and said that he was trying now but was not at all sure of succeeding. Bill remarked that he was quite happy in his present job and would not care to leave it unless it was for something more interesting and something that would bring with it a promotion to the rank of Major.

After he had gone Norman Davis came in with Fred Walcott who has come over from London to see about the arrangements being made for Hoover's visit.

Lunched at the Ritz with Bill Cresson, Lt. Tobin, the Naval Cable Censor and Miss Cheeseborough of San Francisco who is here for the Red Cross.

After lunch James telephoned from GHQ that Nolan wanted a copy of the telegram from Creel to Kerney about the functions of Keeley. I asked Smith to send it down.

James also said that Nolan had told Lippmann that he wished me to be in complete charge of the propaganda business so far as the army was concerned. Lippmann is to come in to see me tomorrow morning.

No other news to be reported from down there, and there will probably be no decision until after the Keeley matter is straightened out.

Hazen, the Oregon newspaper man, came in to see me and see whether he could get any material for some articles about peace moves and the Balkan situation. I told him there was nothing definite to give him and that he ought to go to Switzerland and look round for a general story on the two subjects. He said he would do that later but that I had afforded him enough material for his story and that he would let me have a look at it before sending it. He must be a wonder if he can make anything out of what I told him. He also suggested that he go down to Spain with me when I went but I did not encourage that idea.

Walcott brought in a very interesting Russian named Marcowitz who has just got out of Russia and is filled with information on all sorts of subjects. Frazier and I took him in hand and pumped him at great length and prepared notes as we went along. Marcowitz is also to prepare a memorandum for us on several subjects that we could not deal with exhaustively enough.

Walcott came upstairs with me later and said that he was quite sure I was meeting Hoover's wishes in trying to keep the program for his visit as simple as possible. It seems that he has now got the ear of the President and won his complete confidence. It would be a great mistake to endanger that by letting people make such a fuss over him as to create the idea that he was self-seeking. He has no thought of anything but winning the war and the more he is allowed to devote himself to that subject the better chance he has of success.

Bertaux told me over the telephone that the President of the Republic had planned a lunch for Hoover on Friday and that a reception at the Hôtel de Ville [town hall] was on the cards for Friday afternoon. The CRB dinner was for Thursday night and all of them had to be called off as there is little prospect that he will be here in time for that. I sent a telegram to him asking for a definite statement as to his plans and ideas. Walcott says that if it seems desirable he will go on to Italy but that nothing has been arranged. I consider it highly desirable that he get as much as possible in the way of first hand impression and take them home with him and consequently push the idea as much as possible. Walcott says Hoover may want me to go down with him.

Dined at the Inter-Allied Club as the guest of Col. Cutcheon who was ill and unable to be there. Jaccaci took his place as host. Nitti was the guest of honor and there were several members of his party on hand much dressed up in dinner coats but with very little conversation in any language. I had Major Harjes on one side and a sad-eyed Italian on the other who devoted himself to his food and gloomed all evening. Among the other guests were Bliss, Frazier, McFadden, Stewart, McKehan, Major Smithers, Capt. Jay and a few others.

Dining at the club were Meert whom I had not seen since Belgium, Wickes, Morris, Warwick Greene, Stetson and a flock of others.

Log   Paris. Wednesday, July 31, 1918

Fred Walcott and Walter Lippmann arrived at my office simultaneously this morning with their various affairs. Bade Lippmann and his crew to lunch so as to talk things over and set out with Walcott to make some arrangements for Hoover.

We went first to see Bertaux and drew up a tentative plan which assumed Hoover would get here on Saturday after a visit at Havre. It may be all wrong but if it is it can be changed. There is a luncheon given by the President of the Republic [Poincaré], a reception at the Hôtel de Ville with the inevitable four speeches so that each branch of the public authority shall have a chance to spout, a visit to Marshal Joffre on Sunday morning at eleven, a three days trip to the front and a CRB dinner to which an unwelcome group of Senators and Deputies are to be invited. On top of this Hoover is to set out for Italy to imbibe all the wisdom that can be got in ten days. Walcott said he thought Hoover would want me to go with him but I am not very strong for it at this time of year.

From there to Tardieu who received us at once and announced that he wanted to give a dinner for Hoover on Monday evening. There was nothing to do but agree although we had just gone through the motions of telling him how simple everything should be kept in order to let Hoover work.

From there to the Meurice to engage rooms.

A flock of people waiting for me when we got back to the chancery, among them Pink Simpson just back from London. He did not seem to think that Walcott was in any way authorized to take charge and thought that Hoover might arrive any moment now.

A telegram from Phil [Patchin] saying that Polk felt there was very little use in my continued connection with the Committee on Public Information, that there was plenty of work to be done in Europe where I would have the comfort of making some headway. It ended: "What do you think?" I agree but cannot answer it definitely until I hear from Nolan who got it over the phone as fast as I could pour it out.

Captains Walter Lippmann and Blankenhorn and Lt. Merz to lunch and talk about their business. Blankenhorn got up the trip and collected the personnel and they are about to start on a trip of survey in England, Italy and Switzerland. They quite fell in with Nolan's idea that I should head the organization and Blankenhorn said that he would be delighted to serve under me although the got up the whole show. They are going slow about making up their minds which is sensible and not what we were led to expect by the unfortunate character of their instructions, etc...

After lunch tried to get track of Keeley who was announced as the Am. Representative on the meeting tomorrow afternoon. Nobody has heard of him so it was agreed that in his absence Blankenhorn and I would attend.

Charles Edward Russell came in with Simons and Kopelin, formerly editor of the APPEAL TO REASON[123] who wanted censorship facilities. I called their attention to the press report that Kerensky had landed in New York and they smiled broadly as they had seen him on Monday and held converse with him.

Was kept busy at the Embassy until after five when I fled and returned to the flat to write some urgent letters.

Stetson moved in just before dinner and then went off to dine.

Walter Lippmann came in for dinner and a quiet talk without the others. He is anxious to go over the field of political intelligence which he can do in virtue of his connection with Col. House's inquiry.[124] He agrees that we must have some-

---

[123] *Appeal to Reason* was a weekly left-wing newspaper which was published in the American Midwest between 1895 and 1922. It became the voice of the Socialist Party in American when it formed in 1901.

[124] Group of about 150 American academics headed by Colonel House and was to prepare materials for the peace negotiations.

thing comprehensive in the way of information as to what is going on. I suggested that the inquiry should move a good part of its staff over here and establish an advanced base. I also talked to him at some length about the need for an Inter-Allied Diplomatic Council in Europe where things could be thrashed out directly across the table as our military affairs are discussed. Of course that would not be an easy thing to put over but if the President could send somebody in whom he has complete confidence it would save him any amount. Col. House is too ill to undertake anything of the sort, Lippmann says. Polk is not as well as he should be. Hoover seems to be about the only other really eligible citizen and it would be mighty hard to convince people at home that he could be spared for anything of the sort.

Both Walcott and Lippmann say that Hoover has got very close to the President and has access to him at all times. Pourvu que a dure. [Provided that lasts]

Lippmann brought up again the subject of my taking charge of the propaganda. I held off on the theory that if it is going to be done by the military and done right, it will have an importance that nobody realized now; that a man of the rank of major could not get away with it and that they should pick out somebody to whom they are willing to give the rank of Colonel or Lt. Col. at the lowest.

We talked of the possibility of using Arthur Woods for this. He is a Lt. Col. already and it would not be hard to raise him a peg.

Log   Paris. Thursday, August 1, 1918

Found two telegrams this morning from the Embassy in London. One said that Hoover would leave Boulogne for Paris Friday morning by motor car. The other said that he wanted me to meet him tomorrow morning in Boulogne to accompany him on a visit to the King of the Belgians. The French authorities had a telegrams from their Embassy in London to say that he would land in Boulogne this morning and would be in Paris this evening. They got to work on the telephone to find out where the error lay. On the off chance I sent out and bought my ticket so as to be ready to go.

Simpson came in with a long story from Lewis Richards who sent me the sorrows of [William] Poland and his treatment by Hoover, which seemed to amount to nothing much beyond the fact that Hoover did not give him all the time he wanted to discuss all sorts of matters. Knowing Poland's requirements in the matter of time I am not surprised. Bill Goode, beg pardon, Sir Wm., apparently possessed himself of [Lewis] Strauss and constituted himself manager of the party in London, which he doubtless did in a tactless manner and with intent to hog as much as possible of the reflected glory. Lewis is worried for fear Hoover dislikes

Poland and wants to drop him; he is also in doubt as to whether Hoover wants to see the CRB handed over to the tender mercies of the Wheat Executive. These are some of the things that I am trying to find out and report on while Hoover is in our midst.

A long letter from Ynès in the morning mail. She says that conditions are getting very bad and people rapidly going into consumption. She is no longer allowed to keep my horse but does not say what she has done with it. She now has a pony named RODRIGO with a certain amount of humor. She says that the food situation is awful. Butter 30 francs a kilo. Carrots three francs a bundle, eggs 1.15 each, meat 20 francs a kilo, etc. She says that signs are all over the town *"Vieux souliers, 100 francs la paire" "Excellent foin pour matelas" "Vieux costume, 250 francs."* [Old shoes, 100 francs a pair, excellent hay for mattresses, old costume, 250 francs] They all seem to keep their courage but the strain is getting pretty bad and they are worrying about the general health.

[Lithgow] Osborne also sent me a translation of an article put out by the Germans in the Danish press, copy attached. [See Below] They have pinned me down as the Chief of the British Spies in Brussels at the outbreak of the war. Not a bad advertisement for the book which is just coming out in Danish translation in Copenhagen. The dear old Boche can be depended to do us a favor now and then in spite of himself.

Lambert came in and talked over the arrangements for my little service of intelligence. He is getting to work at once and will begin to deliver at once.

Talked with Nolan over the phone about Keeley, Hoover's trip and the chance of letting him have a military car while he is in Paris. We got cut off in the midst of things but shall resume this afternoon.

Stetson and I lunched together and I hastened back to the shop to meet Lippmann and Blankenhorn and take them to the propaganda conference at Chaix's office. We talked for an hour and a half and had a very satisfactory time. From there I went out and bought some buttons for the Legion of Honor as I was sure that Hoover would not think to put one on and might hurt the feelings of the French who have awarded it to him.

When I got back to the chancery I found Mitchell waiting for me to say that he was off to Archangel but would return at any time that I sent for him. Cresson was also there to see Lippmann. Walcott came in having heard that I might be off to Boulogne but I told him that I would not go.

Bertaux telephoned to say that Hoover had already landed in Boulogne and would be up in the morning, so that there would be no use in my trying to meet him.

Nolan telephoned through from GHQ to say that the General had approved a long telegram to the War Department asking them to request the State Department to lend me to the army for a year to organize the propaganda in enemy countries. He laid it on pretty thick by saying that although the Lippmann-Blankenhorn crowd had made a favorable impression he must have the entire work in the hands of someone whom he trusted and who was familiar with European affairs. He cited me as the man best qualified to have charge of the work and added that he had absolute confidence in me, which was going pretty strong for him. He added that he wanted me to be commissioned as a Major in the National Army which is one rank better than the Reserve. I could not very well say anything about higher rank but perhaps when it has got started they will realize the need for it. His telegram is going and I prepared a message for Phil [Patchin] explaining it, – paraphrase attached.[125] I did not get a chance to show it to the Ambassador as he was busy signing dispatches for the out-going pouch. It will have to go tomorrow after he has seen it.

Guy d'Oultremont came in to see me. He has been made chief of the Belgian Military Mission at our GHQ and is to go down in the course of a few days. I have written letters of introduction to Quekemeyer, Logan, Palmer, James and one or two more. He has lost some thirty kilos since early in the war and looks infinitely better for it. He is much broken up over the death of his father who succumbed after being carried off as a prisoner to Germany. He had a picture of the old gentleman taken while he was a prisoner. It is a loathsome business and I wonder how the Hun thinks he can ever be forgiven by such people.

Hoover is to be the guest of the French Government in rooms they have taken for him at the Crillon. I had to get hold of Walcott by telephone and tell him to cancel the reservations he had made at the Meurice. I fear me he is four-flushing again.

Torrey and Simpson came to dine and we had an old home week.

When Bill Goode became Sir Wm., Shaler is alleged to have asked him whether he should be addressed as Sir William or as Goode Knight. Not bad for the fat gentleman.

A letter from Arthur Page to say that he is taking his father to a rest cure for a couple of weeks and is then coming over here to put himself in my hands to see what he can do.

---

125 No paraphrase is attached in the archival record.

Copy
The Germans in Belgium. German Accusations Against the Former American Secretary of Legation at Brussels.   HHH

BERLIN, Sunday (Privately for the POLITIKEN)
The former American Secretary of Legation at Brussels, Mr. Hugh Gibson, who has recently published a gook call the *Diary of a Diplomat*, has by the Germans been accused of the following:

When the war broke out Gibson was Secretary of the American Legation at Brussels and for some time he was its business manager. He abused this position to carry on espionage for the Allies. He often went from Brussels to Antwerp in the Legation's motor car in order to see the English Military Attaché, Major Fairholme, to whom he gave all sorts of military information as to the German troops and other military secrets. It had been ascertained by the Germans that several of Major Fairholme's assistants handed over their reports to a certain Mr. Babcock in Brussels. Further investigation led to the result that this Mr. Babcock was in the employ of the American Legation. Later on it appeared that Babcock was only a fictitious name for Secretary of Legation Mr. Hugh Gibson, who, screened by his diplomatic invulnerability, personally brought the reports to Antwerp. One of the reports which were handed to him contained a detailed description of the outposts which the Germans had occupied and also information with regard to the strength of the German troops north of Brussels, the number of regiments, etc. The Germans told the American Minister of their observations, but forbore to brand Gibson, because they did not want to compromise the American Governmetn with which they were still on terms of friendship. Gibson had to leave Belgium and return to America because of this espionage for England.

Log   Paris. August 2, 1918

Had a fairly busy morning with nothing particular accomplished aside from a call from Captain Voska who is off on a trouble making mission. More power to his elbow.

A little after eleven Strauss called on the telephone from the Crillon and put all hands on one at a time to say hello. I went down at once and had a little yarn with Hoover.

Taylor's telegram was one day off as they went up to see the King [Albert I of the Belgians] and Queen [Elisabeth] on Thursday instead of Friday and had wanted me to go with them. The King had offered Hoover the Grand Cordon of the Order of Leopold but he declined it. He had, however, given the King a list of people who should have it, at the King's request. He had put my name on the list not knowing that I already had it. At dinner the King announced that since Hoover would not accept a decoration he was going to confer a title upon him and that he was hereafter to be known as: "Hoover, Friend of the Belgians".

Went to the Élysée at 12:30. Hoover and I arrived and found the President and Madame Poincaré lined up with a flock of Generals behind them waiting for us. The President kicked off with some polite talk which I translated rendering the same serviced to Hoover's reply. After this labor had continued for some time Madame Poincaré dropped easily into English and made me feel as though I had wasted a day's work. It was a nice cozy little luncheon of about sixty people, about as sociable as a barbeque. Frank Roosevelt was there and Rublee, Poland, Chevrillon, Bell, most of the Cabinet and an assorted lot of senators, deputies, flower girls, etc. I sat between Clémentel, Minister of Transportation, and Loucheur, Minister of Munitions, and had a perfectly good time.

Soon after lunch Hoover and I made a get away and came back to the Crillon where we were soon joined by Boret and Crespi, the French and Italian Controllers, Chevrillon and Bertaux, to discuss plans. We drew up a tentative programme which was changed several times while being written and will doubtless be changed many times more. At four o'clock I took Hoover to call upon the Ambassador for half hour or so.

At five Daisy Polk with her newly acquired husband, General Count de Buyer who commanded the French Armies on the Soissons and Rheims fronts, and now has a safe billet commanding at Troye. We may stay over night with them on the trip to the front. When they had gone Hoover and I sat down and talked until dinner time.

He says that there is now no government in England; that Lloyd George has kept himself in power by taking into the government every element of opposition as soon as it showed itself; that he now has an inchoate mass pulling in every direction; that there is no discipline in policy and that he cannot steer a course in any given direction. The one hope for Lloyd George seemed to be that the general elections will return him to power and that he will be able to kick out the discordant elements and really rule instead of pussy footing.

After Lord Rhondda's death a small labor man was put in as Food Controller and is now running the whole show for political advantage, concentrating most of his efforts on unnecessary reduction so as to be able to say that the rich are as greatly restricted as the poor, whether the restriction of the rich is of any help to the poor or not. Hoover proposed to set up a powerful interallied food control board with members to represent the various governments, capable of handling the intricate technical problems. The French and Italians joined us in appointing members, but Clynés insisted upon appointing Major Waldorf Astor and a clerk. Waldrof Astor is a parliamentary secretary and could answer questions in the House of Commons, and the clerk to act as personal representative and spy. Hoover refused to accept any such frivolous arrangement and spent ten days out maneuvering the Briton so as to get the right man appointed. They finally definitely named the man he thought ought to represent England and then Clynés refused to have him, said he would have him put on the board as American representative. He then passed this word on to Lloyd George who saw the point and said it would be an outrage to have England misrepresented and the only properly qualified Englishman representing America. He could not, however, force the hand of his own minister, but Hoover did it for him and after ten days' struggle the right man was appointed under duress. Of course, the Italians and French are delighted.

I talked to Hoover at some length about the absolute need for an interallied diplomatic council, or failing that, an entering wedge in the nature of a high commissioner in France with the full confidence of the President. He quite agreed as to the necessity for it, but feared it could not be put over.

Some time ago Colonel House asked Hoover to go to see him in the country and talk about the Russian question. Hoover told him that we must abandon all idea of reconstituting Russia as a fighting element; that our effort must be directed to keeping her from becoming an ally of Germany, or being exploited to Germany's advantage. He said that this could not be done by military expedition, but that we must reconstitute her along lines of peaceful economy and commercial endeavor; that a very small military force of five regiments would be enough to send as a body guard; that they might be massacred, but that he did not think so. Colonel House thoroughly agreed to this plan which was elaborated in considerable detail and said that Hoover was the only man to carry it out. On returning to Washington, Hoover saw Mr. Lansing who also wished the job on him. Justice Brandeis came to see him about it and gave him the same sort of talk. Hoover talked it over at great length with the President who showed interest in it, but said nothing about personnel. A few days later the whole thing was talked over in the Cabinet and to everybody's surprise the President turned to old pink whiskered Redfield and asked him to designate the man who in his opinion was the best qualified to head the expedition under the general direction of John R. Mott of the YMCA Hoover thereupon went to see Lansing and pointed out that he was not looking for any plum as it was a great big gamble with very large chance of utter failure which would cook him and with very reasonable chance that some

Bolshevik would finish him off with a bomb. Hoover said that the advantage of his going was that he could be send as the American Food Administrator as an evidence of the President's desire to avert famine in Russia and help them in regard to the food problem, which has no bearing upon their participation in the war. Lansing said that it was feared that this would be merely looked upon as another Belgian Relief Commission, which would be bad, on the contrary it would be the best possible sort of cover for the sort of work we want to do. However, nothing happened and Hoover came on his trip to Europe. He does not know whether such a mission will be sent. I immediately put in my application to be included in the expedition.

Hoover said that the French Government was going to give the Legion of Honor to a certain number of us who had been instrumental in carrying out the feeding of the invaded parts of France, but that he felt it would be too bad that Chevrillon should not have it as he had done such splendid work. I later took the occasion to speak to Bertaux about the matter saying that while we would all be deeply honored by receiving the Legion of Honor, we felt considerably embarrassed at the idea of receiving it so long as Chevrillon's splendid work remained unrecognized and that anyone of us would gladly waive out decoration if it could be given to him instead. Bertaux said that the reason he had not received it was probably that there was a rule that no French civilian should be decorated during the war, but that it might be possible to appoint him Officier Interprete and give it to him in that capacity. It was agreed that Hoover should make this suggestion to the Prime Minister.

Talked to Hoover at some length about the question of propaganda in enemy countries and he felt that I should not accept the direction of the work with any rank less than that of full colonel, from the point of view of efficiency. As a matter of fact he did not want me to take it at all as he thought I was more free as a civilian and could do anything that came up. He is going to talk to General Pershing about it when he sees him. We talked until dinner and got a lot of things trashed out.

At eight we went to the Cercle Volney where there was a small dinner of the men who had been engaged in feeding the occupied provinces, including Lebrun, the Minister of Blockade, Serruys, Bertaux, Dolléans and others. Some very touching speeches were made by Lebrun, Senator Guerin and others, and Hoover made a very simple reply in which he gave all credit of the work to the French and deprecated the amount of praise and gratitude shown to the Americans engaged in the work. Chevrillon made an excellent translation. After finishing his speech Hoover asked me to translate some more remarks and paid a very handsome and excellent tribute to Chevrillon for his devotion in the work.

Log   Paris. Saturday, August 3. 1918

A rather footless morning largely at the Crillon. Colonel Dawes came in and had an hour or so with Hoover and then Frazier for a few minutes.

Strauss said that he had dinner last night with Walter Lippmann and that Walter was under the impression that I wanted to lay down on the work as I did not wish to abandon my civilian rank. Strauss had talked to Hoover about it and gathered the impression that he was opposed to my putting on a uniform.

At twelve o'clock we went to the Citroën munitions plant and had lunch with over three thousand workmen. We sat in a gallery overlooking a huge room filled with the workmen and had the same meal that is given to them, which costs one franc fifty. It was a splendid meal consisting of hors d'œuvres, a large slice of well-cooked veal with butter beans, a separate course of cauliflower, dessert, cheese and coffee.

After finished lunch Citroën got up and made a few remarks; introduced Loucheur, Minister of Munitions. Lucheur said a few words and introduced Tardieu, who in turn passed the buck to Hoover.

A man with a large brass megaphone stationed himself along side Hoover with Chevrillon as interpreter and what he had to say was translated sentence by sentence and was tremendously well received. When he finished they called for a *bon* which was given with great enthusiasm and we then went out for coffee. From there we then got into motors and went about to see the various cooperative stores and the baby farm which are run by the factory. Citroën takes a great deal more pride in the care of the children than he does in the making of shells, but even at that he has made a huge success as a munitions maker.

Strauss and I ran away early and came back to the Crillon.

Hoover went off at three to the Hôtel de Ville [town hall] and received the homage of the city of Paris. He went with his usual grunt and came home grunting still more heavily. Despite all our efforts to stem the tide of eloquence there were nine full blown speeches aside from Hoover's reply which was extemporaneous and very brief.

While he was gone Horodyski came in to say that he would bring Dmowski in the morning for a long talk and that he himself would come back after lunch. He is more than ever impressed with the opportunities for effective work in Austria toward raising the spirit of discontent. He feels the need of spending money on an extensive scale and I feel free to say that I could not imagine where he would get it. The difference between the tangible and intangible is too great for the ordinary governmental mind and while spending a few millions might put Austria out of business as a governmental power, most of us would prefer to spend hundreds of millions and thousands of lives to put her out by military force. The well known human race has to progress a long way before it will know how to do a job the easiest way.

While Horodyski was here General [Tasker] Bliss came in. Horodyski left at once and I had about a half hours talk with the General while waiting for Hoover to come back. The old General has not been at all spoiled by his successes and has not ceased to be a simple old American soldier just because he has become something of a statesman. He talked very sanely about sending American troops to Italy; the difficulties of keeping them supplied and maintaining moral unless they undertook offensive operations. On the other hand, he seemed to grasp fully the need for reinforcing the Italians so that they could not be wiped out by another Austrian offensive. When Hoover came in they had about a two hour talk about Russia and various other problems. And Hoover had the happy thought of telling the General that the President relied upon him more than on any other one man in Europe today for accurate information and sound advice. The old General was as pleased as punch for he had no intimation from home as to how his information was regarded.

While they were talking I went over to see Frank Roosevelt who, with Livingston Davis, is installed across the hall. Frank was going away in the morning so I got out of dinner at the Volney and went with the two of them to the Café de Paris.

The orderly at the door had a familiar look and hailed me by name whereupon I recognized him as our old friend Stratton of CRB.

Went to dine at the Café de Paris where we got a lot of talking done along the usual lines. Frank says that Colonel House had a very bad break down while he was at the White House and was in bed there for some time with two nurses. Frank Polk has really been quite ill and is in no condition to go back to work. We seem to be wearing out all the good people.

Toward the end of the dinner an officer came over from a nearby table and said that Mrs. Schiller wanted to speak to Frank. He came back considerably disturbed and said that she wanted to go to France some time ago and that after her passport had become confused Senator Knox had pushed the case and had put the matter through for her. She seemed to be very curious about a number of matters which were none of her business and pumped one of the officers with her while Frank was there. One of them, a medical officer, got out his map and showed her the location of his division and brigade headquarters and told her the number of casualties they had had and when they were coming out of action together with a good deal more of such information. Frank thought this was a matter for the Office of Naval Intelligence. Frank is going down to Rome Wednesday to take a look at the naval situation. He has no definite proposal to make as to what ports should be attacked or what ships should be used, but he proposes to convey the impression that we are not altogether satisfied with the lack of offensive spirit manifested by the Italians since we came into the war.

He says that old man Daniels did not altogether approve the idea of his coming over and made the condition that he should not bring a large mission with him. The old man himself is coming over later and does not want the effect spoiled. Apparently the newspaper associations and the censor have been tipped off to avoid any publicity in connection with the visit because there has been none either here or in America. It is rather amusing and at the same time rather depressing.

When I got back to the house I found that James had arrived from GHQ with orders to go back and take over G2[126] D, for about two weeks so that McCabe can go to school.

He said that Nolan was insistent upon my taking over the propaganda business and said he would not sleep until I came there. They are insistent on the taking of a commission. He brought me a copy of Pershing's telegram to the Secretary of War. Copy attached.[127]

SECRET. August 3rd, 1918 (F.) [Foch]
The turn tank by the Malvy Case before the Senate has caused considerable embarrassment among the Judges. The feeling of the majority was that Malvy has been guilty of improper conduct in the discharge of this Ministerial duties, and it was the intention of the majority to condemn him, the penalty in his case ranging anywhere from five years' imprisonment to the death penalty.

The evidence given by the former Premiers does little to alter the basic facts of the case, since they remained very vague about these facts. They sought principally to give him a good general character and to express Ministerial solidarity. This has certainly set in a current of opinion favorable to Malvy. But before a court, oratory does not replace argument. Therefore, Malvy's acquittal is not at all assured.

What embarrasses the Senate now is the form to be given the verdict after the whitewashing attempted by the Premiers. An ordinary Court could go to the extent of an acquittal, while phrasing its considerations so as to give satisfaction to those who doubted of the prisoner's innocence in a case which was not proved either way. The Parliamentary High Court, however, must give a clear, direct verdict, without such attenuations, a man must be declared squarely guilty or guiltless. This increases the chances for the condemnation of Malvy.

The argument for the accused, replying to the requisitory of the Public Prosecutor, will be finished tomorrow, Saturday. The Senate will then rest on Sunday

---

126 G2 refers to the Assistant Chief of General Staff for Intelligence.
127 No copy appears in the archival record.

and resume its sitting on Monday. It is expected the verdict will be rendered on Tuesday.

Nothing can be prophesied about the Caillaux Case[128] until the Malvy Case is ended.

We know little about the German intentions on the battle front, save that the Soissons-Château-Thierry-Marne battle is definitely ended so far as any big attack by them is concerned. We hear no further reports about another concerted movement against the English or elsewhere. Since this attack has not been launched, it is a great pity the English did not take the initiative of attacking. In the future, it may prove they have made a grave mistake by neglecting this opportunity.

Very strong feeling has been roused by the proposed laws for holding Generals responsible before civilian officials. The matter has gone so far, now, that it must be officially fined, but there are reasons to believe it may then be pigeonholed and forgotten as the only solution.

Log   Paris. Sunday, August 4, 1918

Did not get started very early in the morning and came to the hotel only after the party had left to see Marshal Joffre. I had asked Chevrillon to act as interpreter so there was no real need of my going.

Hoover and I went out to lunch together in order to talk out a lot of matters of shop and I took him to the Café de Paris. We talked over at some more length his Russian plan, which seems still to be a possibility. He is going to follow it up when he gets home and if he undertakes it I am to be one of the side people to go along. He has no great enthusiasm about it from a personal point of view as the chances are very poor of ever coming home alive.

He has had quite a lot to do with Henry Ford and has developed quite a high opinion of the old man as an organizer and mechanic. The Aviation people wanted him to undertake the building of aeroplanes on a large scale and he had the sense to hold off on the ground that his factories were incapable of doing the fine character of work required. He said, however, that he could turn out the cylinders for the motors and that the rest of the work could be done by some better equipped factory like the Cadillac. After some arguments he came to Hoover in great distress protesting that he was not a slacker and was not trying to avoid working for the country, but thought he had better specialize on what he could do. Hoover went to see Squier and put up Ford's case with the result he was

---

128 See Biographical Index.

allowed to have his way. However, they said they needed sixty thousand cylinders a month and that he could not make them, although he thought he could. They therefore gave him a contract to make all he could and let other contractors despite his plans. Ford went ahead, however, and turned out ten thousand cylinders a day of better quality than anybody else had thought of making. Later on Ford came around with the idea he could make submarine chasers, the two hundred and twenty foot boat which is needed in large numbers. The Navy people protested that it could not be done and again Ford came to Hoover for help. Hoover went to Daniels and asked him to give the old man a trial. Ford put up his own money and installed the plant that was necessary and decided upon a radical change in the method of ship building. Instead of having a lot of ways and hauling the material of various sorts to each place where a ship was being build, he build long broad gauge railway tracks through his yards; had each sort of material stacked where it was needed; laid the keel of his ships upon six tracks and gradually hauled the train through the ship yards completing the operation as he progressed so that while the paint was being applied to the bow of the ship, the stern was being let down into the water. He is now turning out one ship every two days and says he will soon be able to make ten a day, so that the Navy people are beginning to scream that there will not be any room in the ocean for any other kind of ships unless the old maniac is stopped. However, the old man has now got the bit in his teeth and says that he can build big cargo ships the same way; that he will build car tracks of twenty foot gauge and turn out as many a day as are wanted.

Hoover is rather sorry the old man has got the political bee as he does not think he can get away with anything except his own line of business.

He says that Schwab has given a new impetus to ship building but that the building itself was well underway when he came in and that he is merely keeping up the enthusiasm of his men. The aeroplane production is coming on very well and the liberty motors are entirely successful.

Dmowski and Horodyski came in after lunch for a long yarn. While they were there I went home and packed a bag so as to be ready for our trip tomorrow.

At half past six we shoved off for dinner in the park at Versailles, at the little restaurant that had been picked out by Chevrillon. Those at table included Hoover, Poland, Bell, Walcott, Strauss, Chevrillon, Bertaux, Miss Larner, Madame de Buyer, Wickes, Phil Potter, Sperry, Gailor, Tuck, Simpson, Withington, Stone, Dawson, Robert Jackson, Meert and Richardson. After dinner Hoover gave a splendid talk about what he had been doing since we last met, and most of us were called on to say something. The result was that we did not get back to the hotel until well after midnight. The hotel people had not left any record of my room and I did not get to bed until well after one.

Tuck got in at the last moment after many adventures by land and sea. He is still a captain in the British Army, although he has received his commission in the American Army. However, he has not right to wear the uniform until he has taken the oath, etc. He applied for leave to his and the matter was referred up through the usual channels to his Corps Commander, who turned him down. However, his Brigade Commander sent for him and after some conversation said that he did not really believe his absence would be noticed if he were to go away. Tuck took the hint, put on his American uniform, got on a motor cycle and started for Paris. Every time he was stopped by a British sentry he declined to show his papers save to an American M.P. By the Grace of Heaven there were none present any place he stopped and he got through without having been in jail. We have not heard how he got back.

Log   Troyes. Monday, August 5, 1918

We were all called at five o'clock and got away shortly after six in a number of French Army cars, the party consisting of Hoover, Boret, the French Minister of Food and Supplies, Bertaux, Leval, Major Block, Laroche, Simpson and Wickes. I had a car with Leval. We went through Meaux to LaFerte, the headquarters of the new American First Army, but we got through so early that nobody was about except a few surprised looking sentries. We found out something about our course and picked up Torrey who is now attached to the First Army and shoved on to Chateau Thierry through the country I covered with James and Wilson during the battle; passed the partly ruined village of Vaux and went to the headquarters of General Degoutte who commands in that region. He has six American and four French divisions under his command, and appears to be very live and sensible commander. I had breakfast with him in his little house which is almost intact, although it has a few shell holes in it. Most of the town is pretty badly battered and it is evident that the Germans systematically smashed everything they could lay their hands on before they were driven out. On the way we ran into a troop of some two hundred German prisoners being marched back from the front, a rather bedraggled but cheerful looking crowd.

General Degoutte gave us an officer who took us back through Vaux to Lucy which I had seen while it was being bombarded and thence to the Belleau wood which was a scene of desolation. It was filled with shelters used by the Germans and ourselves. The great part of the trees were shattered by high explosive shells and the ground was strewn with German and American helmets, with shell fragments in between. It seemed like a rather desperate place to hold and still more desperate place to take. Here and there throughout the woods were graves of

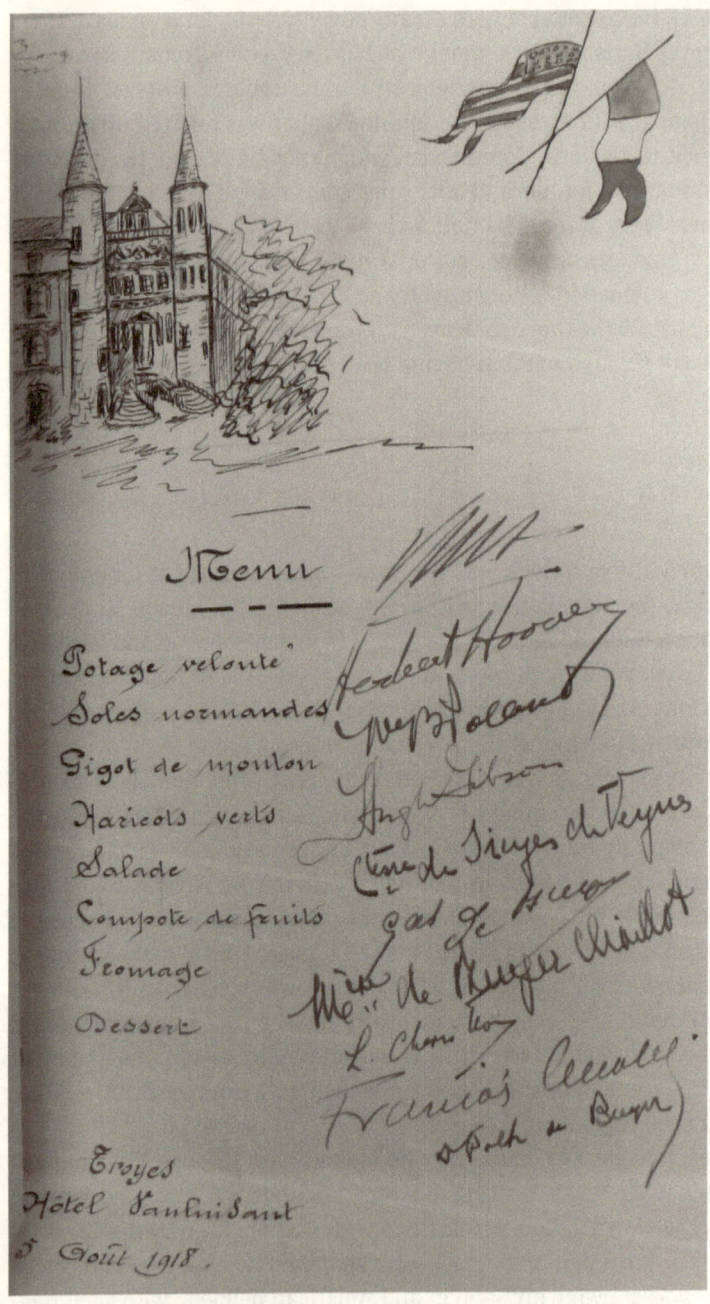

Image 12: Menu from lunch August 5, 1918 signed by Gibson and other guests. (Courtesy of the Gibson Family)

American soldiers with their names and numbers written on the slabs of lead fixed with little crosses over them. We then turned back to the north and east and into Chateau Thierry, thence we crossed the Marne on a pontoon bridge and struck out to east through the country that the Germans had taken when they affected their crossing. There were plenty of captured German guns; large supplies of ammunition, trains standing on the tracks, some of them burnt before being abandoned and one village after another in various stages of ruin. The road between Château-Thierry and Épernay was filled with transports and motor trucks bringing back French soldiers from the trenches. From Épernay we made better time to Châlons where General Gouraud was expecting us for lunch. As we came in I was greeted by Le Neveu, an aide to the General with whom I had gone to school. Gouraud commanded at Gallipoli[129] and at various fronts in France, and has one of the best reputations in the French Army. He lost one arm and one leg in this war but is still going strong. He could not afford many more such experiences. Most of the party was taken to the hotel for lunch and a few of us went to the General's house. After lunch we struck out toward Rheims and went to Mount Senai which is the principal artillery observation post for the Rheims sector. Some of us were taken in a tree where a post had been arranged which commands all of the country from Rheims well to the east. Nearly all the other posts have been destroyed or at least bombarded, but this one has evidently never been observed and we got a rather clear view of all the villages in that district which have figured in the fighting and could follow quite clearly through glasses the lines of trouble marked here and there by the exploding shells of a casual bombardment.

All of the country back of this trough which we came was on the wide Montagne de Rheims, covered with slippery mud and packed with the horses of artillery and supplies. There were enormous dugouts and bomb proof shelters for the men. There was quite an interest manifested in the travelling civilians and the men all looked fairly cheerful, although the life must be vile. The officer who showed us the country from the observation post had been on that duty since November, 1915, and the only pleasure he has had was a few weeks in hospital when he was gassed last year.

We came back and speeded through Châlons and made for Troyes where we found General de Buyer and the Prefect waiting to take some of us to dinner.

---

129 In the Gallipoli Campaign (April 1915 to January 1916), French, British, and Russian troops had attacked the Ottoman Empire in order to win control over the Dardanelles, suffering heavy losses.

The General has a charming old house over three hundred year old with a beautiful façade and well-proportioned rooms which have not been furnished as they deserve. The Mayor came in after dinner but he did not stay long as we were nearly dead for sleep.

Memo from Joffre.   August 5, 1918

As the Malvy trial has developed, it has impressed me more and more as being a matter of politics, and very unfortunate politics. He was accused of betraying to the enemy facts which led to a reverse for French arms at the Chemin des Dames; he was accused of fomenting insubordination in the army. And now we find nothing proved against him beyond the fact that he was a man of weak character, perhaps unfitted for grave responsibility in war time, and surrounded by unworthy people committing improper actions in which his share of responsibility is not made clear. Those who have been called as witnesses have given evidence of a political nature for or against these or those political interests. And, now, after being accused of treason and brought to trial, and after months of waiting, no evidence appears on which a verdict of guilt can be based.

Meanwhile, Daudet, who brought the gravest charges and who has been inaccurate in his statements, goes scot free, although he was deliberately working against the Republic. Not that he seems to have had any plot afoot at the present moment; but his political sentiments are well known, and whatever scandal he can stir up against a Republican Minister furnishes him with an argument to be used sooner or later against the Republican system: "Don't you see," he can say, "that all such people must be swept out of the way?"

The Caillaux case presents itself in a somewhat different light than the Malvy case. The presumptions against Caillaux are graver; whatever the share of guilt of Malvy, it was as instrument for a stronger, brainer man than himself, who may or may not have been Caillaux. However, from all I have been able to hear, there are still no facts proved against Caillaux. He has been kept in prison for months, during which time no revelations have come; the Commission has not yet handed in its report, so it is not even certain that he will be tried; and although he is much disliked, and rightly, for many of his actions, there is a vast difference between the acts he is known to have committed and the charge of treason brought against him. If Malvy is acquitted, it is possible that Caillaux may not be tried at all; but it would be premature to express an opinion to this effect. We must wait and see.

Memo from Joffre. August 5th, 1918

I have received no information tending to show that today's long distance bombardment of Paris coincides with another German offensive. In fact, I doubt whether the Germans are in a position to attempt another big movement. During the last few weeks, many things have altered for the worse, so far as they are concerned.

On this front, they have met with heavy reverses in the course of the Allied offensive, and thanks largely to the work done by the American troops and to the inspiring example the Americans have set by their courage and their dash. The sacrifices of life being made by the Americans is great, but they are right in believing that this is the way to end the war. The Germans cannot hold out indefinitely against such attacks, and our own men, tried as they have been by four years of war, gain a fresh impulse from such a contact.

To the east, Germany is furthermore faced by serious complications. The Russian situation is a distinct menace in its complexity and in its violence. I should not be surprised if Germany were to withdraw a certain number of divisions from this front in order to turn against Russia once more and attempts to straighten out a few of her difficulties there.

Log   Paris. Tuesday, August 6, 1918

Up at seven and off at eight. Most of the party returned to Paris, but Hoover, Boret, Poland, Wickes and I made for Chaumont where we arrived just as the President of the Republic [Poincaré] had finished investing General Pershing with the Grand Cross of the Legion of Honor. Nolan said that everything went very well except that when the President kissed the General some American girl looking out of a window screamed and nearly put the whole performance on the Fritz. I turned over Hoover and Boret to General Pershing and went about my business. I ran into Guy d'Oultremont and introduced him to Hoover who talked to him about his father and mother and cheered him somewhat.

I went about the building seeing people until Hoover was free then took him to see Nolan. They had about an hour's talk to considerable advantage, during which Nolan brought up the question of my commission and Hoover sat on it like a thousand bricks, saying that I would be more useful out of uniform than in it and that they must not press the question. Nolan tried to win him over to the idea by offering to raise the rank to Lieutenant Colonel or Colonel, but we finally agreed to let it go for the present until we saw that it was necessary. Hoover went to lunch with the General while I went to the Intelligence mess with Nolan. Teddy Curtis turned up quite unexpectedly from Evian and joined us so we had a little visit.

McCabe furnished amusement for the crowd of teasing Campanole through the meal and getting a rise every time. Campanole has just been made a Lieutenant Colonel and McCabe started the bull by congratulating him heartily on the grounds that it was a fine piece of propaganda for Italy. When Campanole began to chatter, McCabe said it was too bad he could not speak English, but that it did not matter as he needed no bananas or shoe strings and that he had a shine only a few hours before. When Campanole was about ready to do murder, the party broke up and probably saved McCabe's life.

After lunch I took Hoover away from the General and with Nolan took him on a trip through GHQ, letting him talk to Logan, General Mosely and others. At five o'clock got into our car and started back for Paris, Boret and Leval having gone on before. We reached Nogent about a quarter to eight and had an astonishingly good dinner in a most unpromising little hotel. At midnight we rolled up to the Crillon and I staggered into my happy home more dead than alive at half past twelve by the village clock.

```
Memo from Pershing to G2 jto

PARAGRAPH____
For Chief of Staff [Gen. March]. Reference paragraph 1 your
cablegram 1654 officers appointed for propaganda in enemy coun-
tries have arrived and make favorable impression [Lippmann,
Blankenhorn, Merz]. Their letters from War Department have been
read and thoroughly understood and instruction therein con-
tained will be carried out. Chief of Intelligence Section [Ward]
```

attended conference recently with British, French and Belgian representatives and arranged for a non-administrative liaison committee of all Allies which should lead towards coordination of work in enemy countries. Present method most satisfactory as it leaves us entire liberty of action for conducting our own propaganda which is essentially American and can be worked out more easily by us independently than with outside aid. Importance of this work and responsibility for diplomatic handling fully comprehended and to this end I have taken up tentatively with Hugh Gibson now representing State Department plan for supervision of work of all propaganda in enemy countries. Hugh Gibson now attached to the Embassy in Paris. Has been in State Department work ten years including important work as first secretary at Brussels on outbreak of war and first secretary in London thereafter. Is thought better equipped for this position than anyone else I know over here. I place complete confidence in his ability and judgment and feel that he can properly administer here this most important work. He is willing to accept this position on approval of State and War Departments. Recommend that State Department be requested to grant him one year's leave of absence without forfeiture of rank and that he be commission major National Army as he can do best work as commissioned officer. With this appointment work can progress immediately and within months can forward by courier detailed report of operations to date plans and prospects. Please inform whether this meets with approval of War and State Departments. PERSHING

Log Paris. Wednesday, August 7, 1918

I awoke this morning from sweet dreams of peace to find that James had left, having received hurry orders to proceed to GHQ and take over G2D. Put in the morning at the Crillon where there were visits of all kinds and had lunch with Hoover and McFadden on the balcony. We spent most of the time talking about the need for some central control over American representatives in France. It was agreed that what was really needed was a constantly maintained liaison through daily meetings of the representatives of various governmental bodies and more important still some personal delegate of the President to whom matters should be referred and who could straighten out the greater part of the questions without referring them home. Hoover's chief reason in coming over was to find the solution of this problem and he agreed that the suggestion we made met the situation. He is going to take it up with the President when he gets home.

After lunch Hoover and I went for a walk and bought a large assortment of war medals in the rue de Rivoli, cleaning out the contents of my pocket book. At three Hoover went to see the Prime Minister [Clemenceau] but did not have a very satisfactory time as Boret and Poland went along. The big gun began firing in the morning and kept it up pretty well all day. As Hoover and Boret were on their way back on the rue de la Paix, a shell exploded in the Hôtel de Calais in the rue de Capucines. Hoover gathered up a shell fragment on a slab of marble and brought it back playfully to the hotel. The metal remained too hot to touch for another half hour. We went for another walk and went by the place where the shell had exploded. There was a great hole in the front of the hotel, broken glass and plaster all over the street, and a dead horse with a sheet of canvas over him. It appears that the horse was unhurt by the explosion of the shell, but that an ambulance ran into him and killed him a few minutes after.

We bought a lot of junk to be taken to the boys and got back to the hotel about half past six.

At eight General Bliss came in and we had dinner and a very interesting conversation with lasted until eleven.

Cravath came in to see Hoover on Sunday afternoon and told him that he had been sacked and was leaving for America after a short visit to Italy. He knew that [Oscar] Crosby had done him dirt but he did not know the whole story which is pretty low. It seems that by his insane chatter OTC incurred the dislike and suspicion of both British and French and that they made some remarks in Washington which led to his being had up on the mat by the President to learn what he had to say about being pro-German. He had not much to say the first time but in a day or two it came out that in connection with the Rumely case that Cravath's firm had handled the transfer of the EVENING MAIL.[130] Crosby then went back to the Pres. and told him that the real reason for the uneasiness of the French and British was that they knew of the evil connections of Cravath.[131] Later the President wrote Crosby a letter in which he told him that however unpleasant it might be it was his duty to free himself of even the appearance of evil. Crosby came back to Europe and gave Cravath the sack,

---

130 Cravath's firm represented Edward Rumely, publisher of the *Evening News* in New York, upon his arrest for suspicion of accepting German funds.
131 In the summer of 1918, Edward Rumely, who owned the *New York Evening Mail* since 1915 owner of, was accused of receiving financial support from the German Government. In 1915, Rumely had coopertated with the Cravath Firm.

thus saving his own contemptible skin. Cravath has worked like a dog for him and has used more brains that C can ever command in any other way. Hoover was a good deal aroused by this dirty deal and is going to do something about it when he gets home.

General Bliss says that Foch is now preparing the preliminary plans for the 1919 offensive campaign. He has found it necessary to make heavy demands upon the tonnage of the Allies for strictly military purposes and all our military people are inclined to trim down the demands before passing them on to the civilian branches. Hoover was up in arms at this and told the General that there was no use in trimming down a particle of the demands; that we were now using our tonnage in a way that was certainly susceptible of being scaled down; that we and the Allies would have to get along without things that we now considered necessary to our normal life and that we could be made to do so if it was a matter of life and death. The difference between giving Foch what he asks may readily prove to be another year of the war and the lives of a million American soldiers. We cannot stand for this no matter what deprivation the civil population is called upon to make, and if the need is made clear enough the civil population will increase its output of ships and reduce its demands upon them until the big job has been put over. If there is not enough resiliency in our whole system to make up the full budget of what Foch wants we can better make up our minds now that we can't win and make such a peace as we can get in the fall. Hoover besought Bliss to stand tight for the full list and urge Foch to insist on just what he needed for his task. After the General had gone we sat and talked the matter out and Hoover wrote a lengthy letter to Pershing putting the matter up to him strongly and urging him to stand for no compromise. I agreed to take it to him and deliver it in person.

Bade the whole crowd good bye and came home by the metro as there was no taxi to be had.

Log   Paris. Thursday, August 8, 1918

Have spent a busy day trying to wash the dishes after Hoover's trip. There was an accumulation of letters and telegrams on my desk and a string of callers to talk about all sorts of matters.

Found Coxe waiting for me in the street with the news that he had been transferred to Ward's shop but without a commission. He has not yet been able to see Ward although the latter specially said that he wanted to look the young man over himself. There is altogether too much blockading of chiefs by their subordinates these days.

A letter from [Peter] Jay to say the Ambassador [Thomas Nelson Page] is at Aix. Richardson is away on leave as are a lot of the junior staff, so that he is staying at the shop till all sorts of hours and is weary.

Frank Gunther writes with some price that Ned is away and he is sitting on the lid.

Brought home Southgate to lunch and got back early to the shop.

Telephoned to GHQ and was told that I should go to La Ferté tomorrow to see the General [Pershing]. While struggling with the military authorities to get a car I was told that the General was coming to town this evening and would see me at his house at nine. That saves me a trip.

Talked to James over the telephone. He sounds mournful and bade me go down to see him soon.

Lt. [Jacques] Wittouck came in after lunch to ask what I thought of Heineman. I gave him a rather good bill of health but made it clear that this was based upon my own personal dealing with him and that I could not support a word that I said. It seems the Allies have declined to consider Heineman a good American and would not allow him to come from Switzerland to France. Josse Allard is mixed up with him in a lot of business deals and swears by him. Wittouck, his cousin, is a good deal alarmed for fear this will hurt Allard.

Mitchell came in with word that the money which he had said was being shipped to New York by the Huns is being shipped in the form of French and British War Loans to Buenos Aires, there to be converted into gold or AM securities and sent to New York. He had this first hand from Byrcheff, Chief of the Russian Secret Police until the revolution. I passed it on without loss of time to Nolan.

Stetson brought to dinner a young chap named Paulding who was with Warwick Greene in Switzerland and is now with G2, SOS. He was full of yarns of the people they have to handle including an account of the unvarnished language of Elsie Janis's mother, Mrs. Beerbaum.

At nine went to Gen. Pershing's house where I had to wait some time before the General came in. The party had stopped to dine at Fountainbleau with Boyd's family and was consequently late getting in. The General read Hoover's letter and snorted with pleasure. I added the part that was to be delivered verbally and that was received with equal pleasure. He said he was holding out strong for Foch's full program and that he would not be a party to scaling down on this side. Said he had no patience with the people who said we must not send over any troops that we cannot fully supply with our own tonnage. That might be true if we were advancing across the Sahara for a campaign in Central Africa, but that in a country like France our two or three millions of men would not starve no matter if the Huns sunk all our ships.

The General had 13 Congressmen to lunch yesterday but did not seem disturbed by the number. Said he had given it to them straight from the shoulder.

I was asked to thank Hoover for his letter and say that he had supplied the General with some fresh ammunition. He seemed much pleased with Hoover's stand and said he was a most valuable support for the Army in Washington.

The General leaves tomorrow morning for the La Ferté where he is to take command of the new First Army.

While I was there a phone message came from London to say that Winston Churchill and Lord Weir wanted to see the General on Tues or Thurs. He at 1st said they should see Stettinius and then that he would be glad to see them wherever he might be – but that he could name no place to see them.

Bongy [Bonham-Carter] will probably be over with Weir.

Log   Paris. Friday, August 9, 1918

Got down late to the chancery and had a quiet morning dictating a lot of useless letters.

News came in of the 1st day's success of the British drive on a front from Albert to Montdidier. The advance varies from 4 ½ to 11K and should serve to take the kick out of any German offensive that is planned. 15,000 prisoners have been taken and a large number of guns.

Ben Thaw and Blount came to lunch. Blount wants to come and stay with us and will probably move in within a few days.

When we came in after lunch a phone message was received asking to what hospital Frazier had been taken. It turned out that he had broken his forearm this morning cranking up his car and was at Dr. Taylor's hospital. I talked to the Dr. over the telephone and learned that Frazier was getting on well and would be taken home this afternoon. This will bore him as another Versailles conference is looming up and he will have lots to do.

Gen. Harts came in during the afternoon and we had a little talk. He has come to command the American troops in Paris and bears up under not having a fighting job. Young [John] Jennings is his aide de camp.

Log   Paris. Saturday, August 10, 1918

To my deep disgust got called at seven and made the rendez-vous Place de la Concorde at 8:15: propaganders were waiting and in a few minutes we got started

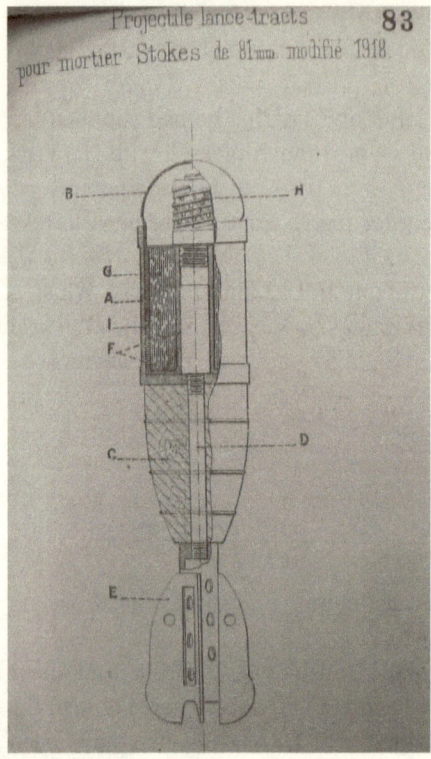

Image 13: Plans of a projectile meant to carry propaganda into enemy territory. This was one of the prototypes Gibson and the others viewed on August 10, 1918. (Courtesy of the Gibson Family)

for Fontainebleau. There were Com. Chaix, Com. Jacquemin, Capt. d'Arenberg, Colonel Brancaccio, a weedy-looking Belgian and several others besides Kenny of the British Mission. I was the only civilian in the crowd.

We reached Fontainebleau at 10.15 and went to the Champ de Tir [firing range] where a battery of 75s was lined up for us. We were shown the working of the new shells that have been made for the scattering of propaganda material and were then taken something over two kilometers away to watch the effect of the fire. We tramped to the top of one of the rocky heights where an *abri* [shelter] had been made for the safe observation of artillery fire, – and as the abri was guaranteed to be entirely safe we perched on top of it and nobody so much as put his nose in it except the telephone operator who passed down the firing instructions to the battery.

The first four shells were duds but after that luck was better and papers, tracts and pamphlets were scattered all over the place. We dictated the elements of fire and found that it was well controlled. The burst could be placed low so as to deliver papers on a given spot. If wide distribution was wanted the burst was placed higher and the papers fluttered over a wide area. Part of the time there was a slight wind and it was surprising how much effect it had on the tracts. The inventor, a little captain, was beside himself with joy, this being his first opportunity to show what he had accomplished.

After 30 shots had been fired at ranges varying from one to four and a half kilometers we went down onto the field and looked for the pieces. The tracts were in perfect condition, the edges of some being slightly ruffles but not enough to matter. The pamphlets on the other hand were shot to bits and some new way will have to be found for delivering them. I don't think it matters much as they are too bulky and a soldier would rarely have the chance to hide such a document from his officers or find the time to read it. In any event only nine small pamphlets can be fired in one shell and that makes it rather cumbersome and expensive method of distribution. What is wanted is a shell that will scatter any number of short tracts containing anything from fifty to two hundred words that are very much to the point.

It might be worthwhile to send over tracts with amusing inscriptions and pictures which would inspire the soldiers to pick up everything that comes along in the hope of more amusement.

At noon we went back to the Hôtel de France et d'Angleterre where we found a big table set out of doors for the crowd of us. One little captain from the Valley of the Rhône got much illuminated on his first glass of Chablis and proceeded to tell droll stories of the "only time he was ever got's". [sic] Of course everybody immediately pledged his health and his [he] became more and more voluble till the end of lunch.

From Fontainebleau we went right after lunch to the Champ de Tir de Montgeron not far from Melun where there were experiments with Stokes guns, rifle grenades and a demonstration of the apparatus for dropping papers from planes and balloons.

Arthur Asquith, a Brigadier-General now, was on hand with his aide de camp Francis Manners. His leg is off below the knee and he gets about with great agility on two crutches, needing no help from anybody. He is only over for a few days and plans to leave Paris tomorrow. He asked me to dine with him but as I was expecting Teddy Curtis I had to say NO.

After watching the firing of the silly looking Stokes for some time we went down into the field of fire and watched the arrivals from a wodden abri which had been built into a corner of the cottage. Arthur and I sat outside and talked until a shell popped uncomfortably close overhead, when we decided that there would be no glory in getting beaned in a demonstration of this sort. Arthur confided to me his conviction that a little High-Explosive would be more effective on the Hun than any about of literature. Who doesn't agree?

Everybody poked about over the field and picked up bits of paper so as to show their interest and then after watching some stunts with rifle grenades we piled into our cars and came home. Colonel Brancaccio landed me at the Embassy where I found a telegram urging me to go over to London Tuesday for a dinner being arranged for Hoover. Sent word that I could not make it and repeated a couple of other cables that had come for Hoover. There was a bundle of proofs of the French edition of my book but I had not the energy to bring them home to read and they shall have to wait for the beginning of the week.

Teddy had not put in an appearance and I have about given up for him this weekend although it was understood that he should come unless he heard from me to the contrary.

I think we shall have to try out the possibilities of making a pneumatic trench gun that could be charged by pressure on a long lever. This could be fired at night, would distribute paper up and down a wide front when the officers are in their dugouts and the men have a chance to pick things up. It would not frighten then men to cover as it would have a noise different from anything else and would be known as a propaganda racket. It should be possible to get a very exact charge so as to plant stuff exactly where it is wanted.

Dinner alone with Stetson and early to bed with the good news of the taking of Montdidier.

Log   Paris. Sunday, August 11, 1918

Got up late after an early to bed and spent my morning writing and tearing up papers.

Davis and Edith Wills came to lunch and stayed to tea for an hour or so afterward.

In the afternoon I wrote a note to Hoover about my talk with Gen. Pershing. A long letter to Phil [Patchin] about possible changes in my work with a boring amount of detail for him to wade through. I also asked for news of Ira [Patchin]. Davis had word that Ira was coming over this month "on diplomatic work". Also primed him to put in a good word for Davis Wills who was left out in the last set of promotions.

Martha McCook and Mrs. Whitridge came to dine and gave us a cheerful evening. It seems the Rome Pages are soon to be in our midst and that Peter [Jay] is growling about being kept in Rome.

Log   Paris. Monday, August 12, 1918

Soon after I reached the Embassy this morning entered to me 1st Lt. Richard Oulahan, Jr. glowing with health. He has been ordered home to act as instructor and is to have leave and promotion on arrival. I sent a telegram to Polk so that he could have the pleasure of telling Dick, Sr. The day the young man was ordered home he received news that he was the father of an 8 pound boy. So altogether things are going his way.

A little later Chandler Anderson came in with Summers of the Munitions Council and I steered them to some preliminary calls.

Lambert came in and said that he would not be able to start to work very seriously before Sept. 1st as every one of the people he wants to engage is out of town. In the meantime he is working out some of the abc's of the socialist and labor situation in France.

Dresel and Gherardi came in and I asked them to lunch but Frazier had got there 1st. I got McFadden and Doc Taylor and fed them instead.

Taylor says Hoover came back delighted with his trip and glad that he got out of going to Italy. He said to me on the side that Hoover considered me "like a brother" and that I was one of his inmost circle of friends. Also that he was a good deal upset because he felt I was wasting my time over here. That he had some work in mind that he felt was just the thing for me and that when he got back to Washington he was going to try to put it over. I don't know what it's all about but I am pleased that Hoover reciprocates to some extent my feeling for him.

Doc [Taylor] says that Crosby has all hands raging in London and that many of them feel that he is really more or less insane. Cravath sailed for home yesterday but we have not heard the end of the matter yet.

Lewis Einstein held me up in the hall and announced that he wanted a commission in G-2 with work in Italy. The Embassy turned him down last May while I was in Rome and it would upset them a good deal to have him in the country. I declined to give him letters of introduction despite his Yiddish insistence. I should think decent Jews would take steps about him. We don't get the blame for all the fault of any casual Christian but every Jew has to take the gaff for Lewis.

A letter from Mrs. [Walter] Page about the missing nephew whom she described as "just fine like a million others." The military authorities are trying to create the impression now that he had fallen into the hands of the Germans, but I can't believe it. She says Mr. Page has gone to Duff House, Banff, for treatment. "He finally broke down, completely, – just tired out."

After lunch Major Coolidge came in under instructions from Harjes and brought me copies of his report on Polish matters as gleaned from the Polish organization here. Have not had time to read them.

Gherardi wants to go down to London next Monday via Boulogne and I have agreed to go with him. He will try to get a Navy car. I called Edward Bell that I was coming and preferred not to have the visit generally known. I ask asked him to tell Arthur Page I would be in London only a few days and hoped he would return with me.

Frazier had a cable from Alice Orr saying that little Arthur had died of infantile paralysis. F. telegraphed and I have spent most of the day on the telephone trying to reach A. and get him up to Paris so that we can tell him here rather than let him learn it at the camp. It is too dreadful to think of poor Alice alone there with her children and Arthur over here. Only this morning I had a letter from him urging me to go down to visit him in and to bring Howard Linn with me, he evidently having just arrived from America.

Dined at the Meurice with Gallavresi, Cerruti (Chief of Italian Military Mission in America) and a Colonel who has been there as purchasing agent. They had no news aside from the rumors of an approaching drive in Alsace to push the Hun back as far as possible toward the Rhine. News had just come in that Lenin and Trotsky have fled from Moscow to Psvok.[132] The 2nd reel will now begin.

From there we went to the Ritz and spent an hour with McFadden, Taylor, Dresel, Gherardi, and Col. Dawes. Gherardi is trying to fix it up for us to fly to Dunkerque in a Caprone. If he can do it we might visit the Belgian front.

Telling of the rough work he had done on the World Trade Board with John Beaver White, Doc [Taylor] said JBW had told Nansen "Your Viking ancestors used to live on fish and you can darn well do it again." Poor Nansen complained to Lansing that this was not diplomatic language.

Doc repeats the rumor that seems to persist that if Mr. Page resigns [which seems inevitable now) Lansing will succeed him, [Newton] Baker become Sec. of State and McAdoo go to the War Dept.

Saw Senator Jim Ham Lewis at the Meurice and had a few minutes talk with him. The poor old gentleman was very tired after a hard trip.

McFadden says Hyde has announced that he is thru with his wife and is going to keep his freedom. There is something the matter with him.

---

[132] These were just rumors.

Log   Paris. Tuesday, August 13, 1918

Word from Arthur this morning that he had already received a telegram from Alice and knew the worst. He says he was only ten days more to finish his course and will then come up to see us.

The morning mail brought me the announcement of the engagement of Cavalcanti to Vera Alves Barbosa of Rio. It will be bad news for Bebeth [de Lynden].

Blount came in this morning and says we are due any minute to start an offensive on the Metz front.

Lunch with Walcott, Chevrillon, Bell and Felder who had an interesting story to tell. He has a job under Office of Naval Intelligence for the duration of the war for $1.00. He went to Switzerland and conferred with Eugene Kahn who proposed that they go into a deal to furnish Germany with a number of things thru neutral countries. He played the venal traitor and agreed to arrange matters. The Col. Godson in Bern horned in and declined to give him a visa back to Paris unless he was fully informed about the whole business. Felder properly refused but it cost him 6 days during which time he was in constant danger of arrest.

The deal seems to involve Otto Kahn, Kessler, and a number of other people and should be followed up. Among other things Kahn said the ship bringing supplies would be notified to German submarines so that they would not interfere with her on the journey. We might have a chance to find out something as to how this interesting game is carried on. Felder does not think much of going back if his liberty is to be endangered by Godson.

Walcott and I went up to see Frank Roosevelt who read the papers and got the point. I suggested that Felder drop his connection with the Office of Naval Intelligence which is the very worst he could have and go to Switzerland ostensibly for Walcott to study vital statistics. Frank agreed. The understanding is that Felder is to get all the material he can and then go back to America to purchase the supplies, charter the ship and go thru the other motions. At the right moment the beans are to be spilled to Justice and the whole show spoiled. Then Franklin Roosevelt comes in and saves Felder from going to jail. I undertook to have G2 tip off Godson to be good.

Frank said he had an interesting time in Italy and got something started. The Italian Navy is fighting every day in the Adriatic and does not like the idea of having their show under a British Admiral at Malta. However they don't object if he will keep out of their pond. So here is ground for agreement with the British and French.

Jay apparently made a bad impression by spilling the beans to the Italians about his secret instructions from home "to back up the British demands."

He [Frank] is convinced that we must send troops to Italy – a minimum of 150,000 and preferably 3 to 500,000. I hope he'll add to the clamor when he gets home.

Carlton Gibson's son came in to see me, accompanied by a Capt. Adams. Also the YMCA Pattison boy who is pretty solid above the collar and wants to be recommended for a commission in G2 – as does [Lewis] Einstein who also came in.

Logan says he will come up tomorrow.

Dined at the Bliss's and found General Lassiter and Stanley Washburn. The General is now artillery commander for the 1st Corps and was rather interesting about the German retreat. He said that in stabilized warfare the Huns got 20 kilometers out of their heavies where we get only about 16 out of ours. During the recent retreat the Germans withdrew their heavies and covered their rear with 77's and machine gun fire so that we had the best of things. He was filled with admiration for the German spy system; said they keep most accurately informed as to our movements and that he would, if he had his way, clear out all the villages behind the line. There are certain villages in easy range that are not bombarded at all while others are reduced to powder – and the only possible assumption is that the unbombarded village is a spy center that they do not wish to disturb.

Stanley Washburn waxed hot over our neglect of Russia, "the deciding factor of the war." When Mr. Root got to Petrograd and sized up the situation, he cabled home that money should be spent freely on propaganda to teach the Russian people the meaning of liberty. He recommended five million dollars for the 1st year. Mott was to put a YMCA hut in each division as a center of propaganda thru motion pictures, news bulletins, speakers, etc. There was to be a school in Petrograd to train 1,000 speakers – a central bureau to receive daily reports as to how material was succeeding in different places and keep it up to high efficiency. A telegram came back saying that the President desired Stanley Washburn to take over the work and that he could have $5,000 a year and one clerk. It never went any further than that. Stanley Washburn was with Root when he reported to the President. Woodrow Wilson told Elihu Root he had not followed his advice about Russia "because its wisdom was not clear to him." Then Stanley charged in and "got severely sat on" as he remarked grimly.

He is strong for a purely military intervention to "form and lead public opinion." I did not insist on the relief expedition idea.

Stanley is a sick man and gets frightfully stirred about these things. He is now going to Lord Northcliffe's place in Surrey "for a rest with a trained nurse and a stenographer."

Somebody telephoned during the evening to announce that "the Americans had captures Mulhouse." Likely!

Log   Paris. Wednesday, August 14, 1918

A quiet morning in the chancery with time to read a stack of information prints and write a lot of letters.

Cerruti came in and got asked to lunch. The party grew until we had Royall Tyler, McFadden and Dresel.

Cerruti says that the great discoveries of Italian iron deposits of which Nitti told Frazier are nothing to get excited about – that the entire deposit is equal to about one year's production from one of the big French mines.

Old-Man-of-the-Sea [Lewis] Einstein came in as usual after lunch with a letter to Nolan and the request that I recommend him for assignment in Italy.

Mrs. Huntington Wilson was announced and turned out to be Hugh Wilson's step-mother, a cheery person who has been driving an ambulance and is now trying to get back to the front.

Dresel came in after lunch to say that the McNally case has come to another deadlock.[133] Van Deman arrived and was soon convinced that McNally should be canned at once. Before he could act, Jerry Gherardi arrived with a special mission from Lanier and Leland [Harrison] and the astonishing news that McNally was supported by the President personally and must not be interfered with. It seems the President was much impressed with McNally's advance information before we came into the war and has considered his subsequent reports from the same angle. Jerry was convinced however that McNally had been guilty of dangerous indiscretion and should be transferred. A recommendation to that effect will doubtless go in from several sources. It is said that the President has annotated McNally's reports in the most flattering terms with sarcastic references to the Legation. It's a great life if you don't weaken.

Van Deman and O'Laughlin are convinced that Mrs. Whitehouse should be limited to running movies and peddling news despatches – and feels that she can't do much harm that way. She still declines to speak to the Minister or Mrs. Stovall.

Dined peacefully along with Stetson and got early to bed.

Log   Paris. Thursday, August 15, 1918

A note this morning from Aunt Leona to say she was coming down the end of this week for her leave. Just my luck to have her come just as I have to go away.

A letter from Walter Lippmann of rather amusing character which is attached.

---

133 See log entry of April 20, 1918.

Felder came in at 11 and I arranged for him to be given a passport for Switzerland and Italy. He brought me a copy of a report from Godson to Mayes saying that Felder has been put on the Italian suspect list because he "had had dealings with a German named Kahn."

Warwick Greene, Stickney, and Campbell-Turner came to lunch. When I told Campbell Turner of Einstein's desire to serve G2, he daned to see him and said nothing would please him more than to have Lewis Einstein as a 1st Lt. under him.

Got Einstein to the chancery at 5 and introduced him to Campbell Turner. *Tableau*! He promptly lost most of his interest in G2 and decided that the only person for him to talk with was Ward.

Soon after I got home Bonham-Carter came in for a visit. He seemed a good deal depressed about the air situation because of the difficulty of getting offensive action from the French. He says their system is wrong because flying men remain members of their old regiment and get no promotions except from the latter. Hence they don't get the sort of men who should go into this work. Among other things they play up the "Aces" and pay no attention to the hard-working patrols and ordinary bombers. The British are trying to get them to detach their air service from the army altogether and make it as completely separate as the Navy. They are trying to use us as a lever and have asked us to help them in their campaign with machines and fliers for bombing German towns. The difficulty is that the French then jump in and say "If you help the English you must help us too." And there is a certain difficulty even for the rough soldiers to turn on them and say: "What's the use? You don't do anything with the help."

The British seem to like Gen. Patrick but say it is a weird thing to give him command where he does not know the first thing about the business he is pitchforked into. They are enthusiastic about Foulois.

Bongy [Bonham-Carter] says Lloyd George is undoubtedly strong with the country and will stay strong while things go well. Bongy does not see the advantage to him of general elections as he believes the House will be returned much in its present form unless there is some clear-cut issue. He believes Lloyd George is expecting some more radical German peace offer in the autumn and that some elements in England will come out in favor of discussion. Then he could knock down the man of straw and secure a strong House. There are several conditional elements in this, including an important figure to come out as a pacifist. They hope Mr. Asquith will be the man but are badly mistaken, as he is a pronounced "bitter-ender," historically he was the 1st to come out flatfooted for the restoration of Alsace as a condition of peace.

Bongy says all feeling in England is strong for continuation of the war until the Germans learn that they can't safely resort to another war.

Arthur Asquith is going to have an artificial leg but learning to use it is painful and he still clings to crutches for ordinary getting about.

Bongy said he would try to arrange for me to fly back from England. Said he hoped I could take a few days off and go down to the wharf.

Dined alone with Stetson who is off for Switzerland tomorrow.

About 11 came the sound of barrage which continued for a quarter of an hour or so before the sirens tuned up. The fire died down and we went to bed while the screaming went on.

Memo from "F." [Foch]   August 15th, 1918

```
The Germans have drawn back slightly, under the pressure of the
English, up in the north. At other points of the line, they seem
disposed to take the defensive on positions carefully organized
in advance. I should not be surprised if they were suddenly to
draw still further back, on the principle of the "Hindenburg
Line" a little later, whenever they feel ready, before winter
comes. They would derive from this the same benefits as before,
but they would need time to build their defenses and to bring back
their artillery and material. In this event, the 1919 campaign
would open with an attack by the Allied troops upon the more for-
midably organized positions yet seen in the course of the war.
    While having become incapable of trying another big offen-
sive on a ninety kilometer front, the Germans are still capable
of directing powerful attacks against any one place, as, say,
Rheims, in the hope of taking it over for prestige. I see, how-
ever, only one real danger in the situation, and that is that the
American Army may seek to act too independently. The method fol-
lowed until now has been precisely the right one, and the Ameri-
can Army jumped into the fray at the very moment when there was a
return to open warfare which allowed them to reveal their magni-
ficent soldierly qualities, but if, an appears possible [sic] we
must return to fortifications and are called upon to attack the
Germans under such conditions, the work must be done mainly by
artillery, as before, and we must not risk disaster by attacking
imprudently in the open.
    ("G."[Gouraud] who was present at this conversation, here
remarked that another danger came from certain elements in
France who protested against the calling out of the 1920 Class
```

and the maintenance of old soldiers under arms, saying, "The Americans are coming in such numbers that we can afford to reduce our efforts." The attitude resolutely taken by Marshal Foch is that France must continue to make her maximum effort, as if there were no one here to help her at all; and if England does as much, and America does as much, then the three efforts united, each supplying its maximum whatever it may be, the war will end satisfactorily. Recently the British Staff approached Marshal Foch to know what reductions he intended to make in the French Army, owing to America's aid; apparently the British were considering a progressive reduction of their effort. Foch protested energetically against any such idea and insisted upon the principle aforesaid.)

G. [Gouraud] August 16th, 1918

At the present moment, French, American, British, and Japanese perfectly agree as to the action being taken in Siberia. But this is limited to assisting the Czech Slovaks, declared to be friends and Allies, and does not go to the extent of helping Russia.[134] This second half of the programme must be applied sooner or later, and the sooner it comes the more valuable it will be. Even if there were to be an overwhelming victory of the Allied arms on the Western front, and peace were to be signed in consequence tomorrow, a condition like that existing in Russia, with Germany remaining master, would be so full of threats that America would not dare call her armies home again.

The most effective action in the aid of Russia would be by selecting some really able Russian General, who inspires confidence to his compatriots, a man like Alexeieff, and entrusting to him the command of all the sound Russian military elements he

---

[134] Before the Russian Revolutions in 1917, the Tsarist Army had taken lots of soldiers of Czechoslovak origin serving in the Austrian Army prisoner. The Bolsheviks did not regard them as enemies and allowed them to evacuate – but on the long road eastwards, on the Trans-Siberian Railroad. Soon, these 'Czech Legionnaires' clashed violently with Red Army units. In May 1918, the soldiers openly revolted and soon controlled large track sections of the Trans-Siberian Railroad. Only in 1920, they were evacuated via Vladivostok.

could grasp together.¹³⁵ The Allies also need to enter Moscow, but they have no intention of laying hands on Russia.

According to the agreement between Japan and the United States, each of these countries was to send 7,000 soldiers and no more. This in itself was not enough even for the limited work undertaken in aid of the Czecho Slovaks. But Japan has already landed 12,000. Her attitude is that she meant "7,000 fighting men," and if these alone were sent on such a journey, not more than 2,500 would arrive; and so 5,000 men "back of the line" were a necessary part of the programme.

Material is not being brought together for further memoranda to be sent to President Wilson about the imperative need for extending Allied action in Russia, but it has not been decided at what moment these memoranda will be drawn up and handed in.

Log   Paris. Friday, August 16, 1918 * Birthday

An unusually quiet day with a flock of callers between 11 and 12.

Chandler Anderson who wanted to find out the whereabouts of his nephew. Located him thru James as being with the 77th Div.

Van Arsdale – the movie man with a trifling errand.

Capt. Colby who has a long tale of woes and wanted to tell me all about it, which he did for half an hour or so.

Dickson of the Embassy in London, who wants to go to the front. Fixed it for him.

Grobet, the Federal Counsellor and Dresel came home for lunch. They leave tonight for Bern and take Stetson with them.

A telegram from Frank Gunther to say he is away on leave. Arthur Page is in Scotland with his father but my message was telegraphed to him. Frank expects me to stay with him Tuesday night at Stanmore. Can make no plans until I get there.

Frazier says Jaccaci's sons who are in the Royal Flying Corps tell the most remarkable stories about the French fliers which in measure bear out Bongy's story. They say these birds construct their machines as much like the Huns as possible and then behave very lumnishly so that they are continually being fired on

---

135 Soon after the October Revolution, a White Movement materialized in Russia. Led by former tsarist officers, its aim was to fight and destroy the Bolsheviks and to turn back the hands of time.

by the British. They seem to delight in nose dives at the British and other threatening tactics.

A birthday note from Aunt Leona with a 100 franc bill. Said she had hoped to be here to stay but had not been able to get her papers fixed. Perhaps that will bring her here after my return from England.

I learn confidentially that bombs fell last night at Créteil and Montmorency.

Davis and Edith Wills came to dine.

Evidently our 1st army is getting ready for something big as the letters I receive refer to the way they are straining at the leash as though I knew all about the preparations.

Two Hun submarines yesterday tossed some gas shells into Charleston and Wilmington, but did nothing but overwhelm some lighthouse men.

Log   Paris. Saturday, August 17, 1918

At 10 o'clock Aunt Leona telephoned to announce her arrival and I promptly claimed her for lunch.

The morning did not produce much of interest. Gherardi came in to say that Capt. Cone had turned down the idea of my flying to Dunkirk because he did not want the responsibility of taking any but Navy people. Pretty cheap inasmuch as they are not shy about asking for help whenever they want it. However I shall growl and probably go on doing anything they ask. Gherardi is sailing away this afternoon.

Blount came in from GHQ where he had found his brother. He is on the upgrade now and due for a month's leave.

I asked him what Senator Jim Ham Lewis had said that was censored from the Chicago Tribune dispatches. He seems to have announced that "McAdoo would come over with the President." Blount was the Senator's conducting officer and was told that the visit was coming; that the Senator had argued on the floor that while he could not come as President, there was nothing to prevent him from visiting France as Commander in Chief of the American Forces.

The English and Italian papers have had dispatches on the subject for some days and now the French papers are coming out and growling that they have not been allowed to say anything about it. If he is coming over it is very poor policy to say anything about it as the Hun would gladly sacrifice a fleet of subs to get him.

Gathered up Aunt Leona at the Champs Élysées Hotel and took her home for a quiet lunch. She looks very tired and has lost a lot of flesh but says she is really well. Her heart is deep in her work and she talks about it with enthusiasm. She now runs a crèche with 39 babies in it.

She has not heard from Warren for months – since last April.

Letter to Mary Gibson. Paris. Saturday, August 17, 1918

... For some time I have noticed that little things have been abstracted from my desk and when I came in this morning the old messenger told me that he had caught one of the scouts in the act of going through my drawers in the early evening when he thought nobody would be there. I sent him up to Caffery and the result was the young man was sacked at once. After lunch he returned with father and mother, father in an advanced state of intoxication, announcing that he was going to thrash C. within an inch of his life for daring to call his son a thief. Caffery being a direct young feller sent for the Marine guard and father was projected into the street more rapidly than he had entered. I heard a frightful row and when I looked out of the window saw what I thought was the murder of an agent de police. Father had him by the throat and was going through the most terrifying contortions. It seems that he was merely describing the outrages of which he had been a victim and was just showing how he had been put out of the Embassy. He then repaired to a nearby wine-shop and soothed his wounded feelings with more drink while son stood watch outside.

Log Paris. Sunday, August 18, 1918

After being pursued by a bear all night got up in time to receive Travis Coxe who came to announce that he had been transferred to G2, SOS and was working a typewriter which pleases him better than what he was doing. The next thing is to get him a commission.

On arriving at the chancery I found Jerry Gherardi looking rather shamefaced. He admitted that when they arrived at the aviation field yesterday afternoon and got all the luggage strapped in a telephone message arrived to say that there was a gale blowing on the coast and that they would not be allowed to start. So he then set out to find a car and the result is that we set out tomorrow morning at nine from the Meurice with Lt. Guggenheim or something of the sort. I knew Heaven was going to punish them for not taking me along.

Got Aunt Leona and Dawson and brought them home to lunch. At three o'clock took them to their various places of abode and came back home to pack. At 5:30 went to the Hôtel Majestic where I met Horodyski and had a little talk with him. He wants me to help him help the Polish Red Cross in getting things out of our Red Cross and I cheerfully undertook to take him to see Dan Pierce and ask what could be done.

Horodyski is much upset about Godson: says he is a blithering fool and that he is messing things up in every direction; that above all things we need a really clever man in his place. I believe Van Deman has done something about it but am not sure that this involved the removal of Godson who certainly ought to be in France commanding a regiment which is his real job.

Horodyski still strong for undertaking some active Secret Service work in Austro-Hungary. He says that conditions are riper every day and that we could get splendid results by the expenditure of a reasonable amount of money. He wants the Department to send me to Switzerland to look over opportunities and dole out the money as it is needed. He can dream on peacefully for there is no earthly chance that they will do anything of the kind.

Dined at Mrs. Whitridges'. Those present, [E.C.] Carter of the YMCA, Ted Roosevelt and his wife, Martha McCook, Lord and Lady Hartigan. Lady Hartigan a great friend of Arthur Asquith. Ted Roosevelt. Jr. so much like his father that I want to hug him. He has two service stripes on one arms and two wounded stripes on the other. His left leg is useless but he is jubilant because he can now put his toe on the ground while navigating on crutches. Was deeply insulted because some evidently well-intentioned soul suggested that he go down to GHQ and become a staff officer. He fairly frothed at the mouth in telling about it.

Just before dinner Blount moved in and settled down. I went out and left him to dine alone.

McFall and Topping came in to call just before dinner and dropped me at my destination.

Log   Campagne. Monday, August 19, 1918

Got started betimes this morning and reached the Meurice before the clock had reached 8:40. Gherardi was smoking at his pipe and we chewed over the morning news until the clock struck when a big open car rolled up and disgorged Lt. Guggenheim who was to be our companion.

We made good time, the speedometer hovering between 40 and 45 most of the time, even when going thru villages. We had two blow outs but otherwise no troubles. Beauvias I had not seen since the beginning of the war and was surprised to see the way the bombs have banged up the place. We stopped only long enough to let the guards look at our passes going in and out and then sped along the good road to Abbeville. About four kilometers outside we had a blow out which had to be repaired in the most cumbersome way, so we walked on ahead and let the car follow us. We broke in the British Officer's Rest House and got a respectable meal wedged in between English, Irish, Scotch, Australians, New Zealanders, Canadians, French, Italians, Belgians and American officers, all of them talking shop at full speed.

At two we were off again and rolled into the dock at Boulogne at sharp half past three with an hour and a half to spare for the five o'clock boat, – only the five o'clock boat was not sailing and we were ditched until tomorrow morning. There was nothing to do about it but swear, so we did and then decided to go up to the flying squadron at Inglevert and see whether they could put us up for the night.

This cheerful place is stuck conspicuously on top of a hill looking over the sea and swept by every wind that blows. Young Lovat,[136] who commands the squadron, is the son of the Judge and a fine looking boy. He took us out onto the field and showed us some newly arrived Capronis [Italian aircraft] which have just arrived. The Italians evidently send them up in bad shape and they have to be practically rebuilt. They even have them painted Italian colors with the Italian insignia on them. Lovat's comment was caustic. There were also a number of Handley-Pages on the adjoining British field and we were also taken to see them. They are monstrous looking beasts, cumbersome and heavy, but are said to be light and easy to handle. Lovat was loud in his praises of the way the British help our people and stay up at nights when we are out to help in handling the return of raiders. It sounded pretty good. The photographs and charts of the work accomplished by this Naval squadron looked encouraging as to what could be expected if and when we undertook work on a larger scale. Our people are peppering Bruges, Ostende and Zeebrugge steadily and seem to be getting results. They keep after the machine shops, etc and the Boche subs in the Canal. They are also using some 1660 pound bombs which blow a whole neighborhood to pieces. They settle into their slings so that it is hard to drop them instantly as is necessary if they are to hit their marks. However it is hoped that some new slinging device will be found to obviate this.

After tea we motored over here to this damp and draughty chateau where another bombing squadron under Major Cunningham of the Marine Corps has its quarters. He was asked whether he would prefer a chateau or huts and chose the first with the idea that his QM was trying to pull over something on him.

Squab Burnham drifted in on his way out to dine with the village priest who has the best food and wine in the neighborhood. New people bob up wherever one goes.

This crowd has a good yarn from Gallipoli. The day after the landing the French slipped down in twos and threes to get a morning dip in the sea. Then came the English but they came in a troop, shouting and turning cart wheels and flapping their towels. The Turks turned loose their artillery and there were five or

---

[136] Maybe Brigadier Simon Fraser (1871–1933), 14th Lord Lovat, but the fact that Gibson calls him "young" casts the shadow of doubt on this assumption.

six casualties. The next morning the French slipped down the same way and got off unhurt. The British learned no caution and came romping down in the same way – but brought some stretchers with them so as to be prepared for the bombardment.

London   London. Tuesday, August 20, 1918

A rotten night. The telephone orderly spent most of his time yelling at various places and then howling up the staircase to wake up the officer who was wanted. Then everybody would get up and run about the house in boots and the echos were enough to wake the dead. The night was what they call a "dud" – no chance for a raid from either side because of the squall that was blowing and the low visibility.

We were called at quarter to six and had breakfast with Rockwood, a Navy Surgeon who kindly offered to pilot us to Boulogne. We might as well have spared ourselves the early rising for after getting to the boat we had to wait for about an hour and a half before she pulled out. The people to stamp our passports did not put in an appearance until just before sailing time so all the brutal soldiery had a chance to get on board and fill all the places. By good fortune Guggenheim and I contrived to get a couple of steamer chairs and shove them under the bows of a life boat. Then the life boat was swung out and we had a comfortable time of it although it was cold and a strong wind was blowing. There were only two other civilians on board but plenty of general and officers of all colors and sizes. When we got into port I had to stay behind with the other civilians until a board of a civilian, a soldier and a sailor come on board to stamp our passes which they did with much geniality. Despite their smiles the train had filled up while they were smiling upon us and we had to wait for the second. Guggenheim skirmished round and got some seats for the Pullman diner so that we had a comfortable meal and a bottle of claret on the way up. I was about all in from lack of sleep, etc., and was glad to snooze for an hour or so before reaching London.

We landed here in the midst of a bus strike and there was some difficulty in getting a cab. We stopped at the Embassy while Guggenheim reported to the Naval authorities and I gathered up my mail and letters. The crowd was in the dining room down below and I did not bother them but ran off for the Ritz to see if I could get cleaned up.

Walter Lippmann came in to see me while I was getting dressed and we had a talk which lasted us for an hour or so. Keeley is leaving for the U.S. to tell them how they ought to run propaganda in enemy countries. He hated his job at first but Walter wrote a speech for him to make at the Inter-Allied conference and he sat next to Mr. Balfour and some other great and mighty to such good effect that he has a headful of it and now proposes to stay at any cost. He is evidently a rounder of the sort that sheds little credit upon us but solid in Washington. He is ready to content himself with staying in London to run things here and sit upon the Inter-Allied conference. I don't care who wears the halo if he allows the work to go on. Walter has seen Willy Tyrrell who has promised to help him and has had a great time with Northcliffe who is evidently getting some things done in good form.

We walked down to the Embassy where I found Blankenhorn waiting for me and ran into all the old crowd who gathered about and welcomed back the prodigal, – Leland Littlefield, Crosby, Beale Davis, Boylston Beal, Buckler and others. Beale Davis is off for Copenhagen this week and is much disgruntled in consequence. I believe it is the best thing possible for him as London is ruining his chances of every amounting to anything. Frank Gunther was not on the premises but I saw him later. Laughlin took me into the Ambassador's [Page] room and stuffed the keyhole and said that he had quizzed the Ambassador's doctor and insisted on knowing just what the situation was; that the answer is that there is nothing organically wrong but that he must have a thorough going rest if he allows the work to go on no matter how long it may take. He will be as good as new if he does take care and won't last at all if he doesn't.

William Tyrrell telephoned and asked me to go to see him at six so I hastened over to see Mrs. Page first and had tea with her and Arthur who piloted me. She looks well and it did my heart good to see that she was no longer worried about the Ambassador. Shoecraft came in while I was there and dropped me at the Foreign Office where I had an hour or so with Sir Wm. who wanted to talk to me about personal matters. He is a good soul and has quite got hold of himself again. After the death of his son he rather went to pieces and took to drinking more than was good for him. Now he is clear eyed and pink cheeked and I was rejoiced.

Telephoned down to the Wharf[137] and was answered by Elizabeth [Asquith] who said it was desired that I go down tomorrow. She telephoned again in the evening to confirm the message from her father to say that I was expected on the 11:40 train.

I dined at the Embassy with Arthur [Page] and Boylston Beal. Mrs. Page dined out and did not return until just as we were ready to shove off for the night.

---

137 The Wharf was the country home of Herbert H. Asquith and his family in Oxfordshire.

Log   The Wharf. Sutton-Courtney. Berks. Wednesday, August 21, 1918

Walter Lippmann came and breakfasted with me and we had some talk about the general features of the work. He is quite set on my being at the head of it and I was equally set that he should run the show. After stalling about it for some time he admitted that the real reason was that Blankenhorn really ranked him and would be the logical head of the show if I was not, and that B. was not capable of running anything. I suggested that he talk with Arthur Page about the possibility of his coming in on the show and marched him down to the Embassy to start him at it.

At the Embassy I found a note from Mr. Asquith saying that he wanted to see me at 20, Cavendish Square either today or tomorrow.[138] Thereupon I telephoned down to the Wharf to make sure that I would not cross him on the way, and when the answer came back that he was expecting me there I had missed my train and had to put it off until three o'clock.

I lunched at the Embassy mess which has been beautifully fixed up and has well served meals. Stockton and Hayden came rolling in as fresh water sailor men and we had a few words.

I caught the three o'clock from Paddington for Didcot and just as the train was pulling out Puffin [Arthur Asquith] stuck his head in the window and when he saw me scrambled in and foregathered. He has not changed a bit and is just as simply interested in everything as ever he was.

Elizabeth Asquith[139] met us at the station and motored us home by a roundabout way which was a relief after sizzling in the train.

The [Asquith] family were all having tea in the Mill House, a new place around the corner which has been fixed up for Bongy and Violet [Bonham-Carter and Violet Asquith] and Cys [Cyril Asquith] and Anne. It is altogether charming. After tea I had a long talk with Mr. Asquith and went for a walk with him thru the grounds of the new place. Then back to the Mill House where all hands were playing pounce, including Lady Tree [Helen Holt] and Cara Copland.

After dinner we went out on the river and reveled in a little moonlight – and coming back at midnight I was ready to turn in.

---

138 Herbert Asquith lived at 20, Cavendish Square.
139 Gibson and Elizabeth Asquith were friends since his posting in London 1916. It is rumored she had a crush on him at that time. By this point in mid-1918, the friendship was restored.

Log   The Wharf. Thursday, August 22, 1918

Got up as late as I dared and even at that was one of the first to appear.

After breakfast some scattered to tennis and others to all sorts of jobs while I settled down in the "BARN" with Mr. Asquith for another talk.

It was so boiling hot that nobody was good for anything and we loafed and talked until after tea which was served in the Mill House.

Then off on the river again returning just in time for tea. And after dinner off again to keep as cool as we could.

In the evening Arthur Page called thru from Winchester to say that he would meet me in London tomorrow at noon and that I was to stay at the Embassy during the rest of my visit to London. Frank is trying to fix it up for us to fly back to Paris.

Log   Hotel Burlington. Dover. Friday, August 23, 1918

This morning we were up and about early and caught at 9:30 from Didcot – Mrs. Asquith, Elizabeth and I. I bade them goodbye and made for the Embassy where I dropped my bag and continued to the chancery to find Arthur [Page].

Got my passport under way and then made for the Foreign Office to have another talk with Tyrrell and Drummond. Both were very cordial and agreed to help me all they could in the matter of political intelligence. Did not see Eustace Percy although I wanted to.

Made for the Admiralty in hopes of finding [Sir Reginald] Hall but he was away and I contented myself with greeting Seracolt and saying hello to Frank Gunther who was somewhat peeved because I had not appeared to go home with him last night.

Thence back to the Embassy where I had lunch with Mrs. Page and Arthur. While we were there Frank telephoned to say that we could not fly to France. Immediately after lunch we set out to find some means of locomotion. As usual our people were not helpful or fertile in ideas and finally we took our nerve in both hands and set sail for the Admiralty to see that gruff old jewel, Sir Douglas Brownrigg. He glared at us when we told our needs, told us to keep our shirts on and began telephoning Dunkirk, Calais and Dover with a few explosions between times at people who called in on his local wire. Within a few minutes he had it fixed that we should go on the 7:50 train to Dover, where he would have us "hooked out by a Naval officer" so that "those bloody soldiers won't bother us". He had rooms engaged for us and passage on the duty destroyer for tomorrow morning. And then he snorted at our thanks and we went our way feeling grateful but inarticulate in the face of his snarls. He is a fine old gentleman.

Dropped Arthur at the house and went my way to polish off the jobs I thought I could attend to by tomorrow morning. Went to 20 Cavendish Square and said goodbye to Elizabeth. Mrs. Asquith had already left for the Wharf. Took Elizabeth to the station and put her on the train at six.

Dined at the Embassy with Mrs. Page who grows more and more dear as time goes on. She told me that the Chief [Walter Hines Page] had sent in his resignations some weeks ago and was now trying to get the President to answer him. He is determined to go home and to go very soon but he does not want to embarrass the President by saying anything about it before the Great White Chief [Wilson] has a chance to pick out a successor. However he will soon deliver an ultimatum and go home anyway.

Frank Hodson was waiting for us at Victoria with the usual flock of satellites touching their caps and sent us off in a reserved compartment which we vainly offered to share with others.

Part was down a young officer got in and actually talked to us as though we were human beings. It was so unusual that we could hardly trust ourselves to converse with him and after he got off the train we agreed that he must be a Hun spy.

At the Priory Station we were "hooked out" by a young Lt. named Morgan who burbled with joy at the thought of meeting us at eleven. He praised the American troops and we did our best to show our admiration of the British, and then the anthem swelled to a chorus over the French, with a grand finale over the prospects of the allied cause. Everything we said to this future admiral he beamed and answered EXCELLENT, in all Caps. I felt like telling him confidentially that there were other suitable adjectives in the English language but it would not have been worthwhile. He took us in a mighty motor to this enormous hotel where we have rooms about the size of our hats.

Morgan was much impressed by Arthur, being his Father's son, and when Arthur's back was turned he inquired in an awe-stricken voice what his rank was. He was obviously disappointed to find that he was not even a Minister, as he put it.

We are off on the destroyer in the morn at 9:15.

And so to bed.

Log   Paris. Saturday, August 24, 1918

We were called at 7:45 and breakfasted in a dining room that looked out over the sheltered harbor of Dover. The little basin was filled with destroyers and monitors and comically camouflaged ships of every size and hue. The torpedo nets at the entrance to the harbor were drawn back and all sorts and conditions of floating contraption was trotting in and out.

Promptly at 9:10, as per schedule, Lt. Morgan came in pronouncing everything excellent, inquired after the disposal of our "gear" and escorted us down through the garden to the dock where he informed us with bated breath that "The Commodore" was waiting to escort us to our launch, – pinnace I mean. The Commodore in turn apologized because the Admiral was off on leave and could not be there to see us off. We being humble souls forgave him for being a mere Commodore and told him so.

A spick and span pinnace sped us out to the P47, a biggish destroyer which had just come in from a long trip and was putting out to sea again at once.

Her skipper, a White Star Line officer "in private life" as he expressed it, stowed our gear and then led us to the bridge so that we could see the show. He got under way and after easing us through the entrance to the harbor went below to wash and change after an all night siege. The Second in Command was also a genial youth. He complained that although he had been on destroyers ever since August, 1914 he had never seen a Hun on the water. He had seen some Hun planes and that was as far as he could go.

We sped across to Calais and then struck up the coast to Dunkirk. The skipper then took us below and produced some splendid whiskey, splendid even to me who never drinks the stuff and never touch anything in the morning. He poured us out a man's sized drink and we got away with it before we picked up Dunkirk. The skipper had married a Los Angeles girl named Fleming, daughter of a newspaperman there. He is a fine little sportsman; anybody who can take the trouble to be civil to utter strangers all morning, after twenty-four hour go, commands my admiration.

We sidled up to the dock at a little behind noon and found Lt. Oosley waiting for us with a Rolls-Royce which he apologized for as being old. It was the Vice-Admiral's car but the V.A. was not there and it was to be used to take us through to Paris. Oosley himself had a wife at Gouffliers and would go with us that far.

First we were taken to the officer where our passports were looked at and another Commodore apologized because there was nobody there with enough rank to receive us. We generously let him off alive and said that in war times when people were busy we were quite prepared to put up with mere Commodores and Rolls-Royces for ordinary jobs and would not insist on all we were entitled to. When alone we dared to look each other in the eye but not otherwise for it would be too much to expect us to keep a straight face when we saw all that was being done for us.

We drove through Dunkirk which is much battered by long range bombardment and by almost nightly raids. Hardly a window in the place, everything being boarded or covered with paper. The hotel where I stayed seemed to be making a feeble effort to show signs of life. We passed the hospital where I left Ynès the night of my arrival in Dunkirk during the beginning of the battle. But instead of streets crammed and noisy with people and horses it was almost a town of the dead. The local Commandant put his mark on our passports and then we sped out on the road to Calais where we drew up at the Restaurant Continental where we fought off swarms of flies and had a lunch that Voisin could have been proud of. This old bird that runs the place is doing it in the best Parisian style, with the best Parisian prices and is said to be getting rich. I can believe it from my personal experience paying the bill.

Oosley is a fine sea going person who in peace times grows wine and olives near Florence. There are all sorts wearing the crinkly stripes in the British Navy. This one talks beautiful French and Italian and is going strong although he longs to go back to his vines and olive trees.

Off to Boulogne which we took on the bias and then thru Étaples to Gouffliers and the pretty little farm house where we found Mrs. Oosley and a couple of nice French women who live with her. The HQ is in a chateau nearby and these ladies have taken the little farm house so as to be as near as possible to their home. One of their husbands has gone over to Montreuil to get Oosley and so we volunteered to take him over to save the poor chap from a longer wait. First we had a bumper of Vermouth in a spick and span garden behind the house and then away across the country through roads that nobody knew, we least of all. The whole country from Boulogne down is solid English camps and hospitals and railroad yards and rifle ranges, and even great yards for the training of trench dogs which we saw in their hundreds. One of the biggest hospitals had been badly bombed by the Boche recently and the ruins stretched far and wide. There was not a particle of doubt that they knew just where they were and what they were doing for they swooped down low and fired at the nurses and patients with their machine guns, while the red crosses were plainly visible. It is too filthy for words and only serves to enrage people. It's too bad we can't be savages enough to do some of that sort of thing to them.

When we got to Montreuil we drew up in an irregular shaped place which went by the name of the square, but there was no friend in sight. Inquiry elicited the information that there was another square and we tried that too. First and last we wandered thru pretty well every nook and corner of the charming old town and saw all its *Sehenswürdigkeiten* [tourist sites]. Then Oosley proposed to have us throw him overboard and let him find his way home. We mutinied however and insisted on delivering him back to his wife, which we did.

From there, after bidding goodbye to our new friends we made through Abbeville on our way to Beauvais. As we started out of the town we were stopped by the arrival of a big batch of Germans, six or seven hundred of them in a bunch. They were evidently of today's harvest for they still looked a bit wild and needed a brushing up. As a whole they seemed fairly husky but certainly looked like a lot of dumb brutes. Perhaps our fellows don't look very beautiful when they get on the other side of the lines but I'd like to bet that they don't look so densely stupid as this crowd. Some were mere boys. Many of them looked like rather delicate clerks, etc. with heavy glasses. Others looked like the off scouring of the slums with every imaginable sort of flat head, chinless face, etc. Most of them had no kit; some of them had retained their tin hats. A few camouflaged rather well so as to conceal them for the first line or sniping work. I was surprised that most of them had only their little cloth caps which do not offer any amount of protection for rough fighting of the sort they have been thru. They had only a handful of men to guard them and I daresay they did not need even those. We sat contentedly and watched them pour in. I would have been willing to have our car delayed as long as possible for the passage of prisoners.

Soon before reaching Beauvais we blew out a tire on a hillside and while the chauffer was changing it we were inspected by a stumpy little *poilu* [French infantry man] who came strolling over from a young steam roller that was smoking peacefully away by the roadside. He was something of a humorist for he called our attention to the fact that *"il ne crevait jamais de pneus"* [he never tires]. He said he had things his own way on the roads, even those road hogs, the trucks getting respectfully out of his way. He was not on his way toward Montdidier and was proceeding at the rate of fifteen kilometers per day. Said that during the fighting recently he was within three kilometers of the frontlines and was plastered with machine gun fire. At about this stage of the game another poilu also wearing the croix de guerre eased into the conversation and proceeded to start arguments about all sorts of things. It finally got down to a debate between the relative merits of the artillery and the infantry. All with much gesturing and raising of voices to threatening pitch, although it was all merely conversational without any real feeling on either side.

"Bah" said the infantryman, squatting down on the ground and suiting the action to the word, "Your artilleryman lives in a funk. He stays miles behind the lines and never gets into things".

"Mince" replied the artilleryman, "We never get a chance to take cover and the Boche gets all the time he wants to spot us and then we are wiped off the earth. But you people hide in holes underground while we stay out in the open and risk our lives to make it impossible for the Boche to come over and cut your dirty throats."

"Ha, but when the time comes we pop out of our holes and go, ZUT, over the top like that, to fight hand to hand with the HUN."

And when we pulled away they had each other by the collar and were talking both at once at the tops of their lungs, alone in the middle of the road miles from a town at nightfall, being intensely earnest about something that they really didn't care a hoot about. They are a wonderful people.

At Beauvais we pulled into a good looking hotel and were offered a chance to dine out of doors if we would sit down at table with some American officers. When I looked at the officers I observed that one of them was Phil Potter as drunk as usual and we decided in favor of dining indoors. A good dinner and away.

The first village we went through we noticed that most of the inhabitants were in the street and many of them yelled at us to put out our lights. Soon they began stopping us whenever we came where there were any soldiers. The chauffeur would obediently put out his lamps and then after a hundred yards turn them on again. After a time he played at being stupid and had everybody pointing into the sky to explain what they meant, that there was a raid and not a sign of light must be shown. This continued to the outskirts of Paris which we found very calm, there having been no signal given here

We rang for some time at our door before Leonia let us in. Nobody else in the place. Logan has not come. Stetson is still in Switzerland and Blount has gone to the country for over Sunday. So unpacked and to bed.

Log   Paris. Sunday, August 25, 1918

Though weary and lazy this morn there was no use staying abed late for noisy workmen arrived at the crack of dawn and began installing direct telephone to the censorship.

After breakfast Arthur [Page] and I went down to the chancery and I found enough mail to sink a ship that had been waiting for me all these days. Nobody about the Embassy so I could not pick up any news.

On the way home Arthur diagnosed Lansing's reason for staying on while the Col. [House] really settles all the important matters. He says Lansing knows he is not big enough for the job. That he is only 75 and that if he is to be used on a 155 gun it can only be by sub-caliber practice.

We lunched alone and then spent the afternoon cleaning up odds and ends of correspondence, etc.

Telephoned through to Chaumont and found that Col. Nolan was anxious to see me as soon as possible. Word has come from Washington that both State and War Depts. are opposed to having me do the job he picked me for and he is up a tree. It has occurred to me that the right thing would be to put Arthur Page in charge of the whole show and let it go with some snap. I said I wanted to go down and take Arthur with me. James telephoned around and the Press Division called up late in the afternoon to say that Bristol would escort us down in the morning and I chose eight o'clock as the time for starting.

Log   Paris-Chaumont. Monday, August 26, 1918

The motor was to have come for us at nine but did not, so I went to the Chancery and let if follow when it got ready.

Tinant and d'Oultremont came in hoping to be presented to the Ambassador, but he was away on leave.

Bristol turned up with Kloeber and Arthur Page at ten o'clock and we got away. Had a blow out in the Place de la Concorde and another shortly before luncheon, which we had at Nangis. Another blow out after leaving Nangis, and a forth about two block from the garage at Troye. It took about an hour to get fixed up there and we got into Chaumont a little before eight. Everybody had left Headquarters so we went to the hotel and had dinner, after which we learned that rooms had been engaged for us at the guest house and went straight to bed.

Log   Chaumont-Paris. Tuesday, August 27, 1918

Got started fairly early and piloted Arthur [Page] up to GHQ where we found Lippmann and Blankenhorn waiting for us, they having come down by the night train. Talked with them and James about enemy country propaganda until eleven when we went in to see Nolan, who has just got his star. There was a fine muddle with all the telegrams sent by Lippmann, Creel, GHQ, and finally the War Department telegram about my participation in the work. We talked until one and then adjourned until after lunch. Went back with Nolan to his mess where we found General King and a few others. James had to leave for Belfort and, at my suggestion, took Arthur Page with him. I decided it best for me to return to England at once so made arrangements to go back to Paris by the afternoon train.

After lunch, at Nolan's request, I prepared a telegram for the Commander-in-Chief to sign, to the Secretary of War on the general subject of propaganda in enemy countries. It was agreed that it might be a good plan for me to go home in the course of the next few weeks, possibly with Lippmann, in order to explain matters clearly. The final decision on this will depend upon developments in the next few days.

We talked until time for me to leave for the train.

At the station I ran into Frank McCoy who has just been made into a permanent brigadier general. He still had the eagles on his shoulder straps but young

Preston, his aide, had fastened the stars on his rain coat, so that you could have your choice. We got a compartment together and dined together. Frank looks very worn and thin. Says he weighs less then when he left West Point. He has made a splendid record, however, and is going strong.

Our train seemed to fly but nevertheless did not get into town until about midnight. The car which Frank had ordered had given us up and was gone away, but young Preston was a resourceful duck and commandeered a Red Cross ambulance which took us and our kit through a drizzling rain to our various homes. Frank is staying with Jim Perkins.

At home I found the lift broken down and had to carry my grand piano and kitchen stove up six flights of stair. Nobody there but Blount, who appeared sleepy-eyed and surprised at having me waltz in at such an hour.

Log   Boulogne-London. Thursday, August 29, 1918

A vile night in the train for Paris. There were four places in the compartment but six people crowded in while plenty of others stretched themselves out on the floor in the corridor and thickened the air as such a crowd can do. Most of them were soldiers getting back to their posts after leave and they found their way out through our compartment so that we were wakened by them at pretty well every station. As we started several people came in and sat down despite the protests of a French captain that all the places were reserved. There was an old civilian who immediately took up the cudgels with him and allowed that the company had no right to reserve places under recent rulings. They went at it hammer and tongs and afforded us a certain amount of amusement. However the night was not replete with gaiety and our bones were stiff as the night drew on.

At five o'clock or so we got into the station at Boulogne and I was fortunate enough to get a porter. Most of the trainload of people went on toward Calais and Dunkirk.

The Terminus Hotel was filled and I was told that if I cared to wait a room would be prepared for me when somebody left. I kept on with my porter and we tried several places, finally being admitted by a bird named Thomas who has a filthy place just off the water front. He came to the door in a pair of trousers and an open shirt and let us in by candle light. Up some dirty stairs which looked as though they had not been swept or scrubbed for weeks into an uninviting room which I would not have stayed in for a minute unless I had been at the end of my tether.

As it was I lay down as I was and rested hard until eight o'clock when I contrived to wash and shave and get away as fast as possible, eluding an insistent invitation to breakfast.

First to the dock with my bag to learn that the ship would not pull out until noon. I left the bag and struggled back to town where I found a 3rd rate place and had some coffee. Thence to the top of the hill for a walk. Bought some papers and sat about on park benches like a tramp trying to keep warm. Loafed up and down the docks looking at the performances of the fishing smacks, the antics of the ships cat, the delivery of provisions by tossing loaves of bread and other edibles onto the fishy decks, etc.

At a little before noon back to the dock where there was nobody ready to sell tickets or stamp passports. I lunched alone in the café and then resumed my wait. Ran into a Naval Lt. Hall and we aided each other to kill the time until we could get on board. At a little before one we managed to get on only to find that all the seats had been prempted by the British officers who had been allowed to go on board as fast as they arrived. Ran into Major Cunningham of the Naval Bombing Squadron with whom we had passed the night and together we hung to rails and otherwise kept ourselves upright during the crossing.

The crossing was rather interesting. There were four or five ships, all heavily camouflaged and bearing all sorts of burdens. We were filled with officers, there being only one other civilian that I saw. One other was filled with British wounded. Two with British troops going home on leave and the last with German wounded who looked fairly cheerful although many of them were stretcher cases. We had destroyers and trawlers and drifters floating about and a silver cigar[140] floating overhead ready to spot the gentle submarine.

As usual all the officers got ashore without difficulty and I came onto the dock just in time to see the first train pull out for London. There was another train soon ready and I contrived to get a place and landed at Victoria at about six o'clock.

At the Embassy I found Ned [Bell] waiting for me with rage in his face because I had not notified him of my coming. He soon allowed himself to be mollified and asked me to stop at his house.

Found a telegram from Mr. Asquith saying that he would be in town tomorrow at 12.15 and wanted to see me at Cavendish Square.

Went over to see Mrs. Page who had some callers but stopped long enough to learn the news of Arthur and tell me of Mr. Page. It seems that a very nice telegram came from the President accepting his resignation and they are going home sometime between the 20th and 25th. Mr. Page will come down in time to do the strictly necessary visits which are to be as restrained as possible, – the King, the Prime Minister and Mr. Balfour. Other people he simply will not see no matter how many noses are put out of joint. There is no time to worry about how they are going to

---

140 Probably a Zeppelin.

feel for he must be kept just as well as possible till he can get home and get to work resting. Mrs. Page had thought they would stop a month or two in New York but he wants to get straight away to North Carolina and so they will do that.

Went to Ned's for a much needed bath and to dress for dinner and then to the St. James' Club for a war time dinner with a bottle of the bhoy which tasted good. Ned looks well and is as full as ever of interest in life.

We yarned about everything until an advanced hour of the night and got to bed at half past one.

Log   London. Friday, August 30, 1918

Got started betimes in the morning despite the fact that I could have done with a reasonable amount of sleep. Saw most of the crowd although Frank Gunther was at home in the country enjoying the flu. Ran into Thomas Nelson Page who dragged me off to walk the streets with him and discuss some of the troubles of the situation in Rome. It seems that Merriam has got on his nerves because of the fact that he has continued logically from the start he made while I was there. He persists in considering himself a commissioner and trying to report to Creel on all sorts of political affairs which are none of his business. The Ambassador wants the COMPUB stuff made a part of the Embassy activities, or at least to have the COMPUB representative impressed with the idea that they are under the rule of the Ambassador. He is right but I don't see any chance of having it done. The COMPUB people in every capital have made a mess of things but there seems to be no idea of putting things right. Thomas Nelson Page asked me to lunch but I had to decline.

Went to Cavendish Square at 12:15 and saw all the family, that is to say, Mr. and Mrs. Asquith and Elizabeth. Stayed on until three and then back to the Embassy.

Telephoned Lewis Richards who came straight up to see me and enjoy a talk. I enjoyed it at least. He is a good deal exercised as to whether Hoover has use for him or is merely keeping him on because he is too kind hearted to throw him out. He has these doubts every little while since 1916 and it is rather hard to know what to say to appease him. He is quite devoted to Hoover but worries a good deal because he has never been given a chance to show what he could do since the early part of his service in Brussels where he undoubtedly did fine work. I must remember to get Hoover to write him some sort of letter which will put his mind at rest and let him settle down to what he is doing now.

After him came Merz who is deep in the work he was left here for. I told him what I had gathered at GHQ as to the general situation and he about died on the spot. He is not particularly interested in the propaganda side of the work but wants to do something big with political intelligence. My opinion of him went up several degrees at this. I am to try to find out something definite as to his future and have him ordered over to GHQ if desirable to learn where he stands.

A good talk with Laughlin who seems to be in a bad way nervously. He demands somebody to act as understudy and take a large part of the burden off his shoulders. His desires inclined towards Joe Grew and me, naturally first toward Joe who would undoubtedly be well suited for the work, better than anybody else I can see. As a matter of fact I suggested Joe when he first brought up the subject.

He is also highly indignant with the Department because they do not understand how to handle business arising under our military service convention with Great Britain. It seems that there is a good deal of trouble because Americans living here have no papers from the Embassy to show that they are not liable to military service or that they have been rejected. The Department will not permit the issuance of such papers though it is hard to see the objection if the people can prove their cases. The Department cannot seem to distinguish between such papers which are merely to put facts on record and the granting of the exemption itself. I promised that I would take the matter up if I went home and get some action along the line he desired.

Dined alone with Ned [Bell] at his house and talked until after midnight.

He told me at last the true story of Stephen Van Rensselaer about whom I have had a certain amount of correspondence. It seems that not long ago DID [Diplomatic Intelligence Division] began picking up code messages from the Hun Ambassador at Madrid [Ratibor] referring to the services which could be rendered by a "neutral diplomat who has recently entered our service." Soon after it was said that he would soon proceed to London and could gather any information that was particularly desired there and the Foreign Office was asked to inform the War Office and the Admiralty so that they could ask any questions they had ready. Among other things it was said that his wife was in London so that he had good excuse for going there. There was a long interchange of telegrams which narrowed it all down to Steve and so DID was ready for him but he never came. He stopped in Paris and has been here ever since trying to get into our G-2 service. It does not look as though he were merely having his leg pulled but the French are now watching him carefully and we may have something to say to the young man before he gets through. It's pretty sickening.

Scholle has resigned from the service and sent announcements to all his former colleagues to the effect that he has opened the practice of international law – whatever that may mean – in Washington.

When we got up this morning we were astounded to read that the police force is out on strike. They made certain demands for an increase in pay and it was eventually granted to them. They then demanded that one of their number who had been suspended for pernicious activities be re-instated. So far he has not been put back and the whole crowd walked out. Of all the outrageous things in the world this is the most topsy-turvy. I expect to see the clergy go out next.

Log   London-Southampton. Saturday, August 31, 1918

Went with Ned [Bell] to the chancery and saw some of the crowd for more or less idle talk.

Went over to see Mrs. Page and get any letters and messages she had for Arthur. While I was there Elizabeth Asquith came in, also Shoecraft.

Called on Admiral Sims before lunch and had a few minutes talk. He was evidently busy and has people waiting to see him so I did not stay as I should have liked. Ran into Stockton and Tobey and other old Navy friends. Quite like old times.

Lunched at the chancery with the crowd and got away early with Ned Bell to Waterloo whence we were leaving by different lines for the country. Frank Hodson was there with all his dignity and was entranced to mingle with Jerry Gherardi, Senator Jim Ham Lewis and other people I knew.

Jerry and I rode down together and had a good yarn.

We were quickly put through the formalities on the dock by the British officials who are always more polite to my mind than any other people in the world. Once on board and settled into a couple of berths in the saloon Jerry and I made our bow to Senator Lewis and tried to go ashore. The man at the gangplank told me flatly that I could not go ashore as it was against all the laws of the land. I growled somewhat and stepped off onto the dock beside him so as to let a lady pass, whereupon he pushed me roughly further onto the dock and I found a landing ticket in my hand. He is evidently a man of experience and manages these things well. I rewarded him with much treasure concealed under the ticket when we returned aboard.

We went up town and looked for food, finally settling on the QUEEN's HOTEL where we had a combination of tea and supper, getting back to the shop at seven.

This little ship, the VERA, is loaded to over flowing, largely with Belgians and with YMCA's of the most offensive fresh type. Several of them have already picked up French girls of doubtful appearance and are making themselves conspicuous. The organization is not gaining any credit by the appearance of these young huskies who look as though they ought to be in the trenches.

We are due to shove off at eight for Havre.

When we left London the police strike was still in full blast and parties of the big thugs were marching about the town trying to look fierce. Whitehall was filled with soldiers with rifles and tin hats who looked effective. The Govt. ought to take all the police and send them to the front and replace them with soldiers who would do the work well and try on no such monkey business as strikes.

Log   Havre-Paris. Sunday, September 1, 1918

Another filthy night with the good ship trying to shake herself to pieces and lots of people sick as they could be.

I got up before daybreak and so contrived to get a wash and a shave. Found poor Senator Lewis with his pink whiskers done up in a silk handkerchief too far gone to get started on his day. After a cup of tea he revived and got ashore soon after we came into the dock.

The American embarkation officer who said he had heard me when I talked at the Princeton Polity Club, came on board and took us off before anybody else. A British Naval Officer also got busy on our behalf and there was a car waiting to take us to the station. The British Naval courier en route to the Gibraltar stood around our neighborhood until I began to get suspicious. Finally he drew near in good stage manner and whispered soft and low: "You're Gibson aren't you?" He looked as though he expected me to give a sign of some sort and after I had failed to understand long enough said that he had been told by the Admiralty to look after me on the trip, but that he had verbal orders that nobody was to know who I was and that my trip was to be put through as mysteriously as possible. Why the mystery I don't know unless somebody was trying to have fun with the poor man. However we went forward to the dinner with the Senator and had some breakfast, leaving him with many mutual expressions of good will, etc.

We drew into the Gare St. Lazare at 12:30 after a trip in which the Senator gave us his views on varied subjects, relapsing into sleep between whiles. I declined a luncheon engagement with him and came on home expecting to find Arthur [Page] and Stetson. They had both gone out to lunch and there was a telephone query for me from the chancery I went down there only to find that everybody had gone. There were a lot of letters including a fat one from Mother.

Lunched alone and settled down in the studio to attend some accumulated odds and ends.

Log   Paris. Monday, September 2, 1918

Came down to the chancery fairly early with Arthur [Page] and found Lippmann waiting. We talked shop steadily until lunch time.

G-2 D has accepted Arthur's services at the rate of $1 per year and he has been given the handling of printing for the propaganda. All other phases of the question are in abeyance pending instructions from Washington. Secretary Baker is now on his way over and we should get some things settled by him.

Townsend and Lippmann came home to lunch and in the afternoon our chatter resumed.

We dined with Martin Egan and Sir Connop Guthrie at Voisin and had more talk.

Log   Paris. Tuesday, September 3, 1918

Down betimes in the morning had a day devoted largely to talk and dictation.

A telegram from Phil [Patchin] saying I should come home as I suggested. I want to wait long enough to see Baker and then get underway.

Cal O'Laughlin came in to lunch and told of his visit to Switzerland. He thinks Mrs. Whitehouse will do well if she is given support. Left me a long report to read on conditions as he found them.

Late in the afternoon ran away as my head stopped working.

Guthrie came home with us for a talk.

Mrs. Whitridge and Miss McCook to dine.

Log   Paris. Wednesday, September 4, 1918

Down to the chancery after ten for sessions with Lippmann, Arthur [Page], Gifford, Arthur Lane and others.

Lunched alone with Stetson. Both of us getting about to the end of our strings in civilian jobs and trying to devise ways of getting into uniform and to the front. Neither of us get any thrill out of the idea of a uniform to do a civilian job and that's what they want both of us to do.

Good news continues to come in. Last night's communique ticked off 10,000 more Huns in British hands and 14,000 in the French nets.

Log   Paris. Thursday, September 5, 1918

Walter Gifford, Director of the Council of National Defense came in this morning to talk about post-war economic problems. Not knowing anything about the subject, I passed him on to Frazier who will probably take care of him. Walter Lippmann and Arthur Page came in and passed a good part of the morning, as usual, talking about propaganda.

After lunch Tom Felder came in from Switzerland with a good bag. By some sort of porch-climbing methods he got away with a large budget of German correspondence, pretty conclusively proving the Boches' intention of using the material in question in Germany, Switzerland being merely a blind. Felder will, probably, have to return to Switzerland to finish tying them up. He is to take a few days off to translate the papers and to prepare a memorandum.

After seeing him went round to the Hôtel St. Anne and signed for our passports to Chaumont.

On the way back stopped at the Ritz and Continental in the hope of finding Martin Egan and taking him home to dine. He was not there, but eventually got him by telephone and he came out.

Letter to Mary Gibson. Paris. Thursday, September 5, 1918.

... Today lunched with the Ted Roosevelts who also bade Martha McCook and DeLancy Jay, the latter with his shattered arm strapped to a board. It was his first time out of hospital and not a success as he had to leave the table to go upstairs to lie down. This sort of thing gets pretty rough on the slacker in civilian clothes and I don't know how much longer I can stand it. Of course they all tell you you are doing more valuable work as a civilian but it looses the power of conviction in time. We shall see what we shall see. ...

Log Chaumont. Friday, September 6, 1918

A little after 7 picked up Walter Lippmann and, together, we caught the 8 o'clock train and had a gigantic sandwich at Troyes. For some strange reason, the train was only an hour late. We were met by Lieut. Bristol who took us straight to GHQ.

We had a long talk with James about various phases of the propaganda question and then went over it all with Nolan from 4 to 6. I submitted my memorandum on Political Intelligence which Nolan approved in principle. It will have to be submitted to the Commander in Chief. Nolan says he will do that at the first opportunity. The only condition was that I put on a uniform and take charge of it, but we left that question in abeyance.

Dined at Nolan's mess. Cabot Ward was there with the General Staff band on his arm and a general air of improvement. After dinner we all went back to GHQ.

I worked with Lippmann on some tracts until after eleven. Arthur Page had started down on the train, but as he had not arrived by eleven, I went back to the guest-house to bed.

Log   Paris. September 7, 1918

Spent most of the morning visiting around GHQ. Had a short talk with Nolan and held him up for Frs. 10,000 for some immediate necessaries. There is plenty more where that came from.

At 12 o'clock lunched with James, Lippmann, Blankenhorn and Arthur Page at the YMCA hut. A stuffy old Colonel came in and complained to the girl at the cashier's desk that he was very much annoyed by the hornets and that something must be done about it. She looked at him unsympathetically and answered: "Yes, this is a very terrible war." Which was all the change he got.

At 1:30 James, Arthur and I set out in a General's car and came through without even a blow up, getting to the Ritz at 6:30.

Found nobody at home so Arthur and I dined together.

Log   Paris. Sunday, September 8, 1918

Came down to the Chancery fairly early and found Senator Hollis on the stairs. He had just received a telegram that his son, an aviator, had been killed and wanted to get any more news that he could.

A note from Ed Bell saying that Crosby is leaving for home, also that he, Bell, has been promoted to Class 1.

At 11:30 went to the Roosevelts where Jim Logan, Martha McCook and Arthur [Page] were gathered together for a trip on the river. As it was raining hard we abandoned that and went to Foyot's to lunch instead. After that came back to the rue de la Pompe and then on to Stetinius's flat in the Avenue Henri.

[Lawrence] Martin for tea. Arthur and I came back to dine there and spent a long evening with Jim Logan wrangling as to whether we should bring over more troops regardless of supplies.

Log   Paris. Monday, September 9, 1918

Throughout the day we have the usual session with Walter Lippmann and Arthur Page.

Mr. Baker arrived here in the morning and came in for a few minutes' talk. Ralph Hayes was with him in a private's uniform and more fuss was made over him than over Gorgas and other generals.

Lunched at Voisin's with Arthur Page and Martin Egan.

Called on Mrs. Whitehouse at the Vendôme and found her considerably cheered about the way her work is going in Switzerland. She came back to the Chancery to send some telegrams and then disappeared into the void.

Maverick brought in Pierre Albin who wanted to tell me how to tell the President how to arrange the war, which he did at considerable length.

Felder came back with the translations and a lot of memoranda of various things he had observed in Switzerland, some very good and some without value!

Walter Lippmann had a talk with Mr. Baker at 3. He seems to have taken it for granted that the army would handle the entire question of propaganda over the lines and surprised to find that there was any question of it. On arriving at Brest he found a telegram saying that the President desired the army to refrain from any activity in the matter. That Lippmann was to report to him and Blankenhorn had been ordered to stop all work.

On reaching Paris another telegram was waiting intimating that the President had been under a misapprehension and that it was all right for the work to go on. The Secretary is going away tomorrow morning but will be back on Wednesday when we are to have the memorandum on the whole subject ready for him. He will then telegraph Washington in the hope of straightening matters. I shall not go home until we have some sort of decision.

Walter and I put in the latter part of the afternoon blocking out our Memorandum and then went to Voisin's to dine with Arthur and James.

Put Arthur on the train for Boulogne and then went home to my deserted dinner party with consisted of Sir Francis Elliot, Craigie, Blount and Stetson.

Log   Paris. Tuesday, September 10, 1918

In the morning Norman Davis came in with Senator Hollis. He was just back from his trip to Spain and ready to set out for England in the evening.

According to him the situation in Spain is very doubtful and he did not know whether to be apprehensive or not. He had talked with Dato at some length and felt that he grasped the significance of the situation quite thoroughly although he is by no means a strong man. Dato said that he proposes to carry out this threat of taking ton for ton of German ships for shipping sunk He was in some doubt as to whether the Ministry would keep its nerve and support him and said that if they did not support him he would resign. Dato seemed to feel that Germany would accede to the [taking] of her ships if a formula could be found to save her face. Dato said the difficulty was increased by the fact that the formula must, at the same time, save Spain's face. There is for Germany the inconvenience of establishing a precedent as regards other neutrals in the same case as Spain.

Germany has, of course, every interest in keeping Spain neutral and preventing her from throwing in her lot with the Allies. Dato and some of the Ministers expressed apprehension as to what would be done by the 80,000 Germans in Spain. Davis called attention to what had been done by the million and a half of them in America. He also tried to make it clear that we do not want Spain to come into the war and send an expeditionary force to France. She could be of more use to the Allied cause by breaking off relations with Germany and then going to work to supply our wants.

In the negotiations about shipping, Germany has laid down the principle that the ships should only be used to South American ports and other places which the German Admiralty will dictate. Davis told Dato that in case they accepted Germany's dictation in this regard, we should be obliged to shut down on supplies of coal, which action would make her ships with just exactly nothing. Dato who, apparently, is something of a philosopher, said he was glad Davis had told him this as it gave him a weapon to use.

Davis also had a very interesting talk with the King [Alfonso XIII] who stands out head and shoulders above his mediocre Cabinet. The King went for him for the way the Allies had tried to browbeat Spain into doing what they wanted. He made the very sound statement that you can make the Spaniard do anything in the world if you go about it in the right way, but that we had taken an overbearing method which is the only one that is quite hopeless. Inasmuch as this is just what I have been preaching for a year I know the King is right. He went on to say that the American problem was relatively easy as Spain had pretty well forgotten the war of '98[141] and there was no real bad feeling left. He said that he and most intelligent Spaniards could understand that the Spanish position in the Caribbean could not be reconciled with the Monroe Doctrine, but he added that he did not see that that gave us any license to seize the Philippines. Davis replied that we had been amply punished for our sins and that Spain had her revenge for, ever since we got them, we had been scheming day and night for a dignified way of getting rid of them.

Davis seemed a good deal impressed with Willard's judgement and the ability to get things done. He put Charlie Wilson on the black list as being an obstructionist.

---

141 The Spanish-American War of 1898 ended Spanish colonial rule on the American continent.

Walter Lippmann, Ralph Hayes and Fred Sterling set off to lunch with me. In the street, we ran into Gil Stockton who is over to pave the way for Admiral Sims and we hauled him along with us. After lunch we came back and pooled all our great thoughts in a memorandum for the Secretary of War on the ever-blooming subject of propaganda.

James and Grant Forbes and Craigie came to dine with me.

Log   Paris. Wednesday, September 11, 1918

By way of a change had a quite morning so had a chance to write a few letters. Chris Herter accompanied by MacEachran and Storey of the Department of State stepped in on their way to Bern to attend the Presidential Conference.

They report that the Department of State is in a hopeless welter, because of the avalanche of work which has hit an inadequate staff.

Perry Arnold came home to lunch with me and I did a little unmalicious gloating. He had spent two months going over my trail trying to straighten out some of the tangles of George Creel's report. He has now thrown up his hands and plans to go back on the ship with me. He appears to have perfectly sane ideas about the work and how it should be done and together we may be able to hammer a little sense into Compub.

Woolley came in with word from the Secretary of War that he had sent W. Lippmann and Ralph Hayes to GHQ to talk to Nolan about propaganda and that the Secretary was writing a letter to the President on the whole subject, and that I should hear from him about it tomorrow.

Dr. Field came in after lunch on his way from London back to Bern. He had some interesting talk with Willie Tyrrell and got some specific instructions from him about the sort of things that [empty space in Gibson's original] Huns that came out across the frontier to chatter about peace terms. Dr. Field was very glad to have something definite to say.

The British authorities also sent him on a trip through the country to gather information and turned him loose in the Prisoner's Camp at Holyport and certain others. The Boche took him for one of themselves and talked with him very freely. Dr. Field thought they were very well treated and said that they had practically no complaints to make. I think it would be a good thing for him to go on a trip through France so as to get some first class knowledge to back up his statement when he goes back to Zurich. Blount is endeavoring to arrange the trip.

Went to see Mrs. Woods and had an hour's visit with her.

Dined with Mr. Stettinius who also had Logan, the Ted Roosevelts, Mrs. Whitridge and Miss McCook. When I came in I found the whole crowd trying to keep from laughing and waiting to see what I would say. It seems they had expected me to dine last night with Mrs. Whitridge though I had not been told. At 8:30 they telephoned to try and find out what was the matter and the maid went back to the drawing room and announced simply: "Monsieur Gibson ne viendra pas." [M. Gibson will not come]

Letter to Mary Gibson.   Paris. September 11, 1918

... Chris Herter turned up this morning with several people on their way to the conference in Bern in regard to prisoners of war. We had a good talk and are to have another tomorrow. I had lunched with Perry Arnold who is over here for Creel and is arrived at the decisions I made some months ago. He plans to go back home next week and ought to be of some use in getting action on a lot of things that have been bothering me. Jack Wheeler was also here from London and I enjoyed a yarn with him. People who do things and don't spend months working up to the point of the action are so rare as to be appreciated when they do appear.

In the afternoon I had a call from Dr. Field, the nice old Quaker whom I met in Zurich. He is coming to lunch tomorrow with Frazier so that we can talk about a lot of interesting things...

Log   Paris. Thursday, September 12, 1918

Censorship called up to say our offensive was launched at daybreak, they had no details as to places and progress made.[142]

Lambert came in in the afternoon with an account of some important article on Spanish neutrality which Censor had stopped. It looked good reading.

Ridgway Knight came in with some green corn [sic] and a small amount of conversation. Felder came in hoping to find Walter but went away to await his arrival. Edith Wills came in to get advice as to whether she should go home or not. She did not want advice as much as a chance to talk it over. The upshot is she will go home if Davis is sent to Russia, otherwise she will stay on with him.

A letter from Peter Jay. He is apparently having rather a bad time with Merriam. That gentleman has not abandoned his uniform as it did not give him suffi-

---

[142] On September 12, 1918, the three day Battle of Saint-Mihiel started. Launched under General Pershing's command, it aimed at pushing the retreating Germans further back. In the eyes of the British and French troops, its success established the AEF as a powerful Allied force.

cient rank. He has taken to calling on the Italian Cabinet Ministers and reporting to Creel on all sorts of political matters.

There has been a bad row with [Harold] Train because Merriam tried to telegraph to Creel a confidential naval matter which he had promised to let alone.

In spite of Jay's definite request Merriam took Edgell to see Gallenga immediately on arrival. Apparently he has run wild during the form of the AEF. He says that the British Government would gladly overlook the irregularity of our making a direct appeal to Ireland but I am not sure whether our Government would countenance it.

Dr. Field and Frazier came in to lunch and talked for some time afterwards.

In the afternoon Charlie Russell came in from Bern and said that Hugh Wilson would come to see me if there was yet time, so I telegraphed him to come at once.

Sir Horace Plunkett rolled in with news from Bob Bacon. He has taken on the Chairmanship of the Irish Committee on War Aims which has nothing to do aside from creating in Ireland an atmosphere favorable to recruiting – a nice simple job. He has worked it out that, as the women are the chief obstacles to conscription because of the opposition of the Church, the thing to do is to get them to serve. Once they are out of Ireland it is felt that most of the opposition will automatically disappear. He says that as [Ireland] has no auxiliary force of women working behind the lines, he proposed to organize a volunteer Irish unit as a result of a direct appeal to Ireland. [Gap in original text] absence of the Ambassador and there will be a fine young row when Mr. [Walter] Page gets back.

Davis, the Solicitor-General, who is here now on his way to the Prisoner's Conference at Bern, has accepted the post of Ambassador to London, but the announcement will probably not be made for days.

Logan came in for me about 7:30 and we went to the Ted Roosevelt's to dine. Just the four of us and Major [original text blank].

It was Ted's birthday, so........

Log   Paris. Friday, September 13, 1918

Quite morning, cleared up odds and ends. Lunched at Embassy with Mrs. Whitehouse, French lady and her daughter whom the Ambassador had met at Aix-les-Bains and George Sharp.

Just before lunch had a call from Maxwell Blake who is up on leave from Tangier, he wants to go to the front for a visit, but visits are being discouraged and General Pershing has given out an order that not a single civilian visitor should be admitted to the zone of the armies until further notice with the single exception of the Secretary of War.

After lunch found Walcott and Bell back from Rome, they are considerably wrought up about the state of the morale both in the army and the civil population and want to do something about it right away. As I have been crying in the wilderness for five months I am quite glad to have someone come and sway the chorus.

Arthur Orr came in late in the afternoon looking very badly but evidently holding himself well in hand.

Dined at home and sent Craigie off to the 10 o'clock train for England.

Log   Paris. Saturday, September 14, 1918

A fairly quiet morning at the chancery with a chance of writing oodles of letters and cleaning up accumulated correspondence and memoranda.

Dr. Field came in in the course of the morning and we had another good talk. He told me of a pathetic talk with the Minister at Bern [Stovall]. Said the old gentleman asked him one day what he considered of interest in the week's news. Dr. Field asked whether he had read a statement of the Turkish Minister that if the Allies would permit it, Turkey would open the Dardanelles and let wheat through for the neutrals. After talking it over for some time, Mr. Stovall led the way into another room to look at a map and "visualize" the situation. First he asked Dr. Field to show him Odessa, "the place where he understood the wheat was to come from." Interested to see that it was on the Mediterranean. Then he asked [about] the Dardanelles. Wanted to know what kind of food could be sent from Odessa and was surprised to know that they had any considerable supply of wheat there. After absorbing this he disappeared to write a dispatch to Washington as the matter was "of vital importance".

Walter Lippmann came back from GHQ without any particular news and came to lunch with me. He said everybody had cleared out of GHQ to go to Pershing's headquarters. Grobet and Maxwell Blake also came to lunch. Blake is a good deal of an ass.

A quiet afternoon at the chancery wrestling with the flu. Felder came in to talk over his affairs and I suggested that he come back on Monday and that we draw up some sort of narrative of his adventures for me to take home to Washington. It ought, as a matter of fact, go to the Department of Justice.

Stopped in for a cup of tea at Mrs. Whitridges and found quite a party, Mrs. and Miss Whitridge, Lady Edward Cecil, Lady Hartington, Lady Edward Cecil's daughter, Martha McCook and a Red Crosser named [Eliot] Cross.

At eight gathered up Mrs. [Eleanor Butler] Roosevelt and took her down to the France et Choiseul where we picked up M. McCook and Miss Morgan and went to the Ritz to dine with McFadden. Started home before ten and deposited the various girls along the line. Then Arthur came on home with me and sat up into the reaches of the night smoking and waiting for the American communique which did not appear until after half past twelve and was not worth reading. Our people evidently far ahead of anything that is mentioned in the official communique but we shall have to wait for real news with such patience as we can summon.

[hand-written note added] Mrs. Roosevelt told me of her Uncle George Alexander who enjoyed himself in his own way. One day they left him at a hotel in Switzerland protesting at the boredom of the place and swearing that he would enliven it. When they returned they found all the heavy British guests crouching behind the furniture on the porch while he harangued them. As they drew near he was saying in the most oratorical way "And we Americans shall never forget that you English have named one of the greatest cathedrals after our martyred President."

Log   Paris. Tuesday, September 17, 1918

Busy morning doing nothing.

Charlie Russell and Brantingham came home to lunch. Brandy has come over from Embassy in London to help George McFadden.

Charles Lyon Chandler came in in the course of the morning with a lot of things he wanted to have done, most of they were things that should be done, but are not likely to be accomplished. He has been ordered by his doctor to go home to America and expects to sail in the course of a week or ten days.

In the afternoon Felder came in and dictated the narrative of his last trip to Switzerland.

As far as I can see it has now become a matter for the Department of Justice to handle and I propose to hand it over to the Department of Criminal Investigation or get the Naval attaché to do it.

Chevrillon and Poland came in to see me late in the afternoon. While Hoover was here he suggested to Boret that he should have a representative at the Food Administration at Washington and Chevrillon has been chosen for the place. That complicates things very much for the CRB in Paris and Poland urged me to prevail upon Hoover to let Chevrillon come back. Poland stayed on to dinner.

Miss Moffat and Scott of the Red Cross also dined with us.

Arthur Orr left this afternoon with General Foulois. Arthur has been appointed Aviation Liaison Officer at Petain's HDQTS.

BRIEF NEWS REPORTS. CONFIDENTIAL
Vol.1. No. 27   Paris. September 17, 1918

From original sources.
The German areoplanes which came over Paris on the night of September 15th dropped in all some 60 bombs in Paris or the suburbs, some of these being time percussion bombs and others incendiary.

The damage done in the course of the first of the two raids was as follows:

In Paris:
    Dufayel Stores: Fire 3 stories demolished
    Boulevard Suchet: One killed
    Rue de Suez
    Rue de Panama
    Pré St. Gervais
    Rue de Steinkerke
    32 bis rue d'Orsel: 7 killed
    Gare de la Chapelle: important material damage
    40 Boulevard Montmorency
    Impasse de la Loi
    Rue Lecourbe: (3 persons killed by French shells)
    Total for Paris: 4 dead [sic], 15 wounded

In the suburbs:
    At Aubervilliers: The general stores containing cotton and food stuffs were set on fire and completely destroyed.
    On the Ourcq canal a barge was damaged.
    At Pantin: rue des Petits Ponts, 2 bombs fell on the railway track, cutting a line, and engineer and a fireman, who had taken refuge under a locomotive tender were seriously wounded. In all there were ten wounded here.
    At Sèvres in the Grand Rue.
    At Gentilly: French shrapnel fell Place de la Fontaine.
    At Vincennes, rue de France: 3 small houses one of which was uninhabited were destroyed.
    At Clichy: French shrapnel fell rue Robert, injured Protestant Church. Another French shrapnel fell 3 rue de Cousin
    At Charenton: in the bois de Vincennes.
    In the course of the second raid:

At Dugny at bomb fell in the yard of a sanatorium and killed a woman, 2 bombs fell on a field.

At Brancy one man was killed

The total killed and wounded in the suburbs is estimated at 2 killed and at least 20 wounded, the total for Paris and the suburbs therefore being 6 killed and 35 or more wounded.

2 German aeroplanes were brought down at Villiers-le-Bel.
The German wireless, dated Nauen September 16th, 2 pm makes the following statement as to these raids:

"By way of reprisals for the continual bombardment of German towns, our bombing squadrons dropped last night 22,000 kilos of bombs in Paris.

Yesterday we brought down 24 enemy aeroplanes and 15 captive balloons."

Signed: Ludendorff

Log   Paris. Wednesday, September 18, 1918

Poor Dr. Field turned up again this morning having been refused a visa by the Prefecture de Police. Their behavior has been getting steadily worse and it was agreed that Frazier should go to the Foreign Office and make a formal complaint.

Lunched with Cabot Ward and talked over various things he wants me to discuss for him in Washington. Among other a rather complicated scheme to cover the Spanish frontier. He has been rather successful in bagging German agents under the guise of Spanish workmen and has succeeded in getting some of his I.P. engaged by the Germans and given full instructions as to how the work is to be done.

After lunch went over to the rue de Calais to see DeLancy Jay with a message from Peter urging him to have Blake examine his arm. He had just had an examination by Lambert. He did not feel inclined to have another, so I did not feel inclined to press the question.

Dined at home. Blount came up and brought his father and Hawes of the Delta Kappa Epsilon.

Before bedtime the censorship rang up to say that the British had attacked successfully west of St. Quentin and had advanced some few miles and taken 6,000 prisoners.

Log   Paris. Thursday, September 19, 1918

Walcott and Bell came in this morning to make arrangements for a courier to take their baggage to England so that they can fly over. Walcott is seeing all the great and the near great and telling them about the dangers of the Italian situation, and I judge that it loses nothing in the telling, but perhaps a little exaggeration is necessary to work people up to the very dangerous situation that exists there.

Lunched at Mrs. Whitridge's with Mrs. Whitridge Senior and Joan, Norman Whitehouse and Clemenceau's grandson, young Jacquemin and his new wife.

In the afternoon, Felder came in and put the final touches to his narrative. The naval attaché agrees with me that it is best to have the case sent to Office of Naval Intelligence so that they can take it up with the Department of Justice if they so desire. I shall stand by at Washington to help out if I can.

Walter Lippmann went to see Lambert and the latter came to see me in the afternoon, considerably excited because he had been pumped systematically, perhaps his knowledge of the situation was not equal to the test, but he objected strenuously to being left to Walter's tender mercies.

Dined quietly at home.

Log   Paris. Friday, September 20, 1918

Put my worldly affairs in order.

Went down to see Mr. Thomas Nelson Page but could not wait so left in the hope that I could return later.

Lunched with Frazier, Mrs. Page, Miss Stanton and McFadden.

Gallavresi came in with an Italian deputy named Balsini. They wanted to convince me that Italy needed help and Gallaversi telephoned the Ambassador to make an appointment for me to see him before I left. I will go tomorrow morning before half past eleven.

Log   Paris. Saturday, September 21, 1918

Arose swearing I would not do any real work all day and would put in my time loafing.

At the chancery found work from Bonin Longare the Italian Ambassador that he was most anxious to see me. Went over to see him at 11 and had a half an hour's talk. It was of course about the need for sending American troops to Italy but he developed, aside from the old stuff, some new ideas. Among other things he said that although Italian moral was bad the Austrians were also in bad care and whoever got started first was likely to come out on top. He is therefore anxious to begin in November when the western front is reduced to a sea of mud. There is another season down there that can be utilized and His Excellency is hammering on that thought. He did not mention any figures as to what Italy's requirements would be but took the sensible stand that we should throw in all we can if we decide to have anything to do with the idea.

He laid great emphasis on the fact that there was no thought of getting aid from France or outwitting her. He said that both he and Orlando had kept Foch fully informed since last March as to their plans and hopes. He added that Foch was now less hostile to the idea than when it was first broached. He was a good deal in the dark as to the present frame of mind of Pershing and Baker.

I made it clear to him that I had no mandate from anybody to talk about the subject in America and no faith that what I said would have any effect. He quite understood but said he would be glad it I would seize any opportunity to tell what I knew of the subject.

Found Walcott and Bell at the chancery. They had hoped to fly to England this morning but it is put off again and they now hope to go tomorrow. Walcott offered to arrange to take me along but I have no great faith that he will do it – or that they will fly at all.

Took Brantingham home to lunch to keep things cheerful to Blount who is laid up with the flu.

Dr. Guthrie came in after lunch and we had a little talk. A rather imposing spiritual advisor who must have been something of a burden at Cherry-heck [sic].

Topping came in with several odds and ends I can attend to for him.

Frazier came in for quite a talk about matters he wanted me to take up with Col. House. Above all he wants him to know something in detail of how the Embassy is running. It seems quite useless to talk about it as they must know – and more talk will not improve the situation. Fred tells me however that Bill Phillips is dissatisfied because he, Fred, has not put everything right. No subordinate can do it and there is no use sending over more underlings in the hope of accomplishing things that can be done only by the Ambassador.

The Ambassador [Sharp] has intimated that he wants Frazier to move up and take Robert Bliss' place – but he has evaded this. If it comes to a show-down he proposes to decline and ask the Col. to have him relieved altogether of chancery duties. This I am to convey.

Late in the afternoon went from the chancery to say good-bye to Edith Wills who is going home. She has been very ill and sees no prospect of getting better as long as she stays on here.

At 7:30 Jim Logan came by and took Stetson and me to the Volney, picking up Walter Lippmann on the way.

The dinner was the biggest thus far held as it was for the purpose of letting the English in on the weekly gatherings. The guests of honor were the Ambassador, the British Ambassador and Tardieu.

I sat at Tardieu's table with Gen. Henderson, Commander of the B troops in the Paris District, Gen. Harts doing the same for the American troops, Sir Charles Ellis, Bennet and Capt. Jackson, our naval attaché. We had a good deal of amusing talk. It was Tardieu's birthday [September 22, 1876] and that gave us a start. He was 42.

Tardieu made a good short speech and was followed by Mr. Sharp who put his foot in as usual. In praising his British colleague he said: "Lord Derby is doing so well that I am sometimes concerned less he surpasses me in popularity." Zowie!!

Pierre Bernus was as well as Carteron with whom I went to school. Among others Dolléans, Bertaux, Chevrillon, Reinach, Beneš, etc.

Home to bed at 12.

Log   Paris. Sunday, September 22, 1918

Frazier called me out of bed at 8 to say that while he was talking with Melville Stone yesterday afternoon, Roberts had come in and announced in some excitement that I was off for American on a special mission for Baker and Pershing to arrange for the sending of 7 American divisions to Italy. Frazier called their attention to the manifest absurdity of it and told them that while I agreed with Mr. Page's views I had no mandate from anybody to talk about the matter.

I got Blount to call up the Censor and order him to kill any story that might be filed about my trip.

Davis Wills called up to bid me good bye.

Craigie came in from London before breakfast on his way back to Bern.

Nothing at the chancery beyond a telegram from Hugh Wilson saying that his wife would reach Paris on the 25th and wanted something in the nature of a car to take her to the hotel.

Put the finishing touches on my office which I have ceded to Overbury as his bureau of accounts was getting crowded. I am to have his old place when I come back.

Spent the afternoon settling accounts and yarning with Stetson and Blount. Blount, Sr. came in also Wickes and Cable (and Fred Sterling after I had gone out).

I got into bed before the train started. Presenting the door opened violently and a large British Colonel surged in, very drunk and threw his kit bag on the floor, proclaiming all at once that he snored dreadfully and was sorry for me and that he had come to Paris with Havelock Wilson and that they had had a top hole meeting and that I was to send him any Americans who needed looking after in London or Scotland, etc, etc, etc, etc… His name was Colonel Murray Baillie and his conversation endless. He sat down upon his kit bag and regaled me with his experiences and views on every known subject. On cavalry, he allowed that there was none equal to the British. Of course, the French and Germans fought pretty well in 1800 "and that sort of thing" and in 1870 "but then they never beat anybody but each other."

Log   Boulogne-London. Monday, September 23, 1918

A wretched night with little sleep. Pulled into Boulogne at 7:45 in a pouring rain.
Breakfasted at the Gare Maritime and put in hours waiting for the boat to go at 11.
About 10:30 Walcott and Bell came along convoyed by Harold Fowler. We got onto the boat too late to get seats, but up-ended our bags and camped on deck. There was a sharp wind blowing a choppy sea and a lot of people were sick.
We rolled into London a little before 4 and I found Arthur Page waiting for me at the chancery to lug me off to stay at the Embassy.
We shopped and talked until dinner time when the Ambassador came in and joined up. He looks very shaky but keeps his spirit. Blessed old soul.
Pennington Sefton came in to dine and stayed until 10.

Log   London. Tuesday, September 24, 1918

Came to the chancery early and spent most of the morning writing telegrams hither and yon.
Shoecraft and Hurley lunched with me.
Soon after we had polished off some after luncheon work a telephone message came from Paris to say that the Dept. had reconsidered its decision and wished me to remain in Paris awaiting further orders. I at once telephoned Phil [Patchin] that unless the Department had some definite work for me to do in the immediate future I felt I should return to Washington because of various matters which required personal discussion. I urged him to reply at once so that I could sail with the Pages as arranged – or return to Paris to await instructions. I can't

imagine what they have up their sleeve – but it must be either that a general shift is imminent or that William Phillips has some idea of sending me to Spain.

At five I pushed off from Victoria [Station] with Laughlin and went to Red Hill where we were met by a motor and taken to the Priory. I had been there before when Mrs. John Gordon had it – but found it much more attractive now. Mrs. Johnson was staying at the house and she and Mrs. Liz Gertrude were gathered round the tea table while the son and heir – a good, solemn youth was gurgling in his nurse's arms.

The four of us dined alone and had a splendid old fashioned time tearing people's characters to bits. And did not go to bed until 12.

Log   Reigate-London, Wednesday, September 25, 1918

At 8 a solemn footman hauled me out of bed and down a thousand halls to a bath quite different from the one I had last night.

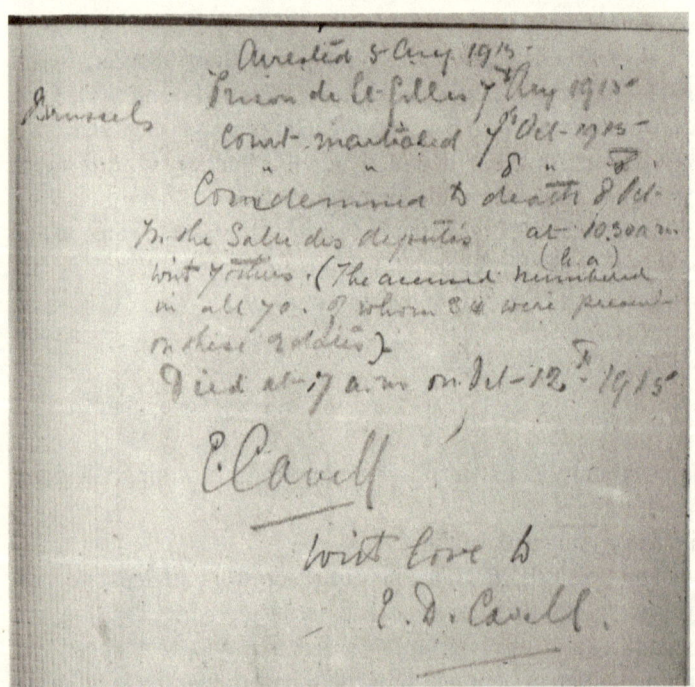

Image 14: The inscription page of the Prayer Book belonging to British nurse, Edith Cavell, who was executed by the German occupation force in Belgium 1915. She gave the book to Gibson during their last conversation during her final moments. He returned it to her family in 1918.

Mrs. Laughlin breakfasted with us and came up to town. Our train was slow but we could not really complain as the G.W. [Great Western Railway] is stopped in large measure by a strike and there is a general tie-up.

Put in the morning talking at the chancery. Gave Miss Cavell's prayer book to Ned [Bell] to be returned to her family.

Lunched at the chancery.

At 3 went up town with Arthur [Page] to help his mother buy some gifts to take home. In Old Bond Street, Mrs. Asquith put her head out of a cab window and hailed me. Puffin was with her. We had a minute's talk and then went our way. Several shopping errands with Arthur and thence to the chancery and home to the Embassy for tea.

Lord and Lady Reading came in to say good-bye. Arthur and I took refuge in our rooms and smoked while they were there.

Pollen broached a new idea to Arthur today. He said our form of Government had been quite changed and that we now did business in exactly the same way as Louis XIV. The only difference was that the President is married instead of having a mistress. There are courtiers more or less *"bien dans la manche du Roi"* [up the King's sleeve]. The only way to do anything is to reach him through one of these. The Ministers do not count unless they are also courtiers. He said this was a recognized form of government if we wanted to have it, but that it certainly was no longer what is set out to be.

Dined with the Ambassador [Page], Mrs. Page and Arthur. His Excellency in good form and evidently on the up grade.

The operations in Palestine are moving along with rapid increases in the number of prisoners.

German officials have started a barrage of speeches to explain away military reverses and there are some strange admissions, such as allusions to the "failure at Verdun" and other regrettable occurrences. I sat up and read them until after midnight. It is a comfort to see the Hun explaining.

Log   London. Thursday, September 26, 1918

Spent the morning at the chancery.

Quite early there was a telegram from Phil [Patchin] saying that Phillips had a mission for me which he considered urgent; that "he thinks he can cable" and that I will probably hear from him shortly. Lord knows what it can be.

Lunched at the chancery. Van Deman was there, back from Holland. He is having a bad time over the need for a passport control office and says the only obstacle is Skinner.

Campbell-Turner also there. He has been made a Major of the General Staff and seems to be doing well. In connection with his famous row with Einstein he says Einstein wrote home to the Department that he had been called a "-------" putting it all down in black and white. The Department ordered Campbell-Turner to apologize in writing which he did in this fashion:

"Sir-

In pursuance of telegraphic instructions from the Dept. of State I have the honor to apologize to you for having called you a "------."

At 4 went up to Sunderland House and saw Cravath for a little talk. In the doorway ran into George Booth and Dakins and had some chat with them. Norman Davis came in and allowed he wanted to see me before I got off for home. Crosby was there but I avoided seeing him.

At 5:30 went to Dudley House with Arthur to see Martha McCook. As we were trying to rouse some answers to the bell, she and Lady Ward came rolling up in a cab and we went in to tea. Mrs. Reid came in and a couple of other ladies who seemed also to be YWCA's. Martha seems to feel that her family may frown upon her returning to Europe and we agreed that a rapid bombardment of telegrams should be sent clamoring for her.

Lord Grey came to lunch at the Embassy today. His Excellency said that once Lloyd George had remarked that he hoped America would come into the war "so that when the peace conference came our calm influence would be brought to bear among all the savages." Mr. Page remarked that he did not think much of that as we would be just as savage as anybody else. Grey smiled slightly and said – "Well, I don't think he really cared so much for that. What he wants was that America should come in."

Dined at the St. James Club with Shoe – Sir Campbell Stuart and Capt. Greer. Home to bed before 12.

Log   London. Friday, September 27, 1918

When I came to the chancery this morning I found a telegram signed "LANSING" directing me to go back to Paris where I would "get instructions thru Ambassador Sharp." Whatever that may mean I can't imagine unless it is that I settle down and do Bliss' work while he is gone, though why they could not say so I don't understand.

Spent the morning writing a long letter to Phil [Patchin] about things in general and particularly about my own work and the urgency of my going home as I recommended.

Made reservations to go back to Paris on Sunday with Arthur [Page] but shall hope that the Dept. will change its mind again and let me sail.

At noon went with Ned [Bell] to the Admiralty to see Hall. Herschell let us in amid rejoicings and there were weird sounds from the staircase whence Gaunt descended in a block and embraced us. He has been knighted and decorated all over and is a tremendous feller. Hall came romping in covered with gold lace and there was another dance. It is the same great crowd and it was a joy to see them.

Hall had just got word from the War Office that the Bulgarian had asked the Br. Gen. command in the Balkans for a 48 hour armistice in order that they might sue for peace. This was not being made public for the simple reason that the brutal soldiery does not care to give the blighters a chance to make a peace. They want to keep fighting them so that Germany will be obliged to support them at enormous expense of man power and money and get more and more deeply involved. The Foreign Office has not, I gather, been informed of this little tidbit.

He [Hall] also had the midday communique which brought our prisoners up to 12,000 and chased the Germans off the map published in this morning's TIMES. The British have attacked opposite Cambrai and seemed to be going strong.

While we were there an officer named WHITFIELD came in, just out of a prison camp in Germany. Strangely enough he was one of the survivors of the Jutland fight[143] whose name came to the Embassy in 1906 and had been taken to Hall by Ned at the time. I remember Ned coming back and telling of Hall's joy that this fellow had been saved. It was rather strong to walk in on him today. He said he had had a rather bad time in some of the 7 camps he had been in and that some of the commandants had been swine. Hall was all for having their names and attending to them at the end of the war.

Hall is coming over to France in October and admitted that he would rather like to see something of our front. I wish to heaven we could give him a fine time. It won't be my fault if we don't.

Lunched with Ned and Etelka and afterwards had a look at the children who are really beautiful. The Muffin is as big as a young house and Virginia just as Evangeline was two years ago. They are good to see.

Spent most of the afternoon grinding out letters to Washington on various matters I had hoped to take up personally. Writing is a poor substitute for talk.

---

143 Most probably Paul Whitfield, lieutenant commander of the *HMS Nomad* which was sunk by the Germans in the course of the sea battle of Jutland in the North Sea on May 31, 1916. He survived and was captured by the Germans.

Late in the afternoon the papers came out with the news of the Bulgarian offer, put out by the Germans with the idea of creating the impression that it had been made by one lone Minister who had no authority from the King or Cabinet and had stirred up a hornet's nest of protest.[144]

Ned and I went over again to the Admiralty to see Hall.

It seems that the Spaniards have been bluffed by Ratibor's threats that Germany would consider as an act of war any action by the Spanish Government in taking Germany's ships to replace those of Spain sunk in the barred zone. Hall just happens to know through having decoded all the messages going from Madrid to the German Foreign Office that they don't intend to do anything at all and that they were only trying it on. Herschell writes a weekly letter to Alfonso and tells him all about everything he is supposed to know about and I doubt not that Her Majesty as been given a line on what the situation really is.

Dined at the Embassy as usual. Early to be after helping Arthur try on his uniform.

Log   London, Saturday, September 28, 1918

Got started early with Arthur and did some shopping in the neighborhood. Tried to find out whether there was any chance that Sims and Mayo were going over to France tomorrow so that we could go with them and possibly reach our destination tomorrow night instead of Monday morning. It was hard to get a line on the subject and nothing was accomplished during the morning.

Had lunch with Lewis Richards at the Carlton. He is pretty tired out with work on the CRB and is anxious to get into uniform. I shall try my level best for him but cannot bet on it.

After lunch Millard Shaler came in and we had a little talk. Mary is on the Isle of Wright with the children.

Jack Scranton called me from Crowborough. He also wants a commission and he wants it right away so that he will not be called under the draft.

---

144 In late Septemer 1918, British and French troops had entered Bulgaria, which haf fought the First World War on the side of Germany and Austria. The Bulgarian Army disintegrated, and a cease-fire was signed upon on September 29.

Log   London-Boulogne. Sunday, September 29, 1918

Got up at the usual hour and had a cheerful family breakfast.

At 11, Arthur and I caught the boat train from Charring and where Frank Hodson had made all arrangement and got us 2 seats in the Pullman for lunch.

Our boat pulled out in a drizzle at 1:20 and into Boulogne at 4. Hodson had a cabin for us on board and an A.P.M. saluting vigorously on the deck. Our bags were whisked over to the station and we were piled into a rattle-trap car which lasted only 100 yards or so and then broke down and landed us in the rain.

We got our sleeper tickets – as arranged by Hodson and then wandered the streets in the rain until we could break into the Phoenix for dinner.

A good dinner amid swarms of British officers and then in torrents of rain to the station whence our train pulled out at 8:27.

Log   Paris. Monday, September 30, 1918

Waked up this morning just as we were coming into the Gare du Nord and by rare good luck found a taxi and got whisked to 147 [rue de la Pompe] where Stetson let us in.

At the chancery found much ribald laughter at my return – and a telegram telling what it was about. I talked to His Excellency [Sharp] about it and found that the job was hardly worth tackling as it merely meant acting as a news scavenger for the Ambassador who would act as censor and would not permit sending of personal letters or impression. After some discussion I wrote a very frank telegram to Polk and Phillips telling them that the job was foredoomed to failure and that I was most anxious to go home and talk things out. They may come back and be abrupt over my insistence, in which case I see no choice but to resign and go into the army. I am willing to go on wrestling with hard jobs – but not with one that is clearly hopeless when taken up. I told them that if they answered at once I might still catch my ship this week.

Peter Jay came in this morning and we had a little talk. He is not coming to stay with me as he wants to be near his brother. He says that when Thomas Nelson Page got back to Rome and found out how Merriam was going on he cut a telegram home saying that either Merriam must be put under his orders or one of them must go home. He put in his telegram that on my arrival I could explain the situation although I did not know all of it.

Altrocchi came up from Rome also and asked me to help him get a commission. I gave him a letter to Cabot Ward and promised to take the matter up with Nolan.

Lunched alone with Arthur Page and spent most of the afternoon picking up loose ends.

Dined alone with Stetson.

Copy of Telegram received from Washington,   September 27, 1918

CONFIDENTIAL
AM Embassy. Paris 5723,   September 26/1pm

Image 15: Polish National Committee in Paris, 1918. Sitting Maurycy Zamoyski, Roman Dmowski, and Erasmus Piltz. Standing Stanisław Kozicki, Jan Emanuel Rozwadowski, Konstanty Skirmunt, Franciszek Fronczak, Władysław Sobański, Marian Seyda, and Józef Wielowieyski. (Public Domain)

The Government of the United States having given recognition to the Polish National Committee and the Czecho-Slovak National Council, both of which have their headquarters in Paris, the Department of State desires to keep closely in touch with them in order that it may be informed of their activities and aspirations, and in turn be in a position to offer such advice and assistance as may seem desirable. Both of these organizations carry on important work, and in this connection the Department of State has instructed Mr. Gibson to return to Paris, and desires him to act as Liaison between the Embassy and the Polish National Committee, and the Czecho-Slovak National Council and informally advise the leaders of both organization that you have been instructed to assign Mr. Gibson to them for this purpose, and should ask them to question him as your representative. On his part, Mr. Gibson should come to know personally the leading Poles and Czecho-Slovaks in Paris. He should report fully to you, and you in turn to the Department of State the opinions of these men, their personal characteristics, ambitions and the relative importance of the positions they occupy. The Department of State desires full information on the respective programs of the Poles and the Czecho-Slovaks: What steps are being taken to carry out their plans; What support is being extended to them from the Governments associated in the war, and what assistance they are looking for from the Government of the United States. Mr. Gibson should bear in mind that the Poles of this country, although nominally represented by Mr. Paderewski, are much divided, and that it has become quite impossible for the Government of the Unites States to form any conclusions in view of the violent dissension among those who regard themselves as the Polish leaders here. Officially, however, the Department of State looks to Mr. Paderewski as the representative of the Polish National Committee in Paris.

The following is confidential: The Department of State is prepared to advance to the Polish National Committee for its maintenance the sum of $30,000 per month for six months, provided this seems really desirable. However, before reaching a conclusion, or advising the Polish National Committee to this effect, the Department wished a report from you on the financial needs of the Committee; how this fund, if advanced, will be utilized, and whether, in your judgment, it should be advanced.

On Mr. Gibson's return to Paris you may show him this instruction, and express to him the Department's earnest desire to receive full information which the Embassy may transmit by mail. If, in your opinion, it becomes desirable for Mr. Gibson to visit Bern or even Rome to ascertain the activities of the Poles and the Czecho-Slovaks, you are authorized to send him.

LANSING

Log   Paris. Tuesday, October 1, 1918

Spent a day at the chancery waiting and marking time for my answer from the Department.

Arthur went out yesterday and found Wm Hackett and Louisa Haydock trying to make arrangements to get married. He agreed to get me as a witness and invited the wedding party to lunch.

At 11 we shoved off to the Meurice of the VIIth Arr. in the rue de rue de Grenelle. There were in our party young Hennen Jennings, Edward Clarke, Arthur and I. Another wedding party was ahead of us and disposed on in short order. The Maire [Mayor] was in his best clothes with his tri-color sash – a good kindly looking man who had a resemblance to the Duc d'Orleans. After going through the ceremony he made a very short quiet speech of good wishes in which he said that he hoped a good omen for their future happiness was to be found in its coming at the time that our armies were marching to victory on every front.

From there to the American church in the rue de Berni where the American religious serviced was held.

Arthur took the bride and groom on to 147 [rue de la Pompe] while I distributed the rest of the party about town in Logan's car which I had borrowed for the occasion.

At 1:15 we had a hilarious luncheon party composed of the bride and groom, Arthur, Stetson, Clarke, Peter Jay, Mrs. and Miss Whitridge. It went off well and we sent the happy pair off at 3 still uncertain as to where they were going.

The afternoon brought news that St. Quentin had been taken by the fzr [French]. Also a cock and bull story that Austria had sent an ultimatum to Germany demanding the acceptance within 72 hours, of President Wilson's 14 conditions. As is frequently the case such instances, it proved that the story came from Warburton's office.

Blount came in to dine and stayed until 11.

Log   Paris. Wednesday, October 2, 1918

Got up early and threw some things out to be packed for a possible trip to America.

On arriving at the chancery found a telegram signed Lansing saying: "Please carry out Dept.'s instructions." If that is the amount of consideration they have to show after 10 year's service I think they can have my resignation. I telephoned GHQ to see if I could reach either James or Nolan and inquire as to whether the offer of a commission was still open. They are both away with troops but may be back within a few days. If the offer still stands, I should like to telegraph back: "Tender resignation to take effect at once. Leaving Embassy today." Bill Phillips is to my mind the greatest curse of the service. He is camouflaged as the great friend and protector of the service and has not enough back bone to stand up for anything. I hope someday to tell him just how I consider him – but it will not be pretty.

The Ambassador took me into the sanctum in the morning and gave me a long a.b.c. talk about the Polish and Czecho-Slovak questions. The announcement that he proposed to send my reports verbatim with such comment as he cared to make.

Lunched with Mrs. Whitridge, who had also asked Arthur and Stetson, Miss Elizabeth Hoyt, Peter Jay and Lord Hartington. A strange mixture but it went well.

An afternoon largely spent in conversing with people who had no particular mandate to win the war.

Martin Egan and his wife came in to call I bade them to dine. Walter Lippmann and Ralph Hayes also came and we had a light and joyful evening.

Log   Paris. Thursday, October 3, 1918

A pouch in from London with 2 letters from Ned [Bell]. One regarding St. Van Rensselaer who has gone home to look for a commission. A copy of one of his letters to his wife now in England, complaining about her failure to send him his allowance. The main part of the story about him may or may not bet true but he is certainly short of money and a general damphool.

Ned also explains at length about the way Andrews uses the Embassy to do his errands and transmit his messages. Took it up with Fred Sterling who promises there shall be no more ground for complaining.

Will Irwin came to lunch with me and unburdened himself. It seems his part of Compub became so important, particularly as the need for propaganding the U.S. disappeared, that Creel, Byoir and Sisson turned envious eyes on his job. The first thing he knew he had been derricked out. He is now over here for the B.M.I. to investigate the principles of propaganda as carried on by the Allied Governments. He is also to send copies of his reports to Compub although Creel scorned the idea when it was put up to him.

He cannot find words adequate to damn Creel on every count.

He advanced his own theory as to the reason for Creel's standing with the President. It seems that every time Creel opens his lips the President roars with joyous laughter – so that Creel is Court Jester and beloved as such.

Will also remarked that Mrs. Whitehouse went home with a knife out for me because she feared I would be placed in authority over her. She has, he thinks, the ambition to be chief of all propaganda work in Europe.

The whole works in Washington and abroad is to his mind utterly worthless and even dangerous.

Wrote Phil [Patchin] a 4 page letter about my interchange of telegrams and my intention as to the future. It got off by this evenings bag via Brest.

A letter from Martha McCook saying she was sorry I was not going along.

Felder came in thinking he was hot on the trail of another plot to smuggle American food through Switzerland into Germany.

The Secretary of War [Baker] and Col. Van Deman are back. The Secretary goes home tomorrow. Van Deman comes to lunch with me tomorrow.

James is to be back at GHQ tomorrow and I may go down to see him on Saturday with Martin Egan.

Mr. Edgar Raikes (cousin of the King's messenger) came to dine. E. is over here at the invitation of the British Ministry of Information but has had little to do. He was full of amusing yarns about his various adventures including looking up his daughter's adopted child in the slums.

Walter Lippmann says that during his trip to our front our people captured the son of Hans von Herwarth. He seems to be quite a youngster – a Lt. in the Prussian Guard.

Log   Paris. Friday, October 4, 1918

Pa [Edwin] Watson came in this morning (now a Lt. Col with Major Shiverick). They are off for the Verdun sector and had only an hour or two in Paris so they did not stay long.

Had a little yarn with the Ambassador who has not yet got around to having me see any of the Poles or Czecho-Slovaks. I might just about as well have gone home to America for all I shall be able to accomplish in this matter.

Frazier handed me a dossier to read in which it appeared that he had written Auchincloss to find out why it was that the US Government was not paying its share of the expenses of Horodyski. Gordon wrote back a flippant letter in which he said that he enjoyed the dinners that Horodyski bought for our people with government money but that he preferred to have it paid for by the British. And intimated that hell would freeze over before Horodyski got any money out of us. Inasmuch as he played Horodyski up strongly and passed him on to us over here it seems a rather strange attitude for him to take to say the least.

He also said that he had not been able to do anything about money for the Polish National Committee. That they had tried hard to get a man in whom Col. House had confidence to come over and look after the administration of that money and get intelligence thru the Polish secret service. Just why the little Colonel should have the handling of it is hard to say. It appears to me that I may unwittingly be working for the Colonel.

Colonel Van Deman came home to lunch and we had a good talk about various matters including propaganda in enemy countries. He has very sane ideas on the whole subject, which is to say that he agrees with us. He is going to dig into the whole matter with a view to trying to straighten it out as soon as Kelley and Creel get over here. I hope he can get some results and that everybody can get to work.

Dined at home with Stetson and Arthur W. Page and got to bed at a reasonable hour.

Log   Paris. Saturday, October 5, 1918

When I got down to the chancery this morning I found a telephone message to say that Clarence Gagnon was very ill and wanted me to take him to a hospital. I learned from the British Embassy that I could take him to the Herford Hospital, 72 rue de Villiers, Levallois-Perret. Went over and found him in his studio being looked after for the time being by a Mrs. McPherson, a pleasant little American painter. He was evidently suffering a great deal but said there was nothing the matter with him beyond a little rheumatism. He had called in a doctor early in the week and had been given aspirin, nothing more. He was convinced that this was wrong and did not want to see the doctor again. He was quite ready however to go to a hospital where he could be warm and have the right sort of food and attention. According to his own story I was not at all sure that I could get him into the British Embassy Hospital so went off to find out about it. Had to walk almost all the way back and landed at the Embassy during the lunch hour when it was out of the question to pursue any inquiries.

During the morning the Ambassador made an appointment for Count Zamoyski, head of the Polish National Committee to come and see me. He came but I explained that I had to go out to look after Clarence and he agreed to come to lunch with me on Tuesday to talk things over. The Ambassador told him of my assignment and added "whatever Gibson says goes". He gave the impression that I was really to exercise some discretion in the matter; it will be interesting to see how long this will last. Dmowski, the regular head of the Committee, is in the US but will be back before long.

Dr. Axson, President Wilson's brother-in-law, came in during the morning and asked to see me to fix up his passport. He is over for the Red Cross, a big, soft-spoken man, who wanted to go to Italy but did not seem to care if he were obliged to wait.

Reggie Townsend came to lunch.

After lunch went over for Clarence and spent a solid hour getting a taxi to take Clarence to the hospital. Finally got a decent driver and got Clarence dressed and into the cab. He seemed to be just on the verge of delirium and not at all sure either in his thoughts or movements. The old concierge was good and helpful and we got away easily.

Dr. Moore received us at the hospital and after one look at Clarence and feeling his pulse, called for a chair and had him carried upstairs. I waited while he made an examination. When he finally came downstairs he looked very grave and said that Clarence had an unusually bad case of flu with bronchial pneumonia to aggravate it. He sent the secretary up to take down all the facts Clarence could tell about himself. He was on the point of going out but the Dr. said that Clarence might no longer be able to talk in the morning and that it was essential to learn everything possible this evening. If he had been taken in hand early in the week instead of being left without care in that wretched studio all the time, he would doubtless have a better chance than he has now. There seemed to be nothing I could do for him so I came away and dropped the Dr. at the Astoria where he also had work to do.

Came by the chancery and gathered up some odds and ends to be attended to tomorrow.

Blount had telephoned that the Central Powers have today made a peace offer. A little after noon a story came thru from Switzerland to say that Germany had made an appeal to the President at the instigation of Turkey for a general armistice with a view to discussion of terms. The censorship had stopped it and forbidden publication but later in the afternoon the news was confirmed and the govt. decided to release it for publication tomorrow morning. The *mot d'ordre* [watchword] was passed out that this was merely a political trick to usher in Max of Baden with the proper setting and rally to his support the discontented elements.

I telephoned the news to the Ambassador and put in a call for GHQ but did not get thru.

Also reported that Ferdinand of Bulgaria has abdicated in favor of his son.

Feeling very groggy with the flu so took a hot bath and got early to bed after setting back the clock for the end of summer time.

Log   Paris. Sunday, October 6, 1918

Woke up this morning and found the papers filled to overflowing with the "peace offer". Sent out and got everything that was printed and put in an interesting morning. Generally little importance is attached to it aside from the political maneuvering idea which was put out by the govt. The OEUVRE alone intimated that it would be well to consider it carefully.

Fortunately the President had twice pronounced himself recently in regard to the reception to be accorded to peace overtures.

Boris has come to the throne in Bulgaria while Ferdinand eclipses himself with a sob manifesto to the people.

The hospital reports that Clarence is about the same and that his condition is very bad.

Spent the whole day in bed and got some reading and writing done aside from have a tremendous visit with Arthur Page and Stetson. Read all of *Philip Dru, Administrator*, published anonymously by Colonel House.[145] Blount came in late in the afternoon and stayed on for an hour or so. Poland came up just before dinner with a mind full of all sorts of things, including ways of winning the war. He was earnest about doing something to make sure that the Hun would not destroy Brussels and other Belgian cities. He made the simple suggestion that we notify Germany that for every city they destroy we would wipe out a German town of corresponding size; that when the time came we should send word to Cologne or Mainz or Heidelberg that the population should clear out so that the town could be bombed off the map at a certain time. I offered objections: 1) that we had not sufficient air supremacy to try anything very fierce, 2) that it was just about impossible to "bomb a town off the map", and 3) that by giving the impressive warning he suggested we would merely give the Huns a chance to bring up all their guns and punish us when we appear. Poland seemed somewhat depressed and said he had not thought of those things. It is something like Frank Page's idea of sending out as many planes as might be necessary and kidnapping the Kaiser. It could probably be done but what would we do with him when we got him?

Poland was also filled with the idea that we ought to be studying the economic problems after the war. He was surprised to learn that the French had people working on these problems and his surprise knew no bounds when I told him that we too were working on them.

---

[145] A futuristic political novel by Colonel House published in 1912, which according to some historians predicted certain features of Woodrow Wilson's policies during his first term as US President. House allegedly had lend Wilson a copy to read on a trip to Bermuda.

Log   Paris. Monday, October 7, 1918

Got up early and trotted down to the chancery to learn what there was to know about the answer to the German peace overtures. To my great surprise I found that the Ambassador [Sharp] has chosen this as the time to go on a trip to the front and that he had taken Dawson with him so that there was not a line of any description going home from Paris. Frazier was active and got Walter Lippmann to help him out by reading the papers and going to see Albert Thomas.

Lloyd George had come over as soon as the news broke and Bonar flew over in a plane so as to lose no time. Orlando was here and had promptly sent for Sonnino who arrived in time for a meeting this afternoon – a meeting at which we were not represented.

The hospital reported that Clarence had made some slight gain.

Stayed at home in the afternoon, wrote a lot of letters and combed out some of the dossiers about Poland. At seven I went down to the chancery in response to an urgent appeal from Fred [Sterling] who had received word that a delegation of French Deputies were on their way up in a state of excitement after seeing Pichon. They were arriving when I came in the door, three mussy looking socialists including Marcel Cachin who is my idea of nothing at all. They had been to the Quai d'Orsay to present the text of the message which the socialist congress had addressed to the President. Pichon had promised them to transmit it but they wanted us to "*prendre acte*" [take note] of his statement so that we would know, evidently so that they could brand him as a scoundrel if he failed to effect the delivery. They wanted to come back later when they could deliver the text to the Ambassador and Fred fixed them with an appointment for noon on Wednesday.

Arthur [Page] brought home Percy Jennings to dine. He is now a Major in the aviation supply service. Blount came in after dinner and spent the evening. We hung upon the telephone to the censorship in the hope of getting some news as to the President's reply, but without avail.

Andrews reports that some wit in England refers to Whitlock's book as IN BELGIUM WITH GIBSON.

Log   Paris. Tuesday, October 8, 1918

Was called early this morning by Horodyski who had just come in from Switzerland and said he would call at 11:30.

The morning brought the news that there was a general attack, one between Cambrai and St. Quentin, one north of Rheims and another in the Verdun sector. All seems to be going satisfactorily.

Brought home Count Zamoyski to lunch with me and talked generalities about the Polish question. He is preparing a map and a memorial designed to enlighten my ignorance and has promised to send me some of the books I want in order to get some of the elements of the question which I am supposed to be an authority on.

Horodyski is wrought up over a story that Hugh Wilson is to be sent to London because that post has nobody that can run the chancery properly and the new Ambassador feels that he needs somebody of experience to help him get started. I don't for a minute believe that he will be moved for any such reason as that but it is quite in the cards that he should leave Switzerland and it would be deplorable. I turned Horodyski over to Frazier with the story in the hope that he might take it up with Auchincloss.

Spent the afternoon hammering away on several dossiers I brought home with me. The telephone rang chimes from time to time but there was nothing of importance and I got thru everything I had ahead of me.

Stetson did not dine at home so Arthur and I dined alone and got early to bed.

Log Paris. Wednesday, October 9, 1918

Blount called me from the censorship a little after nine to read me the text of the President's message in reply to Max of Baden. It was not really a reply but merely an inquiry on which an answer could be based. The more I think about it the better I like it for it puts it up to Max to say what he really meant and whether he has capitulated. Also he has to do some adroit answering as to the charges in the German government.

Blankenhorn came thru from GHQ still filled with enthusiasm as to the effects of propaganda. He had some leaflets that the Germans have been dropping on the allied troops to incite them to clamor for peace. The leaflets are got up on different lines for the different armies. Those for the French emphasize the fact that the Allies has been ruining the country in France and that a continuation of the war will only make things worse in that regard. Nothing of that sort in the leaflets dropped on us and on the English.

Dr. [William O.] Thompson, President of the Ohio State University where Joe Grew and I spoke last January, dropped in this morning. He is on an agricultural commission that is studying the questions of increased production. He has been on the go for some weeks and is about all in. Tomorrow he sets out for the French and American fronts but expects to be back here before long and says that he will come in again. He was enraged by the sight of destruction at St. Quentin and Péronne and says that to his mind the thing to do is to keep all German prisoners after the war for as long as may be necessary to clean up the mess, rebuild the towns and restore the fields to cultivation. That might make a threat that the Huns would listen to.

Peter Jay came up and brought his brother [DeLancy Jay] to lunch. He does not look well but is much more cheerful.

Log Paris. Thursday, October 10, 1918

Went down to the chancery although I had little or nothing to take me there and spent the morning getting out from underfoot of the various people who have adopted my desk as their own.

Frazier said he went out to see Lloyd George yesterday afternoon and as on the previous day had to pursue him about the gold links at St. Cloud in order to talk shop. It seems that Clemenceau, Lloyd George and Orlando have sent a telegram to the President telling him something of their views and intimating that as we are only stockholders in this war anyway it behooves us to consult them before we tell the Huns anything more about conditions. They seem to have been a good deal upset by his having made his preliminary answer without previous consultation with them. Lloyd George asked Frazier whether he knew what Clemenceau thought about the Fourteen Conditions. With a sardonic smile he suggested that it might be worthwhile to ask C. what he thought about them as his views were pronounced.

They all joined in asking the President to send over a diplomatic representative, which probably means that Col. House will soon be in our midst.

In the course of the morning I had a little talk with the Ambassador who is not getting much forrader with presenting me to the people he wants me to deal with. He has been away most of the time since the German note was sent, but has made up for it by writing a twenty page account of the destruction he saw at the front in places that were taken by the Huns as much as two months ago. He proposed to cable it all to the Department for the information of the President but Fred tried to dissuade him by saying that he could achieve his purpose by telegraphing a few lines and then sending on the descriptive material by mail. He was wounded in his finer feelings by Fred's lack of appreciation and I imagine he sent the telegram *quand même* [anyway]. The poor old chap works hard but has no discrimination and exhausts himself just as much on non-essentials as he does on the things that really matter. He read me a long telegram he had sent on Sunday purporting to give the state of the public mind about Max's offer. He had not seen anybody so far as I know but had elaborate analyses of the opinions of various sorts of people, winding up with the statement that all classes had the utmost confidence in the wisdom of the reply that would be made by the President "whose 14 conditions have the unanimous and repeated approval of all elements in the French Govt.", – this at a time when everybody was on tenterhooks lest they might be let down.

He has time to draft long descriptive articles about his trips to the front but no time to pass on material that is brought in by members of the staff. On Oct. 1st Dawson brought in a most interesting memo concerning the terms imposed on Bulgaria by Franchet d'Esperey. It was real stuff furnished him by the Ministry of War but so far not a word of it has been sent. As to the reply of the President nothing has gone in but accounts of complete approval, no mention being made of the not inconsiderable number of articles that have been censored because of their criticism of the answer: also no mention was made of the fact that the order had gone out from the Govt. that nothing of a critical nature was to be printed.

Dropped in to see Edith Wills late in the afternoon but she had gone out.

Blount and Jim Logan came in to dine. Jim was passed over again in the last list of promotions and is still a Colonel. He brought with him Reggie Huidekoper who has just landed and is to be at Chaumont. After dinner Walter Lippmann and Ralph Hayes came in bringing with them George Barr Baker who has come over to straighten out some of the kinks in the cable news situation. He has now been assigned to Admiral Sims' staff in London.

Log   Paris. Friday, October 11, 1918

Spent the morning at home with Arthur [Page] who laid up with a bad cold. There was nothing for me at the chancery so I did not go down to the office.

The advance continues on all fronts, particularly in the region of Cambrai and St. Quentin where the French and British are doing progidies [sic]. We have occupied the whole of the Argonne forest and are on our way to the Ardennes which would complicate things very much for the Boche.

The Secretary's statement which was scheduled for four o'clock yesterday afternoon has not been made. The Reichstag was due to meet this afternoon so there may be an answer to the President almost anytime. Some humorist suggested that the Huns ought to come back and answer the President by saying that they would be glad to enlighten him if he would be kind enough to tell them just what he meant by his Fourteen Conditions which were not at all clear. The papers here and in England are gently pointing the way to us by saying that of course no answer will be made to Germany until after we have consulted with them, and that it cannot be upon the basis of the 14 conditions, which are now out of date.

Went to see Edith Wills who has again changed her mind and now plans to go home about the first of November.

Paris. Saturday, October 12, 1918

Spent most of the day in idle conjecture as to the character of the German reply to the President.

Percy Dodge came in during the morning and spent half an hour or so. He is leaving at once for Serbia and expected to establish his headquarters at Nish, where the Serb armies should be by the time he can catch up with them. He is enthusiastic about the Serbs and about the Yougo-Slav question. He brought out the idea that a large part of the effort that is credited to the Czechoslovaks is really due to the Yougo-Slavs. He says that a considerable proportion of the military force of the Czechoslovaks is made up of Serbs and other Youg-Slav elements; that they found that nobody was familiar with them and that as they wanted to fight in the cause somewhere tacked themselves onto the tail of the Czechoslovak kits and have been fighting for them without getting any credit for it.

The French Government today picked up a cipher message being sent by wireless from Berlin to the German Ambassador at Madrid, advising that all German subjects dispose of their German securities and invest in Allied securities as the jig was up. This holds good whether an armistice is concluded or not, more especially if it is not.

Another message was picked up directing the evacuation of all munitions and supplies in the Laon salient. An answer came back to German GHQ saying that this was out of the question as there was not sufficient transport available.

The Hungarian Premier [Wekerle] has resigned.[146]

The papers generally give us a hint that although the note of the President is all right he will not do anything further or discuss an armistice without acting in harmony with the views of Foch who is the one to dictate the armistice. There is a good deal of talk to the effect that there will not be any discussion, that the Allies have won the war and that they will TELL the Huns what they are to do. There seems to be a certain amount of nervousness lest they be robbed of the fruits of their victory.

The Committee on Foreign Relations of the Senate has come out with a resolution saying that the idea of letting the Germans off now would be abhorrent to any right thinking American; that before anything of the sort can be considered it will be necessary for the Germans to withdraw from all invaded territory, restore Alsace Loraine to France, pay back the five milliards that were taken from her in

---

[146] After the Armistice that sealed the defeat of Austrian-Hungary, Hungary descended into chaos. Indeed, Prime Minister Sándor Wekerle resigned in the course of Count Karolyi's 'Aster Revolution', but only on October 23, 1918.

1870 and make other reparation that is described in detail. [Gilbert] Hitchcock and [Henry Cabot] Lodge indulged in what is described as a DEBATE although it seemed to consist more of a contest as to who could kick the Germans harder.

James arrived late in the afternoon with many interesting yarns as to the past few weeks at the front. He has had a lively time and several narrow escapes. Our people have evidently been up against it but are hammering hard and getting ahead.

Dresel and Blount came to dine and stayed late. Dresel says that so far as he knows there is nothing in the story that Hugh Wilson is to be ousted. He thinks Horodyski is given to sensational stories.

The telephone brought us news in the evening of further gains. A little after eleven word came that the German reply had been received but it was not until after one o'clock that we got the text of the message signed by Solf. The President's reply will show how well he chose his course in the first comeback.

Log   Paris. Sunday, October 13, 1918

Everybody was up early to get hold of the papers and read the German note and the comment of the editorial writers. The note came in so very late that the only comment was necessarily written as a tour de force, but the general trend of it was some misgiving as to what the President would do next. There is a good deal of soreness over the idea that we are preparing to stand between them and their vengeance. It is generally said that nobody on the side of the Allies has ever agreed to the 14 conditions and that they would like to know by what token we assume to settle the war on that basis.

Went down to the chancery in the hope of finding a telegram about Mr. Page but there was nothing all day. In the evening the TEMPS had a telegram from New York saying that he had arrived there dangerously ill and had been carried ashore on a stretcher to be taken to a hospital. I put the paper away so that Arthur would not see it until we got some sort of direct news.

Jim Logan came in to the Embassy very much upset because he thought the war was spoiling our hands.

Walter Lippmann came hope with me because he wanted to see James. He stayed to lunch and on thru the afternoon while James went to Don Martin's funeral.

Late in the afternoon James walked down to the chancery with me in the hope that there might be some message about Mr. Page but still there was nothing. He brought up the subject of my going into uniform and suggested that I get commissioned and go down to GHQ to help him run G-2 D. I should like it very much but don't want to get into uniform just as the war is expiring. If it goes on I shall try to get released from the service and go with him so as to be able to do a days work instead of loafing about the place in a decorative job.

Had quite a party in the evening, Davis and Edith Wills, Miss Larner, Miss Fowler (Harold's sister), Miss Margaret Mayo, and our own crowd. After dinner all hands sat on the floor and sang and spun yarns until midnight. Then the family settled down and shot craps for a couple of hours and the first thing we knew it was two o'clock.

Margaret Mayo says that she will bring her troop up and play for us some evening.

Log   Paris. Monday, October 14, 1918

Got a late start after our dissipated night but even at that found more time on our hands than we could use.

The morning papers show a good deal more soreness about the participation of the President in the show. Even the Ambassador admitted for the first time in my memory that everything was not as lovely as it might be. He asked me what I heard and took my truthful statement better than I had thought he would. At four o'clock he went to see Clemenceau and on his return took to his corner and began writing telegrams, whereupon I fled without waiting to hear what had happened.

Felder brought in a foreword that Meriwether had written for his comic book.[147] It accuses the Ambassador of having confiscated his manuscript and photographs and apparently tells a lot of lies about the entire affair. The Ambassador sent word that he wanted to talk to me about it but as he was snowed up in telegrams I left without attending to it. Tomorrow I think we can settle it by having Arthur Page send a telegram to Dodd Mead[148] to can [stop] the foreword.

George Barr Baker came to lunch.

Vernon Kellogg, Arthur Ruhl and Teddie Curtis turned up from various directions and I bad them all to dine.

Went out late in the afternoon to see Clarence but got there too late to see him and had to content myself with leaving a note for him.

---

147 See note on Meriwether in the biographical annex.
148 Dodd, Mead & Co. was a founding US publishing house which opened in 1839. It focused on history, literature and religion.

Log   Paris. Tuesday, October 15, 1918

When I got down to the chancery this morning found that the DAILY MAIL had a telegram from New York saying that Mr. Page was out of danger and that he would soon be able to leave for S. Carolina. That set Arthur up for the day.

Found a long memorandum from Beneš which he had prepared in response to a telegram from Dr. [Tomáš] Masaryk asking for information about the Czechoslovak movement for Woolsey, evidently in connection with some question of complete recognition. I translated it and prepared a telegram to which the Ambassador insisted on adding the prefatory note HANDED ME BY MR. GIBSON.

Just before noon Frazier got at telegram saying Col. House had sailed with Joe Grew and Gordon Auchincloss. They should be here in a week or so.

The President's reply to Germany came in before they had it at the censorship and for once I was able to give them some news. It takes several readings for a slow mind like mine to take it all in but after I had rubbed it in my hair I decided that it would do. The French did not seem very enthusiastic at first but as the day wore on they seemed to cheer up. I would give a lot to know what Max [von Baden] thinks of it. For him things are getting no better fast.

At one took the Ambassador down to the Inter-Allied Club where Felder had a comic luncheon, consisting of us, the Consul-General [Thackara], Burton of the TIMES, John Page, Tony Drexel [Biddle] and two or three others. I had some talk with Page who is a worthy soul from Louisville.

At half past three went over to see Dr. Beneš who was primed with various things to talk to me about. He had a letter already signed to Mr. Lansing announcing the establishment of the Provisional Czechoslovak Government. They have accredited diplomatic representatives in London, Paris, Rome, Washington, and others are to be chose for Russia, Japan and Serbia. I sent it along as a telegram when I got back to the Embassy, to the considerable alarm of the Ambassador who said that after being called down for the length of his messages he had never sent anything over ten lines.

Beneš seemed more cheerful than I have ever seen him and says that things are going from bad to worse for Austria. The Czech group has withdrawn from the Austrian Parliament after making a definite statement to the effect that they recognize only the Czechoslovak Govt. established in Paris and that they will have no further dealings with the Empire until they talk turkey to them over the peace table. The leader of the Parliamentary group was summoned to see Emperor Charles who asked what he could do to satisfy them. Mr. Leader replied that there was no use in talking about it because Austria had nothing to offer; that in good time Bohemia would dictate her terms and get what she wanted. That in the meantime she was an independent country and that she did not worry a bit as to whether the Emperor recognized her as such or not. It must have taken a good deal of nerve to talk to the Emperor like that even if you felt reasonably sure that he would not exercise his right to have you taken out and shot for a traitor.

Beneš promised to send me all their literature and maps so that I can familiarize myself with the question and know where to begin. Just as a feeler, I asked him to prepare maps showing various populations and the data on which he founded his claims as to various territories as Czech.

Col. Exton and Capt. Edie came to dine. We had plenty of conversation about matters we all had mixed in, McNally, the Duke of Alba, John W. Welkey etc.

Log   Paris. Wednesday, October 16, 1918

A quiet morning at the chancery with nothing to produce interest. I attended to one or two insignificant matters and then went out to the Polish National Headquarters, 11 bis Ave Kleber, to see Zamoyski. He was not there but I had a yarn with a pleasant young fellow who did not give his name but showed me interesting dispatches from Bern as to events of the past few days in Poland. It seems that there has been a big meeting of various elements at Warsaw, where there was more straight talk than has ever been indulged in before. The National Committee in Paris was several times referred to as an accepted fact and there was much cheering at repeated references to an independent Poland of all the Poles, with access to the sea on its own coast. They, as well as the Czechs, seem to be taking courage from the present state of affairs.

Caffery came home to lunch with us.

Arthur [Page] got off a telegram to Dodd Mead telling them that Meriwether's prefatory note was wide of the facts and suggested they should not publish it until after hearing from us. His Excellency [Sharp] was pleased.

Dawson seems to be in disgrace. He urged the Ambassador not to cut or change a statement he had from Joffre and His Excellency finally blew up and roasted him. Among other things he said: "I know what goes on here. I have repeatedly caught you in secret conferences with Sterling and I'm d-d if either you or he can run this Embassy." Oh Lord

Late in the afternoon went across the River and browsed among the book stalls with Arthur, picking up some odds and ends.

Brought Walter Lippmann home to dine. He says Rappard is here on his way to America.

Rappard has had some interesting talks with [Milke] Hindenburg (nephew of the Marshal) who is Minister at Bern. Rappard was told to urge the American "not to push Germany so hard." "Things were going her way already and it was only a question of time." Another by way of threat or inducement. "Things in Germany may go farther than you will like in Switzerland." He also said that the civilians had a steady row with the military and cited as his own grievance that he, an Envoy Extraordinary and Minister Plenipotentiary, was not allowed to go to Berlin to report to the Foreign Office without the permission of the military authorities.

After dinner we had a long session of settling the affairs of the human race. We thrashed out our ideas of the organization of the peace conference, its means of grappling with the many problems that will be put up to it, its publicity and the censorship that should be enforced during the interim before peace is signed. Our war time censorship – for the purpose of keeping information from the enemy and avoiding the loss of American lives – is about all we can get away with under our law. Then there will be no enemy and it is hard to see on what we are to base any restrictive measures. Col. House is already worrying about the publicity end of the conference and thinks of Frank Polk with a proper staff to handle it.

I said something about John B. Moore as one of the legal lights that Walter [Lippmann] said had been tried and turned down by the man who does not forgive.[149]

There is no doubt that the conference will have to be decentralized to a very large extent in order to handle the widely scattered questions.

It is easy to foresee when one goes into the ramifications that are coming that there will be a great mental weariness after a time. Thoroughness will last as long and no longer and the end of the conference will be line the end of a session of Congress with the clock turned back and everything jammed thru without consideration.

Log   Paris. Thursday, October 17, 1918

A quiet morning with no callers and plenty of time to do a little writing and reading. The Czechs and the Poles are cutting up rough and the Austrians have Prague filled up with troops with machine guns and hand grenades. The Belgians are also hanging out their flags and getting arrested for it with the usual enthusiasm. It really looks as though Bruges might be taken by the end of the week and Lille soon after although the Hun will probably make a more determined stand there than elsewhere.

---

[149] It is not possible to say precisely who the "man who does not forgive" is, but perhaps this man was at the highest level of American power (ie. Woodrow Wilson or Colonel House).

Peter Jay came in. He is off for Rome tomorrow or the next day.

Robert Hayden turned up from London on the staff of Admiral Mayo and I brought him home to lunch. He has just come from the Ypres front and says that the whole place is the worst mess he ever saw. He got rather close to Courtrai [Kortrijk] and saw something of the big battle in progress.[150]

The Czechs sent us a copy of their agreement with the British Government which practically recognizes them as an established govt.

Blount telephoned to ask me to a boxing match at the National Sporting Club and in a moment of weakness I accepted.

Ralph Hayes writes me from GHQ to say that Van Deman has telegraphed to the Secretary of War that the whole propaganda matter is a mess and that it is necessary to give us definite instructions as to our powers and duties, that is to say the powers and duties of the army. He also suggested that I be commissioned at once and put in charge of the whole business. I hope they will accept the idea at the Department of State.

Log   Paris. Friday, October 18, 1918

The usual quiet morning with much running in and out by the propaganders. James telephoned from GHQ that Van Deman was calling the Secretary of War along the lines of our suggestions about propaganda and adding a paragraph to renew the request that I be commissioned Major and put in charge of the whole show. I fear we will be turned down unless Col. House gets here in time to put in his word.

The morning papers are flaming with stories of the capture of Lille and Ostende – a great day and the King and Queen of the Belgians went into Ostende yesterday on a British destroyer. The papers hardly tried to describe the demonstrations of the crowd.

Madame Baguès came in with Mme Annie Vivanti Chartres who came up here at the earnest solicitation of Merriam. When she got here she found that nobody had any word of her coming and she has wasted a week. I telephoned James, Blount and others and hope she will be fixed up properly.

Durrel Hall, Arthur Page's bro-in-law, telephoned before lunch and we had him move in.

---

150 Nevertheless, at the Flemish sector of the front, Belgian troops initiated the liberation of their country on October 17, 1918. They were led by King Albert and fought under French command. The day before, they had captured parts of Courtrai.

The usual grind in the afternoon. At 5 took Edith Wills over to Clarence's studio to see his pictures but the concierge had no keys and I had to give it up till I could send out to the hospital.

Nobody in to dine – just for a change.

Telegram from Edward Bell   London, October 18, 1918

SECRET

My dear Hugh:

I have just received the following information, reported to our friends here from Spain, which I think it might be well for you to pass on to American Headquarters in France in case they have not already received it:

"It is reported from a trustworthy source that 200 cards for workmen in France (cartes vertes) which were intended for Spanish workmen in France have fallen into the hands of the German S.S. and that they have been sent to the following address:

  No. 18 Rambla San Antonio
   BARCELONA

It is thought likely that these will be used by the enemy to send agents into France. This information should be sent to all employers of Spanish labor and attention called to the great necessity for a strict examination of all applicants for work for the American Army."

  Yours ever,

                Edward Bell

Log   Paris. Saturday, October 19, 1918

Called up early by Watson who is coming here for GHQ today, Stone taking his place.

Merz arrived from London and was at the chancery when I arrived. He says that the feeling is general that the war is going to end soon by an unconditional capitulation.

The morning papers add Bruges, Tourcoing, Courtrai to the new gains. We are getting as callous to victories as we once were to defeat and it takes a lot to startle us.

The Czechs-Poles, Yougo-Slavs and others are getting rougher and rougher. There is no more Austria and I don't see who the President is going to answer there.

Stephen Bonsal came in off the street to warm himself at my fire but did not produce anything in the way of news or views.

Willy Buckley, just back from Italy with Gompers, where the trip was evidently a great success. Poor Gompers has had a hard blow. As he came off the platform at Turin, after making the best speech of the trip, he was handed a cable announcing the death of his daughter to whom he was touchingly devoted. Buckley is coming to lunch tomorrow.

We had an early dinner because Stetson had got a box to see *Plus ça change*.[151] When we reached the theater after walking to the Etoile to find a taxi we found that "*3 des artistes étaient au lit avec la grippe et on ne jouait pas.*" [3 of the artists were in bed with the flu and they weren't playing] *Gut* [good].

Outside we found our same taxi: driver who was amused at our predicament and agreed to bring us home although he swore he had not dined. He drove us around by way of the Place de la Concorde which was lighted up as in peace times and filled with a merry crowd looking for the hundreds of cannon which Clemenceau has brought to town to cheer his Parisians. It was really a wonderful sight, rows and rows of guns, wheel to wheel, big fellows, little fellows, machine guns, Minenwerfer [mine thrower] and everything else.

Log   Paris. Sunday, October 20, 1918

Got a late start this morning and devoted most of it to reading the papers which were bursting with news and comment.

After lunch went to the chancery where I found nothing of interest.

It was raining steadily and taxis were not performing very freely so I did not go out to see Clarence at the hospital as I had planned.

At 5:30 Arthur, Stetson, Hall and I went round to tea at the Embassy to see Mrs. Sharp who has just come back from America. Miss Letterman was there. I had not seen her for seven or 8 years so we held quite an old home week. After she had gone, His Excellency spun us some stories of his life, including the way he was beset by Webb Hayes and the way Mr. Page had sent a nigger lady[152] with a warm

---

151 *Plus ça change* was a comedic show which opened on September 21, 1918 at the Théâtre Michel in Paris.
152 Rather untypically for him, Gibson uses here unreflectingly this racist term which – sad to say – was the parlance of his time.

letter of introduction. The N.L. wanted all sorts of impossible things and whenever she was refused she told of what a fine gentleman Dr. Page was.

Log   Paris. Monday, October 21, 1918

A day with oodles of little thing to do and nothing that was very thrilling.

Milly and Agnes Fowler came to lunch. The latter drives a 5 ton truck about the country and sleeps in it now and then. She seems to thrive on it although she looked somewhat glum over the prospect of driving the truck and a large trailer from here to St. Quentin, starting tomorrow afternoon.

In the course of the afternoon, John Q. Wedda, a greasy looking Pole, came in. He inquired mysteriously whether I had received any instructions about him from the Department. When he heard there were none he said he had been sent over here to represent the Department and ComPub near the Polish National Committee. He intimated that he would take over the work I am supposed to do in this matter and that he would report to the Dept. direct through the Embassy. I think we shall telegraph and ask for a little news about him. He says he has established offices in the HQ of the Polish National Committee. The only credentials he did show consisted of a carbon copy of a letter from Creel (or Byoir) to Pomeroy saying that this bird was to act as Liaison Officer of the Committee for Public Information near the Polish National Committee. We shall see.

Late in the afternoon I was handed a long telegram from the Department saying that it had been decided to grant a loan to Czechoslovakia and it was necessary for them to receive the texts of the provisions of the Constitution, "Bylaws and fundamental laws" authorizing Prof. Masaryk to contract loans and sign obligations. I made a memo and took it over to Beneš who promised to get after it at once. The Department's telegram was very badly drafted and nobody could tell just what they want. Just to make it easy they say that they must have it not later than the morning of Wednesday, so we have no time to ask.

Beneš handed me a copy of a note just received from Bonin, the Italian Ambassador recognizing the Provisional Government. He was very much pleased with the President's answer to Austro-Hungary.

[Philip] Kennedy, Commercial Attaché in London, and [William] Huntington, until recently so in Russia came to dine – ¾ of an hour late. Huntington is a most amusing chap and gave us some good laughs with his stories and imitations of Gov. Francis, Col. [William P.] Thompson, "Judge" Bailey, Raymond Robins, Gisson, Caldwell, Minister to Persia, etc. His stories of the reigning chaos are enough to turn one's hair white.

Topping is off for Belgium to go with the advancing armies. He had it all fixed up some time ago but Brand Whitlock stepped in and killed it. The Associated Press set is all up again by an appeal to Belgian GHQ and so he is off in a day or two. He swore he was going to "bust Brand Whitlock wide open" in his dispatches but I hope he'll do nothing of the sort. Although right is entirely on his side and this is merely another contemptable attempt of Brand Whitlock to hurt people who served him loyally and well, nobody would ever know it or his stories would be taken as the plaint of a man who was sore for some reason with the great national hero. In the entirely false status he has with the American people, Brand Whitlock has a great deal of power to harm the people under him, and unfortunately he is only too disposed to use it. If it were really worthwhile and I cared to make a great national scandal I could knock him into a cocked hat with the true story of the Cavell case[153] and other places where he was beneath contempt. But I am not willing to have it generally known that an American Minister can be so utterly low. So unless he starts something I shall start nothing against him. If he does crowd me I shall remove the lid and let people see how rotten he is.

And I'm hanged if I can see why he has any desire to harm either Topping or me. We both served him faithfully and well and he ought to be mightily grateful. I saved him more than once from the disaster he so richly deserved but the knowledge only seems to turn him against me. I had often thought of a remark he once made about himself – that when he left Toledo after being Mayor for 8 years there was not a soul to see him off at the station.

Log   Paris. Tuesday, October 22, 1918

With the morning papers came the memo from Beneš. I settled down to thump out my own telegrams, only to learn that my typewriter would not work as Stetson had knocked it over last night and put it on the fritz. Reaching the chancery I found that my stenographer had chosen this time to have the flue. After some time I got Fred's man and dictated my telegrams. Then I put in the rest of the day waiting around to talk it over with the Ambassador. He had General Pershing with whom I had a few words. Then a string of Congressmen and other odds and ends who kept him going strong until after 4:30. It is rum trying to do business that way.

Wanger came in to see me and said that there would be a very interesting test case when Merriam got home and went to the bat. Mr. Page in Rome evidently

---

153 See note on Edith Cavell in biographical annex.

beat him up pretty thoroughly and then got himself recalled. The objection was made that Merriam was interviewing the Prime Minister, Minister for Foreign Affairs and others on purely diplomatic business and then trying to send home telegrams contrary to the view of the Ambassador. Wanger thought this was quite right and that it was up to the Committee for Public Information reps to keep the Government at home informed when our diplomatic representatives did not know what they were talking about. I suggested that perhaps a better way would be to change the diplomatic representative and that until that was done, Committee for Public Information people might safely assume that the President was satisfied.

Stephen Bonsal, Arthur Page and Walter Lippmann were there and Wanger proceeded to lay down the law to them in regard to politics and all other matters and after laying them out flat went his way.

Blount, his wife and their daughter came to dine. A quiet evening and early to bed.

Log   Paris. Wednesday, October 23, 1918

Found a lot of very little things to do at the office and I spent the morning in leisurely before-the-war sort of work.

Guy d'Oultremont and his wife came to lunch and his brother Jean came in after lunch. They are far more cheerful than I have seen them since the beginning of the war. The rest of us were remarking on the pleasure we would have in never playing with the Hun again. Guy looked rather crestfallen and said that with his job he would have to kowtow with frequency in presenting thus to the King. But he gave an amusing imitation of the way he would make faces while they were not looking.

We agreed that we should all go into Brussels as soon as possible with motors loaded with soap and other things our friends there need. As a matter of fact most of them will probably come dashing up to Paris to lay in supplies of things they need and we shall see them all here. It will be a great time.

An afternoon all wasted in stalling and talking to people who had no real business with me. Perhaps when Col. House gets here I can get some of my business straightened out so that I can do some work that gets somewhere.

Guy says that our 2nd Army is going to launch an offensive next week on a broad front and that if successful it will have great influence.

Jim Logan came in beaming to say that he is off for the front to stay. He has been hoping and praying for this ever since we came into the war and at last things are going his way. He ought to be promoted general soon.

Harris (Edward) of the Red Cross came to dine and told us some dismal stories of the way things were going on the front.

Log   Paris. Thursday, October 24, 1918

The usual day of little things with nothing to pay for being tired at its end.

Frazier left for Brest to bring Col. House and his party to town. He has taken for them the house of James Hazen Hyde at Versailles. I don't think very much of having the President's representative lodged in the house of a man who left his country for his country's good, especially as he accepts it as a guest. However it was not my job to decide and I held my peace.

DeLancy Jay turned up late in the afternoon and went with Arthur and me to dine at the Whitridge's. On the way over he remarked about Charley Greenough's affairs that "he knew the ---- well". Then he looked rather remorseful and said; "I should not have said that – I don't know him well.

Mrs. Borden [Florence] Harriman was the only other guest, 3/4/hour late. She was filled up with all the latest news and gossip from home. Among other things she said that soon before she had left George Creel came to her house to see somebody else and remarked that Walter Lippmann had tried to steal his job in Paris "and now Captain Walter Lippmann is on the high seas on his way back to America." He said he had gone straight to the President and had said "Now Mr. President, you have your choice, either Walter Lippman goes or I go ..." and the results was as above stated. She confirms the story that George is court jester and gets away with anything because he makes the President laugh.

Log   Paris. Friday, October 25, 1918

A morning of cleaning up odds and ends and waiting for an opportunity to show some unimportant telegrams to the Ambassador. I resumed this interesting work in the afternoon and carried it on until after five when I got them through.

In the course of the morning, Hinckley came in from Rome and we had an interesting chat. He is coming to lunch tomorrow. Butler Wright also came in on his way to London and we talked for a quarter of an hour or so. I let loose and told him what I thought of the way Bill Phillips had behaved about me and under the vehemence of my onslaught he abandoned all interest in the matter which he had brought up. He and his wife are also coming to lunch tomorrow as are the Andrews.

Woolly came home to lunch with us. Stetson brought Woodell, the Consul-General at Athens who talked well about conditions down there. He said for one thing that the German propaganda, run by the Queen [Sophia of Prussia], was very quiet and skillful and that when the Allies started theirs with Compton MacKenzie as the Chief Devil of the English it all went flooey.

I dined with Davis Wills at the Vernet and then had a little visit with Edith who is in bed with the flu – a mild attack.

Blount was there and walked home with me. We found Joe Green on the divan holding forth about how rottenly everything was going in the army. He is as bitter as ever but seems to be running his job well. He has just been assigned to go with the French group of armies operating in Belgium.

Log   Paris. Saturday, October 26, 1918

Woke up groggy with the flu but staggered down to the chancery to see whether I would be needed in connection with Col. House and the other visiting firemen. Nothing happened all morning and I let them alone as I knew they would be overrun with people who thought they had urgent business with them; and furthermore they knew that they could call me if I was wanted.

It seems Col. House took the same view I did about living in Hyde's house and refused pointblank to go there. The result was that they got into Paris at midnight and went to the Crillon where there was nothing ready for them. They got up bad tempered and Joe and Gordon woke George McFadden up bright and early to see if he could get them a house. They seem to be sore on Frazier which is unfortunate. George got them the handsome house of his kid cousin and there they will remain until they can get something at Versailles.

There was also a tangle about the Colonel's interview with the press so altogether things have not gone very happily for their first day.

The Italians are supposed to have started their offensive yesterday or today.

A large and sumptuous crowd for luncheon and a lot of good talk.

Walter Lippmann and I went down to the Crillon in search of Joe who had been to the chancery looking for me. He was not there but we ran into Gordon [Auchincloss] who looked very glum and said we could not see the Colonel. We assured him that nothing was further from our thoughts. That did not seem to convince him for he went over it several times telling us how busy he was. He was foregathered in the hall with Frank Cobb of the *New York World* and Miss Denten. He allowed that they had had "a hell of an arrival."

Coming back to the chancery we ran into the Col. Admiral Benson and Joe who had been to see the Ambassador. The Col. said he wanted to see us later and Joe appealed to know when he could come and have a meal with us. He is staying with Frazier for the time being but says he will come to us later.

A telephone message came to me to say that Davis will be here tomorrow and wants to get into touch with the Col. at once.

Log   Paris. Sunday, October 27, 1918

Woke up with a good start of flu so took it easy – went down to the chancery before lunch and found little to do.

There was a telegram from Osuský (sent through the Minister at Bern) to say that Staněk and the other Czechs had arrived from Vienna and were anxious to see Beneš. I wrote a note to Strimpl giving him the text of the message and then went my way.

Spent the afternoon translating the Czech Constitution and other documents bearing upon Masaryk's authority to contract loans and read half of the history of Poland sent me by Zamoyski. That and a careful reading of some 15 papers finished off the day.

At 11 the censorship called me up and read me the text of Solf's reply to the President which had been intercepted by the wireless at GH2.

Paris. Monday, October 28, 1918

Prepared a telegram showing the Dept. that Masaryk is President of the C.S.N. [Czecho-Slovak National] Council. The Ambassador signed it after lunch.

Lord Anslow came in during the morning. He has been sent over to represent Northcliffe in Enemy Propaganda.

At noon went over to see Gordon Auchincloss at his request. They are in McFadden's house at 78 rue de l'Université. It looked like the lobby off the Ritz. Sir William Wiseman was there with Lord Reading. Robert Bacon (now a Lt. Col.) and T.B. Mott (a full Col.), Cobb of the *New York World* and swarms of army and navy people.

Gordon [Auchincloss] found a secluded nook and we had 10 minutes talk. Gordon has become a great statesman and told what he would and would not stand in the diplomatic service – particularly that he would not have criticism of Ambassadors and direct communications from subordinates unknown to the chief.

He said Polk has agreed to my coming home – he being away at the time but that Bill Phillips coming back from leave had remarked that I was "wandering about too much" and that I must stay in Paris.

I explained to him the opportunity of building up some real political intelligence and he asked me to make up a memo on the subject.

I also told him something of the futility of my being assigned to the Polish and Czechoslovak questions but his mind was not focused and I gave it up.

The whole place was filled with the evidence of new arrival without any system.

Had a few minutes' talk with Joe [Grew] which was much more satisfactory. As soon as he gets settled we are to get together for a real yarn.

The Versailles Conference has been put off till Wednesday as Orlando will not be here before that. Lloyd George and Balfour will be here tomorrow or possibly tonight.

Wanger came to lunch.

A long afternoon devoted to doing my own typing in the absence of Miss Bennet who took one look at the large supply of work I had set out for her and then went home with a temperature. And after getting everything arranged it developed that the courier could not go till tomorrow night as the day trains have been taken of "because of the flu."

Davis Wills came to dine and I went back with him for a little visit with Edith who is not yet up.

Log   Paris. Tuesday, October 29, 1918

Miss Theodora Dodge turned up this morning – as usual in some trouble and needing help to get out of the work she is in so that she can go into something else.

Joe Grew telephoned he would come to lunch but at the last minute sent word that he could not get away.

After lunch Walter [Lippmann] came in looking weary and we set to work piecing together a map of the former Austro-Hungarian Empire. He seems to have acquired the conviction that the war is over and that the Allies must frame terms that the Germans "can accept." Leave it to Foch and he'll see that they accept them.

He also feels that it is pretty well settled that the peace conference will be here in Paris. He deplored the Italian drive as a needless waste of life "after Austrians have surrendered."

Went downtown with Arthur [Page] late in the afternoon. We indulged in the luxury of a haircut and then left cards of Mrs. Reid, Mrs. Harriman and a note for Martin Egan asking him to dine with us. He phoned later saying that would lunch tomorrow instead.

The 3 Prime Ministers and the Col. [House] were to have had a conference this afternoon – a sort of preliminary canter to the big Versailles show tomorrow. It was to have been help this morning but Sonnino's train was late and it had to be put off.

Log   Paris. Wednesday, October 30, 1918

The morning papers brought the text of [Gyula] Andrássy's abject note to Secretary of State urging him to use his influence on the President to begin negotiation with Austria-Hungary without awaiting the outcome of other pending negotiations. Things are evidently going badly there.

Found word that Clarence [Gagnon] was ready to leave the hospital and at noon I went to get him in McFadden's car. The Dr. told me that they had had a bad time with flu and that a good part of their staff was laid low. Clarence said that 6 men had died in his ward – not a cheerful experience.

Martin Egan came to lunch. He says that there is nothing in the stories that JJ Pershing does not follow Foch's instructions. He says that on the contrary he follows them explicitly even when they are against his own judgment. According to him, Pershing wanted to make the St. Mihiel movement on a larger scale and also the present one. To a layman it looks as though Pershing were right. At any rate, Martin knows what he is talking about and I believe his statement that the two men work in harmony.

Martin says that Foch and Pershing want to impose in the armistice the withdrawal of the German forces beyond the Rhine and the occupation by the Allied armies of the necessary no. of bridgeheads. Haig, on the other hand, in conformity with ideas given him during his recent visit to London is in favor of leaving them on this side of the Rhine – not only so as to make the conditions more acceptable but also "because it would leave the Germans in a less favorable strategic position with their back to the river." It is a quaint conceit but there is this to be said for it that if we could choose the line the Germans could not retire further into their own country without seriously lowering morale at home. It is pretty feeble, however, and I hope we'll make them go as far as we can before we begin to talk.

Last week there was a meeting of the Allied commanders at Senlis to discuss conditions and in the course of it Haig made some derogatory remarks about the "untrained American troops." Pershing objected strongly, Haig later wrote a note of apology and his remarks were expunged from the minutes of the meeting.

Clemenceau, Foch and Pershing are standing out for strenuous and stern conditions and the next day or two will show us who is with and against them.

At 3:30 Walter [Lippmann] and I went 30 Ave Marceau to see Prof. Eisenmann who knows plenty about Bohemia and Poland. He is a bullet-heading little Alsatian who talks well and evidently enjoys it. We kept him going for what I thought a reasonable time and when we got out I was surprised to see that we had kept him an hour and a half.

The Versailles conference was to have been this afternoon but has again been deferred until tomorrow. There was another meeting of the *petit comité* [small committee] this afternoon.

Walter has gathered the idea that the President may come over soon.

In view of my new job Martin Egan insisted on calling me Yougo Gibson.

Log   Paris. Thursday, October 31, 1918

On coming to the Embassy this morning learned that Turkey had signed an armistice last night by which she just about gave up everything except her immortal soul. The only stipulation she made was that no Greek or Italian soldiers should enter her forts. The Allies seemed to be ready enough to agree to this and the signature was rushed thru. There are no further details as yet and nothing has appeared in the papers so far.

Arthur and I agreed to lunch with Martin Egan at Voisin's at 12:45 and turned up in ample time. We waited for half an hour and then ordered our own lunch and ate it. On returning to the chancery we wrote a sarcastic letter to Martin thanking him for his hospitality and urging him to come around for lunch or dine with us.

Some interesting letters from Ned Bell, – one of them about Roy Howard who seems to have gone [nuts] on the idea that we are at swords points with the British and bound to row with them about everything. He is now in France and Ned sent his correspondence on to me so that I would know how to handle him.

Frank Gunther writes that he had been moved to Madrid and wants me to arrange to get this motor thru France. I hope they are not going to break up the old winning team in that Embassy. It is a fine working organization now but there is no telling what will happen if they begin tearing it to pieces.

A disheartening letter from Martha McCook telling of her trip home. Mr. Page was very ill all the way across and there was no nurse sent along although she said that any doctor who would let him start without both a doctor and nurse in attendance should be shot. Both Mrs. Page and [Page] Frank were ill all the way and Martha had to sit up nights and look after the Ambassador. She felt dreadfully about it as she is not trained in that sort of thing and felt that it was wicked to leave her with such responsibility.

There was a meeting of the Prime Ministers this morning and this afternoon at 2:30 there is the long deferred show at Versailles. We should have some news tonight or tomorrow.

Dined at the Ritz with Mrs. Reid who had a real party – Admiral Sims, Jim Preston, Lady Johnstone, the Whitridges, Mrs. Roosevelt, Miss Preston, Perry Osborne and his little cousin Earl, and Mrs. Harriman and Joe Grew, etc. etc. etc.

Log   Paris. Friday, November 1, 1918

News all day in waves, so much of it that we are bewildered and get no sensation out of things that would have done us a world of good a few weeks ago.

Some of the details of the Turkish armistice although a long official statement telegraphed from London was later killed by a telephone message. Austria-Hungary is getting no better fast. Tisza assassinated and Magyar regiments going over to the revolution. Letts, Lithuanians, Croats, Austrian Germans and others setting up governments so fast we can't keep track of them.

Austria proclaiming loudly that she is evacuating Italian territory as fast as she can – and Italy is helping her along. Her plenipotentiaries have been at Italian GHQ since Wednesday but so far no armistice is signed.

British and American Naval units have landed at Pola and Fume and are reports to have reached Laybach although that seems pretty fast going.

We attacked today on a broad front but so far have no news as to the results. The Department has jumped on His Excellency [Ambassador Sharp] for failing to carry out its instructions about establishing a telegraph office in the Embassy with a direct wire to Havre. The urgent instructions on this subject date back to last February so it's no wonder the Department gets sore. His Excellency accordingly said he wanted me to go out and get things started. I went to the Foreign Office and saw the Sous-Directeur Amérique, Mr. Arnavon who agreed to everything and gave me a note to Mr. Villeroy at the Post Telephone Telegraph [PTT].

On my way out I saw Orlando coming out from the morning conference accompanied by Aldovandi. Also Eric Drummond who came out with Bonar Law. I was running to make connection so did not stop to speak to them.

The PTT was closed for All Saints Day but I found a worthy little man named Franck who agreed to go after the matter and give me definitive news tomorrow evening.

Late in the afternoon stopped by to see Edith Wills who has had a long pull. Margaret Mayo was there and we had a few minutes yarn.

Log   Paris. Saturday, November 2, 1918

A morning of misery with the flu. Had about made up my mind to go home to bed when Walter Lippmann telephoned from Col. House to say that there were some things they wanted me to do and asked me to stay on during the afternoon.

DeLancy Jay turned up for lunch as did James and we had a quiet time.

After lunch, Walter [Lippmann] turned up and said that the Col. wanted a memorandum as to the meaning of the President's third point on the "freedom of the seas". It was rather quaint that they had not brought over anything on the subject but at any rate I did not feel qualified to elucidate what the President meant. I therefore gathered up all the documents I could find and gave them to Walter to take away with him. He craftily prepared a short memo neatly sidestepping the whole question by saying that the real meat of the matter was in the last part of the paragraph and that the question of the freedom of the seas could only be determined after the establishment of the League of Nations.

At 5:30 I got into a horse cab and went over to the rue Bonaparte to see Beneš who has just got back from Geneva where he went to see Staněk and the other Czecholosvak deputies who had come out for a conference with him. The leader of the Catholic party was delayed and did not get back there until after Beneš was on his way back. The others signed on the 31st declaration which has not yet been made public approving everything that has been done by the National Czechslovak Council and the Provisional Goverment. They also announce that they will be content with nothing less than the full demands they have made for the complete independence of the Czech countries Bohemia, Moravia, Austrian Silesia and Slovakia. They point out that they are prepared to struggle to that end for this and that any peace which does not give them what they want will leave the menace of future wars. They announced solemnly that there is and never will be any bond between them and the Habsburg Dynasty. Etc, etc, etc.

Beneš said that they had been somewhat worried as to whether these people would be allowed to leave the country and had thought they would come to us and ask us to send over some airplanes to get them and bring them out safely. However, the Austro-Hungarian Government offered no opposition to their coming and when there was delay because of the disorganization of the train service placed motors at their disposal to finish the trip to the Swiss border.

There seems to be the most complete harmony between the parties. After four days of talk the leaders left for Prague and it is proposed to have the Provisional Government follow them soon. Masaryk is still in America but will probably return at once.

Beneš took with him films of the Czech army and showed them to his visitors. From his description it must have been a remarkable occasion when these men first saw their own kind in uniform.

It seems that Bohemia money has lost most of its value. In the country districts there is no more confidence in paper money. These people say that when you go into a country inn and ask for dinner the proprietor agrees to give you so much food for your shirt. You are taken to a back room and remove the garment, button up your coat and eat your dinner in state. Many people now have no clothes save what they actually have on.

There is a good deal of fear that Austria may break out in Bolshevism and steps are being taken to avert it. The Czechs feel that their safety is involved and have agreed to feed German Austria for the next five weeks. They are a little worried for fear this action will be misinterpreted by the Allies. So long as the papers say nothing about it there would seem to be no reason for apprehension and the censorship ought to be able to take care of that.

There is going to be a great need for clothing and other supplies as soon as we get access to the country. Beneš says that they don't need charity and that the banks will take care of the payment without any outside help. It occurred to me that Hoover with his organization would be able to do the trick more quickly and effectively than anybody else and when we get some more data it will have to be telegraphed to Washington for consideration. I fear that the Red Cross will want to send in a large organization and attend to the job whereas what we really need is a lot of old CRB men who will roll up their sleeves and go to work.

If we get in there with the Government, there is no reason why we cannot set the country on its feet and build up a fund of gratitude similar to the one we enjoy in Belgium, but it will mean quick work and no political appointments. It is to be feared that there will be pressure to send some Czech naturalized in the U.S. as Minister to the new Republic. Vopicka will probably want to go there and there are others of the same sort.

Walter Lippmann came to dine in the hope of seeing James who did not return until late. Walter has asked to be detached and assigned to the House Mission and that is where he will go.

The confidential news from our front is good. We have got thru north of Grandpré beyond Buzancy to Fossé and in the afternoon had hundreds of motor trucks loaded with soldiers speeding north without being able to get in contact with the Boche who is evidently retiring as fast as he can to positions which cannot yet be foreseen.

Beneš was indignant because the conditions of armistice with Austria were being drawn up without the Czechoslovaks being heard. He had just been to the Foreign Office to make a formal protest to the effect that the Czechoslovaks were a belligerent govt. with an army fighting against Austria and that they had a right to consideration. They told him at the Foreign Office that the terms were now under discussion, whereas they have really been forwarded. It would have been much easier to have told him the truth and let it appear that he had not been consulted merely because he was absent in Switzerland.

Log   Paris. Sunday, November 3, 1918

Got up late and spent most of the day fighting off the flu.
　　Martin Egan came in a little after noon and stayed on till just before dinner. Arthur brought Miss Fowler, Miss Clark and Capt. Hewitt.
　　Martin says that he does not go in much for the idea of a League of Nations, but that if it must be we should have a National League and a Bush League which can contribute members as they become worthy.
　　Davis and Edith came by in their care with Margaret Mayo and Major Bevan and took me out the Reservoir for tea.
　　We dined alone and early to bed.

Log   Paris. Monday, November 4, 1918

I had hoped to find the Ambassador in this morning but he did not put in an appearance until late in the afternoon.
　　I spent a good part of the day preparing telegrams to Washington about the Czechoslovak situation and reading over various memoranda which had been prepared by Beneš since I saw him on Saturday.
　　The morning papers are chiefly concerned with the Austrian capitulation. The terms are to appear tomorrow and I hear that they are severe enough to give the Boche food for thought.
　　Lunched with Prof. Eisenmann who had rounded up Degay, Minot (interpreter to Lloyd George), Broderick, Lippmann and Stephen Bonsal. We had an agreeable time with good conversation.
　　One of the Frenchmen told a typical story of the Germans at Lille. A young Captain of the German staff came into the office of the Prefect and demanded funds that were still left in the Departmental treasury. When the Prefect refused the soldier boy drew out his revolver and announced that he would kill him. Just as he pressed the revolver to the temple of the Prefect a young Frenchman who was present touched the Captain on the arm and said: "You mustn't shoot him. He is an Excellency." Thereupon the German lowered his revolved, saluted, apolo-

gized and left. And the young Frenchman was the other day made a Chevalier of the Legion of Honor for his presence of mind.

Log   Paris. Tuesday, November 5, 1918

A string of people all morning.

Cabot Ward had a number of questions to talk over and came in at 11. For one thing the English have asked us to step in and assume the policing of the Dutch-Belgian border. They want it to be very strict whereas the Belgians are willing to be easy-going. There is no doubt that the Germans have filled the evacuated territory with their spies and can communicate with them thru Holland unless we keep a strict watch on the border. Ward was a good deal perturbed about it and did not know whether he should put the matter up to Nolan. I advised him to do so by all means as the matter was of the greatest importance and we have a corps of men that could easily be recruited from our intelligence staff who can do the trick well.

Had lunch at Larue's with Walter Lippmann and Willard Straight. Willard is at Foch's HQ and does not like the treatment that is accorded to our people. He says we have our offices at some distance from HQ and usually go in after dinner to have the communique read to us. That nothing else is communicated and there is no general endeavor to keep us posted or to conciliate us. He and others who are in a position to know say that there is a rather raw evidence of the fact that the Allies feel that we have contributed about all that can be expected from us and that from now one we have nothing to say. It looks to me as though that were symptomatic of what is going to happen at the peace conference.

There is no doubt that the Allies are peevish over some of our ideas recently advanced. For one thing, I understand that Col. House broached the idea of the League of Nations to get to work at once and one of the points was that South American was to be asked to join us and help settle the Syrian question. That of course has raised all sorts of a row. There is to be more news on that subject soon.

The terms are supposed to have gone to Germany with a short time limit for their acceptance. They include the evacuation of the left bank of the Rhine, the occupation of 7 bridgeheads and other important places, the dismantling of part of the fleet, an undertaking to restore the devastated regions, certain indemnities, etc.

The French censorship is taking it upon itself to prevent anything about the Versailles conference going to America. I don't see just what right they have to say what our people can have in the way of news if it suits our authorities to let it go, but apparently there has not been enough of a row about it. If the Mission remains here for any time that question will have to be settled and settled right.

Late in the afternoon Beneš sent me the pass [sic] Sychrava, the Czech Chargé d'Affairs in Paris, whom they are sending to Washington on a Mission. Our intelligence people, both Army and Navy, announced that they would not grant him a visa as he was down on the French lists as having been engaged in espionage in Switzerland in 1916. I made a father and mother of a row about it for he had already been granted a Foreign Office visa and has for some time been accepted as Chargé here. After going to the bat on the subject, our people made enquiries of the French and found that there was a slight misunderstanding on the matter as he had been engaged in work against Austria and was o.k. Our suspect lists are wonderful. So far as I can make out it is a sort of certificate of character to be on them. Ryan and Stettinius and others in high authority are on them and I shall be disappointed if I don't find my own name.

James telephoned late in the afternoon to say that General Nolan would come to dinner with me if I was to be home.

Beneš said he would come to dine Friday or Saturday.

Joe Grew is to come to lunch Thursday.

There is a good deal of impatience manifested by people who want to get to work on the pursuits of peace and feel that they cannot build railroads, start steamship lines, etc. until they know just how things are to be settled. It looks as though there would be a lot of pressure brought to bear on the various governments to get some sort of peace signed up as soon as possible to enable them to get to work, and we shall have a patched up affair as in the good old days.

Mrs. Van Rensselaer is in our midst and is to go back to London on Thursday. I am to let Ned [Bell] know about her movements. Ward has received no word about the coming of Steve.

General Nolan and James came to dine and Arthur broke an engagement to stay with us.

The General told us a good deal about the American operations which are going so well. In the course of the evening, he had a long talk with GHQ over the telephone and brought us the latest news of crossing the Meuse and the advance toward Sedan and Mezières. This means that all the southern routes are barred for the Germans and that they cannot get people from one end of their line to the other except by way of Germany and Belgium. To his mind it is the most important battle of the war and is so considered by the Germans who massed their best troops against us and ordered them to hold at all costs. A German officer who was captured some time ago said that we were "in for the greatest blood-letting of the war" and would have to pay high for any advance. Our boys have stuck to it for weeks and have suffered several losses, but the result has been a success that the

French felt they could not attempt as their troops could not stand up against the sort of fierce fighting that would be necessary. Nolan was very much moved as he talked about it and his lips twitched when he spoke of the attempts of various people to rob us of the credit for what we have done as a preliminary to robbing us of our prestige at the peace table. He feels however that the danger is largely removed by the success of this operation.[154]

As a means of getting the world in general to understand what we have done I suggested that he get Marshal Joffre to go up to the front and look over the ground and make a speech or grant an interview on the subject. Also that Foch be taken to see the show, review one or more of the divisions fresh from the fight and compliment them on what they have done.

Nolan swears that JJ Pershing has carried out all Foch's orders with the greatest loyalty and that any stories to the contrary are the basest of lies. He is going to have somebody convey to Foch an idea of the whispering campaign that is going on and ask him to take some action about it.

Arthur had lunch today with Morton Fullerton and Bunau-Varilla. The latter's son was there, fresh from a prison camp in Germany. He told one interesting experience. He said that he had bribed his sentries and others to let him escape and that he was court-martialed for it. He had such faith in his estimate of German character that he wrote home to his mother to send him his full dress uniform. This gorgeous affair reached him a day or two before the trial. He walked into the court room with an overcoat and when he threw it back, the court rose as one man and saluted. From that time on his array saved the situation. The poor fellow who had to prosecute him had had a bad time for each time that he elaborated the high crimes and misdemeanors of the accused the judges looked fondly at his gold braid and shook their heads. Bunau-Varilla pretended that he did not understand German and everything was done through an interpreter. This gave him time to think up the answers to the various questions. When the verdict came and the presiding judge read out the judgment that he was NOT GUILTY, the interpreter started to translate but Bunau-Varilla cut in with a remark that there was no need for him to bother as he understood quite well enough for that. Then he saluted respectfully and he went on his way. His comment was that he knew what would happen in advance; that the German understood the theory of the uniform but that they had no reaction to a gentleman.

---

154 On November 4, 1918, German troops desperately tried to halt an American advance at the Meuse, but were soon driven back by Pershing's forces. Meanwhile, the French and British attacked at the Oise. On November 7, the Germans began their great retreat. Now the Allied forces established daily advances, pushing the enemy back until fighting stopped for good with the armistice of November 11, 1918.

There was also an aide de camp to General Leman. The old gentleman went out the other day and bought a horse for his triumphal entry into Brussels. On his trial trip the horse threw him and dragged him half a block, but the old chap is still in the ring. He says that when they were picked up at the Liege he said to the General: "Mon General, your ribs are broken; they are sticking out and are criss-crossed" to which the General replied: "That's the affair of the German doctor. If he doesn't know enough to fix them it's his business and I'm not going to worry." And he wouldn't.

Log   Paris. Wednesday, November 6, 1918

Went over to see Gordon Auchincloss at 11 but just as I got there he had to go out with the Colonel and did not come back until after noon. I visited in the meantime with Joe but did not learn much. He told me something of the way things were going in the Department which must be getting more and more messy as time goes on.

Among other things he said that the Col. would have liked to bring Frank Polk over on this trip but "it was feared that it would make the mission look too official."

I talked to Gordon at some length about my own affairs. I said that unless there was some real work for me here I would like very much to go to Prague with the new Czech Government. He frowned upon the theory that we did not want to tie ourselves up too closely with "these new fellows" – a quaint point of view without much regard to the President's announced policy on the subject. He finally evolved the idea that I could be of a great deal of use by going to the Embassy at Rome to keep in touch with the movements there and reporting to the Department and the Col. I said that I did not think well of it because of the fact that the Ambassador would be opposed to having anybody in his shop who was on such a mission; that I was trying to get out of a position of just that character now and that it seemed a poor business to step straight into another. Further that I did not speak Italian and that while they were choosing somebody for the job they might as well pick somebody who could speak the comic language. Gordon did not see the force of any of these arguments but agreed to defer telegraphing to Polk.

He said one amusing thing – that he hesitated to make any suggestion that involved my moving as Phillips would be opposed to that on the theory that I was moving too much already. Inasmuch as I was sent over here for that special purpose it makes me rather sick.

Lunched at the Ritz with Lady Johnstone who had the Ronald's and Joe Grew. Mme. Edvina was to have come but telephoned that she could not get a taxi.

An afternoon of nothing worthwhile at the chancery. Senator Hollis came in to see me with a plan to get some of the German and Austrian ships in Spanish ports transferred to Spain so that we can charter them to hasten the repatriation of our troops after the war. I took him up to see the Ambassador who authorized him to see Lebrun about it from the French point of view. He starts in tomorrow and may get some results. He was very successful in his recent trip to Spain.

The censorship reports that the President had answered Germany to the effect that the Allies will make peace upon the basis of his 14 points with a reservation as to the Freedom of the Seas which will have to be discussed and with the understanding that restitution and reparation means that they will pay for everything they have destroyed and carried away. If the Germans are desirous of concluding an armistice with a view to negotiating a peace upon such terms they are asked to make proper application to Foch who will let them know where they get off.

There was also a telegram to say that the Senate and House have both gone Republican. However, this is being held up until there is some confirmation as they still have the memory of a fluke about the election of Hughes two years ago.

The present plan is to have the peace conference in Switzerland, preferably at Lausanne and preparations are being made on that assumption.

Log   Paris. Thursday, November 7, 1918

A day spent mostly contradicting rumor that peace had broken out.

It was around town all morning that the emissaries had arrived at Foch's HQ and late in the morning lots of people knew that the armistice had been signed.

Warburton decided to scoop everybody else and sent a telegram to the War Dept. announcing the signature. Capt. Allen did the same to the Navy. At the American luncheon Club the Consul General [Thackara] got up and said that he was authorized by the Ambassador to announce officially that the Allied terms had been accepted by the Boche and that the armistice had gone into effect at two o'clock. Joe Grew and Walter Lippmann came to lunch. They said that they had stopped in to get me at my office on the way up and that they had answered a telephone call for me from GHQ; that Bristol had told them of the signature and wanted me to phone him at once. I did so at once over the private wire and found that he had merely heard the rumor and was telephoning me for confirmation.

In the afternoon the comedy went on. My telephone rang madly with people who wanted to know all about it and had definite knowledge that it was so because it had been officially announced in the name of the Ambassador. His Excellency nearly blew up and washed the head of the Consul-General [Thackara]. The Consul-General maintained that he had been authorized to make the announcement and the Ambassador swore that he had never authorized anybody to announce anything. Next came a frantic message from Secretary of State [Lansing] saying that the War Dept. was in receipt of a message from Warburton announcing that the war was over and asking for his confirmation. Warburton said he thought he would make a name for himself. He has.

Log   Paris. Friday, November 8, 1918

A day filled with nothing but news of the armistice. The morning papers printed the wireless message from German GHQ and some conjecture about what they would have to say.

During lunch the guns at St. Valérien began firing and we hastened back to the chancery to see whether that meant that the armistice had been signed. There was nothing to it. All that we could get was word from the censorship to the effect that the German emissaries had not been authorized to sign and that they had tried to put over an agreement for a cessation of hostilities while the conditions were being considered. This was turned down cold by Marshal Foch who accorded them 72 hours to send the conditions back to GHQ and get an answer. They were started out in a motor and must be acted upon by noon on Monday. [sic] In the meantime fighting goes on.

A telegram this morning from Hugh Wilson to say that he would be here on Sunday morning and wanted to stop with me. I telegraphed back at once that I should be delighted.

After lunch Eugene, Whitlock's old chauffeur came in to see me and promptly broke into tears. He says that while he was away being treated he was dropped by them and that he was not even given a month's notice or pay. He is here flat broke and trying to find a job. I had to lend him some money to keep him from being turned out of his hotel. He spoke with restraint but it was easy to see that he felt he had been badly treated. He says that the Minister would not even let him remove his belongings as he wanted to keep them as a guarantee that Eugene would return to his service when they got back to Brussels. Of course there may be more to it than appears in his story but it is so much like other things that have happened that it seems quite within the realm of possibility. I telephoned Lady Johnstone and tried some other people to see whether they could not employ him. Lady Johnstone is trying to get a car and if successful will take him. I also sent him to see Blount on the chance that he might be able to do something.

There was a telegram this morning from the Department to say that the United Press had printed a telegram yesterday morning at eleven to the effect that the armistice had been signed and that the whole country set out to celebrate. The Ambassador put me on to find out why this had got by the censor. It developed that the Paris censor had had nothing to do with it as the message started from Brest. Admiral Wilson came back with the statement that he had received word from the Embassy – evidently meaning the Naval Attaches – and that he had authorized the sending of the cable by Roy Howard who was at Brest at the time. The bandmaster got up in the square and made the announcement as official whereupon the town set to work to celebrate. There was a parade, houses were decorated, bands played and airplanes flew over the town until midnight. Altogether it was a considerable sell.

We were have set out today or tomorrow for the front but no car was forthcoming and we have had to abandon it for the present at any rate.

Walter Lippmann came up to dine and discuss the details of a great relief scheme to go to work in Central Europe as soon as possible. I tried to make clear we could not get enough facts about the situation now to make any definite plans. I am for letting a lot of trained men go in to look over the needs and resources of the various countries as soon as travel is possible and then cut our garment according to the cloth. Hoover will probably have to furnish the brains for the task whether he wants to or not and we shall have to impress Poland, Kellogg, Honnold and a flock of others for the hardest sort of hard work.

Apparently there is again some doubt as to where the Conference is to be held.

Log   Paris. Saturday, November 9, 1918

A quiet day cleaning up messes and getting ready to enjoy news when it does come. Spent the morning dictating accumulated correspondence to a real stenographer who came to work for me yesterday.

The morning papers are full of news of disorders in Germany, riots at Kiel and Hamburg and Cuxhaven. The Republic seems to be declared at Munich, the Minister has resigned in Wurtemburg [Württemberg] and hades is popping all over the ex-Empire.

Lunched alone with Arthur.

The TIMES announces the death of Tom Hinckley who was here last week and went to London for a few days leave. He was feeling splendidly when here and nobody could have guessed that he would be snuffed out in this way.

Late in the afternoon word came in that the Kaiser had abdicated, the Kronprinz abandoning his claims to the throne and Max of Baden being placed in the position of Regent. It looks as though it might be true this time although the Kaiser has abdicated in the papers as often as Menolik used to die for the benefit of our breakfast hour. If it has come true at last it means that these fellows will now come sniffling round and whine to be excused from any punishment on the ground that the people who committed the wrong are no longer in power and that the poor innocents must not be punished. And we are just soft headed enough to let them off on the theory that they are at last trying to do right.

The afternoon communique announces the taking of Maubeuge. Four years ago we stood outside our door in Brussels and listened to the roar of the cannon that reduced it when the Hun attacked. Our friends the Guinotte's[155] are probably going through the experience again.

Log   Paris. Sunday, November 10, 1918

Got up late to find the papers filled with the confirmation of last night's story of the Kaiser's abdication. They all take it calmly enough, some of them going in for gentle irony to the effect that this was all that was lacking to complete his resemblance to Napoleon. Strangely enough, although Wilhelm abdicated and his sons waives his right to the throne, nothing is said as to who shall sit upon the tottering throne. It seems to be taken for granted that if the dynasty can hang on it will be the 12 year old son of the Kronprinz.

The news of the interview of Foch with the Boche emissaries at the Château de Francport is classic. For years to come we shall have the picture of Erzberger in his little Tyrolean hat, of Foch's inquirey: "Qui êtes-vous Chacisson" – as much as to say "Look what the cat has brought in" and finally the Hun cowers on his way home with the conditions stopped by barrage from his own guns.

Among the *"personnalités subalternes"* I notice Brinckman who was military attaché in Brussels at the outbreak of the war.

Hugh Wilson turned up from Bern at noon to spend a couple days.

Before lunch I went down to the chancery and found a telegram saying that Hoover was leaving in a few days for consultation with the Allied Governments after which he is going to Austria-Hungary to see to the needs of the civil population. This is better than anything I had dared to hope for. Nobody can do it as he can. My only hope now is to manage to go with him.

In the afternoon the censorship gave me the news that the German courier had only reached German GHQ <u>this</u> morning at 10. That gives them but little time

---

[155] The Guinotte family were Belgians who had worked with the CRB. Charles Carstairs and Teddy Curtis, both CRB volunteers, later married Hélène and Zizi Guinotte.

to get their answer back by 11 tomorrow. And Berlin is said to be cut off from all communication with the outside world.

The Martin Egan's and the Kellogg's came to dine and fell on each other's necks. A pleasant evening. Kellogg said he would send a telegram to Hoover suggesting that he make arrangements for me to be attached to the party before he left Washington.

Mrs. Egan after telling of her trials in getting passports etc., remarked that: "This war is a lot heller than it need be."

Log   Paris. Monday, November 11, 1918

The armistice was signed at five this morning and went into effect at 11. Foch came to town during the morning and spent a good part of the day at the Ministry of War but was not in evidence. The terms were not made public until after Clemenceau had announced them in the Chamber during a scene of historic enthusiasm. Word began to get round during the morning that the signature was an accomplished fact and before long all work had been stopped so that people could celebrate. Flags came blossoming out on all houses and groups of people went parading the streets singing and cheering for Clemenceau and anything else that occurred to them at the moment.

Mrs. Kellogg came in during the morning and we spent a good deal of time trying to get her passes fixed for her trip to Belgium. At lunch time I went to the Interallied Club with George McFadden and found things much as in ordinary times. Lunched with the Ambassador, [Oscar] Crosby, Generals Hart and Dawes, Stettinius, Major Mitchell and several others.

At 2:30 went with Hugh Wilson to the Chamber to try to hear Clemenceau. There was a howling mob and the guard at the door to whom we showed out passes said there was not a chance but "essayez toujours" which we did. We wedged into a solid block of people among whom I found John Loudon, the Dutch Minister of Foreign Affairs, trying vainly to get thru. By vigorous clamor he was successful in getting piloted thru a side door and taken in. We spent half an hour getting thru the door and then found that there was not a chance of getting into the gallery as there was a crowd waiting outside the door of each waiting to take the place of anybody who had the good taste toe die or leave early. We worked out way out and headed thru the Place de la Concorde which was a seething mass of people, the best natured anybody ever saw. They were posted in such a way as to make a sardine look lonesome but everybody was good natured and cheerful. The police were helping where they could but for the most part were letting things go as best they could. Now and then we came on groups that were trundling off cannon they had collected from the Place de la Concorde. There is no telling where they will be found eventually.

George Booth was hanging out the window of the financial mission and bade us in to watch the show with him. From there we worked our way to the cigar shop and laid in a supply. Coming back we ran into Arthur Page and Harold Fowler looking for us and joined them.

During the day Arthur had received a cable to say that his father was coming on well and another to announce the sending of a thousand dollars so he was ready for a party and got two tables at the Crillon. Harold and his sister, Lt. and Mrs. Nichole, Miss Ecklestone, Mrs. Maxwell and Pell were rounded up and we had a quiet dinner.

Got home by metro at 11.

Log   Paris. Tuesday, November 12, 1918

Got up to find the armistice terms printed in extremes. The only thing left out was an article to say that if the allies thought of anything more later that they had neglected they would let the Germans know about it. Clemenceau's remark was about right that they had taken everything but the Kaiser's pants.

Word came thru from Bliss that the Crown Prince [Wilhelm] had been assassinated. There were no details but he said that it was "confirmed by a German newspaper man." And meantime revolution rolls its way thru Germany and thrones are tumbling every which way. Kings and Grand Dukes and Princes are running for the funk holes from one end of Germany to the other and for the first time some of the enthusiasts are beginning to worry about Bolshevism in Germany, a thing they should have thought of some time ago.

The French Ministry of War says that there is a curious general strike in Switzerland, that the Bolshevist have called upon the Federal Council to demobilize the army within a certain time limit, abolish the present General Staff and institute all sorts of reforms. We have no details but suppose the wires are interrupted and that the Legation can't report. Hugh Wilson is leaving with the courier this evening and we should have something soon thru him.

Walter Lippmann came thru from the Mission this morning to talk to me about the possibility of getting on the Hoover trip. I would love to have him go but can't very well hold out any hope. He is thoroughly discouraged with his present work where Gordon Auchincloss evidently keeps him completely outside.

He says that it has been decided to have the President come over for the Peace Conference.

Harold Fowler (now a Lt. Col.) and Miss Ecclestone came to lunch and Harold's sister came in afterwards. They are keen to go to Bohemia or any other interesting place, failing which they are off for home as soon as they can go.

Mildred Bliss back from The Hague for a few days and came in for a few minutes talk. She says they have had a tremendous time and would not have missed it for anything. She has to hurry back as they do not expect to be there much longer.

Log   Paris. Wednesday, November 13, 1918

We felt swindled by the morning papers because they had nothing much bigger than the abdication of the Emperor of Austria. It takes a lot of seasoning to touch our palates these days.

Arthur Page laid up with a touch of flu and spent the day in bed. He has sent his resignation to James and is ready to go home in the course of the next few weeks.

Bigelow from the Embassy in London to lunch. He brought little news with him.

Fronczak came in with a message from the Polish National Committee to the Govt. asking that we hasten to do something for Poland. I let him see that I was utterly disgusted with for their failure to give us the facts about the situation in the country so that we could be prepared instead of coming around at this late day with nothing more than a sob message saying that they were hard up and needed help. I told him that we knew that much without being told or asked to spend good money cabling it in fancy language but that they could do a lot better for their people if they would give us a survey of food conditions and the needs of relief as well as facilities for transport so that we could lay the information before Hoover on his arrival. He got considerably stirred and said that he would go for them at once.

An afternoon cleaning up odds and ends and got home fairly early, leaving a neat desk.

Davis and Edith Wills came to dine and Blount dropped in afterward to see Arthur.

Log   Paris. Thursday, November 14, 1918

Arthur still laid up with the flu. In the morning the doctor came and ordered that a nurse be got for him at once.

A slack morning at the chancery which gave me an opportunity to read up a lot of socialist papers and get alarmed over the bolshevist tendency they preach. It is quite astonishing that the censor should allow the publication of anything of the sort.

The papers in general seem to be worried lest the President should set himself up as the advocate for the defense. They emphasize the need of dealing severely with Germany so that she shall know she is licked. And they particularly resent having us tell them where they get off in all this.

Log   Paris. Friday, November 15, 1918

This morning brought a telegram from the Department to say that I am assigned to Hoover for the duration of his stay in Europe and that I am to proceed to England to meet him on his arrival. He is sailing today on the OLYMPIC and should be in Southampton in about a week.

Joe Grew has been made Secretary of the American Delegation to the Peace Conference and Phil [Patchin] is coming over for the publicity end of it. I hear also that Nemo Harrison will be with us. Joe says it is reported in Washington that Nemo lives on an exclusive diet of birdseed. Willard Straight is also attached to the Mission.

Arthur seems much better but there is still plenty for the nurse to do in taking care of him.

In the afternoon Constantin Skirmunt came in to see me. He is up from Rome to meet Dmowski and was evidently sent to see me and smooth me down about the failure of the National Committee to do business. I assured him that I had no personal feeling about it but that I considered it dreadful that the people who were recognized as responsible for the welfare of the Polish people should show so little interest in what was urgent public business. I had a telephone message from Fronczak who said that there was a mass of statistics ready for me and that he would bring them around tomorrow.

I had a string of visitors including Wanger, Willard Straight, Wedda, Pierre de Wilde, Eugene [Shoecraft] and Cabot Ward.

Ward is undecided as to what he should do now. With the army advancing there will be a lot to do in the German occupied territory. On the other hand there will be a deal to do here in connection with the Peace Conference and he has an organization already built which seems to be the logical way of handling it. The first job is more interesting but he fears that it is not worthwhile trying for it because of the fact that it will undoubtedly be given to a regular officer. I urged him to make the try and see if he could get it.

Ward said he thought we might be able to get the private train used by General Harbord and agreed to look into the matter. In any event he thought we had enough equipment to make up another if we could not get Harbord's.

Walter Lippmann and Lewis Richards came up to dinner. Lewis has just come from Belgium. He stopped in Middleburg to see his villa and brought all of it he could find, – two small pieces of tile. He says that there is nothing left of the place or of Dixmude. Ostende on the other hand is not much damaged and Bruges got off lightly too. He saw Teddy Curtis in Bruges. In fact, Teddy heard he was there and hid behind his bedroom door to pop out at him when he came in, – the old sort of greeting. Lewis leaves with Poland for Brussels on Sunday morning.

The papers report that Rupprecht of Bavaria and von der Lancken are in refuge with Villalobar. It seems a long chance for Rodrigo to take them on when their lives are not really in danger and they are able to escape as other people have done. Evidently they have lost their nerve, unless the reports are altogether without foundation.

Log   Paris. Saturday, November 16, 1918

In the course of the day a cable came from Frank Polk saying that Hoover had asked to have me assigned to him during his stay in Europe; that formal instructions were being sent me but that if I preferred to go home I could telegraph him; in any event to let him know what I wanted to do. He added: "Patchin is going over shortly." It was just like Polk to do a nice thing like that but I always feel helpless in not being able to do anything to show how much I appreciate it. I sent him a telegram at once saying that I was delighted and grateful and that there was no occasion for me to go home now.

Poland, Kellogg, Richards and Rotterdam [Walter] Brown came to lunch and Poland gave us a long account of the problems of the CRB. No conversation is allowed by him on any other subject. I tried to tell him the story of the Polish Professor's book on "The Elephant and the Polish Question"[156] but could not get a word in. He is a devoted soul. The whole party is off for Brussels on Monday morning.

They say that the entrance of the Belgian Sovereigns at Bruges was very flat. It is attributed partly to the fact that the people are dazed and don't realize just what has happened but also to the vigorous propaganda carried out by the Huns. Vandervelde was sent into Ghent two days before the King and Queen to harangue the

---

156 See Log entry Thursday, May 9, 1918.

crowds and prepare a fitting reception. It was better there but still left a good deal to be desired. Now they have gone thru the most disaffected part of the country and from now on their reception will probably be more enthusiastic.

The present plan is for the Government to resign as soon as they get back to Brussels and permit the establishment of a new Cabinet formed by the C.N. [Comité National de Secours et d'Alimentation] people.That would probably mean Francqui as Prime Minister with a live business set who would put the country on its feet. My only doubt is lest Francqui should feel that he has too much to do without tying himself up in office.

Villalobar seems to have come thru the lines to clamor for the sending of troops to Brussels as fast as possible to put down disorders created by the Hun soldiers. I have a shrewd suspicion he may also have been bent on explaining away his supposed protection of Rupprecht and von der Lancken.

Letters from the Duke of [Laurence] Wellington, Friar Tuck and others who are rallying round again for a new job with Hoover.

Walter Lippmann and Charley Merz came to dine. I took all the joy out of their young lives by showing them a telegram just sent by Sisson to Keeley and Lewis announcing that the Foreign Division of the CPI was being transferred immediately to Paris to establish an American HQ for the Peace Conference. CPI is evidently up to its old tricks of trying to run the whole show and George Creel probably is coming with the President to grab off some glory. Now Walter is more anxious than ever to go to Central Europe.

The present scheme of the Col. [House] includes the establishment of a Bureau of Political Intelligence here with Joe [Grew] to run it and Walter [Lippmann] to help and [an] economic unit with somebody not yet chosen as its head, a secretary, etc. with Willard Straight as Liaison Officer to hook things together. There is some talking of having me settle down inside the Central Empires to have general oversight of the various agents who are to be sent there to gather information.

Log   Paris. Sunday, November 17, 1918

Walter [Lippmann] called me early to say that he was worried about Merz and would like to send him up here to sit by the fire. I bade him up and am keeping him over night. Had the doctor look him over and prescribe an impressive lot of stuff for him to take. He has bronchitis.

Late in the morning I was going to the great Te Deum at Notre-Dame but Walter phoned that he had a man just in from Galicia with good information of the sort we wanted. I bade him bring the wanderer to lunch and he came up before noon with Voska and his prize, a little man named [William] Rose who has been in Poland for some years. He is a pious little YMCA Secretary underfed but full of spirit and purpose, but likeable and somewhat pathetic. He told his story in a simple matter-of-face way: "I was on the platform of the RR station in ----. Some of my friends came to me and said I must go out to Vienna or perhaps farther until I could find the Allies and get them to send troops at once to Poland to save us from Bolshevism. I did not know what to do but as I always do in such cases I asked God to tell me and it seems that I should go. S. I set off at once without even time to say good-bye to my wife and without an extra collar or handkerchief."

It was a long story. He found no Allies when he got to Vienna but the "Polish Legation" which had sprung up over night gave him a mission to go on the Laybach or as much farther as might be necessary and fitted him out with an improvised passport in Polish, French and English with a rubber seal stamped upon it. This was a week ago Tuesday.

He went on to Laybach and was disappointed to find no Allies. The Austo-Hungarian army was pouring thru in complete disorder. He said there were thousands, literally thousands of horses running wild in the fields while in this part of the country anything that could stand on four legs was worth 2 to 4,000 francs.

He heard there were American Marines in Trieste and pushed on there only to find fresh disappointment. Finally in Venice, [John] Armstrong, our Consul, took him in hand and shipped to Paris to talk to General Haller. Hearing that I was going with Hoover he chucked his appointment with the General and came here.

He says that the Germans have turned loose over 2,000,000 Russian prisoners who should have been released after the Brest-Litowsk Treaty and are driving them over the border into Poland. He confirms what we have heard from other sources about these poor devils having been systematically educated in Bolshevism by German Government teachers while in the prison camps. They are now turned loose sick and half-starved filledwith the memory of ill-treatment and the inflaming doctrines of anarchy – a menace to the very life of Poland already groaning with suffering and confronting staggering problems.

He says the only hope for Poland and the countries similarly situated is to rush in Polish and Czech troops to form a nucleus of organization around which decent elements can gather. He is also anxious that American troops should be sent in as a concrete evidence that we support them.

I asked him to prepare a memorandum setting forth just what practical steps should be taken and this he has promised to do at once. I also asked him to tell what he could about food and political conditions.

Rose and Voska talked each other down most of the time and both of them had interesting things to tell.

They both had something about the revolution. It seems that the Czechs had everything ready for their bloodless revolution down to the Czech names for the street signposts. As the show began they tore down the old German signs and put up the new ones in Czech – for instance in Prague the Franz-Josef Brücke became the President Wilson Bridge – or its equivalent in Czech and so on.

The revolutionists had the whole telegraph system in their power so that they could play with it and cut or restore communication with any part of the Empire within an hour. At the right points they had the lines fastened together with almost invisible silver wires. These had only to be tightened to put everything out of business and loosened to restore communications.

In the process of dispersing the troops of different nationalities the Czechs were taken to Vienna where the Government could have an eye on them. As a result they were where they could control the situation and when the time came the Emperor had his choice between abdicating and sharing the fate of Nicholas.

I asked Voska what the Czech were going to do with their German population. He answered that they would be left quite free to remain or go to Germany as they preferred. In some alarm I asked how about Bohemia's strategic frontiers if they should decide to go to Germany. He answered quite tranquilly that that was all right; that these Germans were all in business; that they realized the hatred against Germany would ruin them if they went with her, whereas everybody would be glad to trade with Bohemia – that as a matter of fact delegations were already arriving at Prague praying that no attention should be paid to the German propaganda for their reparation from Bohemia. This is a new view of the problem but it sounds reasonable.

Voska says that the new Government will take over the mines, the bathes, the radium mines of Jochiusthal and possibly even the hotels – so that instead of paying taxes the citizen will draw dividends. There are six socialists on the Cabinet so a good deal of this may come to pass.

After Rose left to see General Haller, Voska stayed on to talk about the Hoover Mission. Walter had told him he might go with it for intelligence work and had said I would be in charge of it. I said I could not say anything about it until Hoover had arrived and we knew something about his plans.

He [Voska] stayed and talked at some length about the work. When the war broke out he sold a factory he owned in Kaunas City so as to get funds and started a Secret Service organization to counter German activities. He unearthed a great many German plots and passed on the information where it would do the most good – usually to Gaunt as he said there was always a lead when he told things to the Department of Justice.

He had Czecholsovaks everywhere in munition factories, on interned ships, in German and Austro-Hungarian Consulates, etc. His daughter was confidential secretary in the office Viereck established in the American Importing and Exporting Co. to do Hun dirty work – and under her own name.

His man packed the papers Archibald [Coolidge] carried on his last trip, even to the roll of maps in the sword cane.

Some of his yarns sound so fanciful that they could not be believed but for the fact that many of them have been proved.

Millie Fowler came to spell Miss McCoy and Miss McCoy thereupon dismissed herself as being no longer necessary. We were sorry to see her go for she had made life a lot easier for us. And thank goodness Arthur is o.k. and will be out in 2 or 3 days.

Merz and I dined alone and I put him to bed early after a hot bath and a rubbing with the liniment prescribed by the doctor. A day or two of care will do him a lot of good.

The papers say that Hoover told some Senate Committee that he would be back before Xmas. I don't see how he can do it if he is to spend any time on this mission.

It is also said that Lansing is to head the American peace delegation and that other members will be Brandeis, Root and James Brown Scott.

Log   Paris. Monday, November 18, 1918

A fairly quiet morning at the chancery with only a few visitors.

Lambert came in and talked a little while reaching the decision that his job was about played out. He is coming back tomorrow to be paid off.

Kellogg came in and talked over some of the phases of the trip. He is off tomorrow morning for Brussels where the entry is still delayed because of the delay of the Boches in going away.

Mrs. [Mildred] Bliss came in to say that it would be a good plan to have the President land at Ostende so as to avoid any ruffled feelings which could be caused by his coming first to either England or France. She said that this she knew would be agreeable to both Clemenceau and the British. The Bliss and Garrett families are going to Brussels just as soon as they can and she asked Kellogg to engaged rooms for them as some hotel.

Kellogg came back with Joe Cotton to say that they had figured out that Hoover would reach England not later than Thursday and that it behooved me to get off at once. To make connections I shall have to start not later than Wednesday morning. Sent my passport out to be vised.

Image 16: Reginald C. Foster headed the Informational Mission to Poland on behalf of the American Commission to Negotiate Peace 1918–1919. (Courtesy of the Gibson Family)

At noon went over to see Colonel House who said the Department had approved the idea of establishing an intelligence service in Central Europe.[157] He wants to suggest now that Hoover and I lay the basis for the system and that I remain at the end of the trip at HQ in Vienna to oversee the work of the various agents sent in to gather information. He asked me to talk the matter over with Joe Grew who is laid up in bed with the flu and draw a cable for him to sign. I asked if he would be willing to let Walter go with us and he said that he had no objection.

Reggie Foster and Hech came to lunch. Hech says that Mrs. Whitehouse has resigned and gone to Geneva.

---

[157] The Corps of Intelligence Police was created by the AEF in 1917. General Dennis Nolan led over 400 agents by mid-1918. Although he never donned a uniform, Gibson worked closely with them throughout the war and laid the framework for its work in Central Europe. His work, like that of many others, has gone unrecognized. This organization is active to this day under the name of the US Army Counter Intelligence Agency. "Intelligence 'police' established in WWI American Expeditionary Force" by Lori S. Tagg. https://www.army.mil/article/194191/intelligence_police_established_in_wwi_american_expeditionary_forces.

Arthur Orr came in during the afternoon and said that he was getting ready to move with the French GHQ to Metz in the course of a few days. He has better news from the children, Mimi is beginning to walk a little.

Had a talk with Cabot Ward who was turned down on the proposal to go in and organize the intelligence in the occupied territory. He is now interested in arranging the protection of the Peace Conference and I suggested that he go and see the Colonel [House].

He is also anxious to make some arrangement for our various organizations to tip each other off as the agents they are sending into the Central Empires so that we shall not have to use up so much energy watching each other's people.

I suggested that some understanding be reached immediately among the allies to keep newspaper people of the Central Europe until we have things organized and can handle them. He promised to take it up at once.

Went down to the Ritz to see Joe and found him groggy with flu. He agreed with enthusiasm to the idea of my handling the other end of the intelligence and we drew up a telegram for the Col.

The Col. told me in the morning that he had suggested to the President that he land in France and after the conference go thru the devastated regions in Belgium, then to Italy and finally to England so as to get there as late as possible so as not to be embarrassed by the elections.

Lewis Richards and Walter came to dinner.

Log   Paris. Tuesday, November 19, 1918

Went over to Col. House's this morning at 10 and went over the telegrams that had been exchanged with the Department about the forming of an intelligence system in the Central Europe. Cabot Ward was there and we went over the subject with him. Walter [Lippmann] and I agreed that it would be well to suggest to the Col. that Ward be entrusted with the intelligence end of things here and that some trained man be sent to Vienna to attend to the other end of the work. We drew up a telegram to the Department saying that it would be well to have me remain in Vienna, open the Embassy chancery and have supervision over the various agents sent out.

Joe [Grew] asked that we show him the telegram before submitting it to the Colonel so Walter and I went over to see him at the Ritz. He approved of all our plans and agreed that it would be well to have Walter go along on the trip so that he would know what weight to attach to the material coming out. That will be held in abeyance until Hoover has arrived and we know something more about the plan.

The Delegation to the Peace Conference is taking over the old Red Cross quarters at 4 Place de la Concorde and the members will be housed so far as possible at the Crillon so that our crowd will be pretty well concentrated.

Walter came home to lunch with me. Arthur [Page] was up for lunch in the dining room. Merz was discharged cured after lunch and Walter took his place to get cured of an incipient case of flu.

A telegram from Jim Wadsworth to say that he will be here in a few days and would like to stay with me. I sent word back that we should be delighted whether I am there or not.

Col. [former President Theodore] and Mrs. Roosevelt are on their way over but I gather that it is only for the purpose of visiting Quentin's grave.

Miss Dodge came in after lunch with various plans for going into Belgium. I threw cold water on them by telling her that thousands of Belgians would be unable to get back to their homes for months and that every American that went in kept some Belgian away from his home. That depressed the lady and she left rather sad.

Sent out to get my ticket to leave by tomorrow night's train by way of Boulogne.

Log   Paris. Wednesday, November 20, 1918

Got started fairly early and after looking in at the chancery went down to the rue de l'Université where I found General Nolan and Gordon [Auchincloss] waiting for me.

We went over the telegrams that had already been sent in regard to the Intelligence Service and told Nolan as much as possible of our plan. He quite agreed with everything we had done so far and said he would cooperative in every possible way. He agreed at once to let us have Royall Tyler and several other men we wanted. He said, in fact, that the Commander in Chief [Pershing] had given definite instruction that we were to have just what we wanted. He brought with him a list of 250 officers speaking the various language of the countries we're going to visit and told us to choose the ones we want. I put Trainor to work combing them out and Walter [Goedeke] is to have likely looking candidates produced for inspection.

Nolan agreed with me that it would be better to keep Voska on his present work and keep him entirely out of politics. He is altogether too much given to that sort of thing already and is imagining himself as a leader of the Czech people. He had prepared a long memorandum for Nolan in regard to a plan for intelligence in Central Europe with himself at the head of it, "with a representative of the Committee on Public Information" to accompany him, and the Czechs to handle everything in the countries and in Paris. Probably Stephen Bonsal or somebody of that type will be sent to Prague and will be told to keep a close reign on Voska.

We also talked over the question of protection for the President and for the Peace Conference and as the situation seems to be somewhat vague we decided to put in our telegram a question as to whether the Secretary of War was taking the matter up with the Commander in Chief direct or whether we were to go to work on it with Nolan.

Nolan and I went back to my office and worked on a draft of the telegram. Nolan could not lunch with me as so we arranged to meet again at 2:30 and finish.

I telephoned thru to Ned Bell in London and got him started on finding out when the OLYMPIC would be in. Late in the afternoon he phoned that it would not be until Friday morning so I have plenty of time.

Walter Lippmann, Blankenhorn and Arthur Page were home to lunch. Blankenhorn is trying to get into the work we are starting in some way but I don't know what the answer is.

At 3 Walter, Noland, Van Deman and I went over my draft of the telegram and then took it over to Gordon who made some very pertinent suggestions as to improvements. Again we made a fresh draft and I sent it down to Joe [Grew] to approve as it was done as emanating from him. He was laid up so badly that he did not feel like having any pow wows but was ready to bolster himself up to read and consider whatever we sent.

Told the Ambassador [Sharp] that Dodd Mead would not publish Meriwether's book[158] and was rewarded with a long account of how Meriwether behaved. The old gentleman was a good deal relieved to know that he was not to be held up to ridicule.

Caught the 8:50 after carrying my own young trunk all over the station in a vain endeavor to find my train. After it was supposed to have started I ran into Pink Simpson with Edwards, the Commercial Attaché from The Hague and by Pink's energy I got a porter at the last minute and scrambled aboard the train in a frazzle, only to wait twenty minutes before it pulled out.

Log   Paris. Thursday, November 21, 1918

I was called at about half past four so as to be ready to get off when our foolish train got to Boulogne. It was still quite dark but I was among the lucky ones and got a porter. There were no rooms to be had at the hotel so I curled up in a wicker

---

158 See Log entries of October 14 and 16, 1918.

chair before a half warm stove and did my best in the snoozing line to the tune of snores from a dozen or so officers who were just in my fix.

At half past six we were awakened with the news that breakfast was served so betook ourselves en masse to the dining room where we shivered for half an hour or so before breakfast, consisting of coffee and bread, was produced. It was bitter cold and cheerless but there were several hours to be put in so I set off and walked about town trying to find a barber shop that was open. No such luck so I finally annexed Edwards wandering about forlornly and together we consumed bad coffee in the station café until it was time to start for the boat. Half an hour later, we pulled out and got aboard the Pullman in Folkstone by noon.

Frank Hodson was waiting for me at Victoria with the Embassy car and a note from Laughlin asking me to stay with him. Ditto from Leland [Harrison] and Pennoyer.

Found Ned [Bell], Beal, Leland [Harrison], and other worthies in the mess and had some more coffee with them. Arrangements were made for me to get off on the 7 o'clock with Green and [Harry] McBride to meet the boat.

At 5 went over to the Admiralty and had a talk with Hall. He is going to retire from the Navy as soon as they have washed up the dishes of the war and stand for Parliament. He had been adopted as the candidate for West Fulham but the Admiralty asked him not to stand while he was still Director of Naval Intelligence as they felt he knew too much. So he will now have to wait until the next bye-election. As he has not been to sea for four years he is not eligible for promotion to Vice-Admiral and will gain nothing by remaining in the Navy.

He says that for the most part the Germans seem to be carrying out the terms of the Naval Armistice. He is somewhat concerned over the submarines but has nothing definite on them yet. In the original demands he asked for 160 submarines but the Germans came back and said that they had not that many. Hall then telegraphed Wemyss to strike out the number and write in "all submarines". According to the Huns they are going to be able to deliver about 94 whereas Hall thinks he can account for 184 and has sent a list of those he thinks they still have. It will be interesting to see whether they are trying to flimflam us.

Hall asked me to go down and see the fleet which the Huns delivered today but as I was due to pull out in an hour or two I could not accept. To my sorrow I later learned that I might as well have accepted as Green telephoned that Hoover's boat would not dock until Sunday morning and we shall not have to leave here until Saturday afternoon.

Hall is on the British Commission that is deliberating on the subject of individual trial and punishment for Germans who have been guilty of barbarous acts. He says that the international lawyers who form the rest of the commission feel that these men should be tried by a neutral tribunal for breaches of international law while he feels strongly that where the crime has been against a British subject a British tribunal should handle the case. He feels that he is greatly outnumbered and will have no effect; for that reason he deplores the amount of talk as calculated to make the whole business ridiculous if it is to come to nothing.

His idea is that if the individual is shown to have committed a crime on his own he should be punished by a national tribunal. If he is able to show that he did it under superior orders the tribunal should then proceed to try the superior and establish his responsibility and need of punishment. That seems the reasonable thing to do if there is to be anything of the sort.

Hall agrees that there is nothing in all the talk about extraditing the Kaiser but thinks we should force Holland to send him back to Germany. By all odds we should avoid making a martyr of him. England still suffers from the steps she took against Napoleon but in that case there were infinitely more reason as he personally was far more responsible for what happened than the Kaiser was.

I suggested that Lancken had no legitimate excuse for being at Villalobar's [Spanish] Legation as such asylum could be given merely for the saving of innocent human life. He could have got away as other German officers did but seemingly went to Rodrigo [Villalobar] merely as the more pleasant thing to do. For that reason I should think the Allies could fairly ask that he be surrendered to them and try him for various things he did including his share in the Cavell case.[159]

As I thought I was off to Southampton I had told Laughlin I could not stay with him and then there was a fine time getting a room to stay overnight. We finally got a place at the Cavendish and I went to Leland's to dine with Mrs. Bryce, Monk Jones and McVickar. And home to be at eleven.

Log   London. Friday, November 22, 1918

A monkey and a parrot time which has gone all to pieces. I had a great ringing of the bells without result and finally succeeded in getting breakfast only at half past eleven. The bill was enough to bankrupt me but I was so glad to get away that I did not begrudge them the money.

Made various arrangements on the theory that we were not getting away until tomorrow and had to change them all. News came at noon that the boats would be in tomorrow and we shall have to be at the dock late in the morning. Leland [Littlefield] and Shoe [Shoecraft] suggested that I go down to Brighton with them this

---

159 See note on Edith Cavell in biographical annex.

evening and that we all motor over in the morning in time to meet the boat. So we are off on the 5:45.

Lunched with Laughlin who is planning to take a long leave as soon as the new Ambassador had got settled. He has been convinced that the Department thinks well of him and that he is not dropped from the service.

Jim Wadsworth came in after lunch and may go to France with us on Tuesday. He is going to stay with me in Paris.

Brighton
Got off on the 5:40 train from Victoria with Leland [Littlefield], Shoe [Shoecraft] and McVickar. Frank Hodson was standing on the step of the car chasing off the busses and clearing the way as though for royalty. As usual there was a compartment reserved for us, station officials standing around with their hats in their hands and all the other accompaniments of luxurious travel as arranged by Frank. There were oodles of boxes and baskets and crates containing game and fish and lobsters and drink and the Lord knows what in the usual Littlefield way.

At Brighton we all packed into a one horse hackney carriage and made for Cheasman's the oyster bar which is presided over by five little old women. We dispatched a dozen of the best each of us, with brown bread and butter and then made for the Norfolk Hotel where rooms were ready for us with burning fires. Leland had up the cook and head waiter and explained all the details of food and drink so that such important matters should not suffer from lack of sympathetic treatment.

A bully dinner in our own sitting room with a magnum of the best. And then early to bed.

Log   Brighton. Southampton. London.
Sunday, November 23, 1918 – Father's Birthday

When we got up this morning I found that Leland [Littlefield] and Shoe [Shoecraft] had made a slight mistake in their calculation and that instead of 28 miles we had nearer 70 to do before noon. We got off a little before ten in a comic taxi with a strange man sitting on Shoe's lap and protesting that he had to be of the party "because he knew the road." Shoe's protest that he also knew the road was of no avail and the man insisted on being of the party.

Before we got to Portsmouth one of the foreward tyres came off and went rolling down the road. It took us a good half hour to get things going again and before we had got much further there was an ominous clank and we looked back to see our exhaust pipe rolling on the ground. A carter jumped down and ran toward it while we all stood up and shouted to him not to touch it. Despite our warning cries he seized it in one hand and ran toward us tossing it up and catching it first in one hand and then in the other for all the world like a juggler. It was a comic thing to do and a comic thing to happen but we did not bother to put the pipe back where it belonged and chugged along our way.

We missed the "Floating Bridge" at Southampton and lost some twenty minutes there. And arriving at the dock we learned that Hoover and his a party had landed at noon and left on a special train some half hour before. I was disgruntled but tried to look as cheerful as possible and sat me down with the rest to luncheon at the big hotel, the Southwestern.

I caught a 3:03 train back to town while the others piled back into their taxi and returned to Brighton.

Arrived at the Ritz at 5:30. I was greeted with shouts of ribald laughter.

There was a crowd of people there but the Chief [Hoover] led me into another room and talked for half an hour or so about his problems. He has no very definite plans as yet and will not have until he has talked with a number of people and sized up the situation a good deal.

In the meantime he seems to have arrived at one decision which is that we must have unified control of food and relief work and that as we are to supply 60% of the food and 85% of the money an American should have the supreme command. He does not want to take it himself as he knows just how thankless a job it will be but he thought there might be some American General who could handle it properly, – he had Harbord in mind. I think highly of Harbord but am convinced that no other American enjoys anything approaching Hoover's prestige and that nobody else can get away with the very difficult job.

He has no plan yet as to his trip. Instead of going to Berlin to find out what the Germans want proposes to look after those who have fought for us first and then go to Brussels and let the Germans know that if they care to send out certain people to be chosen by us he will see them and consider what they have to say. He does not propose to let them choose a lot of cheeses and send them along to roar at him or do propaganda but to get some who will do business.

The British want to send a delegation at once to The Hague but he is opposed to that.

We are off to Paris Monday morning.

In the party are Taylor, Cotton, Barnes, [Robert] Taft, Chatfield and one or two others. Hurley has another hunch and is travelling today evidently. Among his people are Tom Logan and Bolling, the President's brother-in-law.

The afternoon papers bring the news of the resignation of McAdoo who says that he can no longer stand the financial strain and must get out by the first of January. He is probably wise enough to know that from now on his job will be a thankless one and that the best thing for him to do is get out and become President of a big trust company at a handsome salary so as to lay something between now and the time that he can come out as a Presidential candidate. As a matter of fact his reasons are probably quite true but there are probably other considerations as well.

I telephoned the Laughlin's and asked them to put me up for the night. Dined with Ned [Bell] and Etelka and walked as the way back to Belgrave House from Chelsea. Found Sir John and Lady Lister-Kaye waiting for their car, and when they had gone sat up and talked to Laughlin until an advanced hour of the night.

Log   London. Sunday, November 24, 1918

Sunday morning went to the Ritz at eleven and spent the whole morning in probatory talk.

Lunched with Taylor, Taft, Chatfield and Jackson at the Hyde Park Hotel.

Kept on talking until five o'clock when I went out to Portland Place to see Mrs. McIlvaine. Mrs. Carter and Lady Atchinson were both there so there was sort of an Old Home Week.

On getting back to Belgrave Hotel I find old man Benson indulging in paroxysms as to whether or not a certain vase was of early or late Ming, and I could not see what it had to do with the price of turnips.

Saw Frank Gunther and his new wife in our old house in Belgrave Street.

The Laughlin's did not come with me but went to dine with Admiral Wemyss who told them about the signing of the armistice. He says that it is quite true that the Huns believed that it was not quite fair to ask them to surrender their ships inasmuch as they had never had a chance to fight. He screwed his eye-glass in his eye and remarked dryly "They had only to come out." He says that the German delegates were apparently stunned by the severity of the armistice terms and wept copiously.

Log   London and Paris. Monday, November 25, 1918

Put in the morning on little errands and went to the train with Hoover at 11:30. There was a crowd at Charring Cross, including Cravath, Frank Gunther, Shoecraft, Shaler, and swarms of others. Poland came dashing in at the last moment, having just landed from France, and was pulled aboard the train although he had no passport. We had with us Norman Davis, Joe Cotton, and Bolling.

At Folkstone we were met by a pleasant mannered old Major who brushed aside all formalities and pushed Poland through despite his lack of passport. We made a flying trip and landed in Boulogne in a drizzling rain at a little after four o'clock. There was one motor for us and certain reservation on the train. We started off a little before five, Hoover, Davis, Taylor and I in the car, leaving the others to follow by train. We stopped for lunch at Abbeville and then began plowing through a heavy fog, which reduced our speed and landed us at the Meurice in Paris at 1:30 am. I went on home with visions of a night of peaceful slumber, only to find a large pair of hob-nailed boots outside my door and a brutal soldier snoring in my bed. I managed to find some sheets and blankets and bedded myself down on a camp cot with an unholy grouch.

Log   Paris. Tuesday, November 26, 1918

Got started betimes, and got landed at the Meurice about ten. There was a talk fest going on which lasted pretty steadily until about four in the afternoon. It was profitable, as we pumped everybody for necessary information, and got it. Gordon Auchincloss came over about twelve and we went over the whole thing with him.

At one pm Arthur Page and I went over to the Crillon to lunch with Walter Lippmann. He is staying there to look after Willard Straight who is desperately ill with pneumonia. Mrs. Harriman was there as a nurse and seemed to be relieved, saying that Willard was better than the day before. He is still badly delirious but they find comfort in the fact that he speaks consequtively [sic] sometimes. Until noon the Doctor had felt that the case was hopeless but now apparently there is some possibility of recovery.

At four o'clock we settled down and Hoover dictated a long memorandum involving the views we had spent so much time discussing, as to how to constitute the food control that would be necessary for the feeding of the Allied, Neutral and Enemy countries. This will be very much condensed and sent to Washington as a telegram before any definite action is taken.

Late in the afternoon, Radović, the former Prime Minister of Montenegro, came in and after hearing what he had to say, I got Dr. Taylor out to talk to him. It seems that the Red Cross has already started a ship from America loaded with supplies for Montenegran prisoners of war. He was anxious to have the ship diverted and sent straight to Cattaro, which Taylor says, can be done if he will give us the necessary facts. The requirements of all the Balkan countries are very modest in amount and very excellently drawn up but in the case of Montenegro the situation is more difficult because of difficulties in transportation.

Radović, who built the Montenegran railroads, says that they are in running order but that they will have to be supplied with 150 tons of coal a month and, that it will be necessary to send twenty-five or thirty motor trucks of two and a half to three and a half ton capacity as well as gasoline and supplies. He is particularly anxious that all supplies sent there be in the hands of an American representative and that this representative get to Cattaro as soon as possible.

The Yougo-Slavs have also brought in a list of their requirements, which will be studied,

Hoover plans to get off commissions to these countries almost immediately with such supplies as can be diverted from the stocks over here. The Red Cross and old Belgian Relief crowd will be drawn upon for this purpose as well as a list of officers speaking the languages, which was furnished me by Nolan.

Kellogg, who has returned from Belgium, brings interesting stories of the last days of the German occupation. He says that the week before the armistice was signed the Reds took over the Government and a little Jew soldier named Einstein, who had been kicked about by everybody, was put in authority. He summoned Von der Lancken and other high officers to his presence. When he entered the room all arose and stood at attention. He sat down, while they remained standing, and told them just where they got off, while they agree with alacrity to everything that he said. Von der Lancken was such an abject beast that one of the other German officers aroused himself to a point where he said that he could not take it that way, and was not a yellow dog like Von der Lancken. It must have been a pretty picture to see that swine kowtowing to Einstein whom he would have ground underfoot a year ago.

I hear that Von der Lancken is now in Berlin as a member of the new Government. I remember a couple of years ago him saying to me that he feared that when after the war was over it would be necessary to grant certain concessions to the people. Now, apparently, there are none more radical than he.

One of the other German officers said that sixty per cent of the German officers were in thorough accord with the new order of things and sympathized with the new movement. When asked about the other forty per cent he dismissed them with a wave of the hand and said that they did not count.

Prince Rupprecht of Bavaria was in a house on the Avenue Louise with a crowd of about 100 men who had remained faithful to him. A crowd of soldiers clamored in front of the house for him to come out and talk. He appeared on the balcony and with his usual tact inquired, "Are there any of my brave Bavarians in this mob?" One of them called out and said, "Yes, there are but they won't do you any good." "Come down into the street and talk to us." At that, a machine gun opened up on the crowd and several soldiers were killed. The Soldier's Council then ordered away the crowd that had been with Rupprecht, and he hid in a coal-hole until after dark, when he ran over to the Legation of Holland and asked for asylum.

Vollenhoven declined to receive him, so his Royal Highness continued to walk to the Swiss Legation where Villalobar took him in and hid him for a day in the cellar. The next night at eleven, he was put into a motor car and Villalobar took him across the frontier into Holland. The Princelings have not shown up very handsomely in their manner of leave-takings.

I understand that the President's party will be here about the 14th of December and that they will be very numerous. George Creel will be among those present, and I can see visions of various members of the party clamoring for limousines, audiences with Kings and Princes, trips to the front, et cetera, until everybody is driven mad. As for me, I hope to be safely in the midst of Balkan turmoil.

Log   Paris. Wednesday, November 27, 1918

Up early and to the hotel where I found that the Chief [Hoover] had gone over to see Gordon. There was no need of my being along so I stayed in and kept house, answering telephones and receiving the odds and ends of people who came. Horodyski came and promised to come back later. Simpson came in with a flock of telegrams and other matters to attend to. Newspaper men galore. All of them choked off.

About half past eleven McFadden telephoned that we were "all" to go to Brussels and that I was asked to arrange the passports. I had some difficulty in convincing him that there was any need for me to know who was to be in the part but I finally got a list which was changed only four or five times. Got all the passports together and had them fixed.

Joe Grew came to lunch and we cornered the Chief to talk about our intelligence system. Frank Cobb of the WORLD came and joined us and vented his rage on pretty well everything.

Went to see Joe in his new quarters during the afternoon. It will be splendid when he gets it going. He had just received a telegram saying that none of the diplomatic officers asked for could be spared and that I alone was available. Several of our officers were approved.

Dined with the Chief, Horodyski and several others. Then home to pack and to bed at the hotel in preparation for a long day.

The Chief went with me to the Embassy to "pay his respects" and we managed to have some talk. He said among other things that he does not want me to go off on this intelligence thing but thinks I should stay with him until his business is fixed. Nothing suits me better.

I found a telegram from [Walter] Brown at the CRB Rotterdam office saying that the German authorities were anxious to come out and talk over their food situation; that if the Chief could arrange to go to The Hague, Lancken and Rieth would come to meet him there and arrange matters. I nearly had apoplexy when I read it but quickly recovered when I thought of the treat it would be to see HCH [Herbert C. Hoover] read it. It was. After he had expressed himself amply he reached for a pencil and wrote an answer to this effect:

"After reviewing the events of the past two and a half years in any language you may select please tell that pair to go to hell personally with my compliments. If I must deal with Germans, it will not be with that pair."

And it was sent clear so that the British censor would be sure to see it.

Log   Paris-Brussels. Thursday, November 28, 1918

Paris-Senlis	23 kilometers
Compiègne	29
Noyon	18
Guiscard	10
Ham	19
St. Quentin	14
Le Catelet	10
Cambrai	8
Valenciennes	33
Mons	21
Soignies	17
Hal	22
Brussels	<u>15</u>
	230

We did not shove off until half past seven because various people were late. The Chief [Hoover] and Kellogg and I set off in one army Cadillac, and Taylor and Poland in the other. It was drizzling as we left town and there was no variation except when it came down in torrents. The roads were slippery and there was a good deal of mist from time to time. Then too the roads were encumbered with lorries and made progress difficult. As a result out trip took us close to twelve hours. We passed thru Senlis and I got my first look at Foch's headquarters. Thence to Compiègne. Before we got there we began to see signs of destruction, villages smashed beyond repair, châteaux battered and shell holes in the fields. Compiègne itself is rather a mess and we had to go a roundabout way to get to the temporary bridge which took us across the river. From there on the country was steadily worse, most of it having been in German possession for varying periods. Noyon was knocked about frightfully but it was nothing in comparison with what we were to see later.

On the roads there were a certain number of refugees working their ways toward their old homes. It is hard to see how they could hope to find anything when they arrived but they seemed to be driven by a sort of dumb animal instinct to go back to the place they belonged in. Some of them we took up from time to time but they had little to say, only a bald statement of how long they had been away from their homes, a conjecture as to whether they would find anything on their return and a helpless evasion of what they would have to do if they found no place to live in. It was particularly pathetic as there was nothing to be done and no way of keeping them from running straight into trouble.

Guiscard, Ham, and St. Quentin were a succession of horrors. In the latter place there was not a civilian to be found although we say a lot of French prisoners returned from Germany standing patiently in front of a soup kitchen set up in a ruin. They were emaciated and drawn and had the brother-to-the-ox look that hurts us to see. They stood there in the drizzling rain as they had nothing else to do in all the long vista of the future, not the sort of attitude that men should have under any civilized circumstances. Another thing to be charged to the HUN.

There is hardly any habitable house in the town. The streets have been cleaned up enough so that a motor can pick its way thru but it will be a long time before civilians will come back. The place was taken some time in September if I remember rightly and as yet there is no one of the ordinary conveniences restored, water, electricity, tram, to say nothing of telephone and such like. There are no plans made for feeding the refugees when they do come back or furnish them with any sort of work that they can do on the ground. It is a dreary prospect.

Out of the town we went into a long stretch of the worst sort of no-man's-land. For miles there was not a field that had been cultivated for years. The country had reverted to its primitive state and looked as though it might be a stretch of Wyoming. The rolling hills were cut with great gashes of trench and communication alleyways, running as far as the eye could see. There was barbed wire but not so much of it as I had expected. There was something hideous about it all, perhaps more because we knew what was behind it than because it was ugly in itself. Piles of munitions and material on every side, – even a few abandoned tanks, one of them standing on end and peering over into a canal as though poised for a dive it could never take. Rows of British tanks lined up spick and span ready for anything from a fight to a frolic. Occasional bundles of men who emerged from dugouts and holes in the roadside to survey us sadly like so many huge chipmunks. And with it all the drizzle, drizzle, drizzle.

The other car broke down as we came into Cambrai so we sat by the roadside and stared at the huge signboard if the *Entlausungsanstalt* [delousing facility] while they were repaired. Then to the officers club where we smacked our lips and asked for coffee only to be told that we could not have any and that the place was reserved for officers. Out we went into the rain and made off along the road until we picked out the half ruined octrol as a lunching place. The town was filled with British heavies who looked as though they were ready for a brand new war. They will have to keep.

We picked up a Canadian officer and carried him on to Mons and another who went there to Brussels.

From the Belgian frontier we found that all railroads had been destroyed as ingeniously as possible. Dynamite was placed so as to bend one end of each rail and we went by mile after mile of track which was absolutely worse than useless until each and every rail could be cut and replaced. It will be a whale of a job but the British are already at it for the lines that run toward Germany.

In Mons the shops looked as though they had been stripped of their stock. There were few brass door knobs but wood and bits of rope did duty for the old splendor.

At Soignies we had a puncture and just outside Brussels another so that we rolled up to the Palace Hotel at seven looking like tramps or niggers, our faces deep with mud and our eyes bloodshot.

I sent a boy off to look for Francqui but he brought back word that Francqui was at Liège and would not be back till midnight. After beautifying ourselves we all dined with Chatfield and Hallowell who has turned up from Boulogne. Sperry rolled in after dinner as did Joe Green and there was quite a reunion which lasted until altogether too late.

Log   Brussels. Friday, November 29, 1918

Got up a little before eight still weary from the trip. Found that Francqui had already arrived and was in session with the Chief [Hoover] so went downstairs and had breakfast with Poland, Smith, Chatfield, Hallowell and Sperry. There was coffee of a sort, bread of a sort, eggs that cost two francs fifty to the hotel, – how much we paid for them there is no telling, and a spoonful of confiture each.

Francqui full of good humor, just back from Spa where he had failed to put over the particular financial arrangement that he wanted for Belgium. According to the armistice Belgium was to be reimbursed for the forced loans, etc. which she has been robbed of by the Huns. In practice, however, it was done with German banknotes which puts Belgium in a bad position for securing ready money and in danger of serious loss of exchange. Of course what was wanted was payment in gold so that the country could start right out and do financial stunts. The Allies and particularly the French feared that this would jeopardize Germany's financial position, and as a creditor felt that this was to be avoided. However other means may be found to ease her through the time of danger. For instance we required 200,000 tons of potash from Germany. We might get the allies to agree that Belgium could pay this for us in German notes and let us effect the payment in gold to her. Other means have been suggested and will have to be worked out.

Francqui was rubbing his hands over the change in conditions and the arbitrary way one can now treat a German official without being shot at dawn. He says the Germans at Spa put in all sorts of appeals and bleats which are referred to Foch. When the decision is returned it is read in open meeting by the French General. The formula is something like this:

"*Les autorités allemandes ont demandé telle et telle choses. La question a été soumise au Maréchal Foch. Sa réponse est la suivante: Non.*" ["The German authorities have asked for such and such things. The question was submitted to Marshal Foch. His answer is the following: No.]

It was decided that the best thing was to have a general meeting of the Prime Minister, the Minister for Foreign Affairs, the Food Minister and Francqui with us and Francqui wrote a note to Hymans asking him to make the necessary arrangements for 11:30. I carried the note to the Ministry and then went on to see Myriam [Reyntiens] who was already about and received me like a long lost brother. Jack [Reyntiens] is back and has gone with our army to Luxembourg. The children were all there and we had a hugging and kissing time of it. They have all grown like weeds and look well. The littlest, Anita, still pretty as a flower.

Ynès [Reyntiens] and Bebeth [d'Aspremont-Lynden] are leaving for Paris tomorrow on their way to Switzerland to look after Ramon [Reyntiens] who seems to have something the matter with his lungs. I went around to the rue du Commerce and was greeted by a small boy who belongs to Adele the maid who also welcomed me as one risen from the dead. I left word that I would try to lunch with Myriam and that Ynès was to be there.

With the Chief [Hoover] to the Legation where Brand Whitlock allowed he was glad to see me and Mrs. Whitlock was nice and asked us to lunch or dine. The Chief chose dinner and we went away with an understanding that we were all to meet at Hyman's at 11:30.

Omer, Gustav, Josef and other servants were beaming and I found Eugene driving the Minister's car as though nothing had happened.

Image 17: Bebeth D'Aspremont de Lynden and Ynès Reyntiens picnicking 1918. (Courtesy of the Gibson Family)

To the CRB offices where we found René Jensen, Baetens, de Wouters and a number of other old friends. We talked steadily on business matters and the details of the future running of the revitailement until it was time to go to the next meeting at the Ministry of Foreign Affairs. The Chief went for the Minister but came back without him as he had not turned up. He appeared a good deal later. I went ahead and explained the delay to the assembled Ministers and Francqui.

The Chief explained what he thought were the alternatives open to Belgium as regards the food problem; either they could continue with CRB and be a distinct entity, or they could set it aside and go under the general arrangement which is about to be set up for feeding the world wherein they would be but one in the crows. He pointed out the advantages of both plans and left the discussion to them. Among other things, he said that our imports of food to the Allies, England, France and Italy had been proceeding at the rate of 1,600,000 tons a month but had to be cut down to 400,000 tons because of the demands of the war upon shipping during this same period Belgium's supplies were not only not cut down but were actually increased from 80,000 to 140,000 tons.

There seemed to be no hesitation among the Ministers as to what they wanted. Hymans said that so far as he was concerned he thought the present arrangement should be maintained. The Prime Minister spoke up and said that they all agreed and hoped that the Chief would continue to help them. They asked for his advice in this but he said it was a matter for them to decide.

They then brought up the subject of the difficult financial situation due to their large oversupply of German marks and the Chief went into that at some length.

At one the Prime Minister [Delacroix] had to go to the Senate and the meeting broke up. Declining an invitation from Francqui I sped to Myriam's where I found the whole family, Ynès, Madame Drugman, Bebeth [Lynden], Uncle Charley d'Assche and René Jensen. We had a splendid luncheon but it all seemed too good to be true. I was a little groggy because they all seemed so well and happy and they themselves are still stunned with the suddenness of it as they had not expected to be released for another year or so. We had so many things to talk about that as is often the case there were long pauses, but we were all happy even if the tears were near the surface.

Their accounts of the departure of the Germans is almost incredible for people who do not know them. Part of them straggled out in utter confusion, others were commanded by their officers after a fashion and others by a mixture of officers and their own Reds. They stole right and left and peddled their booty as they went along. Pictures, linen, cows, sewing machines, and anything else that could be moved. Myriam saw one big gun being hauled by a motor truck and behind it was towed a Victoria whereupon sat an officer with a cage of chickens and ducks, several bundles and a sewing machine.

The château at Waterloo was carefully looted and everything that was not carried away was ruined. Furniture was smashed and windows broken. Even the great marble mantels were broken which must have been a thing that required much effort. The whole place was like a pig sty but Myriam dismissed it as a trifle, saying that she was annoyed her most is that she was unable to get it cleaned in time to receive the swarms of English prisoners that came through within a few days.

Madame Henryx came along late and joined the party. She looks well but isn't.

Ynès [Reyntiens] and Bebeth [Lynden] are due in Paris tomorrow evening and make all sorts of plans about what we are to do there, theatres, etc. I only hope I can be there part of the time to look after them and give them a good time. They must need it after four years and a half of prison.

I came back to the hotel but found nobody here, did some errands, called on Madame de Beughem and Albertine Wittouck.

Ran into Mrs. Brand Whitlock at the de Beughem's door and found the Peñaranda de Franchimont's inside. They created a pleasant atmosphere but immediately launching into eulogies of my book and telling all sorts of stories about how the Germans borrowed it and what they had to say about it. Mrs. Whitlock took it without wincing but I was sorry they brought it up as it evidently annoyed her beyond expression. According to several people they have been at pains to tell people since they got back that they know nothing about me or where I am; that

I am too busy to write to them and they to write me. Rather quaint in view of the fact that we have exchanged letters within the past few days.

Beughem was not there but came around alter to see me at the CRB. I was sorry not to see the nice fellow.

From there to Albertine Wittouck's where there was more affectionate greeting. She looked well and pretty and seemed almost happy although she is worried for fear people are going to be too hard on Austria. I could honestly tell her that Austria would get off a great deal better than Germany and that there was not nearly the feelings against her that there was in other countries. Jean [Wittouck] tried some time ago to get out through the barbed wire to join the army although he is not yet sixteen, but he was turned back. The day the armistice was signed he joined up and is to go to the army at once with the light artillery. The girls were not there but in the entrance I met their old English governess who whooped in a most unusual manner for her and seemed enthusiastic over the idea of having peace at last.

I stopped at Baron Lambert's but he was not there. Left cards and went my way. Looked in at Jean Accent's for some motor goggles and was greeted by all hands, including many that I could not remember, but pretended that I did. Their stock is very low and they don't know when they will be able to get anything more for the customers that will be piling in upon them.

Finally to the Legation to get our passports vised and to have a talk with the Minister. He had gone out but young Swift, his private secretary put some rubber stamps on that were of no use and I went on to the French Legation where I found an unholy crowd waiting in line for passports. There was an old time servant who passed me thru a side door and got me to the Consul who not only stopped swearing at other people long enough to look after my affairs but shook me by the hand and wished me bon voyage.

Thence to the CRB where there was a meeting in progress in the circular corner room. I was filled with curiosity as to what was going on but feared that all hands would get up and shake me by the hand and ask polite questions and break up the meeting, so I stayed out in the hall and talked with Joe Green and Heineman and others who came along. When I saw that the meeting was breaking up I went in and talked with the crowd for a little while, until the Chief was ready to move on to the Legation for a talk with the Minister. Poland and I left him there and went on to Myriam's for a cup of tea and fifteen minute's talk.

Thence back to the hotel to dress for dinner and along to the Legation.

There was an air of cordiality that had been lacking in the morning, perhaps due in some measure to a growing realization of the importance to them of the work I am attached to. However that may be, it was quite like old times with everybody telling stories and cracking jokes...

After dinner the Minister [Whitlock] said that he had had a letter from a spiritualist in Ohio who said that she had had a visit from Miss Cavell who made a complete statement as to her case: "She said all we had written about it was correct save for the fact that she was not shot that morning. She was kept for month before being shot."

While we were there Jean Wittouck came in to see me and I talked with him for a little while in my old office. He is now taller than I am. A few weeks ago he was arrested by the Germans on the charge that he was the leader of an anti-Flemish demonstration down town; for this he was fined 30,000 marks, with an alternative of seven months in prison, – which he did not accept. He is off to the army in a few days and hopes to be in Germany in a few weeks. He is a splendid boy.

We are due to come back here by Friday next. The Chief was anxious to keep away from any sort of demonstration but Francqui and the others said that any such action on his part would be misinterpreted so he yielded as he always does when his own inclinations appear to hurt other people and we are coming back. I was especially included but shall keep well in the background – though I probably shall not have to struggle to get there. The plan is to have dinner with Max and several affairs among le people [the people], after which there is to be a dinner with the King. It will be a very busy time but will not help feed any large part of starving Europe so does not meet with much enthusiasm from the Chief.

The prices here are something fearful. Eggs are three francs each and even at that they have come tumbling down from five. Butter is 25 francs for a kilo. Meat is 12 to 24 and other things in proportion when they can be had.

Log   Brussels-Paris. Saturday, November 30, 1918

Brussels – Mons	54 kilometers
Maugeuge	20
Avesness	18
La Capelle	16
Guise	25
St. Quentin	27
	20
	10
Noyon	10
	10
Compiègne	13
Senlis	<u>32</u>
Paris	203

We were called at 6 and nearly managed to get away by seven as planned. However it was ten minutes late when we pulled away from the hotel. We spun down to Mons thru a fog and reached Maugeuge in good time and there we stopped so that the Chief could have a chance to greet the Mayor [Walrand]. The old gentleman received us at once and told us what he could about the needs of the place which seem to be fairly well kept in view of the difficulties of transport, etc. He was particularly anxious for rice and shoes for the people and was assured that they would be forthcoming. He said they kept about three thousand refugees from ruined towns, a floating population as they were always clearing out without warning to look for their old homes and see what they could find. The Chief is much interested in organizing some immediate relief for these swarms of people who do not seem to be looked after as they should be.

Maugeuge does not seem to have been hurt much in the recent fighting. Most of the damage was done four years ago and begins to wear an air of respectability.

Avesness, La Capelle and Guise were all more or less battered and the roads lined with piles of German material abandoned during the retreat. We rejoined our old road at St. Quentin and sped along in sunshine to Oringy where one of our front tyres went flat and we availed of the opportunity to eat our lunch. When we got to Compiègne we had some tinkering with the bearings as one of the rear wheels and lost half an hour or so but despite the fact we rolled into Paris at a little before four o'clock, having thus accomplished the entire journey in less than nine hours. With luck and dry roads we could undoubtedly improve materially on this.

On coming into the hotel I telephoned to Vilgrain and found that Clemenceau was leaving for London this evening and that he wants to see the Chief at 5:30. Vilgrain came for him and took him away.

Col. House is still in bed and there is no reply from the President as to our general plans. I had our passports vised for London and then learned that until the President was heard from the Chief thought it was much better not to go near London, as we are to be here a few days more.

At the Embassy I found a telegraph saying that Helfferich had been appointed to represent the Austrian Government in regard to food matters and desired to meet the Chief in London at an early date. Lewis Strauss who evidently wants to reduce everything to a system, telegraphed to ask whether he should send Helfferich. The same reply as was sent to Lancken.

Another telegram to say that the President wanted to know before he sailed just how much money would be necessary for carrying out the food plans for Europe. There is no way to give any accurate idea of that but the Chief will have to worry about it until tomorrow and then answer.

Crespi, the Italian Food Minister has arrived and is at the Lotti. He came in before dinner and had quite a talk. He was going thru to London but has now decided to stay on here as all he wanted was to talk to the Chief.

Went up to the House and found that every bed was filled. Jim Wadsworth and Loring are both there and there was no cranny for me. I packed a bag and came back to the hotel. There was not a soul at home so I know nothing.

[Edward] Hurley blew up because he said he had not been consulted in regard to the telegram sent to the President about feeding Europe. He wrote the Chief a fierce letter and has spent most of the evening in loud conversation. The Chief weighed in occasionally with a remark or so which seemed to be effective but Brer[160] Hurley had his feelings hurt despite the fact that he had been fully consulted and was grouchy only because of the fact that he had not seen the draft before it got off. So far as I can make out this administration has been a complete fizzle anyway and it was only the coming of peace that saved him.

Dined with the Chief, Poland and Taft. The evening has been divided between Gordon Auchincloss, Cravath, Hurley and Gibbs and other firemen.

Letter to Mary Gibson.   Paris. Sunday, December 1, 1918

I got up this morning to learn the sad news that Willard Straight had died in the night of pneumonia. He had a long pull but even his magnificent strength was not enough to bring him through. His poor wife is on the other side of the water and could not come over. Walter Lippmann, Martin Egan and Mrs. Harriman did everything that could be done but he was delirious for over a week and there was little hope.

We had a morning of conferences and cleared up some of the business that had accumulated while we were away. Two stenographers gave up their Sunday as they will probably give up others before they get through.

In the afternoon I went out to the chancery and got some of my own stuff and looked in at the flat where there was not a soul to greet me. Arthur is down at GHQ and will not be back till tonight or tomorrow. Jim Wadsworth has been there but was off visiting some New York regiment.

The rest of the afternoon talking to various people, General Dawes, Red Cross people including Colonel [Henry] Anderson, the Italian Food Minister Crespi, and a stream of Belgian Relief people who came, some of them to talk pending busi-

---

[160] Possibly a joke referring to one book in the collection of African-american folk tales published by Joel Chandler Harris, *Uncle Remus and Brer Rabbit*, New York 1907.

ness and some of them to seek new jobs with whatever organization is established. There is a roomful of them now and the air is heavy with smoke and finance.

When dinner time came round there was a roomful of old CRB boys waiting to say a word to the Chief and he bade them all to dine; we sat down fourteen at table quite as in old Belgian days. Most of the crowd were in uniforms, Jackson, Wickes, Leach and one or two other captains, Wellington. Exton and a flock of lieutenants, with Kittredge the sole representative of the Navy as lieutenant junior grade. All this old crowd is coming back and clamoring for work in the new undertaking. A lot have been taken on and there will be more flocking to the standard as soon as they can get leave of absence to get to Paris. The Commander in Chief [Pershing] has laid down the rule that Hoover is to have anybody from the army that he wants and he proposes to reach out and get some real talent. Our forces are moving into Belgium and northern France and before long some of the old crowd will be setting up shop in all sorts of odd corners in order to feed the hungry. The CRB was a big story but it was child's play in comparison with what is being undertaken now and some of these boys are in for a big adventure.

Kellogg and Taylor back from The Hague with news that John Garrett has received a telegram signed HOOVER asking him to head off the telegram which had been sent to Rotterdam concerning the reply to be made to Lancken. It looks as though somebody had committed a cheerful little forgery with a purpose and we got off a message to Garrett to make an investigation. Unless Kellogg and Taylor made a mistake, there may be interesting developments.

Letter to Mary Gibson. Paris. Monday, December 2, 1918

Following the high tradition established since this party started we got up at the crack of dawn this morning and flew at it without waiting for the sun to rise and light our labors.

Mr. Hoover had a flock of people in to see him and then we set out together on some calls. First we went to the Ministry of the Blockade[161] and spent an hour talking to M. Baidoux, Sub-Secretary who is in charge of the sort of matters we are interested in. Baidoux is a helpless cripple who has to be carried to his work but his mind does not have to be carried anywhere. He cannot even reach very far but

---

161 In 1916, a 'sous-secrétariat d'État du Blocus' had been installed within the French Foreign Ministry to coordinate the activities of military, economic, transport, and toll institutions. In 1917, it was transfored into the 'ministère du Blocus et des Régions libérées'

has a most ingenious arrangement of shelves about him so that he can put his hand upon all sorts of papers. His row of bells and telephones are on the edge of the desk and a large drawing board rests upon his lap and the edge of his desk so that he has not to have a step the whole day. We went into the serious questions of feeding and supplying the countries of Europe but even at that there is more to be talked about when we get a chance.

From there to the Élysée Palace Hotel for a talk with Mr. Stettinius and then to General Dawes. You may remember him as the Chicago banker who was such a friend of Arthur Orr and who supported the Chicago Symphony to a large extent. He is General Purchasing Agent for the AEF and as such will have much to do with us. Among other things we were after offices and personnel. Offices we shall probably have in the course of a day or two and personnel as fast as we can pick the men we want.

We stayed to lunch with Dawes and had fried eggs and coffee on his desk.

I then left Hoover at the hotel to talk to streams of people and set off on one of those squirrel-in-a cage activities of mine.

Ynès Reyntiens turned up from Brussels having spent the greater part of two days in rough travel with Bebeth de Lynden. She is on her way to Switzerland to take care of her brother Ramon who was badly gassed and is now going into tuberculosis. He is so miserable alone at the sanitarium that when Brussels was liberated he sent word that either Ynès was to go to him or he would head straight for the health climate of Brussels. She set out with customary nerve and has got this far on her way. She was quite dazed by the different conditions and said she felt like a country cousin, not knowing how to get about or what to do. She had addresses written on little scraps of paper tucked into her glove and spent her time on the metro with her nose flattened against the window pane lest she should go by her station. Bebeth came with her but was so staggered by the change in everything that she settled down at her sister's house and refused to budge until she could get used to it.

I took Ynès and Miss Larner to dine and there was an amount of conversation that made up for part, at least, of the time since we left Brussels.

The restaurants here all closed at 9:30 so we were put into the street at that hour with any amount of things still unsettled and as Ynès felt inclined for dissipation we went to a movie and saw the retreat of the Germans from Brussels, the arrival of Max and the King and Queen and a lot of other things that Y. just lived through. We dropped her at home and managed to get back to the hotel in time to do a little work before turning in.

There are so many things going on that it is quite out of the question for the Chief to go to Brussels the end of this week. He has accordingly telegraphed that he must defer his visit for a week and proposes to go to London on Wednesday morning. At my own suggestion I am staying on here as there is nothing I can do there and I want to attend to starting the offices and getting a house for us all to live in. Taylor and Kellogg are leaving for Switzerland, Poland for Belgium and Bob Taft and I are left to attend to the loose ends.

Letter to Mary Gibson.   Paris. Tuesday, December 3, 1918

This has been a sad day. We laid Willard Straight away among the soldiers in the plot of ground we have taken at Suresnes on a hillside overlooking Paris. The funeral party was small, just the people Mrs. Harriman asked. There were all the old 1718 H Street crowd[162] who could be here, McCoy, Sterling, and Joe Grew. Jim Logan could not get here and Jim Wadsworth had not been heard from since Willard died. Also Mr. Stettinius, Martin Egan, Warwick Greene, Bentley Mott, General Johnson, Peter Bowditch.

The coffin draped in a flag and with his cap and sword laid upon it, was brought down by a guard of soldiers and placed on a motor truck. We followed on foot through drizzling rain to the American church in the Avenue de l'Alma where a fair sized group of friends had gathered. Bishop Brent and two army chaplains officiated and the service was soon over. Then a few of us went out to the cemetery and stayed until taps had been blown. It was a ghastly business to lay away such a man, just coming into his full usefulness and it was a badly depressed crowd that came back to Paris.

I brought Walter Lippmann back with me to lunch as he had been under a bad strain during all Willard's sickness and needed a change.

The afternoon took a busy turn and I went off with Bob Taft to make arrangements for offices and a house. We found a big place in the rue de Lubeck and were told to take it without being able to get the Chief to look it over. The lease is to be signed tomorrow and we shall probably have it ready for occupancy when he gets back from London.

It is almost a hopeless thing to get a house these days as they are being gobbled up by people over for the peace conference. This one had just been on the market and we pounced upon it before it should be taken from us. Hotels are

---

[162] 1718 H Street was a residence in Washington DC rented by a group of bachelors setting out in diplomatic, political or military careers in 1907. 1718 H Street became known as the home to "The Family." As these men married and moved, they kept in close touch. Key members included Hugh Gibson, Basil Miles, and Charles Evans Hughes as well as those mentioned above. The house burned down in 1922, but was rebuilt and hosted parties and discrete negotiations through 1930. 1718 H Street was sold in 1954, the year Gibson died, and the group disbanded.

going like hot cakes. Our Government has requisitioned several of the biggest for various purposes, the Élysée Palace, the Regina, the Crillon, the Louvre and others. The French, of course, have helped themselves generously and now the British have taken over five new ones in the course of the past day or two. The Italians are threatening to take over the Meurice where we are now installed and the British have envious eyes on the Ritz. People are scurrying like rats to new hotels only to be turned into the street to scurry some more. The situation gets worse day by day and there is no telling how acute it will get if this keeps up. I am thinking of resigning from the service and setting up a barracks at 147 rue de la Pompe.

We are probably to have offices in the Élysée Palace and hope to get provisionally installed tomorrow or next day. We shall probably expand as fast as other branches shrink and before long we may have a good part of the hotel. It think the Chief is resigning himself to settling down here for an indefinite time.

Colonel House has been ill for some days, – in fact since before the Chief got here and today he was well enough for the first time to have a talk. That settled some of our perplexities, – but don't worry, there are always plenty more.

In the evening the Chief had Boret, the French Food Minister to dine and I went up to Comtesse van der Burch's (Bebeth's sister) to dine. I was pretty down in the mouth and did not contribute much to the occasion but removed myself at ten and come back to find everybody had taken to their beds dead beat.

The evening paper gives me much pleasures. I see that when the Belgians got to Aix-la-Chapelle they put up an affiche which is an exact copy of one put up by Bissing in Belgium. It states that then notables of Aix will be taken as hostages to be responsible for good order in the town; that they will be changed from day to day; that the inhabitants have until 5 o'clock to turn in all their arms at a given place; that after that time anybody found with arms will be shot; anybody who opposes the Belgian troops will also be shot; nobody must go into the streets after seven o'clock in the evening, and civilians must salute and get off the sidewalk when approaching Belgian officers. It is a perfectly serious document but I am ready to bet the Belgians have been carrying it around with them for a long time praying for the day when they might put it up in a German town.

You will also remember how the Germans imposed German time on the Belgians and bedeviled them about it. On arriving at Aix the Belgians instigated Belgian time in exactly the same manner.

A member of the soldier's council asked to be received by the Belgian commander. The latter sent word back that the soldier's council was "dissolved" and that he recognized nobody save the Burgomaster.

They are running the whole gamut of affiches with which the Huns afflicted us, but seem to be doing it only in the things that do not really go very deep. There has so far been no levying of indemnities, no executions, etc. However, it must be nuts for the Belgians to be able to turn the knife around now and then and hear the victim squeal, – and there is plenty of squealing.

Letter to Mary Gibson.   Paris. Wednesday, December 4, 1918

Up this morning at six in order to have breakfast with the Chief [Hoover], talk to him without interruption and start him on his way toward Boulogne and London. He went off alone by motor and so got away on time, rounding the corner sharp at seven. That gave him ample time to catch the boat at 2:30.

I was too well started to go back to bed, so sat me down before my little typewriter and cleaned up a lot of things, – the which gave me a feeling of self-righteousness. It was well I did it that way for there was not another chance all day.

People began pouring in to talk about all sorts of things and when I transferred my activities to the chancery I found a bunch waiting for me already. Among others was Jim Wadsworth who is in town only for the day before starting off on a long trip through the newly occupied territory. Arthur Page is going with him so as to have a general look round before starting home. I also saw Colonel Moreno who wanted to talk to me about various people I had put it up to the army to show around the American front. The army people are splendid about that sort of thing and whenever I have suggested that it would be a good thing for any reason to take somebody about they have done it and done it well. This week I have Admiral Sir Douglas Brownrigg, British Chief Naval Censor coming over to have a look at our activities and they are receiving him like visiting royalty. Next week I expect to have Admiral Hall, the Director of Naval Intelligence and they propose to treat him the same way. These two men have played the game with us from the beginning of the war and this is the only chance we have to show our appreciation.

My old friend Basil Thomson, Chief of the Criminal Investigation Department of New Scotland Yard, also came in to see me. He is here to make all sorts of arrangements for the Peace Conference and I was glad of an opportunity to have a talk with him. I don't know whether I ever told you about him. He is the son of somebody or other in particular, was at one time Governor of the Fiji Islands and has written the standard book on the manners (if any) and customs of the natives of those lovely islands. He was Senior Wrangler of his university and is a man of high attainments. He is always a surprise as people look for a common policeman and find somebody who would fit nicely into the Cabinet. If he ever writes the stories of his achievements during the war it will make great reading.

I spent a good part of the afternoon straightening out all sorts of minor difficulties in connection with our work here, trying to get some speed into the work that is being done on the house that we have taken and to arrange for proper office and personnel to put in them. I think we shall get well installed in the Élysée Palace Hôtel before the Chief comes back. So far we have got along as well as we could at the hotel and in my office at the Embassy.

And now I am for an early to bed to catch up on some lost sleep.

[Added note found only in Secret Log]
Basil Thomson says that he is arranging to have a regular daily airplane service to England in order to avoid so far as possible the use of telephone and telegraph lines that could be tapped by the French. He spoke of our using them but it would seem best for us to have our own service by plane or otherwise as far as Havre where we can put stuff onto the cable without having it tapped by anybody.

I did not stick to my plans for an early to bed but got Ynès, Bebeth and Bob Taft to dine at the Hotel and then on to the Aepolle to see La Reine Jayeuse. It was pretty rough but we got through it and they all enjoyed the jazz band that played between the acts.

Kellogg and Taylor got off for Switzerland by the evening train.

Letter to Mary Gibson.   Paris. Thursday, December 5, 1918

Another day spent largely in pushing on the reins and trying to get speed into the arrangements for house and offices. We have got a little headway but are not yet through by any means.

The people in Brussels are much upset because the Chief has deferred his visit and today we have been receiving telegrams to say that all sorts of arrangements have been made and that he must come as originally planned. There is a dinner by Max on Saturday and another with the King on Sunday as well as a lot of other things and they are most anxious to go ahead. I telephoned the texts of their messages to London for the Chief and am waiting to hear what he has to say although I am pretty sure that he will feel obliged to stick at his work.

I lunched today with Bob Taft, Capt. Gregory and Poland and set out afterward on business bent. The crowds were dense as we got near the Champs Elysées so we went in the back of the War Industry Board and watched the arrival of the King and Queen of the Belgians who are here on a state visit. We timed our arrival so neatly that we stepped out onto the balcony just as the trumpets sounded, the troops presented arms and the crowds burst into full-throated cheering. The Avenue was lined with veteran troops in bleu de ciel, with steel helmets and long bayonets fixed. The crowd was banked up solidly behind them and was a sight in itself. We looked down upon the red caps and blue caps of officers with the little swirl of gold lace, the khaki caps of our own people, the steel helmets of the mean on leave, the turbans of Indians and the verigated headgear of civilians. The latter made up a good half of the crowd and most of them were in black. You have to see a crowd here to know how deep the war has struck. A single line of lancers spread out across the Avenue came sweeping down from the Étoile. Directly behind them was a carriage with the President of France [Poincaré] and the King [Albert I]. Then another with Madame Poincaré and the Queen [Elisabeth]. Then Clemenceau and the Prince in the uniform of a private of infantry which he has been for over three years. He had no decorations and looked as though he were the real thing and the crowd gave him some real cheering on his own account. Then a few carriages with the suite and the parade was finished. The crowd was enthusiastic as only a Paris crowd can be. The King saluted gravely and the Queen bowed in a gentle shy way that took people off their feet. If anybody is safe in their particular line of business, I should think they would be.

And then it was all over and we went about our business.

Later in the afternoon when I went down to the Place de la Concorde to see Joe Grew, I found the streets packed with people waiting to see the visitors return from the Élysée after paying their formal call on the President and Mme. Poincaré.

The fountains in the center of the Place were gushing away under a full head of steam as they have not done for over four years, glowing with hundreds of concealed lights. Searchlights on top of the Crillon were fixed on the statues of Strasbourg and Lille almost buried in flowers. And the crowd was singing and shouting and generally availing of another opportunity to relieve its pent-up feelings.

After we had finished talking shop, Joe Grew took me through the quarters that have been prepared for the Peace Delegation, showed me the charts of organization, the distribution of space etc. All of this will doubtless have to be changed when the pilgrims arrive for such is always the case. It is an interesting job but I don't envy him a bit and am thankful that I am connected with my present work instead of tagging onto the end of the delegation. Hoover is to my taste.

Before lunch a telegram was received from Whitlock to the following effect:

"For the Ambassador personally. Please see that Hoover gets the telegram I sent him this morning. It is of the utmost importance that he be here for the dinner the King is to give him on Sunday and the ceremonies organized in his honor on Saturday by the City of Brussels.

In the evening the telegram to what he referred arrived as follows:

"URGENT FOR HOOVER FROM WHITLOCK. I have your telegram for Francqui. Your friends here are in consternation. The King gives a dinner in your honor Sunday evening at the Palace. They City gives a reception at the Hôtel de Ville [town hall] at three o'clock Saturday afternoon at which time the freedom of the City of Brussels is to be conferred upon you. All the schoolchildren of Brussels have been invited to the ceremony; at the same time you will receive the degree of Doctor of Laws from the University of Brussels. The Comité National gives a banquet Saturday evening at which all the provincial delegates will be present. A luncheon is to be given on Monday at the Ministry for Foreign Affairs. The complicated arrangements for all these functions have been completed. Permit me as one of your most devoted friends to say that you cannot afford thus lightly to wave aside such honors as the Belgian Nation never showed a man before and irreparably wound the sensibilities of those who in devotion and gratitude are trying to honor you, and I earnestly urge you to reconsider your unfortunate decision.

WHITLOCK
It strikes me as a particularly cheeky telegram to tell the Chief that he has no manners and does not know how to behave himself in civilized society. Incidentally, knowing that he [Hoover] had gone to London it is rather hard to understand why he [Whitlock] sent the message to Paris unless it was so that nothing could be done about it until it was too late.

Letter to Mary Gibson. Paris. Friday, December 6, 1918

I got up early this morning. I've almost got into the habit of getting up early.

First of all I put in a call for London by telephone to talk to the Chief. Then I sat down and waited for it until lunch time which is the usual procedure. Just before lunch time Shoecraft got through to me from the London Embassy with a message from Hoover and I read him the long telegram that had come for Hoover from Whitlock saying that he must drop everything and go to Brussels for the party. And then I spent the rest of the day waiting to hear what Hoover was going to do and whether I should have to spend most of the night in a motor trying to reach Brussels tomorrow at noon.

At four o'clock another call came through with a message for me from the Chief to say that he positively could not get away from the London conference[163] and that it was up to me to see that his decision was understood by everybody from the King down.

I dictated a short memorandum on the subject to give the first person in authority I could find and then went back to the hotel and donned my 1904 frock

---

[163] Hoover was engaged with the Allied Conference of the Committee to Consider Victuallying and Supply of Allied, Neutral, and Enemy Countries in London December 3–7, 1918. His attendance was critical since he would be taking leadership of the efforts.

coat and top hat, so that I might have as little difficulty as possible getting through the police lines. With these badges of respectability and a military car I managed to get through to the Quai d'Orsay where the King and his suite are lodged during their visit to Paris.

I found that a very small reception was being given for the great ones of the land and that the common or garden citizen was not allowed anywhere inside. I inquired for Guy d'Oultremont and one or two others of the King's household who I know and was told that none of them were there. Finally I prevailed upon a young officer to send my card up to any member of the King's entourage who might be free. In a few minutes a young Belgian officer came down looking very bored and said that he could give me only a minute as he was very busy. I tried to tell my tale to him but he could not wait and bade me go upstairs with him and wait while he sought out someone less important who could listen to me.

He went into the great salon where the court was lined up and in a minute came out with a startled fawn expression and the statement that the King had heard I was there and wanted to see me. The Minister of Foreign Affairs [Hymans] and the Belgian Ministers came swooping down upon me, others chased away the rows of duchesses and other face cards who were working their way toward the King and I was led straight to him. He forgot to stand upon his dignity and came part way to meet me, greeting me with a surprising enthusiasm.

He began by saying that both he and the Queen had wondered when I would turn up since I had failed to be on hand for their return to Brussels. He went over all our talks in Antwerp, Malines and the Yser front and remembered things better than I did. And he talked about my hair-breadth escapes in a way that made me shiver, though I confess I don't remember them as having been so bad.

I finally broke in long enough to tell him why I had come although without any idea of bothering him. He listened very seriously while I told him of Hoover distress and his embarrassment at being obliged to defer his visit after arrangements had been made. When I had quite finished the King said:

"Tell Mr. Hoover that I know him so well that no matter what he does I know that his reasons are good and I approve what he does. He has done so much for us that we can never doubt the wisdom or the motive of anything he does. *** And tell him besides that I am only a King and he is a dictator; so he owes me no explanations at any time."

And then we got off on another talk about the first days of the war, etc.

The King looked better than ever, older, a little tinge of grey in his blond hair, deeper wrinkles about the eyes and the same kindly patient look with an added mellowness. And in his plain service uniform he stood out among all the dressy gentlemen who were in the room.

I could see out of the corner of my eye that all the dignitaries assembled were on pins and needles because I had broken up their show. The Chef du Protocol was dancing around the edge of the proceedings trying to attract attention and there was a general murmur that was as near an approximation of a mob scene as was permissible. Of course it was up to the King to dismiss me but he seemed to be settling down for an old home week so I finally took matters in my own hands and told him I was sorry to have bothered him and would go my way. He said all right, and then went right on, saying that I was expected to come to Brussels with the Chief and that they would try to show me that I was looked upon as a friend. "For," he said, "You were a good friend in the very bad days when we needed them worst and although you were neutral we never doubted that you were a friend that we could depend upon. So we want you to come back and enjoy with us the good days of victory even if it is only for a little while." There was more of the same sort but is sounded simple and natural in the way he said it and it was nice to think that he remembered and appreciated.

I had to make another effort to get away, and when I was successful bolted from the room, and it was only when I got half way down the great staircase that I remembered my failure to back out and to bow at the door. Probably all the bigwigs fainted but I imagine the King kept his footing successfully. The picture it suggested made me burst out laughing as I came down the stairs and the startled flunkies probably thought I had been overcome with hysteria in the excitement of having been introduced into the presence of royalty.

I hied me back to the Embassy and got off telegrams to Brussels to explain the situation and another to Hoover to assure him that all was well and that he need not worry about the displeasure of his friend the King.

And then back to the hotel where I dined with Bob Taft and Gregory.

While we were there in came Josse and Antoinette Allard and Gaston d'Ansembourg, all old Brussels friends. They had contrived to get a car and had motored down from Brussels for a few days. They expect to be back home by the middle of this week. They don't quite know where they are but will soon find out.

When Shoecraft called me up he gave me a message from the Chief which requested me to draw up in appropriate language and pass on to the Belgian authorities. I dictated a line in great haste and left the following with the King's orderly and with Hymans whom I saw on returning to the hotel.

"MESSAGE FROM MR. HOOVER TO MR. GIBSON. LONDON, December 6, 1918

Will you please express to the King the grief I feel at my inability to reach Brussels in time to receive the great honors that are proposed.

Only the jeopardy of human life involved in the abandonment or delay of the conference now in progress, upon the settlement of which must depend the whole relief of southern Europe, will prevent my presence.

It would indeed be a great satisfaction and a high honor to me but I feel that I have no right to delay the settlement of this matter for even a single day for any personal interest or satisfaction of my own. I feel very deeply the honor tendered to me by the Belgian Nation, and the loss is my own in my inability to attend.

I am convinced that His Majesty will understand and sympathize with the motives which impel me to take a decision which prevents me from accepting such great kindness from the Belgian people for whom He must know I feel so deep an affection."

Hymans, to whom I showed the foregoing at the Meurice, seemed quite satisfied when assured that the Chief would go to Brussels at some later date. He did not seem to believe that there was any great amount of consternation in Brussels, as he had heard nothing from there, and it would be natural for the Belgians to telegraph him in such an event instead of leaving the whole business to Brand Whitlock. It looks more and more like an attempt of that gentleman to get the Chief into an uncomfortable position with the Belgians.

I got off telegrams on the subject as follows:

American Legation BRUSSELS

ATTENTION WHITLOCK. Your telegram repeated to Hoover in London whither he left several days ago as stated in his telegram of Monday to Francqui. He was constrained to defer his visit to Brussels because his presence was vitally necessary at important conferences involving the whole relief of Europe. He would not have deferred his visit but for the jeopardy to human life involved in the abandonment or delay of the conference now in progress. The matter has been fully explained to His Majesty who quite understands and approves Hoover's motives. Hoover counts upon his Belgian friends also to understand that he would not have asked them to change their plans save under stress of urgent necessity. He feels sure that they all understand and sympathize with the motives which have prompted his decision. He is in no sense lightly waving aside the honor they wish to pay him. He is very grateful and appreciative but feels strongly that he would be remiss were he to allow any personal inclination or interest to interfere with the welfare of these suffering populations. Hoover looks forward to visiting Brussels as soon as he can possibly arrange to do so. SHARP

URGENT
Herbert C. Hoover
Hotel Ritz, London
Saw the King this afternoon and explained matters fully. He thoroughly understands and approves your motives in deferring visit and says that you will be just as welcome whenever you come no matter how often you are obliged to

change your plans. The Ambassador is telegraphing fully to Brussels. Left full message for Hymans who will doubtless explain matters fully on returning to Brussels. GIBSON. SHARP

Letter to Mary Gibson	Paris. Saturday, December 7, 1918

I am coming on so well with the theory of writing you a line-a-day whether there is anything to say or not that I am quite puffed up with myself.

The day has brought in several more telegrams from Whitlock who is having a fit over Hoover's failure to get there for the ceremonies today. It can't be helped in times like these when people are starving and I should think dinners, etc. would take a decidedly second place with everybody.

Bob Taft and I have been spending most of the day pursuing the festive window cleaner and carpet layers of the new house. Plumbers, electricians, coal heavers, tradesmen, scrubbers, and handymen have passed in an unending procession up and down the stairs and the place begins to assume something a habitable aspect. We hope that it will be ready to move into on Monday afternoon but so many of the willing workers are dropping out that I refuse to make my bets. We want to have it in running order when the Chief gets back.

We are also making a brave show of being busy with the new offices so that we can claim more space. The brutal soldiery do not want to let us have anything and apparently we have got to kick up a large amount of dust and convince them that the Food Administrator is on the premises before they will give us room according to our strength.

I finished my days work early today and came back to the hotel to take to my bed and head off a little tough of sore throat. People are careful these days – and it pays. While I was laid up Charley Taft, the younger brother, came romping in to be here over night before going on to Saumur.

I had to climb out of bed to go over to the Ritz to a farewell dinner that George McFadden was giving for himself. It was a whale of an affair with a huge round table in the center of the room where we could have all eyes focused upon us. The guests were Mrs. Leeds, top-heavy with pearls, Lady Johnstone, an old friend from The Hague of whom you have hear before this, Colonel and Mrs. Blake, she formerly Mrs. Mackay, Admiral Long, Major Mitchell, Hoyty Wiborg, Miss Havemeyer, Mr. Stettinius and one or two more. After dinner we adjourned to Mrs. Leed's salon which was large enough to hold us and a numerous cavalry escort. Conversation was correct until Lady Johnstone asked to be taught how to shoot craps. Then we got down on the floor and showed the assembled company which was soon at it in force, – and police conversation vanished for the evening. The carriages had been called for ten but it was a quarter to twelve when the company got up stiffly and stretched itself preparatory to going downstairs. The pikers like myself who started the game were soon cleaned out and then the stakes rose until the malefactors of great wealth among us were going at the rate of a hundred francs a throw while the rest of sat by with staring eyes and luxuriated in such expensive company.

I shall never become a chronic gambler because I never had the least run of luck to encourage me to keep it up.

Letter to Mary Gibson.   Paris. Sunday, December 8, 1918

By way of change I have taken most of the day off to play.

I was got out of bed by Margaret Mayo who wanted to talk about some people who were in trouble. That was for half an hour and I fear she had not much more than the comfort of telling it all to somebody. She got that at any rate.

Then to the house to see how the cleaners were progressing. It would have been better for our peace of mind if we had not gone for there were only three or four people poking about in the whole place whereas there should have been twenty or thirty to make any showing.

From there to the chancery where I found a telegram from the Chief to say that he would be back here late Tuesday night. I am sending a car up tomorrow so that it can fetch him back in good time. That gives us an added day of grace to prepare for him coming.

That finished the day's work and Stetson and I then gathered up Ynès and Bebeth and took them out to Versailles to lunch at the Reservoirs. We had a car that was put at the disposal of the mission and enjoyed a drive through the St. Cloud Forest on our way.

The Reservoirs has gone downhill but still we managed to get through without too much grumbling and then set out on foot to see the Château and park. Neither of the girls had ever been there before and it was good fun. The Château had just been opened for the first time in four years and there was a ravening mob struggling at the door so we contented ourselves with flattening our noses against the windows and then went off and saw the out of door things where the mob was not in the way. Then over to the Grand Trianon, the Petit Trianon and the Haumea which was lovely in the soft grey light. The girls were in raptures about it and it was almost as much fun as the first visit to see them discover the place.

It was as warm as toast and clear and we had just enough time to see everything comfortably before it got dark. Then into the car and back to town stopping at a place picked out by the chauffeur to have tea and thus make a real day of it. The place was on the river and we sat in a little room looking out on the water; we were served in violation of all the rules with butter, sugar, jam and goodness knows what else beside but we were cowardly enough not to denounce them to the police, – and to eat everything that was set before us.

We sprinkled the girls around at their various places of abode and then went to the chancery where I always contrive to find a telegram or two, and then back to the hotel where I found Gallavresi waiting for me. We dined together and talked high politics until it was time to go to bed, – the which I am going to do now with a great deal of enthusiasm.

Letter to Mary Gibson.   Paris. Monday, December 9, 1918

A cussed day of rows and ructions and petty errands that use up the strength and the temper and don't get you anywhere.

This morning we went up to the house all filled up with ideas that we were on the home stretch and that we would be tucked away under its roof by nightfall. Instead we found that practically the entire troop of workmen had deserted, that the expensive housekeep had chosen this moment to have the flu and that even the house agent who had undertaken to see that things were ready had taken to his bed with the same ailment. The rugs were still shy, the silver and linen and dishes had not turned up as per promise; the telephone was disconnected, the electric lights were erratic, the baths had begun to act queerly and the newly engaged chef after one look at the dirty kitchen had burst into tears and rushed from the house never to return. I felt like the Emperor of Germany with my Empire crumbling over my head. The whole day I spent tearing around from one place to another trying to get some action. I succeeded in rousing the poor housekeeper to the point of getting up and tottering about during the afternoon. I saw the agent and threw such a ferocious bluff about breaking the lease and standing for any number of law suits that he rushed off and saw the Princess who has agreed to accept our money and evidently told her such a tale that she is beginning to show some interest. We can't get in in time to put Mr. Hoover in when he arrives but we ought to get there by the end of the week.

Incidentally, a telegram came to say that Mr. Hoover would be here tomorrow and wanted a car to meet him at Boulogne. About the time that we had got that arranged there came another telegram to say that he wanted three cars so we had to start all over again and make ourselves unpopular with the poor men who have to arrange to make a small number of cars do duty for twice as many. After much visiting of Colonels and Generals, we contrived to get it done and sent a telegram to London to say that the stage was set.

So now home to bath and rest.

Bad news from Chaumont to the effect that my good friend Major James has had a bad nervous breakdown and that they are worried about him. It is a shame for he has been getting worse and worse for some time and yet nothing was done to stop him from overwork. Nobody can see him now but as soon as they can I am off to see what can be done for him. If by any chance you see Mrs. James and she knows about this, you can tell her that there are a lot of people here who are very fond of him and will do anything on earth that can be done for him. I saw General Nolan today and he is looking after matters himself with as much interest as though he were James' father.

I have a typical letter from Paul Hammond which was written on October 14 and addressed to Hugh D. Gibson, American Red Cross, Paris. Of course it went to Harvey Gibson who is the Red Cross Commissioner for France and reached me only after having laid about down there for weeks. Paul says that he has had enough fighting and wants a "limousine job". This, of course, was while the fighting was still going strong and his object in writing was to get me to lift him out of his fighting job and land him something here in Paris. He was perfectly frank in saying that he did not want to fight. The signing of the armistice saves me from having to write an embarrassing letter in reply.

[Added note found only in Secret Log]
Walter Rogers is discouraged already and somewhat overcome by the revelation that there is no result over here in all the Creel activity. He does not expect to be able to keep going very long with the Sisson-Byoir outfit and is looking for a place to set up alone. It is amusing how each and every one of Creel's people wants to run a separate show, but I must say I don't blame Rogers. Sisson has taken over the house of the King of Montenegro and is running an establishment such as he never had seen before. He has taken over six military motors and is generally having the time of his life. Bad if Congress were to take a look.

At 7:30 I went to gather up Ynès for dinner. We dropped by to see if we could get Bebeth but she was not there so we went on to the Ritz and dined alone after a visit with Lady Johnstone who was going out with a troop of youngsters and would not dine with us.

Letter to Mary Gibson. Paris. Tuesday, December 10, 1918

Another day of piffling little things.

In the course of the morning I got a telegram to say that Mr. Hoover would not come over until tomorrow. That means more running around to get orders to have the cars wait for him at Boulogne.

Bob Taft and I moved up to the rue de la Pompe so as to make room for the arriving members of the party.

We made several visits to the house and found that our play setting had had its effect and that a good deal is being done to get the place ready for occupancy this week.

We dined peacefully with Stetson and are going to bed early so as to get strong and be able to work hard for our country in the morning.

Letter to Mary Gibson.   Paris. Wednesday, December 11, 1918

Mr. Hoover is due back sometime tonight and then we can look forward to going to work in earnest.

Our house is making such progress that we hope to get into it in time for dinner tomorrow although the cook is protesting loudly that she is not to be judged by what she produced under difficulties.

Leval came in after lunch on his way to Brussels and clamored for a motor to take him and the mail pouches that he is taking with him. You might just about as well cry for the moon as to ask the army to produce another transport as the demands are tremendous. It looks as though Leval would have to travel by train like other people although that seems very hard to him. He has been doing very well in his law practice and is prosperous.

Sidney Cloman has arrived in Paris, having been assigned here from his division, and his office is next to ours in the Élysée Palace. He is now chiefly concerned in getting Mrs. Cloman and their adopted daughter to come over to stay with him but fears restrictions of officers' wives will keep her away.

Taft and Gregory had lunch with Stetson and me in the rue de la Pompe and I go back there tonight to dine with Stetson.

We have had a steady stream of callers on every imaginable sort of business whom we have had to stand off until the Chief gets back with his outfit of experts to discuss matters with them. They look to us to do everything from feeding Russian prisoners in Russia to finding motor trucks to send to Montenegro. It will be a big job whatever we do.

Taylor and Kellogg are being sent into Germany to investigate and report on conditions and in the course of a few days Legg and Taft will probably go to Austria on a similar mission. What the rest of us will do is another story but I imagine we will probably stay in this part of the world for some time to come.

Added Note, found in Log only

As a wind up to our correspondence about the trip to Brussels, Whitlock telegraphed the following:

"Ninth. For Hoover from Whitlock

Your telegram reached me only today, but when your friends did not wish to take NO for an answer I had already taken it upon myself to explain your situation. The invitations to the King's dinner we were able to have withheld and I went personally to the Burgomaster to express your regrets. He very kindly said that he realized the necessity of your continuing the conference and added that the postponement of the reception would have no other than the happy result of giving the city the opportunity to make it more imposing when it is held. Be assured that your friends here sympathetically understand the situation."

Yah!

Letter to Mary Gibson.   Paris. Thursday, December 12, 1918

This has been another hectic day but we have some movement to show for it by way of change.

This morning Bob Taft and I got up bright and early and went down to breakfast with the Chief at the Meurice. We got a good talk with him about his conferences in London and the progress he has made. There were various people in to see him in the course of the morning and at eleven we went to see Colonel House and then Gordon Auchincloss about various matters. From there to General Pershing's with Mr. Hurley. There I abandoned them and went to see André Tardieu. He was out but I made a date to see him in the afternoon and went my way.

We all lunched together at the Meurice, the whole outfit of us, and talked shop until it was time to shove off and see the new offices in the Élysée Palace.

The Chief and I stopped to see Tardieu and got him interested in finding quarters for us, accenting his interest somewhat by saying that it was a good deal of a problem here but that it was easy to get quarters in London and that we might be driven there. It was said somewhat in jest but he rose to the bait and set people off hot on the scent to find us what we wanted.

The President lands in Brest tomorrow and gets to Paris Saturday. There is to be a luncheon for him at the Élysée, given by the Poincaré's at 12:30. I got my invitation yesterday and strange to say I accepted it. The Chief has not yet got his but I have set myself on the trail of those in authority to see that he is bid as it would look queer if he were not. It would bore him to know that he was being taken to a lunch that he did not <u>have</u> to go to, but we sometimes have to do what we think is good for him.

I have a notice also to put on a frock coat and top hat and "find myself at the Bois de Boulogne Station" tomorrow morning to greet the President [Wilson]. It means, according to the directions of the protocol, getting started at 8:15 and remaining in the station for half an hour after the Presidential party has left. We line up and watch them walk by alongside large flocks of French officials and others, so I think I shall omit that and see the procession from our windows in the Élysée Palace.

It is hard to realize even here how much of an impression the President's coming is having on the people here. They look to him to come and straighten out all the troubles of the human race and they are getting ready to give him a reception in proportion to what they expect from him.

This evening we got moved into the new house in the rue de Lubeck and had our first dinner, with many preliminary apologies from the cook that this was not to be regarded as a fair sample of what she could do as it was a tour de force. If this is what she can do when under difficulties, I should not like to face an effort under favorable circumstances. We had a regular banquet which would have got our Food Administrator into trouble if it had been generally known. There were oysters, soup, fish, partridge, lamb with peas and potatoes, salad, ice and fruit. I had to have a session with the housekeeper, butler and cook afterward and explain the simple standard of the household and they are now promised for tomorrow.

Those who moved in for the first day are the Chief, Poland, Barnes, Taft, Gregory and HSG [Gibson]. Tomorrow Taylor may turn up from Switzerland and Cotton and Sheldon are expected from London so we shall probably have a houseful.

Letter to Mary Gibson.   Paris. Friday, December 13, 1918

Another day spent for the most part in our new offices with occasional flittings to look at buildings which may do for our permanent quarters as the ones we have are not adequate for any considerable growth.

This morning there was a pouch with your letter of the 18th when you knew that the armistice was signed. I think we felt a good deal alike at that time. It also brought me your letter of the 19th with the letter to Mr. Hoover from Mr. Brunswig. I don't know yet just what the needs will be but have put his letter on the personnel file so that it will be handy when our needs begin to develop.

I also had nice letters from Anne and from Auntie Jedsin.

I lunched at Bliss's with [Oscar] Crosby, Colonel Van Deman, Frazier, etc.

Dr. Taylor back from Bern with the news that Hugh Wilson is seriously ill with flu. I do hope that nothing will happen to him as he is the sort we cannot afford to do without at this time.

Ned Bell is coming over during the coming week to settle various business matters and will probably stay at the rue de la Pompe.

Frazier says that Arthur Orr is due to go home among the first and will probably leave within a week or so.

Ynès telephoned this evening that she is off for Switzerland tomorrow evening to join her brother. She has been waiting here for the frontier to open and got word today that she had better be getting to Belgarge.

We had dinner at the house and I am getting ready to tumble into bed so as to be ready for a long day tomorrow.

Letter to Mary Gibson. Paris. Saturday, December 14, 1918

This has been a day of wild careering and we are all about dead. The trouble is that work does not abandon its demands just because there are gay doings and functions to go to. You have to do them both and the combination is enough to test the strength of a prizefighter.

We were out of bed at the usual hour and climbed straight into our trusty frock coats and top hats for the day. On arriving at the office we found that genial officials had opened up the entire place to their friends and that our rooms were so packed with strange French people that there was no hope of doing any work and no prospect of seeing the parade later. As the only member of the firm who spoke French, it was my sad duty to get the whole crowd out of the place. This was done only by dint of much conversation, argument, gesticulation and in some cases by threatening to call the Military Police. I'm glad I don't have to turn out indignant old ladies everyday.

When the room had been cleared we tried to sit down and go through some pending matters but were constantly interrupted by young officers who brought in delegations of French friends to whom they had promised seats. They all had to argue as to whether they could dump them on us but we triumphed in every instance and had the place to ourselves for such work as we could do in the intervals.

The Champs Élysées was lined as usual with veteran troops and the crowd was massed solidly behind them. In the street under our window some of the troopers who had duty on foot had turned over their nags to a dozen girls who were perched sidewise on them to see over the heads of the people in front. Hundreds of people had brought out ladders and others had improvised stands by using sawhorses with a few planks laid across them on which they rented standing room.

About a quarter to ten there was a great tooting of trumpets and cheering and the President and Madame Poincaré drove up the Champs Élysées on their way to the station.

Several other times we heard cheering but if we rushed to the window to see what it was about we found that it was only some poor dog running down the middle of the street terrified by the howls of the crowd. This happened several times and seemed to give more pleasure to the mob than anything else that happened all day.

At a quarter past ten we heard the cannon firing salutes and a little later the escort came in eight around the Étoile. There was the usual line of cavalry, then the open carriage with the two Presidents. Ours was beaming and raised his hat in great sweeping gestures while the crowds howled. The enthusiasm was far and away ahead of that for the various kings who have honored us. In the second carriage was Mrs. [Woodrow] Wilson with Madame Poincaré. She had received so many bouquets that only her head was visible. She was radiantly happy to all appearances and got about as much cheering as the President. In the third carriage was Clemenceau with the Ambassador; then Lansing with M. Pichon, then Mr. White with General Bliss and a few more loads of the other members of the party. These were only the face cards. The lesser members had arrived an hour or so ahead by another special train and had been taken direct to the Crillon.

A number of people came in to share our windows, Cotton, Sheldon, Miss Larner, Ynès, Mrs. McCombs and the people from the Committee on Public Information.

The crowd melted away as by magic as soon as the parade passed and we were able to settle down to work until it was time to go to the Palace for luncheon. I went down with the Chief and arrived in good time to see the arrivals of the great. After shaking hands with the President and Madame Poincaré we were bid line up behind them and wait. Everybody was bid and everybody came.

There were Foch and Joffre and Pétain and Bliss and Pershing and Lord Derby and Clemenceau and Viviani, and Loubet and Painlevé and Ribot and the Jusserands and Tardieu and goodness knows who else. I saw a lot of people I had not seen for some time and had some good visits while we waited. Finally came the Lansing's and Mr. [Henry] White and the Grew's and other friends and we had a sort of old home week.

At a quarter to one the President and Mrs. Wilson came in, we were all lined up to shake them by the hand and then went in to lunch, which was in the state dining room, the Salle des Maréchaux. The lunch was in violation of all the rules and regulations of the Food Administration but everybody ate just as hearty as though they were not under the eagle eye of Hoover.

When we got down to the cheese, M. Poincaré got up and everybody else stood. He made a longish speech in which he said he was glad to see everybody on board, – I don't remember much else. After the President's health had been drunk he replied in English, allowing that he was glad to be aboard. Then Bob

Bliss had the pleasure of translating into French what he had said and we sat down and ate our cheese.

After lunch there was more visiting while coffee was served and we got away as soon after the President as we could go without crowding. It was a great sight to see but I should not like to go through with it every day.

Late in the afternoon I got down to the Crillon to see Phil [Patchin] who had been up to see me while I was out. He was completely surrounded by newspaper men who wanted immediate decisions on all sorts of matters he had not yet had time to take up. He was as usual pink and smiling and unperturbed and talked to them as though he had not a care in the world. I bade him up to dine and then went my way back to labor.

At seven I took Ynès down to the train and started her off for Switzerland. The frontier is open and she will get across in the morning. She is badly worried about her brother who is in bad condition and will probably not live very long.

Phil brought a good deal of news from home but there were so many people at dinner that we did not get much chance to talk about anything but shop. We had to go downtown after dinner to see some cable people about facilities for the press representatives and then came back for some more talk with Mr. Hoover. The next day or so will be so busy for Phil that I do not expect to see much of him. The hotel was filled with old friends from Washington, Sydney Smith, McNeir, Macatee, Dave Lawrence, newspaper men, secret service people, Department clerks, visitors of all sorts. It will be as Washintonian from now on as the lobby of the Willard.[164]

Mr. Hoover saw the Secretary [Lansing] at five and told him that he considered it important for me to be sent as soon as possible to Prague. The Secretary said that he would consider the matter for a day but did not commit himself to anything. It would be a most interesting job to [be] the first representative to Bohemia but I don't imagine it will be done.

Letter to Mary Gibson.   Paris. Sunday, December 15, 1918

We hear that this is a Sunday but you would never have known it if you had been able to look in upon us today. We did get up a little later than usual but even at that we were ahead of anybody else in town except the milkman, and after hammering away all day we are ready to go to bed as the clock strikes midnight.

We spent the morning talking over and over a lot of problems that are delaying our relief work. Norman Davis, Joe Cotton, Dwight Morrow and [Oscar] Crosby

---

164 Famous Washington D.C. hotel in direct vicinity of the White House.

were in and the talk went on from nine in the morning until six o'clock when the Chief set out by himself to see several people. At 8:30 he saw the President and told him all our troubles. At eleven he came back with his face wreathed in smiles and we knew that all was well. After hearing the results of his visit we were satisfied with our President. It now begins to look as though the period of delay were drawing to an end and the time of work appearing close ahead.

In the course of the past day or two I have seized every spare minute to scratch off Christmas notes and most of them will be on their way tomorrow. It is a task to do them in times like these and my notes are not long, – but such as they are they were the best I could do under the circumstances.

[Added note found only in Secret Log]
Our friend Lord Reading came through during the morning with a cheeky note to the Chief in which he said that the representative of the three Powers had drawn up a document embodying their view after the Chief's departure. That they assumed that it conveyed his views, over [illegible] at his early convenience as such as he had expressed it was before the preparation of the document and therefore not so formal as it would have been in writing. And all the time he knew perfectly well that the Chief disagreed violently with everything in the memorandum, aside from the fact that he could not have discussed it in any event as the three Powers have not yet had the courtesy to reply to the note of the President of the United States. They are trying to trap the Chief into discussion so that they can continue to ignore the President, – but that is a little too shyster for us to be taken in by it.

The President is ready for anything and is going to have his views conveyed very plainly by Colonel House. He will say that as there has been all this delay in reaching an agreement and as in the meantime there are certain situations in Eastern Europe requiring immediate attention he is directing the Food Administrator to send representatives at once to Vienna and certain other points to proceed with the distribution of such supplies as have arrived at Trieste and may be available at other points; that he trusts the Allies will also sent their representatives to join ours there and help them in coordinating all relief measures. If that does not set them to clamoring for what we want I miss my guess.

Letter from Mary Gibson.　　　　　　　　　　Paris. Monday, December 16, 1918

Another day of running errands and coming home ready to crawl into bed. I have spent a good part of my time trying to get hold of the Serbian Minister [Nikola Pašić] to talk to him about feeding his people, but he has been spending his time going to receptions for the President at the Hôtel de Ville [town hall] and other function. Functions are necessary these days – at least we have to go through that phase – but they certainly do establish a moratorium on business. I have also been running about trying to get quarters for the new organization and find that the problem gets harder every day as the new delegations arrive looking for places to work.

This evening Walter Lippmann and Mark Sullivan came to dine and we have settled most of the general questions that the Peace Conference would otherwise have been obliged to worry about.

My plans are still up in the air but the Chief is to see the Secretary in the morning and get a decision as to whether or not I head off into the wilds. If I do you will have a cable from me long before this reaches you.

Letter to Mary Gibson.   Paris. Tuesday, December 17, 1918

Today there was a pouch which brought me your letter of November 24th which was a little better than the usual time in transit.

This day has been filled with the usual round of conferences. We got into some new offices to begin the morning and that helped us somewhat.

I started off with a conference with the Serbian Minister [Pašić] about relief for his country. There is no end of detail to arrange but in the meantime preparations are going forward and when we do begin actual operations progress ought to be satisfactory.

A little before lunch time, Phil [Patchin] came in and together we went out to Dr. Blake's hospital to see Fred Sterling who is laid up with a succession of carbuncles which make him thoroughly miserable and complicate the work of the chancery. About half the Embassy staff is laid up with one thing or another and it is decidedly annoying with all the things that have to be done in connection with the President's visit.

I went back with Phil to lunch at the Crillon and found a flock of people whom I had not seen before, Mrs. Scott, Moran, Chief of the Secret Service, Stephen Bonsall, McNeir, Stuart Montgomery, Willie Wallace and a number of others. The whole place is in turmoil getting things organized and I did not linger after lunch.

In the afternoon we had visits from Will Irwin, Bicknell of the Red Cross, Norman Davis and others. I went with Norman down to see Joe Grew at the Peace Mission but we had to wait too long and finally gave up. Somebody with a good Prussian taste has lined up a dozen or so orderlies on each floor and just as you heave in sight some sergeant yells SHUN and they all stiffen up like pokers and stand rigid until the next floor yells SHUN. The poor civilian feels like an ass and I served notice that until that sort of monkey business was stopped I should do my business with the Peace Mission by telephone.

We dined peacefully at home and I dressed to go over to the Embassy to a reception being given for the President. But at the last minute I discovered that my dress coat had disappeared completely. I tried on one or two others but they made me look like Uncle Sam with tails that hung down to my ankles, so I abandoned the idea and settled down to hear what Horodyski had to say about conditions in Poland.

[Added note found only in Secret Log]
I gave the Serbian Minister [Pašić] some deep talk this morning on finance. He says that Serbia assumes full responsibility so far as financial matters are concerned for all the Yugo-Slav countries. They are now in process of forming a Yugo-Slav State at Belgrade and he promises to send us within a week all the documents to establish Serbia's responsibility financially for the feeding of the entire outfit. I told him that the program we had elaborated would require ten million dollars a month and that the best thing he could do was to have the Serbian Minister in Washington make application to the Treasury for a loan to that amount. He did not gasp as I had expected him to do when the sum was mentioned and said he would immediately get to work on it. I did not tell him that when he had made his plea with all possible eloquence the amount would doubtless be scaled down to five million cash and five million a month and that sum would be adequate. When I left he seized my hand in both of his and gave me to understand that I was one of his favorite friends.

Letter to Mary Gibson. Paris. Wednesday, December 18, 1918

Another strenuous day – but then all days are more or less in alike in their strenuosity – if there be such a word

This morning we had the usual ebb and flow of visitors and to top it off with I went down to see the Secretary [Lansing] about some of our troubles. He is established in a huge corner room at the Crillon surrounded by palms and statuary and an air of Olympian calm. He has a waiting room about ten acres in extent and two or three youths whose main function is to gaze out onto the Place de la Concorde and entertain the waiting visitors. One of them is Kirk who has been at The Hague and has been assigned down here. Another is Allen Dulles who came up here from Switzerland a few weeks ago and has been held for work in connection with the Peace Mission. They have not got into things yet and probably will not until their business is more organized that it has been so far.

Joe Grew and his wife were waiting outside trying to find transportation to take them off somewhere for lunch and I gave them a lift in the large blue limousine that is now mine. Joe is very sad over the fact that his chief job is to keep everybody happy and that they refuse to be happy no matter how hard he tries. I am just as glad I have not been given his job.

Ned Bell was to have come in with the courier at lunch but missed his connections and did not arrive until evening. I have not seen him but talked to him over the telephone and am to see him in the morning. He will be here only two days and has enough work for a week so we shall probably not play together very much.

I went to lunch with Mr. Hoover and Norman Davis and Clémentel, the Minister of Blockade. We had a lot of things to talk about in regard to our various problems, – that is to say the others had a lot of things to talk about and I had to act as interpreter. That kept us hard at it in a little room at LaRue's until after three, and then we went on to other pow-wows that lasted until seven.

This evening Colonel Joe Boyle turned up from Romania and came to dinner. He has been out in the wilds for more than a year and the last we had heard from him he had been killed by the Bolcheviki. The last he indignantly denies and from his appearance he seems to be telling the truth. He has careered over Russia and Romania and Turkey and goodness only know what other countries and is filled with information of the sort we wanted.

Tomorrow there is to be another series of sessions but nothing startling in prospect.

Added Note, found in Log only

Crosby and Cravath and other Americans have been raising hob with our plans over here by running to the British with advance dope about what we were thinking and planning. In several instances too, Cravath at least has taken it upon himself to tell the British and French that the various provisions of our relief plan presented by the President did not emanate from him but were the machinations of Hoover. That, of course, has not made our task any easier. After we had stood about enough of it I was sent this morning to see the Secretary to see whether he would get the President to authorize him to send out the following confidential note to all American officials over here on special missions:

"The President desires me to say that he had been embarrassed by the fact that certain American government representatives on economic missions to Europe have allowed themselves to discuss economic plans and measures proposed by him which did not directly concern them. Allied officials have in certain instances received the impression that the President's proposals did not represent his own considered views and were subject to comment and discussion. Serious complications and embarrassment have thus been caused to measures which the President attaches the highest importance."

"The President is constrained to request all American officials in Europe to confine their activities entirely to the specific missions on which they were sent to Europe. They must realize that unauthorized discussion by them of questions with which they have no concern can only result in rendering his task more difficult."

"The President has requested me to communicate his views on this subject confidentially to all American officials on missions in Europe."

The Secretary [Lansing] read the whole thing through carefully, smacked his lips, and said he approved of it and would gladly send it when the President had approved it, – but as to getting the President's approval he balked.

The Secretary waxed wroth over the tendency of our officials to become ultra British when they come over here. I made the sage remark that I didn't mind their having enthusiasm if it did not interfere with their pro-Americanism. At that the little man fired up with the statement that it was bound to interfere and so on. He allowed that "it had always been that way with our representatives in England but that it would be that way no more as the new Ambassador knew his way about." He took a sidewipe [sic] at the way Mr. Page had swallowed everything British and sacrificed his Americanism. I restrained myself and did not offer the remarks in reply that suggested themselves but it did stick in my throat to hear that fine old soul criticized. He is so far and away ahead of anything else we have ever had in England or anywhere else that there is no comparison and it is pretty bitter to think that all his fine work is unappreciated. But there was no use in saying anything about it as it would not have been understood.

Letter to Mary Gibson   Paris. Thursday, December 19, 1918

I had no sooner got settled at my desk this morning than Aunt Leona [Wood] called me on the telephone from downstairs where she was trying to get in. I brought her up and we had a little visit. She got in last night and is to be here until Saturday or Sunday for a little Christmas shopping. She is very down in the mouth about the raw deal she got in not being allowed to go to Brussels to see the entry of the King and has resigned from the whole show. I am mighty sorry about it as things had been going well so far and I had hoped that she was to have some adequate recognition. Also I can't help but feel that it was not meant to be so bad as she considers it. When the relief came everybody went a little crazy and the people who had been waiting for four years to get home forgot all about everything except their own desire to be on hand for the great event. All the plans that had been so carefully laid went by the board and there was a free-for-all scramble to get back to Brussels by any available means. Of course it was tough that she should have been left behind to take care of the youngsters while the others careered in but after seeing the way people went off their heads under the excitement I can find some measure of condonement [sic] for them. She doesn't see anything in it but plain cussedness and bad treatment so I did not breathe a word of this for it would have been worse than useless. I wish to goodness that she could have seen the great show as part payment for her devotion but it's all over now and she won't be reconciled.

She says that as soon as the creche is moved she is going home. They are to move somewhere to the neighborhood of Brussels and I am going to give her letters to Myriam and some other friends and ask them to be nice to her, – and I know they will.

She has not heard a word from Warren [Wood] since September but asked me to send a telegram to Mr. Hammond to send him $100 for a Christmas present. She assumes that he is on his way back to the United States with the fleet.

I forgot to tell you yesterday about one thing that happened. Paxton Hibben eased into the office in the uniform of a First Lieutenant. He is in an office alongside ours. Can you beat it? He told Strauss that he wanted to see me as he was an old pal of mine and when he was let in he looked over everybody in the place and then made for Bob Taft and wrung his hand with enthusiasm. It didn't fluster him when he found his mistake but he took me on quand même [anyhow]. He is married and has his wife here in Paris. He told me that he knew my life in Paris must be sad and lonely and that an American home would do me a lot of good, and when I foresaw his asking me to come and live with them forever he came through with a promise that someday he would take me to tea.

I made a quick trip to the Peace Mission in the morning to see about getting some rooms for Mr. Hoover at the Crillon so that he could be in close contact with the members of the Mission. I was turned over to the bright young officer in charge of the allotment of space and after allowing me to tell part of my story he turned loose on me in a way to make my hair stand on end at my temerity at daring to suggest anything of the sort. As an insulter, he was about the most capable person I have seen in my time and when he had quite done I told my story to Joe Grew with the result that his duties were taken over in the afternoon by Captain Patterson whom I knew when he was working with Mayor Mitchell in New York. We had a good session and I imagine that we can have about what we want. It's a great life – if you don't weaken.

I had a look at Ned Bell who was up to his ears in the work that brought him over. Also saw Phil and a few other people and got home to a peaceful lunch with all the crowd.

When we got back to the office after lunch we found all the streets barred off and remembered that we were receiving the visit of the King of Italy [Victor Emmanuel]. The streets were lined with troops in the way that has been done for all the other visitors of his sort and there was a considerable crowd despite the fact that a heavy rain was falling with occasional downpours of hail.

Just before the King came along it cleared enough for the crowd to put down its brolleys [umbrellas] and we had a good view.

This was the first stag party we have had. In the first carriage the King and the President of France. In the Second the little Prince [Umberto II] and then the usual procession of dignitaries. The King looked tired and serious and saluted mechanically. The prince had on a patent leather cap and enormous white gloves and saluted with the greatest enthusiasm as far as we could see him.

When that show was over and the crowd had cleared enough for us to make our way through the streets I climbed into my car for the afternoon round of visits. Twice to the Peace Mission on various matters, to the Embassy, to the Czecho-Slovak Government and finally to the hotel where Aunt Leona is staying for a little visit with her.

I wanted to take her out to dine but had to be on duty as there were a number of things on the carpet where I was needed. Among those who came to dine were Colonel Atwood whom we are sending to Serbia, Dick Oulahan, Norman Davis and Ned Bell. They all cleared out early and then we settled down and wrote a flock of telegrams, etc.

Heaven be praised my job is developing a good deal and I am finding a deal to do as time goes on. If I stay here I can foresee that I shall be very busy in interesting work – which is the one thing I have been honing for.

And now I am ready to tumble into bed so that I can store up energy for another day of the same sort.

[Added note found only in Secret Log]
Hall is going to get out of the Admiralty sooner that he had expected as a result of a row he had had with Wemyss. When the armistice terms were being prepared he went to Wemyss and gave him a memorandum to take over with various matters that would be included. When Wemyss came back Hall went to him and asked whether the terms reported were correct. When they were confirmed he said: "I want to tell you frankly that you have made a silly mess of the whole business" whereupon there was a fine row and the situation is no longer as pleasant for the skipper as it was.

Letter to Mary Gibson   Paris. Friday, December 20, 1918

Another day full of motion – and so full of it that I did not get around to see Aunt Leona.

In the morning the Chief and I went down to the Crillon and picked out the rooms that we wanted and were promised that we should have them within a day or two. A lot of people will have to be kicked out and we shall be just about as popular as rattlesnakes among them.

I ran into Eddie Hood of the A.P. and George Barr Baker and several other people and then came back to the office to take Colonel Atwood and Bob Taft to call on the Serbian Minister [Pašić]. Colonel Atwood is going to Belgrade for us and wanted to get as much information as he could about transport conditions, etc. That kept us busy until lunch time.

After lunch there were a number of people I had to see but this business of having Kings as visitors interfered again with work. Everybody I wanted to see had put on a top hat and gone down to the Hotel de Ville [town hall] to the reception for the King of Italy. Tardieu and the Romanian Minister and several others were away. The Secretary [Lansing] had gone there or somewhere else and could not be seen and I spend most of my afternoon climbing in and out of cars trying to find people that were not in. I finally got some action out of the Tardieu people who have undertaken to try to get us a large building adjoining that of the Peace Mission at 8, Place do la Concorde, now occupied by my friend Major Chaix with the Propaganda Against the Enemy. He must be going out of business now that the armistice has been signed and we want his room. The business that I had with the Secretary I wished on to other people and came away to sign up an accumulation of mail that had gone unsigned all day. It is scandalous the number of letters that have to be written nowadays on all sorts of matters.

At dinner we had Colonel Boyle, Eddie Hood and Dave Lawrence who reported that on her trip over on the GEORGE WASHINGTON had made 17 knots [nautical miles] an hour all the way.

I'll try to do better tomorrow and in the meantime send you all the love there is.

Letter to Mary Gibson   Paris. Saturday, December 21, 1918

Another hectic day in the course of which it was decided that I should leave tomorrow evening for Switzerland on my way to Vienna and Poland with Prague and other places as way stations. I set out tomorrow with Dr. Taylor, Colonel Grove and British and French representatives to foregather in Bern and decide on the next steps.

To begin the morning I had a pow-wow with the Romanian Minister [Brătianu] about matters to be settled in his country. On my way I spied Aunt Leona on the sidewalk and gathered her up to take here to her destination. She has not been able to get her car in shape to leave and will not pull out before tomorrow or the next day.

Just before lunch the Chief had a talk with the Secretary [Lansing] and it was decided that I should go into the wilds without loss of time. That meant that I had to spend the afternoon packing up my office and arranging all sorts of matters at the flat and elsewhere so that I would be in shape to stay away as long as might be necessary.

I had several talks with the people at the Peace Mission as to what they wanted me to do for them. A final talk with Ned Bell who is leaving for London tomorrow.

Jerry Gherardi turned up from the Adriatic where he has been for several weeks. We may kidnap him to work for us. I fetched him home to dine with us and we also had Horodyski.

Late in the afternoon I got in to say good bye to Aunt Leona and give her some letters to people in Brussels so that she will know somebody when she gets there.

I have only vague ideas as to where I shall go and shall probably not be able to tell you very much that is definite before I get beyond communication. However you may rest easy in your mind as we shall have a most interesting time and nobody is going to bother the people that are finding out how to feed them. Remember the old song Do Not Bite the Hand That's Feeding You.

Letter to Mary Gibson   Paris. Sunday, December 22, 1918

We are just getting ready to shove off for Switzerland and by the grace of heaven we hear that a special car has been put on so that we can have sleeper. The British and French representatives are going with us so we have our combined weight to get accommodations as everybody has been sitting up lately we feel lucky.

Have finished a ton of letters per stenography and deposited them at the Embassy, so I leave with a distinct feeling of virtue.

We had a session at the Peace Mission this morning and I gathered a number of useful points – and said good-bye to everybody.

We had 13 at lunch and the afternoon I spent cleaning up the odds things – went to say good-bye to Edith Wills and the Whitridges and Stetson. The Whitridges were out but I saw the others and now we are going to have an early dinner and run for my train.

Dr. Beneš heard I was leaving and sent me some letters of introduction for Prague and a formidable document – one of the first Czechoslovak safe conducts issued for a foreigner. I can add it to my large collection of passports.

Letter to Mary Gibson   Hôtel Bellevue Palace. Bern.
                                               Monday, December 23, 1918

This has been a dreary day without much of interest but we are glad to be here and ready to tumble into bed.

Last night there was a general understanding about our train and the arrangements, as always is the case when they are left to other people to attend to, were only half made. We had two compartments in an ordinary carriage and had to sit up all night, although I felt fortunate enough to be able to stretch out part of the time.

Our party consisted of Dr. Taylor, Colonel Grove, Loree of the Treasury Department (married to a daughter of my friend Baron Moncheur), Chauncey McCormick, Beveridge of the British Foreign Office whom I had known slightly when he was handling the French propaganda in Switzerland. Some cheerful idiot had taken places for us not on the train to Bellegarde but on the one to Pontalier. We had motors waiting for us at Geneva but no arrangements made at Pontarlier and when we arrived – without breakfast at eleven o'clock, there was nothing for us to do but put in the time until the only train left at 3:20. We found our way through a driving rain to the Hôtel de la Poste where we had what Beveridge described as brunch, being a combination of the first two meals. Haguenin is a good deal of a gourmet and provided about 5000 calories for the meal on the theory that we should soon be in countries where said calories would not be so plentiful.

Our train was a Bummelzug [slow train] which stopped at every station and sometimes between stations and landed us at Neufchâtel for dinner in the buffet de la Gare. After an hour's wait we pulled out and landed here at 10:30, twenty four hours on the road and very dirty.

Found Hugh Wilson and several others still waiting for us. Hugh is just getting over pneumonia and looks badly. He is to be off in the course of a few days but was anxious to talk over all the news. I shall have another yarn with him in the morning but just now I am most interested in climbing into bed.

Letter to Mary Gibson   Bellevue Palace Hotel, Bern.
Tuesday, December 24, 1918

– Christmas Eve
I never thought I should be here for Christmas Eve or that I should be spending Christmas talking with Austrians about how their people are to be fed, but that's my fate this year.

We got started early this morning and had a session at the Legation which resulted in arranging an inter-Allied conference at 2:30.

After that I paid a visit to Hugh Wilson who is slowly recuperating from a bad attack of flu and pneumonia and is scheduled for a long rest.

Lunched at Dresel's with Taylor and Herter and Dolbeare. He has a lovely old flat which looks down on the river and on clear days – which come once or twice a year – he sees a lot of assorted Alps in the distance.

At 2:30 we gathered at the Legation again with our Allied colleagues and discussed how we were to deal with the waiting Austrians. There were also some pending questions of immediate relief which we settled in short order and at 3:45 we met the six delegates of the city of Vienna who have been waiting for us here for the past two weeks. They were all dressed in black and looked depressed and underfed. The presentations were formal and only one of them insisted on shaking hands – and there was no saying him nay.

We talked with them in various languages until nearly six o'clock and then adjourned to meet again tomorrow morning at 10 at the Legation. There is to be a second meeting during the morning and another in the afternoon. It is a weird way to spend Christmas but I suppose it is as good as another.

The men who represented the Mayor of Vienna [Weiskirchner] made us quite a little speech in which he besought us to visit the city and convince ourselves at first hand of the need of immediate help. There are several things to be settled first however and it may be some days before we get off. We had set Thursday or Friday for our departure but I begin to believe that it may be a good deal longer.

Ynès telephoned through from Leysin to ask me down there for Christmas with her and Ramon. I made inquiries about cars for the trip but the gasoline shortage is such that I could not make it. The trains were out of the question as there are none now until Thursday, all travel being stopped over Christmas because of the shortage of coal. If we are still here on Thursday, I shall go down to Montreux with the Wilsons's to see a Pole who is filled with information and if there is enough time left over I shall run up to Leysin to spend the night. It would have been fun to be there over Christmas and have a chance to play in the snow for a change.

After our conference was over I went down town with Dresel and did my Christmas shopping which consisted of sending some flowers to Katherine Wilson.

Kellogg and Gregory and Colonel Causey arrived from Paris and we all had dinner together. Afterward we sat down and wrangled till an advanced hour over the financial phases of the relief work. It is very complicated and I have to keep on my toes to stay in the game. If it lasts long enough, which heaven forbid, I may manage to learn something about the elements of finance.

And now at midnight, I'm ready to crawl into bed and get strong and full of health for a day's work tomorrow.

Letter to Mary Gibson   Bellevue Palace Hotel. Bern.
                                    Wednesday, December 25, 1918 – Christmas Day

Here it is Christmas Day – although it does not seem at all like it. I'd give a lot to be at home with you instead of crouching among the Alps.

This morning I woke up with a headache and generally feeling as though I had been on a prolonged debauch. I got up and ate a lot of aspirin and took hot baths and generally groomed myself for an hour or so and before the day had worn on far I felt as though I could lick a small sized policeman. As the day progresses the size of the policeman increases and I am now myself again. And I feel swindled to feel so badly after leading such a sober and upright life.

Horodyski called me up early from Lausanne and said that he was ready to pull out for Warsaw as soon as we gave the signal.

At a little after ten we went up to the Legation and had a long talk with our Allied colleagues about various questions affecting the relief. It was all finished in time for lunch and we did not need to go back this afternoon. The talk with the Austrian delegates was very short and did not need to be repeated after lunch. It look as though the preliminaries to be conducted here could last several days more.

In the meantime I am going down to Montreux tomorrow with the Wilsons to see the well-informed Pole they have on ice for me there. If things are quiet here I shall run up to Leysin and stay overnight or go up to Caux and spend a day in the snow with Hugh Wilson.

There was a crowd at Dresel's flat. He had asked fifty people but the butler came in and reminded him that the lease for the old place prescribed that he could not have more than ten people to a meal – lest the floors give way and precipitate the whole crowd into the river below. He compromised and had only seventeen. There were the Wilson's, the Schelling's, the Exton's, Mrs. Hopkinson-Smith, Taylor, Dulles, Dolbeare, Russell and other of the Legation staff. We have more than the regulation number of calories and a NEGUS[165] prepared by Dresel himself. None of us knew just what that was but we were sure that one of the principal ingredients was alcohol for it kicked like an army mule.

I had a lot to do so came back to the hotel and spent the afternoon writing at various things. I have matters pretty well cleaned up so that I can drive into darkest Europe.

The Minister had had a dinner and dance scheduled for tonight but has come down with the flu and so everything was called off. No other arrangements have been made and we all had dinner quietly together at the hotel, Wilsons, Dresel, Dolbeare, Dulles, Carroll, Russell, and Herter.

Letter to Mary Gibson   Grand Hotel. Leysin.
Thursday, December 26, 1918

This morning we left Bern at 10:30 amid the cheers of the populace. Hugh Wilson was on his way to Caux to recuperate and his new open car was brought out to bear us on our way. It was colder than Greenland and so all the curtains were put on. Mrs. Wilson decided to come with us instead of training down with infant son and nurse. Then her maid had to come along so as to look after things. Fred Dolbeare came in order to produce his pet Pole for me to talk to. Hugh was not well enough to drive so the chauffeur was among those present. All the rest of the passenger space was reserved for me and the baggage. There was my enormous black bag, 2 or 3 more belonging to the Wilson's, one to Dolbeare and one to the maid. By some magic we all fitted in and then from somewhere a huge pasteboard hat box was projected into my lap. And then we shoved off amid my sarcastic protests that we had forgotten the parrot, the canary and the bowl of gold fish.

Nevertheless we made good time and rolled up to the Palace Hotel at Territet a little after one. M. Perlowski was waiting for us and we lunched together, continuing our talk afterwards in Hugh Wilson's drawing room which was large and sunny but furnished nouveau art in a way to make you scream. We talked until four when Perlowski took his leave. He is a keenly intelligent man, who has kept in close touch with affairs in Poland and like most Poles is touchingly concerned in the future of his country. He was able to give me some valuable information about conditions of transport and distribution in his country. He had made me a

---

165 Negus is a hot drink made from port wine, lemon and spices.

Image 18: Leysin, an exclusive ski resort and health spa in the Swiss mountains, as it was in 1918. (Public Domain)

long memorandum on food conditions in Poland which fitted in well with our needs.

Ynès was down for a day's shopping and Hugh's car was sent over to fetch her from Montreux. He then sent us over to Aigle, our old haunt, where we took the rack and pinion road to Leysin. Ynès sailed up in her fur hat with a pom-pom and cheeks like apples. On opening the car door I recoiled from a huge pair of hob-nailed boots evidently belonging to somebody else – but they didn't. Everybody up here wears them for good reason for the ice is slippery as sin – and I soon got my eyes adjusted to No. 12 boots on No. 6 people.

We struck out along the old road to Aigle but at a pace that would have taken our breath away in the old days.

We rolled up just in time to catch the funiculaire. It passes the old château, skirts the hills above the Aigle Hotel and then climbs straight into the heavens for an hour. We looked down on the old place of years ago and could recognize every part of it. – but it is all closed up tight as there are not enough people to fill all the resorts now.

After an hour's climb we stepped out on a level with the roof of the hotel and made for tea. Ramon was waiting for us with a good coat of tan and some color in his cheeks. Far from being hopeless as we had feared he is distinctly on the upgrade and is sure to come through if he stays on long enough and takes some

Image 19: Ramon and Jack Reyntiens, two of Ynès' three brothers, were officers in the Belgian Army. Ramon was gassed and recovering at Leysin. Jack was married to Myriam, but the two were divorcing. (Courtesy of the Gibson Family)

care of himself. Ynès rules him with a rod of iron and he submits with a deal of evident pleasure.

This is really a sanitarium but cheers itself with the name Grand Hotel. The air is supposed to be the best and purest in Switzerland. It is undoubtedly fine but I have never been able to sense the difference in various brands of mountain air. The invalids are not much in evidence and are, for the most part, stowed away in the villas that are sprinkled over the mountainside. A good part of them are men who have had their lungs affected during the war and uniforms are everywhere as most of them are officers and soldiers that have been invalided out of Germany and are therefore internees.

While they are very happy over Ramon they are saddened by the news that the four years of strain have been too much for Myriam and that her lungs are touched. She expects to come up sometime in January and begin taking care of herself, accompanied by the four babies.

After dinner I called up Bern on the telephone and talked to Dr. Kellogg who said that he thought he could arrange to send a car for me on Sunday. Otherwise I should have planned to go back tomorrow.

Everybody is supposed to be in bed at ten no matter whether they are invalids or not, and I am already fifteen minutes over time.

Letter to Mary Gibson   Grand Hotel. Leysin. Friday, December 27, 1918

A wonderful day and I only wish that I could stay on for a month and wax fat and rosy.

There is something approaching a regime even for those who are not patients and so I got some of the benefits. Everybody is supposed to be in bed by ten and you are not allowed to get up before eight. I always wanted to be compelled to stay in bed in the morning.

The three of us had breakfast at nine in Ynès' room, porridge, marmalade, coffee and rolls. This being a sanitarium there are none of the restrictions you suffer under in other places. Butter, rich milk, hot baths, and everything else to make life comfortable.

After breakfast I telephoned Bern for a report of progress and to learn whether I should have to go back this afternoon. Dr. Kellogg said he had arranged for a car to come down for me on Sunday and that there was nothing for me to do in Bern until starting time.

I accordingly dropped all consideration of the troubles of Central Europe and set forth with Ynès and a luge. We hauled it on up the country roads for half a mile or so beyond the hotel and then got aboard. I did not know anything about the roads but undertook to steer and contrived to get through without any casualties. It is not a regular winter sport place and such sledding as you get is on the roads that are used for traffic, through the village and past the big hotels. The roads are thick with other sleds for that is about the only way of getting around. All day long it was like a Hansi cartoon of Switzerland in which he had tried to work in everything he had ever seen. There were hotel porters in uniform with trunks in front of them sledding down to the station. There were old peasant women with prim bonnets and brollies and prayer books sledding down to mass, sporting people from the hotels rigged up to look like magazine ads, poilus [French soldiers] in uniform completely surrounded by whiskers, elderly English governesses sledding all alone in solemn dignity and all the kids of the place zipping along with no concern, chattering at all the people they passed. I whooped with laughter all morning long at the sights we saw and only hope somebody got as much fun laughing at me.

Our first slide was about four kilometers to a place well below the village where we came to a stop. Going back on foot it was a log farther, but we took it easy and got back in time for a second slide before lunch. Going back up the hill the second time was slower still and we were just about able to drag ourselves and the luge into the hotel. Food was administered in time however and we revived very quickly. There were great pitchers of milk and good old fashioned farm food.

And then the afternoon rest. If Sandow himself came here he would have to wrap up in blankets and lie out on the balcony in the sun from two to four without saying a word. There is a law of silence and a riot if anybody speaks. We went through it religiously and I snoozed very comfortably. While I was awake it was fun to watch Ynès who was about as much of an impediment in her speech as Arabella; it is torture to her but if she stays on here she may get used to it.

When we were released at four we got out the luge again and took Ramon for a slide down to the village. It was pretty bumpy for him as he got off and waited for us while we finished the slide, meantime laying in copious supplies for tea, his principal function of the day.

The thermometer was down to zero but for some reason nobody seems to feel cold. When I got up I looked through the window at the thermometer and decided for many layers of sweaters. After a few minutes I began shedding them until I had on only one and was still warm as toast. The snow was dry and powdery and when we ran off the track and landed on our faces in a drift it flew like dust in a great cloud. The whole thing is gorgeous.

Some of the skiing parties were coming in from long hikes, sailing through the town with knees together and feet apart, balancing like birds and steadying themselves with the two sticks they carry. They came swooping down the hillsides, going over banks and through groves, or tearing through the villages where people did not even turn to look at them. I was the country bumpkin and nearly got run over by all sorts of things while standing around with my mouth open.

About the only trees are the mountain ash, without leaves but solidly covered with rich red berries. There are some big black birds that haunt them and that startling red and black against the white of the snow is a real picture.

We made our own tea and yarned on till dinner time. Ramon had been alone here for months and has stored up enough lonesomeness to last him a good lifetime. He doesn't want to be left alone even when he is resting. And he is the best of company with all sorts of experiences which he tells well. He is the rolling stone of the family, the younger of the brothers and the one who had the most money. He has careered around all over the world and seen about as much life as anybody. He has been a lot in Spain with his mother's family and in Mexico where the Iturbide's are cousins of some sort. There he mixed it up with all the revolutionary factions and was on several punitive expeditions against Zapata [Mexican revolutionaries]. He has lived in Habana and San Francisco and New York and

Paris and London and goodness knows where else. The past two years he has been with a battery in Flanders and was there until gassed several months ago. And now he is worrying about what he is going to do when he gets well, for he has made up his mind to that and I think he will come through.

We yarned all evening and now I'm off to bed before somebody comes and scolds me for making a row. And besides I'm so sleepy I can hardly hold my eyes open.

Letter to Mary Gibosn   Grand Hotel. Leysin. Saturday, December 28, 1918

Another splendid day and your son feels himself fattening visibly. We got off this morning on the sled at ten sharp and tried a lot of new roads which led us in the general direction of Cepey. Down near the snow line we found a little hillock shaped like a volcano with almost perpendicular sides. We got the luge up to the top and then cautiously tried the least terrifying side. We went down with a whoop and slid a long way across the meadow which was under about two feet of snow. The second time we tried something steeper and got away alive although the speed was enough to take your breath away. The third time we took our lives in our hands and plunged down the steepest side of all, arriving in a heap or rather several heaps, without any sail across the meadow.

Then we made a snowman – and then we smashed him. And then we set up a small sized Kaiser and knocked his head off with snowballs. And then we had a snow fight in which I got a good deal the worst of it with my ears filled with frozen snow and a lot more down the back of my neck. And then it began to rain and we dragged our way back to the hotel where we waded into lunch in a way to make the stockholders worry about their dividends.

After lunch it began to snow vigorously and there was no use going in and out with the sled. We went through our rest period patiently and then all walked down to the village together to shop, the only other form of sport. I laid in two fine pairs of heavy shoes for plodding about in the snow on my trip and Ynès and Ramon laid in the usual tea stocks.

In the evening we had to dine with us a Miss Dunbar, a little Englishwoman who is here alone and who was good to Ramon when he first came. It must be pretty ghastly to be here without a soul you know, waiting to find out whether you are going to get well or gradually cough yourself away.

This evening Chris Herter telephoned from Bern that there had been a hitch about getting a car for me and that they were worried for fear I could not get back in time to catch our train which is due to leave Bern on Monday at noon. Of course all Swiss trains stop running on Sunday on account of lack of coal, and there is absolutely nothing permitted in the way of motors for hire. I telephoned hither and yon but there was nothing to be done and I called Herter again to say that it was UP TO THEM and that they must contrive to organize a rescue party. He said he would and I am easy in my mind as they can't very well leave me stranded here even if it means stealing a car.

Letter to Mary Gibson   Leysin-Bern. Sunday, December 29, 1918

I'm back tonight at the Bellevue Palace ready to set out for Warsaw in the morning.

 Chris Herter telephoned this morning that he had arranged about a car and the Dr. Taylor was coming down for me at 3:30 which was just in time to catch the afternoon funicular from Leysin.

 It was still thawing hard in the morning and there was no chance of sledding so I took Ynès to the front door of the church and then came back to the hotel for a talk with Ramon. The rest of the morning was the usual Sunday variety, letter writing, reading the papers and looking out the window and abusing the weather.

 After lunch Ramon turned in for his rest and Ynès and I got aboard the train at 2:33. She went down to the village to give me a start and then back through the rain. She is a trump, a good deal the Aunt Leona kind, and that's saying a lot.

 I found Dr. Taylor standing in the rain at the foot of the line, cussing because the car was in trouble and the chauffeur had had to go off to a garage to tinker with it. He had set out at noon and had not had any lunch. He charged like a wounded bull into a patisserie and proclaimed in good healthy language just how he felt and what he would like to do with everybody concerned. After he had unloaded all the strong language he knew, a little Victorian shopkeeper came up and asked in perfectly good English what he wanted. He was not taken aback but sailed into the cakes and tucked them away until I began to worry for his health.

 Then we sat down and waited for nearly an hour for the chauffeur to come back. When he did, the car was snorting and exploding and making a row that brought all the town to the windows to see what was the matter. Despite the row we made good time and landed back in Bern by eight o'clock.

 Cary Coolidge and Dr. Kellogg were waiting for us in the hall with an invitation to go and dine with Chris Herter. We made a quick change and were over at his flat in no time.

 There was no change in our plan and we pull out tomorrow at 12:20, D.V. and the criks don't rise. We are to have a service of couriers from time to time so I shall be able to get your letters and send you a line from time to time. I'm glad of that.

It's just as well I didn't stay any longer or I should have had to get a new outfit. In three days I put on four pounds – which is a wonder for me.

Letter to Mary Gibson   Choo-Chooing Through Switzerland en route from Zurich to Buchs. Monday, December 30, 1918

I don't know where I'm going but I'm on my way.

We had a wild time this morning laying in certain things that we needed for this trip, largely in the way of warm clothes. Then there was a flurry about our passports which got stuck somewhere along the road and did not appear until twelve.

Just as I left the Legation after gathering up my papers, a telegram from Mr. Hoover was shoved into my hands. It said he thought it would be well for me to go to Buda Pesth for certain reasons which he mentioned – and so of course it is Buda Pesth for me instead of Warsaw for the present, although I hope I can get through the Hungarian business in time to push through to Poland to join the others. Anyway it will all be interesting and I do not complain at my change of plans. I shall stay on in Vienna and wait until Taylor arrives and then perhaps he will go with me to Buda-Pesth.

Our party consists now of Dr. Kellogg, Colonel Grove, Lt. Chauncey McCormick, and an orderly, plus Horodyski and Znamięcki who are to labor for us when we get to strange languages, etc. We started in two compartments that had been reserved for us, with a private baggage car loaded chiefly with food and other supplies that we may need if we stay on. I had my own idea of travel at times like these and brought only hand baggage, but the others have a wealth of trunks, etc. I am curious to see how it will all go through.

We reached Zurich at 4:18 and then lay to until 6:30 or so, having to change to a special car that had been reserved for us. Tonight we are to arrive at Buchs about nine and spend the night there. We start on tomorrow at ten and on Wednesday evening we are in Vienna. It's a strange way to begin the New Year. Taylor and his party are due to leave tomorrow and should reach Vienna twenty four hours after us. It will be a real gathering.

Letter to Mary Gibson Special Bummelzug [slow train]
 en route to Vienna – New Year's Eve, 1918

Here is a strange ending to the old year – but an interesting one and one that may lead to relieving a part of the general misery.

Our train yesterday plowed along wearily stopping for long waits at the slightest provocation and finally wheezed into Buchs, the Swiss frontier station a half past eleven. Somewhere along the road while I was pounding out my little screed to you we acquired more Poles who are going through to Warsaw ahead of us. One of them, Gabrinsky, brought me a letter of introduction from Perłowski. He is a splendid looking old gentleman with a white beard and the millions that go with owning one of the greatest zinc mines in Poland.

We found our way through a slight drizzle to a little hotel run by Germans who contrived to put us up after a fashion. Dr. Kellogg and I drew a little room in Scarff Street. There were two beds and two large windows, but when we set about opening them we found that they had been actually built in for the winter and that there was no earthly way of getting a breath of air from outside. We tried the hall air by opening the door for a few minutes but were nearly overcome by it and resigned ourselves to the worst. It was colder than billybedamned and we used our coats and the feather beds that always slide off every time you go to sleep, but somehow we got through the night and lasted until we were called at half past seven.

They gave us a good tuck in before pushing us off into the unknown and at a little after nine we were at the station to attend to the many matters of passports and baggage and the special car that nobody thought would be there for us. Of course, there had been a slip about notifying the customs authorities that we were a mission and consequently had a right to take our plunder through without examination so that set us back that much and we had to telephone to Bern to get orders issued at once. As we had some thirty pieces of hand luggage and a whole baggage care full of food and supplies it would have been a bore to have to go through it all, aside from the fact that we should have lost at least a day in the process.

Fortunately our car had been sent from the Austrian station of Feldkirk and was at the platform. It has three compartments and a large salon where we eat and foregather, so we are very well off. The brave couriers begged not to be left to travel in the ordinary cars and got aboard on the understanding that they will have to sleep on chairs in the salon and keep out of the way when we want to talk. McCormick brought along a full supply of army blankets and pillows so we are going to be far more comfortable than the ordinary traveler.

We pulled out at about ten fifteen and crossed the Rhine while we were still adjusting our bags. We skirted around the northern edge of the Principality of Liechtenstein and in an hour's run made the six and a half miles to Feldkirk where we saw our first Austrians in force. The town has not been occupied and we did not know what would be the attitude toward us. The train had no more than stopped when a man in civilian clothes came out and addressed us through the car window to say that we need not get out and could leave our luggage where it was as there would be no formalities for us. Colonel Grove, McCormick and the other brutal soldiers had meantime been busy getting out of cits [civilian clothing] and into uniform and when they appeared in the corridor the curious gathered and gave them a mild looking over.

After a little, some of us got off and went wandering toward the town to see what we could see. The Colonel and I took a stroll of ten or fifteen minutes in the rain but came back because it was too wet under foot to be comfortable. It was curious to see how the soldiers everywhere avoided seeing us. There was not a salute anywhere and in every instance it was avoided without rudeness. They simply did not see that we were there. One of the few officers we saw glared at us but did it in such melodramatic style that he was only funny.

We had not inquired as to who was running the place but noticed the absence of officers and then that the few there were wore no insignia, but instead a little red-and-white button on the front of the cap, – the emblem of the republic. On inquiry it developed that Feldkirk is run by a deputation of soldiers and sailors who settle questions as they come up by discussion on the station platform or wherever else they may be. They wear red and white brassards on their arms and some of them carry rifles. They seemed to be a decent crowd and were certainly amiable to us. Znamiecki got off with our passports to have the vised but was told "This is a republic and anybody can come and go without passports." He came back with this report but I thought of possible complications further along the line where the authorities might not know of this quaint view of republican institutions, and sent him back to ask them as a favor to put some sort of rubber stamp on our passports. They dug out the old stamp and put it on just to please us.

After we had been in the station for an hour or so, a couple of mild looking little men came aboard and announced that they were members of the Landtag who wanted to greet us and thank us for what America was doing for the Vorarlberg. They told us something of the food conditions in this part of the country and shoved off with protestations of friendship and appreciation.

McCormick then came in and summoned us to lunch in the salon. He had brought along a hamper with aluminum plates, cups, etc. army knives and forks and two kerosene stoves on which the sergeant is to cook our meals on the rear platform, which is fortunately is enclosed. We had corn beef hash with bread and butter and succotash, prunes and coffee. They young man says he has enough to keep up this standard so we are not in danger of suffering for the present at any rate. From the commissary list he showed me, I see a long vista of corn beef and corn beef hash, but that does not worry me.

Our train pulled out about two o'clock and climbed steadily into a raging snow storm which was gorgeous for us but may tie up Dr. Taylor and his party who are due over the same route tomorrow. Late in the afternoon we went through the Arlberg tunnel which took us a good twenty minutes and on coming out ran into a detachment of Italian troops. I did not know they were this far in, but since then we have been running into them at all sorts of little stations. There are also some English troops on board the train moving up the line from a little town they occupy.

The people along the line take only a mild interest in us as they seem to consider our men English.

Letter to Mary Gibson   Hotel Bristol, Vienna. New Year's Day 1919

Happy New Year!!!!!

This has been a long day, spent alternately hanging out of the windows and snoozing and eating.

We got in at a little after eleven, only a few hours late which is nothing nowadays, and are going to tumble into bed dog tired as soon as our mountain of luggage has arrived from the station.

I turned in bright and early last night and was delighted to find that we actually had beds that could be made up although the army blankets that we had brought along came in very handy. Before I had been long in bed, McCormick came and announced that Dr. Kellogg, claiming to be chief of mission, had decreed that midnight would take place at ten and that a bottle of champagne that Horodyski had laid in at Buchs would be consumed at that hour. I refused to stir for any such affair and went peacefully to sleep while the single cork popped bravely as our only evidence of the demise of rotten old 1918. Here's hoping that the baby 1919 may turn out to be a better citizen.

There was nothing to be done this morning and it was cold and clammy so we stayed in bed late and did not gather round the board until after ten. We had passed through Salzburg early in the morning and had foregone the pleasure of seeing it. We dragged along through the country all morning and came into Linz about two. There we got out and tried the station lunch which was not bad for once. There seems to be a sort of standard meal throughout the country, a thick soup of potatoes followed by boiled beef with some speckly potatoes and a synthetic sweet, sometimes a pudding and sometimes a little cake.

The Kroner which is usually worth a franc has gone down to a third of that value, and in many cases prices have gone up ten times, so you can imagine what they sound like until your ears get accustomed to it.

We bought some of the tobacco which is smoked in Austria. It is guaranteed to contain 5 % of real tobacco, – the rest being a mixture of all sorts of leaves. It is very light and fluffy and a pipeful smokes through in no time at all. It is not disagreeable but under no circumstances could it be mistaken for the real thing. It smells like a fire of leaves in the woods when you are cooking a picnic lunch. A penny buys a package that would last a vigorous smoker for a week, and there isn't a headache in barrel of it.

In many stations we found long rows of freight cars that were evidently being gathered together to be sent back to France under the terms of the armistice. In one place there were large numbers of Belgian cars with the royal arms still on them.

For several hours we were in the midst of Mackensen's army on its way back to Germany from Romania. They were a dirty and bedraggled lot, no officers in evidence. They looked at us with idle curiosity but without hostility or much intelligence. Most of the windows in their trains were broken and some had been boarded up after a fashion so that the men inside could not see out and were traveling in dismal boxes. At the rate they were travelling, they may get back home within ten days or two weeks more but it will seem longer.

We lost more and more time as the afternoon worn on and did not come in here until well after eleven. The Polish Consul and a Lieut. of the Polish army were on hand to receive us. We had a mountain of bags to get off and while that was being done stood outside the station and enjoyed the crowd while the crowd enjoyed us. Two good looking Italian officers came swaggering out and climbed into a large car while the crowd look as though it would blow up. They are not really very fond of any of us, but they have a special brand of dislike for the Italians.

The evening papers tell of fighting between the Czechs and the Magyars at Pressburg and of all sorts of disorders at Budapest. Comforting for us who are going there.

Letter to Mary Gibson   Hotel Bristol, Vienna. January 2, 1919

An interesting day.

We were completely dead beat by our journey and Kellogg and I did not budge until ten. We had each a large and comfortable room looking out on the Ringstrasse with a huge salon in between. The hotel seems to be more or less empty and it chiefly filled with British and Italian officers. I rang for hot water and managed to get a large pitcher full by giving up some treasure to the maid. Otherwise there is little to be had for there is almost no coal in the country. Then I rang for the waiter who politely asked what we should like for breakfast. I began with coffee but he countered: *Leider giebts kein kaffe* [Sorry, there's no coffee].

So we compromised on tea. Then I suggested some eggs, but he smiled pityingly and retorted: *Leider giebts keine eier.* [Sorry, there's no eggs]

So I let him bring what he would and we contented ourselves with a slice of some very thin cold meat which could not be identified and some sticky black bread that would do no harm to the toughest ostrich.

The Polish Legation had put a car at our disposal so Dr. Kellogg and I went out for a little ride while Znamiecki and McCormick went off to make all sorts of arrangements about the train to Warsaw. I had succeeded with great difficulty getting a Baedeker [a travel guide] at Zurich and we road around trying to identify things by it. After that had lasted long enough we got out and walked around looking in the shop windows trying to size up what prices were and how people could make shift. There was a good deal more in the windows than we had expected but the prices were high. Perhaps they were largely old stocks that nobody had been able to purchase as often was the case in Brussels. The people did not look over well fed but quite as well as in the North of France. Their clothes were all right and their shoes were in good shape, all of which was exactly the contrary of what we had been told before we came. With prices as high as they are the rich can get about anything they want but it is hard to see how the poor get along. A suit of ordinary clothes costs fifteen hundred to three thousand kroner, one hundred to two hundred dollars. A pair of shoes come to fifty or sixty dollars. And many other things are in proportion.

We saw a crowd gathered round one shop window and in the center of it found Col. Grove and McCormick who were a center of interest. We went into a shop to look at things and thereby succeeded in throwing off the crowd, then continuing our promenade until lunch time.

There are practically no cabs to be found, that is motor taxis. They seem to have plenty of gasoline from Galicia but tyres are things of historic interest. Generally the cabs have old tyres stuffed with anything that will keep them plumped out and are tied round and round with wire or string to keep them from falling off. They are sorry looking spectacles.

Znamiecki needed a fitted dressing case and went into several shops to find what he wanted finally settling on a handsome one for five thousand kroner. It was nothing astonishing at that but the price is something he can always tell about. It must be comfortable to be able to chuck the money around like that.

At one we had lunch in the hotel dining room and fared pretty well. We varied the standard meal by having a herring to begin with. That was followed by the usual potato soup, boiled beef with speckly potatoes and a tasteless cake.

After lunch Dr. Kellogg, Znamiecki and I set out in the car to see the Czechoslovak Legation which we found in a splendid old palace belonging to some Czech aristocrat who has put it at the disposal of the Minister for the time being. The Minister [Tusar] is a little lame man who speaks only German and the Secretary of the Legation indulges in little more. From necessity I am getting to be quite chatty in German although I shall never get thoroughly at home in it if I live to be a hundred.

We made arrangements for our Polish part to have a special locomotive across Slovakia and got all our passports vised, mine included as I did not know but that new instructions might come for me at the last minute as they have a way of doing. It's easier not to use a visa than it is to run around at the last minute and try to get one after everybody has gone to bed.

We had quite a talk with the Minister [Tusar] about conditions in his country and here too. He is very anxious that some of us should go to Bohemia and I imagine that I shall have to do so soon. I should like very much to do so and into the bargain might manage to do some good.

From there we went to the Polish Legation where the Minister [Gałecki] plied us with cigars and talk about the needs of Poland. He has arranged for a special engine from the Polish border to Warsaw so the party will go through practically as a special train.

On coming back to the hotel we found that Dr. Taylor and his party had come in and were bursting with conversation. My orders stand to go to Budapest for a special piece of work and then possible on to Bucharest. If not thither then to Prague and perhaps eventually to Poland although that vista begins to fade. However, there is plenty to be done anywhere and I am not complaining.

While we were talking word came that two gentlemen from the Vienna Foreign Office wished to speak to us and when they were shown up one of them proved to be Baron von Franckenstein who was the Austrian Commissioner in Brussels and the most decent of the whole lot, so decent that the Germans had him removed unless I am mistaken. He and his colleague whose name I did not get have been attached to the Mission to render any service that they can so we shall probably see something of him.

The Polish party leave tomorrow at seven or thereabouts and I leave them to go their way while I go mine. Taylor and I shall probably go down to Budapest Saturday or Sunday and get back during the next week. Further than that we have no definite plans.

Tomorrow morning I shall go over to the Czech Legation and telephone through to Teplitz to the Clary's to learn how they are and tell them Elisalex is all right and is soon going to Switzerland where they can see her if they can get out.

At seven we dined with the Polish Minister [Gałecki] at the Hotel Imperial. There were crowds of people on the streets but they were evidently wandering more or less aimlessly and looked pretty badly depressed. There were few people in the cafes and they looked as though they were sorry they had gone in. The dark shop windows, the dim cafes, the dirty streets and the listless crowd all emphasized our first impression of shabbiness and discouragement. Not much like the dashing nation that plunged the world into war.

The dinner was evidently a tour de force to make a brave showing but in the whole business there was not enough for one person. First we had a Polish drink of some sort with a tiny bit of bread with something nondescript smeared on it. Then a beet soup to vary the usual diet. Then tiny patties with some mushrooms, etc. Then one lone and ancient chicken smothered in vegetable for fourteen people. Finally peaches with some sort of sauce. I think I have a menu which makes it look magnificent but it was really a pathetic showing.

There were two ladies, the wives of the Minister and the Secretary of Legation, the latter a pretty little Greek girl who spoke all sorts and conditions of languages without accent or difficulty. I sat between her and the Minister who lumbered along ponderously in German.

The other guests were the Polish Consul, a General and Colonel of the Polish army, the Lieutenant attached to our mission and ourselves. The Minister made a speech in which he told us how he preferred us to his own family and the Consul followed with a very good little speech in English. He speaks with a strong accent but without mistakes and in a very precise manner which makes it a treat to listen to him. Finally our Lieutenant got up and closed the fireworks with a toast to the American army. Dr. Kellogg braced himself with a whiff at his cigarette and then disposed of the situation with a few words that would not have been better if I had written them out for him myself!

The objectionable couriers have been disposed of and are going back to Paris tomorrow night. One of them was just plain impossible. The other proceeded to open the ball in Vienna with an interview to a perfectly strange newspaper man about what the mission intended to do and what was to be the attitude of the United States towards the German Austrians after the war. Major Peaslee who is to have charge of the couriers arrived with Dr. Taylor and after one look at what appeared in the NEUE FREIE PRESSE he decided that both young men should start immediately for home where they certainly belong.

Our Lieutenant today refused to smoke with us and when pressed for his reasons said that he always avoided it at home for fear of being considered effeminate. All the women at home smoke, he explained, and he felt that he would be rather conspicuous among men if he did. What a world!

Letter to Mary Gibson   Hotel Bristol, Vienna. Friday, January 3, 1919

Today we got down to work in earnest on the Vienna situation.

I began my study of the situation by eating breakfast. Somebody said that breakfast in the public dining room was better than what was served in your own quarters so I went down and got mine there. There is no heating allowed in the public rooms and people were sitting round the tables in fur overcoats for it was bitter cold. I was too lazy to go all the way back for mine so sat and shivered. I had some villainous coffee made of goodness knows what, some miserable fish disguised with a messy gravy and a saccharine tablet plus some black bread that was not fit to eat. I did my duty by it and came away glad to escape alive.

At 10:45 Franckenstein and one or two others came for us in open cars and took us to the Foreign Office to see the undersecretary and several other officials who handle food and other supply problems.

We passed the Palace where revolutionary soldiers with red and white bands on their sleeves stood guard at the great portal and wheezed up to the main entrance of the Foreign Office. We were passed through several rooms to the one where the dignitaries were awaiting us and then settled down for three quarters of an hour of listening to their expose of the food and coal situation which was anything but cheering, – and evidently sincere.

From there we were taken to the Food Ministry where several of the Ministers were waiting to go over the same ground from their own points of view. They had prepared a lot of statistics and we had questions to ask that will keep them busy for some time to come. That kept us going until lunch time when we came back to the hotel and ate our same old familiar meal.

After lunch everybody had some sort of trick to do. Colonel Causey went off to see the stocks of coal. Gregory tackled the finance question and Taylor went into a lot of the statistical end of matters. As the diplomatic member of the party, I trotted off to see the Hungarian, Yugoslav and Czech Legations and make various arrangements. We are to take on each of the three Ministers in turn tomorrow and hear what they have to say about the needs and resources of their countries. True to all the best traditions of their service, there were none of them to be found before five o'clock and I spent most of the afternoon running around from one house to another looking for them.

With the Hungarian whose name is Charmant, I arranged for a special car to take us all down to Budapest Sunday night. When I got back to the hotel, however, Colonel Causey had come in with such a depressing account of the coal situation that we decided it would be better for us to first go to Prague and then to Budapest. That is the present plan, subject, of course, to change.

I had a number of letters to write to Paris and Bern to catch the courier who goes in the morning and settled down in my own salon which is about the size of Madison Square Gardon. Little Cora Corona has worked hard and is entitled to a rest – and so am I.

We dined quietly at the hotel with a growing crowd of British and Italian officers who are rapidly filtering in from various points. We shall doubtless see the French in Budapest.

In spare moments today I have tried to find out something about the form of government here but so far without success. The country seems to be governed by a group of men with no particular organization. They appear to get along pretty well although they represent all parties and at least they have so far succeeded in maintaining public order which is more than can be said for most other places. They consider themselves merely an emergency body and look to have something elected to take their place as soon as possible.

I'll hop to have something less depressing to write by the next courier.

Letter to Mary Gibson   Hotel Bristol, Vienna. Saturday, January 4, 1919

The days go by like the wind and it is hard to remember the things I want to tell you even if I do sit down religiously before my little machine every night before I go to bed and comb out what remains of my mind for the events of the day.

This morning the energetic members of the party were called at six and went out to see the markets. I was interested but my laziness was greater than my interest and I resigned myself to hearing about it from Dr. Taylor when he came back. He was rather downcast when he came in for breakfast, said that there was practically no food offered for sale and that it was so much taken for granted that there was hardly anybody there to buy. There is a certain amount of illicit traffic in food but that does not help the poor. The rich get a good deal in this way and institutions that are able to pay also supplement their regular rations by this illegal method. Professor Pirquet who has a big hospital for tuberculous children told us frankly that he had to get his supplies through the profiteers as his children could not live otherwise. As a matter of fact the working people come out about as well as anybody except the very rich. The factories have found that they have to feed their workmen or they will leave and go to other factories that offer that inducement. So they get free food of the factories plus what they can buy with their wages. The class that is hit hardest is the small salaried clerks and government functionaries. I was talking this morning to a young man who is in the Foreign Office. His is usually in the Consular service and has a small salary. Fortunately he has some means of his own but says that it costs him just three times his salary to keep himself and his wife alive although they live as simply as possible. He says that the Foreign Office maintains a kitchen for its functionaries and that he takes his share home to increase what they are able to get elsewhere. He says he had never given a thought to household matters before but that nowadays he cannot give his whole attention to his work because he is, in spite of himself, trying to devise means to get a little meal here, a few potatoes there, etc. And that is more or less the story that they all tell.

In order to get a proper start Sergeant Cash served me up a good breakfast of real coffee and corn beef hash. And then we were ready to start out. I sent our passports to the Foreign Office to have them vised for Prague and then set out with the others to see some of the public soup kitchens.

We set out in several motors, thereby causing quite a flutter in a town that is not accustomed to seeing anything of the sort. I rode with Franckenstein and another man from the Foreign Office in an open car and nearly froze to death in the cold wind in spite of my fur coat.

First we went to a kitchen in a car barn whence 18,000 people are fed daily. Some three thousand eat in the place itself and the other 15,000 portions are delivered to other centers for distribution. The installation is fine, some forty great kettles holding fifty gallons each, heated by steam, modern machinery for slicing cabbages, potatoes, etc. – but practically nothing in the way of food to work on. Two dishes were being prepared, one a sticky mess called soup of vegetables with a little flour. It had a villainous taste and could not have contained enough nourishment for a meal. The other dish was stewed cabbage plain and simple without any seasoning. It might be all right for those that like that sort of thing, but one taste of each dish was quite enough for me.

Outside in the street there were some fifty people, mostly children, gathered for the meal that would not be served for an hour or so. They looked pinched and weak, blue with the cold and altogether a sight that you would like to forget. So far as we can learn the health of the next generation has been badly undermined and it will take a lot of work and feeding to bring them back to anything approaching normal after the flow of food is reestablished.

From there we went to another kitchen in a crowded quarter. The meal was already being served and the one room was packed with the scum of the city who looked us over like so many men as they gulped down their soup. The soup was the same as in the first place but for tomorrow they had a big pile of bones with shreds of meat hanging to them which are to be boiled with the rest in the hope of extracting some meat flavor from them.

In the next place we visited which was near our hotel, we found them serving the one meat meal of the week. The dish, which cost one krone, thirty heller, was a handful of carrots, turnip and cabbage with a slice of good looking meat about the size of your hand. We went into the kitchen where it was being prepared and I started in the usual business of tasting but pulled up short when I learned that this was horse. It may not be reasonable but I object to eating the poor beast. Some others of the party were not so particular and pronounced it rather good.

The last place we visited was in a big school house whence ten thousand are fed daily. The service was finished and the women were cleaning up the place. They had a fine installation too but the stock of food was alarmingly small and the woman in charge much concerned as to what would happen when it was gone.

One phenomenon that we have noticed before in other places has begun to manifest itself. The more news of our arrival and the hope that something is going to be done has prevailed upon people to bring out stocks of food that had been hidden in the hope of high prices. Prices on some supplies have already dropped ten per cent – but they are still too high for comfort.

One curious thing is that the Government people here persist in regarding their sad condition as if it was the result of a flood or some other calamity for which they were in no wise to blame and they look to us to arrange matters for them as though they were our own people who had suffered from an earthquake. They keep comparing themselves to the people of Belgium and Northern France and do not seem to realize that the suffering of these people were imposed on them from without whereas here the situation was brought about by the Austrian Government itself.

When we came back to the hotel from our morning round of visits, Haguenin and I set out for a walk that lasted us till lunch time and tried to see some way out of the various difficulties that confront us.

At 2:30 the Czechoslovak Minister [Tusar] came to see us and we spent an hour going over the food and coal situation with him. We hope to accomplish something by arranging exchanges between the various countries of the commodities they have to spare. For instance the Czechs and the Poles have coal in abundance. The Czechs and the Hungarians have sugar which they can export. And so if goes on. They are all holding back for compensation and we have got to find some way of getting them to help each other for the time being at any rate. Our problem is not at all simplified by the fact that there are eleven different wars of assorted sizes going on in the general part of Europe. The Poles are fighting with the Germans on one hand the Ukrainian on the other with some sort of spat with the Lithuanians to the northeast. The Czechs are fighting the Hungarians for the town of Pressburg and other places not two hours from Vienna and on the other side are fighting the Germans and have just wrested Joachimsthal [Jáchymov] from them. The Yougoslavs are careering around fighting with anybody that is accommodating enough to fight back and the Romanians are going for the Hungarians for all they are worth. This, of course, quite aside from the general disorder, Bolshevism or whatever you like to call it that prevails every here and there. I want to buy a patch of ground on the far side of Catalina and settle down to forget about it all.

The Czech was the most satisfactory person we have talked to so far and had a mass of information at his finger ends.

When he finished, I went back with him to the Legation to get our passports vised for Prague and took advantage of the opportunity to telephone through to Teplitz and talk to Countess Clary (Resy). It took only about half an hour to get through and I could hear quite as well as on local calls. The lady's voice was as serene as ever and she was full of questions as to her daughter, etc. I got news of them all and asked if there was anything that could be done for them. She answered: "No, everything is very quiet here, thank God!" With fighting going on at Joachimsthal [Jáchymov] there was a good deal of relief in her tone of saying it.

While I was at the Czech Legation the Hungarian Minister was with the Mission telling about Hungarian affairs. He did not wait to be questioned but launched into a long address which he began by announcing he knew nothing about food. He then told of the political sorrows of Hungary and how every man's hand was against her. She is being trimmed on one side by the Czechs, on another by the Romanians while the Yougoslaves are nibbling around the edges. I was sorry not to hear all that he had to say but imagine I shall have all the chance I want when we get to Budapest next week.

The Yugoslav Minsiter was to have come at 5:30 but there was evidently some sort of misunderstanding on his part and we waited for him in vain.

The Food Minister, Lebenfeldt-Russ [Loewenfeld-Russ], had asked to see some of us at 6:30 so Beveridge, the British Delegate and I went to see him. He had a lot of matters on his mind and we talked until after eight o'clock before he allowed us to come home to a late dinner. The foodstocks are alarmingly low and he is terribly anxious to get definite assurances from us as to what he can count on and what he can tell his people in order to quiet them. He says that the poor are becoming more and more convinced that there is a lot of food that they never get a chance at and that the rich have vast stocks which they are holding for themselves. He, like everybody else, is much worried lest there be some little outbreak which may serve as a starter for a general uproar.

While I was at the Czech Legation I saw the commander of the Red Guard who was making one of his periodical visits. He was an insignificant little man of thirty five or so in a khaki uniform without insignia of any sort. He apparently rules the city on his own account, owing no responsibility to the Ministers but working in harmony with them.

After having dinner with Beveridge the lot of us had a long conference as to ways and means. Some food is being started up from Italy as an emergency matter and we are to be back here on Wednesday to discuss finances and other problems that cannot be settled now. We got through a lot and ended in agreement as we usually do. We have a reasonable lot of men on the Mission which is a blessing as we should otherwise lead a dog's life. I don't know whether I have told you who they are. For us we have Dr. Taylor, Lt. Col. Causey (otherwise known as Old King Coal because of his special functions), Capt. Gregory (who is the financial expert), Lt. Caskie, interpreter, and HSG. The British have Beveridge of the Food Ministry. The French sent Haguenin, formerly a professor of the University of Berlin and since the beginning of the war in charge of French propaganda in Switzerland; also Capt. Genestal who is the general expert. The Italians contributed a jolly fat man named Giuffrida who has a brain like a steam engine and a good running mate named Oblieght. Altogether it makes a very good team.

A special train has been arranged to take us to Prague. Our present plan is to reach Prague Monday morning, leave there Tuesday evening, reach Vienna Wednesday morning and remain for the day in order to discuss material that is to be gathered for us in the meantime. That evening we expect to pull out of Budapest and arrive the following morning, Thursday. Thursday and Friday we spend in Budapest and Saturday morning we expect to be back here. There will be more talking to do but all hands expect to start back to Paris on Sunday night. I am torn at present between the desire to go back to see what is going on and my desire to stay in this part of the world for fear of not getting back here again if I get out. Unless there is some reason to the contrary I may decide to run down to Bucharest or Belgrade and then join the Mission in Warsaw, thus getting a fair general idea of what things look like in these parts. I shall be curious to see how much we, any of us, stick to our schedule.

[Added note found only in Secret Log]
The great question that is agitating people is whether or not they are to join up with Germany or try to run as an independent republic. The Socialists appear to be the main element that wants to hook up with the Huns for the reason that they see a chance to increase their party strength in this way. Nearly all other elements

are against it. They would doubtless be more against it if they had any realization of the way they have been done by Germany financially and otherwise. I gather that if the elections were held today they would be for an independent republic, but the Socialists are deferring the elections as long as they can in the hope that they will gain in strength thru popular discontent and suffering thru food shortages, etc. It is a pretty low game but everybody is at it.[166]

I hear this evening that Czernin is coming out to stand for office under the new regime as a liberal! He would not have wiped his shoes on a liberal two years ago but time does bring changes.

The Czechs are getting out their own new money and expect to enter the monetary union with France, Switzerland, Italy and Belgium. As a means of disposing of the Kroner, they have in the country what they expect to round up all there is in the country on a given day, stamp it and redeem it at leisure. Any Kroner are not so stamped will not be redeemed and will have to come home to roost in German Austria.

The financial question is worrying us most and we see no light. So far these people have been unable to produce anything that sounds like real money and we can't quite see what we are to do about it. It has occurred to me that we might get them to take over the art collections and other property of the Emperor and Imperial Family and let us take a mortgage on it for the food we have to send. Under our laws, we can't make them a present of a pound of food and they have got to get something by radical means. This step ought to be popular with the people as showing that they are getting some benefit out of this great wealth that the Emperor held. On the other hand, if the Emperor ever has any hope of coming back, he cannot very well squeal without ruining his chances. He must swallow hard, smile and say that he is delighted that his properties can serve so splendid a purpose as saving his beloved people from starvation. There are elements of humor in it and into the bargain it may do our trick.

Letter to Mary Gibson   Hotel Bristol, Vienna. Sunday, January 5, 1919

This has been a day a clearing up odds and ends and getting thing so shaped up that there will be definite material for us to work on when we get back here on Wednesday morning. To begin with we cleaned up some odds and ends of food in our rooms so as to avoid the horrors of the hotel meal. Sergeant Cash is a real cook

---

[166] Parts of this passage reappear in the memo "Visit of Mr. Hugh Gibson to Countries of the Former Austro-Hungarian Empire", see letter to Mary Gibson, February 5, 1919.

and turns out good coffee aside from being handy with the can opener. Our French gourmets accepted our invitation with touching gratitude and did themselves so well that they did not want any lunch.

Dr. Lorenz, the famous orthopedist came in after breakfast and told us some of the things we ought to do. He had been given the freedom of the city of New York when he was in America and brought his books along to prove it. Have established the facts he deduced from them that it was up to us to see that he got what he wanted. We could not quite follow his reasoning but were glad to hear what he had to say.

There were several people to see me about matters that had to be referred to the Spanish Embassy which is in charge of our interests here. Most of them want to get news from relatives in America or passports to go to America or food because they once knew somebody who had an uncle who lived in America, – North or South. There was one large and indignant lady who forced her way into the room and bearded [confronted] Dr. Taylor with a demand that he arrange to get her sent straight to America. His explanations that he had nothing to do with such matters had no effect upon her and she demanded that he telegraph the President about her case so that she would be taken away. To the explanation that the President had nothing to do with such things, she replied that he "ought to make an exception". To the question why she had not gone to America when the Government told everybody to get out she said that she did not want to and besides she was afraid of the MINES. So far as I could make out she was of Austrian descent and had married an Austrian naturalized American and when he died she settled down here without any care about keeping her citizenship. And now she makes a tremendous uproar because she can't have things done her way. She was a Tartar but the Dr. handled her with skill. I was much obliged to him that he did not pass her on to me as being of the Department of State.

After the Dr. had recovered from this encounter we went out for a walk with Colonel Causey and Gregory. We made the whole tour of the Ring which, as you will remember, is something of a walk. There was a good many people out in the streets for the hand of death seemed to be on the town. It was not so much the swarms of beggars and the pinched and starving faces of the people as the houses and the streets themselves. There is no doubt that whatever happens the bottom has dropped out of this town. For centuries it has been the capital of a great Empire and has exacted heavy tribute from all the countries over which it ruled. Now they have thrown it overboard and the part it has left is the poorest of the lot, with a very small part of the natural riches, no seaboard and a territory smaller than that of Belgium. There is a sort of Homeric justice in that it is clear that people realize it. The brilliancy of the place is probably gone forever and if they tack themselves to Germany it will drop still further.

I don't know whether I told you that everybody has hastened to paint out the Imperial arms over their shops and where they could not be painted out they are covered with sheets of wrapping paper. Even on the Government tobacco shops the k. und k.[167] have been covered while the rest of the sign stands. This is being logical with a vengeance.

When we got back at three we had a snack in our rooms and then separated for our various jobs. Dr. Taylor went out to see Dr. Pirquet's children's hospital while Col. Causey set out to wrestle with the coal people and Gregory and I sat down in our rooms and did correspondence and talked to people from the Ministry of Finance.

We had an early dinner with all the crowd and pushed off for the station with a broad margin of time. We have a special sleeping car which gives a compartment to each of us and therefore I can make as much noise as I like.

We shoved off promptly at eight twenty five and are due in Prague at 6:30 in the morning. Now for a gentle snore.

Letter to Mary Gibson   Hotel U Černého Koně, Prague.
                                          Monday, January 6, 1919

Thank goodness we are here for the change in atmosphere is a joy.

It was still pitch dark when we came in but there was a goodly crowd of officials waiting to receive us. Knowing just what we needed most they led us into the station restaurant while the baggage was being unloaded and gave us real coffee and real bread and sugar. You would have thought we had never seen any of these things before from the way we went for them.

There was a fair sized crowd waiting outside the station to see us and a cheer went up that was a fine effort for that early in the morning. We are divided up among three hotels but they are all within a stone's throw of one another and we can easily get together when necessary. Taylor, Causey, Gregory and I took rooms in this hotel which is the most modest of the lot and set to work to change and make ourselves presentable for our first meeting at nine o'clock. We were called for by a fleet of motor cars and taken through the town at breakneck speed, across the river by the Charles IV Bridge and up the steep streets to the Palace where the new Government has its offices. In the square before the Palace were a number of Czech soldiers freshly arrived from France, with their blue uniforms and steel hel-

---

[167] The abbreviation "k. und k." refers to the German expression "kaiserlich und königlich," meaning imperial and royal, is used to refer to the Court of the Habsburgs and the Austro-Hungarian Empire in particular.

mets. At the door where we got out after winding through several courtyards there were more presenting arms and still more on the staircase. It gave a thrill even to such hardened old people as we were to see these fellows at last having their own way in their own home after all they have been through.

We were shown into the living apartments of the Emperor, splendid great rooms – LOUIS XIV with plenty of gilt and rock crystal chandeliers, and a view over the town that was worth the whole trip to see. The President [Masaryk] and Prime Minister [Kramář] were away but several of the other Ministers came in and met us and led us to an adjoining room where we were to have our conference. There was Staněk, Minister of Labor, formerly leader of the Czech group in the Reichsrat at Vienna. He looks like a burly Judge Stephens and is very much of a man. I think I wrote you at the time that he precipitated events by getting up in the Reichsrat and announcing that the entire group was withdrawing from Parliament without any intention of ever sitting there again. Of course all his friends expected him to go to jail even if nothing worse happened to him, but instead the Emperor sent for him and asked what he wanted. Staněk replied that they wanted nothing the Emperor could give them and that when they did want anything they would see that they got it. And with that he withdrew and brought his hundred and six deputies back to Prague.

The Food Minister [Bohuslav Vrbenský] who was also there was formerly an anarchist but these keen people put him in this responsible job and now nobody is a greater stickler for law and order than he. His name is Vrbenský and he looks the part. He has intelligence and has the makings of a good public servant. And a little while ago he was in jail.

The Minister for Public Instruction was also in jail until a few months ago – Haberman [Habrman] – looks like Gompers on a large scale and knows just what he is after.

Staněk brought in some twenty officials who have to do with matters of food, transportation and coal and introduced them round and then we settled down in the Emperor's drawing room to business. Staněk first made a neat little speech of welcome which lasted about one minute by the clock. Haguenin replied at about the same length and said all that there was to say. Then we got straight down to brass tacks. We told them of the way we had the work divided up among us and they assigned the various people who were competent to deal with the questions in which we were interested. We submitted a few questions on which we wanted statistics or other information and the preparation was got under way at once. The three committees that had been chosen then separated and went to the various offices where they could work to best advantage.

The questions under consideration were all technical and there was no reason for me to sit in so I came back down town and went for a walk to see that things looked like in general. It was a holiday so most of the shops were closed but there were plenty of people about and top hats were more in evidence than they had ever been in France or England since the war began. Some of the shop windows were open and it was easy to see that the situation was far less desperate than in Vienna. Until the crash came the Government in Vienna kept this country stripped so that life would be easy in the capital but in the last few months they were no longer able to impose their little game and the Czechs have recuperated to a remarkable extent. The situation in the country and in the coal mining districts is not nearly so good but we are trying to find a way to help out there, and if they can keep down the Bolcheviki agents who are being filtered in from Russia and Germany they should have a stable government that will be the sort of island of public order for this part of Europe.

The whole appearance of people and things is so much more normal than in Vienna that there is no comparison. There is something very wholesome about the atmosphere that is refreshing and we rather dread to go back to the other.

Our little group rounded up for lunch at our hotel and had a modest meal that would have made the eyes of the Viennese pop out with envy, bread and sugar and two kinds of meat. I don't know whether they were doing something extra special for us but I would not want a better meal anywhere.

A little Frenchman named Paul Rosanin, who is employed at the Ministry for Foreign Affairs came with Colonel Causey as interpreter and joined us at lunch. He was here all through the war and suffered little inconvenience save that he had to report to the police several times a week.

After lunch we had a meeting with the Mission and discussed several phases of the situation in complete agreement. It saves a lot of time if we can settle down in the corner now and then and thresh things out among ourselves.

At four we went back to the Palace and were received by the Prime Minister, Dr. Kramář. He is a fine great gentleman with a kindly smile and great hands as big as the side of a house. To my mind he is the most interesting man I have seen in this part of the world. He is a man of a good deal of means, owning factories in various parts of the country but with it has always been a pronounced radical and has given himself entirely for many years to the Czech national movement. He was for over 25 years a member of the Parliament at Vienna and has spent more than 26 months in jail since the beginning of the war. As you might imagine he feels rather strongly about some things and expresses himself well.

He speaks very good French and after we had settled the business end of our visit we sat and talked with him for over two hours.

He told us of how the Bolcheviki agents were being worked into the coal mining districts and how when the miners were without food and materials for their work they fell prey to the doctrines of the trouble makers. He was intent on ways of ferreting them out and keeping them away. He was not resentful against the miners who went wrong. He was all pity for them. He said he had been urged to send troops to keep them quite but he would not do it unless he had to. His voice broke and he choked as he brought his great fist down on the marble table with a crash that set all the chandeliers to jangling. "I will not shoot down my own people who ought to be fed and cared for instead." He told of his pride in the fact that his country was to be the guardian of order for this part of Europe and wants to help and wants it at once; all he needs is food and some materials for mining and every bit of it he can pay for in cold cash.

As we broke up, the Prime Minister [Kramář] asked us to go with him to a symphony concert and afterward to supper. He apologized for not asking us to his house but said that it was not finished when he was sent to prison and that as his wife followed him to Vienna nothing had been done to it and now it was impossible to have either labor or materials and that he could not have any guests for some time to come.

We joined him at seven o'clock in the great concert hall just across the street from our hotel. It is a splendid great place holding three or four thousand people. Every kind were there, great ladies lit up with diamonds and a goodly sprinkling of Moravian peasant girls in their native costumes which gave the whole house a touch of red and blue. And there were plenty of beauties among them, at any rate from where we saw them. The President and Mrs. Masaryk were in the box just across from us. They had just returned from wherever they had been and he sent word that he would like to have the Prime Minister bring us to see him tomorrow morning at eleven.

The concert was entirely the Slavic dances of Dvořák. Dvořák was a humble musician in the orchestra here and nobody knew anything about him, even that he was writing this music, until there was a concert of it in Berlin and everybody went wild over what he had done. And now Prague stands on its hands to do him honor. The orchestra is a wonder of about sixty pieces and played in a way to keep the audience on its toes throughout a long evening. We sat down at seven and did not get out until well after ten, with only a short intermission after which they played all our national anthems and we had to stand up and take the hand.

After the concert we were led by the lily white hand[168] to another hotel nearby where supper was laid. We realized we were in a Slav country from the leisurely way people kept coming in until nearly eleven when we sat down to table and consumed a long dinner. The new French Minister was among the guests as well

---

168 "Led by the lily white hand" is a self-desparaging expression of Gibson's statue, ie. NOT working with his hands.

as the British military mission, several young French officers who are here with the Czechoslovak legion, the son of the President and most of the Cabinet. The French Minister was on the right of the Prime Minister and for some reason I was on his left. It was a treat to talk to the old gentleman and before I knew it it was one o'clock and I saw that some of the others were drooping. Having been up since long before daylight I was weary myself and excused myself to come back and tick off a line to you preparatory to crawling into my little bed. There were a thousand things of this day that I wanted to tell you but I am too befuddled now to remember them. And anyway this letter is too long, so I cut if as short as it can be now.

Letter to Mary Gibson   Hotel U Černého Koně, Prague. Tuesday, January 7, 1919

I expected to wake up dead tired after our long day yesterday but for some reason I didn't.

At ten o'clock we got under way for the Palace where we had another long talk with the various Ministers who had got together the material we wanted. They are the most satisfactory crowd to deal with I have seen in a long time and I doubt whether there are many countries that have such an able lot of public servants. It give them a fine start and if they can be steered clear of the perils of Bolshevism they ought to have a splendid future.

At a little after eleven the Prime Minister [Kramář] came for us and led us through interminable corridors to the former sitting room of the Empress where we were received by President Masaryk amid the portraits of the thick-lipped Habsburgs. M. is a smallish man, not very impressive, but clearly intelligent and sincere. He wasted little time in telling us he was glad to see us and launched straight into talk about the condition of the country and about its needs. It was just the sort of talk that we wanted and I only wish I could put it all down on paper for it would be worth keeping.

We stayed with him for an hour and a half and when we broke up he kept me behind for few minutes and gave me a few odds and ends that he thought I ought to have to pass on.

Dr. Taylor and I went for a little walk after we left the Palace and ran into young [Jan] Masaryk, the President's son, who accompanied us and dropped into shops to act as interpreter while we bought some maps and other things we needed. Every blessed soul in the place speaks and understands German but it is like drawing teeth to get them to do any business with you if you speak it.

We tried an outside restaurant for lunch and then people scattered their various way for meetings.

Giuffrida, our Italian colleague, has fallen ill of the grippe and has had to go to a hospital so that he cannot go back to Vienna with us tonight. He has a high fever and we are uneasy about him. His colleague Oblieght we left ill of the same sickness in the hotel in Vienna when we came here so there is now no Italian representative with us.

At 3:30 I went by appointment to the house of the Prime Minister [Kramář] to have a real talk with him. He told me yesterday that he wanted to have a real talk and made the appointment.

He has a beautiful house on a high hill near the Palace with what is said to be the finest view of Prague. It is a tremendous place that he was building when the war broke out, and [will be] when it is finished. He took me through the unfinished rooms and showed me the views from the different windows and then out onto the great terrace that looks down upon the river and the town. I have never seen such a view of a town and doubt whether there is another town that could afford such a view. The whole garden was gone to weeds and he was somewhat ashamed of it but explained that when he was sent off to Vienna to prison the place was confiscated to be the home of the military commander of Prague and that his wife had given orders that nothing was to be done to the place. The literal minded gardener took her at her word and did not even pull a weed during the 26 months of his imprisonment. But he saw the funny side of it so well that I doubt whether the gardener got much of a roasting for it.

Then we went into the house and sat down in one of the rooms that had been finished enough to be habitable and had a real talk that lasted until long after dark. We talked about what was to be done in this country, what different elements were trying to accomplish, the relations of the Czechs with the Poles, the Romanians, the Magyars, the German-Austrians, the Yougo-slaves, the Ukrainians and the Germans. The old gentleman knows what he is talking about and had sane ideas on every subject we touched. I should like nothing better than to be locked up with him for some shorter period than 26 months and learn some more. His great concern is for the future of Russia and he talked at some length about what could still be done to save the situation there. He is off to Paris next week by way of Italy and I urged him to lay his ideas before the President as being sound and novel. I only hope he'll get there in time to get a hearing before the show in the big tent.

He [Kramář] told me something of the way the German-Austrians tried to stamp out the national sentiment of the Czechs. Among other things he said that there were about four hundred thousand Czechs in Vienna and that they had never had a school of their own where they could be taught in their own language. He and some friends after a vain endeavor to get a Government subsidy put up the money themselves and built a big school handsomely installed. At first the Vienna authorities refused permission to open it on the ground that it was not up to the building regulations and would be dangerous. After it had been proven that the building went far beyond the requirements, the authorities still held out for seven solid years. He told of the way that Czech mothers came to him and begged him with tears in their eyes to get them some place where their children could be educated as Czechs. Tears came into his own eyes as he described these scenes and then he blazed forth in a fury as he told of going to make a supreme appeal to the Emperor to allow these people to have their school. When he told of being refused curtly he brought down his fist on the table and boomed out: "I said to him 'Majesty, how can you expect people treated as you treat these to have any devotion to you? Do you suppose for a minute that they will fight for you in case of a foreign war? NO, they will fight against you!'" And that was in 1912 and nobody would believe him.

At tea time Madame [Kramář] came in and gave us tea and CHOCOLATE CAKE! So you'll probably think I'm prejudiced in her favor. She is a fine great Russian lady of the old school, and joined into the conversation, making her full contribution.

Colonel Causey finally came for me and brought me back here where I have packed and I'm now waiting for word to move on to the station.

[Added note found only in Secret Log]
In his talk the Prime Minister [Kramář] said that he was very much concerned over the behavior of the Poles who have moved down troops into territory that is recognized as Czech and have occupied it, forcibly taking over the coal mines and certain railroads that are essential to the economic life of the country. There was a distinct understanding with the Poles that both sides should respect the status quo until after the Peace Conference had delineated their frontiers. But the Poles had disregarded this in the most flagrant manner. He says he could send troops to take this back but that he is not willing to complicate the situation any more than is necessary and must look to the Conference to straighten the matter out.

It is astonishing how badly these peoples are informed about one another. In Vienna, they are convinced that Bohemia has a large surplus of coal and that they are holding it back just to make things uncomfortable for German Austria. Here we find that far from being the case, there is almost as great a scarcity of coal here as there is in German Austria and that what has been given has been a positive sacrifice. The trains are running with only a two day supply and unless the labor situation is the mining districts improves soon there will be less and less production. They are in desperate need of dynamite and cables and hoisting machinery and until they get it their condition will be bad.

As to food, they are fairly well off in the city as they have followed the Paris policy of letting the capital have a good supply so as to keep the city population quiet. In the mining districts, there is a bad shortage which must be corrected quickly unless the Bolsheviki are to be given a fair field.

We have wirelessed a recommendation that the Czech Government be given another six thousand tons of fats and lesser supplies of wheat, condensed milk and others supplies.

This afternoon Kramář talked interestingly of the need for forming a cordon of decent nations to divide Germany from the Magyars and the Turks. He is strong for a territorial junction between the Czechs and the Yougoslavs and Romanians. Just how that will strike the Peace Conference is another question.

There was no mention of any sort of understanding with the Poles, whom he described as utterly stupid politically, short-sighted and unreasonable. He repeated what President Masaryk had told us in the morning, that there was a signed understanding between the Czechs and the Poles that the territorial status quo should be maintained. In spite of this, the Czech coal regions and other territory have been occupied by Polish troops without so much as by your leave. They have taken over mines and railroads that are private property and turned a deaf ear to all Czech protests. Masaryk sat down in Washington with Dmowski and Paderewski and drew up an agreement to let territorial questions rest but he explained that when Paderewski got to Poland he was recognized in Posen and denied in Warsaw, so the agreement has no value.

I judge that there will be a reckoning for the Poles when Kramář gets a chance at them. He says that he is unwilling to anticipate the work of the Peace Conference in territorial questions and will not shed blood unless it is necessary. Kramář is leaving for Paris during the course of the next week and proposes to talk out loud about it.

He asked me very pointedly why we had not named a Minister for Prague although the other nations had done so. He pointed out that there were very special reasons for us to be represented and that the Czechs were surprised and disappointed that we had not sent anybody. There was not much to say in reply.

Letter to Mary Gibson   Hotel Bristol, Vienna. Wednesday, January 8, 1919

When we got in this morning I found Professor Coolidge with your letter of December first and a lot of others, as well as the books you sent me for Christmas – for which oodles of thanks. I shall tuck one or two of them into my bag on each trip. They are just what I have been honing for to polish off the day after I get into bed.

I haven't seen THE book in the 75 cent edition but shall send for some copies. Perhaps D.P. and Co. will send me some of them.

We got off from Prague last night at 8:25 by special train and rolled in here at seven o'clock. The Prime Minister [Kramář] came to the train to see us off with Dr. Jaroslav [Ladislav] Novák, his secretary, a tremendously nice chap. There were also a flock of lesser dignitaries and any amount of handshaking which went on steadily and continued right up to the minute the train pulled out.

We had no fixed engagements until three this afternoon and I was able to sit down and talk to some of the Coolidge party and also read my mail and write some letters for the courier who leaves tomorrow at the crack of dawn. Our group got together and conferred over some of the matters we have been dealing with and some of those that are ahead of us.

At three there was a financial conference at one of the Ministries but as I don't shed any great amount of light on such questions I stayed away and went for a short walk instead. Now I'm waiting for the visit of young Reineck, the American clerk who was left here to help the Spanish Embassy look after American interests.

At 9:10 we start off again, this time to Budapest where the Spartakus outfit are raising Cain and making a try at overturning the Government. We are curious to see whether there will be anybody to deal with us when we get there. Gladys Vanderbilt's husband [Széchenyi], whose name I never can spell, came in to see Coolidge today and told him that he gave two days to the existing Government at Budapest before they were thrown out. We may contrive to be there for some interesting times. But I did miss the coup d'etat at Warsaw. It wasn't fair pulling it off when I wasn't there.

[Added note found only in Secret Log]
The news from Budapest is not good. Gladys Vanderbilt's husband [Széchenyi] told Coolidge today that he gave the present crowd two days and that he then expected serious troubles. And he says that the whole business would be kept quiet as a Sunday school with a strong rope and several heavy men at the right end of it.

Our Polish Lt., whom I ran into in the corridor of the Sacher tells me that there has been a serious coup d'etat at Warsaw[169] and that all communication with Cracow has been out. He has been trying to get messages through in order to arrange for the train of the British Mission. The uprising was led by a cousin of his who has been arrested. The uncle of both of them, the Prince Archbishop of Cracow [Adam Sapieha], has held a thanksgiving service for the failure of the uprising headed by his own nephew. Some family.

---

169 The January 4–5, 1919 coup in Poland was an attempt by the Polish National Democrats to overthrow Piłsudski and the government of Moraczewski. It was lead by Marian Januszajtis-Żegota and Eustachy Sapieha. The attempt failed, but by mid-January the leaders were admitted to the coalition governmtne.

Dr. [Otto] Bauer sent word to Haguenin this morning that he was trying to effect an understanding with [sic] but had been warned by the Italians that if he did anything of the sort the food supplies for German Austria would be shut off. H. sent word back that the feeding was not an Italian affair and that is any such threat was made it should be communicated with the Austrian authorities to the Mission. It will be interesting to see whether they have the nerve to do it.

Letter to Mary Gibson   Hotel Astoria, Budapest. Thursday, January 9, 1919

Here is another town to add to our collection and one of the most interesting we have visited, – but oh my! It gives you a headache to think about what is going on.

Last night we had dinner with Cary Coolidge before shoving off and heard something of what he has been learning since he settled down in his listening post. So far as German Austria, his job is the most interesting there is for he has nothing to do but sit still and listen to what people have to say to him.

While we were at dinner news came in that our friend, Dr. Kramář, the Prime Minister at Prague had been shot as he came out of the Palace on his way home to lunch. One shot missed him altogether and the other glanced off a heavy wallet he carried in his breast pocket. Nice times!

We were fixed up with a special train which pulled out of the Ostbanhof at 9:10. Aside from our party, there were two members of the Hungarian Foreign Office who had been sent up to see that the trip was made easy for us. Also Baron Franckenstein and another Austrian who were going down on business and availed of the opportunity to ride in comfort. There is only one regular train a day now and people stand up for the fourteen or fifteen hours that it takes. No wonder that they are anxious to ride on a special train when they get a chance. Two Italian officers were added to our party to take the places of Giuffrida and Oblieght, both of whom are ill, a Major Pintimalli and Lieut. Caricalli.

It is quite ludicrous the way we change all our plans. I had it pretty well in mind to go wither to Warsaw and Bucharest when the rest of the party returned to Paris but yesterday afternoon certain developments made it appear advisable for me to head a mission to Trieste, Fiume, Agram and Belgrade to attend to some matters that are pressing for solution. Accordingly, we have made preliminary arrangements to get off from Vienna on Sunday morning. Colonel Causey and Capt. Gregory will go with me to attend to the technical questions which loom large and really account for most of the work. I shall be partly decorative but may come in useful. In the meantime, Dr. Taylor and the delegates of the other countries are hurrying back to Paris to lay before the authorities what we have learned and our recommendations as to what should be done. I should like to be in on that too, but on the whole it is better to stay on the job down here and go to Paris later when Dr. Taylor and the others have come back to Vienna. In that way we can keep Paris loaded with the latest information we have been able to gather. If time permits, we may push on from Belgrade to Bucharest before returning to Vienna.

Our train eased in here this morning at 6:30 but the Hungarians are a humane people and shunted us into a siding and let us rest peacefully until eight. At 8:30 we were pulled into the station where we found a delegation in top hats waiting to receive us. The Sous-Secretaire a la Presidence [Undersecretary to the Presidency], Dr. Jellinek, headed the delegation and made a short speech in French to the effect that we were welcome and that we should find for ourselves what conditions really were. He added that the Hungarians were not trying to avoid the consequences of being defeated but would accept their fate *avec calme et tranquilité* [with calm and tranquility]. The Burgomeister was also there and several people from the Foreign office and other Government Departments to see us safely landed in our hotel. We were brought here in motors driven by maniacs whose lives evidently seemed precious to some higher power for under no other theory can I explain our getting here alive.

This is really a first class hotel, but we got apologies from everybody because we had not been put up at the Ritz. The reason is that every room in town is filled and they had to do some strong-arm work to find a place for us here. Parts of Hungary, considerable parts, have been occupied by the Czechs, Ruthenians, Romanians, Serbs, and Yougoslavs. From all those districts people have flocked to Budapest until the population has grown from nine hundred thought to a million and a half. It is so bad that the authorities have had to go to all private houses and apartments and requisition all rooms that were not necessary for current needs so as to put refugees into them.

We had just time to brush up and then the coal and food people arrived and we settled to the usual preliminary conferences which lasted until noon.

As my guide I drew a young chap from the Foreign Office. Dr. Baron Tibor von Podmaniczky who is married to an American girl, formerly a Miss Hegeman.

When the pow-wows were over Gregory and I sent out on foot for a tramp down to the Danube. Sergeant Cash, who had read what the papers had to say about disorders here and street fighting, walked three paces to the rear and one to the left with a large automatic strapped to his right leg ready for action. He is a dead shot and seemed much disappointed that nobody tried to start anything.[170]

---

[170] The situation in Hungary was instable. Austria-Hungary had lost the war, and a bourgeois government under Count Karolyi had come to power. January 1918 saw a lot of communist unrest in the streets of Budapest.

We went across the bridge and then turned back and walked through some of the shopping streets before returning to the hotel. There we found our friend Podmaniczky and took him off to lunch at the Ritz. There and everywhere else in Budapest we have been surprised at the amount of English we have heard. The Hungarians did not intern foreigners save in instances where they made trouble and those who could came here from all parts of the Central Empire. They all say that they have been particularly well treated and I have not heard of any of them being bothered because of their nationality. They looked over the American uniforms without any hostility but with a certain amount of interest. There were a few peasants about in their wide skirts but not as many as I had expected and there was little of the Oriental touch that I had looked for.

We had a perfectly good lunch, far better than anything we had seen in Vienna and at a price that seems like nothing when one counts exchange at twenty crowns to the dollar. That doesn't help the poor fellow who doesn't get his money from the outside, however. I enclose the bill of fare of our dinner just to show what we have and you will note that the price was eleven crowns or about fifty-five cents.

We worked all afternoon at the hotel and a little before five shoved off to see Count Karolyi, the Minister President as he is called. He is in the old Chancellor's palace on top of the hill in the same courtyard with the Emperor's Palace. It was too dark to see much but we wound in and out among the courtyards and great portals and rounded into this fine old building where we were handed over to a gorgeous lot of flunkies and attendants of one sort and another dressed in bright red uniforms trimmed with silver lace. They turned us over on the first floor to several functionaries in frock coats who took us through several brilliantly lighted state reception rooms to the place where Karolyi was to receive us. He came in promptly from another room and was introduced but Dr. Jellinek and the Austrians then withdrew.

I had expected to see a wild eyed revolutionary but was not prepared for a very swagger, well-groomed youngish giant who would pass for a Guardsman in London. He is over six feet tall, has quite an English look and wore a smartly tailored grey lounge suit. He has a cleft palate and is rather hard to understand although he speaks excellent English and French and does everything he can do to make himself quite clear.

Instead of asking us to sit down he [Karolyi] squared off and made us a short speech about the situation of Hungary. He ended by saying that he regretted that they could not receive us gaily as "all Hungarians were heart-broken at the fate of their country" but that they would be much obliged for anything we could do for them.[171]

---

171 Having lost the war, Hungary faced massive territorial losses.

He then sat down and talked for over two hours about the situation in general. He did not fail on the side of frankness and made us sit up several times. What he said has been pretty well repeated about town and most of it has appeared in the papers so I don't see why I can't write it.

He [Karolyi] began by saying that when the crash came, the French Commander in Chief. General Franchet d'Esperey, called on the Hungarians to rally around Karolyi as the man best qualified to get good terms from the Allies. Of course, ever since the early part of the war he has fought for the conclusion of peace upon the terms laid down by President Wilson and has proclaimed himself in favor of the Entente.

He says that he signed the armistice agreement in the belief that he would be able to protect the interests of his country better than anybody else, but so far has not got a word in answer to any of the communications he has addressed to the military authorities in regard to the way they are carrying out the terms of the armistice.

He [Karolyi] described at a good deal of length the way that various countries were moving in and occupying portions of Hungarian territory and said that this was not agreed to in the armistice. Today he said that a new complication had been added by the fact that the Ukrainians have moved in alongside the Czechs and occupied a good stretch of territory. From having a population of twenty millions they are now reduced to eight. He says that this precludes them from holding an election as the whole people would not have the opportunity to vote and a Government which is not an expression of the people's will is not worth the trouble of electing. He seems to have no enthusiasm over being President and says frankly that this revolution went further than he wanted as he would have preferred to have a constitutional monarchy with Hungary completely separated from Austria. He did not expect the Hungarians to be ready for a republican Government and feels that the way they have lent themselves to the designs of the Bolsheviki bears out his worst fears.[172]

He then launched into a long explanation of the fact that he had fought against the war in Hungary because he felt that the Allied cause was based upon idealism. But now that he is in the saddle and want to swing his country into line with the Allies, he cannot even get a hearing from anyone in authority in Allied countries. He complained bitterly that so long as the armistice endures we are technically at war and that Hungary must therefore continue to suffer under the disadvantages of that state until peace is signed.

---

172 Soon, the Karolyi government would be overthrown by Béla Kun's Bolshevik Revolution.

He [Karolyi] wound up with a petulant peroration which spoiled what might otherwise have been an impressive utterance. It was something to this effect: "Why do you go on pretending that you are fighting for justice and the rights of small peoples? Why don't you throw off the mask and say frankly: 'We have won and we shall now do with you exactly as we please.' Hungary is beaten and she would have no recourse if such a statement were to be made but at any rate she would know definitely just where she stood. We have been played with and deceived and now our country is being destroyed piecemeal by our neighbors without a voice being raised in protest and without out being able even to get a hearing to tell of what is being done. It is murder!"

Haguenin spoke up very quietly in reply and answered in a masterly way. He said that the charge of inhumanity and evil intent was not very convincing when you remembered that all the Allied Powers had sent a mission before the conclusion of peace to relieve the sufferings of the populations of enemy countries. He inserted a nice note of doubt as to whether the Central Empires would have done as much if the conditions were reversed. He also called attention to the fact that our own countries had suffered cruel injustices during the war and that no pity had been shown them. That the countries which had been defeated could not expect to escape altogether the penalties of defeat and that in any event all these question would be settled at the Peace Conference. It all sounds pretty raw and I have jotted it down but he did it with a fine Italian hand and the effect was good. When he mentioned the coming of the mission, Karolyi threw up his hands in a dramatic gesture and then covered his face, crying out: "Trop tard! Trop tard!" [French – "too late"]

Then he went out and brought in some of the members of the Cabinet who were holding a meeting in an adjoining room and we had a conversational free-for-all with them. There were Baron Ambrózy, the Foreign Minister [Harrer] whom I used to know when he was in the Embassy in Washington, Count Festetics, the War Minister, and the socialist members Kunfi, Jászi, Berinkey and Szende and the President of the Parliament Hock. I had particularly interesting talks with Ambrózy and Festetics and was sorry to leave when eight o'clock drew near and we had to hurry away.

We were all taken down to the Ritz and got through dinner in time to get out before the lights were dimmed at nine. Since the Communist outbreaks of the past few days, all public places must be closed by nine and there is not a drop of liquor to be had at any hour.

And from the Ritz we went back to our own hotel to talk shop and carouse until a late hour of the night. I don't know whether I told you had since we reached Vienna, Beveridge got word that he received the Knight Commander of the Bath in the New Year's Honors List and was therefore Sir William Beveridge. We got up a bottle of fizz and toasted him in a bumper.

And so to bed.

Altogether the situation here is about as bad as it can be. Bolsheviki have been getting in their deadly work here on the demobilized army and the huge mass of unemployed. There are thirty thousand idle men in Pesth alone and the socialist government is paying them fifteen crowns a day each just as though they were working. No wonder they prefer to loaf. But there is a day of reckoning coming. The crops of beets and potatoes and such are rotting in the ground because nobody wants to go to work. They can't give work to all of them in any event until they get some coal to start up their factories and that is our most pressing problem

[Added note found only in Secret Log]
Baron Ambrózy said he would like to talk to me quietly and led me to a sofa at the far end of the room. When he got there he began to stall and said that he had a lot of things that he would like to tell me so that I could report the views of the Hungarian Government when I got back to Paris. I told him to shoot and that I would be glad to repeat anything of interest to Coolidge when I got back to Vienna so that he could deal with it as he saw fit. Ambrózy then said that he hesitated to express any views about such important matters as he did not want to risk saying anything that would not meet with the approval of the President, etc. As a matter of fact, he had not much of anything to say and I gave him up. He has only recently come from the Ministry in Vienna and does not know whether he is afoot or horseback.

Count Festetics, the Minister of War, next came up and introduced himself. He is much worried over the situation and fears that he will not be able to control it. He appears to have more backbone than any of his colleagues and to be more ready to use force to maintain order. The Government is doing practically nothing to keep the Bolsheviki in hand and the leader of the whole movement [Béla Kun], a little Hungarian Jew, recently returned from being a prisoner of war in Russia, does exactly as he pleases. He has caused outbreaks by his inflammatory speeches but the Government has done nothing beyond arresting him for three hours on the second occasion. Karolyi explains that so long as this bird is at liberty they know just what he is doing and can govern themselves accordingly, but if he were to be run out of the country or jailed, others would spring up to take his place and there would be no way of knowing who they were. So the merry Bolshevist has things his own way and whenever he gets the people heated up to a certain temperature, the Government makes them some fresh promises about the division of land and increases the unemployment pension which has reached a ridiculously high level already.

Festetics says that they only hope for maintaining order is to get some Entente troops into the country. He thinks that to maintain order in all the now unoccupied territory of Hungary four or five thousand troops would suffice. He says they would be welcomed by practically all elements and that they would not have to fire a shot.

He says that Hungarian troops have completely lost all discipline and that there seems to be no hope of restoring it. The disaffection spread almost instantly throughout the country and no one seems to have escaped. Even old and trusted non-coms [Non-Commissioned Officers, NOC's] who were looked upon as devoted to their own officers seemed to change completely in half an hour and refused to pay attention to orders.

Festetics says that he does not give any orders unless he is obliged to as they are not obeyed and he only makes himself ridiculous. He said they would prefer to have American troops but that anything else would be accepted "even Italians". That was the impression I gathered from several others who broached the same subject.

The enclosed map[173] was brought me to show just how Hungary was being whittled down. There is no doubt that she is being sinned against territorially. The more we see of the assurance with which the various little neighbors are wading in and helping themselves, the more I am inclined to the opinion that there must be some understanding with the Allies that they are to be given a free hand in disposing of Hungary as they like. If they think they can dispose of the Magyar question by dividing them up in the old discredited way they had better think it over a second time for that won't work anymore.

Everybody we meet is keen to tell us that they are not really enemies and how intensely they have always disliked the Germans. Festetics explained apparently to his own complete satisfaction that while they were all pro-Ally throughout they had been obliged to fight us through the excessive chivalry of the Hungarian character and their exaggerated loyalty to an Ally. They all seem to feel that the past is to be wiped off the slate and that we can make a fresh start with them as complete friends. They don't want to wait for the signature of peace and feel outraged that they are not at liberty to start out for the United States now. I explained to them that our own people were not at liberty to travel freely between Europe and American and they appeared to be astounded. Karolyi said he expected the conference to last a year and that meant that there was no hope of establishing any sort of government that would last in Hungary.

---

173 No map attached in the archival record.

Letter to Mary Gibson   Hotel Astoria, Budapest. Friday, January 10, 1919

This is a hectic day and I only wish we could arrange to stay on here for a little longer for there is a great deal to hear. However, our mission is to get at the true facts in regard to certain things and then fly at the problem of getting the necessary action. Days are precious and the longer we delay in these various places the longer it will be before they get relief.

The crowd went off to the general meeting at the Food Ministry at ten but I stayed away as it was to be more or less technical and I thought I could spend my time to better advantage talking to people. I had a string of them – diplomats, officers, business men and an intelligent little man named Geller who runs this hotel and who ran the St. Regis in New York for eighteen years before the war.

Along about nine o'clock Pink Simpson came in looking like a tramp, nine days on the road from Paris en route to Belgrade where he is to learn 'em all about how to distribute food and clothes according to the best approved Belgian methods. He was a pretty tired boy but we sat up and swapped gossip until lunch time. He has a husky named Cpt. Armstrong with him and also an interpreter and a more disreputable looking bunch you never saw.

At 1:30 Baron Podmaniczky came for us and Beveridge, Gregory, Haguenin and I went home to lunch with him and his wife. She is a big American girl who got married to him just before the war and has been here all the time. It was the first time any Americans had been in her house for more than four years and she made an event out of it by having the drawing room heated and bringing out some maple syrup which was served with synthetic waffles for dessert.

We had to hurry away to get back to the hotel to see various people. There was a steady procession of Socialist Ministers and party leaders all afternoon telling us their different points of view. We divided them up among us and had a session going in each bedroom most of the afternoon as the only way to handle the rush of information.

About three o'clock Count Karolyi came in with Count Szilassy whom he is sending to Bern to act as an informal representative until such time as Hungary can accredit a regular Minister. He stayed on and visited around from one room to another for a good part of the afternoon.

While this was going on there was a big communist meeting taking place not far away and the crowd was so threatening that Festetics had ordered out some of the reliable troops and machine [guns] were posted in the windows of the houses across the street from the hotel. This is the hectic corner of town. Our little drawing room in which I am writing was where Karolyi and his friends planned the revolution. It was from these windows that he made the speeches announcing to the people the overthrow of the Emperor and the establishment of the Republic.

So they provided us with what might be termed ringside seats so that we should not miss anything.

It was strenuous work keeping up with the views of the different visitors and I was glad when six o'clock came round and we were gathered up and put into motor cars to go up to the Palace to have tea with Karolyi and his Cabinet and a few others with whom he wanted us to talk about the situation.

I was packed into a whaling great car driven by a lunatic who was formerly chauffeur to the Emperor. He evidently felt called on to show how Emperors go when there is no speed limit for them, for on the way up the hill he did everything but wrap the car around a tree. But I must say that he did it so well that I was all admiration and forgot to shiver until after we had got home.

The flunkies in Hungarian uniform were out in force and a row of four or five of the great state reception rooms were lighted for us. Countess Karolyi, a good deal of a beauty but looking anxious, was there to serve for us and had several other Hungarian ladies to help her.

There were about fifty men present and they went for us like hungry wolves. I took on a steady succession of them and was backed up into a corner before I got through and was answering questions and asking them until the perspiration stood out upon my brow. There were bankers, professors (lots of them), officers, landed nobles, every sort of white man that the country produces and they all had been coached in advance for the line of talk was the same in each instance. However, it was very interesting to get the point of view of all these different classes of people.

Finally I was introduced to Count Apponyi, "the Grand Old Man of Hungary," and was led off into a corner where there was a collection of maps, and there he proceeded to educate me. We talked for a solid hour and I wished that it could be a lot longer. He is a very splendid old type who ought never to wear anything but a brilliant Magyar costume but who stands out even in our foolish clothes. There were a good many places where I could not agree with him but I was there to learn and held my peace save for asking a question now and then.

I had very little talk with Count Karolyi, who was chiefly busy talking to his many guests and seeing that they were talking to each other. While we were there somebody came in to report that the Communist meeting had drawn a crowd of thirty thousand people and that they had cheerily decided to hang Karolyi. He seemed rather bored as though they were doing that all the time. He says that he receives many delegates every day and that when he walks out into the reception room he never knows whether they are going to hand him a memorandum or a bomb. It must be a nice life and I can't blame his wife for looking worried.

The crowd is clamoring for me to go to dine so that we can be off to the train so this will have to be continued in our next.

Memorandum [included here in Gibson's Secret Log with no date and no signature]

The Hungarian Government wish to thank Mr. Lansing for the opportunity given to them through Mr. Gibson of bringing certain considerations to the notice of the American Government.

We avail ourselves with pleasure of this of American Secretary of State. Quite a number of memoranda dealing with the economical, social and political situation of Hungary have already been handed to the members of the Commission headed by Dr. Alonzo Taylor. We asked for the permission to communicate other material on these problems to the American Government and their representatives at the Peace Conference, and would feel obliged to Mr. Lansing for indicating to us the name and address of the American official to whom communication of this kind may be delivered in the future.

Since we are under the impression that the views of the American Government on the solution of the territorial problems regarding Hungary have been influenced by one-sided information and since we are finally convinced that President Wilson wishes to contribute to the solution of these problems on the basis of un-biased presentation of the facts, we would appreciate an authorization to be given to the American diplomatic agents to enter in direct communication with the official agents of the Hungarian Government in the neutral countries and with the Hungarian officials at the head of or attached to the diplomatic missions of former Austro-Hungary in the neutral states. We, of course, would greatly welcome the sending of an official or semi-official or confidential agent of the American Government to Budapest, who could stay here permanently until the conclusion of peace. We would also feel very thankful to the Government of the United States if it permitted the sending of a semi-official or confidential agent of Hungary to Washington.

If President Wilson deems it possible or useful that a similar kind of contact be organized between Hungary and Great Britain, France and Italy or with all their allies, we would of course immediately appreciate his intervention with the Governments of these countries.

We believe that a careful study of the ethnographical, geopolitical, political and social conditions of all Hungary by an

American Commission, or if President Wilson deems it better, by a Commission of the allied and associated powers would be of the greatest advantage for clearing the views of the President of the United States on the Hungarian problems and ask for the sending of such a Commission to Hungary within the shortest possible time.

We finally venture to recommend the following remarks to the attention of the Government of the United States:

About a month ago, a French paper defined the interests of France in the peace conditions saying that France's interests made it necessary that as many millions as possible of Germans and as many millions as possible of Magyars should be put under the permanent rule of nations which are friends of France. Hungary did not believe this idea was that of the French Government and besides felt so confident in the wisdom and power of President Wilson that she considered it impossible that an idea so monstrously unjust could ever be taken up by her enemies' Governments. But the experience which she has had since the conclusion of the treaty of armistice seems to indicate that France, at least, apparently seems to be inclined to wish to carry out this above-said programme. We wish to emphasize that such a plan would constitute a terrible mutilation of Hungary which would deprive her of the possibility of independent existence and would make her and the parts annexed by her neighbors seats of permanent unrest and irredentistic revolt.[174]

Deprived of her northern and north-western counties of Transylvania, of the Benat and Boczka, of her communications with the Adriatic Sea, separated from Austria by a corridor allotted to the Slav countries, Hungary would be obliged to become either an unwilling ally of Germanism or a hostile vassal state of Bohemia. Many future generations of her people would be filled with a burning desire for revenge. She could never honestly and in good faith become a member of the League of Nations.

---

[174] Irrendentism is a policy advocating the restoration to a country any territory formerly belonging to it, making its context in Hungary a clear warning of future dissension. To be found mainly in Hungary, Germany, and Italy as countries that lost the First World War or were not happy with its outcome, it instigated spirits of discord which largely contributed to the disintegration of interwar Europe.

The Hungarian Government would feel grateful to the American Government if they could be informed about the decisions which the American Government might feel disposed to take in the above said matters.

Letter to Mary Gibson   Hotel Bristol, Vienna. Saturday, January 11, 1919

On getting back to Vienna this morning, I find your letter of December 8th which was brought in by a member of Prof. Coolidge's party and brings me a little more up to date.

It is dreadful about Harvey Thorpe. I did not even know he was headed in this direction. I shall try to write to the Dr. in the course of the next few days.

We got off according to schedule last night, being whisked through the town by our wild drivers so fast that we could only see that there was some sort of excitement and that the police were very active. This morning we learn that the whole Karolyi Cabinet resigned at eleven and that Karolyi is left alone on the lid to handle the entire situation by himself. I feel sorry for him for he is undoubtedly a man of great idealism and splendid personal courage who deserves well of his countrymen and stand a fine chance of getting no reward save a handsome monument some day after he has been made a martyr after some gentleman with whiskers has thrown a bomb at him.

We got here in time for breakfast and spent the morning cleaning up loose ends with the Vienna officials. I had a talk with Coolidge and decided to go down to Budapest on Tuesday. We made our own arrangements to leave tomorrow morning. Taylor and most of the rest of the party go through to Paris to report on the trip. The Vienna Government is giving us a private car in which we shall be very comfortable. It turns out to be the very one in which the Archduke Ferdinand went on his ill-fated trip to Sarajevo in 1914. I don't know if we will go to Sarajevo but if we do I shall resign the leadership of the mission just before we pull into the station.

I called at the Yugoslav Legation and got our passports fixed up. They are also telegraphing all along the line to look after us and make our trip as easy as possible. The Italian Armistice Mission had also visaed us and sent telegrams to say that we are to be given anything we want so our trip should not be too hard.

Coolidge asked us to take along Sherman Miles (now a Lt. Col) and Leroy King who are going to Laybach to stay for the present. They set off with us and may meet us again at Laybach [Ljubljana].

The afternoon was filled with more conferences and the evening session set in right after dinner. We have to be up before six in the morning so I shall not dally to write at much length.

We don't know much about how long our trip will take but expect to be gone for ten days or two weeks before we get back to Vienna. And what may have happened before that is beyond conjecture.

Letter to Mary Gibson					Sunday, January 12, 1919

On the Train en route from Vienna to Trieste.

We're off again digging our way through the snow-covered mountains toward the Adriatic.

I got called at six this morning to see off the other party that is heading toward Paris but even at that I missed Dr. Taylor who is a demon for being on time and had left for the train with almost an hour to spare. If he ever missed a train it will be because the train leaves ahead of time.

Our own train left at 8:10 and even at that hour we found quite a delegation of officials waiting to install us in our car and see that we are comfortable. We are travelling in real state this time in the private car of the old Emperor, the one I told you in which the Archduke Ferdinand left for Sarajevo. I am installed in the Emperor's stateroom which is rigged up to look like the death of little Eva scene in Uncle Tom's Cabin.[175] It is fitted in onyx and bronze, with washstands, radiators, bells and reading lamps and mirrors and thermometers and electric cigar lighters and goodness only knows what else.

I was weary from a bad night's sleep so turned in and got a nap until lunch time. The Imperial crown was so heavily embroidered on the pillow slip as to tickle my ear and the Imperial arms on the china are too brilliant but then these are war times and we must put up with hardships in silence so you will hear no complaint out of me.

We worked our way up to Semmering by lunch time and felt that we were in Switzerland with all the people out doing their bit of winter sports as through there never had been a war at all. Now we are tacking down the long stretches that lie between us and the sea. At Gratz, Col. Causey and I got out for a tramp and saw something of the old town.

We are not running special but are tacked onto the regular train which seems to try hard to take up as much time as possible. We don't care though, for we are comfortable, particularly when we look out and see the poor wretches hanging onto the steps and crouched on the roofs of the cars wrapped up in blankets, try-

---

[175] *Uncle Tom's Cabin* was an anti-slavery novel by Harriet Beecher Stowe, published in 1852 by John P Jewett & Co. It promoted the concept that love can overcome evil.

ing their best to keep warm. There is so little coal that there is only one train a day allowed in any given direction so they have to fight their way aboard or stay home.

We brought along with us Sherman Miles and Leroy King, members of Coolidge's outfit who are going as far as Laybach where we are due to arrive at three or four tomorrow morning. They ought to be darned grateful for having their lives saved. We also took pity on a young ensign named Nicholas who came up to Vienna as a courier and was facing the ordeal of going back by the ordinary route until we saved him. We are due at Trieste at seven tomorrow morning but from what I hear we shall not be there much before noon.

There we have to find out what our plans are. It may be that we can settled our business in short order and shove on to Fiume but the evening train. On the other hand, if we can locate Col. Atwood by wireless we may have to get on an American destroyer and go down the coast to the Montenegran port of Catarro to see him. I shall not be at all disappointed if we do have to go down there for it would be interesting to see aside from the fact the trip is justified by our work.

By the morning paper we see that Karolyi has become Provisional President of Hungary and is going to have a try at running things single handed.

Letter to Mary Gibson   On the Train in the station at Trieste.
                                     Monday, January 13, 1919

The pessimists were right and we did not get in until noon today in a dreary downpour and a cold and clammy breeze. Nobody had been told that we were coming so we worked our way uptown over the broad flat slabs of stone that do service for paving here. At the hotel they said that Col. McIntosh was at his office. At his office they said he was at the hotel, so we trotted back there again and finally found him in deep conversation with a Yugoslav representative from Laybach who was able to tell us some of the things we wanted.

After lunch we paid a call upon the Italian Chief of Staff and after offering our respects, etc. got passes that permit us to travel as we will through all territory occupied by Italian troops.

Then we wasted a good part of the afternoon talking to some people that were brought to see us but had nothing to offer and in some shopping to lay in supplies for our trip. We tramped up and down every street in the town several times and know all we need to know of Trieste in one lifetime. It is all right but I shall not choose it as a place of residence until necessary.

The Italians are here with both feet, and I have never seen so many Italian officers even in Rome. The Hotel Savoia where we lunched and dined was filled with them, plenty of generals and even the Duke of Alba who spent a good deal of time in the lounge looking glum and tramping about while all officers got up from their tables and stood at attention for him. They town is distinctly Italian in every way, streets and signs and the people themselves, although you find that in the shops they all speak German as well as Italian. It has quite a cosmopolitan touch from the fact that there are soldiers and sailors of pretty well all the Allied nations to be seen in the streets and hotels. There were no French in evidence throughout the day and they are said to be the boys that rule the roost at Fiume.[176]

Just before dinner I ran unto a group of old Washington newspaper correspondents who are on a joyride under Italian leadership. They accompanied the President to Rome and dropped off there to see what they could see of this part of the world before going back to Paris. After dinner they came for me one at a time and led me off into the corner to ask for a steer as to the value of the stuff they have been given. It is wonderful to see them in action, trying to size up their material and generally doing it pretty well.

We are going to sleep on the car, the sooner as the heat stopped when the locomotive was disconnected. I suppose our royal and imperial friends kept a locomotive on hand to maintain a proper temperature but in these days coal is too scarce for anything like that and we freeze when the weather man is not kind.

Letter to Mary Gibson   On the car at Trieste. Tuesday, January 14, 1919

This day has been largely wasted. We got up early and went up town to try to find out a number of things but they are all to be found in other places. There was one train out to Fiume at nine and nothing else stirring until five in the afternoon, so we spent the rest of the day sitting around and waiting for the train to go. It was bitter cold and no sun shining until later in the afternoon. We tried to get a motor to take us over to Fiume after lunch as that we could clean up our business there and have the car join us late in the evening. The only one in town belonged to a Colonel Walton of the QMC who is here to receive supplies for us but he is a mess and preferred to send out some of his own officers to collect souvenirs so our day has gone to waste. It makes our blood boil to find a man like that when we have work to do but we had no choice and our work goes over until tomorrow, so that he can have some Austrian helmets to take home.

Colonel McIntosh decided to come along with us and at the last minute Ensign Nichol turned up with two other young officers who had missed connec-

---

[176] The city of Fiume was bitterly contested between Italy and the Yugoslav State.

tions and asked for a lift as far as Fiume so that they could join their ships. It makes a crowd but you can't well refuse people at times like these so we dined ten around our little table.

We gathered some stores off an American ship in the harbor and I took a sack of flour for Percy Dodge who is at Belgrade and has probably not been able to get any for himself.

Letter to Mary Gibson   On the train at Fiume. Wednesday, January 15, 1919

At the end of a busy and largely wasted day I sit me down before Corona to report progress.

We got in here last night at midnight when everybody except these young Naval officers who were going to get off had gone to bed. I had the beginnings of a fine grippy cold and had gone to bed after taking a stiff jolt of quinine and reading THE DOCTOR'S DILEMMA[177] as a shock to my system. This morning I woke up feeling more or less human and the cold is now a matter of ancient history. Nothing like catching them young.

After an early breakfast we shoved off and as we felt it was too early to call on the Admiral [Bullard], we went on board the *Ferencz Ferdinand*, an Austrian ship which had just been completed when the war broke out for the most luxurious sort of travel. She had never been to the sea and has now been taken over as a sort of hotel for our officers who are stationed here. We have four thousand men supposedly belonging to one outfit divided between here and Spalato and Catarro with men in hospital at Trieste and Treviso and Venice and all sorts of other places as far away as Naples.

We had quite a talk with the Colonel [Walton] commanding officer who gave us some good hints we were after and agreed to let us have such officers as we might need for the investigations we are going to make. He was being evicted from the ship today and moving to a hotel. The ship is to be scraped and then used as a transport to take British prisoners home from Germany.

From there we walked back along the dock and went aboard the BRIMINGHAM where we found that the Admiral (Bullard) had gone ashore to be gone some time. We talked to the Captain Hussey, and with Captain Boyd who has come out to relieve him. Then I set off for the Yugoslav headquarters to see what they had to say for themselves and to get our papers in order to go into their territory.

---

[177] Play by George Bernard Shaw (1906) featuring a doctor having developed a pioneering cure for tuberculosis.

The officers on board the ship gave us the wrongest possible information about how to find the blessed place and Colonel Causey and I wandered all over town before we finally found it. At any rate, we saw all we wanted of Fiume and did not need to go sightseeing. It is a rather commonplace town without much color and the most beautiful landlocked bay imaginable. The little strip of the town that runs along the water front is almost exclusively Italian in language at any rate. There seems to be a good deal of difference of opinion as to how much so they are so in spirit or nationality. This strip is bounded by a canal which flows through the town; on its other side you are in Slav territory and neither hear Italian spoken nor see it on the signs.

Under the terms of the armistice the Italians were not supposed to occupy Fiume but were to stop on a range of hills that can be seen to the west of the town. After sitting there for some days they moved in and occupied the whole place, claiming that some Italians had been killed in street fighting and that their presence was necessary to maintain public order. There are also some French, British and American troops that were under the command of the Italian general and they are very much in evidence, especially when it is necessary to quell any sort of uprising. The feeling between the Yugoslavs and Italians leads to riots every blessed day and the streets are steadily patrolled by groups of armed soldiers, usually in groups of eight, two Italians, two Frenchmen, two British and two Americans so as to impress the people with the idea that this is no mere Italian venture. From time to time biggish detachments of Italian lancers parade through the streets just to be seen and guns of various sized are trundled about for the benefit of any ill-advised persons who might be inclined to start something. It is an interesting situation but one would have to have a month available to talk to all the various sets and hear what they all have to say.

The bridge across the canal is heavily held by troops and those crossing from one side to the other are keenly scrutinized.

We all gathered for luncheon at one and Col. McIntosh led us to a restaurant that he had been bragging about for several days. It turned out to be a retched place but we did manage to get some food and clear out. Gregory had stayed on board the flagship while the Col. and I were after the Yugoslavs and had had a satisfactory talk with the Admiral before lunch, getting everything we needed from him.

The Yugoslavs had a large building in the heart of their own quarter to which they had betaken themselves when driven from the palace on the hill by the Italians. It was typically Slav in its dirtiness and the lack of anybody that could attend to your wants. Finally I found a bedraggled little man who spoke German and got him sufficiently stirred to vise our passports. Then he discovered that somebody had gone away with the seal and that he could not finish the job until after lunch. Accordingly we all tramped back there after lunch and got the operation finished, incidentally picking up such information as they were able to give us as to conditions in their country as regards food and coal.

There seems to be nobody here that can help much in our investigations here but we have got what we needed in the way of personnel and have learned just how to go about getting them on the ground when we are ready for them, so our time has not really been wasted.

We tramped around for a little while and then came back to the car to loaf and write some letters. If our energy holds out we shall tramp back up town to dine and pile back on board before the train for Agram [Zagreb] starts at 10:30 or thereabouts. Two of Col. Atwood's men, bound for Belgrade, have turned up here and we had not the heart to refuse them a lift although we now have every inch packed with supplies and shall be badly crowded with them.

Yesterday I forgot to tell you that we picked up an old scallywag named Capt. Stanwood from Norfolk, Virginia, commanding a merchant shop that has just come in with supplies. He is over sixty but went into the Naval Reserve and has been running ships across ever since we came into the war. He is hale and hearty and drinks his liquor straight. With his lunch he had four ordinary drinks of Scotch whiskey in an ordinary tumbler and drank it all off without water or anything else to soften the effect. However, he declined to repeat the dose and said that he knew when he had had enough and never drank to excess. Woooof!!!

Letter to Mary Gibson   Agram (Zagreb) on board the car.
                                         Thursday, January 16, 1919

This is the most interesting day we have had so far on our trip and I only wish we could stay on here for several days. Unfortunately we made too good progress with our work and must pull out by the morning train tomorrow for Belgrade. We growl if we don't make progress and we growl if we do but on the whole I think I like this way best.

Last night we pulled out on time at 10:23 and rolled into bed soon thereafter. The two men from Belgrade were to have come with us but they had to come from Trieste on a destroyer and did not make the connection so we have all the room we need while they plod on behind us in the ordinary train. They may catch up with us tomorrow.

It was hard luck that we could not have done the trip from Fiume here by daylight as it is one of the most beautiful regions in Europe. By daylight, however, we were through most of the mountain country and rolling along between wooded hills that looked like an unkempt Maryland. There were plenty of children out tending flocks of hogs and altogether the country did not look as though it had suffered. When I first looked out the window I stared into the face of a French soldier wearing the croix de guerre who was hanging out of a troop train drawn up alongside us. He seemed about as much amused by me as I was by him and called on all hands to take a look.

Some idiot pulled the danger signal just as we had settled down to running and we stopped at a siding for an hour or so while all the passengers got off and talked about it. It was our first look at them and we got our first glimpse of Oriental color. There were plenty of peasant women with huge bundles on their heads which they continued to tote while they wandered about and gossiped. They wore either black knee boots like Russian peasants or hid sandals or moccasins, and white (by courtesy) skirts with bright embroidery. The men were more occidental but even they had a way of wearing their rags that would have looked unnatural further west.

We were careful to arrive unannounced and so had time to look about a bit before we settled down to our day's work. There was a French Commissaire Militaire at the station to look after French troops in this region and I dropped in for a chat with him. He seemed glad to see some of his own sort and kept a line of people waiting while we talked. He was a young sous-lieutenant [second lieutenant] who seemed cheerful enough in his job. He told me something of conditions and gave me some hints about how we could get hold of the people we wanted.

We all set out together through the modern part of the town which is substantial but dull and disappointing and just as we were about to give up hope we landed kerplunk in the great square, the Jelačićev-Trg, where the market was in full blast. It is a fine old square with good buildings round about and a spirited statue of Jelačić, the Banus or Governor of Croatia who figured in the battles of 1848 and 1849 and became a sort of local George Washington. I could only get a picture of part of the poor modern side of the square but here it is. The booths were spread all over the place and were surrounded by hundreds of peasants, in all stages of native dress, colorful headdresses, embroidered coast, some of cloth and some of hides, the decoration being sometimes in gold thread and sometimes in colored silks. Some of the women wore boleros of solid gilt embroidery which I should have liked to take away from them. It was a great sight and so were the things they had to sell, onions braided together by their strings so as to make necklaces, sweetmeats of all sorts, especially prunes and figs and sections of oranges candied in syrup and spitted on little orange sticks. They looked very tempting but the dirt was too much for us and we lacked the courage to try them. It was all interesting and we would willingly have lingered but duty called so we pushed on up the crooked little street that led to the top of the hill, up some old stone stairs, thru an archway in a tower past a big shrine behind a fine old wrought iron grill and up to the modern palace which was the birthplace and early home of the Yougoslav National Council which was merged only a few weeks ago into the Serbian Govt. The building is now the seat of the local government for Croatia and Slovenia.

In trying to make sure of our way we held up a likely looking officer who turned out to be the intendant of Agram, Emil Rajakavić. He led us straight to Dr. Edo Marković, the food man for the district, and a fine able pair they are. It turned out that we had hit upon just the right man to hold up in the street for he knew or could find out pretty well everything we wanted. We fired questions at the two of them and finally drew up a questionnaire on a lot of matters we had not hoped to get information about and they set a lot of people to work getting information for us. We made an appointment for them to come down to the car at five and tell us everything there was to know about food and coal and transportation problems with all the data they could get ready in the meantime.

And then we set forth with easy minds and took a look at part of the town, falling for the first embroidery shop we saw. Gregory and the others did prodigies of buying and I got one or two little odds and ends. Then when we came to paying the shopkeeper to our thinking tried to do us in the eye on exchange so nothing would suit Gregory but that we should withdraw in high dudgeon and leave all the packages on the counter. This the rest of us did under protest. But after lunch, Gregory's ire oozed out of the tips of his fingers and after we had been to the bank and changed some notes at the good rate, we went back ignominiously and paid for the packages which were still lying on the counter where we had left them. They shopkeeper had a smile in the corner of his eye but said nary a word.

We had a good deal of work to do and did it on the train so we did not get much chance to see the town. At five our men arrived bringing with them two substantial looking citizens rejoicing in the names of Branko Lagjević and Svetozar Delić. The latter seems to be the labor leader of these parts and just about the right sort.

We settled down around the big table in the salon and talked and asked questions until eight o'clock, having a perfect field day and getting the meat of what we were after on our trip. The men were well informed and had gathered a mass of facts and figures that gave us an insight into the subjects we were interested in. With what we have learned here we can make much quicker progress than we had hoped in our visit to Belgrade and altogether we feel much cheered up.

Along toward the end of the proceedings we offered our visitors a drink but all but one of them declined as they don't want to seem to drink much in this part of the country. When the coffee pot appeared, however, they all began to lick their chops as they had seen no real coffee for several years and the way they went for it was a caution. One of them mentioned the fact that they had not seen chocolate for so long that they had forgotten what it looked like. We got out some from our storeroom so that they could refresh their memory but each man put his in the pocket to take home to his children. We inquired how many there were in each family and got them to take a cake of it home for each youngster and I thought they were going to burst into tears of gratitude. We also gave them each a little store of cigarettes and sent them away vowing that we could have anything we wanted in this town.

We did not feel much like dinner but had a cold snack and settled down to combing out the data we had gathered. Presently a locomotive was hitched onto us to give us steam heat, just as a tribute from the station master who had come on board in time to join the revelry. After a bit, a boy came on board with a big bundle containing shiny apples sent by another appreciative citizen and a bottle of Slibowitz, the native liqueur. We had brought along a considerable stock for handing out on such occasions and it is the best thing we have done.

They were all disappointed that we were not going down into Bosnia to see all there is to see there. Perhaps one of these days we shall be able to do that. Nothing would please me better.

[Added note found only in Secret Log]
Both here and in Fiume we have gathered the growing impression that the Italians are carrying on an active campaign against the Yugoslavs regardless of anything that the Peace Conference may decide and in defiance of all the announced feelings of the Allies toward these people.

In Fiume, it was clear to seen that the feeling was very bitter and that even some of the Italian speaking people were not at all keen on becoming Italian subjects. The Yugoslavs are kept pretty close to their own quarter of the town and every day sees its riots and troubles which are put down by force of arms. It is intimated that some of these disturbances are got up by Italian agents, provocateurs in order to justify their occupation. The Americans seem concerned over the fact that when riot duty comes, the Italian general calls out the American troops to attend to it, thus trying to give color to the belief that we are backing up the Italian claims to Fiume even by force of arms. I noticed one or two items in the papers to the effect that the President had pronounced himself as convinced that this part of the coast should belong to Italy whereas I am confident that he has done nothing of the sort. One of our consular agents from the Adriatic coast dropped in at Venice the other day and made a speech in the course of which he said that he had had talk with the President in Paris and that the President had told him that he considered Italy entitled to the whole Adriatic coast. There were several American naval officers present and they made a statement as to the facts which the Admiral has forwarded to Paris.

At Yugoslav headquarters, I asked them to send a telegram ahead to Agram about our coming but they said it was impossible as the Italians had cut all communication and would not allow them to telegraph.

Here, we found the feeling very bitter. When we gathered about the table for the afternoon conference we were first of all asked whether there was an Italian representative among us. When they were told we were all Americans, their relief was evident and one of the men remarked: "We are glad of that for we do not like the Italians. It is too bad, but they have behaved so that we cannot consider them as Allies."

In the course of conversation, they kept recurring to various troubles and shortages that were caused by the Italians. The Yugoslavs had a large supply of coal at Pola which the Italians have taken over; they will not allow any part of it to come to the Yougoslavs, while the situation gets worse and worse through these territories because of the shortage of coal. The need of medicine is desperate while there is in Fiume a large supply of them with the Yugoslavs have bought and paid for but are not permitted to bring out of the regions occupied by the Italians.

They say that the Dalmatian coast is in a desperate condition for food, a report that we had on good authority before we left Paris. It seems that along the coast and on the islands people are dying like flies of starvation. The Yougoslavs have an exportable surplus of food and want to take it to their people but are not permitted to do so by the Italians. They can only deliver it by the coast because there is no way of carrying it through the mountains of Bosnia. Meanwhile the Italians are making small deliveries of food from time to time in return for petitions from the whole population asking that they be annexed to Italy. Once the petition is signed no further shipments are made to that locality and the people are left to starve. Altogether it is about the most revolting story we have heard for a long time, and unfortunately there seems to be reasons for fearing that it is largely true.

One of the young officers from the BIRMINGHAM told an amusing yarn about the propensity of our sailors for drawing the long bow about their exploits. From censoring the home bound mail, he learned that for some of the men, a ship never put out of port that she did not have a brush with a submarine, generally bagging her in the process. Some of these affairs took place at times when the ship was moored alongside the dock in port. There was some tall thinking as to how to stop this sort of thing and the practice finally adopted was to post the original letter on the ships bulletin board under glass so that it could not be taken down. The men usually managed to identify the handwriting and then made life unbearable for the writer. Pretty good.

Letter to Mary Gibson   Friday, January 17, 1919

On the train en route from Agram to Belgrade.

My machine is feeling pretty wobbly in the knees from much thumping and needs an overhauling which it cannot be given until we get back to Vienna. Despite its sad state here goes for the daily gossip.

We were due to start at eight this morning and were only about two and a half hours late. When I made my appearance the Chef de Gare was already at the breakfast table punishing café au lait and army bread. He had come on board to bring us two bottles of Slivowitz, the native brandy, 55 years old and dearer to him than his own children, and Colonel Causey, being from Virginia knew how to appreciate the sacrifice and had set to fill him up with breakfast, a good investment as it proved. The gentleman presented each of us with one of his cards reading thus:

RUDOLF HOMOLA
Glavar postaje

which last we take it means Chef de Gare in this quaint language of the country.

The Director-General of Railroads sent us a little case of cigars made from Bosnian tobacco and some of the other members of yesterday's powwow came down to bid us good bye.

As we were having our breakfast there came a sharp tapping on the window and I looked out on a very grumpy British Captain, followed by eight or ten British, French and Serbian officers. He glared and snarled out: "Hurry up, but your bloody gate open." I explained sweetly about the car but he went off with a threat to find out about it. Soon we saw him and his French colleagues in violent debate with the Chef de Gare, who stood firm as the Rock of Gibraltar, despite his deprecatory gestures. They gave him up at last after roaring at him and presently there was another thumping on our window. Gregory put his head out of the window and was told by the Briton to go and get an officer. Even when he and Colonel Causey explained who they were that was not good enough for him and he called for me. He had brought an officer from the French Commissaire Militaire and bade him "make" me open up. I explained to him that the matter had already been made clear to the officer, that we did not propose to be coerced and finally that it was a matter that did not concern him in any way. I said it as quietly as possible and the Frenchman being a reasonable being agreed that it was a matter of hands off for him.

Even then Mr. Briton was not satisfied but harangued his French colleagues until he got them het up. They had two compartments in the next car reserved for them but that was not good enough for them and they were determined to ride with us. They gave the Chef de Gare another go but he, fortified with our coffee, refused to budge, and finally the whistle blew, the train creaked and we began to move. AND THEN there was the most ungodly row you ever heard, yelling and screaming and running about in all directions. Our French friends had stationed a soldier by the engine with orders to shoot the engineer if he tried to start before they gave the word. They had, of course, neglected to inform the engineer of this cheerful arrangement and when he got the high sign he opened the throttle and pulled away. By the grace of heaven, the French officer yelled in time for the soldier had a bead on Mr. Engineer and was ready to blow him into the next world from ten paces. There was a wild ruction for a minute or so during which the engineer told everybody just what he thought of that sort of train dispatching and then we did get away.

We have spent a whole day plowing along across Croatia and Slavonia, the country getting better and better as we progressed, more and better looking flocks and herds, better soil and great stores of corn and beets and wheat, – just the things we wanted to see.

The towns might have come out of Gorky. All of them lying on the flat plain, the houses of unpainted wood in an advanced state of dilapidation, the streets sometimes a quarter of a mile broad, deep in mud, but with a winding path through the mess on which the wagons had beaten out a way. There were quite as many pigs in the towns as in the country, under the guardianship of grimy brats. The village population usually came down for a look at us and thus gave us a look at them. They seem well fed, probably as well fed as they ever are, but utterly shiftless and hopeless. Their clothes are usually an unbelievable mass of rags and patches which probably have not been taken off since the cold set in. For head dress, either gaudy embroidered handkerchiefs or fur caps. The more dressy ones had fur overcoats with the fur inside and the outer hide embroidered. There was sometimes a sprinkling of fezzes and those [who] did not have high boots wore moccasins and had the calves of their legs wrapped in rags, – perhaps the ancestors of our puttees [Hindu leg covering from ankle to knee].

It has been a bitter grey day with a biting wind and one walk of ten minutes was all we needed by way of exercise. The rest of the time we stayed in the car trying to keep warm, working a little, reading and telling each other droll stories of our infancy.

The railroads have very little coal and that of poor quality mined near the line. It was never used for locomotives before as it is largely mixed with slate and ruinous to the boilers. The result is that we rarely make more than fifteen miles an hour on the level and there are frequent long stops while the engine wheezes to catch its breath.

Letter to Mary Gibson   Saturday, January 18, 1919

SCENE: A room in a private house on a side street in Belgrade. Name of family and street unknown.

From Agram I telegraphed Dodge, our Minister, that we would arrive today and told him to make no reservations, thinking that we would stay comfortably on board the car. They had neglected to tell us in Agram that the big railway bridge across the Save had been blown up by the Germans before they cleared out and that the only way of reaching Belgrade was by a tiny boat from Semlin, the Hungarian village across the river. There was much ribald laughter at the Legation and it will take me some time to live down that telegram. They diagnosed the reasons rightly and had managed with some difficulty to get two rooms for us, one at the hotel and another in a private house under a billeting order from the French Staff. I drew this part of it and it is so uninviting that I sit me down to thump the machine although I fain would sleep.

We were due in Semlin early this morning but crawled along because of lack of coal and at noon had a long wait when the supply gave out completely and more had to be brought from a nearby station. It was colder than yesterday and as some sweep had stolen the rubber connecting pipes from the engine we had no heat and spent the day adding fresh layers of sweaters and finally fur coats, and even with that we were none too warm.

We spent the daylight hours in what the jogguffy [sic: geography] call "the rich plains of Hungary" and they don't exaggerate a bit. We passed an endless review of flocks and herds and corn and beets, great supplies standing in the fields waiting for transport to haul it away. It all hinges on coal and it becomes plainer and plainer every day that our greatest problem is not food but coal to move it with.

The people were more Oriental looking than yesterday. The swineherds along the way looked like the original Tartars from whom they descended, shapeless from the masses of skins in which they were wrapped and motionless as a lot of wooden Indians.

At India, a junction on the grand old Berlin-Bagdad railroad, we made a final effort to get some heat and had the Chef de Gare come aboard for a cup of coffee. He was an intelligent fellow of 27 or 28 and gave us a lot of valuable information about conditions but he could do nothing about heat as there was not a scrap of rubber to be found about his station. He made diligent search and promised to find something to take care of us on our return journey but for the time being there was nothing to do but add our last sweaters and bide our time.

A little before three we eased into the station at Semlin and got our first view of Belgrade across the river, with the fine old Roman fort with its walls battered from the poundings that have gone on pretty steadily for a couple of thousand years or thereabouts.

A fine big Serbian Lt. Colonel named Miloutin G. Néditch came on board and asked if there was anything he could do for us. There was. He got out the station master and arranged guards for the car. He got porters and cabs and telephoned Belgrade to have more cabs meet us and rooms engaged. He convoyed us to the dock and led us to the office of the commandant where we toasted ourselves around the red hot stove until it was time to go aboard. It seems he had been Chief of Staff at Belgrade for a year or so and everybody rushed to anticipate his wishes. He got us and our plunder ashore before the common herd was allowed to stir and into one of the few motors the town can boast which had been sent down for us by the Red Cross.

We were whisked through an exhausted and weary looking town with few window panes intact, no stocks in the shops, a good deal of damage from shell fire in the houses and streets. There were a good many people in the streets despite the bitter cold and you could feel in the air a brave struggle to get things started again.

The Dodges are in the old Turkish Legation, a comfortable modern building which was taken over for them by the Foreign Office as there was no other place for them to lay their heads. Of course, it was treated well during the war as being in the possession of an Ally, although it was evident that somebody has lived in it. After Turkey signed the armistice, however, it was messed up to a certain extent, the window curtains were slashed with swords, the furniture was smashed or befouled and various other things done that were not altogether what you would expect to happen in the home of an Ally. Fortunately, the Huns did not have much time to get in their dirty work as they had to get out themselves, and it must have hurt them to leave the place so nearly intact.

We found Pink Simpson and Colonel Atwood at work in a room downstairs which Dodge has let them have. Dodge came down as soon as he heard we were there and we talked for over an hour or so about all sorts of things. He came back from Corfu with the Serbian Government and had a lot of interesting things to tell about his trip and about the general situation of the country.

Mrs. Dodge bade us upstairs for tea and to see a birthday cake for HPD [Dodge] which had been prepared by the little girl. She came through with the party from Corfu and is pretty weary but still game.

At seven Simpson and Atwood led us gently to the Grand Hotel which seems to be the only place you can get anything to eat. During the occupation, it was the club of the Austrian and German officers and so escaped some of the damage that other places suffered from. Our first shock came when Gregory in his grand manner called for the sommelier. A boy of ten or so with dirty hands and face was sent to talk to us. Gregory, somewhat taken aback but still grand asked for the wine card and was told that there was no such thing. He then asked "What sort of wine have you?" To which the reply was "There are liter bottles, half liters and quarter liters." With a low moan of pain Gregory gave up and we took what was given us. It was BAD, both food and drink and we were glad when we had done our duty by it.

After hearing about our car, Atwood broached the subject of our taking him to Bucharest wither he has to go soon. We agreed to take him if it can be done in any reasonable time although we are anxious to get back to our work in Vienna as soon as may be. If it can be done inside of six or seven days and land us back in Vienna next Sunday without fail, it would be worthwhile for us to do it.

After dinner I was put in charge of an American soldier who speaks this beautiful language and sent out to hunt for my room. It was about fifteen minute's tramps through cobbled streets and a good deal of chatter with passers-by. We found the house with front and back doors standing wide open and the cold wind howling through. The soldier stumbled around in the dark until he found a door bell. Then there was a turning of keys, clanking of chains and drawing of bolts that would have done credit to a melo-drama. Then ensued fully five minutes of conversation after which the door was slammed and the process of locking up gone through thoroughly. Anton groped his way to another door across the hall and there was the same performance gone through while I stood outside and froze slowly. Family No. 2 must have been richer than the first for they had a lot more locks and bolts and their outfit of chains would have supplied the big city jail. They were stronger on conversation too and kept Anton eight minutes by the clock talking about things I could not understand. It was all amiable enough, but he got into the doorway and waved the billeting order and pointed at me, while the family looked sympathetic but raised their hands and eyebrows to heaven, evidently to invoke divine testimony as to their innocence of rooms. When both sides were exhausted, Anton climbed one flight of stairs and the whole show started over again. There the conversation was endless and just as I was getting ready to call off Anton and go back to demand a place on the floor with Causey and Gregory, he came down and said this was the place and that my room would be ready in a minute. The family was assembled to welcome me and then I fled. There is, of course, no fire and the bed is not tempting but at least it has a roof over it and so here goes to try as I can't keep pounding poor little Cora all night.

Letter to Mary Gibson   Abed aboard the car at Semlin. Sunday, January 19, 1919

We finished up Belgrade in a whirlwind rush and tomorrow at the crack of dawn we set out for Vienna by a roundabout way.

I got up and out as soon as I could this morning and met Pink Simpson for breakfast at the Grand Hotel where we had some coffee made of scorched barley and a slice of soggy bread. It was pretty bad but we were repaid when Gregory came in with his incorrigible optimism and began to order ham and eggs and other things that don't exists for breakfast in these parts.

When he and the Colonel had finished what they got, we went off to see the Food Minister, a pinched little man named Yovanovitch [Jovanović] who knows nothing about food but agreed to telegraph for what we want although he was not at all confident about getting it. He says that it takes fifteen days for an answer to a telegram from most of the places we were interested in and that in many of the villages he doubted whether there was a man left who could read and write. This tallied with what Dodge and others had told us about the systematic way in which the Germans have tried to stamp out the educated classes. In every village, they seem to have gathered the Mayor, the priest, the schoolteacher and anybody else of that sort who remained behind at the time of the occupation, and shot them without any pretext that they had been guilty of any offense. About the only educated people left are those who were in the army or those who accompanied the Govt. in retreat through Albania. The stories you hear of atrocities make your blood run cold. The worst of them seem to have been committed by the Bulgarians. An investigation is being carried on by a commission and the things they learn make the German doings in Belgium and France seem like child's play. A brother-in-law of Bill Phillips is on the commission and he was here the other day, having had about all his nerves would stand for a time.[178]

From seeing the Minister we went back to the Legation and talked with Atwood until Dodge came in and suggested that we all go up to the Grand Hotel and have lunch together. There we found Major Ryan, just in from Agram to take over Atwood's job when he goes back to Paris and all of us attacked the usual meal of pork with a soggy cake to follow.

I sat next to poor Mrs. Dodge, who is just about all in. She has no servants and can get none here that will stay for more than a few minutes at a time. There is nothing to be bought in the shops here and they have only what they brought with

---

178 Within their occupation zone of Serbia between 1915 and 1918, German authorities implemented a harsh policy against educated people in order to oppress any national Serbian movement. Although not genocidal by intend, deportation of thousands of people to forced labor in the Reich and the Ottoman Empire resulted in high fatalities.

them on their overland journey from Corfu to Bosnia. They have not had a letter since early November and their last letter from home was dated about the first of October. A courier service is soon to be established for them so that conditions will improve, but they have had a long pull on the ragged edge of the world.

I was determined to see something of the sights so marshalled our party after lunch and marched them off to see the citadel and its view of the Save and the Danube which conflooo [sic] around the island before the fortress. We could not but wonder why the Romans ever left their own perfectly good country to come here but decided that perhaps it was not as bad then as the Germans had not been there to make the place unfit to live in.

That was about all there was to do in the way of sightseeing and as it was cold and drizzly, Gregory and I went back to the Legation to write some telegrams while Col. Causey went off with Caskie as interpreter to find out from the French Staff about our further journeyings. He learned that it would take several days for the trip each way, so that we could not count on being back in Vienna in much under two weeks. That is out of the question for us, so Col. Atwood will have to get down there as best he can. We can't go straight back to Budapest as a tunnel on the main line has been destroyed. We shall have to do a roundabout trip and it may take us three or four days to make our journey. There is only one train a day and that leaves at six-thirty in the morning.

We held a hurried council of war and decided that there was little to be gained by staying over another day. The last boat across the river was due to leave in three quarters of an hour and we made it by record breaking speed, although we did not have an opportunity to say good-bye to the Dodges.

Pink Simpson came down to see us off and nearly wept that he was not going along. He has an interesting problem and wants to stay to settle it but once it is out of the way, he wants to hie [go quickly] him far away and I don't blame him.

After we had got on the boat with the motley throng that was going across, we sat and waited for some time and then a large bandit addressed us all and the swarm began to climb onto another boat that came alongside. We went along and after fifteen or twenty minutes in the rain and wind we were dumped off in the dark on the dock at Semlin. Both there and in Belgrade, I was singled out and seized by the guards while my military friends went on. They had to come back and rescue me each time, and their mere motions were more effective than all that I could say in three languages. It pays to be in uniform these days when you travel.

It was raining cats and dogs, there were no cabs and the station was a couple of miles off in a direction we only knew in a general way. We went in to see our friend of yesterday, the Commandant of the port, but he was not there. We got hold of a passing officer and he dispatched soldiers and telephoned messages for cabs, while we sat down and waited until after half past eight. A Serbian soldier who had worked in the mines at Butte, came in to rescue us about this time and we walked back in to the town and found two cabs which hauled us back to our happy home.

I was near dead with a splitting headache and took to my bed with a stiff dose of aspirin and brandy while the others went off to see the station master and persuade him to hitch an engine to the car and warm it for us. They got him out of bed with a message that they had important matters to talk to him about. When he came down he turned out to be a captain in the Serbian army and a very decent little chap. He gave orders at once for the engine to look after us and accepted an invitation to come aboard for a cup of coffee. Just then his wife came in, a Russian girl from Odessa, and she joined the party. By the time they got on board, I was pretty well cured of my headache but did not join them, getting instead frequent bulletins from the front from Col. Causey and Gregory. Both the guests spoke pretty good French and our brutal soldiers unlimbered theirs so that altogether they had a hilarious party. Sergeant Cash produced dinner and they stayed on and although it is now well after eleven, they are still going strong. They have not had a party for so long that they hate to let it go.

Letter to Mary Gibson   Monday, January 20, 1919
                              On the train en route from Belgrade to Budapest.

Another uneventful day, but a restful one.

We pulled out of Semlin a little after six in the morning and trundled along slowly over the road to Agram as far as Vinkovce where we doubled back toward Zombor and Budapest.

It was interesting to go back over the same ground and see more of it at leisure. With a coal railroad and general transportation expert like Colonel Causey aboard, you can catch a new significance in things you never noticed before and the day was full of interest. For one thing, there were some markets being held at various places and many of the roads were filled with the long horned Serbian oxen and their floundering carts which they dragged relentlessly through the deep mud. I had heard of their doings in Belgrade and was glad to see them in action. It seems that the whole transport service of the Serbian army depends on these beasts. They can get their carts through country that is impassable for any other sort of transport. Motor trucks lie down and sob like children when they see the oceans of mud that pass for roads. Horses flounder and strain and wear themselves out in time, but the calm old oxen plod along and keep at it all day and day after day. When the big retreat began the Germans had it figured out that the speed of the Serbian army would be determined by the speed of the supply column, they came romping up and captured the whole outfit. It worked out quite otherwise, however. The German supply train broke down and they were left helplessly behind until they had requisitioned oxen of their own and built up an entirely new system of their own.

When we came into Vinkovce, it was well after dark and we expected to go on but when we got the station master on board to fill him up with coffee in pursuance of our policy, we found that under the schedule we would have to lay over for about twenty-four hours at Zombor as we would miss the one connection of the day. Our faces fell about four kilometers and our aspects was so pitiful that the Chef de Gare was fired with zeal and of his own accord rushed out and arranged a special engine to take us in time to make tonight's connection and land us in Budapest tomorrow morning. He put a train master on board to see us through all difficulties and came back with the engine. So all is well with us even if we have not much news.

Letter to Mary Gibson	Pulling out of Budapest for Vienna.
	Tuesday, January 21, 1919

We are finishing up our whirlwind trip and if all goes well we shall be in Vienna tomorrow morning.

Last night at a little after midnight, we came into the station at Szabadka – and settled down to stay where we were instead of speeding through to Budapest. When we got up, a gentle snow was falling, our train master had gone back to Vinkovce after arranging for our further movement – and then nothing happened. Following our tradition, we sent Caskie for the station master and wheedled him into giving us an engine for the run to Budapest. He was a little Serbian Captain but had no insignia on and I sounded off wrong by saying that we were in haste to get through to Pesth to talk to Count Karolyi about matters of great importance to Hungary. He did not seem to be thrilled and then I noticed Gregory making faces at me and indicating the man's Serbian cap lying on the couch. I wiggled out by saying that we had come from Belgrade, and that it was also to the interest of Serbia for us to get through as soon as possible. It was feeble but it worked and in short order he had an engine hitched up to us pumping in welcome heat, and within fifteen minutes we were off. It was not very quick going but by three o'dlock we reached Budapest and found that messages had been sent ahead and that we were expected. There were several officers who came on board, offered to do anything they could, arranged for another special engine tonight and placed two motors at our disposal.

We made straight for the Ritz to see Storey and Goodwin and had a good talk with them.

Word came from the Palace that Karolyi would receive us at seven and we settled down and talked until it was time to start.

On the way up the hill, our car blew out its paper tire and we had to walk. I astonished my companions by leading them without a mistake through the tortuous passages and alleys and palaces on the hill and landing them in the front door on time. Karolyi came in quickly and sat down for an hour's talk. I should like to write out the whole conversation but it can't be done. It was absorbingly interesting and gave us a good meal of food for thought. The poor man looks more thin and worn than before, his courage is still good but his patience is getting low.

On leaving him, we came back down the hill and dined at the Astoria before going back to the train. There was a staff of heavily decorated officers waiting to conduct us in state to our palace on wheels, but we did not know it and got in through the same door with the common herd. Just before we were due to pull out, the troupe came dashing up anxiously and showed evident relief that we were not missing.

The station was filled with wretched tired people, sleeping on benches and even on the floor. Leaning against a pillar near the door was a good looking boy of about twenty and with him a pretty girl of seventeen or eighteen; he had his arm around her shoulders and her head was on his shoulder, and both of them were sound asleep. They looked as though they had not another bit of go left in them, not even enough to fall down. The trains were packed, people were hanging onto the steps in clusters and on the little ladders on the sides. And snow and all, they were pulling out for a long night's ride. Just to add a little zest to travel, our friends up country have taken to holding up trains and robbing passengers. A couple of nights ago, the train between here and Vienna was stopped by about a hundred and fifty soldiers who were on board. They went through the pockets of all hands and then took to the jungle. The demobilization here was automatic and the soldiers have kept their arms which makes it a real problem to keep any semblance of order if they want to stir up a fuss.

At the Astoria, we had a table opposite us the most accomplished family of sword swallowers I have even seen. They had forks on the table but used them only as pushers and what they could not do in the way of juggling food on a knife was not worth trying. There was some space between the courses and this they spent busily with toothpicks, going through a sort of drill with military precision. They would have got fat pay at the Orpheum[179] but here they are just doing it all for nothing.

---

179 The Orpheum Circuit was a US American vaudeville and movie theatre chain.

We have not very much to do in Vienna and hope to finish up in a day or two and then fly up to the Bohemian coal fields to see what the situation really is there and how it can be made better. Once we have accomplished that, I think Gregory and I will clear out for Paris, leaving Colonel Causey here to run current business. We want to say our say verbally instead of trying to write a lot of things that can't be written and then come back after three or four days in Paris.

[Added note found only in Secret Log]
Storey showed us the maps with the new lines indicating the advance of the Serbian, Romanian and Czech troops and the lines they are threatening to occupy within the next few days. If they do as they threaten, there will be practically nothing left of Hungary. Coolidge went the other day to see Lt. Col. Vix, Chief of the French Mission which is here to see that the terms of the armistice are carried out. He found that this ogre is a decent little man who is utterly disgusted with his job and is begging to be relieved. He said he was sent here to see that the Hungarians carried out their part of the armistice. No sooner had he got here than all our gallant allies began breaking its provisions and the Hungarians came pouring in upon him with justifiable complaints, but there was nothing he could do. He says the Czechs are utterly unreasonable and that their occupation of the Slovak territory is outrageous but that when he submitted the Hungarian complaint and protest, he was instructed to send the text of a reply stating that the Czechs were re-occupying those territories as a matter of right and with the approval of the Allied Govts. A copy of this most surprising document is attached. Also a copy of the armistice convention. Also a map showing the occupied territories.

[Attachments missing from archival record]

At seven we were received by Karolyi in one of the big receptions rooms of the Chancellor's Palace.[180] He came in looking thinner and more worn and haggard than when we left him two weeks ago. His nose looked as though it had been turned more to one side, his cleft lip seemed more disfigured and his speech was thicker.

He started off without any preliminaries: "The situation is intolerable." and kept coming back to that phrase from time to time, once remarking when he had got unusually indignant: "It is a damned situation." which it seemed to be.

---

180 Parts of this passage reappear in the memo "Visit of Mr. Hugh Gibson to Countries of the Former Austro-Hungarian Empire", see letter to Mary Gibson, February 5, 1919.

Image 20: In the wake of the Great War, after the bloodless 'Aster Revolution', Count Mihaly Karolyi served the short-lived First Hungarian People's Republic (November 1918 to March 1919) as Prime Minister and President. Faced with the myriad problems caused by a lost war, shortages, internal riots, invading neighbors and Allied territorial demands, he fought desperately but in vain to prevent his country's demise into the turmoil of revolution and counter-revolution. (Public Domain)

He seems to lay the whole blame for everything that has happened to Hungary on the French, and said that Berthelot seemed to be a little king and to receive no orders from Paris although Clemenceau was disposed to play fast and loose with his promises and run the whole show for himself. Berthelot seems to have a good deal of authority and to have little patience with Hungarian complaints. Vix admitted as much and added: "*Je ne suis qu'un très petit Monsieur à côté du General Berthelot.*" [I am only a very little Gentleman next to General Berthelot]

Karolyi says that so far as the Bolsheviki menace is concerned it is almost gone. He had gone for them with gloves and has arrested all who come into the country. Vix took one bunch off his hands and has sent them to a safe place. Stringent measures are being taken to keep foreigners from bringing large sums of money into the country unless they can offer a good explanation of the reasons for it. Such sums or check books are taken away from them and held until they can prove that they have legitimate use for them. Coolidge told him in advance of the coming of one crowd of agitators and he bagged the lot as they crossed the frontier from German Austria.

On the other hand, the general situation is getting much worse as national spirit is being roused by progressive encroachments of the Allies. When we were here before, Karolyi had told us that under no circumstances could he do more than protest; that he would not offer forcible resistance or try in any way to anticipate the decisions of the Peace Conference which must solve all territorial difficulties. Today, however, he said that all this had changed; the behavior of the Czechs and Romanians has been such as to stir people to a dangerous degree and that unless there was a decided change for the better, he feared a popular uprising against the invaders. He quite realizes that this means annihilation and severer penalties for Hungary in the end, but says that the people will soon be roused to a point where they will strike out blindly and without reason. He added: "All my life I have been a pacifist and have felt that appeal to force of arms could not be justified under any circumstances, but events have changed that and if the time came when the people took up arms to drive out our invaders, I would take my rifle and join them to the end. We would be put down the first time, but we shall keep on fighting until we get some sort of justice. I don't believe in fighting but we cannot be expected to sit still under such crying injustice."

He went over the old ground of his having accepted power on the theory that he could get good terms for his people and complained that he was still unable to get any intimation from the Entente as to how they felt toward him; he had fought against the war and had preached a Wilson peace because he felt that that would lead to a better established peace than any other arrangement or even than a German victory which he considered a great menace to civilization. He had played square with the Entente and felt that they owed him enough to tell him where he stood. He did not pretend that Hungary could hope to escape the results of defeat by his virtues but he did feel that he was entitled to know whether or not the sword of Damocles was going to drop. He is still trying to keep the people calm with a vigorous propaganda to the effect that as soon as the Peace Conference is really started the President will see that they get justice. In one of his speeches lately he said that the hope for the future of Hungary was to be stated in three words: "Wilson, Wilson, Wilson." The walls of the town are covered with red portrait posters of the President and inscription to the effect that Hungary must have a Wilson peace. I asked Podmaniczky to get me some of them.

Letter to Mary Gibson   Hotel Bristol, Vienna. Wednesday, January 22, 1919

When we woke up this morning we were already in the quiet station at Vienna and we hastened to pile out into the falling snow and come up here to beg for letters from home. ...

I also heard directly from Judge Conrey and wrote to Mr. Hoover to have somebody look the young man over and take him on if he could fit in anywhere. I told him about Judge Conrey and said that there was at any rate that much to be said for the boy although I had not seen him myself for a long time. I don't know much about what the needs of the organization are but imagine they can use a good many youngsters if they are nimble on their feet and in their wits. If I were in Paris I could look into the matter myself, but being so far away I am a good deal hampered. I wrote Judge Conrey explaining the situation and telling him what I had done.

The *Atlantic Monthly* turned up and was mighty welcome although I had to fight Coolidge to keep it. A little home reading before turning out the light at night is a great help to forgetting the troubles of all the world that you don't care to have pursue you all night.

I had a lot of Christmas cards and notes and a few bills just to prove that the New Year was really with us. I drew ten simoleons [dollars] on you to pay my absent dues to the Metropolitan Club and hope it won't put you in the debtor's jail. I doubt whether I have anything in my Washington account and there is no buying of money orders in enemy lands.

Louis d'Ursel has written to announce his engagement and is fairly bubbling with it. He is marrying a Mlle. De Rosanbo, a French girl from Paris. Among other things, he says:

Samedi dernier je lui faisais visite à Paris. Elle m'a montré un livre à couverture bleue, intitulé La BELGIQUE PENDANT LA GUERRE et m'a demandé si je l'avais lu. J'ai dit que non – et que le bouquin m'était tout à fait inconnu. Alors elle m'a fait lire le nom de l'auteur et celui du traducteur et j'ai été stupéfait de voir le nom de mon ami Gibson et le mien.

J'avais presque oublié cette traduction ou plutôt je la croyais si mauvaise que Hachette l'avait jetée au panier. Elle n'est certes pas bonne et je relis certains passages avec gêne.

[Last Saturday I visited her in Paris. She showed me a book with a blue cover called BELGIUM DURING THE WAR and asked me if I had read it. I said no – and that the book was completely unknown to me. So she made me read the author's and the translator's name and I was amazed to see the name of my friend Gibson and mine.

I almost had forgotten this translation or rather I thought it was so bad that Hachette had thrown it in the basket. It is certainly not good and I reread certain passages with embarrassment.]

I did not know the blessed thing had come out yet and shall be curious to see it.

We had a good deal to do during the morning with visitors and other odds and ends. After lunch they went on steadily but I cleared out and went to see the Czech Minister to arrange for our visit to the Silesian coal mines. He was anxious that we should also see the mines in the regions around Prague and urged us to go up tomorrow with him on a special train and do both parts of the business. So we have as usual changed our plans and shall leave in our same old car at four for Prague, taking the Ostrava trip later. This ought to bring us back to Vienna early next week so that we can shove on to Paris and be there by a week from Sunday or thereabouts.

Coolidge came to dine with us and we had a long evening's talk comparing our information and finding that we were in complete agreement on all essentials. He is a very satisfactory citizen.

He told us that the other day he looked out of his office window and rhapsodized over the Church of St. Stephen over the way, the history it had seen in the making, and wound up: "And to think that from the towers of that church the Viennese watched the two invasions of the Turks!"

Somebody asked if it was that old and he replied: "Why, it's Gothic."

Major Martin, a literal minded map maker who came with the outfit, thought heavily for a little and then said: "Oh, I see. I thought the architecture was Gothic. You mean it was built by the Goths."

The congregation will now be dismissed with the benediction.

[Added note found only in Secret Log]   Vienna, January 22nd

Dr. Schwarz-Hiller came in this afternoon and broached the questions of getting Entente troops sent to occupy Vienna. He said that he was not officially authorized to make any observation on the subject and that he would prefer not to have his name connected with any recommendations that were made in regard to it, but the unrest was growing very rapidly on account of the increase in unemployment, the food difficulties and the coal shortage; that Bolshevist agitators were filtering in from Russia with very large sums of money, and that trouble was possible at any time.

I pointed out that the Czech and Hungarian Governments had managed to deal with these people by the simple expedient of arresting them on arrival and handing them over to the Chief of the Armistice Commission, Colonel Vix, who seemed to have somewhere to put them, and that the Bolshevist danger had largely disappeared in both these countries. To this, Schwarz-Hiller replied that this was not so easy for Austria, as she was the center where about fifteen languages converged, that her frontiers were not adequately guarded, and that she could not adequately police them; that even if a severe control were exercised in the railway stations at Vienna by police agents speaking fifteen languages, the problem would not be adequately met as one of the favorite tricks of these people was to come across the frontier on foot, ride most of the way to Vienna by train, and get off between stations a few miles outside the town. He had many good reasons why the Viennese were unable to help themselves, but said that a few entente troops would be able to hold the situation in hand. He asked if I would communicate these views to the Peace Commission. I replied that I would give them benevolent consideration.

Letter to Mary Gibson　　　　　　　　　　　　　Thursday, January 23, 1919
　　　　　　　　　　　　　　　　　On the train en route Vienna to Prague.

The old train is lurching and the typewriter does not answer to her helm as she does in port but I sit me down nonetheless to tick out the doings of the day.

As a matter of fact, we had not done much but clear up odds and ends and get away from Vienna again.

I spent the morning reading Coolidge's dispatches and was glad to find that there was no disagreement between us. I am particularly glad because the same character of reports coming in from different sources has a cumulative effect.

We had a meeting with the Vienna authorities which took us until nearly two. Then we snatched a hasty lunch and dictated furiously to a stenographer until it was time to rush for the train, leaving Caskie behind to sign our names and bring on the mail tomorrow when the courier comes on.

The Czech Minister and his wife and the Director General of Railroads are travelling up to Prague in their own car which is tacked on behind ours. We had them in to dinner and got a good deal of information, the which leaves me rather exhausted as it all has to be done in German and both Gregory and the Colonel are rapid fire questioners and as you may imagine my German vocabulary on technical matters is not all that it might be. However, it is increasing rapidly and will soon leave my general vocabulary far behind. I can rest myself by chatting about gradients and equipment and means of increasing the output of steam coal, etc, in a way I could not have done at home a year ago.

[Added note found only in Secret Log] January 23rd

Tusar says that he is sitting on the Liquidation Committee at Vienna and is expected to supply most of the backbone required for the proceedings. The government of German-Austria is nursing its position in view of the approaching elections and is doing everything possible to avoid antagonizing any faction.

The Labor groups are being conciliated by receiving unemployment allowances. Some 40 to 60,000 officers of the Austrian Army, which has now been completely demobilized, are receiving full pay although in the nature of things they cannot render any service in return. The officials of the War Office at Vienna have made a formal proposal to the Liquidation Committee that their work be so arranged that the adjustment of affairs shall occupy the space of one year, during which they shall continue to draw full pay. Everybody agreed that this was ridiculous and that the work must be finished as soon as possible, but the onus of saying so was wished upon Tusar.

Letter to Mary Gibson Friday, January 24, 1919
On the train in the Wilson Bahnhof at Prague.

Our special train from Vienna turned out to be a special freight train. As a matter of fact, we picked up some freight cars and shuffled them along the line, finally getting here at eleven.

We had sent word ahead that we were coming to talk coal so there were a flock of coal people to meet us at the station besides a group of officers bearing the compliments of various people.

We headed through a gentle dry snow to the Ministry of Public Works where we went into the figures of production and distribution of all the mines. There is a slight improvement since we were here the last time but I think we can get still more improvement without very much effort. We've got to get it for the coal question overshadows all others and if we can't increase the output enough to supply the minimum needs of this part of Europe, we might just as well give up any other activities.

We had lunch at our old hotel and remembering the good ham and eggs, we had a meal of them. We got away with a double portion each and had nothing else. The bill was a trifle under two hundred kroner, – in normal times about forty dollars. All the rest of the day, Gregory has murmured from time to time in a sepulchral voice: "Give me forty dollars' worth of ham and eggs." It has come true at last.

After lunch we had a long talk with the deputies from the coal regions of Kladno and Orsava. They were good hard-headed citizens who talked business and knew it from experience. It was decided that the party would go to Kladno tomorrow and Sunday, leaving for Ostrava Sunday evening.[181] As I don't feel that I can render much service looking over a coal pit, I am going to run up to Teplitz to see the Clarys and stay overnight, coming back in time to catch the train for Ostrava.

George Creel and his retinue have been here from some days and left yesterday evening for Vienna. George has cut a wide swath here and has promised to arrange all the problems confronting the Czechs.

My machine has nervous prostration and I shall have, if I keep thumping it any more before having it repaired.

[Added note found only in Secret Log]   Prague, January 24th

George Creel, Sisson and Byoir have been here for several weeks and left today after having carried on a press campaign of remarkable character, probably with the aid of [Emanuel] Voska. All the articles herald George as Secretary to the President of the United States and give the impression that he is a member of the Cabinet. In one of the interviews printed in today's paper, George says that there is no question that the Peace Conference must give the Germans of Bohemia to the Czech state; also, that he has made careful inquiry in the Slovak countries and that he finds great devotion to the Czech State and only hatred for the Hungarian oppressors.

George has made a good many speeches since he has been here, assuring the Czechs that they are the favorite child of the Allies and that they can get away with anything, including murder. Since our last visit there is a distinctly more aggressive tone to the Czech attitude and from what we can gather it is, in some measure at least, attributable to George's propaganda.

Letter to Mary Gibson   Schloss Clary, Teplitz. Saturday, January 25, 1919

A long and interesting but on the whole a saddening day but I want to sit me down and tick our some lines about it before I turn in.

Dr. Eugen Durych, the man from the Ministry of Public Works who was assigned to look after us undertook to get me up here and back to Prague in time for our train tomorrow afternoon and said he would come for me at half past

---

[181] The coal mines of Kladno were near Prague, those of Ostrava in the Cieszyn region which by that time was disputed between Czechoslovakia and Poland.

eight. He gathered up Gregory and Causey at the same time to take them to Kladno but on the way took me to the Masaryk Bahnhof and introduced me to a special train which the Government had arranged to take care of me. It was rather overwhelming but there was nothing to do but get on and sail away in solitary grandeur in a big steel compartment car behind a snorting engine.

We pulled out at nine sharp and I put in my time reading the *Atlantic Monthly* and trying to follow our course by the Baedeker. As we went through Theresienstadt, I observed a lot of troops line up for review and the local dignitaries in top hats ready for action. I supposed they were waiting for some visiting dignitaries but when we came into Lobositz, the same scene was repeated and the guard came in to say that I was supposed to come out and be polite. Word had evidently been sent down the line and all hands had turned out to do honor to the visiting "mission". While the guard was still breaking the news, the hero of the Merry Widow or his twin brother came pirouetting in and began saluting with enthusiasm – meanwhile firing at me in Czech. He had soft black knee boots with buff bloomers that hung over their tops, a white silk shirt and buff bolero with red silk tassels around the edges, the whole crowned with an Astrakhan cap.

He was a Sokolist and evidently master of ceremonies for he introduced ten or a dozen of the local firemen who came on board at his heels. One of them represented the municipality, another the Czech population, another the miners, and so forth. They all had something they wanted to say about the needs of the district and were disappointed when they found that I could not get off and spend the day learning about the situation first hand. It was finally arranged by compromise that they should send me a written statement of their needs and resources and then I was required to come out and "review" the detachment of troops and shake hands with some of the people who had not got on the train and look agreeable to the crowd that stood banked up behind the troops and uttered many and strange friendly cries. All the time, Danilo was hopping about and saluting and sputtering Czech in snappy military sentences. Then the engineer came to the rescue by pulling the throttle and I scrambled aboard while the colors were dipped in salute and the crowd waved its hats.

From there down the valley of the Elbe, past Schreckenstein, an old chateau belonging to Prince Lobkowicz and into Aussig which is the junction for Teplitz. In the station there was another crowd and a group of officers. A Colonel came on board accompanied by a younger officer who proudly introduced himself as an interpreter in French. He had never got through Aunt Louise's seventy lessons and could only sputter. The Colonel shifted for himself in German and we got along all right. He asked me out to meet the officers of the 8th Fusilier Regiment, which has recently been stationed at Aussig and I went out for another handshaking match. There were some twenty of them and they were a good-looking crowd.

When we had shaken hands round, the interpreter reminded me that French was his chosen weapon, so I gave him a chance to show off while they hooked on a new engine. Then we cleared out at once with all hands saluting furiously and the crowd giving its imitation of a mob scene.

From there on to Teplitz we were all the time amid coal mines and factories, most of them working and passing trains of coal headed south which was a cheering sight.

At 11:30 we came into the station at Teplitz and found the Chef de Gare on hand with his state uniform on. He herded me into the Imperial waiting room despite my pleas to be allowed to go straight through. Once inside, he explained that a terrible thing had happened. The Mayor, the Bezirkshauptmann [district commissioner] and other authorities had planned to meet the train at noon and he had not been able to reach them with the news that we would get in at half past eleven. He was much worried as to what he should do. I think his impulse was to lock me up in the waiting room and keep me until they could arrive and bid me welcome. I solved it by saying that I would go on and that he could tell them that the train had got in ahead of time – to which he agreed. I finally got outside and found Sophie [Clary] in an old fur coat running around trying in vain to find me while a groom held an impatient horse that objected to freezing no matter if matters of protocol were being involved.

The castle is in the town, and of it, so it was only a few minutes' drive straight into the Middle Ages. The castle faces on a little square and you can dive into it from any side. On the side away from the square, the property begins and stretches off to the mountains and around the town in all directions as far as the borders of Saxony.

Count [Siegfried] and Countess [Therese] Clary were waiting for us in the hall and welcomed me as though I were a long lost son. After showing me my room, which was on the second floor and several kilometers away, we went down to see the old Prince [Carlos] and Princess [Felicia] Clary and her sister Princess Radziwiłł who is staying with them.

They are all a nice simple lot who pounced on the first outsider they had seen for several years and nearly tore him to pieces in the anxiety to hear what was going on. The Prince looks like a gentle Hindenburg, if you can imagine such a thing, the same fierce mustaches and bristly hair but kindly eyes and altogether a good sort. The Princess, who is about seventy, looks like Rosa Bonheur, stiff collar, man's vest and a bunch of keys at her belt. Princess Radziwiłł is more placid and mild but flairs up if anybody fails to say frequently that Poland is the best country in the world and that they rather prefer it to their own. After we had talked a little I went off with Count and Countess Clary and talked shop as I knew that they were posted.

Image 21: The Clary Family (1923). Seated Siegfried and Terese with children Hieronymus, Marcus and Karl, Standing from Left- Sophie, Alfons, Lidwina, Elisalex, Paula, and Marcus. (Courtesy of the Gibson Family)

This is quite a coal producing center but the production has fallen off badly and the lack of coal is a constant menace to the peace of this part of Europe. Food and coal keep working round and round in a vicious circle. The miners don't get enough to eat and their strength is depleted and so they are not up to their hard work and without coal there is no way of transporting food and so on indefinitely. The lack of food brings on dropsy and other diseases and altogether the situation is bad. The only treatment for these diseases is food and the problem is bad. Countess Clary was finally charged with handling this problem and got the authorities to set aside certain stocks of flour for the purpose, procured by cutting down the ration of the healthier classes. The sick people have to be passed on by two doctors and given a certificate that they have such and such a disease requiring a special ration and then they come to Countess Clary for it. For some time she was able to give them a kilo of flour a week but lately it has been harder to get and she has had to cut the allowance to half of that, and of course the results are bad. She showed me her account books with the names of the individuals, details of their cases and separate entries and receipts for every pound of flour she has given out.

The children are suffering too but as they are not allowed to dispose of the milk from the cows on the estate the family could not do anything for them until

Countess Clary went out through the country and gathered up all the goats that money would buy. She as a big flock of them in the park and doles out goat's milk for the children who need it worst.

We had a long talk on these matters then and later and the details were not pleasant to hear. There is a terrifying lot to be done before people can even begin to take care of themselves.

We were all marshalled for lunch and though there was an army of flunkies to serve, they were not overworked. There was a vegetable soup which was passed three times, some veal with little speckled potatoes and as dessert some speckled apples. There was a matting cover for the table and paper napkins. And it was, I imagine, a particularly good meal for the visitor. After lunch, I produced some Corona Coronas which the King had given me in Prague and you should have seen the eyes stick out. They had not seen anything remotely resembling a real cigar since the first year of the war and were almost pathetic in their delight.

The whole family was smoking cigarettes made with a mixture of strawberry and other leaves and offered them with apologies. I don't go in for cigarettes myself but fortunately I had brought along a big bundle of them from our stores in the hope that they might be acceptable. They were greeted with whoops of joy from the whole family who fell upon them with enthusiasm and soon had the great room grey with smoke.

While we smoked, the Princess got out some of the treasures of the place. The prize exhibit consists of a bronze casserole and a bronze vase both found in a pile of stones near the older castle on the hill behind this one. With them they display articles and pamphlets printed in a great row that Mommsen and some other savant had as to the origins of the two pieces. Mommsen maintained that they were undoubtedly Roman while the other bird said it was only necessary to look at them with one eye to see that they were Etruscan. Both went into raptures over them and said that they were altogether wonderful. To look at, they were beautiful but the archeological end of it was beyond me.

Then there was a Roman alabaster vase built for the ashes of somebody's little boy. The inscription is clearly legible, – the first time I have ever been able to figure out an old Latin inscription for myself so I thought it was a splendid thing. It had been given to one of the Clary's by Catherine of Russia.

There was also a big silver goblet which Peter the Great drank his brandy out of and which he left as a gift when he came to visit. A huge silver tankard, set with old enamel medallions was a gift by the Elector of Saxony from the Royal Treasure. Also a tremendous ceremonial sword which would require two men and a boy to carry given by an allied prince in the days when the Clary's were still a ruling family. And so on for an hour or so with promised of more to come later. The endless corridors of the castle are ordinarily filled with a collection of armor which is said to be one of the finest in existence, but when the Czech troops were sent round to gather up all the arms in the country, it was thought wise to put the collection away lest some literal peasant soldier might feel obliged to carry off cross bows and morning stars and battle axes. The walls are still pretty well covered with thousands of hunting trophies and the place does not look altogether bare.

By the time we had got through looking over the Sehenswürdigkeiten [sights, collections], the carriage was announced and Countess Clary and Sophie took me off for a drive behind a pair of horses that were probably one of the finest but now are pretty well run down from lack of proper food. Everything here runs back to food. The miners can't work because they have not enough food to keep up their strength. The horses in the mines and elsewhere are weak from lack of proper food. The children are sickly and dying because they can't get enough to eat. And the mothers are in a worse state because they give all they can get to the children and go without themselves. It's the same for the cattle and even the game on the estate has to be thinned more and more as time goes on because otherwise it would starve. Every topic of conversation leads back to the same subject.

It was four or five degrees below zero and we needed all the covers we could get. Each of us had a fur bag which we had to climb into before sitting down and then we were packed in with more fur rugs. And at that we did not have too much.

We drove out through the town and along the frozen country road toward the Saxon frontier between coal mines and factories which interested me particularly. After half an hour or so we came to what is known as Uncle Carlos' Church and it was a surprise in several inches of snow, a graceful Italian Renaissance church which Prince Clary picked up bodily from an island near Venice and transplanted here, – twenty years work and a pile of money went into it. It is the pride of the old gentleman's heart; the rest of the family feel that the church is out of place and the idea a poor one, but they have never spoiled his pleasure in it by telling him so. As a matter of fact, it is a combination of two churches which he purchased and dismantled, taking the best parts of each and fitting them together. The stone work is finely carved and the white and pink marble are lovely but this climate is playing havoc with stains and scars and in time it won't be so lovely. We opened the front door and went through the whole place, every detail having been worked out with care to avoid the gaudy.

From there we drove through the forests belonging to the property to a keeper's lodge where it was thought we might see a stag or two. As a matter of fact, one of them was lying on the grass near the keeper's house and instead of scampering at our approach, he got up and came to us looking for something to eat. He had a fine spread of antlers with sixteen points and the prudent Countess Clary bade us keep away from him lest he brain us, which he could do with no effort.

The keeper came out and bewailed the times and the difficulty of feeding his game. To celebrate the occasion, he got from his house a pint or so of chestnuts and poured them out into the feeding trough, having to fight off Mr. Stag with a long stick while he did it. The poor beast was frantic with hunger and trembled so that he could hardly eat.

We talked to keepers and beaters here and there and found them all depressed and shaking their heads over the need of killing some more game soon. They are a feudal crowd and seem to take no joy in their republic. All they could say about it was that a lot of Czech officers of the occupying forces had come onto the property and shot WITH RIFLES which certainly is not done in our best families. The Government at Prague gave prompt order to stop that sort of thing but the keepers were shocked in all their finer feelings and refuse to get over it.

We came back by Kitties' "circus route" and got in for tea with the whole family. And then I made my second home run of the day. They have not had a good tea for a long time and now drink a mess which they try to fool themselves into considering tea. They mix equal parts of tea leaves and strawberry leaves and boil the mixture till the hands fall off the clock. The result is an essence like the coffee essence we used to have in Central America. Before I left the train this morning, I stuffed into my bag several packages of tea and brought them along. When I produced them you would have thought I had presented each member of the family with a diamond stomacher, – gold and precious stones would not have been half so welcome.

After tea we spent half an hour looking through parts of the castle that are open. There is a chapel which holds a thousand people, a big library with fine carved old bookcases and ceilings, a theater to hold three hundred and fifty people and with a regular sized stage. There is a summer dining room opening onto a terrace at the far end of one of the wings that looks upon a large pond now covered deep with ice. There is a great two story Louis XV state reception room that is the best thing in the castle and there are innumerable reception and ball rooms and living apartments for a town. I haven't a very clear idea of the plan for the place was started in the middle ages and has been added to up to 1751 when there was a lot added. It wanders all over the neighborhood, up hill and down, around courtyards and ponds. There are straight staircases and round staircases and long easy staircases so that you can get your horse in the corridor on the second floor and set out upon your ride. It is big beyond anything of the sort I have ever seen and yet it is easy to live in, or would be if you had the wherewithal to keep it up. The Clary's have, and in addition to this they have a great palace in Vienna and another in Venice and a few scattered places throughout the Empire.

After tea we scattered and I sat down at my Corona and thumped out a questionnaire for the local authorities as to conditions and needs.

I had got out of the habit of dressing for dinner lately but was firmly put into a dinner coat by a stern flunky [servant] who discouraged my attempts at conversation and devoted himself to making me as beautiful as possible. I hope he was satisfied. I so far forgot myself as to ask if the "Prince" had gone down, and was told with a heavy emphasis that His Serene Highness would be down in two minutes. After that I kept my chains on for fear of skidding when I talked to the proud slave.

For dinner we had a different vegetable soup which was also passed three times, some beef croquettes with spinach and the same speckled apples. I brought out my last three cigars as a ration and was sorry I had not invested heavily. After dinner Count Czernin and Count Chotek came in and snorted with jealousy when they sniffed the real tobacco. Count Czernin sat down next to Count Clary and made him blow smoke in his face till Princess Radziwiłł told him he was "offul disgusting" and must stop.

I had a long and interesting talk with Count Clary about political affairs and then one with Count Czernin. A few months ago, I should have scoffed at the idea of sitting down and talking with him. Too bad it won't all bear writing about.

When we had done the whole family gathered about the table and we played a foolish card game I can't remember the name of. It was much like *trente et un* [thirty one][182] and is a sort of freeze out. Everybody buys three chips for fifty heller (about two and a half cents at present rate of exchange) and the survivor takes the pot. It took until after eleven to hand over the bowl full of iron money to Princess Radziwiłł and go our separate ways to bed.

Our poor friends are really pathetic. They don't know yet what has happened. For seven or eight centuries they have lived their own way and nobody questioned their rights, and now everything is kicked over at once and they can't grasp it. Furthermore, they know that things were right as they were and they can't conceive that anything can be right if there is change. They can't even see the possibility of future good in the things that are happening now; that is about all that anybody could reasonably ask them to see now, for the general state of affairs is not cheerful. The Republic has abolished their titles and forbidden them to wear decorations and has stopped the entail which has held the great estate together through the centuries. They all mourn the thought that it will have to go to pieces, even those who would profit by the division, for it is a thing of tremendous pride to them. They have a family flag that has always flown over the castle when they were in residence and they have been forbidden to fly it any more. And of course, they don't know but that before long a radical government may decide to expro-

---

182 French card game similar to to Twenty-One.

priate their whole place. But they don't seem as much concerned over that as over the passing of the old regime. They were in it up to the end as Countess Clary was on duty with the Empress to the end. She did not appoint a Grande Maîtresse during the war but took Countess Clary to perform the same duties so she got a look at the last days of the old system and it is interesting to hear.

Alphy is not here but returns tomorrow so I shall miss him. They are very proud of him. He was at the front from the beginning to the end of the war, and was the first officer to get the Golden Tapferkeitsmedaille [bravery medal], the highest decoration for valor which could be given only to private soldiers. In 1917, however, it was awarded to him and one officer has since received it.

Letter to Mary Gibson   Sunday, January 26, 1919
                                        On the train en route from Prague to Ostrava.

The Big Show is on the road again and here goes for the daily bulletin, – but after the sock-dollager I wrote yesterday this won't be so long.

When I was wakened up this morning by the Stern Flunky [servant] stoking the fire in my family-mausoleum-white-tile stove I found that the bottom had dropped out of the thermometer and that snow was falling fast.

All hands were present for breakfast, having already been to church. Afterward we sat round and gossiped until it was time for me to go to my train at ten.

I landed back here at a quarter to one without having to receive any delegations and found the car had been moved over from the Wilson Bahnhof and was just opposite where I got off. I learned from Anton that the party was all up town and tracked them to our old hotel where we had lunch together and talked shop busily. King was there and Reggie Foster down from Warsaw and a Capt. John Karmazin who had just come from Ostrava after many adventures and wanted to tell us all about them. It made interesting hearing and we stayed on for some time after lunch listening to what both of them had to say.

At 5:40 we shoved off and about two AM we are dropped off at our destination ready for a day's work tomorrow. We shall probably be in Vienna Tuesday morning and leave almost immediately for Paris so as to be there by the end of the week. We've got lots of things to tell and we hope to find people with enough time to listen to us.

My old machine is going groggy again and has to be handled tactfully but I hope to get it on its feet again in Vienna or Paris so that writing won't be quite so much of an ordeal. Spending so much time on trains, I am nearly helpless without it as I have a lot of writing to do and stenographers are not to be had.

[Added note found only in Secret Log]   Prague, January 26th

On returning to Prague today I found Reggie Foster and Fred King waiting for me with an account of what has been happening for the past few days. On Thursday last, four Allied officers, French, British, Italian and Lt. Voska for the Americans, appeared at Karwin in Silesia and ordered the Polish Commander on behalf of the Entente to withdraw his forces within the space of two hours. If the ultimatum was not complied with, Czech troops were to attack. The Polish Commander replied that he could not take any action in the matter without orders from Warsaw but that he would immediately communicate with Warsaw by telephone and make a reply. Within one hour and a half, although no reply was received from Warsaw, the Czech troops advanced, attacked and drove out the Poles, killing some and taking a number of prisoners. As soon as the occupation had been effected a proclamation, copy of which is attached, was posted in Karwin, signed by the Entente officers, including Voska, proclaiming to the inhabitants the necessity for the occupation of the coal regions by the Czechs and urging the people to obey the new Czech Government.

On hearing of these developments on Thursday night, Paderewski asked the members of the Entente Missions in Warsaw to proceed to Karwin and inquire into the matter. Schelling, who was dining with Paderewski, said that he could not go but suggested the sending of Foster. Commander Rawlings, Royal Navy, came for the British and there were also French and Italian representatives. After some parley with the Czechs and some rather lively repartee, they were allowed to cross the lines by daylight on Saturday and interviews the Entente officers who had issued the ultimatum.

On being questioned as to the authority under which they had acted, the French, British and Italian officers said that they had taken their orders from the Czecho-Slovak War Office, under which they were assigned. Lt. Voska, having the same question put to him, said that he had acted under instructions from Captain Voska (his father) representing the American Peace Mission in Paris. The young man was not content with joining in the issuing of the ultimatum but took part in the battle and displayed with evident pride empty cartridge shells which he had fired at the Polish troops.

Both the French and American representative are to all intents and purposes Czechs and the Polish Commander made the somewhat justifiable mistake of thinking they were Czechs officers in Allied uniforms. He accordingly so reported to Warsaw and Paderewski had replied that he should "meet violence with violence" and arrest those people for transportation to Warsaw. Rather loose orders were issued and Captain Karmazin, a perfectly innocent bystander, was pulled out of his room in Karwin and marched through the streets to Polish headquarters, after which there were no apologies. Karmazin had come on to Prague to see me and was highly indignant, thinking his arrest much more important than the general situation.

Letter to Mary Gibson On the train in the station at Ostrava.
  Monday, January 27, 1919

Living on the train as we have for the past few weeks I expect to wake up some morning in a conductor's uniform. It looks as though the train life might last for some time longer but I shan't mind as I am getting quite used to it and am so comfortable that I almost enjoy it.

When I woke up this morning, we were here in the station with the thermometer at several degrees below zero and ice all over the place. A director of a group of mines named Pfeifer came on board early and had breakfast with us while he explained the local situation. The Czechs have advanced into the territory formerly held by the Poles and there has been a bad amount of bloodletting. There was the usual talk about *franc tierurm* [sniper activities] and necessary executions, etc.

At nine we piled into waiting motors and went uptown, stopping at military headquarters to see Lt. Col. Ghilain, a French officer commanding the Czech troops in this district. We asked him whether we might go to Karwin, another great mining center near here, and he promised to find out and let us know. There is so much fighting going on in the neighborhood that he could not tell us at once where the line ran. Later he sent word that we could go through to Karwin as the district had been pretty well cleaned out by the Czech troops and the fighting was on the other side of the mines we wanted to visit. He said he had expected to walk into the district without opposition and was surprised when he found strong Polish forces standing against him.

From his office we went to the director's room of one of the big coal companies to meet the managing directors of the region and representatives of the workmen. We had them all into the room at once and went to it, our talk lasting until a quarter past one. For the mine owners, there appeared four or five old style hard shell bosses, and for the miners five good men and true, only one of whom had any evidence of brains though one had a handsome celluloid collar with stripes in many brilliant colors.

We broached our questions without preliminaries and said that we wanted to know what was needed to increase at once the output of coal so that an adequate supply could be sent to the neighboring countries that stand in need of it. The workmen undertook to answer first, and their spokesman, a clean cut citizen with a big handsome head, said what we have heard so often before, that it was first of all a question of food so that the miners could get back their strength, they also needed clothing and shoes as well as certain materials which were exhausted. He stated it all well and reasonably and when he had finished what he had to say he stopped.

Then the German director of one of the mining groups spoke up and before he got through his first sentence we saw we were among the hard-shell crowd who do not know the world has moved. He said that food was of course desirable as all good things were desirable but that they would not effect any improvement in the situation, – that what was needed first of all was discipline and respect for authority. The workmen had got the idea that the change of regime had landed them in heaven and they were disposed to lie down and let their employees wait on them. He growled and scolded and when he had finished his long harangue we were no forrader than we when we began.

He was particularly bitter because the workmen had demanded the dismissal of a number of engineers and foremen against whom they lodged complaints. He admitted as though it were not really a consideration that these people had perhaps been 'a little rough' with the miners but hastened to add that they could not be handled otherwise. The workmen retorted that it was not a matter of being 'a little rough' with them, that while the mines were under military rule during the war the engineers and foremen had been unjust and brutal with military support and had enforced their will by having workmen they did not like taken off to the army. The director answered that this was not true; that the military authorities were responsible for anything that was wrong but that they had made the engineers and foremen sign all orders as though they were their own. The buck was passed back and forth for some time but on the whole the workmen seemed much more reasonable and even tempered than their bosses. The spokesman said that the workmen were as anxious as anybody else to maintain order and to prevent the spread of Bolshevism. He said that they had by their insistence got rid of a crowd of men who were causing great discontent and whose maintenance in authority was calculated to breed Bolshevism. He said the workmen in the district realized that Bolshevism would bring them only suffering and sorrow and that in their own interest they wanted the district to prosper and increase its output in an orderly way.

Then there was a long bicker as to how labor disputes could be settled without letting the companies impose unjust foremen or allowing the workmen to crowd out any man who might not be a Chesterfield.[183] It was interesting but

---

[183] Probably a reference at Philip Stanhope, 4th Earl of Chesterfield (1694–1773), British writer and politician who became famous for his short administration of Ireland in 1745/46, where he successfully fought corruption and opened schools and factories.

depressing to see how far apart the two sides were, and as Harry Lauder would say the directors were farther apart than the workmen. The upshot was that we all concluded that it was up to the Government to establish some organization to settle such questions and enforce its decisions.

To finish Gregory made a few remarks on the practical side of the question which were translated into Czech and I wound up with a little speech to the effect that the whole working population of this part of Europe was dependent on the work of the coal districts and that both directors and workmen had both a responsibility and a great opportunity; that future developments in the countries of the old Dual Monarchy would be the direct result of what happened here and that the outside world would be forced to measure its sympathy for the new Czechoslovak state according to the will it manifested to restore normal conditions and help its neighbors to do the same. It may sound rather exaggerated but it's all true.

From there we went to the Witkowitz Works where we were expected to lunch with the Director General, Herr Sonnenschein, who we discovered was a Hun who became a Czech a couple of months ago in order to safeguard his properties. We learned it too late to do anything about it but at any rate we got a good lunch.

Immediately after lunch we piled into open motors under piles of furs and mufflers and made for Karwin where we arrived at dusk and went to the head office of the company. There we talked for an hour about the possibilities of getting an increased output, and incidentally warmed up from a bitter cold drive. The place was working normally enough to all appearances and no one would have thought that only yesterday there was fighting going on in the streets and people being killed all around.

We got back to Ostrava at six and stopped at the office where we gathered up our papers and were given some of the decorations which the Austrian Govt. got out to jolly along the workmen who did well. There are three classes of the same decoration and I got specimens of them all. They are now forbidden by the Republic so we were free to help ourselves from the pile in the office.

After what he have seen here it seems better for us to go back to Prague and try to get the Govt. to see things our way before setting out for Paris, so tomorrow morning we expect to wake up in Prague instead of Vienna, going on tomorrow night and reaching Paris a day later than we had originally planned.

Letter to Mary Gibson.   On the train en route from Prague to Vienna.
Tuesday, January 28, 1919

A busy day with important results and we are ready to turn in and try to find repose from the cares of this ridiculous world.

We got in here this morning from Ostrava at 10:30 and hastened to get in touch with the various people we wanted to see. Stnaněk, the Minister of Public Works, was at Kladno but came in to see us and foregathered at 3. We also had an appointment with the President [Masaryk] at 4.

At three sharp we went to our conference with Staněk who had also called in Dr. Oberthor, the man in charge of coal distribution.[184] We presented our views and finally smoked out an admission that took our breath away as to the steps that were to be taken soon. It gave me a fluent use of German and I painted pictures that would have burned canvas and then without much hope we went up to the hill to see the President. We gave him the same story and had a general talk with him about the situation and then went our way very much depressed.

From the Palace we went to the Parliament to see Vrbenský, the former anarchist who is now Food Controller. From him we got some comfort and had the satisfaction of throwing a scare into him about what was going to happen next. There seems to be nobody so nervous about a disturbance of public order as a converted anarchist.

When we got back to the hotel we found little Durych waiting to tell us that he was sent by Staněk to say that the unfortunate decision would be reconsidered and that we could go our way in peace.

So with good spirit we sat down with King to a dinner of ham and eggs and watery Pilsener beer.

And then straight aboard the train which pulled out at 9:40.

Letter to Mary Gibson   Wednesday, January 29, 1919
                                     On the train leaving Vienna for Paris.

We got into Vienna this morning in a driving snowstorm and came up to the hotel in broken down cabs because we had not been foresighted enough to telegraph ahead for our handsome motors.

Gregory and Causey had a lot to do seeing their various technical playmates and left me to go their various ways. I was loaded up with information which I wanted to pass on to Coolidge so I went down to his office and talked to him until nearly lunch time. He came back to the hotel and had lunch with me so as to talk some more.

---

184 Parts of this passage reappear in the memo "Visit of Mr. Hugh Gibson to Countries of the Former Austro-Hungarian Empire", see letter to Mary Gibson, February 5, 1919.

We were expecting to pull out for Paris tomorrow evening but when we came in this morning we found a basketful of telegrams from Hoover which had been repeated to us from Trieste and Belgrade and other places too numerous to mention saying that he wanted to talk to us at once and that we were to return as soon as possible. His word is law, so we told the railway people that we wanted to get off at once and that we could start as soon as they could back our car around to the Westbahnhof. They explained why it would be impossible to do for some time but finally arranged to get us off by a special train at 9:40 and we made our own arrangements accordingly.

Late in the afternoon I went around and called on Djina Apponyi. I did not know whether she would care to see an enemy so I had Caskie telephone her and inquire. She sent back word that I was under no circumstance to leave town without coming to see her. She greeted me like a long-lost brother and we had a little chat which consisted

[end page 2, page 3 missing from file at HIA, continuing with Page 4]

Albertine [Wittouck] and gave her some good news. Madame Frischauer's chief worry now is that she will never be allowed to return to Paris where she had spent all her life until the war broke out. As a matter of fact she is only technically an Austrian and it is pretty hard luck on her, but there are several other people who have been put to some inconvenience as a result of the unpleasantness.

Coolidge had a lot of things on his mind so he came and dined with us and stayed on until it was time to start for the train. I am loaded up with enough messages for the Peace Commission to keep me talking steadily for a week and I don't want to stay more than a few days if it can be avoided.

[Added note found only in Secret Log] Vienna, January 29th

Coolidge is a good deal concerned over the way his boundary between the German Austrians and the Slavs has turned out. [Sherman] Miles and [Frederick] King arrived the other day in Marburg and when their presence was known the Germans of the locality gathered to make a demonstration. Miles and King retired in good order to the hotel dining room for lunch, thinking that the demonstration would die down. On the contrary, the crowd gathered in front of the hotel and went on howling until the Slovine troops opened fire on them, killing ten and wounding sixty.

Coolidge urged me to impress upon the Commissioners in Paris the need of a Minister in Prague, and the necessity for withdrawing Voska, and the need for making all arrangements necessary to send Austrian munitions to the Poles.

Letter to Mary Gibson   Hotel Victoria, Zurich. Thursday, January 30, 1919

A long day but not very full of incident.

I was aweary when I woke up and lay abed looking out the window for an hour or so at the passing pageant of the snow-covered mountains, the castles on the mountain tops and the little village churches with Oriental minarets which looked as though they had been put up just for my benefit.

I finally did manage to get up when Sergeant Cash put his head in my door and announced that he was going to produce hot cakes for breakfast. While we were still at table, we drew into Innsbruck and I looked out the window in the face of Ernest Schelling who left Vienna yesterday morning on his way through to Paris. He [Cash] hauled him [Schelling] aboard and regaled him with coffee and conversation and spent a most interesting morning listening to what he had learned in Poland. He was chiefly filled with the doings of the Bolsheviki which we have been hearing about all along the line in terms that would make your hair curl.

One of the stories we got at first hand not long ago was of some peasants on a big estate near Moscow. They had been stuffed by one of the Bolshevist agitators with the theory that nobody had a right to live unless he worked and that those who had managed to beat the game so far by living comfortably without manual labor should in all justice be made to suffer now to make up for it. When they got back to the estate, one of them was struck with the great thought that there was in the stables a stallion who had never worked, so after he had enunciated his great idea to his pals they all proceeded to the stable, communicated the theory to the stallion as though he could understand it, then led him outside and tied up all his feet so that he could not move no matter how hard he struggled, and skinned him alive. While the operation was going on they carefully explained to the poor beast that he had never worked and that he had always lived in luxury and that now the day of justice had come he must begin to suffer. To my mind that is one of the very worst of hundreds of stories I have heard and so far as we can learn it is absolutely true.

One of Schelling's stories which he had verified was when the Bolsheviki decided that a number of people in a village should be punished. They took them out when the thermometer was below zero, stripped them and tied them to trees. Then they pour water over their heads slowly until they were nothing but pillars of ice.

They varied the procedure with one fat man by slitting his stomach open and building a fire in it.

A little while ago we got a rather more complete story which is worth ticking out. There was a woman travelling in Russia with a considerable amount of money which she had put in her stocking. While she was waiting in a station, she noticed that a man on a bench opposite her was watching her intently. After a bit she went to sleep and when she woke up, the man was just walking out the door. She instinctively reached for her stocking and cried out that the money was missing. The Soldiers' Council was called and she explained what had happened. The man was held and searched and a little more than the missing amount of money was found upon him. He could give no good account of it although he protested that he had not stolen it. The soldiers hear what both sides had to say and then took the man outside the station and hanged him. A few minutes afterward, the woman screamed again, this time that she had made a mistake and that the money was in her other stocking. There was another sensation, again the Soldier's Council was called, and this time it was decided that the woman was at fault for having accused the man falsely. She was therefore thrown into a river and allowed to drown. Although the crowd approved all that had happened so far, they then clamored that the chief of the Soldier's Council had been hasty and had not weighed the evidence as he should. He was therefore brought to trial on the spot, found guilty and hanged – all this taking place in the space of an hour. And then the sensations of the day were over in the town and affairs went their normal course.

We managed to do a lot of work during the day. Our special train had gone out of business at Innsbruck and we had been tacked onto the end of the regular train which dawdled along through Tyrol. It was fun when we slowed up on work long enough to look out the windows for the whole landscape seemed to be filled with Italian soldiers trying to learn how to ski on the steep hillsides. You can imagine the scene. I would have given my eyes for a chance to get out and play with them. The little taste I had of winter sports has just whetted my appetite for more, but there is no telling when, if ever, I shall ever get another chance to be irresponsible in that particular way.

At a few minutes after six we came into Feldkirch, the Austrian frontier station where we wangled an engine out of the local authorities and got them to telegraph ahead that we were coming and that the Zurich train was to be held for us. When we got into Buchs we found a bucket brigade formed to hurry us off. The car we had telegraphed for had not reached Buchs but Schelling's car was there and we were piled into it and rushed off over the roads of ice to Sarganz where the train was being held for us. We slipped and skidded most of the way and there must have been some divine intention that we should reach our destination for there is no other explanation of the fact that we arrived intact. The train had been waiting for us forty minutes and pulled out as soon as our belongings could be piled aboard.

At 10:45 we came into Zurich and walked across the street to this hotel so as to be ready to climb aboard the morning train for Bern at 6 sharp. If we can possibly do it we are going to make straight through to Paris, but we shall probably have to stay overnight in the capital and reach Paris Sunday morning. My fellow travelers have ordered up some hot chocolate and now invite me to partake before we tumble into bed.

Before we close for the night, I must tell you the bon mot of Mr. Balfour about the entry of Liberia into the war. She [Liberia] decided to make war upon Germany on the night of the 10th of November and telegraphed the news in felicitous terms to the British Foreign Office. Mr. Balfour read the telegram carefully, walked over to the window and looked out musingly for a time and announced seriously: "I fear we shall have to raise the entrance fee."

Letter to Mary Gibson   Hotel Beau Rivage, Geneva. Friday, January 31, 1919

This morning we were called at a little after five and made the six o'clock train without any trouble although we felt like Christian Martyrs. The trains are slower than any I have ever seen anywhere and if there is any merit in running slow these engineers should get high pay. However, despite all they could do we did get into Bern at a little before eleven and piling all our stuff into a taxi, made for the Legation and got our passports under way for the necessary visas. By the grace of heaven we found that a courier was leaving for Geneva by motor at two o'clock and that he could take us. Our passports were put through in record time and we made our connections all the way through.

I had lunch with the Legation crowd plus Taylor and Kellogg who were there on their way into Germany together. Dr. Field who is going to Munich was also there and we learned a lot of news that we had missed by being in the train.

We shoved off promptly on time in a little Dodge car which carried Gregory and the courier and the chauffeur and me and all our baggage and the big pouch. As you can imagine there was not much room for us to frolic around in but we did manage it and considered ourselves lucky not too have to miss an entire day. We did not slow up all the way, though part of the trip was through snow and ice and we pulled up before this hotel a little after six which is remarkably good running.

I found telephone messages from the Legation at Bern and from the Consulate here and was kept busy for some time getting them straightened out. Then I called up Ynès at Leysin and gave her news of the Clary's and Djina Apponyi and learned what they have been up to. Jack [Reyntiens] is there now with them and Myriam is going up toward the end of the month, so there will be quite a reunion of the family. Ramon is making rapid progress and they are much cheered about him.

We have not been able to make any arrangements about sleeping cars on the train and have very little chance of getting anything as the trains are crowded these days and people feel fairly lucky if they can stand up in the corridors. However, we shall use bribery and corruption and see what we can do for ourselves.

Letter to Mary Gibson   19 rue de Lubeck, Paris. Saturday, February 1, 1919

Here we are more dead than alive, but glad it's no worse.
 We set out from Geneva last night at 9:57 and got into the French station at Bellegarde at about eleven. There we had a long wait while the authorities combed out the crowd in a new and aggravating way they have evolved to eliminate the Bolsheviki and other undesirables that are trying to get in. We suffered none on the inconvenience save that of waiting a long time before our train was made up, but even at that we were peevish and when there was nothing doing for us in the way of sleeping accommodations, we began to feel badly treated. With the aid of Captain Wetter, the courier, and some judicious tipping, Gregory got a seat in a first class compartment and sometime afterwards I was led to a second class compartment and sandwiched in between some genial soldiers who had had too much to drink and a poor little nurse who was very much frightened and somewhat amused by the uncensored remarks of our companions. The compartment was so overheated that the soldiers had to get off every few minutes and get a drink to cool themselves off and each time when they came back they were perceptibly gayer. I suggested that perhaps they would not be so warm if they opened the window but this was met with such withering scorn that I kept quiet and let them go their own gait. After several sorties, they say that the train was about due to start so they laid in a goodly supply of wine and made merry until after half past two, with songs and jokes and attempts to make the rest of us join them. They were perfectly good natured and amusing until the night wore on and I wanted to doze. A Belgian woman with a little girl was wedged in with us in the last minute and added to our membership. The little girl was about five and pretty as a red wagon. The soldiers promptly turned their batteries on her, making her flowery speeches and drinking her health with exaggerated gallantry. She fairly basked in it and did not close her eyes a minute as long as they kept it up. She hardly answered back at all but fairly beamed at them all the time and paid no attention to her mother's orders that she lean back and go to sleep.
 At half past two, Gregory came and tapped on the window for me to come out. The corridors were so packed with people that he could not work his way through and I had a beast of a time getting out. Gregory had managed to get one couchette and this we proceeded to utilize for both of us, each with his feet neatly planed in the other's face. The couchette was narrow and we had to sleep carefully on edge so as not to fall off, so altogether there was less sleep than there would have been

sitting up, but at any rate it gave us something to think about and we got through the night some way.

The train is due early in the morning but as usual we were a little late and did not get into the station until nearly twelve o'clock. Fortunately, the courier was able to pack us into his little Dodge and delivered us at the house a little before one.

Bob Taft and Lewis Strauss came up to lunch with us as soon as we had managed to get a bath and shave. Then we hastened down to the Crillon where the Chief was waiting for us with all his afternoon engagements cancelled so that he could talk with us. We dug in and talked a blue streak until long after dark. And it was satisfactory.

When we slowed up a little I went up to the Embassy where I found that no telegram had ever come from us and my mail was still going through to Vienna. There are probably several from you and goodness only knows when I will get them.

I went up to the rue de la Pompe and saw Stetson who has been in bed for some time with a bad back which he strained playing golf. I only stayed a few minutes and then hastened back down to the Crillon to foregather with Phil [Patchin] and Joe Grew and others who wanted to hear what I had brought back and tell me their own gossip.

One of the tidbits they had to communicate to me was that while I was away in the wilds and unprotected, the French Government had made me a chevalier of the Legion of Honor. They had turned over the decoration to Hoover who had it in his desk and handed it over with all the honors of war amid the cheers of the populace.

Edgar Rickard is here and was with us at dinner as well as Claire Torrey, George Barr Baker, Will Irwin and other firemen. We sat round and talked until eleven when I declared my independence and made for my room.

And now I am near dead for sleep and propose to get some as soon as I can. Good night.

Letter to Mary Gibson   Paris. Sunday, February 2, 1919

Nothing startling today. I spent the morning in the offices at the Hôtel de Crillon and at noon set out to meet Schelling who was coming up on the Bummelzug [slow train] from Switzerland. It was frightfully delayed and did not come in until nearly half past one. Schelling is on the verge of going into pneumonia and for that reason I was anxious to get him and see him safely into a room at the Crillon where he could be looked after.

Once having placed him, I gathered Phil [Patchin] at his place and we went out to lunch together and had a talk that lasted until after three.

Then back to the office and unloaded to a stenographer until it was time to come home to dine and now to bed.

Letter to Mary Gibson   Paris. Monday, February 3, 1919

I spent the greater part of the day at the Hôtel de Crillon talking to all sorts of people.

In the course of the morning, I went over and had yarns with Beneš, the Czechoslovak Minister for Foreign Affairs about some matters in which the Chief was interested, and among other things, I gave him some impressions of my trip which were of considerable interest to him. Horodyski, who left for Warsaw again this evening, took me over so we could talk on the way.

I lunched with Joe and Alice Grew in their apartment at the Crillon and had a good talk with Joe about matters that interested us both. The result was that I spent the greater part of the afternoon dictating telegrams and memoranda for him to submit to those in authority.

I had an invitation to the Chamber of Deputies to hear the President's [Wilson] speech on the occasion of his reception but could not get away to go although I should have liked to do so.

This evening we had Schelling and Madame Baetens from Brussels to dine and heard a good deal of good talk.

Tomorrow morning I am summoned to appear before the Commissioners to give my impressions of my trip and be questioned by them as to conditions in the Central Europe. It is a formidable array of slaves to take down what you have to say, etc. but I refuse to prepare anything in advance.

[Added note found only in Secret Log]
Hoover went down this morning and told the Secretary [Lansing] that he considered it highly desirable that we should have as soon as possible some sort of accredited representative at Prague, and that he should not be less than a Minister Plenipotentiary. He suggested that I should be sent there. The Secretary said that without congressional action he could not send anyone higher than a Diplomatic Agent.

I talked to Joe [Grew] about the matter at lunch and impressed upon him that while I should like to go there myself I felt that it was highly desirable that it should be done with as much show as possible and that I should not mind in the least if they should choose somebody that they were willing to make an Envoy

Exordinary and Minister Plenipotentiary at once. He said that he thought there would be no objection to putting me in on that scale. He asked me to draft a letter for the Secretary's signature for authority to instruct the Deptartment to ask Congress for the needed legislation to create Legations at Prague and Warsaw. He further suggested in the letter that pending the passage of this legislation that I should be sent to Prague as Diplomatic Agent with the temporary rank of Envoy Exordinary and Minister Plenipotentiary. It now remains to see what the President will say.

Late in the afternoon I went in to see the Secretary [Lansing] and told him that if it was all the same to him I would prefer not to unload before all the Commissioners they whole story of George Creel and his doings; that I felt it concerned him more closely than anybody else and that if he wanted to do anything about it he could take it up with the President [Wilson]. When he had heard the story at length, he asked me to prepare a memorandum for him and said that he would take it up with the President as he considered it a shocking affair.

Letter to Mary Gibson   Paris. Tuesday, February 4, 1919

There is nothing to report today that would startle the town but it has been busy nonetheless.

I was slated to appear before the Commissioners for a hearing at 10:30 but when I got to the trysting place, I found that various things had come up that prevented a full meeting and that they had adjourned it for the present. However, they propose to take me on one at a time and so far as I am concerned, that is far more satisfactory.

There being nothing else pressing that required my attention, I cleared out with Gregory and spent the morning shopping for him and for myself.

We had a late luncheon at Voisin's with Captain Craven (USMC), a cousin of Gregory. The place was filled with people I wanted to see and talk to, and it was an easy way of polishing off a number of things. Ted Roosevelt was there, the first time I had seen him since he lost his father.[185] He is pretty deep in the dumps but is coming on pretty well. He went back to the front much too soon and his leg got a great deal worse so that he had to be detached from his regiment and brought to the hospital here in Paris. It is believed that with treatment he will come through in good shape and that he will recover the full use of his leg. I also saw and had

---

[185] Referring to the death of his father Theodore Roosevelt, 26th President of the United States, on January 6, 1919.

little talks with Jim Logan, Schelling, Dresel, Leland Harrison and a flock of others.

After lunch I went up to the Embassy where I saw the Ambassador [Sharp]. He has just come back from American where he went on the death of his brother. He has now resigned and is going home for good as soon as he can arrange it. The poor old man is pretty well down in the mouth.

At four I went into executive session with Dresel, Dolbeare, Dulles and Royall Tyler to tell them all that they ought to know about our trip. They were filled with curiosity and when I tried to make it short and to the point, they clamored for more so that I spun it out for an hour and a half.

At six I went to Mr. [Henry] White who had broken off some dates and settled down to hear all that I had on my mind. I talked to him for an hour and a quarter, and am to have another talk as there are other things that he wants to hear about at greater length. These days the Commissioners are not in the habit of talking to people at such a length of time, and the observant news hounds of the press were thoroughly intrigued and convinced that there was some deep and dark significance in what I had to say.

Coming out from that talk, I ran into Jack [Frank] Fremont who has just been ordered here and is to be with the Peace Mission for a time at least. He has been commanding the destroyer flotilla at Brest but when they were sent home he came up here and is now hovering around in a job which he has not been able to define. He doesn't know whether he belongs to Admiral Benson or Admiral Wilson but bears up bravely under the uncertainty.

We dined at home and have broken up early to turn in for a night's sleep. I am aweary and if as not seems probably they want me to be here about ten days from now for a decision and have no need of me in the meantime, I am thinking seriously of going off to Switzerland and playing in the snow for a week. I picked up enough flesh there last time to carry me through the Austrian trip and if I could have a week of it I could prepare for a siege of months. I did not get really tired so long as we were on the go, but now I have let down and feel as though I could never get rested enough. A couple of days in the snow would put that right as rain, however, and I am for it if it can be arranged.

[Added note found only in Secret Log]   February 4th

The Secretary [Lansing] has received instructions from the President to ask Congress for appropriations for the creation of Legations with full Ministers at Warsaw and Prague. He has also telegraphed to ask for blank commissions to be sent here so that appointments can be made without loss of time when the appropriations have gone through. The Secretary did not put my name up to the President because he thought it would be better to wait until the whole matter was settled.

Letter to Mary Gibson   Paris. Wednesday, February 5, 1919

A busy day but not much to chronicle. I put in the greater part of the morning dictating a report of observations on our trip for the information of the Secretary [Lansing]. It was easy going for me and the stenographer kept up so easily that I burbled on without pause. The result was that I unloaded a very long memorandum which it took her all afternoon to thump out. She had not finished it when we left the office this evening although she had done sixteen pages. It looked as though she had eight or ten more.[186]

I went home to lunch with Kirk, who had acquired a gorgeous pleasure palace in the rue de Belle Chasse. His mother was there just out of the hospital after a motor accident in which she was sliced in to little bits. Her face is a mass of scars and she is undergoing a daily treatment of being burned with some electric flame which is supposed to make her face melt and flow together again. Alice Grew went over with us and there were also a couple of young British officers who had not anything to say for themselves.

In the afternoon, I came home and did a lot of quiet work in the library. It is hopeless to try to do anything in the office as there is such turmoil. I made good progress until Will Irwin came in also with the idea of laboring quietly and then sat down and talked a blue streak until it was time for me to dress for dinner and go out.

I dined at the Crillon with the Secretary and Mrs. Lansing who had also invited Vance McCormick to hear the moving lecture on conditions in the Central Europe. Allan Dulles was also there. The Secretary was in unusually good form and talk was fast and furious until half past ten when I adjourned to Phil's room for a few minutes and then came back home. I found Friar Tuck and one or two more friends in from CRB posts and we sat and talked until too late.

This place is Mecca now, and everybody seems to breeze through at one time or another. This afternoon, I ran into Eustace Percy who is here with the British Commission and a new wife. I am summoned to see them and shall try to go soon.

---

[186] The report was later published as memo "Visit of Mr. Hugh Gibson to Countires of the Former Austro-Hungarian Empire" in: The Foreign Relations of the United States. Paris Peace Conference 1919, vol. XII, Washington: US Government Printing Office, 1947, pp. 228–239.

[Added note found only in Secret Log]   Paris. Thursday, February 6, 1919

McCormick was perturbed at dinner over the fact that the Committee on Reparation had no lawyer on it, – at least on the American part of it. He said that the others had good legal talent and had been framing up their plans for some time. They came to the first meeting with all sorts of final proposals embodied in memoranda and the poor Americans could not even figure out what they were driving at. We are now fighting a defensive warfare to keep from having something big put over on us. The American members have not yet been given any definition of what constitutes reparation and don't know what they are trying to get.

The Secretary [Lansing] spoke quite freely about the way the other delegations are trying to put things over on us and the manifest effort of the French to weaken the President by playing up in the press the opposition to him at home. He wound up by saying that we had as many tricks in our bag as they have in theirs and that we can play them some tricks that will make them pretty sick if they force matters while the President [Wilson] is at home.

They both seem to feel that the storm will break when the President starts for home. They have been chiefly concerned with the way Clemenceau has given in to the President but feel that that phase is rapidly approaching its end. He has made up his mind that Germany is to be completely crushed and he will not willingly have any truck with any scheme that does not involve wiping Germany off the map.

[Added in pencil]
The Secretary spoke of the way the new Congress is going to wade into the war activities of the Government. [Vance] McCormick took comfort from the fact that most of the big jobs have gone to Republicans, Stettinius, Schwag, Baruch, etc. and that Republican Congressmen will not feel inclinded to make capital out of any failures to be found in their doings. The Secretary [Lansing] said: "Yes, we were very wise to put Republicans in these places." He added: "They won't even feel much like going very strong after Hoover."

Letter to Mary Gibson   Paris. Thursday, February 6, 1919

A day of seeing lots of people and talking about all sorts of things without getting anywhere in particular.

Haven't you got your Christmas message from me at all? I sent you one from Bern through the Legation and the Department so that you would be sure to get it. I sent several others the same day about various matters, including one to

Mrs. Page about the death of Mr. Page, and I am wondering whether she got it. I have written to ask Arthur about it and shall ask the Legation at Bern to make inquiries.

In the course of the morning, Chatfield and Jensen came in from Brussels. It was the first time Jensen had been out since before the war and he did not quite know where he was. Both of them are going back tomorrow night and Mr. Hoover and I will probably go to Brussels with them. The roads are covered with ice and motoring a slow and doubtful business, so we shall probably go by train to Lille, getting there Saturday morning and motor thence to Brussels, a matter of three hours.

I lunched with Gregory and George Baker and Colonel Whitney, Chief of Staff for the District of Paris.

Just before lunch, I dropped in to see Wickham Steed of the *London Times* who is laid up in bed and wanted to talk to me about our trip to Austria. He has specialized on those countries for the past twenty years and probably knows them better than any other English speaking man. I gave him some new ideas and he certainly gave me a number. On the whole it was a repaying visit. Also saw Willert, the *Times* Washington correspondent who is here for a few days.

[Bob] Taft is coming down with a bad cold so late in the afternoon I took him home and started on a course of hot baths, aspirin and bed which ought to give him a grip on the situation.

I was due to dine with Mrs. Whitridge but it was called off at the last minute much to my relief as I am weary and more inclined to dine at home and crawl into bed early – which is the next thing on the programs.

Letter to Mary Gibson   Paris. Friday, February 7, 1919

Woke up to find us under a still heavier layer of snow and put in the morning shopping and doing odds and ends for Hoover. We had expected to get off for Brussels this evening but late in the afternoon, just as we were making the final arrangements, word came that the President wanted Hoover to appear tomorrow before the Peace Conference in regard to a very important matter, so we had to call it off. We shall now try to get away tomorrow by motor at noon if possible, otherwise on the night train.

Late in the afternoon, the Secretary [Lansing] told me he would have work for me to do soon but that in the meantime, it would be well for me to clear out and get some rest. If things are quiet when I get back from Brussels, I shall probably run down to Leysin and play in the snow until I am sent for. There is nothing doing here in the way of rest for everybody wants to talk to you and can find odds and ends of jobs to be done. So heroic measures are necessary and although I am tired of travel another night of it won't set me back so much after all. However, I shall have no belief in leave until I am gone.

Will you look around the library and see if you can find my shorthand book, and if so send it to me through the bag? I find it most useful these days to make all sorts of notes in shorthand and am lacking a few things that it would be very useful to know. If you don't find it, don't bother.

We all sat down and dined early in our going away gowns and then, after seeing Chatfield and Jensen off for Brussels, we settled down for an evening of work. Tomorrow night we shall probably spend on the train.

Letter to Mary Gibson   Paris. Saturday, February 8, 1919

This morning I got up early to see Edgar Rickard off for London and home but even at that I missed him and had a long day ahead of me. There was plenty to do, but none of it worth recording.

Hoover's meeting took place at 10:30 and we thought that we might manage to get off by noon so one of the President's cars stood before the Crillon with our baggage on it ready for a speedy get away. However, they did not finish at the morning meeting and the Chief had to appear again at 3:30 so there was no hope of getting off before 8:50 when a pokey train for Lille pulls out of the Gare du Nord.

I lunched with Phil [Patchin] at the hotel and heard such gossip as he had gathered. He hopes to have Polly come over the end of the month. George McFadden blew in while we were at lunch and we had an old home week. He is here to stay but does not know just what he is going to do. Hoover wants him for the financial end of the food business, but Vance McCormick also has covetous eyes on him and it is hard to tell which will be most tempting to George. William Allen White and Prof. Herron were also there being guyed gently about their mission to Prinkipo. Also Mark Sullivan who is running the press end of our Peace Commission.

It really looks as though we should get off this evening and get to Brussels tomorrow afternoon.

Letter to Mary Gibson   Hôtel Métropole, Brussels. Sunday, February 9, 1919

Although our plans looked wobbly for a time we finally did manage to get aboard the train last night a few minutes before it pulled out for Lille. It must go by way of

Nice and Bordeaux and Havre for we moved along pretty steadily and yet did not reach Lille until nearly eleven this morning, although in normal times it is only a matter of two and a half hours.

Tuck met us with a navy car at the station and after administering coffee to us in the CRB house, we were started off for Brussels. At the house, we found a group of navy officers who are putting up barracks for us to house the population in and also Mrs. Kellogg who is moving in a mysterious way her wonders to perform. She is very mysterious about it and is having the time of her life.

There were two navy cars for us, that is to say one for us and the other for our luggage and we were informed by the young officer who drove us that he was a terror. He came back to pack us in with rugs and asked whether it would not be well to get one of his men to sit in the back seat so as to keep us from being tossed about, but we refused although impressed by the reckless way he was evidently getting ready to drive. Then to our astonishment, he drove about as fast as I could have done and we were nervous all the time because we feared that something might run into us from behind. The luggage car left us far in the lurch but at any rate we did get in at a little after three.

Honnold, Shaler, Baetens, Van Bree, Gutterson, Chatfield, Jensen and other local firemen were waiting for us and we settled down and talked shop until after five when we set forth with George Baker to pay a duty call at the Legation. We found them at tea surrounded by George Creel and Rutger Jewett. Later Villalobar came in and greeted me as his long lost brother, assuring me at length of his undying affection for me, which was rather amusing to all present.

At seven we got back to the hotel where Francqui was waiting for us by arrangement and took us to dine at Helder's. It was full but quiet and we had a chance to talk over a lot of matters of importance. The crowd had gone to the opera and I was bid to hear Madame Edwina sing but was hauled off to the Ministry of Finance to talk with the Prime Minister [Delacroix] about all sorts of things affecting Belgium in this settlement of the big show. I acted as interpreter and it was enough to keep me awake to have to catch the abstruse technical talk and get it into another language, but when we finished I was surprised to find that it was after midnight.

Lettert to Mary Gibson On the train en route Lille-Paris.
Monday, February 10, 1919

We had a lot to do today so I crawled out at the crack of dawn, that is to say at seven-thirty which is when it cracks for me, and got a few odds and ends done preparatory to getting a glimpse of some of my friends.

I found Myriam [Reyntiens] up and about and had about ten minutes talking to her and the children before dashing off to see Madame Wittouck to give her some news of her sister whom I had seen in Vienna. There I had just about five minutes and then joined the Chief at the CRB offices for a meeting.

We were summoned to appear at the Palace at 11:30 and went over to the minute accompanied by Francqui. One wing of the palace has been cleaned up and is quite habitable. There were very few flunkies in evidence, not more than three or four at most. One lone aide de camp took us in charge and led us to the King's [Albert I] study where he received us at once. His Desk was covered with papers and looked like the desk of a busy man but he laid everything aside and settled down to talk to us. He is more shy than ever if that is possible and his shyness worked on Hoover until it got perfectly painful, but after a half an hour they both thawed out and from that time on things were easier. There was plenty to talk about and plenty of things on which the King wanted the Chief's advice, so once started they did not run down. We had said we were anxious to get off early so as to catch the train from Lille, so at a little after noon the King got up and led us upstairs to the family dining room where the three of us had lunch with him. It was a good lunch, but very simple. Three servants in plain black liveries served the lunch and after serving left the room until the King rang for them to come back with the next course. Here is the menu which Francqui lifted with the true collector's instinct and which he handed over to me afterward.

The King was chiefly interested in the principles to be decided by the various committees of the Peace Conference and about the measures he should take to bring down prices in Belgium and make living more bearable for his people. He seemed to be posted as to the prices for all sorts of foods and necessaries of all kinds and to have ideas as to how they could be brought down. He was anxious for outside advice on all these matters and he got enough to keep him thinking for some time as Hoover has been devoting a good deal of thought to how Belgium should be got back on her feet.

The Queen [Elisabeth] was away at La Panne, so we did not see her. The King said: "Tomorrow I shall get in my areoplane and fly to La Panne to see my wife." He always speaks of her still as "my wife" which would be frowned upon in most kingly families. The young prince he refers to as "my boy". But I'll bear up even if he does not observe the protocols as rigidly as he might.

When luncheon was finished we went into another room and had our lunch and the King told us that when we felt we had to leave to make our connections, we could start. He came downstairs with us and bade us goodbye at the door, and then made for his office and interrupted work.

We stopped for a minute at the Legation to get our passports and I went around the corner for a minute to Myriam's to see Madam Drugman who was there for lunch. There I also found Bebeth de Lynden and several of her uncles and brothers and Captain Best and Genevieve de Bauer. I had only time to look at them and fly.

Shaler came with us and we had only one motor, so we were wedged in tight with baggage and rugs and lunch hampers and goodness knows what else. It was a glorious day and we made tremendous time over the country roads in spite of the fact that they were filled with British transports wandering in all directions. At the CRB house in Lille, we found Poland and Tuck and Kruger and others waiting for us and after hearing what they had to say about the Paris roads, we decided not to push on by motor but resign ourselves once more to the doddering train. If we had to come to Brussels very often, we shall certainly exert influence to have a through night train from one capital to the other so that we shall not be obliged to waste so much time getting about.

Fortunately we got a couple of compartments on this train and have been able to dine quietly out of our lunch hamper and have a comfortable talk.

For some strange reason although the Paris-Lille train is always one or two hours late, the Lille-Paris train seems to get in on time. We should therefore get in tomorrow morning at about 6:50 and have a real day ahead of us. If I can manage it, I think I shall clear out for Switzerland in the evening, but I still knock on wood.

Letter to Mary Gibson   Paris. Tuesday, February 11, 1919

A long day and I am off this evening to roll in the snow at Leysin and wax fat in preparation for the work that is being got ready for me.

Our old train ambled in this morning on time at 6:50 so that we got a good running start before the other members of the community were astir. The thermometer was at 12 below zero, so we were glad to find our cars waiting for us and did not enjoy even the short wait we had while the luggage was being piled aboard.

At breakfast the TIMES disclosed the formal engagement of Elizabeth Asquith which caused me to indulge in confidential celebration. Someday I shall tell you the whole story. It won't bear writing but this is the best news I have had for many a long day and I feel correspondingly cheered. Hoover happened to know the whole business and when he saw the news he joined in the party – just the two of us.

I had a good morning with a first rate stenographer and got my correspondence cleaned up preparatory to leaving. Dropped in to see Joe [Grew] and Bill Bullitt and had lunch with Phil [Patchin] and on all hands was ordered to get out of town and stay out until sent for. I am pretty near dead beat and shall enjoy hav-

ing leave, particularly as it is forced upon me. Ynès and Ramon and Jack [all Reyntiens] are all at Leysin and have been urging me to go, and as they are the only people I k now who are able to play with me besides liking them tremendously I hie me thither with enthusiasm.

In the course of the afternoon I had a hurry call from the Chief to say that he had agreed to receive Albert Thomas and the interallied group of socialists who are gathered here. He wanted me to be there and serve as interpreter so I went up to the new office in the rue de Bassano and stood by for trouble. About fifteen of them turned up with Thomas in the lead and when they had settled down, Thomas opened up as spokesman and said that they were concerned about keeping alive after the war the various bodies for the control of commodities such as the Wheat Executive, etc. Hoover told them that he thought it was a very poor idea and that they had had worked great hardship on the consumer and should be abolished as soon as possible in the interest of all concerned. We had it back and forth for an hour or so and Hoover advanced several ideas these people had not thought of as to how they could attain their ends. Their eyes opened and when the time came for them to go, Thomas said on behalf of the group that although they had visited all the allied statesmen in Paris, this was the first time they had received any useful and constructive advice. They are coming back to see him again and it looks as though they might be set in the right tract to accomplish some useful things. Thomas is a most attractive citizen with very blunt manners and a splendid power of simple statement. I was sorry when the meeting was over although it kept me on the jump.

From there I had to rush back to the house to get a bite before starting for the train and found Will Irwin alone to have it with me. And now to say goodbye to the crowd gathered downstairs for a meal at a more reasonable hour.

Letter to Mary Gibson   Grand Hotel, Leysin. Wednesday, February 12, 1919

I wish you could be up here and seen this gorgeous place under a meter or so of snow. And I'm the gladder to be here because it means the end of travel for a time and particularly of last night's beastly ride. There was a tangle about the tickets as usual and when I got to the station I found that I had nothing but a seat in a carriage with five other people, three French officers, and Italian officers and a comic Czech who was evidently a courier bound for Prague. However I was too enterprising to go back and make a fresh start so I settled down as comfortably as I could and passed a wretched night. To make matters more charming, the pipes froze in the night and there was no water in the morning. Also we managed to lose two hours in the course of the night and did not turn up at Bellegarde for breakfast until half past ten. There we were put through in short order and fussed around for an hour or so while other people were being put through and asked all sorts of questions.

I was to have gone with the courier (Young Sperry) as far as Lausanne where the Legation was to have sent a car for me to bring me to Aigle. But when we got in we learned that the roads between Bern and Lausanne were so deep in snow that the cars could not get through. By the skin of my teeth, I caught a train heading for Lausanne and there made another close connection for Aigle which brought me to the foot of the funicular just as the one train I wanted was ready to pull out. As there is only one train a day each way and as connections are usually missed with enthusiasm, I was more than lucky. At Leysin Village, I found Ynès waiting, she having luged down that far to meet me and ride back.

We had a hearty tea which did me good and by the time we had finished chattering, it was time to dress and go down to dinner. I had not seen Jack since the first months of the war when he was on the Yser and he has been pretty well everywhere since then – the Congo, and up and down the Western front for over four years. So there was plenty to talk about.

At dinner there was a Mrs. Ward who is a sister-in-law of John Ward in London, a Miss Dunbar a good soul of an English old maid whom I knew here before and several miscellaneous people including a young French aviator and an American named [R.T.] Goode.

We did not talk long after diner as I was dead beat and ready for my little bed. And I don't think I shall lie awake and worry about insomnia.

Letter to Mary Gibson   Grand Hotel, Leysin. Thursday, February 13, 1919

A day of strenuous rest with little to report.

I was pulled out of a sound slumber at half past eight after ten and a half hours of sleep feeling as though I had had a week's leave already. It was frozen hard outside and the thermometer in my room stood at a little over zero until the windows had been closed for some time.

In the morning we got out the luge and did some tall sliding until lunch time. In the afternoon we rested hard as required by the rules of the establishment until four o'clock and then we climbed the hills behind the hotel for three quarters of an hour to a place whence we could see the Lake of Geneva just as the moon was coming out. It was freezing hard and when we started down on the luge, we went like the wind far beyond the hotel and almost to the village to a place where unsportsmanlike people had thrown shoes on the road to keep the likes of us from careering to the public danger.

We all dined together and then I fled to the security of my chamber to do some odds and ends of writing that have hung over from the supposed complete clean up I did in Paris before I started.

Letter to Mary Gibson   Grand Hotel, Leysin. Friday, February 14, 1919

Resting is the hardest work I know but when it is done this way you feel comfortably tired at the end of the day and glad you have done all the exertion.

Goode, the American of whom I have spoken has invented a new sort of winter sport which is making him immortal, although all sorts of small boys have done it for years all over the United States. He has made a chariot consisting of four barrel staves strongly fastened together; there is a hole through them at the front and through which a steel bar is inserted as a brake and there is also a piece of cord by which you can haul the precious thing up the hill. It rejoices here in the name of tonneau. You carry this two hours tramping up the mountain and when you can't stagger another step, you sit down on it and before you know it you are back at the hotel covered with snow and wishing you were back at the top to do it over again. The joys of the sport were described to me, but I did not get very enthusiastic about them. However, a party was arranged for this morning with Goode, Jack and Miss Dunbar. Ynès was not feeling up to it and did not come along. We set out at ten, climbed until after twelve, then set out and climbed some more till we got about as high as we could get without wings. The snow had fallen in one layer after another and a crust had frozen on each. We sank to the knee through the upper crust but the others did not budge; otherwise it would have been all up with us. On the last stretch toward the top, we were out in an open sweep of snow when the whole thing settled with a roar and we expected to be deposited at the edge of the lake. But that was all that happened and when the roar was well digested, we sat down upon our tonneaux and went off like the wind. I soon found that the break was not needed and that we could steer with hands and feet and I came down like a cyclone with my eyes and ears full of snow and my insides full of satisfaction. About half way down, we entered a dense pine wood with a much steeper slope and a thick crust on the snow so that our speed got to be that of an express train. We came swooping down little gullies, bouncing into holes, dashing around great trees, always within an inch of being dashed to bits but never quite making it. I haven't yet figured out how the steering is done but it evidently is done instinctively or I should not now be in our midst.

After I had been beaten with sticks and brushed for a little time, most of the snow was got off me and I set off on the luge down to the village to see what had to be done to my passport by the Bureau des Étrangers [Foreigner's Office]. It turned out that nothing had to be done, but leave it there and tell them the day before I wanted to leave, so that is done.

Among the papers I brought from Paris is a long letter from old Mr. Charles W. Farnham who says toward the end:

"Hugh Gibson, you are coming back to a different America. You are coming back to an America from which 'the Colonel' and 'Teddy' and 'T.R.' are gone.[187] I wrote to my boys the other day and said it seemed almost as though Santa Claus were dead, or there were no more Hamlet – something so much more than the mere death of a human being. I had occasion to write to Mr. James M. Beck the other day and in reply to a question from him as to whom the West might favor now that Theodore Roosevelt is dead, I named a lot of men and discussed them, but I was stumped as to Mr. Hoover's polititics..."

And further on he [Farnham] says:

"Mr. Hoover made a great hit when he sent word to those German Generals to go to hell. He will cuss himself into the White House if he don't watch out."

Right after dinner, there was a movie show in the hotel and all hands gathered for it. I looked in for a minute with the family and hangers on, but it was not thrilling and I feared I should disgrace myself by falling asleep so came back to my room to tick out a letter to you which I find better fun than a movie even if I haven't anything to say.

Altogether I had six hours of active sport today, but a hot bath at the end of it and plenty of loafing have me feeling like a fighting cock. I have drunk so much milk that the cow has evidently complained at the office and I was told that I would have to slow up as I was exceeding my ration. In this bully air, you don't care to smoke and you get nothing but simple food and the richest of milk so I don't see how people can help getting well.

Letter from Mary Gibson   Grand Hotel, Leysin. Saturday, February 15, 1919

Another day of strenuous ease.

When we got up this morning it was to find a message from Ynès that she was not well and that we should have our breakfast without her. Jack and I accordingly did ourselves as well as we could in my room and then went forth in search of adventure. We climbed to the top of Le Chamois and luged down to the public danger and as we went through the village were seized with the idea that we

---

[187] Referring to the death of Theodore "Teddy" Roosevelt, 26th President of the United States, on January 6, 1919.

should be more of a public menace if we had a bob sled instead of a luge. The culprit who rented it to us said that the best thing for us to do was to go right on down from the front of his shop. I got out in front and took the wheel and Jack sat behind with the breaks and irresponsible enthusiasts gave us a running start. We went down the hill like nothing that ever was and the first thing I knew we had in front of us an acute turn which brought us almost back on our tracks. I had no idea of how to negotiate it but threw my whole weight on the wheel and skidded round it at top speed in style that would have made most professionals jealous. It was a pure fluke but we got respectful way made for us by everybody on the road and decided that we were experts in the noble sport. We did not dare go round that turn again for fear we would make a mess of it and ruin our reputation, so took the bob sled up to the top of the hill above the hotel and played there by ourselves until lunch time.

At four Count Terlinden and his sister Baroness de Coninck came up for tea from Montruex, Ynès got up and we foregathered for much talk about Belgium in the war time and other gossip. Marie de Coninck knows Aunt Leona and was enthusiastic about her and her work.

Tonight there was a masked ball on the ice at one of the hotels a little lower down the mountain and we went down for a look, Ynès and Miss Dunbar and Goubault, a young French aviator and Bergon a Chasseur Alpin. It was pretty dismal and the ice was spoiled by falling snow but the music furnished by the village band was so excruciating that we were repaid for the effort and stayed out until half past ten which was enough to get us sat upon by the hotel management. However, we did get in without being reprimanded and while the others are regaling themselves with some hot tea, I sit me down to give you this thrilling narrative of the day's work.

Letter to Mary Gibson   Palace Hotel, Montreux. Sunday, February 16, 1919

I woke up this merry morn in Leysin with the full expectation of being there for another week at least before easing back into the turmoil and strife of the peace conference where there is no peace. But just as we were all going into lunch, Hugh Wilson called me on the telephone from Bern and said that he had a telegram from the Peace Commissioners saying they wished me to return to Paris at "my early convenience." On Sundays, no trains run in Switzerland, but Hugh said that he would send a car for me and get me to Bern tonight. I gathered all my belongings together, got my passport back from the Bureau des Étrangers [Foreigner's Office] with great difficulty and left Leysin amid universal sorrow by the 6:21, reaching Aigle in a drenching rain at half past seven or so. The car was there but the chauffeur said that the high country near Bern was too deep in snow for us to get through and that we could not think of trying it by night. He therefore recommended spending the night in the village and going on tomorrow morning. I got no thrill out of the idea and we compromised on going part way and stopping for the night here. I found Terlinden and his sister Marie de Coninck sitting down to dine and joined them. Mr. [John] Jackson (my onetime chief in Habana) and Mrs. Jackson were nearby and joined us after dinner for a talk that lasted until after eleven. The place was only partly filled but it was an amusing crowd. There was an old lady giving a party at the next table. She is a daughter of Merebeer, 86 years old and spends all her time here giving dinners. She saves her strength by staying in bed until five in the afternoon and has a fresh zoo to entertain her every night. Tonight she had a brother of the Khedive of Egypt, a couple of Russians and a Czech. What they all found to talk about it is hard to imagine but they seemed to be having a fine time. At another table was the newly deposed Archduchess of Luxembourg who did not seem to be fading away over the loss of her throne, and there were several other near royalties scattered about over the room; most of them, according to Marie de Coninck, don't pay their bills and are practically obliged to stay on here by the management on the hope that somebody will leave them money so that they can make some sort of settlement. What a joke it would be on the hotel if any of them were to up and die!

I have an idea that when I get back to Paris I shall be put to work for a time and then sent back to Bohemia or some such place, but I am game for anything. I should have enjoyed having a little more leave and a chance to fatten up for the slaughter but after so much experience I ought to know better than to expect it. However, I shall know more about my fate when I get back to Paris.

Letter to Mary Gibson   Bellevue Palace Hotel, Bern. Monday, February 17, 1919

Travel is slow these days and we shall not be in Paris until Wednesday morning.

I was ready to start early this morning but the chauffeur did not turn up until a little after nine, having some repairs to make to his car. We made good time until we got about half way when speed became dangerous on account of the ice on the roads. Once we skidded on approaching a railroad crossing and turned all the way around. However, there was no harm done and the chauffeur refused to get excited enough to put on his chains. Half an hour later in coming down a hill we skidded again and swung around in the same way on a bad corner, knocking down a tree and with the back wheels hanging over a sheer drop of about fifteen feet. By the grace of heaven a rocky bump on the edge of the precipice and the fallen tree kept us from going over or you would have had the pleasure of buying a new car for Hugh Wilson for it would have been good bye in all probability for all hands. It was raining in torrents and I declined to add anything to the weight lest the car should decide to go over the side. I stood in the rain and got soaked. The chauffeur and Schelling's chauffeur who had accompanied us from Montreux went into the village and got some chains from the blacksmith and fastened them to the front axle and a milestone which was standing obligingly across the road. I timidly suggested once or twice that we and the crowd gathered round about could hoist the car back onto the road but all those present treated the suggestion with scorn for an hour or so. The village horses could not do anything as they were not shod for work on the ice and we finally got to the point where I was bold enough to issue some orders to the free born Swiss. I put them all to work and gave a hand at the front wheel myself, and we had the car out in no time as we could have done at once if I had been a little braver.

The rest of the trip was pretty rough with slushy snow and pelting rain but we did draw up at the hotel as everybody was coming out from lunch convinced that we were buried in some crevasse along the way.

I spent the afternoon at the Legation talking shop with anybody who would listen and completing arrangements for our trip. We are going by way of Bellegarde, starting tomorrow morning at seven fifteen, and getting to Paris twenty four hours later. Katherine Wilson is going with us as far as Besançon, where she is to meet her brother whom she has not seen for three years.

Had dinner with the Wilson's and Herbert Parsons, who is here as Asst. Military Attaché and has just been ordered home to his intense relief. This will teach members of Congress to go interfering with wars. Mrs. Hopkinson-Smith was also there and I sat with her for a minute.

Letter to Mary Gibson Tuesday, February 18, 1919
On the train en route from Pontarlier to Paris.

The more travel I get the less I want. We decided to come this way partly because Katherine Wilson wanted company on her trip to visit her brother at Besançon and partly because there was doubt as to whether the motor [could] get through to Geneva. Accordingly, we set forth this morning at a quarter past seven almost before daylight and made the run to Neufchâtel. The chauffeur was a conservative and got us there with more than an hour to spare. We sat down and killed the time with converse and coffee at a hotel across the street from the station.

Thence we made the half hour trip to La Verrière, the Swiss frontier station where we put in something over two hours waiting for the little jerkwater that was to take us across the frontier to Pontarlier, the French frontier station. Fortunately, we had brought lunch with us and ate in a dingy bar across from the station along will all the station employees and town bums. It was as cold as Greenland, snowing slightly and all outdoors was covered with such a layer of ide that there was not use trying to walk anywhere.

At Pontarlier, we had our only fun of the day when the *douanier* [customs officer] asked me to open my bags and I declined on high diplomatic grounds. He pulled his diplomatic knowledge on me and said that only Ambassadors were entitled to the privileges of free entry and I challenged him. By that time, there was a group of merry villagers and people off the train busy trying to understand how anybody could be so altogether foolish as to think he could get by the customs without opening his baggage. We had it back and forth several times and he got so impressive about his written instruction that I demanded to see them. He went off and remained a long time, going through the motions of hunting for his instructions and wondering what he was going to do next, for of course, he had nothing but his own bluff to cover up the bull he had made. We had more than two hours to wait for our train and were content to be patient no matter how long it took him, and after he had used up all the time he dared, he came back with the most conciliatory manner and said that he found that the instructions he had received had a special exception for American diplomats, which was not so bad considering although there was not a word of truth in it. We were just as sweet as he was and parted with much evident regret on both sides.

It was raining in buckets and we could not wander the streets much so we tried a café until the bad air drove us out and when we could finally get into the train three quarters of an hour before it started, we climbed in gladly and here we are waiting for our get away.

Next day. The day's travel did not improve much as we went on. We had a French officer, a civilian, an American courier and ourselves in the compartment to start with. At nine or so, we put Katherine [Wilson] off at Mouchard whence she had to find her way alone to Besançon, and while we were doing that a giantess with a boy of six and a baby worked into the vacant place. She filled all our places with her luggage and children and proceeded to hand a little hammock across the compartment from one baggage rack to the other and install the baby in it. She spent most of the night getting up to look at the baby and walking on our feet and sitting down all over us and turning up the light when we were asleep and dousing as soon as we got awake enough to read. The windows and doors had to be kept shut because otherwise there might be a *courant d'air* [draft] and the atmosphere was thick enough to eat with a fork. Needless to say, sleep was just about out of the questions and we got off the train with wrath in our hearts. How dare people have children anyway.

Letter to Mary Gibson   Paris. Wednesday, February 19, 1919

Hugh Wilson and I got off the train this morning at about eight and found two cars waiting for us. We were sociable enough to ride up in one of them and let the other follow. I left him at the Crillon and came on up to the house where I found the family waiting for breakfast and sat me down in my seat to hear the gossip and breathe fresh air.

The Chief [Hoover] had some news of what I had been called back for, – an assignment which everybody considered most complimentary but which I considered bad tactics. The Chief agreed with me and I sat down and blockaded the Secretary [Lansing] until I saw him and had the opportunity to place my views before him. He quite agreed with me and said that the whole business was called off. So after all I might as well have remained in Switzerland and gone on playing. They are quite willing for me to go back again and start playing but now that I am here I shall stay and attend to business as there is always plenty to be done. I have got superstitious about leave anyway.

In the course of the day, I had good talks with the Chief, the Secretary, General Bliss, Mr. White, Vance McCormick and Barney Baruch as well as a lot of the lesser lights. Prof. Herron, Phil [Patchin], Joe Grew, Bullitt and Taylor and Kellogg and Gherardi who have just got back from Berlin filled with rage against everything German and the Hun way of trying to do things. They evidently get more and more insufferable as time goes on. I'm glad I did not go to Berlin as was suggested. I thought at the time that it would not do, as I am in too great danger of apoplexy. From all they tell me, I know I was quite right.

Early in the morning, we got word of the attempt on Clemenceau and I went around in the course of the afternoon and left cards and signed his book. It must be wonderful to live to 78 and then have to be shot to make any impression. The old gentleman was disgusted and wanted to go back to his office when the first dressing was completed, and they had to keep him at home almost by force.[188]

I have no plans yet of the next few days beyond the fact that the Chief has some negotiations he wants me to undertake for him. I don't know how long they will take or how much there will be waiting for me when they are out of the way.

You speak of having perhaps missed some of my letters in December. You can always be sure for I have made a point of ticking off something, no matter how little, every blessed day for the past few months. As a matter of precaution, I have been keeping a carbon so that I can always send you anything you miss. It is the

---

188 On February 19, 1919, Clemenceau was injured by anarchist Emile Cottin, who had fired at his car. A few days later, though, Clemenceau returned to his office and resumed state business.

only way I can be sure of writing for unless I do it every blessed day as regularly as shaving or bathing it is bound to slip.

Letter to Mary Gibson　　　　　　　　　　Paris. Thursday, February 20, 1919

I had hoped there might be mail in today with letters from you, but there was nothing of any description and hope is deferred for a day or two more.

The day has been interesting but I have not had much work to do. The Chief has been active and I have stayed about in the offing to hear what he had to say each time he came in. He injected some new rules into the game that have the old players rubbing their eyes. I don't quite get over rubbing my own, although I expect him to do all sorts of impossible things. He has done some of them today and has gone peacefully to bed leaving most of the Great Ones sitting up trying to figure out some way to beat the game.

I had lunch with Phil [Patchin] and George Baker and as there was nothing pressing to do I went off afterward with Phil and we drove as far as Versailles so as to have a good talk.

This evening Jerry Gheradi came to dine and talk about his trip to Berlin. He is still inarticulate with rage against the Huns and their cheeky ways of trying to put things over even now. The Germans in defeat seem to enrage all our people more than they did in more prosperous days. I am more and more glad each day that I did not go to Berlin as suggested.

I may go up to Spa in the course of a few days with Dr. Taylor in pursuit of some finances. It would be an interesting trip and will not last long under any circumstances, so I don't worry about my angelic disposition.

Although I have nothing to do for the moment, I am rather glad I got called back for it is hard to be away at this time. Just being here gives me the feeling that I am not neglecting any possible chance to be of use.

[Added note found only in Secret Log, hand written in pencil]
The Chief threw a bomb into the Italians this afternoon in a meeting with Crespi and Nitti. He told them we had gone into the relief business for everybody and that we attached just as much importance to our efforts on behalf of the Czecho-Slovaks and Yugoslavs as those for the Italians; that the Italians had played politics and were interfering with our work in an intolerable way and that the time had come to come to an understanding. He said the American people wanted to be helpful but that they were not going to fight for the opportunity. The US is self-sustaining and has plenty to do for some time taking care of itself. He wound up by saying that unless Italy immediately ceased her obstructionist tactics and

set to work to help us in every way, he would have to recommend the immediate stopping of all advances to Italy.

The 2 ministers were petrified with astonishment and exclaimed that he could not mean this as it would involve the starvation of the Italian people. The Chief replied that he quite realized this and deplored it sincerely but that we could not be expected to be more concerned about the matter than the Italian Government. Crespi in a panic said: "Tell me the American program. I'll propose it and support it." The Chief replied that it was a little late in the day to be coming out with this sort of thing and that about the only thing for them to do was to see that all support was given our people by the Italian authoritites.

Crespi called up in the evening and said: "Can't we 2 get together and settle this?" but Hoover said the matter was out of his hands now having been referred to the Peace Commissioners. Crespi is doubtless burning the wires to Rome.

Letter to Mary Gibson   Paris. Friday, February 21, 1919

Another Mr. Micawber[189] day which I am finishing up in bed trying to decide whether I have the gumption to get up or whether I shall lie me down and enjoy a little grippe. If there were more things which had to be done at once I should undoubtedly decide to stay on my feet, but for the next few days I can see nothing to do but wait for something to turn up.

This morning I had a long talk with Dr. Beneš, the Czechslovak Foreign Minister, and then came home to lunch with Poland and Torrey. About four o'clock I gave up and climbed into bed where at least I can keep warm. The Berlin Vienna crowd are having dinner tonight and I was bid as the representative of Brussels. It would have been fun to see the old crowd gathered together, but that will have to wait over for another time.

I hope to get up tomorrow morning and go after such work as I can find. There is no fun being an invalid these days with M. Clemenceau occupying the center of the stage and attracting all the attention and sympathy.

[Added note found only in Secret Log, hand written in pencil]
This morning I went to see Dr. Beneš and told him something of the way the Chief had laid down the law to the Italians. He was visibly pleased and relieved.

---

189 Wilkins Micawber was a character in *David Copperfield* by Charles Dickens (1850). This optimistic clerk had the belief that "something would turn up."

He said they had had great trouble with the Italians and although they had stocks of food at Trieste, they had not so far been able to get them started. Meantime conditions were getting worse in Bohemia and he had telegrams from Masaryk saying that he was much concerned over the maintenance of public order. Certain elements have been kept quiet by repeated assurances that food was on the way, but these assurances were losing some of their force and the only thing that would help now would be some evidence that shipments were arriving. Beneš felt that even small shipments would have an effect out of all proportion to their size, but that further delay would be fraught with much danger.

He also brought up again the question of using the Elbe. In order to bring in their requirements of 100,000 tons per month from Trieste, they would require 2,000 cars in service – which they cannot secure. On the other hand, they have a good number of ships of about 800 tons burden which they could use to bring supplies up the Elbe from Hamburg.

The Chief on my return said he had referred this matter to the British Admiralty and saw no reason for an unfavorable decision. He had me send word to Beneš that he should despatch Czech representatives to Hamburg and Rotterdam (so that we could communicate with through the latter) and added that we could immediately divert cargoes from Rotterdam.

I also told Beneš that the Bill creating a Legation at Prague had not passed Congress as reported in the papers here; that it might be some time before it was passed but that once this was done, an appointment would be made as soon as possible.

Letter to Mary Gibson   Paris. Saturday, February 22, 1919

Nothing startling in the way of news as I am still lolling in beds of ease trying to get rid of the misery in my bones before it develops into anything worse. It is so comfortable doing nothing that I may decide to become bed ridden.

There has been nobody of note to see me and the Chief has not yet come in at this writing so the day has been dull but for the reading of some of Alfred Noyes' *Walking Shadows*,[190] rattling good yarn.

Will Irwin has left for England with the newspaper man's hope for trouble and stories. I hope he won't get any, not that I have it in for him but because we have enough trouble already to keep us busy for some time.

---

190 A short story collection that British writer Alfred Noyes (1880–1958) published in 1918, containing diverting spy tales.

Letter to Mary Gibson   Paris. Sunday, February 23, 1919

I am still in bed – or as one of the more technical reporters says this morning in his story about Monsieur Clemenceau "le decubitus dorsal prolonge". There is nothing really the matter with me but I feel wuthless and don't have to get up unless I want to – so I don't.

Our family has scattered to all quarters of the city and none of them came in until evening. I crawled out for dinner and then got back into bed after listening to the day's gossip.

Carlton Gibson and his son came in to see me in the course of the afternoon as did Blount and Roye. Colonel Atwood who was feeling seedy himself, came in and stood by while I consumed some lunch and then crept back to his own hole.

Letter to Mary Gibson   Paris. Monday, February 24, 1919

Another day devoted chiefly to trying to get the misery out of my bones and without much effect even for that. I got out and paid visits to the Embassy, the Food Council and the Peace Mission, seeing a swarm of people and not learning much.

Miss Larner was back after a month's leave in the South of France and ready to start in again.

I had a session with Blount who has had an assignment that he does not like and wants to join the Hooverites. It looks are though we had him cornered and I hope so for he is a useful citizen who is not afraid of hard work.

Frank Schell turned up after lunch, a Major in the Air Service, and claimed me for dinner. I was too low for that sort of thing, but had a little visit with him in the office. Frank is now on his way to the replacement depot at Gondrecourt and expects to be sent home soon.

Davis Wills called up on the telephone to announce that he and Edith were back from their trip to the South of France and that Edith was laid up with something resembling flu. She had just finished writing a play and Margaret Mayo has carried it off to London to see if she can place it.

Hugh Wilson is staying here for a week or so and I managed to have a little talk with him. He is being held to take the place of Chris Herter who is ill. As a matter of fact, pretty well everybody <u>is</u> ill and work suffers in consequence.

I was too worthless to work, so came back after lunch with Phil and George Baker and settled down to read Rose's *Life of Napoleon*.[191]

---

[191] A monumental two volume biography of Napoleon featuring new material from British official records, authored by John Holland Rose and first published in 1901.

Arnold Whitridge, who went to Berlin with Gheradi, was due in Munich yesterday or the day before, and was told by Dr. Taylor to go to the Hotel Regina. This morning's papers announce that there was a sharp fight in taking the hotel with three people killed and eighteen wounded. I telephoned around during the afternoon trying to get some news for Mrs. Whitridge, but could not get anything very comforting until late at night when we learned that Whitridge and his companions had gone to the old Hotel Vierjahreszeiten where nothing happened.[192]

Rutger Jewett, B. Whitlock's publisher, came to dine this evening. He has been spending some time at the Legation in Brussels.

Letter to Mary Gibson   Paris. Tuesday, February 25, 1919

Another deadly dull letter for I have hardly stirred all day long. It has been rainy and cold and as I had no special call upon my services, I stayed in the house all day and read and wrote. My only comfort is that I got a number of letters written and am keeping fairly abreast of my obligations.

In the afternoon Philip Brown came in to say goodbye before starting off for Vienna whither he is going to lend a helping hand to Coolidge. He has been lecturing in the occupied regions of Germany to the American troops and is loath to leave that work. He has been over for the YMCA and wears a uniform all his own without any distinctive marks of that pious organization. I don't blame him for the camouflage if he can get away with it, for Y men are about as popular as rattlesnakes with the men. Philip does not know what he is going to do when he gets to Vienna but I have a feeling that he will be planted in Budapest.

I had lunch alone at the house and did not see a soul of the family until dinner time when they all came trooping in together. Dr. and Mrs. Kellogg came in to dine and she told the story of how she got to Brussels before the Germans had left. It was a great story and as you can imagine it lost nothing in the telling. She started from Calais and begged rides from lorries, motors, wagons, anything on wheels until she got beyond Dunkerque. There she was fortunate enough to find a car that was going to Bruges and they gave her a ride after she had displayed letters from Mr. Hoover and her credentials as a member of the CRB. From there the car moved on toward Ghent, but when they stopped at Belgian GHQ, she was lifted out and told that she would have to go back as she had broken all possible

---

192 During the German November Revolution of 1918, Independent Social Democrate Kurt Eisner proclaimed in Munich the 'Free State of Bavaria'. On February 21, 1919, he was assassinated by a right-wing terrorist, which the following days triggered a general strike and the declaration of state of siege over Munich.

laws and that anyone else in her place would be punished severely. However, she wheedled them into good humor and in the real Belgian way they set about finding some way to get her into Brussels through the lines. A car came out from Brussels with two German officers to discuss armistice matters and when the car started back empty, the Belgians waylaid it and sent her in state. She was there several days before the Germans left, saw some of the little revolution, the entry of the King and Queen, the departure of the Hun army and the official reception of [Adolphe] Max by the Echevins. It was a tremendous experience and she told it well.

There is to be a meeting at Spa Sunday or Monday and I may go up with the Chief. It will be decided in the course of the next day or so. Unless the conference has something definite for me to do, I think I shall start out a week from Friday on the new Paris-Bucharest train that is being run by the War Office and go to Bucharest and Constantinople with Dr. Taylor to find out just what is really going on down there. There may be some side trips but we are not planning beyond those two places just now. I should like, if possible, to come back by way of Poland and see something of how they are getting started. I hope nothing will interfere with this and that any regular job will be kept waiting for the few weeks necessary to get this glimpse of the Near East.

Letter to Mary Gibson   Paris. Wednesday, February 26, 1919

Today the postman repented of his evil ways and disgorged your letters of February 2nd which beats any recent record all to pieces.

I don't wonder that you are ready to resign from the Commission – and goodness knows you are entitled to get out whenever you like without reproaches from anybody. I shall rejoice when I hear that you have thrown it over and let somebody else take a turn at it.

I have hardly had a letter of any sort for days and thought that this pouch would bring me a lot. There was a big bundle of letters but most of them were dodgers telling me that for five dollars I could get a system of improving my memory one hundred percent in two weeks or a thousand percent in six months – or that for a similar amount some philanthropist would show me how to make my employer come across with an increase of thirty to one hundred percent in my salary. Another bird had a fine system for training children and would send it to me on approval for the asking. I was also asked to join a Travel Club which has ten thousand members and hopes to double the number by 1919. A society for the protection of the rights of authors against unscrupulous publishers was ready to receive my two dollars and take care of my rights for me. Several magazines explained that they were practically making me a present of [it] by letting me have a year's subscription for $ instead of the old price of $. I wonder if there is any other country in the world that has so many dodges for getting your money away from you.

The only other real letter I had was from Martha McCook, who is pining away at the Everglades Club at Palm Beach and wishing she was back here at work. The doctor would not let her come back to her old job with the YMCA which was altogether too strenuous, and her New England conscience won't let her ask for a passport for a job that isn't really essential, so she is staying at home and glooming. It is too bad as she is the sort that is needed here to raise the average. She is depressed by the state of mind of the idle rich at Palm Beach and remarks:

> "We are in an extreme pre-war atmosphere here and it's the hardest thing in the world to find anyone who cares two straws about the Peace Conference or anything European. Almost every man I've talked to seems to be anxious to get the peace signed soon and to let Clemenceau get what he wants so that Germany will be well tied up – and then for us to mind our own business again in the U.S.A. It may be that these men I have seen are all low-brow reactionaries, but they seem to come from every part of the country and it's been interesting to try to explore and see what they think. They are all much more interested in the effects of National Prohibition and in the readjustment of labor conditions and of their own business than they are in any of the questions the Peace Conference is struggling with – and they seem to be afraid that if we keep on advising and insisting on what we want done over there we shall have to take a part in making it work. These are just the stay-at-home men – though most of them have been working hard on war jobs – and I'd love to know what is the feeling of the men who are over there and have been doing the fighting – and if their horizon is wider than their relations here at home. Etc. etc..."

Do you get as much gloom over the state of mind at home?

A not very busy day with no thrills. I lunched with the Chief who had been at a long meeting with the Commissioners and wanted to talk about it.

During the day, it was reported in hushed tones that Joe Tumulty had telegraphed the President: "Hurry home. Fear a republic is about to be declared."

I shall try to get a copy of the greatest book on the war as published in French. The publishers tell me it is going very well here, but they have not yet touched Belgium or Switzerland where they expect to make their great killing. They got out a very respectable looking little volume but of course there is not much money in it as it retails for three francs fifty.

Hugh Wilson came out to dine as I wanted the Chief to know him. He is going back to his post the end of the week.

The Chief has decided that Taylor and I had better start for Bucharest and Constantiople next week unless Mr. Lansing has something definite he wants me to do in this part of the world. There are a lot of things down there that we don't know much about, and the only way to find out is to go and see. We shall make a flying trip of it and try to get back here within three weeks of our departures which is pretty good going for these times.

Letter to Mary Gibson   Paris. Thursday, February 27, 1919

Not because there is any news but because this is another day, I sit me down before the machine and tick out a few lines to go off by tomorrow's bag.

    I had lunch today with Dresel and Sheldon Crosby who has been transferred from London to Rome and is on his way to his new post. He is quite cheerful about it as the staff in London has been dispersed to the four winds. Frank Gunther has gone to The Hague; Pennoyer goes to Lisbon to his great disgust; Crosby to Rome and Morgan to Copenhagen. Ned Bell asked for a transfer some time ago so of course he didn't get it. Laughlin is moving off to the Riviera for a long rest with the John Ward's and Ned is staying on as the only experienced member of the staff. I should think the new Ambassador would feel rather uncomfortable at having his staff shot to pieces like that.

    So many things have come up to be attended to here that it seems unlikely that Taylor and I can get about to Bucharest before a week from Tuesday, though we may manage to make it a week from tomorrow. The sooner we get away the sooner we get back. That seems to be the basis on which we do most of our business these days.

    Herbert Stabler has come over to the Conference and sailed in to see me just before lunch. That leaves just about nobody in the Department aside from Polk and Phillips. The center of things has certainly got to this side of the water.

    Clemenceau got out this afternoon and attended the meeting of the Big Ten. Just nine days from the time he was shot till he was back at the table directing the big show. Not bad for seventy-eight.

    The family gathered for dinner as usual but with no outsiders. After dinner, the Chief got a talkative streak and spun yarns all evening about his experiences in China before and during the Boxer outbreak. Someday I'm going to conceal a stenographer behind an arras (whatever that may be) and get a shorthand account of the way he tells these things. All you would have to do would be to listen long enough and you'd have a ready made book.

    I forgot to say that in the course of the afternoon, I stopped to see Clarence Gagnon. I had not laid eyes on him since he came out of the hospital and wanted to know how he was. He has put on weight and seems well and prosperous. One of his big Canadian pictures was purchased as a wedding gift for Princess Patricia and Clarence's name looms large in the descriptions of the gifts. That ought to help him some. He is working hard on woodcuts and thinks he has a grip on something new and worthwhile. He has been trying to get to this point for several years and has always been just out of reach of what he wanted. His spirits are now high as he feels he has arrived. I hope he has.

Letter to Mary Gibson   Paris. Friday, February 28, 1919

Another month ends today and we set out tomorrow on summer time, which has its comic element inasmuch as we are wearing fur coats and wondering how we are going to last until it gets comfortably warm.

I lunched with Stetson at his flat and had a good talk with Blount who was also there. He has been made aide d'camp to General Harts, commanding the American troops in Paris and is disgusted with the valet work he has to do. We are trying to get him for our work which is good deal more to his liking.

Most of the CRB boys are in town for a meeting and came to lunch at the house. I came back here to see them after lunch and found most of them still here – Curtis, Tuck, Gailor, Dorsey Stephens, Brown, Exton, and a few others. They are to be here until Sunday.

In the afternoon I went savaging for news but without success as I found everybody away. With Committee meetings going on from ten in the morning until midnight all the people connected with the Conference are way from their offices most of the time and one never sees them.

In the evening, there was a tangle about the number of people expected to dinner and as I could foresee a food shortage, I gathered Bob Taft, Hart and Gutterson and we went down to Foquet's and dined among the bright lights and the vampires. And at that we got back in time for the evening's conversation. Tooey and Herbert Bayard Swope were among the unexpected guests and furnished much conversation.

A note from Jack Reyntiens this evening to say that he and Ynès are coming up to meet Myriam here during the first days of March. I am afraid I shan't see them as I shall probably have set out on my travels.

Letter to Mary Gibson   Paris. Saturday, March 1, 1919

No letters today from anybody but I hope for a bag from Washington on Monday with a budget from you.

I have not laid eyes on the Chief all day and don't know what he has to report as the day's gossip. I came down to breakfast after he had gone out and missed him several times at our various offices. He did not come home to dine and now I am off to bed with my curiosity unsatisfied.

I had lunch with Joe and Alice Grew and Mrs. George McFadden at Voisin's. Mrs. McFadden is giving a big dance at the Ritz on Monday and I felt very aged explaining that I did not go to dances. I am getting so old and crabbed that I resent being asked to go out into the world after dark for company and amusement.

Edith Wills is off for the United States tomorrow and in obedience to orders, I went around after lunch to say goodbye. She has written a play and is hoping to market it and get rich and live happy ever after. Perhaps – and then again perhaps not.

We had a small family for dinner tonight but much wrath about the doings in the various meetings that had been attended. They are so many small councils and committees and commissions and boards that there is none so poor he can't have a seat or two. I have kept off all of them with nimbleness and get my pleasure from listening to my friends snorts when they come home.

It looks as though Hugh Wilson was to be brought here from the Legation at Bern. He will like it very much as he has had a long pull with much drudgery in his post. It seems that one of the chief reasons they were hesitating about it was that they understood that I was opposed to having Hugh leave Bern. After I had made my point of view clear, the telegrams were sent off. And what amused me was that under no possible conditions could it be considered any of my business.

I see the Senate has approved the nomination of Hugh Wallace as Ambassador here. I think he will do well despite the criticism one hears. He is a very human citizen who plays the game and ought to take well. The only thing I have heard against the Wallaces is that Mrs. Wallace speaks GOOD French. That is against all our hallowed traditions – but then in these times I suppose we are casting off more and more the bonds of tradition and this sort of thing is to be expected.

Tomorrow we set up summertime so we get an hour less sleep this night.

Letter to Mary Gibson   Paris. Sunday, March 2, 1919

Some kind soul at the Embassy sent me this morning the mail from my box. There was nothing from you – only a letter from Myriam Reyntiens to say she would be here on the seventh with either her mother or Bebeth and asking me to get her some rooms in a good hotel – than which there is no thing harder these days. I shall have a try tomorrow but am not very hopeful.

We put in a morning at the offices just as on week days and when lunch time came round I took the Chief and Jim Logan down to Voisin's where we were fortified for the afternoon with much food. At the next table were the Laughlin's just in from London on their way to the Riviera for a rest. Laughlin is about all in and said that as he felt now he would throw a bottle at the head waiter for two sous. I offered to put up the two sous [hundredth of a franc], but he evidently did not mean it literally.

We went back to the office at the Crillon and pretended to work for a time when we adjourned to the rue de Bassano offices and made another try which lasted until after five o'clock. Then, although the weather was wretched, we climbed into the car with George Baker and drove out to Versailles. I led my unwilling charges around to the front of the chateau and made them look at it so as to improve their minds and then let them come home which they did as rapidly as possible.

The Seine is higher than I have seen it for many years and there were great crowds out watching the angry waters. The quais were inundated and piles of gravel, coal and other precious materials were being swept away downstream. Strange to say I haven't yet heard anybody say that the Bolsheviki were responsible for it.

Melville Stone was asked to dine but did not show up so we had a strictly family affair and now I am ready to climb into bed for a night's sleep.

The Queen [Marie] of Romania has set out from Bucharest after sending word to the Chief that she was coming here to see him. The lady knows what she wants and if she doesn't get it, it won't be for lack of trying.

Letter to Mary Gibson   Paris. Monday, March 3, 1919

Another dull day and no letters from you – but there are hopes for the morrow.

This morning I got an S.O.S. from Mrs. McFadden asking me to lunch at the Ritz. The Grand Duke Alexander [Mikahilovich] had asked himself and had suggested some names of people he wanted to meet. It must be quite a convenience to be an Imperial Highness and be able to do that sort of thing. The other guests were Joe and Alice Grew and the Brambilla's, so it was good fun. I had not been to the Ritz for a meal in so long that I had forgotten what it was like. Everybody in the world seemed to be there and none of them seemed to be in any hurry to get away. The Grand Duke did not afflict us with his views as to how Russia was to be saved, though I believe he has designs on me to the extent of telling me what he thinks about it all. He did tell something of their life after the revolution which I should have liked to have him amplify. It seems that he and his family and several of the other Grand Dukes and their families were on an estate in the Crimea with the Empress Dowager. They were not bothered, but once a week some soldiers came and paraded them all, men and women, on the lawn to call the roll of the Imperial family. Of course, they never knew when they were going to be taken out and shot, and most of them never took off their clothes except to change. The Empress Dowager, however, allowed that this was a bore and that anyway she would not be any deader in her nighty than if she were all dressed up, so she set out living more or less normally and the rest gradually came to follow her example.

Conversation after lunch drew out interminably. The Grand Duke was having a fine time and as Imperial Highnesses don't have to work, he was in no hurry. At last, Joe and I could stand it no longer and broke all the laws of the Medes and Persians by saying a firm goodbye and clearing out to work.

I forgot to tell you yesterday that Honnold told me in the morning that the Guaranty Trust Company would like to have me join their staff and go to work for them over here without delay. I showed only a moderate interest and did not even ask about the sordid details of remuneration, etc. I have had previous feelers from them and when I get ready to really go to work, they will most likely be the people privileged to work with me. The President of the Company, Hemphill, is a friend of mine and is the one primarily interested in giving me a job. It is one of the best New York banks and all the people I have seen that work for them are enthusiastic about the treatment they get. I don't see any use in showing special interest just now because I could not throw up government service until after the dishes are washed; and when that time comes there will be such a demand for people that there ought to be chance to pick and choose.

Francqui came down from Brussels and was here to dine tonight. The Chief was so busy telling him about what had happened that he did not get much of a chance to tell us what had been going up there. He is here for various financial questions and will probably be in our midst for several days.

[Added note found only in Secret Log, misdated February 3; correction to March 3 made in pencil by Gibson]
There was a pleasant row at the Supreme Economic Council this afternoon when it met at the Ministry of Commerce. One of the French delegates got up and read a long wheeze that was to be sent to Germany ordering her to produce so many thousand tons of coal per month for the use of the Allies. He said that this had to be done, that France was not disposed to discuss the question and that "this was an ultimatum." Lord Robert Cecil, with an ominous gleam in his eye, asked all those present who were not actual delegates should leave the room. When the meeting had been reduced from sixty odd to about twenty, he opened up in very definite terms. He said that Great Britain, at any rate, was not disposed to accept ultimata from her allies; that if the French had anything of this sort that they wished to have done, it was proper for them to set forth their vies in the form of an argument but that he would decline to receive anything in the character of an ulti-

matum. He further pointed out that if the situation was as desperate as the French seemed to consider it, they were always at liberty to announce that they withdrew from the alliance and desired to go it alone. This seemed to throw considerable emotion into the situation.

The Chief then proceeded to analyze the subject. He pointed out that this was a purely selfish French measure. By a few questions, he got the French to bring out the fact that the United States could not use any of this coal, that England did want any of it and that it was all to be used by France.

He further pointed out that we had from the beginning been for a relaxation of the blockade which would have tended to correct the situation of which the French now complained in Germany. The French wriggled and squirmed and tried to avoid coming to general principles for they do not wish a general relaxation of the blockade, but only such half way measures as favor their short-sighted needs of the day. The Chief also pointed out bluntly that there was a persistent effort to misrepresent the American attitude toward this whole matter and that we were not disposed to stand for much more of it.

The next round comes tomorrow morning.

Letter to Mary Gibson   Paris. Tuesday, March 4, 1919

I have puttered about busily all day, but blessed if I can give account of having accomplished anything.

I lunched with Dresel and Leland Harrison amid the idle rich and talked a large amount of shop.

The afternoon I spent visiting with the Czechoslovak Government and talking over some of their troubles. Beneš was not at his Ministry but I had a lengthy yarn with his second in command, Strimpl, and from there went to the Hôtel Lutetia where I had a good talk with the Prime Minister Dr. Kramář. He is a repaying citizen who knows what he wants and keeps after it. I am going back soon to have a meal with him.

His Chief of Cabinet, Dr. Novák, was also there and we had a half hour together on various odds and ends. And thus most of the afternoon was scattered away.

Chauncey McCormick came to dine and brought with him [Herbert] Ward, the British sculptor with whom he is staying. The Chief was not at home but we sat about and talked until my eyes began to close when I excused myself and came up to bed.

The Chief has been tormented with ulcerated teeth ever since he came over and is now in the midst of his fourth attack and looks pretty badly run down. I am now threatening to chuck the trip to the Balkans and take him off for a few days rest which is what he needs worse than anything else. He has not had a minute of real relaxation for months and it is undoubtedly beginning to tell on him. We can't afford to have him put out of commission at a time like this.

We are anxiously awaiting word as to what Congress has done on its deathbed. There are a lot of things that interest us in our daily work, and we are going to be hampered if some of them have not gone through.

[Added note found only in Secret Log]
The Chief yesterday went for the Italians for the way they were treating the Czechs and was most emphatic. Before he had got very deep into it, Crespi came out with a letter which the Czechs had addressed to him thanking him for all that the Italian Govt. had done for them. Of course, this cut the ground out from under the Chief's feet and he had nothing further to say.

Accordingly, he addressed a note to Beneš saying that he had seen this note and that inasmuch as the Czechs were satisfied, he assumed that there was nothing further for us to do in the matter.

After lunch I went over to the rue Bonaparte and followed this up with some more-in-sorrow-than-in-anger talk. Strimpl did not know much about it but brought in Major Hierflinger, a Czech officer who was evidently responsible for the letter and for the assumption that the Italians were doing all they could. I developed in conversation with him that the Italians had cut off all direct communication by way of Laybach for Czech shipments of food. They had, however, allowed them to send trains by way of Udine to such an extent as might not interfere with other work on the line. Theoretically, he said they should be able to send five trains a day by this route but on being pressed admitted that they had not been able to send more than one or two trains a day. Thus their gratitude to the Italians is for allowing them to do something they don't need to do, don't want to do, and something that in no way meets their needs. He felt rather sheepish by the time he got through.

The only adequate way of dealing with the situation is to send food up the Elbe from Hamburg and I told Strimpl to have his people make a direct application to this effect to Marshal Foch and he promised to do so. I told him that we should support their request so as to help it through.

He also brought up the question of their desperate need of American raw materials, particularly cotton, and the problem as to how they could pay for it. I sent him to see McCormick and Davis about the two questions.

From there I went to the Lutetia and set the whole question before Kramář. He was at first disposed to dismiss the way they had let us down as of no importance, but seemed to attach greater importance to it after I said that in view of this sort of thing, Mr. Hoover would not be disposed to make any further representation on their behalf until assured that they would stay put. I made it quite clear that we had no special interest in pushing the food through to them and if they did not want it enough to stick to their guns, we had plenty of other things to occupy our time.

After we had finished this pleasant business, he brought up the troubles they were having with the Poles and said that they were in many ways worse than the Germans. He said that Czech prisoners taken in the fighting at Teschen had been abominably used and that the feeling in the country was very high. I had not mandate to discuss the question with him and though I did not agree 100 %, I listened and let him have his say.

Letter to Mary Gibson   Paris. Wednesday, March 5, 1919

I had a fruitless morning at the office with a meeting of all the organizations at 11. From there, the Chief and I went down to the Crillon and stayed until lunch time working over various odds and ends. I gathered up Phil [Patchin] and Dr. Taylor and led them out to lunch at Voisin's thereby squandering a shameful amount of money in times when it should be spent for more worthy purposed than filling up the insides of dainty eaters. However, I was too lazy to even try to think of any more sensible place to lunch and so old Mrs. Voisin got our money.

In the afternoon it turned beautiful and anybody with an ounce of gumption would have seized the occasion to break away from work and go forth to breathe the fresh air and watch nature get ready for spring. However, I was worthless and came home early, first loafing about trying to read an improving book, and then by taking to my bed for a couple of hours before dinner. The village worthies are having a lot of fun worrying about whether I should or should not go to Constantinople on account of my well-known health, but I maintain that I feel so rotten only because I am not doing anything and that when I begin to get some action I shall feel like a fighting cock. I have been through this so often before that I recognize all the symptoms. Accordingly we shall probably set out on Tuesday next by military train which takes only through passengers for Bucharest. Monsieur Clemenceau has promised the Chief that we should have four places without fail. We are going to take Chauncey McCormick along for company and as bodyguard. Also either a servant-cook or a stenographer – thus far we have not been able to make up our minds as to which should go. Now if we can get two extra places we shall take them both together with [Herbert] Ward, the sculptor, to let him sculp and draw pictures and write propaganda when he comes back. That will make an adequate party.

Heinz, who is our commissioner in Constantinople, will come up to Bucharest to meet us – in fact he is already on his way. After we have cleared up the local situation, we shall shove on to Constantinople and then come back to Sofia as nobody knows just what the Bulgarians are up to.

Mr. and Mrs. Honnold come to dine and immediately after dinner the Chief went back down town to row with more people. He does not often continue his labors into the night, and it is a good rule for him to stick to.

Letter to Mary Gibson   Paris. Thursday, March 6, 1919

I puttered around at the office this morning and attended a meeting at eleven. We have decided to move the offices to the Avenue Montaigne so that my new shop is to be occupied for just two or three days. We have handsome new quarters that are just being evacuated by the army and there is adequate room for all hands.

Lunched with Dresel and Major Kuntze at the Travellers Club which was as empty as the tomb.

Late in the afternoon went out with Chauncey McCormick to see Herbert Ward at his studio. An uncanny place filled from floor to ceiling with African weapons which he collected years ago when he careered through those parts with Stanley. In one room, he has some thirty-six hundred knives and axes, each of which has accounted for at least one human life. If there be such things as speaks, that out to have been them.

Amid this welter of death, he has full sized reproductions of his various statues which are in the [Musée du] Luxembourg and other respectable places. They are all of African niggers and all right for a public museum, but I didn't buy any to send home for you to put in the library.

McCormick is anxious to have Ward go with us on our trip to Constantinople and he is going if he can get Lord Derby to get him a place on the train.

Before we left, he gave me a copy of his last book, *Mr. Poilu*.[193] There was another which he said "kept Stanley from being buried in Westminster Abbey."

A letter from Teddy Curtis asking me to be his best man when he gets married to Zizi Guinotte in July or August. As I was best man at the wedding of her sister, Helene, I seem to be getting to be a habit with the Guinotte family.

---

193 In 1916, Herbert Ward had published a book with notes and sketches on the French soldiers (commonly addressed to as "poilus" [French: hairy ones]) at the fronts of the First World War.

[Added note found only in Secret Log]
The matter of the way Italy was behaving was put up to the President the other day by cable and he came back without delay, authorizing us to lay down the law to them and say that unless there was an immediate mending of their ways we should shut off all shipments of food and all loans. The Secretary [Lansing] was to have informed them of this in the meeting of the War Council this afternoon, but as usual he didn't do it and left it up to the Chief who sent for Crespi and broke the news to him after dinner at the Crillon. He began by saying that we had warned them of our apprehension as to the effect of the Italian attitude toward the smaller nations but that nothing had been done about it; that public opinion in America was now dangerously aroused and we did not know whether we could control it. This last was by way of getting back at the eternal Italian wheeze about not being able to do anything they ought to do on the ground that they were afraid of public opinion. Crespi was appalled but there was nothing he could do but promise to get to work at once and try to remedy the situation.

In the meeting at Spa yesterday, the Germans took the strongest stand they have yet tried. They said that we should have their merchant ships when they were assured that they would have an adequate supply of food – and that until such assurances were forthcoming the ships would stay just where they are.

It now remains to be seen whether we are going to let a beaten enemy get away with such talk. If they do it once, we are in for a hellish time with them. All they need is to see that such tactics work once and we shall have them trying it on all the time.

Letter to Mary Gibson   Paris. Friday, March 7, 1919

A strenuous day but without much result to help along the peace.

The morning in a hurly-burly of meetings and talk. I lunched with Phil [Patchin] at the Crillon and listened to his views on how to remedy the ills of the world. There were a flock of correspondents who swooped upon me every time I showed my head because they knew that I had made a flying trip through the Yugoslav country and must therefore be an expert on all questions pending between the Italians and the Yugoslavs.

Late in the afternoon I went around to the Brighton to see Myriam [Reyntiens] who had got in from Brussels, much depressed by what she had seen coming through the devastated districts. It's curious how little idea people have got from their own imaginations as to the horror of those regions. No matter how sensitive and sympathetic they are none of them seem to grasp it until they actually look upon it.

Myriam has come down to meet Jack [Reyntiens] and break to him the news that she is going to get a divorce. It is a long story and he has behaved most abominably. She has gone through a good many years of it but has now come to the conclusion that there is no kindness to anybody in going on with it. Jack and Ynès are expected tomorrow and she is going to have her talk out as soon as she can. She has laid an elaborate plan of deception so as to have an opportunity to talk things over first with Ynès, as she is very fond of her and dreads a situation where she is faced with divided loyalty. I have no doubt as to Ynès standing by Myriam through thick and thin, but it wasn't my business to say so and I have left it to her to state her own position. I was told the whole story from beginning to end, partly to get advice on some minor matters but more, I am inclined to believe, for the comfort of telling it all to somebody. I have grown to be more and more of a *paño de lagrimas* [shoulder to cry on] as time goes on and spend a lot of time these days listening to peoples' troubles.

I went back to the Brighton and dined with Myriam, Miss Hughes, a nurse who came down to look after her, and Captain Best of the British Intelligence Service. The disagreeable subject was not mentioned and we had a pleasant enough time. I cleared out early so that the travelers could go to bed and when I got back to the house found the Chief just back from dining at the Embassy. He was deeply aggrieved as he always is when he is forced to go out to dine but soon got to feeling better when he got entrenched behind a cigar and launched into talking shop.

Letter to Hugh Gibson   Paris. Saturday, March 8, 1919

Another lively day with unexpected developments.

I broke away from a meeting this morning to go down to Gare de Lyon to meet Ynès and Jack and get them installed in their hotel so that Myriam's deep plans could begin to work on them. They were dead beat from the trip and I dropped them and made back for the Crillon where I foregathered with the Chief and others until lunch time when I had a bite with George Baker and Jim Logan, who has just come back from his mission to Spa where the Huns refused to hand over their merchant shipping.

As we were getting up from table in the office, Myriam telephoned dramatically that she and Miss Hughes had strayed out from the hotel on an errand and had run plumb into Jack and Ynès. Of course all bets were off and she had to tell Jack to come and see her at the hotel. She asked me to get there first and charged me with the pleasant task of going over to the other hotel and breaking the news to Ynès. Of course there was nothing to do but go to it, and I did but it was not the sort of job one would choose. Ynès took it with a stiff upper lip and announced at once that she knew it would have to come and that naturally she would move right over and stay with Myriam. I dropped her at the door and let them have their talk and their cry – and then went back to my neglected desk.

They asked me to go back and dine this evening but I had had about enough going for one day and begged off so that I could stay at home and recuperate.

And just to make it unanimous, there was not a particle of mail for me that was worth reading.

There was only a handful of the family to dine tonight, the Chief, George Baker, Colonels Barber and Atwood and HSG [Gibson]. We sat round and discussed the meetings of the Supreme Council and the Council of Ten[194] until my eyelids began to droop and I fled to the sanctity of my room to tick our a few lines on the old ice wagon before turning in.

Letter to Mary Gibson   Paris. Sunday, March 9, 1919

A fairly busy day but no large amount of news.

Franklin Day got back this morning from Berlin and I rounded him up to lunch with Mr. Hoover and give his impressions. He has had a tremendous time but is almost too tired to talk about it.

I labored over some drafting in the afternoon but caved in toward five and came home to loaf until dinner time, when by request I took Jack Reyntiens out to dine. It wasn't alluring job but he behaved well and I lasted until half past nine which is when the restaurants close.

Then I hurried back to the house as Goode had arrived with his fellow Knight Beveridge and was talking food problems with me not there to listen. I got in a couple of hours of it anyway and am now ready to turn in.

---

194 From January 1919 onwards, the Council of Ten was a meeting of the chiefs of states of the United States, Great Britain, France, Italy and their foreign ministers, joined by two representatives from Japan. Since it was soon regarded as too large to handle urgent affairs, the Council of Four (David Lloyd George, Vittorio Emanuele Orlando, Georges Clemenceau and Woodrow Wilson) – also referred to as the Supreme Council – was invoked in early March 1919. It met until Wilson's departure in late June 1919.

Letter to Mary Gibson　　　　　　　　Paris. Monday, March 10, 1919

Another strenuous day with certain developments.

I spent several hours in the morning with Dr. Taylor trying to straighten out the matter of our accommodations on the train leaving tomorrow night for Bucharest. While I was at it, I got word that Joe Grew was anxious to see me and when I got through I went down to the Crillon to see him.

Joe said that Congress had failed to act on the Bill for creating a mission to Prague but that it was necessary to get somebody there and that it had been decided that I should go in the only capacity possible, that of Diplomatic Agent with the rank of Minister Plenipotentiary. I was to start as soon as possible and choose anybody I wanted to go with me.

After taking Counsel with myself, I got off a telegram to Mr. Page in Rome saying that I should like to have Arthur Lane as Secretary of Legation, if he had no objection to my asking for his assignment. I am also to take a Military Attaché and as many clerks, etc. as I need. These I have not yet picked out.

It will be an interesting job and it is well to have the rank although I may lose that when Congress creates the rank regularly and a permanent appointment is made. Phil [Patchin] and I had lunch together at the Crillon and talked over the details of the job.

Late in the afternoon, I took Dr. Taylor by the lily white hand and led him to the Ritz where we were told that the Queen of Romania wanted to talk with us. To our surprise, we found most of the old ladies and social climbers in Paris lined up to see the Queen in a big downstairs room. It was clear that we could not hope for anything more than a chance to shake hands with the Queen and as that was not what we were after, we looked over the assembled company and then cleared out and went to the Crillon where we had more important things to do.

In the evening we had a gathering of our own to dinner – Thomas Lamont, Albert Strauss, Allen Dulles, Fred Dolbeare and Bowden.

Letter to Mary Gibson　　　　　　　　Paris. Tuesday, March 11, 1919

This morning I found that there was some doubt as to whether Congress had acted on the Prague Mission Bill. We got off another telegram to Washington to find out about it and in the meantime I gave up my place on the Bucharest mission and shall stay here to await further news. The President will be here on Thursday or Friday and may be able to enlighten us.

Myriam came in to see me in the course of the morning and told me some more of her troubles. They are evidently being straightened out to a certain extent and she seems a good deal less unhappy, although looking very much worn.

I lunched with Phil Patchin at Voisin's and we had some more talk

During the day I went three times to the Czechoslovak Government and talked with Beneš and others about the means of getting to Prague. They threw up their hats with enthusiasm over the idea of my going there, for it was what they had desired and asked for. As far as I can discover, I cannot get away before next Tuesday so I have some time to make my preparations.

In the afternoon, Ynès came in after looking for me in my various offices and said that she wanted to talk, so I put her into a car and we went out through Bois [de Boulogne]. What she wanted to tell me was that she was engaged to Goubault, the young aviator who was at Leysin. I am a little worried about it as he is a good deal of a kid and has never done anything but fight in this war. He did that very well, in fact distinguished himself but he is a lot younger than she and has no particular prospects. I didn't volunteer any views on that subject, however, and gave as much comfort as I could. I hope she is not throwing herself away for she is a rare soul and deserves the best that this life can give her. They have no plans about when they are to be married but if all goes well it will probably be in the course of the next few months. He is off to see his family and she is going up to Brussels to make some arrangements before going to the South of France with Myriam. That family is certainly in a state of flux.

The Chief is going up to Brussels tomorrow night with Admiral Wemyss and others to meet the German Delegates on the question of feeding Germany. They asked for another meeting in Spa but the Chief thought it was time for a little poetic justice and summoned them to Brussels where they can make their plea in one of the very rooms where they used to browbeat us. We got off a telegram to Max to ask him to provide a suitable meeting place and it promises to be a satisfactory occasion. I really ought to stay here but the temptation is strong and I may motor up tomorrow so as to be there and incidentally to gather together all my belongings and bring them back. It would be lifelong satisfaction to see the meeting.

Letter to Mary Gibson   Paris. Wednesday, March 12, 1919

There was nary a letter from you today although I had my hopes high for a pouch. The only letter I did get was from Aunt Leona, who is at Inverness with Warren and seemingly more happy than she has been for a long time. She is going back to her work for a time and speaks of my sailing in to see her. If present plans work out I fear there is little chance of seeing her before I get off to the wilds, as much as I should like it.

Image 22: Ynès Reyntiens, here in Archachon in 1919, was a friend of Gibson since his Belgian days. He was acquainted with her entire family and aware of their war-time resistance activities. Ynès and Gibson married in February 1922. (Courtesy of the Gibson Family)

I am rather up in the air so far as nothing definite has come yet from the Department as to whether Congress has created a Legation at Prague or whether I must be sent in some improvised capacity or incapacity. A telegram came in this afternoon and everybody who read it jumped to the conclusion that the post was created and rushed about saying so. When I went in to see it in Joe Grew's office, I found that after skillfully skating all around the subject, the message wound up without telling anything at all. It was cleverly done if the purpose was to avoid telling us what we wanted to know. Joe has sent another message to see if he can find out where we are and until the answer comes I am just as much up in the air as ever.

I don't care to go ahead and make final plans until I know for sure whether I am going in some permanent capacity. If so, I shall require a considerable outfit and a lot of supplies that I don't want to spend money on unless it is really necessary. I shall hope to know something definite by Saturday.

This morning I had a nice telegram from Arthur Lane to say that he would be delighted to go with me to Prague. He wants to know when he should start and I shall hope to be able to tell him in a day or two. He has quite a little establishment in Rome and will need some time to settle it up unless he does the usual married man's trick and leaves his wife behind to do the work. I am glad he is to be had for he is a hard worker and would be really helpful.

The Chief and I had a party at the Crillon today – to talk shop, of course – with Dr. Kramář, the Czech Prime Minister, Dr. Beneš, the Minister for Foreign Affairs and Dr. Preiss, the President of the biggest bank in Prague. We had some ideas to enunciate as to how the industrial life of the country could best be stimulated and work provided for the people. They were enthusiastic as to the suggestions and Dr. Preiss is starting for Prague by the first train on Friday to get things started.

Late in the afternoon, I ran away for a little while and had tea with Myriam and Ynès. M's affairs are getting straightened out to her satisfaction and she is off to the south of France for a rest of a couple of months. Ynès is going back to Brussels to pack up and then will join Myriam for as long as she stays away. I fear Ynès' affair is not going at all well, and that she is in for a lot of unhappiness. This is a rottenly complicated world.

I am going along on the Mission to Brussels, being slated as "Diplomatic Advisor" whatever that may mean. We shall only be away a day or two which does not matter as there is nothing I can do until we hear definitely from the Department. I shall get some satisfaction out of seeing the Germans in their new role at Brussels. And as you can imagine, I shall not fail to report fully from the spot.

Letter to Mary Gibson   Brussels. Thursday, March 13, 1919

Back here again playing with the Hun but the sensation is more agreeable than it ever was before.

We left Paris last night at eleven on a special train with the Delegates of the Allied Governments, the whole party numbering about twenty five with all the underlings.

The British Delegation was headed by the Frist Sea Lord of the Admiralty, Admiral Sir Roslyn Wemyss, who was also to preside over the plenary sessions. The Chief heads of our delegation and the French and Italians have less conspicuous representatives. Lamont goes with us to handle the financial questions involved and for shipping questions we have Robinson of the Shipping Board who is a great friend of Rob Frick and seems to know his way about in the dark.

The railroad now runs through the old devastated regions where every inch of the line had to be completely rebuilt on ground that was still feeling pretty nervous and the result was that the old ship rolled across country in a way that made sleep very poor. I got a little of it but could have done with more. Just to conform to the conventions, we managed to lose an hour or so on our schedule and limped into the Gar du Midi at 10:30.

Fred Chatfield and Baetens were at the station to meet us and there was an assemblage of French and British uniforms to meet their delegations. We made for the Metropole where rooms had been engaged for us and where we found almost half as many as had been promised us.

Francqui came down to lunch and brought us up to date on a lot of pending problems.

At two o'clock we went to the Astoria for our first meeting with the Germans. It had originally been intended to hold the meetings at the Hôtel de Ville [town hall] or some other public place for theatrical effect, but the Belgian authorities seem to have been against having so many Huns walking their streets and set aside the ball room of the hotel for the purpose. The Germans kept this hotel requisitioned all through the war as headquarters for their officers and there was never any room for Belgians or other non-Huns.

When we arrived, the Germans had already gone into the conference room and were waiting for us. When we had counted noses, we lined up and marched in. The seventeen Germans were standing on one side of a long table which stretched down the center of the room. They stood there looking at nothing at all and proffering no salutation. We gave no sign of seeing them, but when we had all lined up behind our chairs everybody sat down.

The whole proceeding was utterly matter of fact and there was no expression of emotion by anybody, no eloquence, but for some reason the air was charged with electricity. I suppose everybody realized the significance of the occasion which was probably the most important since the signing of the Armistice. All remarks were made in an impersonal and detached way and addressed to nobody. When a remark was finished, it was translated and then the reply was made slowly and translated back.

By way of opening the ball, Admiral Wemyss read a prepared memorandum which in effect asked an assurance from the Germans that they proposed to carry out Article VIII of the Armistice. When they had signified through their chairman, Dr. von Braun, their intention of doing so, the Admiral read another memorandum giving in short, terse sentences the exact terms of the Allies for furnishing food to the Germans – German merchant shipping to be delivered at once, German gold and other assets to be placed at our disposal at once and food to be sent to Germany as soon as these conditions had been complied with.

Braun said that the points were of such great importance that he would like an opportunity to discuss them with his colleagues before going over them with us. At his request, they were accorded half an hour to discuss the memorandum and we sat down and smoked until they were ready.

At four o'clock we all filed in again solemnly and lined up as before to listen to a running comment from Braun on the terms of the memorandum, each comment being translated from German, first into English and then into French. When he had his say, the Admiral announced that the detailed discussions would be referred to three subcommittees, on Food, Finance and Shipping, which were immediately appointed and went to work in the various hotel dining rooms which had been set aside for them. I sat in on the Food Committee which was presided over by the Chief. There the procedure was the same as in the big meeting, but we managed to get a good deal more speed into the work and finished before the other committees had got very far. This was merely a preliminary session to run over the questions and report the difficulties in the way. At seven we had another full meeting where all the committees made their reports and certain questions were put over till tomorrow when the subcommittees get together at ten. We broke up at eight and withdrew to a small room where we tried our hand at drafting some memoranda for tomorrow's meeting.

I came up for air during the meeting of the subcommittee and as I came out into the lobby, I saw bearing down upon me a beaming individual whom I mistook for a Belgian named Winspeare. He called on heaven to witness how delighted he was to see me and how happy we all were that we were living in such happy days instead of the unhappiness of the past four years. I agreed with him cordially, wrung his hand and assured him that I was delighted to see him – but as I was doing it my smile froze on my face and my words stuck in my throat for I recognized him as none other than that complete swine Baron von Schroeder who had been such a skunk to Lewis Richards and others of my friends. I had never seen him before out of a Hussar uniform and he certainly had me. I mumbled some lame excuse about having mistaken him for a friend and retreated with as much show of dignity as possible, and but I kicked myself afterwards. To think of me embracing a Hun that I dislike more than I do most of them!!!!!!!

Among others in the gang, I recognized Merton who had been assigned to the CRB and has been just about as disagreeable as possible. He came round and tried to shake hands, but I kept both my hands full of papers in an ostentatious way and had the same success as Grant Watson [No success at all]. Most of the German delegates were anxious to shake hands with our people when they had anything to say to them but so far as I observed, nobody slipped but me.

We did not have our dinner until nine and are dead beat. The Chief and I dined together and Lamont and Robinson came in for a few minutes talk while we were at it. And now to bed to be ready for the battles of the morrow.

Letter to Mary Gbison   On the train Brussels-Paris. Friday, March 14, 1919

We have finished our work and are bringing home the bacon with a certain amount of satisfaction. The previous mission that went to Spa failed to get what they were after and we were not at all sure that we would be any more successful, save that we could not face the idea of coming home empty handed.

I was up at a little after seven after really sleeping and got to work with the Chief. He felt that he could do with a day's rest and we got off a courier with many massages to be telephoned to Paris from Lille, among them one to have the Chief's car sent up for us to go back in on Sunday. He thought he would like to avail of this opportunity to see the Ypres Salient, but it will have to be done some other time. As the day wore on, he saw less and less attraction in the idea of spending an idle day in Brussels waiting for the car, and by late afternoon he was all for coming back with the rest of the crowd.

We put in a long morning, with one plenary sitting and a long go with the subcommittee, which let us out a little after one. The Chief went up to the Legation and I contented myself with leaving a card and going down to lunch at the Monnaie with Fred Chatfield.

At three, there was a meeting with the Belgian Food Minister and then the subcommittee got back to work. As I was not needed, I set out in one of the cars and looked in upon a number of people, not as many as I should have liked. I saw Madame Drugman and was able to give her good news of Myriam. Bebeth was there, all a-flutter over the news of Ynès' engagement and filled with misgivings. Ynès turned up later and went with me over to Albertine Wittouck's but she was not at home and I could only leave a card. I looked in and saw Guy and Adrienne who are in the throes of getting their house ready for Norman Armour, the new Secretary of the Legation, who has just arrived. From there to see Myriam's baby Anita, who has been laid up with the measles so that the other children had to be moved away. She was almost moved to tears at the thought of so much attention being paid her, but as shy as usual she had very little to say. After that I dropped in a minute to see Charley d'Assche who offered to sell me his palace for two million francs to be used as a Legation. The poor old man does not look as though he had long to live and I am sorry for he is a fine old soul. There were a lot of people I wanted to see but there was to be a plenary meeting at half past four and I did not want to be late. I might just as well have continued my pilgrimage indefinitely for the Boches had got into all sorts of wrangles and we paced the lobby until nearly eight before the financial outfit were ready to report. We were tired and grumpy when we did get in, and did not waste much time. After a pitiful bluff of not accepting the conditions, the Germans signed and we all scurried around to make our final preparations and get away. The train had steam up and when the last one of us climbed aboard, she pulled out and here we are on our way back to brag about what we have done.

It occurred to me that as we had two baggage cars on out train for buffers, I might seize the opportunity to bring back my plunder which has been here since 1916. I asked the Major in charge of the train and he said they would be delighted to have me bring along anything to the limit of the two cars. Chatfield got things down and aboard, five big cases and three small ones. It would have been hopeless to get them down any other way for a long time to come, so I am delighted. I dread to open them and see the ruin wrought by three years.

We had telegraphed from Paris for George Baker to come over to Brussels from London and join us for the conference. His message was delayed but he finally got into an airplane this afternoon. We found out quite by accident that he was there and got him aboard the train at the last minute. Airplane trips are getting so commonplace now that nobody gets in the least excited about them anymore. The front page of the *Daily Mail* has an advertisement of a regular air passenger service between Paris and Brussels, and I hear it is doing so well that the service will have to be increased.

Letter to Mary Gibson   Paris. Saturday, March 15, 1919

Our train got in this morning at a little before eight and we were at work in our offices before the morning was well started.

I found at Joe Grew's office a telegram from the Department saying that the Bill providing Legations for Prague and Warsaw had passed. It is quite probable that the President will want to make his own appointments and therefore I am going slow on any further preparations. There is nothing to be done until the matter has been put up to the President and he is so busy these first days of his return that I don't imagine he would be thrilled by the problem of what I am going to do. S. I shall settle down for a few days and possess my soul with as much patience as possible.

At the house we found John Beaver White and Prentiss Gray both just arrived from the United States. Prentiss wangled a trip on the [USS] *George Washington*[195] and came over with the President. They are setting out on their travels in the course of a few days. Later in the day, Colonel Causey turned up from Vienna and Trieste with all sorts of troubles bearing upon his work and all sorts of stories about how the troubles originated.

I lunched with the Chief, the new arrivals and George Baker at the Crillon and talked shop. Later I toddled home and engaged several orderlies in unpacking and repacking the belongings I had brought back from Brussels. I am very pleasantly disappointed as to the condition of the things. Practically nothing is really spoiled or broken and I must hand it to old Gustave that he packed them all beautifully. I am repacking them so as to be able to leave as much stuff as possible here in Paris if I do start out again for another spot.

I hear that Wallace Young has been appointed Consul at Prague.

Letter to Mary Gibson				Paris. Sunday, March 16, 1919

In the morning, I pottered about in our new offices and in the Crillon where I yarned with Joe Grew, Dulles, Herter and Dolbeare. I tried to get to see the Secretary [Lansing] as Joe thought it would be good thing, but he was just going out so I forbore.

I lunched with the Bliss's – just the two of them and had a really good time. They have both been laid up most of the winter with touches of the flu but are now on the upgrade.

Late in the afternoon, I went out with the Chief, George Baker and Bob Taft for a drive in one of our new Cadillacs. We went out through Bois [de Bologne], St. Cloud to Versailles and beyond, getting back about half past six.

Bob had got a box at the Opera Comique for the *Tales of Hoffmann*[196] and we all went, even the Chief enjoying it and coming away whistling the barcarole. I believe there is a low plot of some sort to get him out on that sort of parties every now and then.

---

[195] The *SS George Washington* was a German built ocean liner connecting the USA and France since 1909. On April 14, 1912, it had sent an iceberg warning to the *RMS Titanic* which soon after sank at the designated spot. At the outbreak of war in 1914, it had been interned by the then neutral United States. In 1917, as *USS George Washington*, it transported US-American troops to the Western Front. After the Armistice, it moved more than 80,000 passengers – the most prominent being US President Wilson – between the two continents.

[196] Opéra fantastique by Jacques Offenbach (1819–1880).

Letter to Mary Gibson   Paris. Monday, March 17, 1919

There was no pouch from Washington today and consequently no letters from you. I got nothing all day but one letter from Djina Apponyi which came through our Legation in Bern, asking me to take her some packages which had been prepared for her in Switzerland with clothing for her baby, etc.

I spent most of the day pottering about trying to find out if and when I was to go to Prague. The President is still swamped in big things and nobody wants to bother him with my affairs, so I am still biting my fingers and honing for a little certainty.

I lunched at Voisin's with Mr. Stettinius and the Chief – and strange to say we talked shop. Mrs. Harriman was there with Dorothy Cane and allowed that she was coming out to dine with us at the house tomorrow night. It seems that George Baker had a burst of speed and decided that we needed some feminine society. Mrs. Harriman is going home in the course of the next ten days.

Yesterday Dr. Kramář sent over and asked me to go to see him, but I was not able to make it. This afternoon, I went over but he was not in. I had a yarn with Novák and thus showed my honorable intentions. From there I went on to Clarence's studio which is just around the corner and returned to him the bundle of etching which I have been lugging around with me for the past five years. He is just out of the hospital where he went for a slight operation on his throat, but says that he is now quite all right.

I shall probably blow up unless I get some sort of settled job soon so don't be surprised if you hear of my explosion.

Letter to Mary Gibson   Paris. Tuesday, March 18, 1919

No letters from home but now my hopes are fixed on tomorrow.

I am much bored by the failure to get around to settling my affairs. I don't want to undertake a number of things that should be done at the ARA because if I do, I am more than likely to have to lay them down unfinished and go my way. I don't want to go to Joe Grew and start giving him a helping hand for fear I shall get stuck there. So there is nothing more for me to do but loaf about waiting for a decision, doing such little odd jobs as I can sandwich into each day. If and when the decision does come, I shall give three rousing cheers whatever it may be.

I spent a good part of the day at the Crillon trying to push on the reins but without any results. I led Joe Grew out to lunch at the Ritz where we saw a lot of people and got something remotely resembling a meal for something closely resembling a small fortune. Joe is about as anxious to get me off as I am to go, but I don't notice that anything happens.

This evening Willy Buckler and Mrs. Harriman came to dine and there was a large amount of conversation which lasted until after eleven. And now I am off to bed to dream that I have a steady job where I can work all day and don't have to eat my heart out sitting around.

Letter to Mary Gibson.   Paris. Wednesday, March 19, 1919

What is the matter with Gifford Pinchot?[197] I can't understand his attacking the Chief who has done more than one favor for him. If you get hold of any of this material, I should like to have a look at it. A lot of people are getting excited about the possibility of Hoover and are beginning the bomb throwing to spoil his chances. If they only knew how little enthusiasm the gentleman has for the job, they could save themselves a lot of trouble. Nothing but brute force would lead him to touch the job. He has had a long season of public service and knows just about how much satisfaction there is in it. Furthermore, he has neglected his personal affairs since the day the war broke out and his one selfish desire is to get back and straighten out his business so that he can have something in the bank to pay his taxes with. He does not care a hoot for the sensation of having people bow down before him because of his job and that cuts out one of the most compelling motives that usually drive men into public life. I think he would make a first class President but I don't for a minute think he would take the nomination unless there were some great crisis to convince him that it was his patriotic duty. He has enough sense to know that he has made one of the few great reputations to come out of the war and that further public service won't add any luster to it. I wish some of the mud-slingers could realize this.

I also have two letters from Arthur Page, one bringing a welcome check for $606.18 for all sorts of odds and ends of royalties. Just to make it seem bigger, he sent it in the form of a check for "three thousand two hundred ninety six francs ninety four centimes." It comes in very handy just now when I may have a good many things to buy and unless you need it, I shall salt it down in my account here. If you do want it, telegraph and I'll shoot it along. I can make out all right, so do as seems easiest to you.

---

197 Gifford Pinchot, head of the US Forest Service 1905–1912, was highly critical of what he perceived as Hoover's autocratic manner in running the Food Administration and the ARA. See Kendrick A. Clements, *Life of Herbert Hoover: Imperfect Visionary 1918–1928* (Palgrave, 2010) and Hoover Too Autocratic," *New York Tribune*, April 17, 1920.

Among other things, Arthur says:

"The other day a writing friend of mine asked me if I had any material on Mr. Brand Whitlock, as some of the Minister's friends had asked him to act as a publicity agent to sort of spread the name and fame of that gentleman abroad from the housetops and see whether the Presidential lightning would strike. I told him I didn't have any information but if he was going to make any money out of the proceeding, it was all right to go ahead, but he must look upon it as a purely temporary operation for it wasn't a job that would last long. I struck some people in Washington the other day who didn't know I had ever discussed such a matter and they told me that there were only two people whose heads stuck above the common herd at present, and they were a certain Food Controller and a certain ex-Secretary of the Treasury.[198] My on private opinion is "The Great White Chief" is going to run himself, for he has pruned off all the other shoots on the tree in order that all the sap may run up the main stem."

I knew Brand Whitlock had it in mind but did not suppose anybody was going to spend real money on it this far ahead.

I have put in most of the day in the same old way, trying to find out what the Powers want me to do, but so far I am as completely in the dark as I was yesterday. I get called into various offices each day and told that the situation is such that it is vitally important that somebody should go to Prague at once. I agree. There it ends. To begin again the next day.

I lunched with Mr. Henry White who had asked in Eynac, one of the younger deputies. He is blessed with the esprit vif and talked well, mostly about politics in France. He was in the flying business through most of the war, piloting bombing planes and talked well about it, chiefly about the exploits of other people.

A family dinner tonight with Mr. Albert Strauss as the lone guest. We are a strong lot for staying at home evenings.

Late in the afternoon, I dropped in on the Whitridge's for a cup of tea. Miss Hare was there very much interested in getting "tickets" to see the signature of the Treaty! I don't suppose more than a hundred thousand other people have had the same idea – and none of them will manage to get squeezed into the gallery at Versailles to see the performance. The Gallerie des Glaces[199] is a great room, but I doubt whether all the principle members of all the delegations can be got into it.

I know I shan't be there, so I refuse to worry about the others.

---

[198] Herbert Hoover and William Gibbs McAdoo.
[199] The famous Hall of Mirrors were the Versailles Treaty was signed on June 28, 1919.

Letter to Mary Gibson   Paris. Thursday, March 20, 1919

Another boring day with very little done to justify me for eating three meals.

Joe Grew summoned me to help him prepare some shells to be fired at the Commissioners about the urgent need of getting people to Prague and Warsaw. I ground out a memorandum for him and that was about the only thing I did.

Arnold Whitridge came in growling about being sent into Germany to act as G-2 [Intelligence] to the Third Army. He would like to go to Prague and if I go I may ask for him as Military Attaché.

Colonel Buckey, from Rome, also eased in and allowed that he ought to be made Military Attaché there – not that he would care to go there, oh no – but because it would be a fitting recognition of his public service in discovering the Czechoslovaks long before anybody else knew how to pronounce them. He admitted that they admired him more than any other living man and said that he was really considered the FATHER OF THEIR COUNTRY, which is going some. He said it would be a great thing for me to go in with the prestige of his name, etc., etc. It must be wonderful to feel like that about yourself.

Cartier, the Belgian Minister at Washington, arrived today and came to dine. He has come over to be present in Brussels during the visit of the President. Needless to say, he has not been home since before the war and is in a hurry to get there.

Wellington has also arrived and was brought up to dine. He is the father of a bouncing boy born shortly before he sailed. He has a bad case of it, going around with pockets full of snap shots of the boy and describing him in the terms one usually employs about the fish that got away.

It is colder than Greenland and rains every time you go out. The buds have come out on the trees and are now getting the most uncomfortable time they are ever likely to have. There is snow in the south of France and I should not be surprised to see some here.

Letter to Arthur Bliss Lane   Paris, March 20, 1919

I had hoped to telegraph you something definite before this as to our common plans but so far nothing has developed. Each day I get up with high hopes that the Powers that rule over our destinies will settle things one way or the other. Each morning I hurry down to the Crillon and put in a busy day trying to find some way of hastening a decision, and each night I drag my weary way homeward with the same amount of knowledge that I set out with in the morning.

I am told today that the Commissioners are going to "take the matter up" tomorrow and consider making a recommendation to the President "in the premises". If they do, that's that. If they don's we are just as far ahead as we were before.

Seriously, I do believe that something will start tomorrow and that within a day or two we shall know where we are. I am quite shameless in pushing the matter because I feel so strongly that somebody ought to go to Prague and go at once. Trying to force a decision in this way may destroy my own chances of going, but that is one of the penalties of taking this European situation seriously.

We have been having some comic correspondence with Phillips about you. Mr. Lansing's telegram to the Ambassador was merely by way of inquiry before asking the Department to make the assignment and consequently the Department had not heard anything about either of us going to Prague. Phillips was equal to the occasion however and came at us with a telegram saying that Mr. Page told him that Gibson wanted you to go to Prague to open the Legation. He tactfully inquired whether it would not be better to have the Legation opened by a Minister and added as a sop to us that you could if so desired, go along as Secretary of Legation. Not having heard of my going to Prague, he probably assumed I had taken charge of the diplomatic service in Europe and would make wholesale transfers unless locked up soon. However, I drafted a telegram which the Secretary sent explaining matters and then other helpful citizens got to work and so far as I am able to learn two other messages have gone explaining things – and some of the explanations are more or less correct. At any rate, Phillips cannot complain that we don't answer his telegrams.

Jay's man-eating telegram never came but I did get a very nice letter from him in which he mourned your loss and wrote you an unsolicited testimonial I should have been proud to have.

I am maintaining a peaceful blockade of all those in authority and as soon as there is a word of news, I shall pass it along by telegram.

And I hope it won't be much longer.   Yours, [Hugh]

Letter to Peter Jay   Paris, March 20, 1919

I was delighted to get your good letter of March 16th particularly because you do not tear me limb from limb for asking for Lane.

As Lane has probably told you, things have assumed a different aspect since my telegram was sent and there is now a good deal of doubt as to whether I shall go to Prague at all. I was going on the theory that Congress had not provided for a regular Legation; that being assumed the Secretary wanted to send me as a Diplomatic Agent until the next Congress should pass the necessary legislation. Fortunately, we found out that the legislation did get through at the last minute and that the post can be filled with a regular Minister. It may be that in view of the urgency of the situation, they will want me to go in temporarily as Agent and let the Minister come romping along at his leisure. However, that is yet to be settled and until it is settled, I am making no plans.

You ask about transfers and promotions, but so far as I have been able to observe there have not been any since the cataclysm which disrupted the London Embassy. For the immediate present, there is nothing extensive in prospect but the minute the Peace Conference is over, I look for an epoch-making upheaval and am particularly anxious to dig in before it comes.

The Diplomatic & Appropriation Bill created four new posts, four, COUNT THEM, Warsaw, Prague, Belgrade, and Sofia. There are also two other vacancies, La Paz and Bankok, so perhaps there will be a chance for some promotions inside the service. I very much hope there will be something of the sort; otherwise I look for acute discouragement among the best elements in the service and some wholesale resignations.

The Constantinople matter was settled by giving to the War Trade Board delegate the title of Commissioner [Heinz]. I don't know whether he had ever been in that part of the world, but he seems to be doing well and is having help from Admirals and other high dignitaries.

I was slated to start for Bucharest and Constantinople last week, but the Prague matter came up a few hours before the train was to start and I was ordered to stay behind. So far as I can make out now, I might as well have gone and had a look at that part of the world.

Yesterday afternoon, I got a burst of speed for the first time in many moons and went to the Whitridge's and clamored for tea. Whitridge was mourning the fact that he has just been ordered to Germany as part of the G2 [Intelligence] outfit of the Third Army. He gets off next week.

We sorrow that there is no immediate hope of seeing Miss McCook over here.

Is there any chance that you will come up here while the Conference is on? If you do, head this way and I am here, do send me a blast in advance. I have given up my flat and am living with Mr. Hoover but dare say I could contrive to find a place for you to lay your head.

My very best to all the family.   Yours, [Hugh]

And I'll say thanks about Lane even before I know whether I am going and whether I can have him.

Letter to Mary GibsonParis. Friday, March 21, 1919

No letters and no excitement today. It is still as cold as Greenland and we are wearing heaving coats and sniffing at the calendar.

I lunched with the Whitridges' with Miss Hare, Col. Mott, George Howe and a French girl whose name I didn't get. She is a neighbor of ours and I have seen her before. She sports a Croix de Guerre with a palm and two stars and a couple of other war medals, so she must have had her share of the big show.

The Commissioners have addressed a memorandum to the President about the Prage business and I hope that something will be done soon so that I can either go or settle down to something steady here. The Kellogg's are back and he wants me to go with him to Warsaw on Thursday. If nothing better develops in the meantime, I may do it. Mrs. Kellogg is going home very soon and says she may see you.

I pottered around the Crillon the usual amount today with the usual amount of success. Early in the afternoon I got discouraged and came home to write letters and try to keep warm. I have abandoned all pretense of doing anything constructive at the ARA until I get a decision one way or the other as to my fate.

Letter to Arthur Bliss LaneParis, March 21, 1919

The mail room at the Embassy yesterday disgorged your letter of March 7th and I was even more pleased with it than with the princely check which accompanied it. Don't misunderstand me and feel that it would be more tactful to hold back further checks for I have no feeling against them.

I think you have it right about the next President. A lot of people like Brand Whitlock will put their heads up just long enough to get them knocked off and along about Convention time, it will be observed that there ain't but one candidate. As to the well-known Food Controller [Hoover] you mention, nothing but physical violence would drag him into the arena. In the first place, he has an abnormal dislike for the *souplesse dorsale* [flexibility, back-bending] with which he would be surrounded in the office. In the second place, he has enough sense to know that he has made a whale of a reputation in his present job and that the Big One could not add to it and might on the contrary, land him in the scrap heap. In the third place, he has now neglected his business for more than four years and has a not unnatural desire to pick up some of the pieces and put them together. The business has suffered a lot and won't get well until its papa devotes his own attention to it. So, I don't believe that he will have any truck with the idea unless some crisis develops where persuasive friends can convince him that it is a public duty for him to go to it – and I don't see much chance of that.

I don't know anything about the chances of the other gentleman you mention but should not like to put very much on his name [McAdoo].

But if we can get along without any Government at all as at present, why should we worry?

I have the same disease that you report as afflicting all other returning heroes. I have made up my mind that nothing will do for me but an island where I can go swimming and raise chickens and vegetables and keep everybody off but those I ask to come and stay. And I will pay expenses by writing blood and thunder stories quite as good as those of CLEEX,[200] and they will be published by Doubleday, Page & CO. and I will amass riches and live happily ever after. You are all invited to come on the first expedition and stay always. Soon after I had announced this plan, I got an intimation from Spa that there was an island that I could get on advantageous terms, namely and to wit HELIGOLAND.[201] I steered clear of that, I also wanted a place in the sun, with a green brolly. Keep your eye open for the right place. It sounds fine just now, but I am ready to bet that the place would be for sale cheap within three months.

The past few weeks have been full of movement as far as I am concerned but rather barren of news. I have commuted between Paris, Bern and Brussels with occasional trips in this fair land. Most of the time I have been on a leash, ready to start at a minute's notice to Prague, Bucharest and Constantinople. Last week I was going to the two last named places but a couple of hours before the train left, the Secretary [Lansing] sent for me and said he wanted me to go to Prague instead. I let Dr. Taylor go off alone weeping bitterly and since then I have sat here waiting for someone to give me the word to start for Prague. Each morn I raise and go down to the Crillon and try to get things settled and each night I crawl back to my lair having got just exactly nowhere. Even at this moment, however, I believe the Commissioners are sitting on my case, having abandoned Europe to its fate while mine is regulated. I hope and pray that they will decide the matter once and for all for I am growing old in uncertainty.

The other day, I could not stand the suspense any longer, so burst from my cell with a hell of a yell and went to Brussels for the parley with the Huns about their ships. It was worth the journey, particularly for those of us who had been there before under different circumstances. As you will remember, the first mission which went to Spa failed to get the ships and it was decided we must bring up our heavy artillery – which explains how I got in. Admiral Wemyss presided as it was a matter involving salt water. On his right at the conference sat Hoover. On

---

200 Cleex of Scotland Yard is a character in the stories by T.W. Hanshew.
201 Heligoland is a small archipelago in the North Sea and part of the German state.

his left was Sir Joseph Maclay, the Shipping Controller. We got Francqui in as Belgian representative merely for the poetic justice of the thing. It was at our behest that this meeting took place in Brussels as it seemed a more fitting place for the Huns to make their supreme appeal for food.

There were seventeen people in the delegation of baby-killers and we had a few more on our side. The proceedings were conducted according to the most approved methods of wooden Indians. All remarks were addressed to the empty air which immediately resounded with the death cries of many languages as they were massacred by the interpreters. The first big meeting broke up into three subcommittees on Food, Shipping and Finance, and I may say that we polished off the food hounds hours before either of the other committees came up for air. The Huns evidently have not read the public prints with any care for they do not seem to understand that they have been licked. They looked dejected enough but kept talking about German credit and the future of German trade relations and all sorts of comic things of that sort. They made several bluffs of breaking off the negotiations because of the severity of our conditions, but we showed no interest in this and they came through just in time to sign up and get a late dinner on the second day.

The only disgraceful incident was supplied by me. Between meetings a beaming individual bore down upon me, pouring out greetings and calling on heaven to witness how splendid it was that we should meet in such happy times after all we had been through together. I wasn't quite sure who he was and is the rule in such cases, I was twice as cordial as normal. I wrung his hand and assured him that I was delighted to see him after we had all succeeded in knocking the block off the filthy Huns. I thought he looked a little queer at this, and suddenly my words stuck in my throat for I recognized him as Schroeder, a horrible little swine who had been unusually obnoxious all through the war. I made it plain that there had been a mistake and turned my back on him, but at that I shall go down to the tomb regretting that I did not recognize him and insult him in the first place. My only excuse is that I had never seen him in anything but a Hussar uniform and that he was an entirely different looking specimen in cits [civilian clothing]. And think of the little hound talking about those happy times. Blah !!

However, we got their bally ships and are going to give them the food that they would have had a long time ago if the Americans had had their way. That is, unless the sailors continue to hold up the ships in German ports.[202]

Nothing much to report of what is going on in the Peace Mission. Joe Grew is all wore out. Leland has a fresh supply of bird seed and is chirping contentedly.

---

[202] A revolt of sailors in Northern Germany had triggered the November Revolution.

Phil Patchin is in the depths and allows that the war was preferable any day to this peace. Ralph Hayes is getting over a bad case of mumps and has acquired enough strength to send me a daily bulletin of foolishness, nonsense and verse, etc. I don't know what he does the rest of the time, but he has an office in the Crillon. All other members of the Mission are recovering from Sam Blythe's article about them in the *Saturday Evening Post*. What was the matter with Sam aside from being turned out of his room at the Crillon and having to show a pass at the front door?

Pooh[203] is getting ready to sail for home in the course of the next few weeks. He will doubtless see you and give you a lot of the recent gossip.

If you see Martin Egan, please tell him from me that he is a porch climbing robber. He carried away my two most cherished possessions, the life of the great little man and also the g.l.m.'s magnus opus. If returned, no questions will be asked. If I can get up sufficient energy, I shall write and insult him personally.

Everybody in the diplomatic service is watching anxiously to see what is to be done with the four new posts that were created by the Diplomatic and Consular Appropriation Bill which was passed and signed on March 4th. Four – count them – four, Warsaw, Prague, Belgrade and Sofia. There are also two more posts vacant, Bangkok and La Paz. This seems to be the last call for promotions during this Administration for there is little likelihood of so many posts being vacant again. There is a great deal of discouragements and unless there are at least one or two promotions of service men in filling these six posts, I look for wholesale resignments when the Peace Conference in over. That is not so bad for the immediate future for I suppose the service can struggle along somehow without several of us, but it will mean that the service will form now on attract an even less suitable lot of men than it does now and that ten and fifteen years from now we shall not have proper crews to man our Missions while other countries will have increased their lead on us.

Telephones ring, slaves enter from time to time, children fall down stairs and anyhow I am in no stated to recall the numbers of things I have meant to tell you. I'll make another try some soon day, and in the meantime with all sorts of messages to Mollie and the youngsters, I am Yours [Hugh]

---

203 It is not clear who Gibson is referring to here.

Letter to Colonel William Causey. Paris, March 21, 1919

I had hoped to be in your midst before this but one complication after another has arisen and it looks as though I might not get to Prague after all. I shall probably be waiting to greet you here with a long white beard when you return to Paris.

In the meantime, will you have somebody fire along the letters that have been awaiting me in Vienna. Don't bother for the present about sending back my bag and other junk. I may manage to get to that general part of the world and attend to that end of things myself. However, I should like to see the letters.

If by any chance you see Mrs. Egan, please tell her to let me know when she can be expected through Paris. I think there is a good story on ice for her here, one that would interest her and incidentally help out our Uncle Samuel.

It has turned cold as Greenland and we have reverted to fur coats. The buds all came out the foolish things do each year, and then the cold comes along and nipped them the way it does nearly every year. I pray for summer so that I can be comfortably warm while I am praying for winter so that I can be comfortably cool, if you know what I mean.

My best to anybody who remembers me. Yours [Hugh]

Letter to Mary Gibson Paris. Saturday, March 22, 1919

The pouches continue to come in empty. So far as I am concerned the Government might as well save itself the trouble of sending them.

Most of the day I have spent in the Crillon talking with various people and trying to understand the details of the work done by the Commission on Czechoslovak boundaries. Heaven be praised I was not put on any boundary commission for it is enough to drive one raving mad.

I lunched at the Kirk's and found there the Bucklers, the Dulles', and Mrs. John Garrett who is just down from The Hague.

Tomorrow we hope to clear out, all of us, and go for a day's motoring with a visit to Rheims and the Chemin des Dames.[204] If we stay in town there is plenty for the Chief to do, but if he goes away it all waits over until the next day, so off we go.

---

[204] The Chemin des Dames (French: Ladies' Path) is a striking mountain range in the triangle of the cities of Laon, Soissons and Rheims in northern France and had been an attractive excursion destination since the 18th century. It also saw some of the most fervent battles the First World War, causing the destruction of most villages along its track.

Letter to Edward Bell   Paris, March 22, 1919

Phil [Patchin] has let me read the letter you wrote him about my going to Prague and the means that should be used in communication with that charming city. The whole matter becomes of academic interest because of the fact that I did not get away after all.

Those in authority here thought that Congress had failed to pass the Diplomatic and Consular Appropriation Bill and that consequently there was no provision for a Minister at Prague. Feeling that somebody should be there, the Secretary [Lansing] ordered me to go as Diplomatic Agent. In the course of the necessary arrangements, I learned that the Bill had passed and that there was nothing to prevent the sending of a regular Minister. So my trip was called off and all hands are now busy respectfully wondering who is to be sent.

If I get anywhere near the gent who does go, I shall make some remarks on the subject of codes.

The new Bill creates four new posts, as you have probably observed, Warsaw, Prague, Belgrade and Sofia. Aside from there, there are vacancies at La Paz and Bangkok. Here's hoping that there will be something in the nature of promotions from the service. It will be pretty discouraging unless some of the Elder Statesmen get a boost. There will probably be a decision as to some of these posts within the next few days.

I was delighted to see that Hall got away with his election.[205] Eustace Percy seems to have the same sort of ambitions and has gone home to have a try.

I had hoped to get over to see you before this, but have been rottenly seeding since I came back from my interrupted leave in Switzerland. I revived enough to go up to Brussels and see the Huns give up their ships. I nearly had a dangerous relapse due to the fact that I mistook a demonstrative Hun for somebody else and shook him warmly by the hand before I recognized him. The only thing that saved my health was the fact that I insulted him immediately afterward in public. And he was one of the swine we had all sworn to be particularly insulting to at the first opportunity.

I saw Lundy when he went through here on his way south. Lunched with [Sheldon] Crosby when he was here but have not seen any of the other wanderers. I hate the thought of the Embassy now that all hands have been scattered.

Is there any prospect of you coming over again soon? I hope to be here for some time but if nothing better develops I may pull out for Warsaw next week to

---

205 Reginald W. Hall was elected to the British Parliament in early 1919.

be gone a month or so. To my sorrow, I was pulled off the Constantinople train just when I thought that trip was a sure thing.

Let me have some news of you and your flock when you have the time to write.

When you do, I'll send you the best Limerick yet. Yours [Hugh]

Letter to Mary Gibson   Paris. Sunday, March 23, 1919

We have had a long pull today but I sit me down nonetheless to thump out a few lines before I tumble into bed.

We got off this morning in two cars at nine, Hoover, John White, Bob Taft, George Baker, Cols. Atwood and Barber, and HSG [Gibson]. The cars, Cadillac limousines, are brand new and in perfect shape. We went over familiar country through Meaux, Château-Thierry, and then along the south bank of the Marne to beyond Jaulgonne where the Huns first crossed. There we crossed the river and struck out for Rheims. At half past one, we drew up by the road on the side of the hill dominated Rheims and had our lunch with the Cathedral and all the Rheims country as a setting. After we had polished off the elaborate meal that had been packed in our hampers, we drove on to the Cathedral and had a good close range look at it. It was somewhat different from our last visit when we sat in the top of a tree and divided our thoughts between the sights before us and the chances of the Huns spotting us and landing a shell in our midst. On the whole, I prefer this way of sightseeing. It was surprising to all of us to see how little the Cathedral was damaged. Most of the statutes on the façade have all the edges knocked off them, a good many have their heads missing and a great part of the decorative designs are worn down as though with extreme old age. There is one great piece missing from the northern tower and the roof has suffered badly, although it is now patched up with some temporary makeshift. The people of the neighborhood frankly believe that the preservation of the church is miraculous. They point out that everything else in the neighborhood is a complete wreck and that more shells burst around the cathedral than anywhere else in town. It is a fact that even when the bombardment was at its worst, it was reasonably safe to sleep in a house a few blocks to one side or the other of the line of fire. And there is something ghostly about the place that is far more impressive than the churches that are completely destroyed. I hope that they will not try to restore the place as it was before the war. It will require very little work to make it structurally safe, and its battle scars are surely a part of its history that should be kept.

There were a few people in the square, British, French and Americans, officers, red crossers, YMCA, etc, who had come from Paris or nearby towns. A few people of the town are back on the job and had set up little booths before the Cathedral doors to sell post cards and photographs. One of the more enterprising ones had gathered up a lot of German steel helmets and had them for sale. Many's the yarn that will be built up around these hats bought four or five months after the Boche threw down his arms.

From Rheims we struck across country down the Vesle, through Fiames and up to the Chemin des Dames. That was about the most complete and utter mess I have seen yet. Broad stretches of country where the shell holes overlapped and it was hard to distinguish one from another. The earth was so foul with gasses and other poisons that there was practically no grass growing and it is said that there is no prospect of any for a long time to come. We got out and walked now and then to let Barber explain some phase of the operations, but we walked gingerly for the ground was littered with hand grenades, shells and aerial torpedoes. There were wires buried in the ground connected with the Lord knows what and there were helmets, boxes and cases scattered all over the place filled with April fool tricks for the unwary. I am glad this was a wary crowd for the fool killer has been busy in all this district for months. Every day we have fresh stories of people who have been killed on the battle fields through trying to pick up things that looked innocent and were loaded for bear, or who had tripped over some harmless looking bit of wire. The toll of children is heavy and the grownups don't seem to know much better. I suppose the farmers of the region will go on plowing for years, occasionally being spattered all over the landscape through deplorable effectiveness of modern explosives. I'd like to see them put the German prisoners to work picking up all the litter so that white [changed in pencil to "other"] people may be saved. We climbed around over some of the forts for half an hour or so and then got underway for home just before five. We bore off for Soissons, but just as we came in sight of the Cathedral towers, we were held up by sentries who sent us by another road on a wide detour. I did not hear what they said to the chauffeurs, but we soon saw the reason for it. When we got out into the open country, we could look back to the road we should have taken, we saw a big fire burning near where we would have passed. As we were sizing it up, there came a loud explosion and a big cloud of yellowish smoke. Then another and louder explosion, and a cloud of black smoke. A few seconds later, a star shell[206] went off and the brightly burning light went sizzling up into the sky and came lazily down through the smoke. We doubled back and passed within a quarter of a mile of the fire just before we got into town. Presently, I began to feel a burning in my

---

[206] Type of ammunition which produces a shower of stars in order to illuminate enemy positions.

head and without warning let go a prodigious sneeze. While I was recovering, Bob Taft reached convulsively for a handkerchief and did the same just before Colonel Atwood loosed off a rip snorter. The chauffeur and orderly on the box began and new came into town sneezing away in chorus. By the time we came to the Cathedral, we had to stop and get out. There we tramped up and down for a few minutes making an awful row. When we got back to town we found the other's car had had the same experience and that everybody was a little blear eyed. The first explosion was evidently some gas shell and we got a little whiff of it as we drove by. At present, we do not intend to ask for permission to wear wound stripes. Prentiss Gray is back from Brussels but I have not seen anything of him so far. John White goes back to London in the morn, and thus our family changes from day to day.

Tomorrow I resume my guard at the Crillon with the same old hope of getting something decided one way or the other.

Letter to Mary Gibson Paris. Monday, March 24, 1919

Another day and a pouch day at that, but with nothing from you. I didn't have a thing worth reading and am consequently disgruntled.

Our little whiff of gas yesterday lasted us all until today. I wheezed through a good part of the night, nothing painful but just a little trouble in breathing. This morning we all had slight sore throats which wore off toward mid-day. It was just as well that we did not dally by the roadside and watch the fire. But it is a great thing to have been gassed on the battlefield if you don't have to be too precise as to dates.

I lunched with the Chief and Oswald Garrison Villard who has just come back from Germany with his usual sympathy for them and some remarks that got under our hide. After we could stand it no longer, the Chief and I opened up on him and let him have both barrels. He took refuge in agreement and then we changed the subject but some of the things I am sure he will remember for some time.

The President has not yet been able to settle my little troubles but it is hoped that he will do so soon. With the lid blown off Hungary, it is more urgent that ever that somebody be got to Prague before the lid blows off there too.[207] The Central European countries seem to be in for it but there are a number of things we can do

---

207 On March 21, 1919, the Hungarian Bolsheviks under the leadership of Béla Kun had overthrown the Karolyi government and proclaimed a Hungarian Soviet Republic on about a quarter of the country's prewar territory. It should last only 133 days.

to stem the tide if we get people on the ground at once and I am all for speed, even if it means that somebody else is sent.

The Chief dined out tonight and we were not numerous at table, Atwood and Barber and Hart and Taft and I. And now I am ready for an early to bed.

[Added note found only in Secret Log] March 24th

Allen Dulles led me gently by the hand into a quiet room this afternoon and after some preliminaries said that it had reached the Powers that I had a sister who had vigorously attacked the President thereby prejudicing my chances of being made Minister. He inquired as to the real facts for the friendly purpose of smoothing out difficulties. After I said my say, he said he had already told them – whoever them may be – that he thought I had no sister and that it was all cock and bull stuff. People seem to have little to do these days.

Letter to Arthur Beaupre Paris, March 24, 1919

I had a letter from Mrs. Beaupre a long time ago – so long ago that I am ashamed to make it any more definite – and ever since then I have planned to sit me down and try to write a decent letter. But these days are just about as bad as they can be for letter writing and I have neglected everybody.

If you had seen the way I have been flying about, I don't believe you would be very severe with me, however. Since the beginning of this year, I have been six times in Vienna, three times in Prague, twice in Budapest, twice in Brussels, twice to Switzerland, and have been to Trieste, Fiume, Agram, Belgrade, Ostrava, Kharwin, Telplitz and goodness only knows how many other places. And between times, I try to blow up and do nothing until it is time to set out again. In the charming month of January, I spent twenty-two nights in the train. Travel is not up to its peace time comfort over here these days but even at that the travel did not bother me so much as two people who remarked to me separately on the occasion of my last return to Paris: "How do you manage it to be always on these joy rides, pretty soft!" It took two men and a boy to hold me until they had been carried to a place of safety. Of course, it is all very interesting and I would not miss it for anything on earth, but just the same I shall heave a sigh of relief when it is all over and I can settle down to some quiet job that lasts so many hours a day where you are sure nothing will happen to surprise you. I think I shall take an oath never to amount to anything once peace has broken out. My present leaning is toward a small island off the coast of Lower California where I can raise vegetables and chickens and have only friends come to stay and help tear everybody else to pieces. You and Mrs. Beaupre are invited to come by the first boat and remain always.

And at that the charm of the place would probably wear out for all hands in a few months and we should be wondering how Broadway looks.

But if you do see any good looking island off the coast of Florida that is for sale at a price within the reach of a poor diplomaticker, you might let me know.

I have been away from the haunts of men so much lately that I have not seen much of anybody that could supply me with gossip but nonetheless there are a good many of our old friends floating around this part of the world from time to time.

Norman Davis is a great man and sits in the seats of the mighty, holding forth learnedly and well on subjects of finance. I have seen a good deal of him because everything overlaps onto finance and we have to work together on some new problem every week.

Sanborn is stationed in Spain, but comes up here about once a month and is seen flitting by in the distance. He was a Captain not long ago but now I understand he is a Major. He has done a great job in Spain since we came into the war; he was the chief purchasing officer for the AEF in Spain.

Poor Cecil Carter died in Madrid just a few weeks ago. He had been stronger than ever in his life, but was taken with the influenza and snuffed out in a few days. He came over in the beginning of 1916 and went through the mill in an O.T.C. When he died, he was a Captain.

Travis Coxe is still in Paris, I believe. He enlisted when we first went into the war and came over about a year ago. He was a corporal at last accounts. I was rather peevish with him because he could just as well have had a commission in a place where his French and Spanish would have been of some use, but he got hold of some comic idea that it was his duty to enlist and that if he was worthy of it promotion would be forced upon him. They put him to work as a telephone operator and there he stuck until we contrived to get him a job thumping a typewriter and writing foolish things on little cards to be filed in an index. It is harder for a man in his position to get a commission that it would be to get into the Kingdom of Heaven, and I fear me he will go home as Corporal Coxe. And he might have been some real use if he had gone into the Intelligence Section with a commission. He paid his first call on me one Saturday morning at breakfast time when I had a flock of officers up from GHQ. The concierge made him come up the service staircase instead of using the lift and the servants put him in the kitchen and sent me word that there was a soldier there who wanted to see me. They could not quite make out what had happened when they saw him rescued and brought in to breakfast with his elders and betters. We rubbed that in on him hard.

Harry Maude is here but I have not seen him very often. He is gorgeous as a Colonel on the Staff; with red bands on his cap and gold lace all over his person. He has a very nice flat on the rue de Rivoli with a view over the Tuilleries and dispenses hospitality with much enthusiasm. I am getting too old and feeble to get out much evenings and have not been to see him for many months. He has done good work and won the DSO.

Major Chase came in one day a few months ago and I sent him off in the direction of his desire, but have never seen him since. He has been here several times but I have always been away from Paris and have missed him. Mrs. Chase travels with him all the time which is quite an achievement in these days of passport restrictions.

Edward Bell I have not seen for some time. He came over the latter part of December for a few days in order to tell the Peace Conference how to accomplish its tasks, but I went off in the midst of his visit and have not been over to look him up since. He never fails to speak of you and Mrs. Beaupre and talk over all sorts of things I had forgotten. Habana days seem to have a special flavor for him and he treasures every detail and paints me pictures of old times as though I had never been there. He was the only member of the London Embassy Staff who asked to be moved after Mr. Page's resignation – and in accordance with the best traditions of our service he was almost the only one who was not moved. The others have been scattered far and wide over the globe but E. Bell stays put.

That is about the only move that has taken place in the service for many months. Frank Gunther has gone as First Secretary to The Hague. John Garrett is going straightway off on leave and let Frank try his hand at being Chargé. Pennoyer – I don't know whether you ever knew him – is sent to Lisbon. Sheldon Crosby goes to Rome as First. Beale Davis to Bucharest and Morgan to Copenhagen. That is a pretty good upheaval for one lone post.

In all probability there will be something epoch-making before long for there will be a lot of young secretaries turned loose when the Peace Commission finishes its work. In the last Dip. & Cons. Appropriation Bill, Congress created four new posts – four, COUNT THEM – Warsaw, Prague, Belgrade, and Sofia. In addition to that there are vacancies in to other charming places, La Paz and Bangkok. Out of that it is hoped that there will be one or two promotions from the service. If not, I fear that discouragement will be so general as to cause wholesale resignations. That would not be so bad just now because the service could probably stagger along without its Elder Statesmen, but it would mean that a less suitable lot of men would be attracted from now on and that ten and fifteen years from now there would be no decent force of Secretaries. On the other hand, a very few promotions would serve to carry things one for some time and keep us hoping.

Not long ago Paxton Hibben came in to see me one day. He told the clerk that let him in that he was an old friend of mine and when he came in he walked straight up to Bob Taft who was sitting across the table from me, and wrung him warmly by the hand to the amusement of said clerk. He is a first lieutenant and has something to do with financial matters. He is under Col. Sidney Cloman, who you doubtless remember. He (Pax) has married and his wife is here in Paris. He had come in to tell me that he had a "real American home" the like of which did not exist in Paris; that he knew how lonesome it must be for me here not knowing many people and with nowhere to go, etc. etc, etc. I thought he was going to ask to at least to come and live with them always, but after he had gone through a long preamble he said that he would come in some afternoon and take me home to tea. I may add as a matter of information that he never came back.

Wallace Young's name showed up the other day in a telegram somewhere about the shop as having been appointed as Consul at Prague. He was for several years at Carlsbad and ought to be glad to go back to that general part of the world. I had a hard time to tear myself away from Prague when I was there – I liked the people better than the place. Wallace always was lucky.

Willy Wallace turned up here some months ago to my surprise and disgust. He has been a Major in the Intelligence Service but stayed in Washington at the War College until the Peace Conference began. He is always amiable when we meet but he does not bother me by following me about and urging me to spend my spare time with him. He seems to be just the same as when we knew him, only more so.

My previous job blew us with the Armistice and while I was trying to make up my mind to ask for what I wanted, along came a telegram from the Department asking me if I would like to have it. Hoover had asked me detailed to work with him while he was over here and the Department gave me the chance to say whether I would care to do it. I got off a quick reply to say that was exactly my job and then hurried off to meet the gentleman at Southamptom. Since then I have stayed with him save when on trips into enemy country. I would not give up these months with him for any of the other jobs I could have had, or for the whole lot of them. I have always thought a great lot of him, but the more I see of him the higher my opinion goes. Of course, the food job is inseparable from political and diplomatic questions and the gent is wise enough to know that he doesn't want to get tangled up in details of things. S. I sit by the fire and put on the breaks occasionally or undertake to do some small job that I could handle more easily than anybody else around the shop. And while I am sitting by the fire, I acquire a liberal education free.

One of the latest stunts was to go up to Brussels to get the German ships and make the arrangements to feed the Huns. A previous mission sent to Spa for this same job failed and came back to Paris. Then the Huns sent word that they wanted another meeting and would make their supreme appeal for food. H. is not theatrical but he decided that it was time for a little poetic justice and sent word to the Germans that they could do their little food talk in Brussels. Last week we went up with a lot of big artillery from the other Allies. The British sent Admiral Sir Roslyn Wemyss, First Sea Lord of the Admiralty and a Lot of Other Things Like That and also Sir Joseph McClay who lent an air of dignity to the proceedings. Aside from Mr. Hoover, we had Thomas Lamont for Finance and Robinson for Shipping.

When we reached Brussels, we got hold of Francqui, Chairman of the Comité National, the Belgian organization which had worked so hard on the feeding problem all through the war. We announced to him that he was Belgian delegate to the conference and he chuckled so hard over the idea that we feared he was going to do himself injury.

The delegation of babykillers [Germans] was seventeen in number and when we arrived in the ballroom of the Hotel Astoria where we had been herded, they were all lined up on one side of a long table. We lined up and took our places on the others side and then, without any sign or any bowing or smiling, we all sat down at once just the way they do in the *Minstral Show*[208] Each side had its interpreters who worked hard and the whole procedure was stereotyped and impersonal. Our remarks were addressed to a spot in the middle of the table. When they were concluded they were rapidly translated into the horrible language of the Hun. The Hun reply was then shot at the same spot on the table, whence it was gathered up by our interpreter and given to us in an occidental language. Of course, there was not much speed in this sort of procedure, but it made people very careful what they said; not a word was wasted, and furthermore it gave you plenty of time to be thinking up your next point.

On the Boche side of the table we recognized some of the very swine with whom we used to have to deal in the old days during the war. One of them was [Richard] Merton, the big metal man, whom we had had assigned to Brussels because we thought he was decent and would help us in our work. Instead, he was one of the most cussed citizens in the whole place. Since getting licked, however, he has evidently forgotten all about that and came up wagging his tail and holding out his hand for a shake. One after another of us put our hands behind us but that didn't seem to keep him from trying it on the next one he met.

---

208 Popular American entertainment show in the 19th century where blackfaced white actors mocked people of African descent.

Late in the afternoon of the first day, I came up for air and went out into the lobby where there were a number of curious Belgians watching the show. A man came bearing down on me from the crowd holding out both hands and calling on heaven to witness how happy he was to see me here in these happy days and how grand and glorious it was that we should meet again under such conditions after the dark days we had gone through together. I did not quite place him and so, of course, I was double cordial, wrung his hand and assure him that I was delighted to see him again, etc., etc. And while I was in the midst of this, the spectators say that my smile froze on my face and the words died in my throat, for I suddenly recognized my friend as Baron von Schroeder, one of the most utterly contemptible little Huns we had had to deal with during the war. I was then as insulting as possible under the circumstances, told him that I should not have shaken his hand if were not for the fact that I had thought he was a Belgian friend, turned my back on him and made my getaway with as much dignity as possible after the break I had made. It pleased the Belgians to see me shaking hands with a Hun, for they knew my feelings pretty well. I had never seen the little beast before save in a Hussar uniform.

But in spite of my performance, we got the ships and undertook to feed the Huns as soon as they could carry out their part of the agreement. Needless to say, they are not doing it and are evidently disappointed because we don't row them about it. As soon as they get their internal troubles straightened out, they will probably get their ships out to sea and that will relieve the whole situation more than any one thing that can happen.

Yesterday being a Sunday, Mr. Hoover and Bob Taft and George Baker and I ran away and played hooky, taking a trip to Rheims and to the Chemin des Dames. I have been spending a good part of my time during the past year trotting around on the front, but I had never been actually on the Chemin des Dames and I'm blessed if I knew what a real blown-in-the-bottle battle field was like. One particularly unpleasant thing about it was that the ground was littered with hand grenades and torpedoes and all sorts of baby mines and traps and you were always tripping silly little wires that came from nowhere and disappeared nowhere. I have seen enough of that sort of thing to be deathly afraid of it and fortunately our crowd was sensibly timid and picked its way with care. Every day has its list of casualties – curious idiots who want to pull wires out of the ground or unscrew the caps on unexploded shells or open hand grenades. There seems to be nothing on earth can stop them and more than one of the poor devils of conducting officers have been killed or seriously hurt. If I were dictator, I'd send all the Hun prisoners out and drive them from one end of the old battle line to the other, pulling up wires, gathered the unexploded shells and grenades and making the country safe for God-fearing farmers. Poor old Mr. Farmer is going to have a bad time for some years; every now and then he will run his plow into a dud and they will be picking up pieces of him for weeks afterward.

Coming back we passed an ammunition dump that had caught fire in a field and was celebrating uproariously. Sentries stopped us some distance away and sent us by another road which skirted the field at a quarter of a mile or so. First there was one explosion which left a big cloud of yellow smoke. Then another which covered the whole field with black smoke – a high explosive – then a star shell which ambled around through the heavens burning brightly and settled down as though it had all the time in the world. Soon after we passed, I leaned back and turned loose a tremendous sneeze. Everybody else laughed and then they began one at a time to do the same. At last we had to stop the car and get out and stamp around sneezing and weeping and beating ourselves on the breast. And most of the night we sat up and wheezed and wondered what had happened to us. This morning all hands have sore throats and are preparing to offer thanks that we did not follow my suggestion and stop in just the wrong place to watch the fire. If we had, we should probably have been very interesting cases in the hospital. As soon as I can get down town, I am going to sport a wound stripe.

In my TOWN TOPICS list I forgot to say that not so very long ago I saw old Waffleiron [Charles de Waepenaert] the Belgian Minister at Habana. He was with his wife at Laussane where he seemed to be quite happy. I was passing through and stopped there for lunch.

A couple of weeks ago I saw the [John] Jacksons in Montreux where they are now living. He is very much down in the mouth and I think he begins to realize his mistake in not having gone home to offer his services when we came into the war. Altogether, his position is not very enviable.

I have just had a letter from Miss Wright who used to be in Habana. She has been for several years in Madrid and has turned out a couple of volumes of a history of Cuba which is said to be good – though I'm blessed if I see why anybody should want to read a history of Cuba, let alone write one.

My Mother is still in California but does not stay put very long. She has been going altogether too hard and at last accounts was laid up to pay for it. I have tried to scorch her with orders to take care of herself, knowing in advance that my words will have no effect aside for easing my pent-up feelings.

When you have the time and inclination, do write me a little news of yourselves. It would do me a world of good. My address is always the Department. I have not adopted any over here because I am forever moving and it is so much simpler to have everything come through once funnel.

Give my best love to Mrs. Beaupre and believe me always yours, [Hugh]

Letter to Mary Gibson   Paris. Tuesday, March 25, 1919

Still no news as to what I am to do by way of a job.

    I have spent a long day wheezing around the Crillon talking to people who said they wanted to talk but seems to have little to say. I took the Chief and George Baker to lunch at the Meurice and afterward we sat down and talked for a few minutes with the Norman Davis' and de Cartier who were having their coffee. It sounds very leisurely, but as a matter of fact the Chief had some things he wanted to talk to Davis about.

    No sound the last day or two from Dr. Taylor and his crowd. It would be great to be in that part of the world now that Hungary has blown up and I might as well have been there but for the fact that Joe Grew had a bad hunch. Unless something happens pretty soon I am not sure but that I shall make a run for Bucharest in the course of the next week. Of course the blow-up in Budapest has cut off direct communication and the train now goes by way of Luliana and Zagreb.

    Dr. Kellogg got off this evening for Warsaw, but I could not make it to go with him.

    Secretary [Josephus] and Mrs. Daniels got here this morning but I have not seen them. George Baker had to get out of bed before daylight and stand about on the station platform for over an hour waiting to give them a welcome from the second rank behind his chief Admiral Benson.

    Nobody to dine tonight but Lieut. Irving who is an aide to Cary Grayson and a great friend of George Baker.

    Phil [Patchin] has word that Polly is coming over in a couple of weeks so he begins to blossom again.

Letter to Mary Gibson   Paris. Wednesday, March 26, 1919

Just the usual amount of news, to wit none at all.

    I put in the morning at the house thumping my own typewriter and just as I was beginning to wonder whether it was worthwhile to go down to lunch, there came a telephone call from Dresel to say that Coolidge had arrived from Vienna and was bursting with news and a natural desire to see me. I hurried down and had lunch with him and Allen Dulles at the Crillon. He had all the latest news about the situation in Vienna as affected by the Budapest blowup and also some direct news from Budapest itself. Philip Brown went down last week to see the Hungarian show first hand and he is still there. Nicholas Roosevelt was also there and they decided that it was best for one to stay and one to get away with the news, so Philip Brown is watching the show of his life. I don't believe he is in much danger though I should not like to be a Frenchman or Italian in the same place.

This evening we had a real party as everybody had invited a guest or two without telling anybody else. I had asked Coolidge and Dresel. George Baker had bid Frank Simonds the correspondent and his wife, and the Chief had summoned Mr. and Mrs. Oscar Strauss. We were thirteen at table but I don't believe it was noticed by anybody but George Baker who was the last to come in and made awful faces at me with a view to getting advice as to whether he should stay or go.

Talk waxed fast and furious after dinner and the guests did not go until after eleven.

Letter to Major A.L. James   Paris, March 26, 1919

For lo, these many weeks I have planned to sit me down and write you a proper letter, but my execution as not been up to the level of my good intentions. However, it looks now as though I might be setting forth on my rambles again soon so I want to get something on paper that will stir you to letting me have some news of yourself. I haven't had a word from you since you got home and should mightily like to know how and where you are.

Our old crowd of playmates is pretty badly broken up. Arthur Page, as you know, went home immediately after the death of his father in December and is now back at work on the magazine. His father's death was a dreadful blow to him, and as it was in lesser degree to all of us, and it is best that he should be back at work.

Stetson is getting ready to go home in the course of the next couple of weeks – being one of those who is born lucky. I believe he is only going home for a visit and will soon be back in our midst.

Blount is still here. He got collared by General Harts as an aide but did not seem to bloom in the job although he did it well and to the entire satisfaction of the General. Finally after much palaver we got him pried loose and have put him to work under Mr. Hoover. He is looking after visiting firemen and has taken two important parties to Belgium. He handled the job to the Queen's taste and got the maximum results out of the trips. And strange to say, he seems to enjoy it, though I can't conceive of anything more awful as a steady job.

I ran into Cutcheon the other day when he was down here from Spa. He sports gold leaves now and is another of those rare people who is enjoying his job. To hear him talk you would think that the one sorrow of his life was his inability to live with us at 147 [rue de la Pompe].

General Nolan spends a good part of this time here in Paris nowadays but I have hardly laid eyes on him as I have been away most of the time myself.

Col. Van Deman is at the Crillon doing his old job and I see him nearly every day.

Magrudder is here with General Harts but I don't know what his job is.

We pried Logan loose from his job and he is now running the shipping end of the American Relief Administration. He has got a fine hold on it and after seeing what he could do, Mr. Hoover has given him a free hand. We have also got Col. Barber who says he knows you – but then he may be only bragging. He is a priceless citizen and an addition to our family.

Walter Lippmann went home while I was away from Paris and I have not had a sound out of him despite the fact that I have sent him several insulting messages through other people. Merz went about the same time and they are both, I believe, spreading the gospel. Ralph Hayes is here, sometimes sitting at a desk at the Crillon and sometimes piloting distinguished visitors about the battlefields. He is now off with Attorney-General Gregory. Like a lot of others, he wants to go home. ...

I came back to Paris the first of February to report and get a breath of air – and have not been back since though my trunk has been packed most of the time and I have had reservations on nearly every train that has pulled out in an easterly direction. I am still about to start but goodness only knows when I shall actually get under way.

After about a week's wait, my accumulated weariness began to get in its work and I blew up. The Peace Mission then canned me for the time being and ordered me to go off to Switzerland and rest for several weeks. I trotted off enthusiastically to Leysin to roll in the snow for that indefinite period – and just as I was getting into it, at the end of the third day there came a telegram urging me to hurry back to Paris. I made a return trip which would have looked all right in a ten cent melodrama, but left a good deal to be desired in the way of ease and luxury, and since that time I have hardly stopped long enough to catch a breath.

There has been some fun in it all, especially in going as part of the Armistice Mission to get the German ships and listen to their plea for food. ...

Letter to Lady[209]   Paris, March 26, 1919

... Our friends the Belgae are coming on fast. The people are managing to find work of some sort as rapidly as possible they are getting ready to resume nor-

---

209 Most likely Willa Alice Page, as Gibson refers to her this way in other correspondence. See Biographical Index.

mal life. There are now less than a third of the war time number of people in the free soup lines and the number is going down every day. As soon as they can get in some raw materials, the number will drip still farther. If they can keep free of any sort of social upset, they should be the first people in Europe to get on its feet.

Hoover and I had lunch with the King on one of our recent trips, just the three of us, and had a good talk about what is going on. He knows just what he is after and is anxious for good ideas as to how to go about it. He has developed enormously during the war and if he has a chance to govern his country, will do it well.

Poor old Brussels itself is pretty out at the elbows and it will be some time before it gets back to its immaculate appearance of before the war. The papers seem to be hipped on the fact that the whole town is given over to merry making and dancing and the consumption of champagne. If it were true, I should understand it and sympathize for if the Belgae want to dance and get drunk and howl they are entitled to do it. But they don't. There are some loud resorts maintained for the British and Canadian officers where such doings are to be found, and that is what most visitors see during a one or two day trip, but so far I have been unable to find any Belgian houses where they have the money or the inclination for such performances. Most people who go there are indignant because they don't find women and children dying of hunger in the street. They have been under the impression for four years and more that people were starving in Belgium and when they don't find the streets littered with corpses they feel as though they have been swindled and want their money back. It never seems to enter their pure minds that we spent a prodigious amount of effort to prevent these people from starving and spent an enormous amount of our own and other people's money to that same end, and that it would reflect little credit on us if they had starved. GOSH!!!! ...

Letter to Mary Gibson   Paris. Thursday, March 27, 1919

... I broke away from my labors this morning and went to Dresel's room for the morning conference. We had Nicholas Roosevelt, just back from Budapest to tell us what he had seen. He is an observant fellow and gave us an hour of good talk on things we wanted to know about. After that Coolidge retained me as adviser for some time and the morning was gone. It seems to me that I spend an increasingly large proportion of my time listening to people's perplexities and giving advice. If they like it, I suppose it's all right, but it does put an awful hole in your day.

Lunched with Ellis Dresel at the Inter-Allied Club and talk shop.

This evening we had another real party which grew from independent invitations. There were the Bucklers, General Carson, Judge Parker and Senator Hollis and Mr. Johnson of the Liquidation Board. That added to our own family made us just thirteen at table as we were last night.

[Added note found only in Secret Log]   March 27th

Joe [Grew] told me this afternoon that Buckler had been offered the Mission to Poland but had not accepted until he could find out whether we intended to have some sort of policy toward the Bolsheviki. In the evening, Buckler showed me the letter he had written to Col. House and it was not what our Commissioners are accustomed to. B. said that although he was greatly honored he could not see that there was any purpose in his going unless we had something definite in the way of a program and policy; with Russia and Hungary gone and Germany on the toboggan and Bohemia tottering, he could not see any hope for Poland if we were to follow the policy of drift that has been ours so far. He said that he did not care to ascent the pyre, etc. DRIFT and PYRE were his own words.

Bill Bullitt is back after talking with Lenin and gathering first hand impressions of the Bolshevist state of mind. He had breakfast this morning with Lloyd George and has been thick with the Commissioners. The general talk is that he has brought back proposals that would enable us to conclude some sort of arrangement with the Bolshevists and L.G. is leaning that way. Wickam Steed is all stirred up about it and says that he will snort fearfully in tomorrow's *Daily Mail* so as to stiffen his back bone.

The Chief has come home with some new thoughts on the Bolshevist questions and is embodying them in a memorandum for the President. He begins with the statement that there have been grievous injustices to the lowest classes in all the countries that have been affected and also in England which he deems right for upheaval. If we were to send an army of occupation into Hungary, it would in effect be for the purpose of forcing the peasantry back into their old position and consolidating the rich landowners in their old privileges. The whole thing has got to work itself out and the best thing we can do is keep clear of it. For one thing, if we do go in it we will be not only under the military domination of the Allied Powers but also under their political domination – and their political ends are at radical variance with ours. Our soldiers would soon find out the true state of affairs, and we should have great discontent at home at our doing the work of other countries. Further it would entail an occupation of the Lord knows how many years and would cost a great many lives.

The constructive part of the idea is this. He says that each side is now frightened to death of the other and that if we know how to avail of that opportunity, we can perhaps get something done. He proposes to send a neutral who could command the confidence of both sides to Petrograd to talk to the Bolsheviki, tell them that he thinks he might secure from the Entente a contract to supply Russia with food supplies if the Bolsheviki would undertake to refrain from military aggression or foreign propaganda. That, at least, would tend to keep the trouble localized and if food could be got in to them, it might in time stir the orderly classes to take some steps to straighten matters out. The Chief thought of Nansen as a suitable person and spoke to the President about it today. The President authorized him to broach the matter to Nansen and it is to be done tomorrow morning at nine.

One of the things that [Nicholas] Roosevelt had to say this morning was that Garbai in the new [Hungarian] Government was a Christian. Someone asked him how that happened and he replied quite seriously that the crowd of Jews who have seized the power thought that there should be a representative of the Christians in the Govt.

Practically all the worst and most powerful of the Bolsheviki and the like are Jews and this is bound to react on them before long. Some Government is going to see in this a way of taking its people's mind off other troubles and turn them loose on the Jews. Just as likely as not, the war will wind up with a gigantic pogrom. I notice that the Czech newspapers are already intimating that it would be just as well to keep an eye on the young girls during Passover because of the danger of ritual murder. This may be with the consent of the Govt. for they have enough troubles to require a red herring of some sort.

Letter to Mary Gibson   Paris. Friday, March 28, 1919

A letter today from Aunt Leona who is back in Brussels sooner than she had expected to be. Warren has gone off to sea and she is running the hospital while Miss Upton is in England looking into methods of running institution such as theirs. She (Aunt Leona) is to have a decoration from the Queen of the Belgians; the audience was fixed while she was away but they are not trying to arrange another so that she can receive it properly. I am mighty glad they have recognized her work from the top. The Belgians have decorated very few people for that sort of hard work, although they have had to give the usual number of decorations to those who collected funds and gave parties, etc. It pleases me a lot more than if I had received it myself. Aunt Leona said that she had been to make a courtesy call on Brand Whitlock and adds: "I was glad I wore my fur coat." In four or five weeks, she expects to come to Paris to see if there is any work in jewelry making that interests her before she makes definite plans about going home. She went to see Ned Bell when she was in London and he was nice to her and fixed up her passport which she had allowed to expire; gave her a letter which let her pass ahead of the crowd at the Consulate General, etc. – for all of which she was as usual pathetically grateful.

Spent the day trying to reduce to writing what we think about Bolshevism. It was finally got onto paper but what the result will be is another question. The Chief has written an essay on the subject which goes to the President today as a letter. It is an overpowering question an as nobody knows anything about it there are many minds.

The following today was produced as an ODE to COLONEL HOUSE

"Wholly unquotable
Always ungoatable
Secretly notable
Silence's spouse.

Darkly inscrutable
Quite irrefutable
Nobly immutable
Edward M. House."

I await an opportunity to read it to the Colonel as I know he would enjoy it.

I led Joe Grew and Phil [Patchin] out to lunch today and together we mourned over the human race.

Spring refuses to come. We have varied all day between bright warm sunshine and snow with a little rain between times. It can't be beat and the boys of the AEF will probably go through life believing that it rains all the year round in "sunny France."

Wallace Young turned up this evening from Sweden on his way to Prague as Consul. I had him come out to dine and we had a long talk about things in general. He does not want to go until the Minister goes, whoever said Minister may be, but he is to see the Secretary [Lansing] in the morning and get his instructions.

Copy of letter from Hoover to President Wilson.   28 March 1919

Dear Mr. President:
As the result of Bolshevik economic conceptions, the people of Russia are dying of hunger and disease at the rate of some hundreds of thousands monthly in a country that formerly supplied food to a large part of the world.

I feel it is my duty to lay before you in just as few words as possible my views as to the American relations to Bolshevism and its manifestations. These views at least have the merit of being an analysis of information and thought gleaned from my own experience and the independent sources which I now have over the whole of Europe, through our widespread relief organization.

It simply cannot be denied that this swinging of the social pendulum from the tyranny of the extreme right to the tyranny of the extreme left is based on a foundation of real social grievance. The tyranny of the reactionaries in Eastern and Central Europe for generations before the way, and the suffering of their common people is but a common place to every social student. The situation was thrown into bold relief by the war and the breakdown of their reactionary tyrannies. After fighting actually stopped on the various fronts, the famine which followed has further emphasized the gulf between the lower and upper classes. The poor were starved and driven mad in the presence of extravagance and waste.

It is to be noticed that the Bolshevik ascendency or even their strong attempts so far are confined to areas of former reactionary tyranny. Their courses represent the not unnatural violence of a mass of ignorant humanity, who themselves have learned in grief of tyranny and violence over generations. Our people, who enjoy so great liberty and general comfort, cannot fail to sympathize to some degree with these blind gropings for better social condition. If former revolutions of ignorant masses are any guide, the pendulum will yet swing back to some moderate position when bitter experience has taught the economic and social follies of present obsessions. No greater fortune can come to the world than that these foolish ideas should have an opportunity somewhere of bankrupting themselves.

It is not necessary for any American to debate the utter foolishness of these economic tenets. We must all agree that our processes of production and distribution, the outgrowth of a hundred generations, in the stimulation to individual initiative, the large equality of opportunity and infinite development of mind and body, while not perfect, come about as near perfection as is possible from the mixture of avarice, ambition, altruism, intelligence, ignorance and education, of which the human animal is today composed. The Bolshevik's land of illusion is that he can perfect these human qualities by destroying the basic processes of production and distribution, instead of devoting himself to securing a better application of the collective surplus.

Politically, the Bolsheviki most certainly represent a minority in every country where they are in control, and as such they constitute a tyranny that is the negation of democracy, for democracy, as I see it, must rest on the execution of the will of the majority expressed by free and unterrified suffrage. As a tyranny, the Bolshevik has resorted to terror, bloodshed and murder to a degree long since abandoned even amongst reactionary tyrannies. He has even to a greater degree relied upon criminal instinct to support his doctrines that ever autocracy did. By enveloping into his doctrines the cry of the helpless and the downtrodden, he has embraced a large degree of emotionalism and has thereby given an impulse to his propaganda comparable only to the impulse of large spiritual movements. This propaganda, however, in my view, will stir other populations only in ratio to their proportions of the suffering and ignorant and criminal. I feel myself, therefore, that the political danger is a direct factor of the social and political development of the population which they attempt to impregnate. Where the gulf between the middle classes and the lower classes is too large, and where the lower classes have been kept in ignorance and distress, this propaganda will be fatal and do violence to normal democratic development. For these reasons, I have no fear of it in the United States, and my fears as to other countries would be gauged by the above criterion. It is possible that the Soviet type of government might take hold in some other countries as a primitive form of democracy, but its virulence will be tempered by their previous degree of political subversion.

There remains in my mind one more point to be examined, that is as to whether the Bolshevik centers now stirred by great emotional hopes will not undertake large military crusades in an attempt to impose their doctrines on other defenseless people. This is a point on which my mind is divided with the evidence at hand, and it seems to me that the whole treatment of the problem must revolve on the determination of this one question. If this spirit is inherent in their doctrine, it appears to me that we must disregard all other questions and be prepared to fight, for exactly the same reasons that we entered the European war against Germany. If this is not the case, then it appears to me that from an American point of view we should not involve ourselves in what may be a ten-year military entanglement in Europe. The American people cannot say that we are going to insist that any given population must work out its internal social problems according to our particular conception of democracy. In any event, I have the most serious doubt that outside forces entering upon such an enterprise can do other than infinite harm, for any great wave of emotion must ferment and spread under repression. In the swing of the social pendulum from the extreme left back toward the right, it will find the point of stabilization based on racial instincts that could never be established by outside intervention.

I think we have also to contemplate what would actually happen if we undertook military intervention in, say, a case like Hungary. We should probably be involved in years of police duty, and our first act would probably be in the nature of things make us a party to reestablishing the reactionary classes in their economic domination over the lower classes. This is against our fundamental national spirit, and I doubt whether our soldiers under these circumstance would resist infection with Bolshevik ideas. It also requires consideration as to whether or not our people at home, on gradual enlightenment as to the social wrongs of the lower classes in these countries, would stand for our providing power by which such reactionaries held their position, and we would perchance be thrown into an attempt as governors to work out some social reorganization of these countries. We thus become a mandatory with a vengeance. We become, in fact, one of four mandatories, each with a different political and social outlook, for it would necessarily be a joint Allied undertaking. Furthermore, in our present engagements with France, England and Italy, we become a junior in this particular partnership of four. It is therefore inevitable that in these matters where our views and principles are at variance with the European Allies we would find ourselves subordinated and even committed to policies against our convictions.

In all these lights, I have the following three suggestions:

First: We cannot even remotely recognize this murderous tyranny without stimulating actionist radicalism in every country in Europe and without transgressing on every National ideal of our own.

Second: That some Neutral of international reputation for probity and ability should be allowed to create a second Belgian Relief Commission for Russia. He should ask the Northern Neutrals who are especially interested both politically and financially in the restoration of better conditions in Russia, to give to him diplomatic, financial and transportation support; that he should open negotiations with the Allied governments on the ground of desire to enter upon the humane work of saving life, and ask the conditions upon which ships carrying food and other necessaries will be allowed to pass. He should be told that we will raise no obstructions and would even help in his humanitarian task if he gets assurances that the Bolsheviki will cease all militant action across certain defined boundaries and cease their subsidizing of disturbances abroad; under these conditions that he could raise money, ships and food, either from inside or outside Russia; that he must secure an agreement covering equitable distribution, and he might even demand that Germany help pay for this. This plan does not involve recognition or relationship by the Allies of the Bolshevik murderers now in control any more than England recognized Germany in its deal with the Belgian Relief. It would appear to me that such a proposal would at least test out whether this is a militant force engrossed upon world domination. If such an arrangement could be accomplished, it might at least give a period of rest along the frontiers of Europe and would give some hope of stabilization. Time can thus be taken to determine whether or not this whole system is a world danger, and whether the Russian people will not themselves swing back to moderation and themselves bankrupt these ideas. This plan, if successful, would save an immensity of helpless human life and would save our country from further entanglements which today threaten to pull us from our National ideals.

Third: I strongly feel the time has arrived for you again to reassert your spiritual leadership of democracy in the world as opposed to tyrannies of all kinds. Could you not take an early opportunity to analyze, as only you can, Bolshevism from its political, economic, humane and its criminal points of view, and, while yielding its aspirations, sympathetically to show its utter foolishness as a basis of economic development; show its true social ends; rap our own reactionaries for their destruction of social betterment and thereby their stimulations of Bolshevism; point, however, to the steady progress of real democracy in these roads of social betterment. I believe you would again align the hearts of the suffering for orderly progress against anarchy, not alone in Russia, but in every Allied country.

If the militant features of Bolshevism were drawn in colors with their true parallel with Prussianism as an attempt at world domination that we do not stand for, it would check the fears that today haunt all men's minds.

Faithfully yours, Signed: Herbert Hoover

Letter to Mary Gibson   Paris. Saturday, March 29, 1919

This morning I got a surprise and shock in the form of a telegram from Phillips saying that you had not heard anything from me since my letter of January 15th and wanted inquiry made as to my whereabouts and welfare. I went hotfoot down to the Embassy to find out what was the matter for I have ticked out something to you every blessed day and have sent off a budget whenever there was a pouch.

In the course of my inquiries, I found that the Ambassador had received a telegram from his mother the other day saying that she had heard nothing from him since January – and he writes regularly twice a week. Norweb, one of the other Secretaries, said that he had had an inquiry from home as his family had had nothing for more than eight weeks. I suppose there are others and an inquiry is now underway to get all the ammunition possible so that we can get off a general blast to the Department on Monday asking for an investigation. I telegraphed Phillips at once with a message for you and asked him to look into the disposition that had been made of my letters. It is evident that something strange has been happening. There is a long hiatus since the last pouches were received here and we are wrought up about it. I think that until it is straightened out I shall send your letters by open mail.

It is a shame that there should have been any such delay for there is nothing to do with the maid when it arrives but drop it in the post and let it go its way. I am mighty sorry but hope to hear soon that you have got all the back numbers.

We had a farewell party for the Ambassador [Sharp] today. First we went to his house at noon and had our picture taken in a group, some twenty or thirty of us. From there to the Inter-Allied Club where we had lunch and a speech by Bob Bliss to present a big silver cup which we had got as a farewell give to the old gentleman. He was immensely pleased and it all went off very well.

Most of the day I spent in the usual treadmill work at the Crillon and at six knocked off and came back to the house.

Tonight we had George and Mrs. McFadden and Fred Walcott and Munn to dine. Kittredge came in during the meal so that we had a goodly crowd. Just before George started up, General Pershing summoned him downstairs in the Ritz and had pinned the Distinguished Service Medal on him in recognition of his work for the AEF during the war. He was as pleased as a small boy.

Letter to Mary Gibson   Paris. Sunday, March 30, 1919

We had our plans for a day in the country today, but never got off. First Francqui arrived last night and asked that the Chief go down and breakfast with him in order to talk shop. That put off our going for a time. Then when we woke up in the morning we found that snow was falling smartly and it did not look much like the sort of day you would like to sit on the grass and eat sandwiches. So we kept on puttering about the office until lunch time and gave up the idea of being rural. The Chief, George Baker, Bob Taft and I went down to La Perouse and had a matter of fact lunch just like anybody else.

I am feeling pretty worthless so about four of the clock I got into my downy and had a good nap, not getting up till after seven. I then dressed like a professional beauty and went over to dine at the Kirk's, having let myself in for that dissipation some days ago. They had the Bullitt's, Mrs. Garrett, the Lithgow Osborne's, and Colonel Poillon who used to be Military Attaché at The Hague. After dinner the Minot's and Fred Dolbeare came in and the gramophone was turned on and the more ambitious people danced. I was content to sit in the corner with the Elder Statesman and listen to chatter on how to run the world.

Letter to Mary Gibson   Paris. Monday, March 31, 1919

Today's mail brought me an envelope of printed matter on Americanization for you, but not another thing. The Ambassador got off a telegram this morning to the Department to stir up the question of what has happened to all the letters we have written. They must have been piled up on the floor somewhere until somebody could find time to dump them in the open mail and we want to find out who is at fault. It makes me mad when I think of the amount of thumping I have done in order to make sure of sending you something at every possible opportunity.

I found a message from Marian Littlefield when I got in last night saying that she was at the France et Choiseul. I went around there twice but she was out buying gowns. Leland did not come with her as he is moving the dog and other belongings to the country.

I lunched with the Chief plus Francqui, Jaspar and de Cartier who has just been up to see the Cardinal about going to America. It looks as though he would get away toward the end of this month for several weeks in the United States. What a time he will have!

Spent the afternoon drafting a lot of stuff and came home just in time to dress for dinner. As guests we had the Robinsons, Lewis Richards (who flew over from London today after missing his train), Kittredge; the Lamonts were coming but evidently misunderstood or forgot.

Letter to Mary Gibson   Paris. Tuesday, April 1, 1919

I put in the whole day working in various parts of the Crillon and did not get home until just before dinner.

I lunched with Wallace Young and Allen Dulles and improved the shining hour by talking large amounts of shop. Wallace like me is held up here indefinitely although he is bursting with anxiety to get to his post.

We had the Lamont's to dinner this evening. They were to have come last night, but there was some sort of misunderstanding and they took a rain check. Prentiss Gray got back this evening from Brussels steaming and snorting about the behavior of one of our friends whom he dislikes with enthusiasm and energy. Lewis Richards was also here so we had a full house.

Letter to Arthur Bliss Lane   Paris, April 1, 1919

Your letter of March 27th came along yesterday but so far there is not a thing to be said in enlightenment.

I still go through my daily round of going down to the Crillon and haunting the offices of those in authority but no results are to be observed. Forty or fifty years from now I shall doubtless be trailing my long white beard up and down the corridors and having the boy scouts pointing me out as the old codger who has the delusion that he is going to Prague.

The whole matter is up to the President and has been for some time. He has several pounds of memoranda on the subject reposing on his desk and they go right on reposing while he worries about things that are of more importance to other people.

The minute there is a sign I shall see that word goes to you. AND I HOPE IT MAY BE SOON.

Letter to Mary Gibson   Paris. Wednesday, April 2, 1919

As my letters are going to you by open mail until I find out what has been happening in the Department, I shall drop something in the box every day so as to catch anything that is going out.

This day has brought nothing very thrilling. I spent the day pottering about the Crillon doing odd jobs. I lunched with Horodyski at the Ambassadeurs and heard his lengthy tale about what is going on in Poland. He was very interesting about it but it is a depressing story.

After lunch I went over and had a talk with Beneš and the rest of the Czech Government. They too have their troubles as always and added to the gloom of the day.

The King of the Belgians flew down from Brussels yesterday afternoon and is staying out at Versailles so as to preserve some measure of privacy. He came in this morning and has spent the day seeing various people. Tomorrow he is to see the President at two and probably after that will fly back. He is doing altogether too much but some day his machine is going to be smashed and he with it and then people won't think it so fine.

Tonight Irving and Cartier and Count de Chevigné came to dine. Cartier went away after dinner carrying under his arm the copy of my book which Arthur had bound for the King. The other gentleman who should have delivered it would probably have kept it a century so I accepted C's offer to hand it over.

Tomorrow I am breaking into society. I take Marian Littlefield out to lunch and in the evening I dine with Count de Chevigné who lives around the corner. This is the first time that I have shone at two functions per day for some time.

Letter to Mary Gibson   Paris. Thursday, April 3, 1919

Still no pouches in from the Department and I hardly dare think of the mountains of mail that will come to me when they finally do turn up. None of us have been able to understand why, with ship sailing nearly every day, no pouches seem to have been sent for weeks together.

As usual, the day brought forth nothing very startling. I had some things to do at the Crillon just in time to see the King of the Belgians come in to see Colonel House. There was a fair sized crowd gathered outside the hotel but there was no cheering and only a little thread of hand-clapping.

I picked up Marian Littlefield and took her to lunch at Foyot's across the river. She had a bad attack of flu several months ago and since then has been at Monte Carlo recovering. I thought she had just come over from London. They have had to give up the Dower House at Sonning where they have lived for several years as the owner has come back and claimed it. Now they have bought the Manor, a big place on a hill dominating the village and the river, fifteen acres of ground, old trees and all the makings of a splendid place. They are both spending all their time and money buying furniture and fixings for the house and expect to be kept busy for months to come getting it ready to live in.

This evening George Baker and I walked all the way around the corner to dine with Chevigné. He also had bade Cary Grayson and told us it would be a man's dinner. Just before he went home last night, he inquired mildly whether we would mind if his wife was there. Accordingly, I went around in a dinner coat and to my horror found that they had a party of sixteen, all of them dressed within an inch of their lives. It was all French and good talk at that. I enjoyed yarning with [Louis de] Broglie and with the editor of the *Journal des Débâts*. At eleven we broke up and walked around to the White House with Grayson before coming home to bed. The Place des Etats-Unis is quiet as the tomb, with policemen at each end to keep people and motors out, sentries in comic little striped boxes before the door, and secret service men sprinkled along the way like roses on the path of the bride. I fear I couldn't sleep if my friends kept it that quiet for me.

Letter to Mary Gibson   Paris. Friday, April 4, 1919

... I have as usual put in a good part of the day at the Crillon doing "things". This morning we had the customary meeting of what we call the "rational nucleus" and then I went over to Voisin's to lunch with Teddy Curtis, Madame Guinotte and Zizi (Teddy's finacée). They are to be married in July and I am summoned to act as best man. If I am in this part of the world of course I shall do it. They are to be married at the Château de Mariemont which the Guinotte's inherited on the death of Raoul Waroqué and will be general rejoicings. The whole family is here for some time as Hélène, the daughter who married Charley Carstairs, is expecting an addition to the family any day now.

Mrs. Steve Slocum, was at a nearby table lunching with Marian Littlefield and Bessie Stabler. I walked up the Champs Élysées with Mrs. Slocum afterward and was sorry to hear that Herbert S. was passed over altogether in the promotions to Brigadier-General. Of course they are very bitter about it and blame all sorts of people who probably had nothing to do with it. It seems to be that if Mrs. Sage had left me eight millions or so, I should not worry much about anything. But people never seem to be that way.

Tomorrow I am going to pick up and play hooky for the day. Marian Littlefield and Miss Waterbury are anxious to see a battlefield and I can't think of a better way to return some of their kindness than to take them up to the Belleau Wood or the Chemin des Dames. I have asked Fred Dolbeare to go along and have annexed an ARA car. I have sat around here day after day waiting for a decision in my case and perhaps if I go away for a day it will be taken. *Ojala*! [God willing]

The President is laid up with a cold today and people seem to be worrying for fear it will turn into flu. It would be a calamity to have him incapacitated now with so many vitally important things that only he can decide. It gives me the shivers to think of it.

Letter to Mary Gibson   Paris. Saturday, April 5, 1919

I am well-nigh asleep but here goes for a few lines before I topple off my chair.

Our joy ride got off this morning promptly at nine with the most beautiful spring day so far. There was bright sun all day and most of the day we did not need coats at all. Coming in toward evening, they were comfortable but not really necessary, the which is a welcome change after all the overcoat months we have been through.

The best part of the trip was that none of the three people have been anywhere near the front before and everything was new and deeply interesting to them. When we got to Meaux and they say the first ordinary ruined houses, I thought they would fall out of the car. The sight of an old farmhouse that had been the HQ of Pershing's 1st Army caused immense excitement and when we came to the destroyed villages before Château-Thierry, I thought they had exhausted their sensations.

From Château-Thierry we took the road on the north bank of the Marne which I have never been over before through Brasles, Gland and Jaulgonne, thence to Fère-en-Tarenois through the woods which were splintered and filled with shell holes. The woods are still filled with piles of shells and other munitions and the merry little hand grenade is everywhere underfoot to trap the unwary.

There was a climax when we came into Fismes, which is really about as bad as any town that is recognizable. As we drove up the main street, we came on a group of four or five American soldiers and a couple of blue jackets. We stopped to get some oil for their car and Marian [Littlefield] and Miss Waterbury improved the shining hour by learning their life history and photographing them with all the youngsters of the place who clung to them. They belonged to a Registration Unit, their job being to find the graves of American soldiers, record their exact location and where possible move them to the cemeteries which we have established in the neighborhood. It's not very cheerful work and they were not very cheerful boys, but they seemed glad to talk to some of their own people and loaded the girls up with violets and daffodils which they had already gathered.

From Fismes we struck out eastward along the Vesle and kept going strong until lunch time when we picked out a likely place by the roadside and opened our basket under a big tree. We chose a very hectic ex-battlefield with a fine collection of loot ready to hand. The front of the car was loaded up shell cases, helmets, and other junk to be taken back to England. In prowling around, we found the emplacement of one of the very big guns, with narrow gauge tracks running up from the road for ammunition, deep dug-outs for the crews, store houses and dumps complete. There was also a big plant for the manufacture of the camouflage screens used along here on the roads. There seems to have been a considerable amount of ordinary hard work about this war.

In the neighborhood there were big parties of Hun prisoners at work clearing the fields. I did not get a sight of how they go to work but every now and then we heard and saw big explosions where a lot of ammunition went up in smoke without accomplishing its aim in life. The fields that were dry enough were being burned off and the prisoners stood at a respectful distance and watched the occasional grenade or star shell go pop. Most of the men were in the new violent green uniforms furnished them by the French, all with a big P.G. [*Prisonnier de guerre*, Prisoner of War] stenciled on the back and front – reminiscent of the old conundrum about how to spell blind pig.

After puttering about for an hour and gathering all the truck anybody wanted, we went on to Rheims. The Cathedral received respectful attention but deeper sorrow was lavished on the Hôtel du Lion d'Or across the street where Marian used to stay with Leland and where they had acquired lasting memories of the place to be taken back to Leland so that he might realize how dreadful the war had been.

We tried a new way back, going all the way down to Épernay, thence along the south bank of the Marne to Château-Thierry and then to the Bois de Belleau. I had not been there for some time and should hardly have recognized the place. The wood is thick with underbrush, the rifle pits are half covered over and thousands of visitors have worn paths through the place from end to end. There is hardly a scrap of shrapnel or a rifle bullet left on the ground where there was once enough loot to equip an army. There were a couple of officers puttering about trying to establish the lines of various operations but they were discouraged by the fact that a lot of landmarks used at the time had disappeared, fields of wheat, trees, overturned wagons, etc. They are doing this for history and knowing their difficulties, I shall just omit any reading on the fight of the Marines in the Bois de Belleau. From there we came back through Lucy-en-Bocage, la Fère-Sous-Jouarre and Meaux, reaching Paris at about half past seven, just in time to get a tub and cascade down the stairs in time for dinner.

Letter to Mary Gibson Paris. Sunday, April 6, 1919

Another day of playing in the country.

There were so many things requiring attention in town that we agreed the simplest thing was to run away and let them settle themselves. We set off at ten with the Chief, Bob Taft, George Baker and HSG [Gibson] in one car and several other firemen in another; I am sort of vague about them because their car lay down by the roadside and died just outside of Paris and we never saw then again until we found them at the table on our return.

We went up through Senlis where we saw a prize collection of tanks, on to Compiègne and did not stop until we came to Mont Renaud just this side of Noyon. It was an interesting place so we abandoned the cars and tramped to the top. It was a symmetrical hill with a big retaining wall around the top and a tuft of woods to top off. There had also been a chateau but that had gone and there was little sign of it. The whole place was like a Gustave Doré drawing of trees in torment and the earth was churned up like a raging sea. On the sunny side, we found two graves of French soldiers. One of them was marked with a cross bearing his name and rank and the grave was covered with fresh flowers. The other evidently had not been identified and on the cross was only the inscriptions, carved with a knife: "*Ici repose un soldat de la Patrie. Français découvrez-vous; c'était un brave.*" [Here rests a soldier of the Fatherland. French people, take of your hat; he was a brave man.] And I should think he would rest about as comfortably under that as though his name and number were regularly on record.

Most of the earth was so befouled with gas and other poisons from the shells that nothing would grow. But here and there we found little patches where the grass had come up and where violets were thick and fragrant. Of course we gathered a lot of them and of course they faded before we had gone ten miles and we had to throw them away.

A little beyond Noyon we stopped by the roadside for lunch and to give our companions a chance to catch up with us. Then on to Laon through a broad belt of country where the Germans had systematically destroyed everything before retreating. There were entire villages where you could clearly see how the destruction had been carried out. A separate explosion had taken place in each hour and you could tell from the position of the fallen walls their sequence and relative violence. Of course, this is simpler and less costly than destruction by artillery fire and wherever the Hun could use it, he did. Many of the villages were so completely destroyed that there was not a single refugee to be seen. And that's saying a good deal for when there are a few fragments of wall left, you always find a lot of hopeful people trying to build some sort of lean-to and set up the old business of living. When you think what this means to thousands of poor people and how unnecessary it was, it makes you see red.

We climbed up the hill in Laon and found the streets filled with people, many of whom had been there through the war. One man came up to answer the chauffeur's questions about the road to Rheims and although he professed to speak English, he talked mostly German, and the people round about looked at him with amusement as though they all understood.

We made off on a filthy dusty road to Corbeny and there turned off to Craonne. We knew it was Corbeny because there was a big sign stuck up in the sea of bricks to tell us so. Otherwise there was nothing to distinguish it from almost any other place along the road. Now we were in one of the most hotly contested portions of the line and the country showed it – patches of woods torn to splinters, fields cut to cat's meat and ponds turned to vile smelling pools. We drove up the side of the hill where the white chalk undersoil had been whipped up till the whole hill stood out glaring and here the chauffeur stopped and told us we were at Craonne. We looked about trying to find the village and could hardly believe him when he told us we were in the middle of it. There was <u>nothing</u> to show that there had ever been a village. No matter how much a village is hammered by artillery, there always remains some fragments of wall. Even with internal explosions and artillery combined, there is always the mass of broken bricks to show that something had happened. But here there was nothing at all, not even bricks or the red tinge of brick dust to give a hint. Here and there we saw some big blocks of shaped stone which had been worked into the defense of the place and we were at liberty to assume that they had been parts of the village before the smash. I did not suppose it was possible to wipe out a place as completely as this no matter how much effort was put into it.

We clambered to the top of the hill and sat in the sun looking over the desolate country round about. It was about as depressing as anything I have seen yet, miles of country utterly abandoned, forests destroyed, numberless lines of

trenches picked out in white across the valleys and hillsides, great irregular patches of white to show hotly contested points which had been hammered hard by the artillery. The soil was so poisoned that there was hardly a green thing growing in the neighborhood and the feeling grows in your bones that the country itself has laid down and died. Although it was sizzling hot in the sun, we all kept quiet and I know I shivered and was glad to get away.

We came back down to the Aisne and thus back to Soissons, Villers-Cotterêts, Senlis and Paris. Our new cars and good drivers are a delight and we made gorgeous time all the way back. For long stretches at one time we got up to over seventy without discomfort.

In the woods this side of Senlis, we had a puncture and while the wheel was being changed we gathered a mass of daffodils which are now in the drawing room as evidence of our day in the country.

Letter to Mary Gibson　　　　　　　　　　Paris. Monday, April 7, 1919

Tonight we had big dinner to look after a big party of Congressmen who are over to see what they can see and I was kept fairly busy all day attending to various details of this and a trip to Belgium which was have arranged for them tomorrow. We had the following:
　[William A.] Ashbrook, [D] Ohio
　[Burton L.] French, [R] Idaho
　[William R.] Green, [R] Iowa
　[Ladislas] Lazaro, [D] Louisiana
　[Addison T.] Smith, [R] Idaho
　[James P.] Glynn, [R] Connecticut
　[Porter H.] Dale, [R] Vermont
　[C. William] Ramseyer, [R] Iowa
　[William W.] Hastings, [D] Oklahoma
　[Thomas T.] Connally, [D] Texas
　[Walter H.] Newton, [R] Minn.
The local talent was recruited as follows: Mr. Hoover, Norman Davis, Mr. Peden, Dick Oulahan, Bob Taft, Col. Barber, Col. Atwood, George Baker, Kittredge, Hart, HSG [Gibson].

As you can see, that made a good sized dinner table but it was well arranged and went off very nicely. The Chief gave them a talk after dinner, reviewing all relief activities and trying to foreshadow some of the things we must expect to deal with in the future. When he tried to sit down after half an hour, they protested vigorously and he went on for fifteen minutes more. It was one of the best things I have ever seen him do, and the Congressmen were deeply impressed.

We send them all off tomorrow morning on a specially conducted trip and hope to make them happy.

Letter to Mary Gibson   Paris. Tuesday, April 8, 1919

A society day for the old man but no letters.

I spent the whole morning at home thumping out a lot of stuff that I could do best without a stenographer. At one I went home with Norweb to lunch at his flat and see his seven months old son whom I have missed before. Commander Mayse was also there and we had a good quiet time.

There was enough at the Crillon to keep me busy through the afternoon and then I had to dress for dinner and go over to the de Montille's. I stopped at the Crillon and went over with Joe and Alice Grew so as to have moral support for the long drive. The other guests were some of the fringes on the Montille family, and Mr. and Mrs. Birch he being our Minister to Portugal. He is a rather ponderous old party with a pink face, white hair, and fire-escape whiskers and a general air of 1840. He has a kindly twinkle in the eyes and I should think he would need it in his post.

Bertie Goelet was giving a dance at the Jeu de Paume and on the way home I dropped in for half an hour just to make it a complete day. It was not very thrilling and I came home and got into bed sometime after eleven.

Phil [Patchin] is deep in despond because the President has put his foot down on any more wives coming over. Polly was to have sailed tomorrow and although the matter was brought up to the President, he declined to make an exception. It is pretty rough as they have been separated for a long time since the war began to say nothing of the fact that Polly didn't see such a lot of him while he was in Washington and working night after night. As soon as he can decently do so, I believe he will ask for permission to go home.

Letter to Mary Gibson   Paris. Wednesday, April 9, 1919

Today has been the usual grind.

I lunched with Clare Torrey at the Meurice to meet his brand new fiancée – a Miss Sombodyorother whose name I didn't get. She seems to be very nice, is working for the YMCA (which will not be used against her under the circumstances) and seems to be strong for Clare. He is bringing her up to the house to dine tomorrow evening.

Late in the afternoon I got out and left some cards. Ran into Laughlin and has a little talk to him about all sorts of things. He expects to return to the United States in the fall to stay for some time. I am glad of it as he has been away from home far too long through no fault of his own.

The Marquis d'Assche has been in town for a couple of days and has pursued me all over the place but always missed me. He came to the house just before I got in and I turned around and went down to his hotel in the hope of finding him.

I also got energetic and signed the book at the President's house which is right around the corner from us.

Before lunch I went down to see Cabot Ward at his request and yarned about all sorts of things. He has a periodical desire to tell what he has on his mind and I always strive to oblige.

Myriam Reyntiens has come to town for a day or two on her way back to Brussels and I am trying to get her on the telephone to bid her for dinner tomorrow night. The Continental where she is staying is notorious for having only a quarter enough lines and they always ring busy. And if you send a note, it is never delivered. I don't know anything to do but to put up large posters in the street after the fashion of the suffragettes.

Dr. Leach got in tonight just in time for dinner having flown from Lille late in the afternoon. All the fellows who has taken to that mode of travel as too stuck up to ring on the ground anymore and even scorn the best limousines.

Lewis Richards got in by lowly train and came to dine. He is off to London tomorrow morning but will be back on Monday next for a few days.

Letter to Arthur Bliss Lane   Paris, April 9, 1919

Your letter of the 4th reached me several days ago, but I have delayed answering it in the hope of having something definite to say.

1st. I don't know what to say about planning to take the family in during the summer but I am going ahead making my plans as though things were to be reasonably normal. The next few weeks ought to tell the story, and if we get through the middle of May without a complete blowup I shall feel fairly comfortable about the future. By that time we shall have a flow of food assured and some raw materials beginning to arrive and that ought to turn the scale. I hope very much that things will be calm enough to incline you to bring them in. Our friends are right that it looks pretty dark just now but all sorts of forces are beginning to work for good as well as evil and we may get the situation on its feet yet.

2nd. Topsy still lives though she is getting old and feeble. The poor old thing has travelled a good deal between here and Bern and has taken a trip to London now and then. She is a good soul and worked hare when she was young.

3rd. Would you be willing, le cas échéant, to substitute Warsaw to Prague? I don't know what will happen but it may be that the former will be the interesting place. Let me know how you feel about it so that I can be ready in case of emergency.

4th. I accept the bet of a <u>good</u> dinner that you and I will be in Prague before July 15th. If I lose, I shall be glad to pay and if I win I shall need the fortification of food and drink.

The most important pending matter goes up to the President periodically but so far he has not handed down a decision. I am praying that he may do so soon.

Needless to say, you will hear all about it as soon as possible after he does hand down his judgement on the matter.

Letter to Mary Gibson   Paris. Thursday, April 10, 1919

The best of birthdays to you. I'm sorry not to be with you on this one but hope I may by the time April 10 rolls round next year. The cable I have sent takes all my love, a supply to see you through the year.

I found this morning your letter of March 11th which shows that there is no particular sequence in the arrival of pouches.

You would be amused if you could see the job that has been given me. I have been made chairman of the Interallied committee to determine the ownership of the Austro-Hungarian merchant ships as between the Italians and Yugo-Slavs. The other Powers will probably put on naval officers but they asked that we assign an officer of the Department of State to preside over the deliberations. At any rate, I may learn something about merchant ships.

I went home to lunch with Joe Grew to see the children who have just arrived from America. They are a good lot and enjoyed being named THE BIG FOUR. The name fits and besides think of the standing one gets by going about Paris talking casually about lunching and dining with the Big Four.

This afternoon Dr. Kellogg got back from Poland with a lot of interesting talk. A lot has been accomplished and he is reassured about the food but there is so much remaining to be done that it is rather overwhelming.

Also had a long talk with Fred King who is just back from three months in Prague and hopes to leave for home in the course of a few weeks. One could easily spend all waking hours in profitable talk with returned travelers but there are other things to do and the traveler gets sadly neglected as a rule.

Znamięcki also came in to see me for a few minutes. Paderewski has taken him on as a sort of exalted private secretary and he is in the thick of things.

This evening I fetched Myriam Reyntiens from the Continental for dinner and found that we had a real party. Clare Torrey brought Mrs. Halley to whom he is engaged to present her to the house. Dr. Kellogg came in to get acquainted all over again. The Chief brought home Francis from Stockholm and McKnight who is coming to our organization. Bob Taft brought Major Benson and Lt. Klotz, and we had the usually number of our own people and sat down sixteen. ... After taking Myriam home, I found the Chief sitting up on an important piece of drafting and have been thumping at it until after one, so GOOD NIGHT!!!!

Letter to Mary Gibson   Paris. Friday, April 11, 1919

Spring has gone flickering again and we are back in wintry weather. There seems to be little hope of any real summer for a time yet.

As usual I have put in my day trying to clean up odd jobs and get some news as to what I am to do next. I got up at seven so as to go over the draft of the Chief's letter before he got down and with the help of George Baker in doing it. The frightful strain of getting up at any such hour had to be compensated for, however, and I came home later in the afternoon and took a nap.

I lunched with Phil [Patchin] and Wallace Young at the Crillon and talked a lot of shop. Phil is still down in the dumps because Polly is not coming but I hope he will stay and see the show through now.

The Chief went out to dine and pretty well everybody else seems to have been struck with the same idea. I had Fred King come up to talk about affairs at Prague and Dr. Kellogg came in with his budget of Polish news.

Just as we were finishing dinner, I was summoned by telephone to see Colonel House and had a short talk with him about my affairs. There was some sort of meeting at which the President was present, probably the League of Nations but the Colonel led me into another room and talked until I felt uncomfortable about taking so much of his time and eased myself out. I hope to see him again tomorrow.

The Chief told me the other day a story with a strong flavor of tragedy that could be made into something big by Edith Wharton or somebody with her ability. In his London office, he had a bank messenger who was something of a personage in his own class. He had served many years in the army and was finally retired with the rank of Sergant-Major and a pension. His pay and pension together enabled him to look after his family comfortably and he was contented. When the war broke out, he was well over age but volunteered and was put to work in an instruction camp as drillmaster. He drilled troops for some time and was finally sent to the front. There, by sheer ability and merit, he was pushed ahead, first to be a Lieutenant and then gradually promoted until he became a Major. So long as the war lasted, he got on swimmingly, was wounded three timed and decorated about as often. But when he was discharged, he found the other side of the picture, and came to see the Chief. He said that as a major nobody would give him a job as messenger, that that sort of job was reserved entirely for ex-non-coms. On the other hand, he had no training to fit him for a job that was up to his rank. He couldn't afford to stop and do nothing for now he had no pension. And he was flat up against it. There was a lot more to the story but that's the gist of it. When he had finished telling it, he stood up by the desk and said: "And now, in God's name, what can I do?" The Chief thought about it and finally told him that there was only one thing to do, and that was to pull up stakes and go to British Columbia to some small town where they would be glad to have a major in the British army whether he dropped his aitches or not, and where he could hope to become somebody in the community. Telling the old boy to leave England at his time of life was a shock to his imagination, but he took it standing up and is going to bundle up his whole family and take them off to British Columbia.

[Added note found only in Secret Log] April 11th

Colonel House wanted to tell me that the President had decided to appoint me Minister to Warsaw and that the papers would be signed almost at once. He had just sent a telegram to the Department saying that I was to go to Warsaw, Dick Crane to Prague and Norman Hapgood to Copenhagen. These are to be made as recess appointments. I was asked to say nothing about it until the President could complete the signature, etc.

Letter to Mary Gibson[210] Paris. Saturday, April 12, 1919

Nothing startlingly new today save the interruption of Doc Taylor from the Balkans by way of Rome. He came boiling in while I was thumping my typewriter and after shaving and making himself beautiful, I took him down to the new offices.

---

[210] Letters to Mary Gibson (but not the log material) hereafter are published at the first pages of the follow-up edition *An American in Warsaw. Selected Writings of Hugh S. Gibson, U.S. Minister to Poland 1919–1924*, ed. by Vivian Hux Reed, et al, Rochester, NY: University of Rochester Press, 2018.

He is sizzling with information and indignation about all sorts of things and in view of his sputtering, I understand why he is famous as a professor of fizzyology.

When he found me here he snorted with rage that I had not gone with him as there were lots of things I could have done to advantage and they had to go undone. Poor Ward was very ill and had to come back. Chauncey McCormick got a telegram that his wife had had a bad nervous breakdown and he had to abandon the trip and return to the United States, so all the latter part of the trip the Doc was alone.

I spent the afternoon in the Crillon going over all sorts of little things. Late in the afternoon, Colonel House sent for me to present me to Paderewski and a little talk about Poland. P. told something of what our people were accomplishing in Poland and was moved to tears in telling about it. We get lots of kind words about what our people do, but it is rather refreshing to see that much real feeling about it.

This evening we had as guests Mr. [Henry] Morgan, our Consul-General at Antwerp and his wife.

[Added note found only in Secret Log]   April 12th

The Chief told me confidentially this evening before dinner that he had been sent for by the Great White Father [Wilson] and offered the job of running Constantinople. It seems that Turkey is to be more or less completely dismembered and that Constantinople is to be left out of the wreck and placed under the mandate of the League of Nations. America is to take the job and the Chief was chosen to handle it. He shivered at the thought as I did for him. All our people seemed to think that it would be a great opportunity of running a rich state, etc. not understanding that with all the wealth of the Empire taken away, Constantinople would be as poor as a beggar. Just because wealth sails by from the Black Sea ports does not mean that any of it will stick to the city and it looks like a poor job to us. I hope the Chief won't touch it.

The Colonel said he had written another note to the President urging him to act at once on the appointments. Frank Polk has telegraphed urging that any action to be taken be taken at once so that it will not be irritatingly near the convening of Congress.

I told the Colonel that I had received a note from Ned Bell to the effect that Stephen Leech was now in London on his way to Warsaw as Minister. The French have already beat us to it by getting the first Minister but we should not repeat the mistake we made in Prague of letting everybody else get ahead of us.

The Colonel promised to hurry the matter along.

Letter to Arthur Bliss Lane   Paris. April 12, 1919

Congratulations on the healthy, screaming daughter. I hope she is still healthy but the screaming has stopped. You don't say whether father and child are doing well. My best wishes to the Mother.

As usual, we are just on the verge of deciding what we are going to do. I am sitting on the edge of my trunk ready to lead on the train.

Dr. Taylor came barging in this morning, snorting and rampaging about his trip, and I was able to gather that he had seen you and didn't altogether approve of you.

I don't take any stock in the stories of danger in going to Prague or Warsaw. As a matter of fact, the wife of British Military Attaché in Prague is now here on her way to join her husband, who she has already seen once since she married him – in 1914. It must be awful to have nobody out there but a perfectly strange man.

I renew my promises to write as soon as there is any news.

Letter to J. Butler Wright at American Embassy, London   Paris. April 12, 1919

Thanks for the large White Paper on Bolshevism. I opened it once or twice and was overcome by the fumes. I have sent for my old gas mask, however, and shall really sit down and read it at the first opportunity. I hope in a day or two to be able to write you some news about developments in regard to that same matter. In the meantime, thanks.

Letter to Capt. Joseph C. Green, ARA Bucharest, Romania   Paris. April 12, 1919

Your letter of March 22nd came in some time ago, but I put off answering it because I was hoping to have some sort of news to give you. As there seem to be no prospected of anything ever happening, however, I send this along just to let you know that I still live.

Doc Taylor came barging in this morning, sputtering about everything that is happening between here and Bucharest. I begin to understand why they call him a Professor of Fizzy-ology.

If he didn't tell you about his interested audience with the Queen, there is no use my doing it. At the Chief's request, I went to the Ritz and explained to an imposing lady in waiting just who the great Doc Taylor was and suggested that the Queen would possibly like to give him the privilege of a talk with her. She allowed as how she would and suggested he come at six. I poured the Doc into a frock hat and plug coat and led him around, to find that it was a tea party for about 200 old ladies, who were trampling each other to death in the rush to get somewhere near the "Que-ween". After about 10 minutes of looking at their backs as they struggled, I said I would leave for two pins and the doctor reduced the price fifty percent, so we left without having seen anybody and it took all Phil Patchin's available supply of gin to get the doctor so that he was at all articulate again.

Write us a little gossip when you get a chance.

Letter to Mary Gibson					Paris. Sunday, April 13, 1919

No news yet but symptoms of it at almost any moment.

It was a Sunday, but we did not get off to the country as we planned to do. It was biting cold and rainy and nobody budged from the warm fireside. The others spent the whole day at the office but I stayed in until after lunch and had Fred Dolbeare and Dresel come up to lunch with me to talk shop.

I saw Colonel House during the afternoon and had a little talk about my plans. I don't believe anything is settled until it is settled but there ought to be some sort of decision as to my plans within a day or two at most. I am as usual impatient to be off to the job if I am to have it. If I get what now seems to be on the ways it will suit me a great deal better than the Prague job, although goodness knows that was tempting enough. It will be so much good luck that it taxes credulity and I hardly dare think about it until it is really nailed down. If it goes through, I shall hope to send you a telegram very soon.

Late in the afternoon, we pushed off from the office and went for a drive in the Bois and the general direction of Versailles. By that time the sun had come out brilliantly and there were crowds of misguided people walking about on their own feet. I suppose it's all right if they care for that sort of thing, but it is dreadful to think of the great volume of effort that goes into propelling people through the Bois. Yesterday's expenditure, if it could be harnessed, would drive all the ships of the American Navy half way round the world.

We got back in time to dress and stand by for the arrival of Secretary Daniels and Admiral and Mrs. Benson. The Secretary [Lansing] did not drink any cocktails before dinner but managed to do his share of the talking without having his tongue loosened in that way. The Secretary made off early as he had an ear ache and an engagement to start for Chaumont at six in the morning.

Secretary Baker arrives tomorrow.

Also another troop of Congressmen.

Fred King has brought me an ad from the Schenectady *Gazette* which makes one wonder where out mid-Victorianism has gone: "Young lady wants housekeeping in bachelor's home; no objection to children. Box 17-R, *Gazette*."

Shockin' I calls it.

Letter from Ellis Loring Dresel to Gibson   London. April 13, 1919

Dear Hugh,

A small bird whispered the news to me yesterday, but it was a very discreet bird and in accordance with his wish, I have kept quite mum. However, this does not prevent me from congratulating a) the American people, b) the Polish people, c) the Diplomatic Service, d) last but not least, yourself as a most exemplary appointment – the best wishes, long life to Your Excellency and other greetings. The heavy responsibilities you will bear will not succeed in flooring you for a minute, as all your friends will agree. Ever most cordially yours.

Ellis Loring Dresel

Letter to Mary Gibson   Paris. Monday, April 14, 1919

In conformity with my traditional habit, I have spent the day in trying to get some definite news as to what I am to do next. All I need in the world now is a signature from the Great White Father [President Wilson] and then I can set out for a new job – but thus far there has been no signature from the GWF.

I lunched at the Kirk's with Myriam Reyntiens, Allen Dulles and two or three other people.

In the afternoon, Colonel House sent for me and said he was désolé because I had not been asked to a dinner he was giving this evening for Paderewski. He had taken it for granted that I was asked and when he found out that my name was not on the list it was too late to make any changes because the whole table would have to be reseated. When I had convinced him that I was not injured in all my finer feelings, he asked me to come in afterward and I agreed.

After going around for several days with a secret locked up in my head, it was rather comic to come into the reception and be greeted by all hands with congratulations over my appointment as Minister to Poland. I began with Alice Grew who was standing near the door of the Salon des Aigles talking to Colonel House. When I came in Paderewski he threw up his hands and cried: "Ah, here is the new Minister to my country" and then proceeded to make a regular speech. Madame Paderewska also allowed to all those round about that I was going to Warsaw and in about two minutes there wasn't a soul in the room who didn't know about it. It seems the Secretary had gone through the formality of asking P. whether I would be persona grata. It has to be done as a matter of form but is usually done in writing. He neglected to say that the matter was still confidential and P. spread it as rapidly as possible because he wanted a Minister appointed and being happy about it wanted to tell everybody. So it's a secret no longer, and very soon I ought to be able to telegraph you.

The Secretary was very nice about it and said things in public about the appointment that I could not have improved upon myself. Colonel and Mrs. House and Mrs. Lansing and Mr. White and a swarm of other people laid themselves out to be nice and when the reception was over all the service people present adjourned to Leland Harrison's room for a stirrup cup – Caffery, Harrison, Phil [Patchin], Whitehouse and a flock of others. And now home at a late out and to bed.

There was not much of a crowd at the reception, but in the course of the evening I did see and talk to John and Mrs. Garrett, Mrs. and Miss Willard, Miss Hemp from Rome, Sonnino, Willie Tyrrell, the Brambilla's, Miss Hare, General Harts, Poillon, and the Bliss' and some others. And between times, I had the best and most satisfactory talk I have had with the Secretary [Lansing] so far.

Letter from HG to Peter Jay   – Confidential Paris. April 16, 1919

Here is a matter on which I should like to have an expression of opinion from you.

Miss Larner, who was in charge of the Legation at Brussels from the outbreak of the war until after I left, has been here in the Embassy for something over a year. She has been in the Department for eight or ten years. Her work here will naturally end about the end of this summer and in the nature of things she would go back to the Department. However, she said the other day in talking to me that if she could be useful, she would like very much to go to Rome. I told her that I would broach the matter confidentially to you and ask whether there was any use in her raising the question.

I don't know what you need in the way of help, but I know that if ever I had the chance I would snap her up. To begin she is real people – Larner's of Maryland – and she is so very real people that she never has to emphasize it and is strictly business when business is on the boards. She knows all the ropes of the Department and the foreign service and there is no need to educate her as to procedure. I used to pass on about nine-tenths of the work of the Brussels Legation to her, and she did more of the work that I got credit for. She has French and Spanish at her finger tips and does some German. And she gets on with people.

Will you let me know whether on the basis of the foregoing you think there would be any chance for her to be considered for a place in the Rome Embassy. I would be grateful for a frank expression from you.

P.S. As I thump this out, the telephone rings to say that the President has just signed my commission as Minister to Poland. As you can imagine, I am delighted with the post and its opportunities – even if it is not that complete rest I was going to take on the signature of peace.

Letter to Ralph Van Deman Paris, April 19, 1919

General Staff
4, Place de la Concorde
Dear Colonel Van Deman:

I have tried to get you today at unseemly hours and have not had any success. I wanted to say that it looks as though I might get away on Tuesday evening and that I am still hopeful of getting a Military Attaché lined up by that time.

Do you suppose there would be any possibility of getting Frank McCoy? I don't know whether he would care for the job and whether the fact that he is a permanent Brigadier General would be against him, but the more I see of what is going on in Poland the more I am convinced that we need a very sound, dependable man with a good deal of authority. If he is to lay down the law to the Poles and the Ukrainians on one side, the Germans on another, the Czechs on another, and possibly the Bosheviki here and there, he will have his hands full and need a pretty level head.

I hear out two friends of whom I spoke to you the other day are actively clamorous for the place and I hope there will be no such slip as to let them go. I like them both, personally, but feel sure we should be in a mess very soon after they got there.

I shall keep on your trail until I find you and hope for good news.

Telegram received by HG 4/19/1919 from Edgar Rickard April 10th

Delighted to hear of your promotion. Both Governments concerned in your new job are to be congratulated. AMRNFA

Letter to Wm. Cullen Dennis   Paris, April 19, 1919

No. 3, Fang Chia Yuan
E. City, Peking, China

... I had mightily hoped that I should get to Peking to see you all while you were still there and enter Chinese society under your auspices, getting acquainted with Chop Suey and other dignitaries and learning to eat Li Hung Chang, Wu Ting Fang and other native dishes. I fear me now, however, that there is little prospect of this as our great and wise President has made his name and fame secure by appointing me Minister at Warsaw and I shall probably spend the next few years in a fierce endeavor to maintain the requisite amount of human life in my system between the insults of the Bolsheviki on the one hand and the Huns on the other. From this, you will know that I shall appreciate all the news you can send. Send it through the Department or to the Embassy, Paris, whence there is a pouch to Warsaw.

    Our old friend MAH is in our midst, dressed in the simple garb of a Major in the American Army but looking nonetheless like a Presbyterian friar. I come upon him in the halls with great frequency and he never fails to fall upon my neck and assure everybody within hearing distance of his quavering voice that he found me in the gutter and raised me up and up and up, until I started in at the bottom of the diplomatic service, where he in his wisdom was able to place me.

    Your friend, Mr. Charles R. Crane, is also in our midst. As a matter of fact, I have spent most of the afternoon on a pair of roller skates just one lap ahead of messengers, orderlies and telephone calls saying that he wanted to see me. I shall not fail to act upon your suggestion to get him to do some of his inimitable little stories when occasion offers. His son, Richard, has just been made Minister to Prague, so Uncle Charles will probably be my next door neighbor and pay me frequent visits, telling me droll stories of his infancy and otherwise whiling away long winter evenings.

    If you really do leave Peking next winter, and if the Bolsheviki have ceased from troubling, and if the Finns, the Estonians, the Letts, the Ukrainians and others are at rest, why not come back such a way as to finish a trip around the world and stop off and pay me a visit in Warsaw? Don't fail to bring the children! All my reading about Poland tends to show that they are very useful to throw over to the wolves while sleighing in the country, thereby saving the life of a large man in a fur overcoat and cap who holds the reins.

    I have not had a sound out of Reuben since slightly after the flood, but now and again I hear that he is prospering and waxing fat. I shall write him an insulting letter and suggest that he reciprocate.

    For the love of Heaven, do sit down and let me have some news from time to time, and in the meantime believe me

Letter to Thomas Gregory Paris, 19 April 1919

American Food Mission
Trieste.

I have hoped to see you bob up here any time and have put off writing on that account. That is to say, partly one that account, for to tell the truth, most of it has been pure laziness.

Sergeant Cash breezed in some time ago and has been busy getting his discharge and passport so as to go home by way of England. We fought shoulder to shoulder in certain hostilities that occurred here and, as usual, Victory perched upon our banners. He should be back today or tomorrow as a civilian ready to go to England to visit his family before going home to America.

We hear all sorts of vague reports of you bobbing up in Bucharest, Budapest, Teheran and Vladivostok and other quaint places, but haven't had a very clear idea of what you are up to. When you get a chance, sit down and tell us something about it.

Doctor Taylor is once more in our midst, after having absorbed all the information and stimulants between here and the Black Sea, and is gradually getting to a point where he is more or less articulate. Usually upon his return from a trip, he is about as satisfactory as a conversationalist as a bad shellshock case, but after he has trimmed his mustache and put both feet on the floor, he does deliver the information.

Doctor Kellogg pussy-footed in from Warsaw with an encouraging account of what was happening there. He has left for home with Mrs. Kellogg.

I am off in a few days for Warsaw, where our wise President has appointed me Minister. If you can, oil up the Slivovitz and have her hauled up to Warsaw and pay me a visit. That is, pay me a visit if I have a house, and if I haven't a house, I will pay you a visit on the Slivovitz. What could be fairer than that? On the lever, I think you really should come, for you certainly cannot pretend to know anything about conditions in Central Europe unless you have been everywhere, and so far as I know, you haven't tackled Warsaw yet.

Letter to Lou Henry Hoover Paris, 19 April 1919

I have become rather discouraged about trying to write to anybody because we have been sending everything by pouch and discovered the other day that our letters were taking from 30 to 60 days between here and California. We have now decided to patronize the open post and I hope for better luck. This is just for a try out.

There is nothing special to report but that is because our whole life is like a three ring circus and we had all strained an eye trying to watch the performing elephants in one ring and see the fat lady fall off a trapeze in another.

Our heavy artillery is usually unlimbered at eight in the morning and pounds away until eleven or so in the evening. The Chief sticks pretty regularly to his 10:30 grand disappearance act, which he accomplishes with his never-failing technic. Usually he gets away with it boldly, but last night some of the guests, after saying goodbye, lingered to chatter outside the door and he had to climb up the back stairs, looking as though he had been robbing a hen roost.

Although he has had a strenuous time, he is standing it very well. Along toward Saturday night he usually begins to look weary, but I try to make a practice of taking him off somewhere on Sunday and he comes back like an elastic band. Tomorrow being Easter Sunday, we are surely going to haul him away and the prospects are for a gorgeous day.

We are getting more frivolous as time goes on and go in more and more for society. Since I last wrote, we had a charming function for 13 Congressmen with an equal number of local firemen. The events of the evening will be described to you with appropriate gestures upon our return to the United States. After they had been given the requisite number of calories, the Chief got up and gave them a little talk on things in general and food relief in particular. After about 20 minutes, he paused and allowed that he had talked about enough, whereupon thirteen booming Congressional voices protested with evident feeling and demanded that he go on, which he did for another half hour. The M.C.'s were really deeply impressed and allowed that perhaps the gentleman was competent to run his job, along with several other observations of a complimentary nature.

We followed up the good work by sending the thirteen on a trip through Belgium and Northern France in our own cars, convoyed by our own people and educated as to the significance of things in general. It was the best investment we have made to date, for each and every one of them will go home and speechify about what he has seen and heard and what the King and the Cardinal and the Burgomaster had to say and what disorderly, destructive people the Germans are.

There is another party due now, a Committee on Military Affairs, and we are going to put them through the same mill.

By way of breaking up the talk of shop in the evening, we have taken to bidding various people to dine. Among those out society editor has recently noticed are Mr. and Mrs. Honnold, Mr. and Mrs. Morgenthau, Mr. and Mrs. Oscar Strauss, Mr. and Mrs. Morgan, Mr. and Mrs. Peden, Mme. Reyntiens and Mrs. Halley.

The last named is about to commit matrimony, the part of the other part being Clare Torrey. The event is to take place on the 29th at the house, at 4:00 pm. friends invited, no flowers. The bride is to be given away by the Chief. Torrey has given himself away from the beginning. She is really very nice and just the right sort for him. You could fire a 9" Howitzer just three inches from her left ear and she wouldn't jump.

The other evening a cullud gemmun [sic, colored gentleman] rang the doorbell and allowed that he would like to play his guitar for Mr. Herbert Hoover. He was installed just outside the dining room door and warbled well and enthusiastically until I brought him into the room, where he thought he had a chance to show off. To our surprise and horror, he then burst forth in imitation of Harry Lauder and would not desist from Scotch songs for the rest of the evening. Fortunately, he thought our mirth was occasioned by the songs themselves so he came back a second time.

Another evening we had a Jazz band of eight pieces – American boys who have just been demobilized and are seeing the world before they go home. They played on every kind of thing you ever saw and made a row like nothing on earth. The Chief sat through dinner with a look of acute misery on his face which those who understand his inner soul were compelled to explain was his customary way of expressing rapture and appreciation of the beautiful. The rest of the family had so much fun out of it that it was hard to make the boys go home, even after they had been fed, and they had to be ejected so that the Chief could go to sleep.

We have even gone so far now as to set up a piano, which is very decorative, but I don't know whether it has any insides or not.

Doctor Taylor has come boiling back from Bucharest and other points as explosive as usual and, having blown off steam for three or four days, is now ready to take on anything that offers. Doctor Kellogg has polished off his Polish business and is not on his way back to American with Mrs. Kellogg.

I have been sitting around here for weeks and months and years waiting for some kind President to make up his mind as to what I was to do next. Now I am approaching the time of life where I can no longer bear the hardship of travel, it has been decided to send me as Minister to Poland. I am off some time this coming week. If my previous record is to be continued, you will know from the outbreak of hostilities that I have arrived. And me expecting to take a complete rest when Peace was signed!

I hope that when you have the time and inclination you will let me have a little news from home, for, as I remarked the other day to Messrs. Morgenthau, Strauss and Frankfurter, it would be a Christian act.

My address as always is either Department of State, Washington, or America Embassy, Paris. There are pouches to Warsaw from both places.

Letter to Mary Gibson   Paris. Wednesday, April 23, 1919

Last night the Chief had a dinner in his rooms at the Crillon for Paderewski. The guests were Henry White, George Baker, Dr. Taylor, Col. Barber, Tom Lamont, Norman Davis, Vance McCormick, and HSG. Paderewski let himself out in his best style and all the men present were very deeply impressed by the fact that he is really a statesman as well as a musician, which seemed to surprise all of them. He talked in a very dispassionate and restrained way about questions that get everybody excited these days, and went over patiently some of the Polish problems that have been explained over and over for months.

After dinner we settled down to talk and General Bliss and Admiral Benson came in and joined us. We kept at it until midnight.

Paderewski stated that he felt the most difficult questions for Poland from now on were her economic problems and that he was anxious for a good American financial advisor to tackle the currency and exchange questions, etc. Mr. Hoover suggested the name of Fred Kent, which was warmly seconded by McCormick, Davis and Lamont. They agreed to send him a telegram urging him to come over as a volunteer for as long as might be necessary to solve Poland's immediate financial problems. I very much hope he will come as these questions are far beyond my depth, and I know he can have an extraordinarily good and wholesome influence.

In the course of the evening in talking of the feeling in Poland toward the President, Paderewski told of a village now in dispute between the Poles and Czechs which had raised a fund and sent the Priest and an old peasant all the way to Paris just so that they might look upon the President and go back and tell the villagers about it. Mr. White spoke up and said that was not the whole of the story; that these old boys had come to the Crillon and asked to see him, that they had explained to him how the money for their trip had been raised by popular subscription, and that they desired to but look at the President so that they might return home and rejoice the hearts of all the merry villagers. He was greatly touched and had taken the matter up with the President who immediately asked to have them sent up to see him. Both of the men had been in America and spoke fairly good English. Once they got in the room with the President, each of them took him firmly by the hand and stroked it while they filled him up with a carefully rehearsed lot of talk to the effect that their villages should belong to the Poles instead of to the Czechs. It was a very shrewd and clever way of doing it, as if they had asked to see the President to discuss this matter he would certainly have referred them to somebody in the Peace Commission, but there was no escape for him once they got it. He was touched and amused and sent for Mrs. Wilson to come and talk to the old men. They gained their point for he promised to look into the special claims of their own villages and when they go home they will be real heroes.

We talked of the possibility of an agreement of some sort between the Poles and Czechs in regard to the Teschen territory. Paderewski said that such an agreement might be possible if some time were allowed in which to arrange it. He said that both sides had such high feeling in regard to the matter that any decision reached by the Peace Conference or by mutual agreement would cause popular uproar and possibly trouble and that it was very desirable that no decision be announced for some time to come.

Mr. Hoover said out of the clear sky that he thought he could arrange the matter. That he was Director of General Relief in Europe and administrator of railroads and that the Teschen district might be turned over to him to administer so that he could increase the coal output and thereby handle the Relief and Railroad situations adequately; that he would do this for several months during which time the Poles and Czechs could do their best to come to an understanding.

Paderewski burst out enthusiastically that this was just the thing and that he was prepared to sign any document submitted by Mr. Hoover along those lines and that he thought the Czechs would look at the matter in the same way.

We undertook to take the matter up with the Czechs, so I went over in the morning to Beneš and brought him to the Avenue Montaigne to talk to Mr. Hoover. The little man was in no conciliatory mood, however, and gave us a long talk about the rights of his people, the general inequity of the Poles and a lot of generalities in regard to ethnography, economics and the price of food. We did not get anywhere with him, but Paderewski took up the matter with the President today and he has promised to lay it before the Council of Four and if they approve, Beneš will probably agree.

Letter to Mary Gibson   Paris. Thursday, April 24, 1919

This was a very busy day with very little that was definite, but a great deal of detailed preparation for getting away.

Right after breakfast, Paderewski's secretary came in to see me and said that Paderewski wanted me to dine with him in the evening at Voisin's.

I lunched with Dr. Taylor, George McFadden, George Baker and Irving at the Escargot because the Doctor was determined that before I left I should eat some snails and take away that happy memory with me. He ate them by the dozens and scores, but I dropped out after about six. They are not cheap, but as Sam Weller said "They are filling at the price."

George McFadden is going home to build a house and told me casually that if I found some tapestries that would do for his dining room, and if I could get them cheap, he would like to have them, but not to spend more than twenty or thirty thousand dollars for them.

In the afternoon I had a long talk with Admiral Benson, chiefly about an idea he has about the world being reformed by giving it a little spiritual bump on the head. I am afraid the Admiral is an optimist about the well-known human race.

Col. Farman came in for lunch and said that he had definite instructions from GHQ that he was to proceed to Warsaw as Military Attaché. He is busy getting assistants, clerks, orderlies, chauffeurs, etc. and hopes to come up by the next train on Tuesday.

He has been liaison officer at Foch's Headquarters for over a year and has a very fine reputation among the men I know in the regular army.

Horodyski came in to see me in the afternoon to say that he had a telegram from a lot of Poles in America saying that they had raised the money to buy 80,000 tons of condensed milk for distribution in Warsaw to certain classes of the working population and that they wanted it handled by the new American Minister as one of his first official acts. Horodyski is to deposit the money here, Col. Grove is to deliver the milk in Warsaw. The Poles have already given up the money, and so far as I can make out all I have to do is to write a letter generously giving away the milk.

I went down to Voisin's a little after eight and found Horodyski waiting. Paderewski and Madame Paderewska came in a little late closely followed by Mrs. Schelling, and we had dinner together in a small room upstairs, talking about everything on earth except music which seems to have been laid away for good.

Mrs. Schelling started in calling me "Mr. Minister" with great unction every time she spoke, until I snorted and Paderewski arose and said he was glad he saw somebody who felt the way he did; that every time anyone called him "Mr. President" he wanted to laugh and, of course, he could not laugh so it just bored him. That disposed of Mrs. Schelling for the rest of the evening.

Log   Paris. Friday, April 25, 1919

The day which as E. Bell would say "has been as busy as a one-armed paper hanger." I went down to the Embassy and bade everyone goodbye, some of them several times, and I ambled around the Peace Commission and saw all the people who were to be found.

I lunched alone with Mr. Hoover and had a lot of good talk about things which we had not been able to talk about at our cozy little dinners of 12 to 20 that are the rule.

I had two nice telegrams from the Poles in America which came just before I left so that I did not have a chance to answer them. The telegrams are as follows:

> "You will carry with you into Poland the heartfelt wishes for success from four million Poles resident in the United States. They have every confidence in the success which you will achieve. Your record in Belgium has encouraged them to believe that America is securing a trained representative and that Poland is gaining in you a strong friend.
>
> John F. Smulski Chicago Ill., President Polish National Department of America"
>
> ----
>
> "Permit us to congratulate you upon your appointment as first United States Minister to Poland. We wish you success in cementing even more securely spirit of Brotherhood between the two nations.
>
> Polish National Alliance, K.Z. Zichliski, President"

I got off to the Station with George Baker and Arthur Lane at six, and foregathered at the Gare de Est with the rest of the party. There were a number of people there to see us off, including Sczrinski and Perlowski and several other Poles, Hugh and Katherine Wilson, Teddy Curtis (who had flown down from Belgium especially to say goodbye and expected to fly back in the morning), Stockton, Dulles, and a number of others.

Paderewski sent his Aide, Major Ivanowski, to look after us on the trip and see to our comfort. He availed of the opportunity to bring his wife along, an American. When not busy freeing Poland, Ivanowski is an artist and did a series of pictures that Century published several years ago under the titles "Shakepeare's Heroines," "Heroines of Fiction," etc. He is altogether a fine fellow. Znamiecki had planned to go last Tuesday, but put off his trip so as to go with us.

Although we sent down our baggage right after lunch, it was discovered just before time for the train to start that it had not been weighed. As we had 34 pieces, this was something of a tragedy and Znamiecki and I set off at a run to find the Station Master and to get him to hold the train while our stuff was put on. We found the little man very red and perspiring near the engine quite unprepared to hold the train. Znamiecki got more and more exited and gradually raised me in rank to an Ambassador and explained how horrible it would be it the train got off without my belongings. Two minutes more and I would have been President of the United States. However, he agreed to wait a few minutes and everybody rushed, pulled and pushed until we finally got the stuff aboard. Then three-quarters of an hour later, the train pulled out.

Log   En Route through Switzerland. Saturday, April 26, 1919

After the wild rush of the last few days we have had a quiet time. We reached the frontier at five o'clock and O'Neil and Lane got out to see that there was no trouble about our baggage, and then we all set to and slept late. We got thru Switzerland in short order and crossed from Buchs into Austria a little after two o'clock making the run to Innsbruck by dark. Switzerland and the Tyrol were under fairly heavy snow and the ride was gorgeous.

Yarned about Poland a good part of the day with Znamiecki, Iwanowski, etc.

Log   On train, Vienna-Warsaw. Sunday, April 27, 1919

I always have tangles on coming into a town in a train. We got into Vienna on time at 9:40 but there was nobody to meet us and we all got in cabs and went to the Hotel Bristol only to find Gregory, Col. Godson and others had just left to await our arrival. However, I passed the shining hour by having a talk with Coolidge until a message came from the North Station to say that Gregory and other local firemen had followed us there where we were to take the train out and would wait for us there. We found Schutzenhoffer waiting for us at the Station entrance and the others on the platform.

Gregory had a lot of things he wanted to talk about and was much upset because we could not stay over a few days. He had arranged a special train to take us off to Warsaw but we felt in as much as all arrangements were made for us it would not do for us to change out plans at this late date, so he talked as fast as he could and said he would come up to Warsaw within a week or two to have things out. He has done a great job and I hope he will stick it out until it is finished.

Col. Godson had got word some time ago that he was to proceed to Warsaw and establish a Military Attachés Office. In Vienna he heard I was coming and assumed he was to be the Military Attaché so sat down with his aide, Dewald, awaited my coming. He was much depressed may when he found out that somebody else had been appointed as he was thrilled with the thought of serving in Poland. The Poles would have liked it too.

We spent the afternoon going through Bohemia and reached the Polish frontier at about eight where there everybody dutifully got off and put their feet on Polish soil, though it seemed like any other sort of soil.

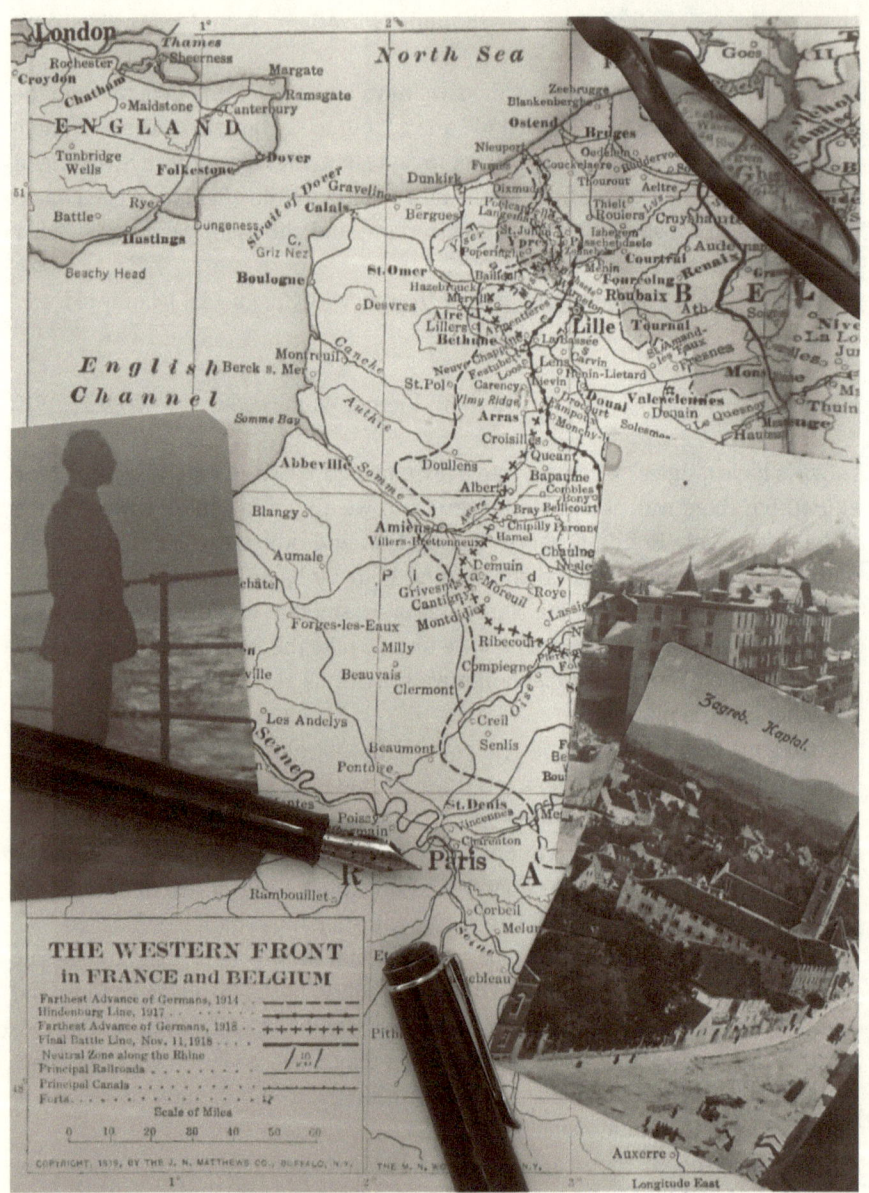

Biographical Index

A

Abbott, Frank Frost (1860–1924) was an American classical scholar who taught at the University of Chicago, then Princeton. He retired in Europe. 130

Ackerman, Carl W. (1890–1970) was an American journalist covering the war on behalf of the *New York Times*. 37, 39, 41, 44–46, 59, 91, 94, 95, 104, 129

Acton, Lady, Dorothy Lyon. (1876–1923) was married to Lord Acton. 102, 120

Acton, Lord, Richard Lyon-Dalberg-Acton (1870–1924), a British diplomat who had served as secretary at the British Embassies in Berlin 1896–1902, Vienna 1902–1905, Madrid 1906–1907, The Hague 1909–1910, then First Secretary and chargé d'affaires at Darmstadt and Karlsruhe in Germany until the outbreak of war. He was counselor of the Embassy in Bern 1915–1916, Consul-General in Zurich 1917, and the first British Ambassador to newly independent Finland in 1919. He retired in 1920. 103

Adams, Capt. 300

D'Addoni. 125

Alba, 17th Duke of, Jacobo Fitz-James Stuart y Falco (1878–1953) was a Spanish aristocrat, diplomat and politician. From 1902, he served as Lord of the Bedchamber to King Alfonso XIII and as Foreign Minister 1930–1931. He was drawn into Gen. Franco's camp when his brother was murdered by communists in 1936, and represented Franco in London 1936–1939. He served as Spanish Ambassador to London 1939–1945. Throughout his career, he was a proponent of cordial British-Spanish relations. 364, 500

Albert I, King of the Belgians (1875–1934) reigned in Belgium from 1909 to 1934. He and his family formed a firm friendship with Gibson during his tenure in Brussels 1914–1915, which continued through the reign of Albert's son Leopold III (1934–1951) and into that of his grandson Baudouin (1951–1993). 261, 271, 275, 366, 427, 554

Albert I, Prince of Monaco (1848–1922) was a political reformer as well as an oceanographer. 223–225

Albin, Pierre (1872–1922) was a French international policy specialist. 329

Aldrovandi-Marescotti, Luigi (1876–1945) was an Italian politician and diplomat who worked with Sidney Sonnino representing Italy at the Paris Peace Conference. Later he was Ambassador to Argentina 1923–1926 and Germany 1926–1929. He also served as a Senator 1939–1944. 140, 145, 176, 378

Aldrich, Chester Holmes (1871–1940) was an American architect who served in the American Red Cross in Italy from 1917–1919. Later he became the director of the American Academy in Rome, 1935–1940. 121

Alexander, George Beatty (1849–1927) was the paternal uncle of Eleanor Butler Roosevelt. 335

Alexeieff, Alexei (1880–1917) was a Russian general who was thought to have been killed in Baden-Baden because of his extensive knowledge of the Middle East. 304

Alfonso XVIII (1886–1941) King of Spain from birth to 1931. 330, 344

Allaire, William H., Jr. (1858–1933) was an American army officer serving as the Provost-Marshal General of the AEF in France in June 1918. In July he was attached to Douglas Haig's headquarters of the British Expeditionary Force. From August to November he commanded an infantry brigade before doing special duty in Paris until June 1919. 202

Allard, Josse (1868–1931) was a Belgian banker and businessman. The bank which bears his name played a role in developing many Belgian, colonial and foreign companies. He sat on the board of seventy companies and was a director of the Belgian Railway Bank. His business expanded greatly after the war was over. 292, 430

Allen, Capt. Jerome Lee (1891–1947) was an officer in the US Navy since 1908. During 1918–1919, he had charge of radio use for the US Naval forces in European waters under Admiral Sims in London. Later he served as Communication Officer at the Paris Peace Conference 1919–1920. He continued a long distinguished career in the Navy. 386

Altrocchi, Rudolph (1882–1953) was an Italian-born scholar of Italian language and literature who received his PhD from Harvard in 1914. During WWI, he served in the AEF managing propaganda and liaison functions. Later he taught at Columbia, the University of Chicago, and became chief of the Italian Department at the University of California at Berkeley. 85, 119, 120, 122, 127, 133, 147, 153, 347

Alvord, Benjamin, Jr. (1860–1927) was an American Army general serving with the AEF in France. 51

Ambrózy, Gyula (1884–1954) was a Hungarian lawyer and politician with the Ministry of Justice 1914–1921. Later he served as Secretary of State 1938–1942. 490, 491

Amette, Léon-Adolphe (1850–1920) was a French Catholic cardinal who served as Archbishop of Paris 1908–1920. 82, 223

Anderson, Chandler P. (1894–1953) was an American lawyer who served as the first Counselor of the US State Department 1912–1913. During WWI, he was assigned as a legal adviser to the Embassy in London. 297, 305

Anderson, Henry W. (1870–1954) was an American lawyer serving as Red Cross Commissioner for the Balkans. He commanded the American Red Cross Commission to Romania during WWI. When Romania surrendered to Germany in March 1918, the Anderson fled the country in a dramatic train escape that took him through revolutionary Russia in the throes of civil war. He developed a close friendship with Queen Marie of Romania before returning to the US in 1920. 420

Anderson, Isabel W. P. (1876–1978) was an American heiress from Boston who married diplomat Larz Anderson, who had served as Minister to Belgium 1911–1912, and very briefly as Ambassador to Japan (1913). Isabel also wrote several books, mostly travelogues, poetry and children's books. 51

Anderson, T. Hart was an American diplomat serving as 3rd Secretary to the Embassy in Rome 1916–1919. 126, 135–136, 159

Andrássy, Gyula, Jr (1860–1929) was a Hungarian politician who represented Austria-Hungary in 1912 in unsuccessful diplomatic negotiations to avoid the outbreak of the Balkan War. He served as Foreign Minister briefly from October to November 1918. 376

Andrássy, Katinka (1892–1985) was a Hungarian aristocrat, granddaughter of Gyula and daughter of Tivadar, who married to Mihály Karolyi in 1914. After the political turmoil in 1919, she lived in France. 494

Andrews, Mme. 67

Andrews, William Whiting "Bill" (1875–1957) was an American diplomat who served in Panama 1911, Romania 1912, and Paris 1915. 32, 99, 170, 176, 181, 212, 218, 221, 230, 351, 356, 372

Anslow, 1st Baron of, Tonman Mosley (1850–1933) was a British businessman, politician and. He was chairman of the North Staffordshire Railway Company 1904–1923. 374

Anthoine, François (1860–1944) was a French army general who served as chief of staff to Pétain. 197

Antonelli, Étienne (1879–1971) was a French economist who served as assistant military attaché in Petrograd in 1917 and reported on the Russia Revolution. 255, 256

Apolloni, Adolfo (1855–1923) was an Italian sculptor who had immigrated to the United States in 1879 and returned to Italy in 1883, after the death of his wife. He was a member of various art academies and circles, director of the Circolo Artistico Roma. He was nomination senator in 1919 and the following year served as Mayor of Rome. 133, 159

Apponyi, Albert (1846–1933) was a Hungarian nobleman and politician serving as the head of the Hungarian delegation to the Paris Peace Conference in 1919. Previously he served as the Minister of Religion and Education in Hungary 1906–1910. He made several speaking tours of the US and describes his impressions in *The Memoirs of Count Apponyi* (1935). Although nominated for a Nobel Peace Prize on five occasions between 1911 and 1932, he was not selected. 494

Apponyi, Djina. 540, 543, 593

Armour, Norman (1887–1982) was an American diplomat who served in Russia 1916–1918. After the collapse of Czarist Russia, Armour remained as part of a limited staff in Moscow. He was later arrested before making his way to Sweden or Finland. He snuck back into Petrograd and helped Russian princess Myra Koudashev escape. They married in February and he was then assigned to Brussels as Secretary 1919–1920. Later he served as Ambassador to Haiti, Canada, Chile, Argentina, Spain, Venezuela and Guatemala. 47, 121, 590

Armsby, Cornelia Wicker (1884–1969) was an American socialite and golfer who spent much of her adult life in Europe. She and her brother, Gordon Armsby, shared a house in Paris with Gertrude Tower. 185, 194, 236

Armstrong, John Samuel, Jr. (b. 1888) was an American diplomat serving as Consul in Venice 1918–1919. 396

Arnavon, Mr. 378

Arnold, Perry Bernard was an American businessman and publisher who worked with Creel's ComPub in the New York office. 331, 332

Arthur, Prince, Duke of Connaught and Strathearn (1850–1942) was the son of British Queen Victoria. He joined the Royal Corps of Engineers in 1868, serving in South Africa, Canada, Ireland, Egypt and India until 1890. He served as Governor General of Canada 1911–1916. 204–206

Ashbrook, William Albert (1867–1940) was a US Congressman from Ohio. 633

Asquith, Arthur M. "Puffin" (1883–1939) was a British army officer in the Royal Naval Land Division and son of Herbert H. Asquith, former British Prime Minister. He fought on the Western Front in France from 1916 to December 1917, when he lost a leg due to severe battle injuries. He served during the rest of the war in the Controller of the Trench Warfare Division of the Ministry of Munitions. He married Betty Manners in 1918. 121, 295, 303, 308, 312

Asquith, Cyril "Cys" (1890–1954) was a British barrister and judge. He was the son of Prime Minister Herbert Asquith, and married to Anne Pollack. 312

Asquith Bibesco, Elizabeth (1897–1945) was the daughter of Herbert Asquith. She and Gibson struck up a friendship when he was posted in London 1916–1917. She was a writer, and performed readings for the servicemen. Gibson and Elizabeth Asquith were friends since his posting in London 1916. It is rumored she had quite a crush on him at that time. Her sister-in-law recorded in her published diaries that Elizabeth hopefully announced her engagement to Hugh Gibson in 1916, but it was not true and no such marriage took place. In 1919, she married Prince Antoine Bibesco, a Romanian diplomat posted in London. Subsequently, Elizabeth published several works. She died of pneumonia in Romania during WWII. 311–314, 322, 324, 555

Asquith, Herbert Henry (1852–1928) was a British liberal politician who served as Prime Minister 1908–1916. 122, 302, 312, 313, 321, 322

Asquith, Margot Tennant (1864–1945) was married to Herbert Henry Asquith in 1894, his second wife, and became step-mother of his five children. Her daughter, Elizabeth, was born in 1897 and her son, Anthony, in 1902. 313, 314, 322, 343

Astor, Waldorf (1879–1952) was an American-born British politician and newspaper publisher, as well as the eldest son of William Waldorf Astor. He served in Parliament, 1910–1918 and served as Parliamentary Secretary of the Ministry of Food in 1918. From 1919–1921, he was Parliamentary Secretary to the Ministry of Health. 276

Atwood, William G. was a US Army colonel assigned as technical adviser to Yugoslavia. He reported on the resolution of the Yugoslav-Italian border disputes at the Treaty of Rapallo in 1920. 448, 449, 503, 512–515, 568, 583, 605, 607, 608, 634

Auchincloss, Gordon (1886–1943) was an American diplomat serving as an assistant to Frank Polk, State Department Counselor 1917–1918. He was later as secretary to Col. House in Paris 1918–1919. He married Janet House, daughter of Col. Edward House, in 1912. 195, 216, 352, 357, 363, 373, 374, 385, 391, 401, 402, 408, 410, 420, 437

Austin, Mary Hunter (1868–1934) was an eccentric American novelist and preservationist of Indian and Spanish culture. 14

Autrand, Auguste (1858–1949) was a French lawyer and senior official serving as Prefect of the Seine district 1918–1922. 178, 222

Axson, Stockton (1867–1935) was an American professor of English serving as the national secretary of the American Red Cross in 1917–1919. He was the brother of Ellen Axson Wilson, Woodrow Wilson's first wife. 353

B

Bacon, Robert (1860–1919) was an American diplomat who served as Secretary of State in 1909. He was commissioned into Pershing's staff in 1917 as Chief of the American Military Mission at British GHQ in France. 333, 374

Baetens, Fernand was the Belgian head of the CRB office in Brussels 1917–1919. 415, 553, 588

Baguès, Madame. 202, 366

Baidoux, M. 421

Bailey, James G. was an American diplomat who served as Secretary of the Embassy in Petrograd, Russia in 1918. 369

Baillie, Colonel Murray. 341

Baker, George Barr (1870–1948) was an American journalist who served as Naval Censor in New York, attached to the force commander in European waters. He worked for the Commission for Relief in Belgium in 1916. In 1919 he was attached to Hoover, then director-general of relief under the Supreme Economic Council of the Paris Peace Conference. 23, 224, 359, 362, 449, 544, 552, 554, 564, 567, 574, 581, 582, 590–592, 604, 612–615, 625, 631–633, 637, 649–653

Baker, Newton D., Jr. (1871–1937) was an American lawyer and politician, and the Secretary of War from 1916 to 1921. 37, 41, 42, 44, 48, 49, 51, 52, 72, 117, 144, 259, 267, 298, 326, 329, 339–340, 352, 641

Balfour, Arthur James (1848–1930) was a conservative British politician who served as Prime Minister 1902–1905, First Lord of the Admiralty 1915–1916, and Foreign

Minister 1916–1919, and Lord President of the Council 1919–1922 and 1925–1929. As Foreign Minister, he issued the 1917 Balfour Declaration, supporting the establishment of a national home for the Jews in Palestine. VII, 11, 178, 321, 375, 543

Ballard, Captain. 197

Ballin, Albert (1857–1918) was a German shipping magnate and inventor of the concept of the cruise ship. He ran the world's largest shipping line, the Hamburg-American Line. 169

Balsini, Deputy. 338

Barber, Alivn B. (1883–1961) was in the US Military Corps of Engineers 1905–1917, then served on the general staff for the rest of WWI. From January to August, 1919, he was in charge of transportation and distribution of supplies for the ARA. He then headed the ARA operations in Poland until 1922. 583, 605, 608, 617, 634, 650

Barnes, Howard R. (b. 1877) was an American diplomat who clerked for the State Department in the codes department for 10 years. 47, 188, 200, 406, 438

Barrès, Maurice (1862–1923) was a French writer and politician who supported the Union Sacrée (urging the left wing not to obstruct the government during the war years) political truce concept. 222

Barry, Griffin was an American journalist who worked with the CRB in Belgium. In Rome, he was a Special Assistant on the Foreign Relief Staff of the Red Cross. 159

Barthou, Jean Louis (1862–1934) was a French politician of the Third Republic and Prime Minister briefly in 1913. Later he served as Foreign Minister in 1934. He was killed by a Bulgarian revolutionary on October 9, 1934. 175, 184

Barton, Mrs. 156

Baruch, Bernard M. (1870–1965) was an American financier and statesman who chaired the War Industries Board as of January 1918, and was awarded an Army Distinguished Service Medal for his contributions to the mobilization of US forces. He was an adviser to President Wilson during WWI, Economic Adviser to the American Commission to Negotiate Peace in Paris 1919, and again as advisor to President Franklin D. Roosevelt in WWII. President Truman appointed Baruch as the US representative to the United Nations Atomic Energy Commission in 1946. 214, 216, 550, 564

Barzini, Luigi, Sr. (1874–1947) was an Italian journalist, who arrived in Paris on August 20, 1914 to find that the trains to Belgium were still running, so he went to Brussels and was able to write a series of first-hand articles. 195

Bass, John F. (1866–1931) was a noted American war correspondent. 117, 118, 120, 122, 123, 127, 131

Bates, Blanche (1873–1941) was an American actress, born in Portland, OR. She married George Creel, head of the Committee for Public Information in 1912. 180

Battista della Chiesa, Giacomo (1854–1922) was Pope Benedict XV 1919–1922, the man Gibson refers to as 'the Pope'. 62, 104, 123, 128, 131, 139, 143–144, 150

Bauer, Genevieve de. 555

Bauer, Otto (1881–1948) was the Austrian Foreign Minister from January to November 1919. 486

Beal, Bolyston A. (1865–1944) was an American lawyer serving at the US Embassy in London. With Littlefield and Buckler, he inspected Camp Douglas and reported to Ambassador Page. 311, 403

Beaupre, Arthur M. (1853–1919) was an American diplomat who served as ambassador to several countries, including Cuba 1911–1913, where Gibson worked under him. 608–614

Beck, James M. (1861–1936) was a political acquaintance of Gibson and his mother in California. 558

Becket, Mrs. Lucy (1884–1979) was married to Otto von Czernin, an Austro-Hungarian diplomat during WWI. They divorced in August 1914. 120

Bell, Edward "Ned" or "Ed" (1882–1924) was an American diplomat who served as secretary of Embassy in London where he dealt with British intelligence. He was involved in the issues surrounding the 1917 communication between Germany and Mexico (the Zimmermann Telegram) which pushed the US into WWI. He was married to Etelka and they had three children. 39, 71, 105, 143, 153, 233, 235, 275, 282, 292, 298, 299, 321–324, 328, 334, 338, 339, 341, 343, 345, 346, 351, 367, 377, 383, 402, 403, 407, 439, 445, 447, 448, 450, 572, 604, 610, 621, 640, 652

Beneš, Edvard (1884–1948) was a Czech politician serving as Secretary of the Czechoslovak National Council in Paris. Together with Tomáš Masaryk, he was instrumental in founding the Czechoslovak state in 1918, and he acted as its Minister of Foreign Affairs 1918–1935, Prime Minister 1921–1922, and President 1935–1938, 1939–1945 (in exile), and 1945–1948. 4, 232, 340, 363, 364, 369, 370, 374, 379, 380, 381, 383, 451, 546, 566, 567, 577, 578, 585, 587, 628, 651

Bennet. 340

Benson, Major. 638

Benson, William Shepherd (1855–1932) was an American naval admiral who acted as Chief of Naval Operations 1915–1919. After his retirement from the Navy he accepted a position on the US Shipping Board. 373, 407, 548, 615, 642, 650, 652

Berdan, Mary Kimbal (1835–1924) was an American widow who had been married to Civil War General Hiram Berdan. 126, 130, 132, 133, 146

Berinkey, Dénes (1871–1944) was a Hungarian politician who served as Prime Minister/Minister of Justice briefly under Karolyi, from January 11 to March 21, 1919. 490

Bernstorff, Johann Heinrich von (1862–1939) was a German diplomat who served as Ambassador to the US 1908–1917. 98

Bernus, Pierre (1881–1951) was a Swiss-born French historian in the French infantry from 1914–1916 when he was badly wounded and awarded the Croix de Guerre. Later he worked as a diplomatic information agent for the Ministry of Foreign Affairs. 340

Berthelot, Henri Mathias (1861–1931) was a French army officer charged with helping to rebuild the Romanian Army between January and June 1917, which entered the war on the side of the Allies in 1916. However, the Russian Revolution led to another Romanian defeat in December 1917. In July 1918, Berthelot was a key figure in the Third Battle of the Aisne. He was tasked with bringing Romania back into the war in September 1918, and helped defeat the Hungarians and Russian Bolsheviks during 1918–1919. After the war, Berthelot served as military governor of Metz 1919–1922 and Strasbourg 1923–1926. 209, 520

Berthot. 218, 251, 252

Bertie, Francis (1844–1919) was a British diplomat and Ambassador to France 1905–1918. 91

Bertraux, Félix (1882–1948) was a French chemist who translated for the Ministry of Culture on occasion. 269, 272, 275, 277, 282–283, 340

Besnard, Paul-Albert (1849–1934) was a French painter who was a founding member of the Société Nationale des Beaux-Arts in 1890 and co-founded the Salon des Tuileries in 1923. 120, 228

Best, Sigismund Payne (1885–1978) was a British Secret Intelligence Service officer during both the first and second world wars. In 1917, he was based in Rotterdam to handle intelligence networks in German-occupied Belgium. Later, in 1938, Best renewed his intelligence work with Claude Dansey's 'Z' organization. He was kidnapped and held in Nazi custody between 1940 and 1945. His memoirs are published under the title of *The Venlo Incident* (1950). 555, 582

Beughem de Houtem, Ferdinand de (1861–1926) was a Belgian diplomat and grandmaster of the house of Queen Elisabeth of the Belgians. 417

Beughem de Houtem, Irone Hare de (1885–1979) was an American who married Viscount Ferninand de Beughem de Houtem in 1909. She was a friend of Gibson and corresponded with him. 416, 595, 599, 644

Beveridge, William (1879–193) was a progressive British economist who helped mobilize manpower during WWI. In 1918, he was made permanent secretary to the Ministry of Food. His public service continued through WWII. 451, 473, 474, 490, 493, 583

Bicknell, Ernest P. (1863–1935) was an American who worked with the Indiana and Chicago Boards of Charities 1894–1907. In 1908 he assumed the roles especially created for him as National Director of the American Red Cross. During the war, he served as Deputy Commission to France and Commissioner to Belgium 1917–1918. During 1918, he also served as Special Commissioner to the Balkan States. In the following years he was Deputy, Acting, and then full Commissioner to Europe. He also served as Director of the Rockefeller Foundation War Relief Committee. He was decorated by Belgium, France, Montenegro, Serbia, Russia, Greece, and Poland. His memoirs are recorded in *Pioneering with the Red Cross* (1935). 443

Biddle, Anthony Joseph Drexel, Jr. (1896–1961) was born into a prominent Philadelphia banking family and enlisted Army man during WWI. Later he went into diplomacy, being appointed Minister to Norway 1935. He served as Ambassador to Poland from 1937–1943, but fled the country with the Polish Government when the Germans and Russians both invaded in 1939. He continued to represent the US to Poland, along with the small democracies whose governments-in-exile were centered in London. After the Tehran Conference in 1943, Biddle resigned from the diplomatic service and rejoined the Army as a Lt. Colonel on the staff of Dwight Eisenhower 1944–1955. His last post was as US Ambassador to Spain in 1961. 180, 363

Biddle, Edith Frances (1881–1938), daughter of Arthur and Julia Biddle, worked at Galworthy House (a hospital for wounded Belgian soldiers) in London during the war. She was later decorated by the Belgian Government. 230

Biddle, John (1859–1936) was an American Army officer and Superintendent of West Point Academy 1916–1917. In 1917–1918, when General Tasker Bliss was in London, Biddle acted as US Army Chief of Staff in Washington DC. Later he took charge of American troops in Great Britain and Ireland. 166

Bigelow, Glenna Lindsley (b. 1876), was an American nurse serving in France. She later wrote *Liége on the Line of March: An American Girl's Experiences When the Germans Came Through Belgium*. 194

Birch, Thomas H. (1875–1929) was an American manufacturer and aide to Governor Woodrow Wilson 1912–1913 then Minister to Portugal 1913–1922. He was married to Helen Barr Birch. 635

Bissing, Moritz von (1844–1917) was a Prussian general who was appointed Governor-General of German occupied Belgium 1914 until his death in 1917. Among many other infamous deeds, he signed the death warrant of Edith Cavell. 424

Black, William Murray (1855–1933) was an American Army general who trained nearly 300,000 engineers for various military tasks in Europe. 51, 52

Blair, Seymour. 47, 51, 182

Blake, Dr. 337

Blake, Maxwell (b. 1887) was an American diplomat serving as Consul General in Tangier 1917–1922. 333, 334

Blankenhorn, David Ferguson "Young Blankenhorn" (1886–1969) was connected with the War College of Los Angeles and Athletic Director for Cal Tech in 1926. 13

Blankenhorn, Herber Holbrook (1884–1956) was an American Army officer assigned to the military intelligence and propaganda divisions of the Department of War and the General Staff of the AEF. With few instructions and little direction, he and 28 men improvised to produce and distribute three million copies of over twenty separate leaflets in enemy territory. Later, he provided similar services during WWII. 17, 258, 266, 270, 272, 273, 288, 311, 312, 319, 328, 329, 357, 402

Bliss, Mildred Barnes (1879–1969) was an American heiress, art collector and philanthropist. She married her stepbrother, Robert Woods Bliss a diplomat, in 1908. They lived in Paris 1912–1919, where Robert served as Counselor of the Embassy, and she immersed herself in the art world. During the war, she served with the American Red Cross. Following the war, the Blisses purchased Dumbarton Oaks in 1920, which they ceded to Harvard University in 1940. It became the site of the Washington Conversations on International Peace and Security Organization meetings in 1944. The Charter of the United Nations emerged from these meetings. 72, 392, 398

Bliss, Robert Woods "Bob" (1875–1962) was an American diplomat and philanthropist. He served as the counselor of the Embassy in Paris 1916–1919. Later, he was chief of the Western Europe Division at the State Department (1920–1921), Assistant Secretary of State (1921–1923), Envoy to Sweden (1923–1927), and Ambassador to Argentina (1927–1933). After retiring, he co-founded of the Dumbarton Oaks Conference in 1944. 32, 39, 72, 76, 79, 82, 86, 91, 163, 164, 170, 174, 180, 182, 223, 237, 248, 269, 300, 339, 344, 391, 438, 441, 591, 626, 643

Bliss, Tasker H. (1852–1930) was the US Army Chief of Staff for the AEF in France. He was appointed as the American Permanent Military Representative to the Supreme Council and was active in the Paris Peace Conference as a plenipotentiary. 37, 69, 72, 188, 189, 222, 248, 252, 279, 290, 291, 440, 564, 650

Block, Major. 283

Blount, Daniel Lynds (b. 1884) was an American army officer who had volunteered in the CRB in 1914. When the US entered the war, he joined the army and became aide de camp to General Harts, commander of American troops in Paris. During spring and summer 1918, he was assigned to the censorship office. After WWII, Blount served as vice president of the American Chamber of Commerce in Paris (1945). 215, 222, 242, 245, 252, 293, 299, 306, 308, 318, 320, 329, 331, 337, 339, 340, 350, 354–357, 359, 361, 371, 373, 387, 392, 568, 573, 616

Blount, Richard Allen was the younger brother of Daniel Blount. 215

Blowitz, Henri de (1825–1903) was a Bohemian journalist famous for obtaining the text of the Treaty of Berlin (resolving the Russo-Turkish War of 1877–1878), and publishing it at the very moment it was signed. 60

Blythe, Samuel George (1868–1942) was an American journalist who wrote for the *Saturday Evening Post*. 601

Boardman, Mabel Thorp (1860–1946) was an American philanthropist who worked with the Red Cross in the United States after 1904, when she ousted Clara Barton from the leadership role. She imposed new emphasis on management, expansion and professionalism. 75, 120

Bobrinsky, Georgiy (1863–1928) was a Russian general who served as the Governor of

Galicia and Bukovina 1914/15. He was the great-grandson of Catharine the Great. 136

Bohn, Frank (1878–1975) was an American socialist who advocated for industrial unions and served as National Secretary for the Socialist Labor Party of America 1906–1908. As his politics became increasingly nationalistic and the US entered the war, Bohn went to work for COMPUB in France and Switzerland. 81, 91, 94, 96, 97, 101, 102, 143, 180, 258

Bolling, Raynal (1877–1918) was an American lawyer who became an early Army aviator and was sent to France to lay the groundwork for the AEF air services as part of the Signal Corps in May 1917. He was killed in action over Amiens on March 26, 1918. 71, 143, 406, 407

Bolo – See Pasha, Bolo.

Bonar Law, Andrew (1858–1923) was the British Chancellor of the Exchequer 1916–1919 and later Prime Minister 1922–1923. 356

Bonham-Carter, Ian M. "Bongy" (1882–1953) was a British officer in the Royal Air Force. Later he served as Duty Air Commodore in the Operations Room of RAF headquarters during WWII. He was married to Violet Asquith. 264, 293, 302, 303, 312

Bonheur, Rosa (1822–1899) was a French realism painter and pioneer of women's emancipation. 528

Bonsal, Stephen (1865–1951) was an American journalist and diplomat serving in the AEF. During the Peace Conference, he served as private translator for President Wilson. He published *Suitors and Supplicants* in 1946. 368, 371, 381, 401, 443

Bonzano, Giovanni (1867–1927) was ordained a cardinal in the Roman Catholic Church and served as the Papal Delegate to the US 1912–1922. 145

Booth, George Macaulay (1877–1971) was a British businessman and a director of the Bank of England. 344, 391

Boret, Victor (1872–1952) was a French politician serving as Food Minister. 275, 283, 287, 288, 290, 335, 424

Boris III (1894–1943) ascended to the Bulgarian throne upon the abdication of his father, Ferdinand I, in 1918. 355

Bourgeois, Maurice J. was a French army officer in the Air Service who served as aide-de-camp to Pétain. One of Gibson's former instructors, he received a Distinguished Service Award from the US. 178

Bovet, Pierre (1878–1965) was a Swiss professor of physiology at the University of Zurich. 108, 110–112, 169

Bowden. 263, 583

Bowditch, Edward "Pete" (1881–1966) was an American army officer and diplomat. As part of the AEF in France, Major Bowditch was the personal aide-de-camp to Gen. Pershing. Earlier he had served in Manchuria, and later as a member of the Harbord Commission in the Philippines. He continued to work with Pershing during the inter-war years and served in WWII until 1943. 198, 423

Boyd, Carl (1879–1958) was an American army officer serving on Pershing's staff. 199, 252, 264, 292, 501

Boyle, Joseph W. (1871–1923) was a Canadian entrepreneur in the gold fields of the Yukon, earning the nickname "Yukon Joe." He was an early associate of Herbert Hoover and Lord Beaverbrook. At the beginning of the war, he outfitted a 50 man Yukon Machine Gun Company. Although he was named a Lt. Colonel, he was deemed too old, at 47, to lead the company in battle. Through his connections in London, he was appointed in June 1917 to conduct a private mission to Kerensky's provisional government in Russia. In one daring episode, he rescued the Romanian treasure from Moscow, making him a national hero in Bucharest. He became a close friend of Queen Marie, who nursed him personally when he suffered a stroke in 1919. 445, 449

Braconnier, Léon (1850–1935) was a Belgian Commissioner in Kasai (now the Democratic Republic of Congo), where he expanded crops and attempted to improve living conditions. 229, 230

Brainard, David L. (1856–1946) was a US Army general who had explored the artic, fought in the American Indian Wars, the Spanish American War, and later in World War I as military attaché to the US Embassy in Portugal. 24, 26, 29, 30, 166

Brambilla, Guiseppe (b. 1879) was an Italian diplomat who served as Counselor of the Italian Embassy in Washington, DC. In 1917, he married Julia Meyer, daughter of former US Ambassador to Italy 1901–1904. 125, 129, 130, 140, 143, 156, 157, 575, 644

Brambilla, Julia Appleton Meyer (1886–1979) was an American married to Guiseppe Brambilla, Counselor to the Italian Embassy in Washington, DC, 1917. 121, 125, 140, 143, 155, 157, 575, 644

Brancaccio, Col. 294, 296

Brandeis, Louis D. (1965–1941) was an American lawyer and judge who wrote many famous opinions while serving on the US Supreme Court 1916–1939. 241, 398

Brantingham, Francis E. "Brandy" was an American observer who toured the Holyport camp in Britain for German prisoners of war. His report was given to Ambassador Walter Hines Page on October 31, 1916. 241, 261, 335, 339

Brătianu, Ion I.C. "Bratino" (1864–1927) was a Romanian politician who served as Prime Minister for five terms between 1909 and 1927. He was especially known for his role from November 1918 to September 1919 and leading the Romanian delegation to the Paris Peace Conference. 450

Braun, Magnus von, Sr. (1878–1972) was a German civil servant and Chairman of the delegation to Hoover's food meeting in Brussels in March 1919. He later served in Poland. 587

Brent, Charles (1862–1929) was the chief chaplain for the AEF in Europe 1917–1918. As an Episcopal Bishop, he presided from the American Church in Paris. 423

Bréton, Guillaume was the son of Louis Bréton, who partnered with Louis Hachette in the development of one of the largest French publishing companies, Maison Hachette. When his father died in 1877, Guillaume became a partner at Maison Hachette. 85, 86, 223

Briand, Aristide (1862–1932) was a French politician who served as Minister of Justice for several terms between 1908 and 1915, Prime Minister between 1909 and 1926, and later as Foreign Minister from 1926–1932. 174, 175, 184, 209, 260

Bridges, Thomas (1871–1939) was a British army officer who had been involved in the early battles of WWI. In 1917, he was military attaché of the Balfour Mission to the US. When he returned to the front in France, he was severely injured on September 20, 1917, losing a leg. He recovered and went on to serve as military attaché in Greece, the Balkans, and Russia (where he was responsible for the evacuation of the British Mission). Later, he served as Governor of Southern Australia 1922–1927. 199

Brinckman. 389

Bristol, Lt. 185, 319, 327, 386

Broadhurst, Hugh Hunt (1880–1973) was an American army officer who served as Provost Marshal for the Second Division. 190

Broderick. 73, 381

Brown, Arnold and Ida. 227

Brown, (Albert) Curtis (1866–1945) was an American journalist writing for the New York papers from London. 87

Brown, George Rothwell (1879–1960) was an American newspaperman from Chicago serving as a war correspondent for the *Washington Post* 1913–1917. He wrote a column called "Postscripts" until 1929 when he went to work as a political writer for Randolph Hearst. 72

Brown, Louis Francis (d. 1925) was the manager of Burton Holmes' Travelogues 1897-1925. He is credited with coining the term "travelogue." He submitted a plan to the Secretary of War and the Signal Corps for training camera men for making still and motion pictures of the US Army more adequate and comprehensive. 266

Brown, Philip Marshall (1875-1966) was an American professor working with Coolidge's mission in Hungary. 569, 615

Brown, Walter Lyman "Rotterdam" (1865-1966) was an American relief worker who served as director of the CRB activities in Rotterdam July 1916-September 1919. By 1921, he directed ARA activities in Europe. 394, 411

Brownrigg, Douglas Ereemont (1867-1939) was the British Chief Naval Censor 1914-1919. 313, 425

Brunswig, Lucien Napoleon (1854-1943) was a French born American druggist. He founded the Bergen Bruswig Corporation in 1887. He wrote a series of essays describing the war damage in France, and followed the rehabilitation facilitated by Hoover. 438

Bryan. 57

Buat, Edmond (1868-1923) was a French general who commanded the 33rd Infantry, 17th Army Corps and 5th Army between February and June 1918. 254

Buckey, Mervyn Chaudos (1873-1940) was an American Army colonel serving as Military Attaché at the Embassy in Rome 1917-1919. 134, 141, 147, 148, 152, 154, 155, 159, 165, 186, 596

Buckler, William H. "Willy" (1867-1952) was an American diplomat and archeologist serving as a Special Agent at the US Embassy in London 1914-1918. With Beal and Littlefield, he inspected Camp Douglas and reported to Ambassador Page. Later he served as a staff member to the American Commission to Negotiate Peace. 311, 594, 603, 619

Bucklin, George A., Jr (b. 1875) was an American diplomat who served as Consul at Bordeaux 1914-1919. 31, 232

Bullard, William H.G. (1866-1927) was a US Navy Admiral serving as commander of the USS Arkansas as part of the British Grand Fleet during WWI. He was an expert on electrical systems and radio communication. Later he served as Director of Naval Communications. 501

Bullitt, William C. (1891-1967) was an American diplomat and writer who is remembered for his special mission to negotiate with Lenin during the Paris Peace Conference in an effort to normalize relations with Bolshevik Russia. He later served as US Ambassador to the Soviet Union (1933-1936) and to France (1936-1940). 18, 555, 564, 619, 626

Bunau-Varilla, Philippe (1859-1940) was a French engineer and soldier who had worked with Theodore Roosevelt at the Panama Canal. As a French officer, he lost a leg at the Battle of Verdun. 384

Bundy, Omar (1861-1940) was an American army officer serving as commander of the 1st Brigade of the 1st Expeditionary Division in France 1917. For his service, he was made a French Legion of Honor Commander and awarded the French Croix de Guerre with Palm. When he retired in 1934, the US honored him with a Distinguished Service Medal. 191

Burnaby, Algernon Edwyn (1868-1938) was a British landowner, soldier and Justice of the Peace. He was married to Mina. 126

Burnaby, Mina (1882-1952) was the daughter of Florence [Mrs. Thomas Nelson] Page and her first husband, Henry Field. She was the niece of Marshall Field. Mina was married first to Preston Gibson, then to Algernon Burnaby. 125, 126, 150

Burnham, Squab. 309

Burton, Pomeroy (1869–1947) was a British newspaper magnate who took over *The Times* in 1908. He also managed the *London Daily Mail* and was affiliated with Lord Northcliffe. In October 1918, he was in Paris as part of the British Mission to the US. 45, 363

Busch, Elise "Lilly" Eberhard Anheuser (1844–1928) was married to Adolphus Busch (1839–1913), the German-born founder of Anheuser Busch beer. 39

Buyer-Mimeure, Daisy Polk de (1874–1963) was an American relative of Frank Polk who was active in relief work in France during WWI. She was assigned to the reconstruction of the first village French, Vitrimont, with use of American aid. There she met her future husband, de Buyer, and married him in Vitrimont on September 12, 1917. She was named a Legion Chevalier in 1920. 275, 282

Buyer-Mineure, Robert LMJ de (1855–1919) was a French aristocrat and Army general in WWI. He married Daisy Polk in 1917 and retired shortly after their wedding. 275, 285

Byoir, Carl R. (1888–1957) was an American reporter serving with Creel's CPI 1917–1918. In 1930 he established a successful public relations firm and helped establish the March of Dimes foundation. 351, 369, 435, 526

Byran, Albert F. (1869–1929) was an American Army officer. 41

Byrcheff. Chief of Russian Secret Police. 292

Byrne, James was an American lawyer serving as Deputy Commissioner of the Red Cross in Rome. 146, 148

C

Cable, Philander L. (1891–1940) was an American diplomat serving as secretary in Paris since 1917. 340

Cachin, Marcel (1869–1958) was a French socialist politician who represented the Seine in the Chamber of Deputies 1914–1936. In 1917, he travelled to Russia where he supported Kerensky's provisional government and denounced Lenin and Trotsky. 356

Caffery, Jefferson (1886–1974) was an American diplomat serving as secretary to the Embassy in Paris in 1918. Later he would return as Ambassador, 1944–1949, after serving in several Latin American countries. 32, 67, 85, 170, 185, 219, 237, 307, 364, 644

Caillaux, Joseph (1863–1944) was a French politician who served briefly as Prime Minister of France (June 1911-January 1912). He favored a separate French peace with Germany, at the expense of Britain. When Clemenceau came to power, Caillaux was tried for treason because of these views. After serving his sentence, he was rehabilitated in the 1920's. 44, 183, 184, 281, 286, 287

Caldwell, John Lawrence (1875–1922) was the American Ambassador to Persia (Iran) from 1914–1921. 369

Campbell, Charles, Jr. 214

Campbell-Turner, Arthur (1880–1963) was an American Colonel in the AEF. 90, 302, 344

Cambon, Jules Martin (1845–1935) was a French diplomat who would serve as chairman of the Commission on Polish Affairs in 1919. 222

Camoneli, Major 48

Campanole, Nicholas W. (1881–1955) was an American army officer under Gen. Pershing in both Mexico and France. Later he served as Gen. Patton's chief of staff in WWII. 69, 231, 232, 246, 288

Cane, Dorothy 83, 593

Cannon, James, Jr. (1864–1944) was an American bishop of the Methodist Church 1918–1944 and well-known temperance leader. He later visited Poland in 1920. 172, 173

Caricalli, Lt. 486

Carpenter, Jeanne was a Red Cross volunteer who was a leader in American municipal policy. She published, with Wm. Parr Capes, "Municipal Housecleaning: Methods and Experiences of American Cities in Collecting and Disposing of Municipal Wastes" in the October 1918 issue of *American Society of Mechanical Engineers Journal*. 30, 166

Carr, Wilbur John (1870–1942) was an American diplomat who served as director of the Consular Bureau from 1909 to 1924. He was instrumental in reforming the US Foreign Service, favoring professionalism to domestic politics. He served as Assistant Secretary of State 1914–1937, the as the US Minister to Czechoslovakia 1937–1939. 118, 127

Carrell, Alexis (1873–1944) was a French surgeon who won the Nobel Prize in Physiology in 1912 for his work with vascular suturing. 86, 90

Carrigan, Clarence (1880–1929) was an American diplomat serving as Consul in Lyons 1918–1920. 232

Carroll, Charles (1885–1921) was heir to a prominent New York family who served with the Red Cross in Italy and France. 233, 235, 454

Carson, General. 618

Carstairs, Charles (1886–1919) was a volunteer in the CRB where he met and married Hélène Guinotte in 1916, with Brand Whitlock serving as best man. 214, 217, 389, 629

Carter, Alice Morgan (1865–1933) was married to American diplomat and banker John Ridgely "Jack" Carter (1862–1944). while he was posted as the Secretary of Embassy in London 1894–1909. He then served as Minister to the Balkan States (1909–1911). He retired from the Foreign Service and joined the J.P. Morgan & Co. bank in Paris. 63, 180, 407

Carter, Arthur Cecil (d. 1919) was a British army officer serving in Spain. 266, 609

Carter, E.C. was the Chief of the YMCA attached to the American Expeditionary Force in France. 308

Carter, John Ridgely "Jack" (1864–1944) was an American diplomat and banker. After serving as Secretary of Embassy in London 1894–1909, he served as Minister to the Balkan States (1909–1911). He retired from the Foreign Service and joined the J. P. Morgan & Cie bank in Paris. 14, 174 180, 216

Cartier, de Marchienne Emile (1871–1946) was the Belgian Minister to the US 1917–1927 and to the UK 1927–1946. 15, 16, 596, 615, 627, 628

Carton de Wiart, Adrian (1880–1963) was a Belgian-born British Army officer who married Austrian aristocrat Friederike "Chauette" Fugger von Babenhausen in 1908. By the end of the war in 1918, Carton de Wiart had lost one arm, one leg and an eye in battle, was promoted to General and was awarded the Victoria Cross. After the war, he served as head of the British Military Mission in Poland, 1919–1922. After retiring in 1923, he remained in Poland until the new threat of war loomed in summer of 1939. An ardent anti-communist, he again took up the task of heading the British Military Mission in Poland when the Soviet Union invaded from the east. After Poland fell, Carton de Wiart served in Northern Ireland and Yugoslavia, spending 1941–1943 as a Prisoner of War in Italy. Between 1943 and 1947, he represented Winston Churchill in China and Southeast Asia. 62

Casement, Roger David (1864–1916) was a British diplomat and an Irish nationalist. He served in various posts as Consul from 1891 to 1913. During WWI, he attempted to garner German aid for the 1916 Easter Rising attempt at Irish independence. The incidents Gibson describes happened between October 31, 1914 and Casement's execution on August 3, 1916. 212

Casenave, Maurice (1860–1935) was a French diplomat who served as the French Financial Commissioner during the war.

Subsequently, he served as the High Commissioner of the French Government to the United States from 1919 to 1922. 15, 16, 164

Cash, Oliver H. was an American army officer serving with the ARA relief to Central Europe. 471, 475, 487, 516, 541, 647

Caskie, Lt. 474, 515, 517, 524, 540

Cassatt, Robert Kelso (1873–1944) was an American banker from Philadelphia, a partner in Cassatt & Co. 163

Castle, William R. Jr. (1878–1963) was a Harvard educated American diplomat who was the assistant chief of the Western European division of the State Department from 1918 to 1921 when he became the chief. Later he served as Assistant Secretary of State 1927–1929, briefly as Ambassador to Japan in 1930, and Under Secretary of State in 1931. 8, 89

Causey, William Bowdoin (1865–1936) was an American army officer serving in the Corps of Engineers. After the November Armistice, he was charged to managing transportation for ARA relief to Central and Eastern Europe. Much of his work involved the movement of coal, earning him the nickname "Old King Coal." He later served as Technical Adviser to Austria in 1920. 453, 469, 470, 474, 476, 477, 479, 483, 486, 498, 502, 509, 513, 515, 516, 519, 527, 539, 592, 603

Cavalcanti de Lacerda, Felix de Barros (1880–1950) was a Brazilian diplomat who had served in Brussels as the person in charge of Portugal's interests. He was later Ambassador to Vienna 1922–1929 and then became Foreign Minister 1930–1934. He married Vera Alves Barbosa of Rio. 299

Cavell, Edith (1865–1915) was a British nurse who served in Belgium during the first year of the war. Although she helped soldiers without discrimination, she was found guilty of helping 200 Triple Entente soldiers escape from occupied Belgium. Gibson was active in trying to stay her execution and one of the last persons to see her. She was executed by the German authorities on October 12, 1915. 342, 343, 370, 404, 418

Cecil, Robert (1864–1958) was a British lawyer, politician and diplomat. During WWI, he served in the Red Cross as well as holding various public offices, including Minister of Blockage 1916–1918. His work on the League of Nations earned him a Nobel Prize in 1937. 576

Cerretti, Bonaventura (1872–1933) was an Italian archbishop of the Roman Catholic Church who served as Undersecretary of State for the Vatican. He had been the auditor of the apostolic delegation to the US 1906–1914. 128, 144, 145

Cerruti, Victorio (1881–1961) was an Italian lawyer and diplomat. Between 1908 and 1915 he was assigned to the Italian Legation in Vienna. During WWI, he was assigned to the Supreme Army Command. Later he served as Ambassador to Russia 1927, Brazil 1930, Germany 1932 and France 1935. 298, 301

Chaix, Edmond A. (b. 1866) was the French Minister of Propaganda Against the Enemy. 217, 244–246, 272, 294, 449

Chamberlain, George Earle (1854–1928) was an American attorney who served as the Governor of Oregon 1903–1909, and then Senator from Oregon 1909–1921. Among other activities, he served on the Committee of Expenditures in the War Department. 52

Chambrun, Charles de (1875–1952) was a French diplomat in St. Petersburg in 1914, then in Athens and Vienna. Later he represented France in Ankara (1928–1933) and Rome (1933–1935). He was the brother of Pierre de Cambrun. 50

Chambrun, Pierre de (1865–1954) was a French aristocrat, lawyer and politician. He served as legal counsel at the French Embassy in the US 1892–1897, and returned to Washington as part of Viviani's diplomatic mission in 1917. Later, in

1925, he came again to Washington with Caillaux to discuss French war debt. He was the brother of Charles de Cambrun. 50, 191

Chandler, Charles Lyon (1883–192) was an American diplomat and businessman. He acted as Consul in various Latin American countries 1908–1914. He worked as an agent for the Southern Railway 1914–1918, and then served briefly as vice-Consul in Bern, Switzerland in 1918. Later he worked as foreign trade manager for the Corn Exchange Bank of Philadelphia 1918–1942. 78, 335

Chanler, Beatrice (1881–1946) was the former wife of William Astor Chanler (1867–1934), with who she shared three children. They divorced amicably in 1909. He inherited the Vanderbilt Hotel in New York in 1913 while she created the elaborate frieze for the lobby. He supported boxer Frank Moran as the "great white hope" against Jack Johnson. She owned the flat in Paris where Mrs. Sanger and Mrs. Linn stayed. 34

Charles I of Austria (1887–1922) was the last Emperor of Austria and last King of Hungary and Bohemia. He reigned from November 1916 to November 1918 until the Armistice disbanded the Austrian Empire. 363

Charmant, Oszkar (1860–1925) was a Hungarian lawyer, journalist, notary public and diplomat who served as legal adviser to Mihály Károlyi during the Daisy Revolution in Budapest. He was sent to Vienna in 1919 as Special Envoy of Károlyi's government. 470

Charpentier, Captain. 198

Chartres, Annie Vivanti (1866–1942) was a British-born Italian writer who support Irish independence and assisted the Irish delegation at Versailles in 1919. 366

Chase, Major. 610

Chatfield, Frederick H. (1874–1936) was an American working in the Food Administration and serving as director of the Brussels office of the CRB. 406, 407, 413, 551–553, 588, 590, 591

Cheeseborough, Edit, was an American golfer from Los Angeles working in Paris with the Red Cross during the war. 268

Chevrillon, André Louis (1867–1953) was a French writer and professor at the Naval School at Lille University. He had worked with the CRB in Belgium, and later married a Polish woman in 1919. In 1934, he wrote *The German Threat* which was banned in France in August 1940 by the occupying German regime. 85, 215, 218, 275, 277, 278, 281, 282, 299, 335, 340

Chéroux, Adolphe (1857–1934) was a French politician serving as City Councilman for Paris, 1894–1934. 222

Chevigné, François de (1882–1962) was a French aristocrate. 628, 629

Chotek von Chotkowa und Wognin, Wolfgang (1860–1926) was a member of the Kinsky clan to whom the Clary's were also related. 533

Churchill, Winston (1874–1955) was a British military officer and politician. In Asquith's government, he served as President of the Board of Trade, Home Secretary, and First Lord of the Admiralty. From early 1915 to early 1916, Churchill oversaw the Battle of Gallipoli, which was a disaster for the British and caused Churchill to resign his governmental positions. Much later, he became one of the most famous of British politicians when he led Britain during WWII. 60, 122, 293

Cigogna-Mozzoni, Carlo (1867–1928) was an Italian engineer, artillery soldier, and aristocrat. 76

Citroën, André-Gustave (1878–1935) was a French industrialist of Belgian and Polish heritage who owned a munitions plant near Paris. 278

Clarke, Captain Edward Denman (1898–1966) was born in Finland, but served in the British Royal Air Force 1916–1919. He earned a Military Cross for conspicuous bravery. Later he managed Saunders-Roe Ltd. on the Isle of Wright. 26, 350

Clary und Aldringen, Siegfried von (1848–1920) was an Austrian diplomat. His final post was to Brussels where he served from 1902 to 1914. He delivered the Austrian declaration of war on August 28, and handed his legation to the US legation where Gibson, was second in command, because the American Legation was still neutral while Austria and Belgium were belligerents. The connection between Gibson and the Clarys, however, went much deeper than international relations. He was married to Therese Radziwill. 468, 526, 528, 529, 530, 532, 533, 543

Clary, Elisalex (1885–1955), Siegfried's daughter, was the best friend of Ynès, Gibson's future wife. Because Ynès' mother died in childbirth and her father in 1913, Siegfried and his wife acted as second parents to Ynès, who became part of the family – and this extended to Gibson in time. Elisalex later married Guy de Baillet-Latour, organizer of the 1936 Olympic Games in Berlin. 468, 529

Clary und Aldringen, Maria **Carlos** (1844–1920) was "Prince Clary" from 1894–1920. He was married to Felicia Radziwiłł (1849–1930). 528, 531

Clary, Sophie (1891–1961) was the daughter of Alfons and Therese Clary, and sister of Ynès' friend Elisalex Clary. 528, 529, 531

Clary, Terese Kinsky von Wchinitz und Tettau "Resy" (1967–1943) became Countess und Aldringen when she married Siefried in 1885. As mother to Elisalex, Alfons and Sophie Clary, she also "mothered" Ynès and welcomed Gibson to the family. 473, 528–532, 534, 543

Clayton. 267

Clemenceau, Georges (1841–1929) was the French Prime Minister 1917–1920. He believed and fought for total victory over and harsh peace terms for the Germans, and attained both of his aims with the Allied triumph over Germany in November 1918 and the subsequent Treaty of Versailles. 44, 66, 69–71, 162, 174, 175, 178, 184, 189, 195, 208, 209, 213, 222, 247, 290, 338, 358, 362, 376, 390, 391, 398, 419, 427, 440, 520, 550, 564, 566, 568, 571, 572, 583

Clémentel, Étienne (1864–1936) was a French politician who served in the National Assembly 1900–1919 and the Senate 1920–1936. During the war, he served as Minister of Commerce, Industry, Posts and Telegraphs 1915–1919. His duties included managing the French part of the blockade. 275, 445

Cloman, Sidney A. (d. 1923) was an American army officer serving as Assistant Finance Officer, member of the Board of Contracts and Adjustments, and chief of Administrative Liaison Bureau, December 1918 to May 1919. 436, 611

Clynés, John R. (1869–1949) was a British trade unionist and politician. He served as Minister of Food July 1918 to January 1919. 276

Cobb, Esther Ellen (1887–1970) was an American opera singer and actress who used the stage name Cobina Wright. She married American novelist Owen Johnson in 1912, but they divorced in 1917. During WWI, she performed for French and American troops in Europe. 235

Cobb, Frank Irving (1869–1923) was an American journalist for the *New York World*, in Paris to interview Colonel House. 373, 374, 410

Cobb, Irwin Shrewsbury (1876–1944) was an American author on staff at the *Saturday Evening Post* since 1911. He was famous for writing about the 369th Infantry Regiment, the "Harlem Hellfighters," who were assigned to the AEF and attached to the French Army in April 1918. This regiment was made up of primarily African American and Puerto Rican soldiers who faced significant discrimination, but fought with valor. 75

Coffin, Howard E. (1873–1937) was an American engineer and industrialist who served on the Naval Construction Board in 1916 and chaired the Aircraft Production Board in 1917. He was replaced by John Ryan in April 1918. 18, 42, 86

Colby, Capt. 305

Colletti, Madame 125–127, 157

Collins, Dr. 148

Collins, James Lawton (1882–1963) was an American army officer who graduated from West Point in 1907. He served with Pershing in the Philippines and sailed to France in May 1917 as his aide. In September, he was an observer at the Battle of Verdun. By May 1918, Collins was appointed secretary of Pershing's General Staff. He later served as military attaché in Rome 1928–1932. 199

Colonna di Paliano, Stefano (1870–1948) was an Italian aristocrat. 157

Cone, Capt. 306

Conger, Arthur L. (1872–1951) was an American Theosophist who served in the US Army as Chief of the Intelligence Division of Pershing's GHQ at Chaumont. Later he served as Military Attaché to Berlin and Bern (1924–1928). 50, 51, 191, 243

Coninck, Marie (Terlinden) de (b. 1891), was married to Jean de Coninck de Mercken (b. 1890). 560, 561

Connally, Thomas T. (1877–1963) was a US Congressman from Texas. 633

Conrey, Nathaniel P. (1860–1936) was an American lawyer, judge and professor of medical jurisprudence. He served three terms as Los Angeles County Superior Court Judge between 1900 and 1913. He moved on to the California Court of Appeal in 1914 as Presiding Justice. He served on the Supreme Court of California briefly before his death. Conrey knew Gibson from Los Angeles, and asked him to look out for his son, David W. Conrey who had enlisted in 1917. David Conrey did end up working for Hoover's ARA by 1919. 522

Coolidge, Archibald Cary (1866–1928) was an American historian from Harvard University and director of its library from 1910 to 1928. Being a scholar of international affairs, he also served as a Foreign Service Officer and edited the foreign policy journal *Foreign Affairs*. He served as secretary of the Legation in St. Petersburg (1890–1991), secretary to the Minister in Paris (1892) and secretary of the Legation in Vienna (1893). In 1918, he was assigned to a special mission in Russia to report on the situation there. In 1919, he headed the "Coolidge Mission" to observe political conditions in Austria, Hungary, and neighboring countries for the Paris Peace Conference. In 1921, Coolidge negotiated for the ARA and helped organize humanitarian aid to Russia. He was also one of the founders of the Council on Foreign Relations. 206, 214, 216, 218, 297, 398, 460, 484–486, 491, 497, 499, 519, 520, 522–524, 539, 540, 569, 615, 616, 618, 654

Copland, Cara. 312

Cortesi, Salvatore (1864–1947) was an Italian-born American who wrote for the Associated Press. He was married to Isabella Lauder Cochrane of Boston and father to two sons, Arnaldo and Roger, both of whom became journalists for the Associated Press. 118, 121

Cotillo, Salvatore Albert (1886–1936) was an American politician serving as Democratic State Senator from New York. He studied economic conditions in Italy at the behest of President Wilson. 182, 183

Cotton, Joseph Potter (1875–1931) was an American lawyer and politician serving as the Chief of the US Food Administration's Meat Division during WWI. Later, he as Under Secretary of State 1929–1931 in the Hoover Administration. 398, 406, 407, 438, 440, 441

Coudert, Fred (1871–1955) was an American lawyer who joined the family firm, Coudert Brothers', with an expertise in international law. The firm represented the French government when it arranged in 1915 to borrow $500 million from private U.S. banks, and helped the Russian and Italian governments as they sought to purchase U.S. supplies and weapons after they joined the Allied nations in their fight against Germany and the other Central Powers. They also consulted with President Wilson on how to deal with the Mexican Revolution. 174

Couget, Joseph Fernand (1866–1950) was a French diplomat who served as French consul general in Beirut 1910–1916, chargé d'affaires in Mexico 1916–1920, and ambassador to Czechoslovakia 1920–1926. 16

Cowden, Elliott Franklin (1891–1976) 235

Coxe, Francis Travis (1889–1973) was an American diplomat who had served with Gibson in Cuba as 2nd Secretary of the Embassy. During the war he was a corporal in the telegraphic section of the AEF. 162, 165, 171, 245, 254, 266, 291, 307, 609

Craigie, Robert Leslie (1883–1959) was a British diplomat, then assigned to Bern, but who would go on to become British Ambassador to Japan 1937–1941. 103–104, 329, 331, 334, 340

Crane, Miss. 85

Crane, Charles Richard (1858–1939) was a wealthy American businessman and Arabist. He was the son of Richard Teller Crane, and father of Richard Teller Crane II. 645

Crane, Richard Teller II "Dick" (1882–1938) was an American manufacturer, son on Charles Richard Crane, who served as Minister to Czechoslovakia 1919–1921. 638

Cravath, Paul Drennan (1861–1940) was an American lawyer who represented many prominent east coast companies during the early years of the 20th century. His firm handled the transfer of ownership of the *Evening Mail* when its publisher, Edward Rumely, was arrested for accepting German funds in July 1918. He was strongly pro-British and advocated for the United States to enter the war to defeat Germany and create a robust alliance for the postwar period. He was one of the founders of the Council on Foreign Relations in 1921. 48, 51–53, 57, 61, 238, 248, 290, 291, 297, 344, 407, 420, 445

Craven, Thomas Tingey (1873–1950) was an American Navy officer who commanded the gunboat Sacramento during WWI. After the November 11, 1918 Armistice, he became the director of Naval Aviation. He went on to several commands, including serving as the Director of Naval Communications. Gibson is mistaken that Craven was in the Marine Corps. 547

Creel, George (1876–1953) was an American investigative journalist. After being involved in the presidential re-election campaign of Woodrow Wilson in 1916, Creel sent Wilson a brief in March 1917 detailing both the desire of military leaders to have strong censorship and his own proposition to direct the press. By April 1917, Creel's idea was embodied into the Committee on Public Information (CPI), with Creel as its head. Their mission was to administer voluntary press censorship, boost US morale and develop propaganda abroad. 37 divisions were created encouraging thousands of civilians to speak out while only repressing material the Committee believed to be dangerous. While this worked reasonably well on the domestic front, the freewheeling and divergent persons making claims in Europe caused many of the problems Gibson was tasked to resolve. The CPI was official dissolved on Armistice Day, November 11, 1918. 4, 11, 10, 14, 16–18, 22, 34, 37, 43, 52, 63–64, 68, 71, 72, 76, 82, 85, 90, 94, 102, 119, 129, 135, 161, 162, 175, 180, 195, 198, 202, 203, 231, 236, 259, 266–268, 319, 322, 331–333,

Biographical Index — 673

351, 353, 369, 372, 395, 410, 435, 526, 547, 553
Crespi, Silvio (1868–1944) was an Italian politician serving as Food Minister. 275, 420, 565, 566, 578, 581
Cresson, William Penn (1864–1932) was an American architect and diplomat who served as chief of the military mission with the Belgian army during the First World War. 46, 202, 206, 254, 260, 268, 272
Croisset, Francis de (1877–1937) was a Belgian/French playwright and opera librettist. 222
Crosby, Jeanne Bouligny (1865–1934) was married to Oscar Crosby. They have one daughter, Juliette (1895–1969). 176, 185, 195, 201
Crosby, Juliette (1895–1969) was the daughter of Oscar and Jeanne Crosby. Later she married Arthur Hornblow, Jr. 212, 234, 237
Crosby, Oscar Terry (1861–1947) was a West Point graduate who served in the US Army Corps of Engineers 1883–1887. Between then and 1915, he directed the Potomac Electric Power Company of Washington DC and wrote several books. In 1915, Crosby became director of the CRB and traveled in Belgium and France. He served as Assistance Secretary of the Treasury 1917–1918, President of the Inter Allied Council on War Purchases and Finance 1917–1919, and United States Special Commissioner of Finance in Europe 1918–1919. Oscar was married to Jeanne Bouligny. Their daughter was Juliette. 37, 55–57, 182, 195, 216, 290, 390, 438, 441, 445
Crosby, Sheldon Leavitt (1879–1936) was an American businessman and diplomat posted as Secretary of the Embassy in London 1917–1919. Previously he served in Bangkok, Madrid, and Vienna. 59–61, 164, 235, 297, 311, 328, 344, 572, 603, 610
Cross, Eliot Buchanan (b. 1883) was an American architect and engineer in the Construction Department of the American Red Cross June 1916 to September 1918 in France. In October, he travelled to the US to purchase materials for France which were unnecessary due to the Armistice of November 1918. He married Martha McCook on September 15, 1920. 334
Crozier, Philippe M. de (1857–1944) was a French diplomat who served as Ambassador to Denmark 1902–1907 and Austria-Hungary 1907–1912. 72
Cruger, Alexander P. (b. 1886) was an American diplomat assigned to Le Havre, France 1918–1919. 18
Cunningham, Alfred A. (1882–1939) was an officer in the US Marine Corps 1909–1935. Under his command, the 1st Marine Aviation Force coordinated forty-three raids with the British and French and fourteen independent raids. The Forcey also supplied 2,600 pounds of food in five separate drops. His service earned the Navy Cross. 309, 321
Curtis, Edward "Teddy" (1891–1983) was an American friend of Gibson's who served in the CRB. He married Zizi Guinotte in Belgium in 1919. Later during WWII, he served as military attaché in Vichy, France. 64, 94, 231, 288, 295, 362, 389, 394, 573, 580, 629, 653
Cutcheon, Franklin W. (1857–1942) was an American army officer stationed with Col. Dawes at Pershing's headquarters. 214, 269, 615
Czernin von und zu Chudenitz, Ottokar (1872–1932) was an Austro-Hungarian diplomat and Foreign Minister 1916–1918. 61, 66, 120, 475, 533

D
d'Arenberg, Capt. 294
d'Ansembourg, Gaston Comte de Marchant et (1891–1957) of Luxembourg and Ambassador from to Belgium in 1919. 430
d'Aspremont-Lynden, Elisabeth "Bebeth" (1883–1947) was a close friend of Ynès

Reyntiens. XV, 299, 414–416, 422, 424, 426, 433, 435, 555, 574, 590
d'Aspremont-Lynden, Marie Henriette (1886–1969), younger sister of Bebeth, was married to Jean van der Burch. 424
d'Assche, Charles "Charley" was a family friend of the Reyntiens'. In 1919, he hoped to sell his Brussels home to the US as a Legation for $2 million. Meanwhile, he leased the property to the American Legation during the tenure of Brand Whitlock and Gibson. 416, 590, 636
d'Esperey, Franchet (1856–1942) was a French army general who was defeated at the Battle of Chemin des Dames in May 1918, but later commanded the allied army at Salonika. 197, 359, 489
d'Hauteville, Paul Grand (b. 1875) was an American diplomat who retired from his position as Secretary of the Legation in 1908. 100
d'Oultremont, Guy (1882–1927) was a Belgian army commander 1914–1918 serving under Pershing at General Head Quarters. He received the Army Distinguished Service Medal in 1919. 243, 273, 288, 319, 371, 429
Dakins. 344
Dale, Porter H. (1867–1933) was a US Congressman from Vermont. 633
Dangaix, William J. (1864–1943) was an American businessman who was the General Agent for Southern States Agricultural Insurance Co. and President of Birmingham Savings bank. He acted as Foreign Agent of the War Trade Board 1918–1919. 91
Daniels, Josephus (1862–1948) was a prominent American naval officer who served as Secretary of the Navy 1913–1921. 17, 172, 280, 282, 615, 642
Danielson. 67, 5, 87
Danilo. 527
Dato e Iradier, Eduardo (1856–1921) was a conservative Spanish politician who served three terms as Prime Minister, 1913–1915, June-November 1917, and 1920–1921. 242, 329, 330
Daudet, Léon (1867–1942) was a French journalist, politician and Deputy of Paris 1919–1924. Earlier he had campaigned vigorously against alleged German involvement in French business and politics and pointed the finger at Malvy (French Minister of the Interior 1914–1917, 1926) and Caillaux (Prime Minister of France 1911–1912) who were charged with treason and temporarily exiled. 286
Davis, Captain 98, 100
Davis, Livingston "Livy" was special assistant, and old friend, of Franklin Roosevelt's who accompanied him to Paris. 279, 286
Davis, Norman (1878–1944) was an American diplomat, businessman and president of the Trust Company of Cuba 1902–1917. During WWI, he served as financial adviser to the Secretary of the Treasury, William McAdoo, on issues of foreign loans. He was responsible for the finance section of the American Commission to Negotiate Peace in Paris 1919. Later he chaired the International Federation of the Red Cross and Red Crescent Societies 1938–1944 and was president of the Council on Foreign Relations 1936–1944. 248, 264, 268, 329, 330, 344, 407, 408, 441, 443, 445, 448, 577, 609, 615, 634, 650
Davis, Robert Beale, Jr. (1884–1929) was an American diplomat transferred from London to Copenhagen in August 1918. 311, 610
Davison, Henry Pomeroy (1867–1922) was an American banker with the J.P. Morgan Company who served as chairman of the War Council of the American Red Cross in 1917–1918 and founded the Red Cross Societies in May 1919. 75, 95, 121
Davison, Major. 246
Dawes, Charles G. (1865–1951) was an American banker, diplomat and a colonel in the AEF 17th Engineers 1917–1919. He was

decorated with the Distinguished Service Medal and the French Croix de Guerre. He later served as Ambassador to Britain 1929–1931 and Vice President of the United States 1925–1929. 197, 199, 238, 278, 298, 390, 420, 422

Dawson, Warrington "Pa" (1872–1962) was an American diplomat serving at the Embassy in France. He compiled political intelligence for Ambassador Sharp during his tenure in Paris. 34, 37, 57, 59, 65–67, 69, 73–75, 85, 87, 88, 90, 151, 161, 165, 174, 175, 178–180, 182, 184, 206, 207, 209, 219, 231, 232, 237, 241, 252, 253, 258, 282, 307, 356, 359, 364

Deland, Margaret (1857–1945) was an American novelist of the school of literary realism. She did relief work in France during WWI and awarded a Legion of Honor cross. 48

Day, Franklin "Wolfram" (1893–1958) was a German-born American diplomat. After serving at the Legation in Bern, he became Secretary to the US Mission at Berlin after the Armistice. Later he worked for the Equitable Life Insurance Co. 583

Débeney, Marie-Eugène (1864–1943) was a French general who commanded the troops during the Battle of the Somme and then chief-of-staff for Petain in 1917. He participated in the Battle of Amiens under Haig, and at Cambrai where the Hindenburg Line was broken in October 1918. 253

De Broqueville, Charles (1860–1940) was a Belgian politician who served as twice as Prime Minister, 1911–1918 and 1932–1934. 202, 233

De Garmendia Julio (1898–1977) was a Venezuelan writer serving in the Venezuelan Embassy in Paris in 1918–1919. Later, in 1972, he won the Venezuelan National Literature Prize. 197

Degay. 381

Degoutte, Jean (866–1938) was a French army general who replaced Duchêne after the Battle of Chemin des Dames. Later he served as commander of the French Army of the Rhine 1919–1925. 283

De Guiche – See Armand de Gramont. 222

De Kay, John Wesley (1872–1938) was an American entrepreneur, nicknamed the "Sausage King" of Mexico due to the success of his "Popo" brand. He was also a writer and eccentric socialite who supported Mexican President Victoriano Huerta. 105, 108

Delacroix, Léon (1867–1929) was a Belgian lawyer and politician serving as Prime Minister November 21, 1918 to November 20, 1920. 416, 553

De Ligne, Charlotte de Gontaut-Biron (1852–1933) was married to Charles-Joseph de Ligne (1837–1914) and a friend of Gibson's since 1914. 155

Delić, Svetozar (1885–1967) was a Croatian communist who helped found "Napred," the Yugoslavian communist party in which he held a high rank. He is known for being the first communist mayor of Zabreb, but his tenure lasted only three days, April 16–19, 1920. 506

Demeny, General 67

Dennis, Wm. Cullen (1878–1962) was an American lawyer and professor of law. He served as Assistant Solicitor to the State Department 1906–1910, and as Agent of the US in the Chamizal Arbitration with Mexico 1910–1911 and in the Costa Rica-Panama Boundary Arbitration 1911–1913. He was legal advisor to the Chinese Government in Peking 1917–1919. After acting as US agent in several more arbitrations, he practiced law privately and then became president of Earlham College in Indiana 1929–1946. 646

Derby, Edward Stanley (1865–1948) was the British Secretary of War 1916–1918, then Ambassador to France 1918–1920. 92, 222, 340, 440, 580

Derby, Richard (1881–1963) was an American surgeon who was married to Ethel Roosevelt (1891–1977), the daughter of Theodore Roosevelt and sister of Kermit and Quentin. 245

Deschanel, Paul (1855–1922) was a French politician serving as President of the French Chamber 1912–1920, with a role on the Committee of Foreign Affairs. He briefly served as President of France from February to September 1920. 222

De Traz, Robert (1884–1951) was a Swiss military writer from Geneva. 109

Dewald, Jacob R. (1894–1986) was an American army officer who served in Europe during WWI and then in Austria. 654

De Wilde, Robert-Pierre (1883–1947) was a Belgian General. 393

Dexter, Fletcher (b. 1885) was an American college professor and later as Consular Agent in Vevey 1915–1916, and Lausanne, Switzerland 1916–1918, where he remained as Vice Consul until 1924. 94, 178

Dickey, Donald Ryder (1887–1932) was an America natural scientist who amassed the largest collection of bird and mammal specimens in the US. He was also active in his community serving on the boards of museums and hospitals as well as a director of the Pasadena Branch of the Pacific Southwest Trust & Savings Bank. 13

Dickson, Samuel S. (b. 1895) was an American diplomat serving in London 1917–1919. 305

Dmowski, Roman (1864–1939) was a Polish politician who headed the Polish National Committee in Paris. His ultra-nationalist notions about a renewed Polish state was at odds with those of General Josef Piłsudski which included a wider, more federalist view. While Piłsudski became First head of State of independent Poland in November 1918, Dmowski worked behind the scenes, officially serving only briefly as Minister of Foreign Affairs in 1923. 4, 278, 282, 348, 353, 393, 484

Dockweiler, Isidore B. (1871–1947) was an American lawyer and Californian politician. He helped to secure California's vote for President Wilson, who offered him the post of Secretary of the Interior. Dockweiler declined, instead serving on the Board of Indian Commissioners 1913–1920 and on the Board of Directors of Security First National Bank 1922–1947. 20

Dodge, Geoffrey (1887–1941) was an American designer who worked with Robert Bliss in an administrative position during his tour in Argentine 1909. When war broke out, he moved to Paris to work for various wartime charities, including the American Red Cross. He became a chevalier in the French Legion of Honor and received the Serbian Cross for his wartime relief work. As a designer, he help Robert and Mildred Bliss decorate their Paris apartment and Dumbarton Oaks. 217

Dodge, Henry Percival "Percy" (1870–1936) was an American diplomat, Ambassador to the Serbs, Croats and Slovenes 1910–1926 and Denmark 1926–1930. 360, 501, 511, 512, 514, 515

Dodge, Theodora. 375, 401

Dolbeare, Frederick R. (1885–1962) was an American diplomat in Vienna, Bern, Paris, Warsaw, Berlin, London, Ottawa and Istanbul between 1915 and 1928. He was responsible for matters pertaining to Russia and Poland for the American Commission to Negotiate Peace in Paris 1919. He moved to Poland under Gibson later in 1919. Later he joined the Henry Schroder banking firm, which he represented to the Thai Ministry of Foreign Affairs, 1935–1940. 95, 105, 452, 454, 548, 584, 592, 626, 630, 642

Doleant. 215, 218

Dolléans, Édouard (1877–1954) was a French historian who specialized in the labor movement. 228, 277, 340

Draper, of the Associated Press. 56, 239

Dresel, Ellis Loring (1865–1925) was an American lawyer and diplomat and attaché to the US Embassy in Berlin 1915–1917.

Upon the US entry into the war, he was temporarily assigned to the Embassy in Vienna. During the war, he worked in Bern, Switzerland, with the Legation, the Red Cross and the War Trade Board. Later he led the political information section of the Paris Peace Conference and US Commissioner in Germany 1919–1921. 95, 98, 100, 170, 297, 298, 301, 305, 361, 420, 452–454, 548, 572, 577, 580, 615, 616, 618, 619, 642, 643

Drugman, Sidonie Marie Louise Catoir married Hubert Drugman (1854–1907) in 1883. She was the mother of both Myriam (who married Jean Marie "Jack" Reyntiens in 1908) and Adrienne (who married Guy Reyntiens). Her home was located at 19 Boulevard de Waterloo in Brussels from where resistance work was reported to take place (See Kenneth Baker, *The Obscure Heroes of Liberty*, 2018). 416, 554, 590

Drummond, James Eric (1876–1951) was a British politician and diplomat, and the 7th Earl of Perth. He was a member of the Balfour Mission to the US in 1917, and a British delegate to the Paris Peace Conference 1918–1919. Later he served as the first Secretary-General of the League of Nations 1920–1933 and Ambassador to Rome 1933–1939, before becoming the chief adviser of the Ministry of Information 1939–1940. 137, 139, 149, 313, 378

Dubail, Augustin (1851–1934) was a French general serving as the military governor of Paris 1916–1918 after being fired by Joffre over the disaster at Verdun in March 1916. 196

Dubost, Antonin (1844–1921) was a French politician serving as President of the Senate 1906–1920. 222

Duchêne, Denis Auguste (1862–1950) was a French army general who defied Pétain's orders during the Battle of Chemin des Dames in May 1918 allowing the Germans to come within reach of Paris. 197

Duke of Genoa, Tommaso of Savoy (1854–1931) was an Italian aristocrat who managed the civil affairs of Italy throughout the war. 157

Dulles, Allen Welsh (1893–1969) was an American lawyer, diplomat and 2nd Secretary at the US Legation in Bern in 1918. He was responsible of matters pertaining to Austria-Hungary and the Balkans for the American Commission to Negotiate Peace in Paris 1919. While assigned to the US Embassy in Istanbul in 1921, he helped expose the *Protocols of the Elders of Zion* as a forgery. He became director of the Council on Foreign Relations in 1927 while becoming increasingly interventionist in relation to events in Germany. In 1941, Dulles was recruited to the OSS by William Donovan and returned to Bern. After the war, he became deputy director of the CIA in 1951, served as Director from 1953–1961, and intervened in Latin American affairs as part of US Cold War policy. 95, 103, 105, 444, 454, 548, 549, 584, 592, 603, 608, 615, 627, 643, 653

Dumont, Frederick F.T.F. (b. 1869) was an American construction engineer and banker who served as US Consul in Guadeloupe 1911–1912, Madrid 1912–1914, Florence 1914–1919, Dublin 1919–1920, and then as US Consul-General in Frankfort 1924 and Havana 1929–1932. 118

Dunbar, Miss. 459, 557, 558, 560

Dunlap, Robert H. (1879–1931) was an American officer in the US Marine Corps. He advised Admiral Sims, who proposed that an Allied amphibious operation could be successful. He later attained the rank of Brigadier General. In 1931, he returned to France to study Strategy at the French War College, but perished while attempting a rescue of a French woman trapped after a landslide. 153, 197

Dunn, James Clement (1890–1979) was an American diplomat, one of the "Family" who shared living quarters when in Washington, served in several key roles over his career: He was the first US Chef of Protocol (1928–1930), chief political advisor to the Berlin Conference (1945), and Ambassador to Italy (1937–1952), France (1952–1953), Spain (1953–1955) and Brazil (1955–1956). 47n

Durand, Edward Dana (1871–1960) was an American economist who directed the US Census 1909–1913. He was a professor of Economics at Stanford University. In 1917, he joined the Food Administration under Herbert Hoover. After the war he was assigned as an adviser to the Polish Ministry of Food. Later he served as a member of the US Tariff Commission 1935–1947. 164

Durych, Eugen. 526, 539

Dvořák, Antonín (1841–1904) was a world-famous Czech composer. 480

E

Earle, Homer P. (1869–1946) was a Stanford University professor of Romantic languages who translated documents for the State Department, especially during the Spanish-American War. 21

Ecker – See Egger. 109

Ecklestone, Miss. 391

Edelman, Samuel (b. 1885) was the vice-consul in Geneva 1917–1919. Previously he has served in Constantinople, Jerusalem, Aleppo, and Damascus. 92, 94, 178

Edgell, George H. (1887–1954) was an American scholar of Fine Arts from Harvard University. He was a Visiting Professor at the American Academy in Rome. He worked with ComPub, serving as US Commissioner to the Inter-Allied Committee for Propaganda into Enemy Countries at Padua in 1918. 333

Edie, John Rufus, III (1870–1946) was an American naval officer serving in France 1918. 364

Edvina, Mlle. 385, 553

Edward VII (1841–1910) was the King of the United Kingdom 1901–1910. 44, 60, 224, 321

Edward Albert (1894–1972), Crown Prince of the United Kingdom, Prince of Wales, was a Colonel in the Welsh Guards during WWI. He was crowned King of England on January 20, 1936. His reign lasted less than one year, ending with his abdication on December 11, 1936. He was subsequently known as the Duke of Windsor. 157

Edwards, Paul Leroy (b.1882) was an American businessman serving as Commercial Attaché and Representative of the War Trade Board at The Hague. 402, 403

Egan, Martin (1872–1938) was an American newspaperman who negotiated with the Japanese Government to help the Associated Press achieve an outstanding "beat" on the Russo-Japanese War (1904–1905). Between 1910 and 1938, Egan was associated with JP Morgan and Co. He interrupted this tenure to serve as one of General Pershing's top civilian advisers for public relations and propaganda during 1918, bringing him into close association with Hugh Gibson. He was married to Eleanor Franklin. 187, 190, 198–200, 218, 262, 263, 326, 327, 329, 351, 352, 375–377, 381, 390, 420, 423, 602

Egger, August (1875–1954) was a Swiss lawyer, judge and professor of law at the University of Zurich. 109, 113, 169

Ehrensvärd, Johan Albert (1867–1940) was a Swedish diplomat who had served as envoy to Belgium and the Netherlands 1908–1910, to the US 1910–1911, and to Switzerland 1915–1918. From 1911 to 1914, he served as the Swedish Foreign Minister. He was married to Marna Münter, remained in politics, and became a political commentator. 102

Einstein. 409

Einstein, Lewis D. (1877–1967) was an American historian and diplomat. After graduating from Columbia University in 1899, he served in several posts in the Middle East and Latin American. As early as 1913, he foresaw that German dominance would pose a threat to the US. In Constantinople, he recorded the massacre of the Armenians and the Gallipoli Campaign in *Inside Constantinople: A Diplomat's Diary During the Dardanelle* in 1915. Later, he served as Ambassador to Czechoslovakia 1921–1930. 297, 300–302, 344

Eisenmann, Louis (1869–1937) was a Professor of Slavic Studies at the Sorbonne University in Paris. 376, 381

Elisabeth of Bavaria (1876–1965) was Queen consort of the Belgians 1909–1934, and Duchess of Bavaria by birth. During the WWI, she often visited the front lines and sponsored a nursing unit. She was a friend of Ynès Reyntiens and Hugh Gibson. 275, 427, 554

Elkins, William Oliver "Willie," Mrs. Burton (1888–1932) was a society woman from Santa Barbara, California. She was also prominent in France, where she worked in a children's hospital during the war. She married amateur golfer James Cresson Parrish in 1922. 221, 235

Elliot, Francis E. (1851–1940) was a British diplomat, Ambassador to Greece 1903–1917, and Deputy Controller of the Foreign Trade Department at the Foreign Office until his retirement in 1919. 329

Ellis, Sir Charles Drummond (1895–1980) was an English physicist who served as a cadet in the Royal Military Academy who happened to be on holiday in Germany when WWI broke out. He was interned at Ruhleben, where he had enough freedom to study and develop a laboratory in a stable where he able to study the photochemical process. He later worked on nuclear fusion and was knighted for his service in WWII. 340

Eltinge, LeRoy (1872–1931) was an American army officer and Deputy Chief of Staff, May 1918-June 1919. 200

English.

Erskine, William A. (1871–1952) was a British diplomat and counselor to the British Embassy in Rome. Later he would serve as Minister, then Ambassador to Poland 1928–1934. 126, 157

Erzberger, Matthias (1875–1921) was a German politician from the Catholic Centre Party who spoke out against the war as early as 1917. In 1918, he was designated as the authorized representative of the Reich Government to sign the Armistice between Germany and the Allies. He served as Minister of Finance 1919–1920. In August 1921, he was assassinated by a right-wing terrorist group. 389

Eustis, William Corcoran (1862–1921) was from a prominent Washington DC family and served as personal secretary to Gen. John Pershing during WWI. 217

Evans, Vernon (1893–1987) was an American army officer from 1915 to 1954 who arrived in France in November 1917. Later he taught at various military academies and at Georgetown University. During WWII, he served in Burma and was awarded the Distinguished Service Medal. From 1948 to 1951, he was chief of the Military Mission to Teheran. 193

Exton, Charles Wesley (1872–1964) was an American Army officer in France 1917–1919. Later he served in Chemical Warfare Service 1923–1936. 51, 77, 200, 364, 421, 453, 573

Eynac, Laurent (1886–1970) was a French lawyer and politician, served as a deputy in the Haute-Loire 1913–1935, held several ministerial positions during the interwar years, was vice president of the French Union 1947–1958, and sat on the Economic and Social Council 1959–1964. 595

F

Fabry, Jean (1876–1968) was a French army officer, journalist and politician who later served in the Chamber of Deputies 1919–1936 and several other government posts. 34, 66, 87, 180, 182, 206, 210, 222

Fairholme, W.E. was the British Military Attaché in Paris 1909–1912 and Antwerp 1914. Gibson records five visits with Major Fairholme in *A Journal From Our Legation in Belgium*. In each case, Gibson mentions the information learned from him, but never mentions passing information to him. 274

Farman, Elbert E. (1886–1982) was an American army major who served as Gibson's military attaché in Poland 1919–1923. 651

Farnham, Charles W. published *Theodore Roosevelt, 1858–1919: A Memorial* in 1919. 559

Farrar-Smith, Stuart (1874–1951) was a US Navy Captain serving in the Naval Construction Corps. He was the son of Civil War hero William Farrar-Smith. 41, 121, 147, 236

Favre, Madame. 98

Fay, Father, was a friend of F. Scott Fitzgerald and a Catholic priest who nurtured Fitzgerald's writing. He served in the Red Cross during WWI. 139, 150

Felder, Thomas was an American Naval Intelligence Officer operating in Switzerland. 299, 302, 327, 329, 332, 334, 335, 338, 352, 362, 363

Ferdinand I of Bulgaria (1861–1948) was a member of the Saxe-Coburg family and ruled Bulgaria from 1908 until his abdication in 1918. 354–355

Ferguson, Harley B (1875–1968) was an American army general and the engineer in charge of raising the USS Maine in Havana (1910–1912) while Gibson was stationed in Cuba. 52–53

Ferretti, Giovanni (1792–1878) was Pope Pius IX who reigned from 1846 to 1978. 62

Festetics, Sándor (1882–1956) was a Hungarian nobleman and politician who served as Minister of War December 1918 to January 1919. He later espoused Nazism and Zionism as a solution to the Jewish problem. 490–493

Feyler, Col. 109

Field, Herbert Haviland (1868–1921) was an American zoologist who represented the US on the National Research Council in Zurich. 101, 106, 109, 110, 169, 170, 331–334, 337, 543

Fife, George Buchanan (1869–1939) was an American newspaperman and war correspondent working with the Red Cross in Bern. During summer 1918, he worked closely with Whitehouse and Compub. 183

Fiori, Robert de (1854–1933) was an Austro-Hungarian lawyer and journalist, born on the Italian-Slovenian border. He was a correspondent of the *New Free Press* in Rome 1881–1914. In June 1918 he became a lead agent for the German Foreign Office for talks with George D. Herron. Considered one of the most intelligent German agents, the information Herron gleamed from de Fiori was highly prized by the Allies. 239, 240

Fisher, Colonel, was a British representative to the committee on propaganda to enemy countries. 244

Fleiner, Fritz (1867–1937) was a Swiss jurist credited with being the father of modern administrative law in Switzerland. 110, 112, 169

Foch, Ferdinand (1851–1929) was a French general who served as the Supreme Allied Commander during the First World War from March 1918 to January 1920. 44, 48, 50, 54, 69, 70, 78, 150, 209, 229, 254, 280, 291, 292, 303, 304, 339, 360, 375, 376, 382, 384, 386, 387, 389, 390, 411, 414, 440, 578, 652

Foerster, Freidrich Wilhelm was a German academic who taught history and pedagogy at the University of Munich. He was an ardent pacifist and a long-time friend of Herron's, and thereby provided many of the contacts for Herron. Foerster acted as an adviser to Kurt Eisner, a Bavarian politician opposed to the war, and published his account in *Mein Kampf gegen das militaristisch und nationalistische Deutschland* in 1920. 112, 239

Focqué, Mr. 214

Forbes, James Grant, II (1879–1955) was an American businessman who was born in Shanghai. The Forbes family amassed a fortune from the opium trade and merchant banking. 167, 331

Ford, Henry (1863–1947) was an American industrialist and founder of Ford Motor Company. Although he was known for his pacifism during WWI, he also promoted anti-Semitic material through a series of articles in *The Dearborn Independent* newspaper, which Ford owned. He ran for a Senate seat in 1918, but lost despite the support of President Wilson. 281, 282

Foster, Reginald "Reggie" Candler (b. 1889) was an American army lieutenant who had served in the Red Cross before American entered the war. As a member of the American Commission to Negotiate Peace, he headed the Informational Mission to Poland 1918–1919. He was the first American to assess and report on the conflict in Teschen (Cieszyn). 399, 534, 535

Foulois, Benjamin D. (1879–1967) was Chief of the Air Service for the American Expeditionary Force and a member of the Joint Army and Navy Aircraft Committee in France in November 1917. After Armistice Day, November 11, 1918, he served on the Supreme War Council. 33, 41, 42, 78, 86, 87, 147, 162, 257, 302, 335

Fowler, Emily "Millie" (1879–1960) and Agnes Fowler (1893–1976) were the sisters of Harold Fowler. 369, 381, 398

Fowler, Harold (1886–1957) was a British solider and banker. Just before the war, he served as secretary to Ambassador Walter Hines Page in London. He joined the Royal Flying Corps in 1916, downing a German plane in February 1917 and joining the US Army Air Service in April. Upon the signing of the Armistice on November 11, 1918, he flew his biplane through the Arc de Triomphe in celebration. Between the wars, Fowler worked the New York Stock Exchange. During WWII, he was the military attaché in London and served as an intelligence officer for the RAF. 235, 341, 391, 392

Francis, David Rowland (1850–1927) was an American politician who served as Governor of Missouri 1889–1893, Secretary of the Interior 1896–1897, and Ambassador to Russia from May 1916 to November 1917. 369, 637

Franck, Harry Alverson (1881–1962) was a self-educated American travel writer. His *A Vagabond Journey Around the World* (1910) sold well. He continued traveling and writing throughout his life. During WWI, he served in the cavalry and with the Ninth Air Force in France during WWII. 75, 78, 176

Franckenstein, Georg Albert von (1878–1953) was an Austrian diplomat who had served in Washington, DC, St. Petersburg, Rome as well as Japan, India, and Great Britain. During WWI, he was the Austrian representative in German occupied Belgium until being transferred to the Caucasus in 1918. After the war, he was a member of the Austrian delegation at Saint-Germain. Later he was the Austrian Minister in London 1920–1938. He opposed Nazi regime which forced his resignation. After WWII, he participated in Austrian politics. 467, 469, 471, 486

Franklin-Bouillon, Henry (1870–1937) was a French far right politician. 222

Francqui, Émile (1863–1935) was a Belgian businessman, diplomat and politician. As a young Belgian officer, he served in the Congo Free State under Leopold II, King of the Belgians. In 1896, he was assigned as Consul to China where he met, and competed with, Herbert Hoover. His financial career began in 1902 with various banking and mining ventures. As head of the Comité National de Secours et d'Alimentation, he worked closely with Hoover's CRB during WWI. This was the beginning of a collaboration with Hoover on a humanitarian effort comprehensive humanitarian effort which fostered an academic and practical cooperation between Belgium and America. 2, 395, 413–416, 418, 427, 431, 553, 554, 576, 588, 601, 612, 626, 627

Frankfurter, Felix (1882–1965) was an American lawyer who co-founded the ACLU, lobbied for recognition of the Soviet government by the US, and took up the Zionist cause. He served as an Associate Justice on the US Supreme Court 1939–1962. 648

Franz Ferdinand of Austria (1863–1914) was the heir apparent to the throne of the Austro-Hungarian Empire. His assassination on June 28, 1914, triggered a series of alliances and conflicts leading into World War I. 497, 498

Fray. 169

Frazier, Arthur Hugh (1868–1963) was an American diplomat who served as Secretary of Embassy in Paris 1915–1918, designated as Counselor in June 1918. He later served as Chargé d'Affaires in Austria 1921–1922. 32, 33, 39, 60, 61, 67–69, 72, 76, 85, 86, 163, 164, 166, 170, 174, 178, 180–182, 184, 187, 188, 202, 213, 220, 221, 230, 235–237, 243, 251, 260, 268, 269, 278, 293, 297, 298, 301, 305, 326, 332, 333, 337–339, 340, 350–352, 356–358, 361, 363, 364, 372, 373, 377, 381, 383, 384, 388, 391–393, 420, 438, 439, 628

Fremont, Francis Preston (1854–1931) was the son of Jessie and John Fremont, US General, California Senator, and presidential candidate. In the course of the log, Gibson refers to both "Jack" [John Charles, Jr.] and "Frank" [Francis Preston]. Because Jack died in 1911, it is likely Gibson is mistaken here and that both refer to Frank. But there are some official records that list "J.C. Fremont" as having served at the Peace Conference in Paris. The Fremonts and Gibsons were family friends, and Jessie Fremont lived her last days with the Gibsons in Los Angeles. 548

French, Burton L. (1875–1954) was a US Congressman from Idaho. 633

Frick, Rob. 587

Frischauer, Franziska (1873–1945) was the daughter of Heinrich and Margarethe Brandeis of Austria, and sister of Albertine Wittouck. She married to Austrian lawyer and journalist Berthold Frischauer and they lived primarily in Paris. Berthold served as a travel companion for Austrian Crown Prince Rudolf before he represented the *New Free Press* in Paris, which advocated for Alfred Dreyfus. Berthold became the editor of the *Neue Freir Presse* after their return to Vienna. 540

Fronczak, Franciszek E. (1877–1955) was a Polish activist in the US and a member of the Polish National Committee in Paris. 348 photo, 392, 393

Fueter, Eduard, Sr. (1876–1928) was the editor and chief editorial writer on foreign politics for the *Neue Zuricher Zeitung* from 1912–1921. 108, 109, 113

Fuller, Samuel was an American banker from New York serving in Rome as head of the Department of Administrative Affairs for the American Red Cross. 148, 167

Fullerton, William Morton (1865–1952) was an American journalist and foreign correspondent for *The Times* in Paris 1890–1910. He authored a number of books and articles while serving as an officer in the US army during WWI. After the war, he wrote for the French magazine *Le Figaro* for the rest of his career. 233, 384

Funk, Ilo Clare (b. 1889) was an American from Colorado serving as vice-consul in Milan, Italy, in 1918. 115, 118

G

Gabriński, Stanisław (1858–1940) was a Polish politician. 462

Gagnon, Clarence (1881–1942) was a Canadian painter from Quebec. 74, 220, 353–354, 376, 572

Gailor, F.H. was a former CRB volunteer. 282, 572

Gaisford, Hugh William (1874–1954) was a British diplomat serving as British Secretary to the Vatican. Later he was British Consul in Munich 1925–1932. 133, 139, 144, 145, 155

Gałecki, Kazimierz (1863–1941) was a Polish lawyer who was the last Minister for Galician Affairs in the Austrian Government in 1918. He briefly served as Minister to Vienna from January 1 to March 31, 1919 and voivode (governor) of Krakow 1921–1923. 467, 468

Gallavresi, Guiseppe (1879–1937) was an Italian historian. 174, 195, 212, 243, 298, 338, 434

Gallenga-Stuart, Romeo (189–1938) was the Italian under-Minister of Propaganda 1917–1919. 122–124, 250, 333

Garbai, Sándor (1879–1947) was a Hungarian socialist politician in favor of merging his party with the Communist Party in 1919. He was Prime Minister from March to August 1919, but held little power as Béla Kun, as foreign minister, was the true leader. 620

Garfield, Harry Augustus (1863–1942) was an American lawyer and academician. He was the president of Williams College 1908–1934 and supervised the Federal Fuel Administration during WWI. 213

Garrett, Alice was married to John Garrett and socialized often with Gibson's group. 602, 625, 643

Garrett, John Work (1872–1942) was an American who served as Ambassador to the Netherlands in 1918. He resigned in 1919 to join Robert Garrett and Sons Investment Bankers in Baltimore. He was married to Alice Garrett. 87, 103, 398, 421, 609

Gasparri, Pietro (1852–1934) was an Italian cardinal who served as Secretary of State for the Vatican from 1914 to 1930. 118

Gaunt, Guy R. A. (1969–1953) was a British Navy admiral who had served as a military attaché in the US in 1914. During the war, he worked as an intelligence officer and liaison. He was knighted in 1918. 345, 397

Gavronsky, Jacob O. was a Russian socialist active in the revolution and collaborated with all the main leaders. In 1917, he headed the Press Section at the Russian Embassy in London and promoted the idea that the Bolsheviks would ultimately betray the allies. 246, 247

Geller, Mihály was a Hungarian businessman and the first general manager of the Danubius Hotel Astoria in Budapest since 1914. He had previously worked at the Waldorf Astoria in New York. 493

Genestal, Capt. 474

Gertrude, Liz. 342

Gherardi, Walter R. "Jerry" (1874–1939) was an American naval intelligence officer who had served at the US Embassy in Berlin 1914–1917. Between April 1917 and August 1918, he took command of a transport ship, the USS Dekalb. He was assigned to Paris August 1918 to February 1919. Between 1919 and 1935, he filled various administrative roles in the US, including Aide to the Secretary of the Navy and Chief of the Navy's Bureau of Hydrography. 297, 298, 301. 307–308, 324, 450, 565, 568

Ghilain, Lt. Col. 536

Gibbons, Floyd Phillips (1887–1939) was an American journalist and war correspondent for the *Chicago Tribune* during WWI. He lost an eye while rescuing an American soldier injured in the Battle of Belleau Wood (June 1918), and afterwards wore a distinctive eye patch. 90, 244, 256

Gibbs. 420

Gibbsons, James (1834–1921) was the Catholic Archbishop of Baltimore 1877–1921. 150

Gibson, Carlton. 300, 568

Gibson, Francis Asbury (1857–1902), Hugh Gibson's father, was a bank manager in Los Angeles, California. 1, 2, 405

Gibson, Harvey Dow (1882–1950) was an American businessman serving as Commissioner of the American Red Cross in France during the war. In 1931 he became president of Manufacturers Trust Company and served as Red Cross Commissioner in Great Britain. 435

Gibson, James McMillan (1910–1966) was the step-son of Mina Burnaby. 126

Gibson, Mary Kellogg (née Simons, 1885–1930), Hugh Gibson's mother, was a trained teacher who worked tirelessly for the improvement of the conditions faced by immigrant women in California. 1, 2, 5, 8, 11–22, 24, 31, 83, 307, 327, 332, 325, 420, 421, 423, 425, 426, 428, 432–439, 441–444, 446, 449–454, 457, 460–462, 464, 466, 469, 470, 475, 477, 481, 484, 486, 493, 497–501, 503, 509, 511, 514, 516, 517, 519, 522, 524–526, 534, 536, 538, 539, 541, 543–547, 549–553, 555–562, 564–570, 572–575, 577, 579–581, 583–585, 587, 591–594, 596, 599, 603, 605, 607, 615, 618, 620, 625–630, 632, 634, 635, 637–639, 642, 643, 650, 651

Gibson, Preston (1880–1937) was a prominent American society figure and playwright. He was one of the first American volunteers to the French army where he served 1916–1918, earning the Croix de Guerre for bravery. He married Minna Field (1882–1952), niece of Marshall Field and step-daughter of Thomas Nelson Page. 68, 75, 178, 217, 320

Gibson, Ynès – see Ynès Reyntiens, who married Hugh Gibson in February 1922. VII, XV, 2, 8, 81, 243, 272, 315, 414–416, 422, 426, 433, 435, 439–441, 452, 455–460, 543, 556–560, 573, 582–583, 585–587, 590

Giers, Mikhail Nikolayevick von (1856–1942) was the pre-revolutionary Russian Ambassador to Italy 1915–1917. 171

Gifford, Walter Sherman (1885–1966) was an American businessman and diplomat. During WWI he served as the Supervising Director of the Committee for Industrial Preparedness, Director of the Council of National Defense, and Secretary of the US representation on the Inter-Allied Munitions Council. Later he was President of AT&T 1925–1948 and Ambassador to Britain 1950–1953. 326

Giuffrida, Vincenzo (1878–1940) was an Italian politician who was put in charge of food supply during war-time Italy and who developed a series of services to help manage the war economy. He went on to become one of the central figures of the new technocracy in Italy. 474, 482, 486

Gisson. 369

Glynn, James Peter (1867–1930) was a US Congressman from Connecticut. 633

Glynn, John Lyles Jr. (1892–1938) served in the US Army 1918–1919. Later he practiced as a prosecuting attorney, judge and state representative in South Carolina. 237

Glyn, Elinor (1864–1943) was a British novelist of romantic fiction who also wrote articles for Randolph Hearst, including *Cosmopolitan Magazine*, after 1919. 167

Godson, William F. H. was an American Army officer assigned as Military Attaché in Bern. He was awarded the US Army Distinguished Service Medal on July 9, 1918. He was transferred to Military Intelligence in Washington in September 1921 and sent to Poland to investigate the Wilno issue during the Polish Soviet War. 98, 100, 103, 183, 299, 302, 307, 308, 654

Goedeke, Walter J. was an American diplomat who moved from the State Department to Intelligence. In 1918, he was assigned to Pershing GHQ, where he was charged with examining passports for possible forgeries. 41, 87, 251, 401

Goelet, Robert Walton "Bertie" (180–1941) was an American financier and real estate developer in New York. He served as director of Guaranty Trust Co. and Union

Pacific Railroad Corp. He married Anne Marie Guestier in 1921. 634

Gompers, Samuel (1850–1924) was an American businessman and labor leader who founded the American Federation of Labor. He was in the tobacco business and known for his cigars. He served in the Labor Section of the American Commission to Negotiate Peace in Paris 1919. 368, 478

Goode, R. T. was an American businessman of the Paris branch of Packard Motors. 556

Goode, William "Bill" (1875–1944) was the principal British Director of Relief and primary British representative on the Supreme Economic Council. 271, 273, 583

Goodwin, Philip L. (1885–1958) was an American architect who served in the US army during WWI with the American Commission to Negotiate Peace. He was assigned as a lieutenant to the Coolidge Mission in Budapest from, Budapest January 1919 to March 1920. Later he designed, with Edward Stone, the Museum of Modern Art in New York (1939). 517

Gordon, George A. (1885–1959) was an American lawyer and diplomat who served in the US Army assigned to France after participating in the Poncho Villa Expedition. After the war, he was on the staff supporting the American Commission to Negotiate Peace and at the Paris Peace Conference. Later he was both Ambassador to Haiti (1935–1937) and the Netherlands (1937–1940). During WWII, Gordon worked for the State Department designing foreign policy and internal reorganization. 24, 352, 373

Gordon, Mrs. John 342

Gorgas, William C. (1854–1920) was the Surgeon General of the US Army 1914–1918. 329

Gorky, Maxim (1869–1936) was born Alexei Maximovich Peshkov, a Russian writer and revolutionary of humble beginnings in whose novels the lower strata of Russian society feature prominently. He was nominated for the Nobel Prize several times. 510

Goubault. 560, 585

Gouraud, Henri Joseph Eugène (1867–1946) was a French army General who commanded the Fourth Army on the Western Front. His celebrated successes include the defensive tactics used during the Second Battle of the Marne, July 15-August 6, 1918. On November 22, 1918, he entered Strasbourg and overthrew the Soviet government forming there. Later, he served as the Military Governor of Paris 1923–1937 and on the Supreme Allied War Council 1927–1937. 285, 303, 304

Gramont, Armand de (1879–1962), the Duc de Guiche, was a French aristocrat, scientist and industrialist. Upon his father's death he became Duc de Gramont. 222

Grant, Ulysses S. III (1881–1968) was an American Army officer serving on the General Staff in France. He was the grandson of US President Ulysses S. Grant. 44

Grasty, Charles Henry (1863–1924) was an American journalist, war correspondent and newspaper publisher in Baltimore. After retiring in 1915, he went to Europe as a war correspondent on several trips between 1915 and 1918 when he published a book, *Flashes from the Front*. 57, 180

Gray, Prentiss (1884–1935) was an American businessman who had volunteered in the CRB before serving as Hoover's assistant in the US Food Administration. Later he became president of J. Henry Schroder Banking Corp as well as several other successful and lucrative companies. 592, 607, 627

Gray, Violet G. was an American librarian at the Friends Library Germantown Philadelphia. She was to take charge of the Information Files for ComPub in Paris June 1918, but decided to remain in the US. 61

Grayson, Cary T. (1878–1938) was an American Navy Rear Admiral, surgeon, personal aide to President Wilson 1916–1921 and chairman of the American Red Cross 1935–1938. 615, 629

Green, Joseph Coy "Joe" (1887–1978) was an American diplomat who served in the CRB 1915–1917, in the Press Division 1918, and ARA in Romania and Caucasus 1918–1919. His posts in the State Department included the chairmanship of the Armaments Commission (1944–46), US Mission to observe elections in Greece (1946), director of the Foreign Service Board of Examiners (1952–54) and ambassador to Jordan (1952–1953). 39, 42, 43, 46, 48, 64, 65, 71, 74, 77, 84, 87, 238, 373, 403, 413, 417, 641

Green, William Raymond (1856–1947) was a US Congressman from Iowa. 633

Greene, Warwick (1879–1929) was an American military officer, pilot and press officer in the intelligence section. In the spring of 1919, he led a US mission to Latvia to report on Bolshevik activities in the Baltic. 269, 292, 302, 423

Greenough, Charles Pelham "Charley" (1844–1924) was an American lawyer prominent in Boston. 372

Greer. Capt. 344

Gregory, Thomas C. "Tommy" (1899–1933) was an American army officer charged with directing ARA relief in Central Europe after the November Armistice. He also served as Assistant Director of Relief on the Supreme Council, under Hoover. He recorded his adventures in "Bolsheviks and Archdukes: The Personal Story of a Westerner who Acted as Receiver for Europe's Oldest Empire" in *Sunset Magazine*, 1920 (Vol. 44, pp.25–28) 426, 430, 436, 438, 453, 469, 474, 476, 477, 486, 487, 493, 502, 506, 509, 512–517, 519, 524, 525, 527, 538, 539, 543, 544, 547, 551, 617, 647, 654

Greppi, Guiseppe (1819–1921) was an Italian nobleman, politician and diplomat. He joined the Diplomatic Litigation Council in 1902. In 1912, then over 90 years old, he served on the Commission for the examination of Italian sovereignty in Libya and the ratification of the Treaty of Lausanne with Turkey. 153

Grew, Alice Perry (1883–1959) was married to Joseph Grew and a good friend of Gibson's. 546, 549, 574, 575, 635, 643

Grew, Joseph C. (1880–1965) was an American diplomat who was serving as chargé d'affaires in Vienna when the US declared war on Austro-Hungary in April 1917. In 1918, he was appointed secretary of the US Commission to the Paris Peace Conference. Later he served as Ambassador to Denmark, Switzerland, Turkey, and Japan 1932–1941. He and other foreign citizens were interned by the Japanese until July 1942. Grew then served as Under Secretary of State 1944–1945. 47, 189, 323, 357, 363, 375, 378, 383, 385, 386, 393, 395, 399, 400, 402, 410, 423, 427, 440, 443, 445, 447, 545, 546, 555, 564, 574, 575, 584, 586, 591–593, 596, 601, 615, 619, 621, 635, 637

Grey, Edward (1862–1933) was a British diplomat who served as Foreign Minister from 1905 to 1916, and then as Ambassador to the United States from 1916 to 1920. 2, 344

Griffith, Captain 47

Griscom, Ludlow (1890–1959) was an American ornithologist. His uncle, Lloyd Carpenter Griscom (1872–1959), an American diplomat, served as Ambassador to Iran 1901–1902, Japan 1903–1905, Brazil 1906–1907, and Italy 1907–1909. During WWI Ludlow served as Adjutant-General of the AEF. 266

Grobet-Roussy, Henri (1864–1930) was a Swiss metallurgist who directed the *Usines métallurgiques* in Vallorbe since 1899. He was trained in Basel and New York, and served on the legislative council 1912–1922 and 1024–1928. He was also the director of the Swiss Import

Trust during WWI, 1915–1918. 181, 305, 334
Grove, William Remsburg (1872–1952) was an American army officer who had been decorated for his service in the Philippine-American War in 1902. In 1918, he headed the ARA relief mission to central Europe with a group of about twenty officers. He settled in Poland and began operations there, renting the Zamoyski's Blue Palace which would become the home of Gibson's Legation by summer 1919. 449, 451, 461, 463, 466, 652
Guggenheim, Harry Frank (1890–1971) was an American businessman, diplomat, publisher and aviator. He joined the US Naval Reserves in September 1917, serving in France, Italy and England. Later President Hoover appointed him to the National Advisory Committee of Aeronautics where he served 1929–1928. Guggenheim founded *Newsday* newspaper in 1940 and won a Pulitzer Prize in 1954. 307, 310
Guillaumat, Adolphe (1863–1940) was a French army general who replaced Dubail as Military Governor of Paris in June 1918. 196
Guinotte Family worked with the CRB in Belgium during the war. Two CRB volunteers married their two daughters, Hélène and Zizi (Charles Carstairs and Teddy Curtis respectively). 389, 580, 629
Gunther, Franklin Mott (1885–1941) was an American diplomat who was assigned as Secretary to the US Embassy in London in 1918. He was transferred to The Hague in early 1919, and later served as US Minister to Egypt (1928–1930) and Romania (1937–1941). 14, 37, 39, 68, 292, 305, 311, 313, 322, 377, 407
Guthrie, Connop (1882–1942) was a British merchant banker serving in the British Ministry of Shipping 1916–1918. 326
Guthrie, William Norman (1868–1944) was an American clergyman and professor at the University of Chicago 1911–1937. 339

Gutterson, Herbert L. (1881–1940) was an American businessman who later supported the Walter Hines Page School of International Relations at John Hopkins University. 553, 573

H

Habrman, Gustav (1864–1932) had been for many years of the Czech textile union, the second largest union in Bohemia. From 1907 onwards, he was a member of the Austrian Diet (for the Czech Social Democrats). During the First World War, he was one of the main figures of the 'national wing' of the Czech Social Democracy, which drifted away from the Habsburg Empire and aimed to build up an independent Czechoslovak State. After this goal had been achieved, he served Czech Minister of Education 1918–1920, Minister of Social Affairs 1921–1925, and as a deputy of both the lower and upper chambers of the Czechoslovak Parliament until 1932. 478
Habicht, Lt. Colonel. 108, 113
Hackett, Chauncey was an American officer in the aviation section of the Signal Corps. 202
Hackett, William was an American army officer in the 1st Division 1917–1918. His experience is retold by James Nelson in *Five Lieutenants: The Heartbreaking Story of Five Harvard Men Who Led America to Victory in World War I* (2012), which contains a wedding picture of William and Louisa Haydock. 350
Haguenin, Émile (1872–1924) was a French literary scholar and diplomat who had taught at Friedrich-Wilhelms-Universitat Berlin 1901–1914, when he returned to Paris. In 1915, he undertook a diplomatic/intelligence mission as the Director of the Press Bureau at the French Embassy in Bern, Switzerland. From there, he led unofficial talks with both French and German scholars exploring the possibilities of a compromise peace throughout 1916–

1917. He participated in the Reparations Committee in 1919 and headed the social economic section of the French Embassy in Berlin. 451, 472, 474, 478, 486, 490, 493

Haig, Douglas (1861–1928) was a senior Scottish officer in the British Army who commanded the British Expeditionary Force from 1915 to the end of the war. 45, 215, 376

Hall, Durrel was the brother-in-law of Arthur Page. 366

Hall, Lt. 321

Hall, Reginald W. (1870–1943) was a British Naval officer and director of Naval Intelligence 1914–1919. He served a term in Parliament from 1919–1923 and in the British Home Guard until his death. 136, 313, 345, 346, 368, 403, 404, 425, 448, 604

Haller, Józef (1873–1960) was a general in the Polish Army. Between 1895 and 1906, he served in the Austrian Army, and then worked with Sokół, a paramilitary organization supporting Polish independence. In the First World War, he commanded one brigade in the famous Polish Legions which fought within the ranks of the Austrian Army. In 1917, Haller and his unit defected in Russia and he travelled via Vladivostok to Paris. There, on behalf of the Polish National Committee he created the 'Blue Army,' which mainly consisted of Polish former prisoners-of-war, in July 1918. He and his men went on to fight for Poland on the Ukrainian front and during the Polish-Soviet War. Later, Haller served as a deputy in the Polish Sejm and as Minister of Education in the Polish government-in-exile 1940–1943. 396, 397

Hallowell, John "Jack" (1882–1927) was an American businessman. He worked with the CRB in Belgium and the ARA after the war, as well as in other parts of Europe. He was decorated by Albert I, King of the Belgians, for his efforts. 413

Halley, Mrs. was engaged to Clare Torrey. 637, 647

Hamilton, Richard M. "Little Alexander" was an American diplomat who served as Vice Consul in Le Havre 1918–1919. 30, 31, 35, 172

Hammond, Paul. 435, 447

Hanna, Edward Joseph (1860–1944) was an American archbishop of Roman Catholic Church in San Francisco 1915–1935. 144

Hansi – See Waltz, Jean-Jacques

Hapgood, Norman (1868–1937) was an American journalist and diplomat who served as Ambassador to Denmark in 1919. 637

Harbord, James Guthrie (1866–1947) was an American senior army officer who went to France in April 1917 as Gen. Pershing's chief of staff. He took over the Services of Supply in 1918, achieving great success. In 1922, Harbord retired from the army and became president of the Radio Corporation of America. He campaigned for Herbert Hoover in 1928. 191, 251, 394, 406

Harjes, Herman Henry (1875–1926) was a French banker of the Morgan-Harjes Bank in Paris. He served as a Major in the French Army during WWI. 50, 65, 69, 84, 182, 238, 269, 297

Harrer, Ferenc (1874–1969) was a Hungarian politician who served as Minister of Foreign Affairs in 1919. 490

Harriman, Florence Jaffray (1870–1967) was an American suffragist and social reformer. When the US entered WWI, she directed the Women's Motor Corps in France. She was married to J. Borden Harriman, cousin of Averell Harriman. Later she would serve as Ambassador to Norway 1937–1940. 372, 375, 378, 408, 420, 423, 493, 593, 594

Harris, of the Red Cross. 216, 372

Harris, Edward (b. 1891) was a young American private in the Army who reported his war experiences in Saint Mihiel and Meuse-Argonne primarily in letters to his mother, Millie Harris. 372

Harrison, Leland "Nemo" (1883–1951) was an American diplomat serving in the State

Department's Bureau of Secret Intelligence 1916–1918. He was then assigned to the American Commission to Negotiate Peace in November 1918. Later he served as United States Assistant Secretary of State 1922–1924 and Ambassador to Sweden 1927–1929. Uruguay 1929–1930, Romania 1935–1937, and Switzerland 1937 to 1947. 34, 47, 393, 403, 404, 548, 577, 601, 644
Hart, General. 390, 573, 608, 634
Harte, Archibald Clinton (1865–1946) was an American volunteer for the YMCA. Along with Dr. Mott, he planned to start a mission in Palestine since 1906 but the needs of other countries and the Great War delayed the effort. When Palestine came under the British mandate following the war, the YMCA, under Harte's leadership, began. 87
Hartigan, Lord and Lady. 308, 351
Harts, William Wright (1866–1961) was an American army officer who had commanded the Sixth Engineer Regiment and the British Fifth Army before taking command of the District of Paris from 1918–1919. From 1919 to 1920 he was the Chief of Staff of the American forces in Germany. Later he was military attaché to Paris 1926–1930. 293, 340, 573, 616, 617, 644
Harvey, George Brighton (1864–1928) was an American journalist and business magnate. He served as Ambassador to the United Kingdom from 1921–1923. 73
Haskell, Lewis W. (1868–1938) was an American lawyer and diplomat. After serving a term in the South Carolina legislature, he served as Consul in Salina Cruz, Hull, Belgrade and Geneva (1915–1924), then Algiers and Zurich. 92, 94
Hastings, William W. (1866–1938) was a US Congressman from Oklahoma. 633
Hauzeur, Louis was a Belgian mining engineer with extensive interests in Spain and Africa. 233

Haven, Joseph E. (1885–1937) was an American diplomat who served as Consul in Turin 1916–1920, then in Trieste 1920–1922 and Florence 1923–1937. 120
Havemeyer, Miss. 432
Hawes, James Anderson (b. 1861) was an American lawyer. Among his many services during the war, Hawes was a war correspondent for the US and British Armies as well as the US Navy. He was General Secretary of the Delta Kappa Epsilon fraternity and editor of the *DEKE Quarterly*. He was in France to organize services for DKE members serving in Europe. 337
Hay, Ian was the pen name for British General John Hay Beith (1879–1952). He was a school master and soldier, novelist, playwright and historian. His first novel, *Pip* (1907), was successful enough to allow him to retire from his teaching position. The war brought soldiering, and his stories of army life in *The First Hundred Thousand* (1915) was a best-seller. 49
Hayden, Robert. 312, 366
Haydock, Louisa Lowe (b. 1890) married American army officer William Hackett on October 1, 1918. 350
Hayes, James Webb (1856–1934) was an American businessman and soldier as well as the second son of President Rutherford B. Hayes. During WWI he served as a special agent for the State Department in France and an administrator on the Italian front. 223, 224, 368
Hayes, Ralph (1894–1977) was an American businessman who served as Assistant Secretary of War under Newton Baker. Later he was Vice-President of Transamerica Corp and Coca Cola. 51, 329, 331, 351, 359, 366, 602, 617
Hays, William H. "Will" (1879–1954) was an American politician who chaired the Republican Party 1918–1921. He served as Postmaster General 1921–1922 and chairman of the Motion Picture Producers

and Distributors of American 1922–1945. 267
Hazen, David W. was an American newspaperman from Portland, OR, who wrote for the *Telegram*. He was attached to Oregon troops in France from 1918–1919. 171, 268
Hazen, Lt. 136
Hearley. "little physchologist" 155
Hech. 399
Heguenin. 100, 101
Heineman, Dannie N. (1872–1962) was a Belgian-American engineer and businessman, and managing director of Sofina. Later, during WWII, he was instrumental in persuading Luxembourg to admit 100 Jewish families fleeing from Germany. 76, 292, 417
Heintzelman, Stuart (1876–1935) was an American Army officer who would be responsible for planning and executing the St. Mihiel Offensive, September 12–15, 1918. 84
Heinz, Howard C. (1877–1941) was an American businessman, son of the founder of H.J. Heinz Company. Just after WWI concluded, he served in the Balkan States representing the American Food Commission, then the ARA. Later he became director of the Pennsylvania Railroad. 580, 598
Helfferich, Karl Theodor (1872–1924) was a German economist and politician who figured as Vice Chancellor to the German Empire in 1916/17 and was involved in the peace negotiations at Brest-Litovsk in early 1918. After the war, he became a strong opponent of the Versailles Treaty, especially concerning the German reparations, and a figurehead of the antidemocratic German National People's Party. 419
Hemmick, W.A. was an American clergyman serving as a chaplain attached to the US Army in France during WWI. 79, 87, 248
Hemphill, Alexander J. (1856–1920) was an American businessman who was president of Guaranty Trust 1909–1915. He was on the boards of many other companies and charitable organizations, including serving as treasurer of the Commission for Relief in Belgium. 576
Henderson, David (1862–1921) was a British Army officer of the Royal Flying Corps. 340
Henry, Prince of Prussia (1862–1929) was the younger brother of German Kaiser Wilhelm. He served as a naval commander in the Baltic from 1914 to 1917.
Henryx, Madame. 416
Herron, George D. (1862–1925) was an American clergyman and social activist who was a kind of self-designated diplomat. In November of 1917, Herron was invited to address a conference of key American decision-makers in Paris under the auspices of Ambassador Sharp. After that meeting, Herron began making written intelligence reports to the American Legation in Bern, as well as to the British. These reports were based on a series of agents sent to seek him out by the German Foreign Office He was greatly disappointed in the Treaty of Versailles and predicted that peace would last no longer than a generation. 61, 68, 93, 94, 99, 101, 169, 239, 552, 564
Herschell, Richard Farrer (1878–1929) was a British politician serving in the Royal Navy's code breaking section. He had served under Asquith as government whip of the House of Lords 1907–1915. 345, 346
Herter, Christian A. "Chris" (1895–1966) was an American politician who volunteered for the CRB before marrying heiress Caroline Pratt in 1917. He served as an attaché to the Embassy in Berlin. The Germans arrested him as a possible spy. He went on to be part of the US delegation to the Paris Peace Conference and assisted Hoover in providing post-war relief. After serving five terms in Congress, Herter served as Secretary of State 1969–

1961. 331, 332, 452, 454, 459, 460, 568, 592

Hervé, Gustave (1871–1944) was an ultranationalist French politician who had formerly espoused pacifism. 106

Herwarth von Bittenfeld, Hans (1871–1942) was a German military officer, diplomat and publicist. During the war, his task was to monitor how Germany was being presented in the foreign press. He headed the military division of the Federal Foreign Office 1916–1918. He later served in a similar function under the Nazi regime. The son whom Gibson notes as captured could have been Hans, Jr. (b. 1898) or Heinrich (b. 1901). 274, 352

Hibben, Paxton P. (1880–1928) was an American diplomat in St. Petersburg, Mexico City, Bogota, The Hague, and Santiago, Chile. He served in Armenia on a military relief mission and in the Red Cross assisting in Russia during the famine of 1921–1923. As a journalist, he wrote as a correspondent throughout WWI. 447, 611

Hierflinger, Major. 578

Hinckley, Thomas (1888–1918) was an American Foreign Service officer who served in San Salvador, Vienna and Rome between 1912 and 1918. He died of the flu on November 6, 1918. 123, 127, 133, 152, 153, 372, 388

Hindenburg, Captain Milke von was the German Envoy and Minister to Switzerland in 1918, and was the nephew of Paul von Hindenburg. 364

Hindenburg, Paul von (1847–1934) was a German general who, together with Erich Ludendorff, headed the Supreme Army Command which towards the end of the First World War assumed quasi-dictatorial power. In the Weimar Republic he became President twice, and in his latter term he was instrumental in empowering Adolf Hitler and the Nazi Party. 108, 303, 528

Hitchcock, Gilbert (1859–1924) was a US Senator from Nebraska serving of the Committee for Foreign Relations. 361

Hoagland, Herbert C. was an American movie distributor and general manager of the Selig Polyscope Company. He was the originator of the film newspaper *Pathe Weekly* in 1911. In 1918, he served on Creel's Committee for Public Information. 231, 233, 267

Hock, János (1859–1936) was a Hungarian Catholic priest and politician. Between November 1918 and March 1919, he served as chairman of the Hungarian National Council. He lived abroad from 1919 to 1933. Upon his return to Hungary, he was tried on charges of national libel contained in his published articles and imprisoned for a year. He was pardoned in 1935. 490

Hodson, Francis "Frank" served as the Chief Clerk at the American Embassy in London for over thirty years. 314, 324, 347, 403, 405

Höfer, Anton (1871–1949) was the Chief Quartermaster for the Austro-Hungarian army during the war and continued heading the food bureau 1918–1919. Gibson appears to have mistaken him with Lebenfeldt-Russ.

Hollis, Henry F. (1869–1949) was an American politician serving as Senator from New Hampshire 1913–1919. He represented the US at the Interallied War Finance Council. Later he served on the US Liquidation Commission for France and England in 1919 and was appointed to run the International Bank of Bulgaria in 1922. 248, 328, 329, 386, 619

Holmes, Elias Burton (1870–1958) was an American traveler, photographer and filmmaker. He coined the term 'travelogue'. 266

Holt, Hamilton (1872–1957) was an American educator, editor and politician. 172

Holt, Helen Maud (1863–1937) was a British actress married to actor Herbert Beerbohm Tree, later becoming Lady Tree. 312

Homola, Rudolf. Station master in Agram. 509

Honnold, William Lincoln (1866–1950) was an American mining engineer who had experience in the US, Mexico, Canada, and South Africa. In 1915, he was appointed as London director of the CRB and transferred to New York in 1916 to direct the whole operation until 1918. He founded the Anglo American Corporation of South Africa with Ernest Oppenheimer in September 1917. Later he served at the Claremont Colleges, Pomona College and as a trustee for the California Institute of Technology. He also served with the Metropolitan Water District of Southern California, chairing the Engineering Committee from 1930–1933. 388, 553, 576, 580, 648

Hood, Edward M. "Eddie" (b.1872) was responsible for White House and governmental department reports for the Associated Press. 449

Hoover, Herbert Clark (1874–1964) was an American mining engineer. Orphaned at age 9, he was educated at Stanford University and created a successful worldwide business. Approached by the Belgians on October 20, 1914, Hoover began his public service career by agreeing to lead the Commission for the Relief of Belgium. He quickly became known as the "Chief." His success led to the formation of the American Food Administration in 1917 and the American Relief Administration in 1919. He served as US Secretary of Commerce 1921–1928, and was elected as the 31st President of the United States, serving from 1929–1933. After losing the 1932 presidential election to Franklin Roosevelt, Hoover became a leader the loyal opposition and devoted much of his energy to humanitarian work during World War II and beyond. He and Gibson became acquainted that fateful day in 1914, and remained fast friends for the rest of their lives. Also known as 'the Chief." 1, 2, 4–8, 14–16, 19, 22, 57, 63, 99, 164, 181, 211, 215, 238, 246, 251, 252, 261, 263, 267–279, 281–283, 287–293, 296, 297, 322, 335, 380, 388- 400, 403, 406–411, 413–438, 440–443, 445, 447, 449, 450, 461, 522, 540, 545, 546, 550–552, 554–556, 559, 564–567, 569–573, 575–583, 585, 587, 589, 590, 592–595, 598–600, 603, 605, 607, 608, 611–613, 615–621, 625–627, 632, 634, 638–641, 648–651, 653

Hoover, Lou Henry (1874–1944) was an American geologist and mining engineer who married Herbert Hoover in 1899. She served as the national president of the Girl Scouts of the USA from 1922 to 1925. She served as First Lady of the United States in 1929–1933, during which time she gave regular radio broadcasts. The Hoovers had two sons, Herbert Charles and Allan Henry. 15, 16, 19, 22, 647

Hopkinson-Smith, Mrs. 453, 562

Horodyski, Jan Maria (1881–1948) was a Galician Pole who was part of the Polish Military Mission in the United States in September 1917. M.B. Biskuski describes him as "young, ambitious, unscrupulous" but a "devout Polish patriot who, sometime in 1915, became a British agent supplying valuable intelligence regarding the labyrinthine world of nationality politics of Central Europe to the Foreign Office. In exchange, Horodyski became an ever more trusted advisor regarding things Polish in London." ("Canada and the Creation of a Polish Army, 1914–1918," *The Polish Review* (Vol. 44, No. 3, 1999), p. 351) According to Joseph T. Hapak, Horodyski was a "shadowy figure who had advised Paderewski and the Polish Falcons of America for the past year on the possibility of creating a Polish Army" and a friend of Alexander Znamięcki ("The Polish Military Mission, 1917–1919," *Polish American Studies* (Vol. 38, No. 2, Autumn 1981) p 26). He orchestrated the rapprochement between Dmowski and Paderewski, coordinating with the British and Americans, per Piotr Wandycz in *The United States and Poland* (Cambridge: Havard University Press, 1980) pp. 116–118. His thoughts on how Europe should be run when the war concluded are laid out by Paul Latawski in "Count Horodyaki's Plan To 'Set Europe Ablaze' June 1918," *The Slavonic and East European Review* (Vol. 65. No. 3, July 1987, pp. 391–398). 4, 46, 57, 60–63, 93, 96, 98, 104, 116, 122, 123, 127–131, 134, 136–140, 143–145, 147, 149, 150, 153–155, 249, 278, 279, 282, 307, 308, 352, 356, 357, 361, 410, 444, 450, 453, 461, 464, 546, 628, 652

House, Edward Mandel (1858–1938) was an American businessman, Politician and diplomat. In 1893, he was appointed to a military staff with the title of lieutenant colonel. Although he had no military duties, the title stuck and he was known as Colonel House since that time. After moving to New York, House became a close friend and adviser to Woodrow Wilson and helped him become elected as President of the United States in 1912 and 1916. House spent much of 1915–1916 in Europe, trying to broker peace through diplomacy. During the American involvement in the war, House had a dominate role in shaping policy, prepared the constitution for the new League of Nations, and helped draft the Treaty of Versailles. Wilson and House grew apart over various aspects of foreign policy and House was sidelined in after the Paris Peace Conference in 1919. 39, 44, 60, 61, 68, 138, 235, 259, 270, 271, 276, 279, 318, 339, 352, 355, 358, 363, 365, 366, 371–373, 375, 379, 382, 395, 399, 400, 419, 424, 437, 442, 619, 621, 629, 639, 640, 642–644

Howard, Henry (1843–1921) was a British envoy to the Vatican, the first in over 300 years, during the war years of 1914–1916. Although he retired in 1916, he remained in Rome until his death in 1921. 130, 141, 146, 148

Howard, Jesse, was the daughter of Henry Howard. 132, 141, 146, 148

Howard, Roy Wilson (1883–1964) was an American newspaperman with the E.W. Scripps Company serving as War Correspondent in 1917–1918 in France and was president of the United Press. 377, 388

Howe, George. 599

Howe, Thorndike D. (1881–1934) was an American Army officer charged with the postal service in France. 188

Hubbard, Capt. 48, 132, 188

Hughes, Charles Evans (1862–1948) was an American politician who served as Governor of New York (1907–1910) and Associate Justice of the Supreme Court (1910–1916). He narrowly lost the 1916 US Presidential election to Woodrow Wilson, and went on to serve as Secretary of State (1921–1925) and Chief Justice of the Supreme Court (1930–1941). 47n, 423n

Hughes, Everett S. (1885–1957) was an American army officer who graduated from West Point in 1908. He arrived in France in 1918 and served at the Office of the Chief of Ordnance. Later, Hughes was active in WWII as Chief of Ordnance for the European Theater of Operations United States Army in 1942. He was awarded the Legion of Merit on two occasions as well as the Army Distinguished Service Medal and the *Croix de Gruerre* from both France and Belgium. 199, 386

Huidekoper, Reginald "Reggie" Shippen (1876–1943) was an American lawyer serving as a judge advocate in the US Army 1917–1919. Later served on the War Contract Adjustment Board November 1919-July 1920. He was married to Bessie Cazenove Dupont. 359

Hunt, Edward E. (b. 1885) was an American journalist who authored *War Bread: A Personal Narrative of the War and Relief in Belgium* in 1916. 52, 53, 215, 228

Huntington, Arabella (1851–1924) was one of the wealthiest American women of her time. She was married to railway tycoon Collis P. Huntington (1821–1900) in 1884, quickly becoming a avid art collector. After Collis' death, Arabella married his heir and nephew, Henry E. Huntington (1850–1927) in Paris in 1913. Together, Arabella and Henry founded the Huntington Library, Art Museum and Botanical Gardens in San Marino, California. 74, 301

Huntington, Constant Davis (1876–1962) was an American publisher. He married writer Gladys Parrish in 1916 and together they moved to London. Huntington opened the London branch of G.P. Putnam's Sons publishing company. 258

Huntington, William C. was an American who served in Russia as the Commercial Attaché in 1919 before returning to Washington to run the bureau there. 231, 369

Hurley, Edward Nash (1864–1933) was an Irish-American businessman who helped Tomáš Masaryk in the foundation of the Czechoslovak state in 1918. He chaired the US Shipping Board and served on the American Commission to Negotiate Peace in Paris 1919. 420

Hurley, William L. "Bill" was an American journalist working with the US Embassy in Rome. 117, 120, 122, 437

Hürlimann, Edwin (1880–1968) was a Swiss manager who joined the Swiss Reinsurance Institution in 1904. He became chairman of the board in 1919, and director-general from 1930–1960. 109, 113, 114

Hussey, Charles Lincoln (1870–1934) was a US Naval Admiral who commanded the *USS Birmingham* during WWI and was awarded the Navy Cross for his service. 501

Hutter, Dr. Charles 30

Hyde, James Hazen (1876–1959) was an American businessman who the inherited majority shares in The Equitable Life Assurance Society of the United States in 1899. By 1905, he was accused of corporate crimes, which led to his resignation and move to France. During WWI, he converted his Paris properties into Red Cross hospitals and volunteered as an ambulance driver. He received the Grand-Croix of the Legion of Honor for his service. He remained in France until Nazi Germany invaded, returning to the US in 1941. 68, 73–76, 79, 83, 162, 166, 170, 172, 182, 185, 214, 216, 217, 221, 256, 298, 372, 373

Hymans, Paul (1865–1941) was a Belgian lawyer, politician and professor serving as Minister for Foreign Affairs 1918–1920, and again in 1935–1936. He served as the 2nd president of the League of Nations 1920–1921, and again in 1932–1933. 414, 415, 429–432

I

Ickes, Harold LeClaire (1874–1952) was an American lawyer and reporter for the *Chicago Tribune*. After working on the presidential campaign of Charles E. Hughes in 1916, Ickes volunteer with the YMCA attached to the 35th Division of the AEF in France. Later, he served as Secretary of the Interior 1933–1946. 175

Iddings, Lewis M. (1850–1921) was an American diplomat serving as Counselor to the Embassy in Rome and involved in relief work in Rome during the war 1914–1918. He was married to Louise Belden Iddings. 130, 133

Infanta Eulalia (1864–1958) was the aunt of Spanish King Alfonzo XIII. 242

Ivanowski, Zygmunt (1874–1944) was a Polish artist and military officer who served as aid to Paderewski 1918–1920. 652

Irving, Alexander D. (1873–1941) was an American Naval officer serving under Admiral Cary Grayson as a junior aide to President Wilson during the Paris Peace Conference. He handled presidential mail and translations, and worked closely with Hoover. 615, 628, 651

Irwin, William H. (1873–1948) was an American journalist who covered the San Francisco earthquake of 1906. He published articles for Collier's Magazine between 1906 and 1914, sometimes in a muckraking style. He was one of the first American correspondents in Europe, and crossed Gibson's path in Belgium, where he served on Hoover's Commission for Relief in Belgium (1914–1915). He was chief of the foreign department of Creel's CPI in 1918. 17–19, 21, 22, 66, 68, 76, 78, 80, 82, 91, 105, 117–119, 123, 126, 133, 135, 139, 143, 146–148, 156, 162, 183, 195, 203, 204, 266, 351, 443, 545, 549, 556, 567

Iselin, Major. 98

Iturbide Family. A political force in Mexico during the 19th and 20th century. 458

Iwanowski, Zygmunt (1874–1944) was a Polish artists who married Helen Moser, an American, and they moved to New Jersey. He joined Haller's Blue Army in 1917. In 1918 the Iwanowskis accompanied the Paderewskis on their return to Poland and Zygmunt became Paderewski's aide. He had been assigned to help Gibson get settled in Poland. 654

J

Jaccaci, August (1856–1930) was a French art historian and muralist who wrote, together with John La Farge, one volume of what was to be a series entitled *Noteworthy Paintings in Private Collections* (1907). 269, 305

Jackson, John Brinkerhoff (1862–1920) was an American diplomat who first served in Berlin in 1890. After serving in various post in Europe and Cuba, he resigned in 1913. Then he volunteered as a special agent of the Department of State at the American Embassy in Berlin. During 1914, he reported on the status of German prisoners of war in England. Later, at the Embassy in Berlin, he was in charge of the British section. After his retirement, he settled in Montreaux, Switzerland, where he died in December 1920. He was married to Florence Baird Jackson. 561, 614

Jackson, Capt. 340

Jackson, Robert Appleton was an American army volunteer who graduated from the French Artillery School in Fontainebleau, France. He served at the General Headquarters for Artillery for the AEF and received several medals for his distinguished service. 56, 282

Jacquemin, Georges was a French army officer who served with the US Signal Corps in 1918. 218, 294, 338

James, Major A. L. was an American army officer who served as Chief Military Censor in 1918. He was a friend and occasional roommate of Gibson's. 176, 180, 182, 185, 190, 202, 214, 221, 234, 244, 245, 249, 250, 266, 267, 268, 273, 280, 283, 289, 292, 327, 328, 329, 350, 352, 361, 366, 379, 380, 383, 392, 435, 616

James, Henry III (1879–1947) was an American writer and nephew of novelist Henry James. During the war he served in the AEF and the War Relief Commission. He was a member of the delegation to negotiate peace at the Versailles Peace Conference 1918–1919. Later he chaired the Teachers Insurance and Annuity Association (1928–1947). 48

James, Lucy Wortham (1880–1938) was an American philanthropist. She married Huntington Wilson in 1903, but they divorced in 1915. Gibson worked under Wilson in Washington in 1911 and they became friends. 87

Januszajtin-Żegota, Marian (1889–1973) was a Polish Military commander who worked with Sapieha in an attempted coup d'etat in January 1919. 485

Jarotsky, Thaddeus von was a Prussian general in WWI who commanded German troops that entered Belgium in August 1914. 108

Jasper, Henri (1870–1939) was a Belgian politician who served as Minister of Economic Affairs 1918–1920, Foreign Minister 1920–1924, Prime Minister 1926–1934, and Minister of Finance 1932–1934. 626

Jászi, Oszkár (1875–1957) was a Hungarian social scientist and politician who served as Minister for National Minorities October 1918 to January 1919. In 1925 he immigrated to the US and taught history at Oberlin College. His *The Dissolution of the Habsburg Monarchy* was published by the University of Chicago Press in 1929. 490

Jay, DeLancy K. (1881–1941), younger brother of Peter A. Jay, was an American lawyer and army officer. His arm was injured during his service with the AEF at Chateau du Diable in August 1918 and awarded the Distinguished Service Cross for extraordinary heroism. 199, 246, 269, 327, 337, 358, 372, 379

Jay, Peter Augustus (1877–1933) was an American diplomat serving as counselor of the Embassy in Rome 1916–1919. He later served as Minister to Romania 1921–1925 and then Ambassador to Argentina 1925–1930. He was married to Susan McCook. 117, 119, 121, 125, 127, 132–134, 139, 140, 141, 145, 146, 149, 150, 152, 154, 156–158, 216, 292, 296, 299, 332, 333, 337, 347, 350, 351, 358, 366, 597, 644

Jay, Susan Alexander McCook (1879–1977) was the sister of Martha McCook and married to Peter Jay. 122

Jellinek, Dr. Arthur (1852–1929) was a Hungarian lawyer, and member of parliament. 487, 488

Jennings, Hennen (1854–1920) was an American mining engineer who worked primarily in South Africa. He served as a consulting engineer to the US Bureau of Mines 1915–1918. 350

Jennings, John Coleman (1873–1949)) was an American army officer of the aviation section of the Signal Corps serving as aide de camp to Gen. Harts in Paris as of August 10, 1918. He was later attached to President Wilson's party before being discharged and returning to the US in July 1919. 293

Jennings, Percy (b.1886) served in the British Royal Air Force 1918. Later he worked as an insurance agent. 356

Jensen, René was a friend of the Reyntiens family and Hugh Gibson. 415, 416, 551–553

Jessé-Curélly, Gaston (b. 1876) was a French diplomat who was charged with the foreign press in 1918. Between the wars, he acquired Château de Chamerolles from the Lambert family but lost it again during WWII. During the war years, he served as French Ambassador to Paraguay 1937–1942. 85, 184

Jewett, Rutger Bleecker (1867–1935) was an American publisher. As Editor-in-Chief of D. Appleton Company since 1911, he produced the work of Edith Wharton as well as Brand Whitlock. 553, 569

Joffre, Joseph Jacques (1852–1931), a Freemason, was the French Commander in Chief 1914–16. In late 1916, he was promoted to the rank of Marshal and leader of the Supreme War Council in 1918. 34, 35, 43, 45, 69, 154, 165, 167, 172, 174, 175, 178, 195, 206, 207, 210, 217, 219, 222, 223, 252, 253, 260, 262, 265, 269, 281, 286, 287, 364, 384, 440

Johnson, Harry Hubbard (1895–1987) was an US Army general who arrived in France August 1918. He later served in WWII and then worked for Gulf Oil. 429

Johnston, Mary (1870–1936) was an American novelist who focused on women's rights. Her best known work is *To Have and to Hold* (1900). 49

Johnstone, Antoinette "Nettie" Pinchot (d. 1934) was an American heiress, daughter of James W. Pinchot of New York, who married British diplomat Alan Vanden-Bempde-Johnstone in 1892. He served as Ambassador to the Netherlands and Luxembourg 1910–1917. 378, 385, 387, 432, 435

Jones, Monk. 404
Jovanović, Miloje (1875–1953) was a Serbian politician who was a member of first the Progressive Party and later the Yugoslav Democratic Party. Having studied political science in Germany, he earned a reputation as an excellent financial expert. He served in the first Yugoslav government as Minister of Nutrition and Reconstruction, December 1918-February 1919, and then became a state senator. 514
Jusserand, Jean Jules (1855–1932) was a French diplomat who served as Ambassador to the United States from 1902 to 1925. He was married to Elisa Richards. 18, 20, 85, 440

K

Kahn, Eugene J. was an American stock broker and a cousin of Otto Kahn. 299
Kahn, Otto (1867–1934) was a German-born American businessman and investment banker. He joined Kuhn, Loeb & Co. in 1896. Later he was also a director for Equitable Trust Co. of New York and the Union Pacific Railroad. 178, 183, 184, 299, 302
Karmazin, John (1884–1977) was a Czech-American engineer and businessman who worked for International Harvester in Chicago. In early 1918 he joined the US Army, Military Intelligence Division. After the Armistice he worked with the American Committee to Negotiate Peace, offering various intelligence reports about developments in central Europe. 534–36
Karolyi, Katinka Andrássy (1892–1985) was married to Mihály Karolyi. 494
Karolyi, Mihály (1875–1955) was a Hungarian aristocrat and politician who participated in government since 1910 as a Member of Parliament. During the war, he led a small maverick faction and made contact with Allies diplomats in Switzerland. In January 1918, he proclaimed himself a proponent of Wilson's Fourteen Points, quite against the empire and Hungarian government opinion. By October 1918, Karolyi formed an opposition council and became Prime Minister until January 1919. Heading the almost bloodless 'Aster Revolution', on November 16, he proclaimed the Hungarian Democratic Republic and himself as provisional president. He was formally recognized on January 11, 1919. It lasted only until his ousting in March. Karolyi spent from July 1919 through WWII exiled in France and Britain. He returned to Hungary in 1946 and served as Ambassador to France 1947–1949. XV, 360, 487–494, 497, 499, 517–521, 607
Keeley, James (1867–1934) was an American newspaper editor and publisher of the *Chicago Tribune* 1898–1914. He personally reported on the war from Europe and served as a US representative to the Interallied Conference on Propaganda in Enemy Countries. During the 1920's, Keeley was vice president of the Pullman Company. 266, 268, 270, 272, 310, 395
Keene, Francis B. (1856–1945) was an American diplomat after serving in the Wisconsin State Assembly from 1899–1901. He was Consul in Florence 1903–1905, Geneva 1905–1915, and Consul General in Zurich 1915–1917 and Rome 1917–1924. 109, 119, 120, 126, 146
Kellogg, Charlotte Hoffman (1874–1960) was an American social activist and author. She was married to Vernon L. Kellogg in 1908. During the war years and the CRB activity in Belgium, she studied issues affecting Belgian women at the request of Albert I, King of the Belgians. She published *Women of Belgium: Turning Tragedy to Triumph* in 1917 and *Bobbins of Belgium* in 1920. Also in 1920, she published a biography of Désiré-Joseph Mercier entitled *Mercier, the Fighting Cardinal of Belgium*. In 1921, Charlotte began a friendship with Marie Curie, helping to

fund her work and translating Curie's book *Life of Pierre Curie*. After her husband died in 1937, Charlotte served as co-director of the Commission for Polish Relief and chaired the Paderewski Testimonial Fund. In addition, she published *Jadwiga, Queen of Poland* (1936), *Paderewski* (1956) and *Prelude* (1960). 390, 553, 569, 599, 647, 649

Kellogg, Vernon Lyman (1867–1937) was an American entomologist and evolutionary biologist. He taught at Stanford University from 1894 to 1920. He took a year, 1915–1916, to serve which he spent as the director of the CRB in Brussels. Although initially a pacifist, Kellogg soon was shocked by the German creed of survival of the fittest and advocated US entry into the war. After the war, Kellogg served as Chief of the ARA mission to Poland 1917–1919. He returned to the United States where he led the National Research Council in Washington, DC. 61, 138, 362, 388, 390, 394, 398, 409, 411, 421, 423, 426, 436, 453, 456, 457, 460–462, 464, 466–468, 543, 564, 599, 615, 637, 638, 647, 649

Kelly, Captain 205, 222, 267

Kelly, Shaun, was a Commissioner of Deeds in Paris. He was the son of a former American Embassy Counselor who practiced law in Paris during the war. 24, 30

Kemin, Anna, was a Lithuanian propagandist. 213

Kemp, Miss 126

Kening-Kenynsch, Madame Anna. 85

Kennedy, Philip B. was an American who worked with mineral problems for the War Trade Board, as well as his duties as Commercial Attaché in London. He also coordinated work between the embassy and the American Chamber of Commerce in London. In July 1919, he was appointed Director of the Bureau of Foreign and Domestic Commerce. 369

Kenny, Captain, was a British representative to the committee on propaganda to enemy countries. 244, 294

Kent, Fred I. (1859–1954) was an American banker. The majority of his career was with Bankers Trust Company in New York. He also served as deputy governor of the Federal Reserve Bank 1917–1918 and directed the division of foreign exchange and served on the reparations committee. 650

Kerensky, Alexander (1881–1970) was a Russian lawyer and revolutionary. After the February Revolution, from July to November 1917, he served as the Minister-Chairman of the Russian Provisional Government. His government was overthrown by the Bolshevik October Revolution and he went into exile in Paris and New York. Although his permanent residence was in New York, Kerensky spent much of his time in Palo Alto, California, teaching Russian history at Stanford University and contributing to the Hoover Institution's large and growing archives on Russia. 228, 231–234, 244, 246, 247, 260, 270

Kerney, James F. (1873–1934) was an American journalist who edited *The Trenton Times* between 1901 and 1920. As a trusted friend of President Wilson, Kerney was sent to France to coordinate public information during the American war effort. He later served as a Special Ambassador to Haiti, continued his work as a journalist, and published *The Political Education of Woodrow Wilson* (1926). He was married to Sarah Mullen. Together they had six children, Mary being the eldest. 35, 37, 39, 42–45, 63, 64, 71, 72, 74, 75, 78, 79, 82, 88–90, 117, 135, 139, 142, 161, 162, 166, 167, 176, 180, 182, 185, 202, 211, 214–217, 227, 231, 234, 244, 245, 255, 257, 259, 266, 268

Kessler, Harry (1868–1937) was an Anglo-German writer and diplomat involved with Eugene and Otto Kahn's deals to get goods thru Switzerland for Germany. 299

King. American Intelligence Officer 94

King, Campbell (1871–1953) was an American army Brigadier General and Chief of

Biographical Index — **699**

Staff of the 7th Army Corps, later the 3rd Corps. 59

King, Colonel 54

King, Frederick R. (1887–1972) was an American architect who served in the US Army during WWI. Fluent in French and German, he worked with Benes and Voska in Czechoslovakia after the Armistice. 535, 539, 540, 637, 638, 643

King, General. 319

King, Leroy was an American professor of Slavic languages at the University of Missouri who was serving in the Army and assigned to Coolidge's mission with Sherman Miles. 497, 499

Kirk, Alexander Comstock (1888–1979) was an American diplomat assigned to The Hague as 3rd secretary to the Legation. In 1919, as private secretary to Lansing (US Secretary of State) he was active in the Paris Peace Conference. Later he served as Counselor in Rome 1932, Moscow in 1938, and a senior officer in Berlin under Ambassador Hugh Wilson 1939. He was Ambassador to Egypt 1941–1944 and Italy 1945–1948 before retiring. 103, 444, 549, 603, 626, 643

Kittredge, Tracy B. (1891–1957) was a volunteer in the CRB and continued to work with Hoover as the war ended and the ARA began. 421, 626, 627, 633

Klobukowski, Reinach. 222

Kloeber, Charles E. (1875–1925) was an American newspaperman who served as Chief of the Associated Press 1912–1918. Later he was correspondent from Vienna 1919 and Japan 1924. 319

Klotz. Lt. 222, 638

Knight, Daniel Ridgway (1839–1924) was an American artist living in Paris. For his wartime activities, he was awarded the Cross of the Legion of Honor. 332

Knox, Philander Chase (1853–1921) was the Senator from Pennsylvania 1917–1921. Earlier he had served as Secretary of State 1909–1913. 279

Kohl, Mary Elizabeth "Bessie" (d. 1949) was an American singer who married Charles Frederick Kohl of San Francisco in 1904. They were separated by the time she volunteer to sing for the troops in France with the Red Cross in 1916. She later married, successively, Comte de Lambertye and Comte de Thiene. She died in Monte Carlo. 177, 182

Kopelin, Louis was an American socialist who edited *Appeal to Reason* from 1913. In July 1919, he published an article entitled "Why Wilson Fell Down." 270

Kozicki, Stanislaw (1876–1958) was a Polish politician and a member of the National Committee in Paris. 348 photo

Kramář, Karel (1860–1937) was a Czech politician who led the Czechoslovak National Committee in Prague since October 1918. He served as the first Prime Minister from November 1918 to July 1919. 478–486, 577, 578, 587, 593

Kruger. 555

Kun, Béla (1886–1938) was a Hungarian communist revolutionary and politician. During the war, he had been a prisoner of war in Russia where he became fluent in Russian and met Lenin as well as other leaders of the Bolshevik party. During 1918, he fought for the Bolsheviks, returning to Hungary in November with other Hungarians communists and a large sum of Soviet money. He was imprisoned by Karolyi in February 1919, but orchestrated a merger of the Communist and Social Democratic parties, which succeeded in overthrowing Karolyi's government. The Soviet Republic of Hungary was announced in March 1919 with Kun becoming People's Commissar of Foreign Affairs and defacto leader. This lasted only until August. Kun then became a prominent Comintern operative until his arrest in Vienna in 1928. He was killed during the Great Terror in Russia in 1938 or 1939. 489, 491, 607

Kaufman. German Secret Service 258

Kunfi, Zsigmond (1879–1929) was a Hungarian politician who served both Minister of Labor and Welfare and Minister of Croatian Affairs November 1918 to January 1919. 490

Kutz, Captain J. O. 30

L

Laboulaye, André Lefebvre de (1879–1966) was a French diplomat who served as Second Secretary at the Embassy in Washington, D.C. (1912–1919), and later served as the French Ambassador in the same Embassy (1933–1937. 18

Lagjević, Branko was a wholesaler and landowner, born in Gladoš near Stara Pazova (Southern Hungary until 1918, today the Vojvodina-part of Serbia). He had a large estate which he managed to industrialize by building power plants, steam mill and a cannery. He lived in Zagreb where he was a member of the Serbian Business Society 'Entrepreneur' of the Serbian Bank and of the board of the Zagreb Stock Exchange. 506

Lahm, Frank Purdy (1877–1963) was an American aviation pioneer and officer in the US Army Signal Corps and later Army Air Force. 80

Lambert, Henri (1862–1934) was a Belgian engineer who owned a glass works near Brussels. He was a prolific writers on political philosophy, favoring individualism, free trade, and international peace. XV, 2, 65, 81, 82 164, 174, 202, 206, 258, 260, 272, 297, 332, 337, 338, 398, 417

Lammasch, Heinrich (1853–1920) was an Austrian jurist specializing in criminal and international law. He was a member of the Hague Arbitration Tribunal and briefly served as the last Minister-President of Austria in October-November 1918. 93

Lamont, Thomas W. (1870–1948) was an American banker, a partner in J.P. Morgan & Co. since 1911. With Norman Davis, Lamont served with the American Commission to Negotiate Peace and represented the US Treasury at the Paris Peace Conference in 1919. They were charged with determining what reparations Germany had to pay. Lamont drew up the plans for both the Dawes and the Young Plans for reducing German debt. As a member of the Council of Foreign Relations, he was an unofficial advisor to Presidents Wilson, Hoover and Roosevelt. Later he served as chairman of the Commission for Polish Relief in 1939. 584, 587, 590, 612, 627, 650

Lancken-Wackenitz, Oskar von der (1867–1939) was a German diplomat who governed Brussels during WWI and garnered Gibson's ire in 1914–1915. 103, 394, 395, 404, 409, 411, 419, 421

Lane, Arthur Bliss (1894–1956) was an American diplomat serving as Secretary of the Embassy in Rome in 1918. When Gibson was assigned as Minister to Poland, he recruited Lane to be Secretary in Warsaw 1919–1920. After a successful career, Lane returned to Poland as Ambassador in 1945. He resigned in 1947 in protest over the lack of US support for free Poland and became a founder of Voice of America. 122, 123, 126, 136, 147, 150, 155, 159, 326, 584, 586, 596–599, 627, 636, 641, 653, 654

Lang, Major. 235

Langdon, Russell Creamer (1872–1963) was an American army officer who earned the Distinguished Service Cross for his service in France, 1918. 190

Langhorne, Marshall (1870–1942) was an American diplomat who served as secretary of the Legation at The Hague. 103

Lanier, Charles D. (183–1926) was an American banker and railroad executive who was close to J.P. Morgan and worked with him on several international ventures. 301

Lansing, Robert "the Secretary" (1864–1928) was an American diplomat serving as Secretary of State 1915–1920. He was married to Eleanor Foster. Their daughters as mentioned as "the Lansing girls." 175, 203, 232, 276–277, 298, 318, 440, 596, 599, 603, 620, 641, 643,

Larner, Caroline (b. 1869) was an employee at the US Embassy in Paris 1918–1919. She worked with Gen. Tasker Bliss and shared an apartment with Gibson's Aunt Leona Wood. 23, 27, 29–32, 282, 362, 422, 440, 568, 644

Laroche. 283

Lassiter, William (1889–1959) was an American army officer who served as military attaché in London in 1916 and then led several offensives in France during WWI. He later served in Panama, Chile and Hawaii. 54, 300

Lathrop, Julia Clifford (1858–1931) was an American social reformer, especially in the area children's welfare and education. She served as director of the US Children's Bureau from 1912–1922 as the first woman to head a federal bureau. 79

Lauder, Harry (1870–1950) was a Scottish comedian. 648

Laughlin, Irwin Boyle (1871–1941) was an American diplomat who served as a secretary at the Embassy in London from 1912–1917, then as counselor until 1919. He later served as Ambassador to Greece (1924–1926) and Spain (1929–1933). He was married to Therese E. Iselin. They had two children. 39, 98, 262, 301, 311, 323, 342–343, 403–405, 407, 527, 572, 575, 636

Lawrence, David (1888–1973) was an American newspaperman with the *New York Evening Post*. Having taken a class from Woodrow Wilson at Princeton University, Lawrence was instrumental in keeping Joseph Tumulty on Wilson's staff as chief of staff in 1916. 441, 449

Lay, Harry Randolph (1878–1932) was an American serving in the Marine 4th Brigade. He received the Navy Cross on July 17, 1918. 191

Lay, Tracy Hollingsworth (b. 1882) was an American reporter and department store manager who became Deputy Consul in London 1912–1914, Vice Consul in Paris 1914–1915, and Consul 1915–1919. Later he served as Consul in Munich 1923–1925 and Buenos Aires 1926–1928. 183

Lazaro, Ladislas (1872–1927) was a US Congressman from Louisiana. 633

Leach, Charles Nelson (1884–1971) was an American physician, educated at Stanford University, and recruited by Hoover to serve in the CRB. He remained in Belgium after the US entered the war with the American Ambulance Corps near Paris. He served in the ARA in Vienna and Budapest during 1919. During WWII, Leach again served in Europe, working on nutrition in Holland and providing health care for the survivors of Bergen-Belsen concentration camp. 421, 636

Lebenfeldt-Russ – See Höfer

Lebrun, Albert (1871–1950) was a French politician serving as Minister of Liberated Regions and Minister of Blockade 1917–1919. Later he served as President of the Senate 1931–1932 and President of France 1932–1940. 228, 277, 386

Lee, Ivy Ledbetter (1877–1934) was an American publicity and public relations expert who served as Assistant to Chairman of the Red Cross, Perkins. She earned the reputation of "Poison Ivy Lee." 75, 79

Leech, Stephen (1864–1925) was a British diplomat who served as Minister in Cuba when Gibson was assigned there in 1912. 639

Leeds, Mrs. 432

Legg. 436

Lehr, Louis. 238

Leigh, Mrs. Roland. 24

Leishman, John G.A. (1857–1924) was an American businessman and diplomat who had been Ambassador to Switzerland (1897), Turkey (1901–1909) Italy (1909–1911) and Germany (1911–1913). He was the father-in-law of James Hazen Hyde. 73

Leman, Gérard (1851–1920) was a Belgian army general who commanded the area near Liège in 1914. He was injured, taken prisoner by the Germans and held until 1917. He was welcomed home to Belgium as a hero. 385

Lenin, Vladimir (1870–1924) was head of Soviet Russia from 1917–1924. 247, 298

Le Neveu. 285

Leonard, Private. 237

Letterman, Miss. 368

Leval, Gaston de (1871–1944) was a Belgian lawyer who served as Legal Counselor to the American Legation in Brussels during the first years of WWI when Gibson was Secretary. They worked together on behalf of British nurse Edith Cavell. 283, 288, 353, 436

Leverier, M. and Mme. 67

Lévy. 101

Lewis, James Hamilton "Ham" (1863–1939) was an American lawyer and politician who served as Senator from Illinois 1913–1919 and again 1931–1939. Between 1921 and 1925, Lewis was part of the US delegation to the League of Nations conferences to settle war damage claims. 298, 306, 324, 325

Lewis, Roger L. (d. 1936) was an American journalist with the Associated Press during WWI. 182, 213, 214, 218, 227, 241

Leygues, Georges (1857–1933) was a French politician who later served as briefly Prime Minister from September 1920 to January 1921. 74

Lichnowsky, Karl Max (1860–1928) was a German diplomat born in the Upper Silesian area that was hotly contested after WWI. He strongly objected to what he called "Germany's efforts to provoke war." 99

Lichtenberger, Emile A. (1870–1940) was a French historian specializing in socialism and a novelist known for his works for youth. From 1914 to 1916, he worked with Gen. Gallieni, the military governor of Paris, and the Gen. Gouraund for the organization of the Polish Legion. 218

Lindsey, Benjamin Barr "Ben" (1869–1943) was an American judge and social reformer from Colorado. He was married to Henriette Lindsey. 90, 172–173

Linn, Howard (1885–1970) was an American businessman, a graduate of Yale University (1907) and a real estate investor. When the US entered the war, Linn shipped out for France as a Captain in the US Army Signal Corps, Aviation Section in April 1917. 14, 15, 23, 165, 167, 181, 189, 298

Linn, Lucy McCormick Blair (1886–1978) was an American socialite and philanthropist with an artist flair. She founded the Junior League of Chicago in 1912, opened *Au Paradis* (a chic retail shop), and married Howard Linn, son of grain merchant William Linn of the Chicago Board of Trade, in 1914. Both were friends of Gibson's. While Howard was in France, Lucy raised funds to benefit victims of war, especially for Children of the War Zone. 14, 15, 23, 27, 30–35, 41, 57, 65, 67, 83, 85, 87, 162, 164, 167, 174, 181–183, 185, 189

Lippmann, Walter (1889–1974) was an American journalist and political commentator who co-founded *The New Republic* in 1913. During WWI, he was commissioned as a captain in the army in June 1918. He was assigned to the intelligence section of AEF in France. In October, he was assigned to the staff of Col. House and attached to the American Commission to Negotiate Peace until 1919. He assisted in drafting Wilson's Fourteen Points speech and was sharply critical of George Creel. After WWII, Lippmann advocated respect for the Soviet sphere in Europe. In 1962, he was awarded the Pulitzer Prize for International Reporting. 258, 262, 263, 266, 268–273, 278, 288, 301, 310, 312, 319, 325–329, 331, 334, 338, 340, 351, 352, 356, 359, 361, 364, 365, 371–373, 375, 376, 379, 380–382, 386, 388, 391, 394, 395, 397, 400, 402, 408, 420, 423, 443, 617

Lister-Kaye, Sir John Pepys (1853–1924) was a British peer and Groom in Waiting to King Edward VII. He married to Maria de la

Natividad Yznaga (1859–1943) in 1881. 407

Littlefield, Leland H. was an American diplomat serving as Special Attaché to Ambassador Walter Page. With Beal and Buckler, he wrote a report on an inspection conducted at the prisoner of war camp Douglas, Isle of Man, May 1916. 301, 311, 404, 405, 627, 631

Littlefield, Marion Hazard (1873–1964) was married to Leland H. Littlefield, who had served as Special Attaché to Walter Hines Page in London 1916–1918. 627–31

Lloyd George, David (1863–1945) was the British Prime minister from 1916 to 1922. Previously he has served as Chancellor of the Exchequer under Asquith 1908–1915 and Minister of Munitions 1915–1916. During the Paris Peace Conference, Lloyd George clashed with Clemenceau, Wilson and Orlando by demanding moderation and favoring German interests in the drawing of new Polish borders. 136, 139, 150, 171, 178, 209, 221, 222, 247, 266, 275, 276, 302, 321,344, 356, 358, 375, 381, 583, 619

Lobkowicz, Ferdinand (1850–1926) was a Czech nobleman and politician who served as the highest marshal of the Kingdom of Bavaria 1907–1913. As a member of the Czechoslovakian House of Commons, he focused on agrarian and economic issues. 527

Lodge, Henry Cabot (1850–1924) was a US Senator from Massachusetts who served as Chairman of the Senate Foreign Relations Committee 1919–1924. 361

Loewenfeld-Russ, Hans (1973–1945) was a public servant at the Austro-Hungarian Ministry of Economics in Vienna starting in 1898. After October 1918, he was State Secretary in the Office of Public Food and a main character in the Austrian fight against hunger immediately after the war. In 1926, he published a book on the state's effort to feed the population of Austria-Hungary during WWI. 473

Logan, James A., Jr. "Jim" (1879–1930) was an American Army officer who served as chief of the US military mission to the French army 1914–1919. 47, 187, 188, 198–200, 263, 273, 288, 300, 318, 328, 331, 333, 340, 350, 359, 361, 371, 423, 548, 574, 582, 617

Long, Andrew T. (1876–1943) was an American Admiral serving as Naval Attaché to the Embassy in Paris. 175, 432

Longare, Lelio Bonin (1859–1933) was an Italian diplomat serving as Ambassador to Paris 1917–1921. 176, 248, 338, 369

Lopp, George Washington (1865–1955) was an American resident of France since 1894. He was a dance instructor who introduced the cakewalk. During the war, he drove ambulances for an American unit. 164

Lorin, Henri (1866–1932) was a French geographer and sociologist who specialized in colonial questions. He participated in the peace treaties and interallied commissions in Paris at the end of WWI. He served twice as a deputy 1919–1924 and 1928–1932. 256

Loree, Robert F. (1889–1979) was an American businessman who worked in the Foreign Department of Guaranty Trust Co. since 1914. He was assigned to London 1915–1917. In August 1917, he moved to Paris where he assisted Oscar Crosby and other members of the US delegation to the Peace Conference. He married Alix Moncheur in 1913. 451

Lorenz, Adolf (1854–1946) was an Austrian orthopedist who had trained in Vienna as a surgeon. But due to an allergy to the carbolic acid routinely used as a disinfectant, he focused on treating patients without cutting the skin. By 1901, he was known as "the bloodless surgeon of Vienna." After attending an American Medical Association meeting in 1903, he helped found what later became Good Samaritan Hospital and Baylor University in Texas. He was nominated for a Nobel Prize in 1923. 476

Loubet. 440

Loucheur, Louis (1872–1931) was a French politician serving as Minister of Armaments in 1918. Later he served as Minister of Reparations and as an economic adviser in 1919. 215, 275

Loudon, John (1866–1955) was a Dutch diplomat serving as Minister of Foreign Affairs 1913–1918. His aim was to keep the Netherlands strictly neutral. Although the Dutch cabinet approved, this policy brought him into conflict with Queen Wilhelmina. Later he was ambassador to Paris 1919–1940. 390

Lovat, Lord (1871–1933) was Simon Fraser, 14th Lord Lovat. 309

Lowry, Mr. and Mrs. She is the sister of Norman Armour. 121, 132

Ludendorff, Erich (1865–1937) was a German general who claimed victory at Liege and Tannenberg. From 1916 to 1918, he served as Quarter-Master General for the Paul von Hindenburg's Supreme Army Command, a body which towards the end of the First World War assumed quasi-dictatorial power. From his experience he developed the theory of "Total War" which he published in 1935. 239, 337

Luxburg, Karl von (1872–1956) was a German diplomat who served as chargé d'affaires in Buenos Aires, Argentina during WWI. During the summer of 1917, he sent secret dispatches to Berlin urging that neutral Argentine ships should be destroyed. This led to his dismissal and Argentina's entrance into the war. 99

Lygon, Henry (1884–1936) was a British officer with the Royal Flying Corps before being placed as an intelligence officer in Paris and Rome. 129, 152, 154, 160

M

McAdoo, William Gibbs (1863–9141) was an American lawyer and politician serving in the Wilson Administration as Secretary of the Treasury 1913–1918. Later he served as Senator from California 1933–1938. He married Wilson's daughter, Eleanor, in 1914. 164, 216, 298, 306, 406, 595, 600

Macatee, Robert Berry (1891–1974) was an American diplomat serving with the American Commission to Negotiate Peace 1918–1919. He later served as Vice Consul in Geneva 1920–1923, Consul in London 1923–1929, Belgrade in 1938, and Consul General in Jerusalem 1947. 441

McAndrew, James W. (1862–1922) was an American army general serving in France as chief of staff 1918–1919. 199

McBride, Harry Alexander (1887–1961) was an American diplomat serving as vice-Consul in London. Later he would serve as Consul in Warsaw during Gibson's tenure 1919–1920. In 1921, he was the chief of the Visa Office at the Department of State. 409

McBride, James Harvey (1849–1928) was an American nerve specialist physician who founded The Southern California Sanitarium for Nervous Diseases in 1904, where he served as medical director until 1918. He had served as an expert witness in the trial of Charles Guiteau, assassin of President James Garfield in 1881. In 1918 and after, McBride worked with Mary Gibson on California state policy to address the needs of immigrants, particularly women. 19

McCabe, E.R. Warner (1876–1960) was an American Army officer serving on Gen. Pershing's staff in France 1917–1919. He later was Military Attaché in Prague 1920–1922 and Rome (1924–1926, 1932–1933). He served as Chief of Military Intelligence for the General Staff 1937–1940, and taught military science at other times Gibson occasionally misspelled his name "McKaib." 47, 48, 53, 56, 76–78, 84, 199, 211, 265, 267, 280, 288

McCarthy 86

Maclay, Joseph Paton (1857–1951) was a Scottish businessman and public servant who served as Minister of Shipping 1916–1921. 601

MacCloskey, Mangus (1874–1963) was an American army officer who commanded the 12th Field Artillery Regiment during WWI. Later he served as superintendent of Cook County Hospital in Chicago 1938–1947. 191–193, 234

McClure, Sidney Samuel "SS" (1857–1949) was an Irish-American publisher who became well known for his investigative journalism. He established the McClure Syndicate in 1884 and launched *McClure's Magazine* in 1893. 125, 126, 130, 136, 137, 149

McCombs, Dorothy Williams married William Frank McCombs (1876–1921), an American lawyer who served as chairman of the Democratic National Committee 1912–1916. 206, 440

McCook Cross, Martha (1883–1957) was an American who worked with the YMCA in Rome. She was the sister of Peter Jay's wife, Susan McCook Jay, and married architect Eliot Buchanan Cross in September 1918. She was active in politics and later campaigned for Herbert Hoover's presidential election. 150, 152, 154–155, 156–157, 159, 223, 230, 250, 296, 308, 326–327, 328, 331, 334, 344, 352, 377, 571

McCook Jay, Susan (1879–1977) was the sister of Martha McCook and married to Peter Jay. 85, 154–157, 159, 223, 326, 331, 598

McCormick, Anne O'Hare (1880–1954) was an American (born English) journalist and foreign correspondent for *The New York Times*. She was the first woman to receive a Pulitzer Prize for a major journalistic category in 1937. She was married to Francis H. McCormick. 85

McCormick, Chauncey (1884–1954) was an American businessman with International Harvester. During the war, he offered his connections to for humanitarian aid for refugees. In 1918, Hoover sent McCormick to Poland to organize aid there. 87, 202, 451, 461, 576, 578–579, 639

McCormick, Harold Fowler (1872–1941) was an American businessman and chairman of the board for International Harvester. 96

McCormick, Vance (1872–1946) was an American businessman and politician who chaired the Democratic National Committee and the War Trade Board 1916–1919. He was appointed as head of the American delegation at the Treaty of Versailles by President Wilson. 195, 549, 552, 564, 650

McCoy, Frank Ross (1874–1954) was an American Army officer who commanded the 165th Infantry Regiment in 1918. From 1918–1919, he directed transportation for the American Expeditionary Force in Europe before leading the American military mission to Armenia. He later served during WWII and on the Far Eastern Commission tasked with the fate of postwar Japan. 47–51, 93, 187, 319, 320, 398, 423, 645

McDougall, Mrs. 75

MacEachran, Clinton Edson (b. 1887) was an American diplomat who served as private secretary to several key State Department figures before becoming the chief clerk for the American Commission to the American-German prisoner of war conference in Bern, Switzerland in 1918. He went on to serve as a special drafting officer to the American Mission to Negotiate Peace July-December 1919. Later he was consul-general in Halifax, Nova Scotia 1937–1941 and as a special agent for the Department of State 1943–1945. 331

McFadden, George (1873–1931) was the representative of Trustee Penn Mutual Life Insurance Company in France. He served on the United States Food Administration and War Trade Board, as well as consulting with Oscar Crosby of the Treasury Department. He was made Honorary 1st Secretary of the Embassy in Paris and served as an economic adviser during the peace negotiations. He was one of the two American civilians on the Armistice Commission and was part of the American Commission to Negotiate Peace. He was awarded the Distinguished Service Medal by General Pershing in 1919. 39, 44, 45, 82, 87, 102, 103, 105, 132, 163, 164, 167, 169, 170, 174, 179, 181, 183, 188, 189, 195, 197, 200, 201, 202, 206, 211, 212, 218, 221, 223, 230, 235, 238, 246, 248, 269, 289, 297, 298, 301, 334, 335, 338, 373, 374, 376, 390, 410, 432, 552, 574, 575, 626, 651, 652

McFall, Burge. Associated Press 239

McGovern, Miss 30

MacGruder, John (1887–1958), a Major in the United States Army, was assigned to the 102nd Field Artillery 1918–1919. Later he attained the rank of Brigadier General in 1940, serving as Deputy Director for Intelligence of the Office of Strategic Services (1943–1945). His last official position was Director of Strategic Services for the War Department, 1946. 48, 78, 84, 187

McIlvaine, Annie Wilson (1878–1919) was a friend of Gibson's. 407

McIntosh, Joseph W. (1873–1952) was an American businessman and army officer who had served as vice president and treasurer of Western Stoneware before the US entered WWI. From 1917 to 1920, he served in the army in France and the Balkans, part of that time acting as a translator for the American Commission to Negotiate Peace in Paris. During 1919, McIntosh worked for the ARA, supervising food distribution to civilians in Austria. Later he served on the Federal Reserve Board 1924–1928 and directed W. J. Wollman & Co. in New York, Pure Oil Co. in Chicago, and First National Bank in Miami. 499, 500, 502

McKehen. 269

MacKenzie, Compton (1883–1972) was a Scottish author, political activist and news broadcaster who served in British Intelligence in the Mediterranean during WWI. He founded the Aegean Intelligence Service in 1917 based in Greece. At one point he was offered the presidency of Cerigo (Greek island of Kythira) but declined the honor. He was awarded the Greek Order of the Redeemer in 1919, and published his *Greek Memories* in 1932. 373

McKenzie, John. 155, 157

McKnight, James Stuart (1884–1950) was an American lawyer who served in the National Guard during WWI. He married actress Anita King in Paris in March 1919. He worked with the ARA from November 1918 in Europe and Russia. Later he was elected to the city council of Los Angeles 1931–1932. 638

McLane, Allen, an American wanting to serve as a pilot, was recommended by Gibson to work with Merriam in Rome. 147, 159

McMillan. 123, 126, 152

McNally, James Clifford (1865–1920) was an American diplomat who served as Consul General in Zurich, Switzerland. He was married to Agnes Keane McNally, and their daughter Madeleine (1896–1960) was married to Andrew Gordon of the German Navy. These relationships caused some consternation. 39, 93, 94, 96, 98, 102, 109, 236, 301, 364

McNally, Madeleine (1894–1960), was James McNally's daughter who married to German Lieutenant Fritz Menzing. However, Madeleine's grave indicates she was the wife of US Marine Major Andrew L.W. Gordon (1897–1973), making it likely that she had a first and second marriage. 93

McNeir, William (1864–1952) was an American, Chief of Bureau of Accounts of the State Department, serving as Disbursing Officer for the American Commission to Negotiate Peace in Paris. 441, 443

MacPherson, Margaret Campbell (1860–1931) was a Canadian painter. 353

McVickar, Lansing (d. 1945) decorated for actions in battle October 4, 1918, as part of the of the 1st Division AEF. 404, 405

McWilliams, Roy was the US Consular Agent in Biarritz, France, in 1919. He was promoted to Vice Consul 1924–1932. 67

Mackensen, August von (1849–1945) was a German field marshal during WWI. He was suspected of disloyalty to the Nazi regime before and during WWII. 465

Mahan, Frederick A. (1847–1918) was an American engineer and soldier who served in the Army Corps of Engineers from 1867 to 1894. He was military attaché in Copenhagen 1898–1900. After his retirement, he settled in Paris during the war years of 1917–1918 where he served as military attaché. 39

Malvy, Louis (1875–1949) was a French politician who served as Interior Minister March 1914 to August 1917. When it was discovered that the *Bonnet Rouge*, a newspaper subsidized by Malvy, was receiving German funds, he was charged with treason, along with Joseph Caillaux, in 1918. Malvy was later acquitted, but found guilty of negligence and exiled for five years. Later he served in the same role from March to June 1926. 280, 281, 286, 287

Mangin, Charles (1866–1925) was a French general known as "the Butcher" for his believe in all-out war. He was successful in the battles of Charleroi and Verdun, but the Nivelle Offensive in the spring of 1917 damaged his reputation. Later, Mangin became a member of the Supreme War Council and was inspector general of French colonial troops. 253, 265

Manners, Betty (1889–1962) was the daughter of John Thomas Manners-Sutton and sister of Francis Henry Manners-Sutton. She married Arthurs Asquith in 1918.

Manners, Francis Henry, the 4th Baron Manners of Foston, (1897–1972) served as aide de camp to Arthur Asquith. Asquith married Manners' sister, Betty Manners. 295

Manzoni, Silvia Alfonso y Aldama (b. 1858) was Cuban heiress who first married José Emilio Terry y Dorticos (1853–1911), of the wealthiest families in the world at that time. The Terry family of Cienfuegos, Cuba, had a hand in all forms of business including sugar, slaves and electricity. Silvia then married Italian Count Gaetano Monzoni (1871–1937), Director of Political Affairs at the Italian Foreign Ministry 1913–1920. 124, 146

March, Peyton C. (1864–1955) was an American army officer serving as chief of staff 1918–1921. He was in conflict with Gen. Pershing over the level of independence of the AEF. He published his memoirs, *The Nation at War*, in 1932. 252, 288

Marchienne – See Emile Cartier de

Marconi, Guglielmo (1874–1937) was an Italian engineer and inventor who developed the radio. He was awarded the Nobel Prize in Physics for his contributions to wireless telegraphy in 1909. 143

Marcowitz. 268

Marie of Romania (1875–1938) was born into the British royal family and married Ferdinand I of Romania in 1893. She became Queen consort of Romania in 1914. During WWI, she and three daughters served as nurses in military hospitals. She arrived in Paris on March 9, 1919 to represent Romania at the Paris Peace Conference. Later, she had many dealings with Hoover and Gibson over the next decade. Due to her relationship with railroad baron Samuel Hill, there is a museum in her honor on the banks of the Columbia Gorge in Washington at Maryhill. 575

Marion, Frank J. (1869–1963) was a pioneering American film maker who worked for the Committee for Public Information under George Creel. He was assigned to Spain and Italy. 37, 43

Marjoribanks, Dudley, 3rd Baron of Tweedmouth, (1874–1935) was a British army officer who served in the early battles of the war in the Royal Horse Guards 1914–1918.

Marković, Edo (1885–1939) was a Croatian economist, patriot and public official who headed of the Land Supply Inc. in Zagreb 1915–1918. Between 1910 and 1934, he served as the Deputy Director General of the Yugoslav Bank in Zagreb. From 1934 to his death, he was the General Director of the Privileged Society for the Export of Agricultural Products in the Kingdom of Yugoslavia in Belgrade. 221

Marquesson. 260

Marshall, Horace Brooks "Lord Mayor" of London (1865–1936) was the Mayor of London 1918–1919. 238

Martin, Don (d. 1918) was an American journalist covering the front in France for the New York Herald. His reports were detailed, accurate, and evocative. He died of influenza on October 7, 1918. 361

Martin, Lawrence (1880–1955) was an American geographer who volunteered to serve in the military. He instructed in map interpretation and served in Military Intelligence. He served on Coolidge's mission and assisted in the redrawing of boundaries after the war. Later he worked in the Office of Geography at the State Department and then heading the Geography and Maps Division of the Library of Congress. 328, 523

Martin, William (1888–1934) was the Chef de Protocol at Versailles. 40, 87

Martini, Ferdinando (1841–1928) was an Italian journalist and professor at the University of Pisa. He served as Governor of Eritrea 1897–1907. 110

Masaryk, Jan Garrigue (1886–1948) was a Czech diplomat and politician, and son of then-President Tomáš Masaryk. Jan served as chargé d'affairs to the US 1919–1922. He later served as Foreign Minister 1940–1948. 481

Masaryk, Tomáš (1850–1937) was a Czech politician who is credited with being the founding father of Czechoslovakia. He served as its first president from 1918 to 1935. 4, 363, 369, 374, 379, 478, 480, 481, 484, 527, 539, 567

Masi, Henri Armand de (1890–1981) was aide to Gen. Brainard. He had written Hearst, but returned to the *Chicago Journal*. In 1915, he published *Who's Who in Motion Pictures*, using material he obtained first had while acting as director of publicity for the Essanay Company. He was married to Martha Wiotte. 24

Mason, Frank Earl (1893–1979) was an American journalist. During the war, he served as an Intelligence Officer and a military observer in Berlin in 1919. He served as president of the International News Service during the 1920's and as vice-president of NBC 1931–1945. In 1946, he accompanied Hoover and Gibson on the famine survey trip commission by President Truman. He was married to Ellen, both long-time friends with Gibson. 22

Maude, Harry was a British Army officer granted the Distinguished Service Award on July 6, 1918 by the Americans for his service in the procurement of food and necessary supplies in France. 103, 234, 236, 238, 252, 266, 610

Maura, Antonio (1853–1925) was a Spanish politician who served several brief terms as Prime Minister between 1903 and 1922. 242

Maverick, Robert (1881–1954) was an American businessman and diplomat, a graduate of Princeton, who was president of the San Antonia Express. After holding various posts Belgium, Switzerland and Serbia, he served as military attaché at the Embassy in Paris 1918. 257, 329

Max, Adolphe (1869–1939) was a Belgian politician who was mayor of Brussels 1909–1939. He refused to cooperate with the German occupation early in the war and was held in captivity until his escape in 1918. 358, 570

Maximillian von Baden (1867–1929) was a German prince and politician acting briefly as Chancellor of Germany October-

November 1918. He played a pivotal role in moving Germany from the old regime into a democratic government. 354, 357, 358, 363, 418, 422, 426, 585

Maxwell, Mrs. 212, 391

Mayes. 302, 634

Mayo, Henry Thomas (1856–1937) was a US Navy Admiral, Commander in Chief of the Atlantic Fleet. 366

Mayo, Margaret (1882–1951) was an American actress and playwright who entertained troops in Europe. 346, 362, 378, 381, 433, 568

Meert Family – Frederick (Fritz) Meert (1873–1951) was an American volunteer with the CRB in Belgium. He was married to Gertrude in 1898, and they had three daughters, the eldest Constance. 34, 269, 282

Mendl, Charles (1871–1958) was a British actor who starred in *Notorious* in 1946. 235

Meneval, Napoleon J.E. (1849–1926) was a French baron and diplomat who served in Rome, Berlin, Belgrade, Madrid and Florence. 74

Menocal, Mario Garcia (1866–1941) was the president of Cuba 1913–1921. 68

Menton de Horne, Frédéric "Fritz" (1875–1940) was a Belgian aristocrat who spent 16 days in German custody during the invasion of Belgium in 1914. 218

Mercier, Désiré-Joseph (1851–1926) was the Papal Nuncio to Belgium where he was noted for his resistance to the Germans. He was a close friend of Gibson's during his tenure in Belgium, 1914–1915. 145

Meriwether, Lee (1862–1966) was an American diplomat serving as special assistant to Ambassador Sharp 1916–1918. In 1919, he published his memoirs as *The War Diary of a Diplomat* (Dodd, Mead and Co., 1919). 176, 362, 364, 402

Merode, Jean de (1864–1933) was a Belgian aristocrat who had served as Grand Marechal of King Albert I's court, receiving the title of "Prince de Merode" in 1928. 229

Merriam, Charles E. (1874–1953) was an American political scientist who taught at the University of Chicago, beginning in 1900. He was active in local politics and became an advisor to Presidents Taft and Wilson. In 1917 he joined the US Army Signal Corps and volunteered to serve on The Committee on Public Information. From April to September 1919, he was the American High Commissioner on Public Information in Rome. He continued his tenure at the University of Chicago until 1940. 23, 72, 85, 91, 104, 117–120, 122, 123, 126, 127, 129, 131–33, 142, 146–148, 151–153, 155, 158, 182, 183, 231, 250, 322, 332, 333, 347, 366, 370, 371

Merry del Val, Alfonso (1864–1943) was a Spanish nobleman, born in London. He spent his career as a diplomat, serving as Spanish Ambassador to London from 1913–1931. 2

Merry del Val, Rafael (1865–1930) was a Spanish Roman Catholic cardinal and secretary to the Supreme Sacred Congregation of the Holy Office 1914–1930. 62

Merton, Richard (1881–1960) was a German industrialist and politician who served on the front in WWI as adjutant in military administration in Belgium. He insisted on state food enforcement and curtailment of corporate war profits. He was a member of the German delegation to the peace negotiations at Versailles and found the treaty disappointing. 589, 612

Merz, Charles "Charley" (1893–1977) was an American journalist dedicated to the American ideal of democracy as the Washington correspondent for the *New Republic*. During the war, he worked in military intelligence, bringing him into Gibson's sphere of influence. It was Merz and Walter Lippmann who compiled the press coverage survey of the Russian Revolution in 1917 in which they were very critical of the *New York Times* coverage of the events. 258, 270, 288, 322, 367, 395, 398, 400, 617

Meyer, Albert was a Swiss politician and journalist who served as editor of the Neue Zűricher Zeitung from 1897–1915. He served in various political positions after the war. 113

Micheler, Joseph Alfred (1861–1931) was a French general during WWI. 209

Mikahilovich, Alexander (1866–1933), Grand Duke of Russia, was the brother-in-law and advisor to Tsar Nicholas II. He was also a naval officer, explorer and author who published his memoirs *Once A Grand Duke* in 1933. 575

Miles, Basil (1877–1928) was an American diplomat who served as Chief of the Far Eastern Division of the State Department and American Commissioner on the International Chamber of Commerce in Paris. 47, 48, 423

Miles, Sherman (1882–1966) was an American army officer who was military attaché in the Balkans 1912–1914. During the war, he was a military observer in Russia until 1916. Then as part of the General Staff, he was an observer at the Argonne Offensive in September 1918. He was assigned to the peace negotiation team in 1919 and accompanied Coolidge on his assessment trip through the former Austro-Hungarian Empire and made reports back to the negotiators at the Paris Peace Conference. By 1940, Miles was the head of the Military Intelligence Division of the Army, but resigned after the communications debacle preceding the Japanese attack on Pearl Harbor. 497, 499, 539

Millais. 185

Mills, Ogden L. (1884–1937) was an American lawyer who served in the American Expeditionary Force in France, 1917. Later he became the US Secretary of the Treasury in Hoover's cabinet 1932–1933. 51, 161

Minot, Grafton W. (1892–1983) was an American diplomat and assistant to Joseph Grew on the general staff of the American Commission to Negotiate Peace at the Paris Peace Conference in 1918. He also served as interpreter to David Lloyd George. 381, 626

Mirbach, Wilhelm von (1871–1918) was a German diplomat who was active in the Russian-German negotiation at Brest-Litovsk. In April 1918 he was appointed Ambassador to Russia, but was assassinated at the German Embassy in Moscow on July 6, 1918, by revolutionaries attempting to drive a wedge in German-Russian relations. 246, 247

Mitchel, John Purroy (1879–1918) was an American politician who served as Mayor of New York City 1914–1917. 153, 154

"Mitchell" was a jockey in Paris who provided information to Kerensky. 232, 244, 246, 247, 258, 272, 292

Mitchell, William Lendrum "Billy" (1878–1936) was an American Army general who was regarded as the father of the United States Air Force. On April 24, 1918, he made the first flight by an American officer over German territory. By the end of the war, he commanded all the American air services in Europe. 86, 87, 244, 390, 432, 447

Mommsen, Theodore (1817–1903) was a German historian and politician who won the Nobel Prize in Literature in 1902. 530

Moncheur, Ludovic (1857–1940) was a Belgian Baron who served as Ambassador to London 1917–1927. 451

Money, Leo Chiozza (1870–1944) was an Italian-born British politician and journalist who served as Lloyd George's private secretary 1915–1917. His political career was effectively ended when Lloyd George was ousted in 1922. 261

Montgomery, Stuart was a Harvard-trained American Army officer who worked on the Russian Section of the American Commission to Negotiate Peace under Robert Lord in Paris 1918. 443

Montille, de. 635

Moore, John Bassett (1860–1947) was an American lawyer and authority on international law. He was the first American judge to serve on the Permanent Court of International Justice. Moore was known for his pragmatic approach to international relations and his support for arbitration and negotiated peace. He favored American distance from European affairs and did not shy away from the expansionism inherent in American history. These traits irritated many fellow lawyers and diplomats rushing to Paris as peace became a real possibility. 96, 354, 365

Moraczewski, Jędrzej (1870–1944) was a Polish socialist who served as Prime Minister briefly from November 1918 to January 1919 485

Moran, William H. (1864–1946) was an American intelligence officer who served as Chief of the US Secret Service from 1917 to 1936. He was appointed by President Wilson and served under Harding, Coolidge, Hoover and Roosevelt. 443

Mordecai, Randolph J. (d. 1949) was an American charged with running the American Relief Clearing House (ARCH) which dealt with the war refugees in Europe. 79, 85, 87, 211, 216

Morel, General 146

Moreno, Aristides (1878–1955) was an American army officer on Gen. Pershing's staff. He was decorated with a Distinguished Service Medal for his work in counterespionage on behalf of the AEF. 75, 188, 425

Morgan, Gerald (1879–1948) was an American journalist and war correspondent who served in the AEF as Press Chief. 53, 56

Morgan, Henry H. (1860–1933) was an American diplomat who served as Consul-General in Antwerp 1918–1919, Brussels 1919–1920 and Buenos Aires 1924. 572, 610, 640, 648

Morgan, Lt. was a British naval officer. 314, 315

Morgenthau, Henry Sr. (1856–1946) was German-born American lawyer who became wealthy from real estate. He served as Ambassador to the Ottoman Empire 1913–1916. He attended the Paris Peace Conference. In the summer 1919, he conducted what came to be known as the Morgenthau Commission to investigate anti-Jewish pogroms in Poland. He was married to Josephine Sykes. 647–648

Morris, Major 51

Morris, David Hennen (1872–1944) was an American lawyer and diplomat. Well educated with considerable inherited wealth, Morris raced thoroughbred horses and was vice-president of Southwestern Railway Co. Later, he served as US Ambassador to Belgium 1933–1937, between Gibson's terms in that position. He was married to Alice Vanderbilt Shepard. 24, 269

Morrow, Dwight (1873–1931) was an American businessman and diplomat, and the father-in-law of Charles Lindbergh. He was a partner in J.P. Morgan bank and served as chief civilian aide to Gen. Pershing. He later served as Ambassador to Mexico 1927–1930 and US Senator from New Jersey 1930–1931. 163, 263, 441

Mosely, George (1874–1960) was an American army officer serving as chief of staff for logistic at Chaumont. 288

Mott, John Raleigh (1865–1955) was an American serving as the International Secretary of the Young Men's Christian Association (YMCA). His work earned him a Nobel Peace Prize in 1946. 86, 87, 88, 116, 120, 185, 276, 300

Mott, Thomas Bentley (1854–1929) was an American Army officer who had served as military attaché in Paris for 20 years (1884–1914). He retired from the US Army in 1914, but was recalled in 1917 to serve on General Perishing's staff where Mott represented the staff of Marshal Foch. 47, 50, 51, 72, 88, 374, 423, 599

Mountbatten, Leopold "Batty" (1889–1922) a British army officer and grandson of Queen Victoria. In 1918, he served in Paris as an aide-de-camp on staff for the War Office. 178

Muelhon, William was a German businessman who led the Krupp's Munition Factories and wrote about German culpability in the war. 99

Munn, Charles Alexander, was a junior attaché in Paris. 625

Murray, Alexander, 1st Baron of Elibank (1870–1920) was a Scottish liberal politician who served under Asquith. He was forced to resign when implicated in the Marconi scandal in 1912. 190

Murray, Arthur Cecil, 3rd Baron of Elibank (1878–1962) was the younger brother of Alexander. He was an officer in the British Army and served as Military Attaché in Washington 1917–1918, after being awarded the Distinguished Service Order for his service in Belgium and France in 1916. 189, 341

N

Nansen, Fridtjof (1861–1930) was a Norwegian explorer of the Polar region. From 1921 to 1930, he served as the League of Nations High Commissioner for Refugees, and was awarded a Nobel Prize for his work. He despaired over the prospect of feeding Russia in the post-war, post-revolution days. 298, 620

Nasmith, Charles R. (b.1883) was the American Consul in Brussels. 20

Néditch, Miloutin G. 512

Neefs, Cyriel (1899–1976) was a Belgian technical teacher who served as an excavation worker during WWI. After the war, he joined the Christian Workers Organization, which he chaired from 1292–1944. He was active in the resistance movement during WWII. Later, he served as a provincial senator 1946–1965. 242

Neefs, Gommar, was the father of Cyriel Neefs. 242

Nettleton, George Henry (1874–1959) was an American academic who directed the Yale Bureau in Paris in 1917. He became Chair of Yale's English Department 1921–1931 and Dean of the College 1937–1938. 152

Neville, Colonel 237

Newcome, William A. (1b. 866) was an American Foreign Service worker who served as clerk at the Embassy in Rome from 1912–1917. He later served as a passport agent in New York and San Francisco. 119, 158

Newton, Walter H. (1880–1941) was a US Congressman from Minnesota. 633

Nichol, Ensign. 500

Nichole, Mrs. 391

Nikola I (1841–1921) was the ruler of Montenegro from 1860 to 1918, when his country was incorporated into Yugoslavia. 60, 132

Nitti, Francesco S. (1868–1953) was an Italian economist and politician serving as Minister of Finance 1917–1919. Later he served as Prime Minister 1919–1920. 243, 248, 269, 301, 565

Nolan, Dennis E. (1872–1956) was a Brigadier General in the US Army. During World War I, he organized the Intelligence Section of the AEF (the first American military combat intelligence office) and served as Chief of Military Intelligence after the war. 3, 4, 42, 46, 48, 49, 51, 53, 65, 154, 156, 159, 178, 185–189, 200, 211, 218, 231–233, 235, 239, 241, 243–246, 251, 258–263, 265–268, 270, 272, 280, 287, 288, 292, 301, 318, 319, 327, 328, 331, 347, 350, 382–384, 401, 402, 409, 435, 616

Northcliffe, Lord, Alfred Harmsworth, (1865–1922) was a British newspaper magnate and publisher of the *Daily Mail* and *the Daily Mirror*. As an early developer of popular journalism, he set the trend towards sensational topics. He served as British Minister for Propaganda in 1918 and helped further the career of Lloyd George. His efforts drew a German assassination attempt for his anti-German propaganda during WWI. 151, 300, 311, 374

Novák, Ladislav (1872–1946) was a Czech politician who helped organize the engineering industry. He served in the National Assembly from 1920–1935, and was the Minister of Industry and Trade 1921–1925. 485, 577, 593

Norweb, Raymond Henry (1895–1983) was an American diplomat serving as second secretary at the US Embassy in Paris 1917–1919. Later, he served as Ambassador to Peru 1940–1943, Portugal 1943–1945, and Cuba 1945–1948. He was married to Emory Mae. 67, 223, 625, 635

Nye, Joseph M. "Bill" (1887–1985) was the first American to hold the position of Chief Special Agent for the State Department Counterintelligence, 1916–1920, and held the title of special assistance to the Secretary of State. He reported directly to Lansing. Nye was directed by Lansing to tap the telephones of the German Embassy in Washington, with the interception of the Zimmerman telegram being one of the primary results. Nye was therefore able to brief Lansing ahead of time as to the topic of the German ambassador's call on January 31, 1917. 175, 206

O

Oberthor, František (b. 1878), was a member of the Board of Directors of the Czechoslovakian Cooperative Bank in Prague. After 1919 he was head of the coal department of the Ministry of Public Work and attorney to Dr. Otto Petschek, the largest Czech coal magnate. In the 1930s, he acted as president of the Czechoslovak Bank and a vice-president of the Czechoslovak Chamber of Commerce in Prague. He owned the Radíč Castle south of the Czech capital. 539

Oblieght. 474, 482, 486

O'Laughlin, John Callan "Cal" (1873–1949) was an American journalist who contributed to the *Army and Navy Journal* and was commissioned to serve as aide to Gen. George Goethals. Previously he had served as US Assistant Secretary of State in 1909. 232, 236, 262, 326

Onou, Alexander Mikhailovich (1865–1934) was a Russian diplomat serving as Chargé of the Legation in Bern 1918 after completing an assignment as Counselor of the Russian Embassy in the US 1917. 100

Oosley, Lt. 315, 316

Orlando, Vittorio (160–1952) was the Prime Minister of Italy 1917–1919. 76, 157, 171, 176, 221, 222, 250, 339, 356, 358, 375, 378, 583

Orr, Alice was married to Arthur Orr, American pilot and diplomat. 33, 298, 299

Orr, Arthur (1885–1933) was an American diplomat began his career as a pilot during WWI. Later he served in various diplomatic posts in Berlin, Paris, London, and on the Board of Trade. 33, 35–37, 69, 183, 265, 334, 335, 399, 422, 439

Ortiz, Rafael. 222

Osborne, Alexander Perry was a Lt. Colonel in the US Army who served as head of the Bureau Reciprocal Supply, with authorization to negotiate the purchase and transportation of necessary supplies. 34, 41, 57, 90, 174, 244, 378

Osborne, Lithgow (1892–1980) was an American diplomat serving as secretary at the Legation in Denmark. He worked with the American Commission to Negotiate Peace in Paris 1919. Later, he served as Ambassador to Norway in 1946. 272, 626

Osterrieth, Leon (1870–1924) was a Belgian cavalry officer who headed his country's Mission to the US in August 1917, to which Gibson was attached from the State Department. He was awarded the US Army Distinguished Service Medal in 1918 for his meritorious service to the US during WWI and Acting Military Attaché to the Belgian Legation in Washington. 20

Osuský, Štefan (1889–1973) was a Slovak lawyer, diplomat and academician. After studying in the US for ten years, he earned a JD degree in Chicago. During his American sojourn, he was active in expatriate organizations and returned to Europe as vice-president of the Slovak League. Between 1917 and 1918, he was the director of a Czecho-Slovak news agency in Geneva which brought him into contact with the American Legation in Switzerland. Later he served as Czech representative to the UK, secretary-general of the Czechoslovak delegation at the Paris Peace Conference, and Ambassador to France 1921–1939. 374

Oulahan, Richard V., Jr. (1893–1961) was an American army officer and journalist. He was the son of war correspondent, Richard V. Oulahan of the *New York Times*. In 1919, Oulahan, Jr. was added to the advertising staff at the *New York Times*. 297, 448, 634

P

Pacelli, Eurenio (1875–1958) was an Italian Catholic church statesman who was undersecretary of state of the Vatican during WWI. In early 1917, Pacelli was consecrated as Archbishop and appointed as the papal nuncio to Germany. Later, in March 1939, Pacelli was elected Pope Pius XII. 61, 98, 104

Paderewska, Helena von Rosen Górska (1856–1934) was a Polish social activist. She was first married to Władysław Górski in 1873, and then remarried to Igancy Paderewski in 1899. She co-founded the Polish White Cross during WWI and fostered young Polish-American women volunteers in the Polish Grey Samaritans just after the war and into the Polish-Soviet War. She was first lady of the second Polish Republic from January to December 1919. 651

Paderewski, Ignacy (1860–1941) was a Polish pianist and statesman. Recognized for his musical genius worldwide by the beginning of WWI, Paderewski was active in advancing the cause of Polish independence. When the Allies were uncertain of both Piłsudski and Dmowski, Paderewski emerged as a statesman who could command the respect of all parties. He served as Poland's first Prime Minister and Foreign Minister from January through December 1919. Upon being ousted from the Polish government, he returned to his musical career. He was married to Helena Górska. 4, 349, 484, 535, 638, 640, 643, 644, 650–53

Page, Arthur W. (1883–1960) was the son of Walter Hines Page (US Ambassador to London 1913–1918). After graduating from Harvard College in 1905, Arthur worked for his father's publishing business, Doubleday, Page & Co. He edited several magazines, particularly *The World's Work*. He went on to become VP for Public Relations in 1927, and then VP and director of AT&T from 1927–1947. 13, 22, 23, 25, 41, 42, 78, 162, 261, 273, 298, 305, 311–314, 318, 319, 321, 324–329, 335, 341, 343–348, 350, 353, 355, 356, 359, 362, 364, 366, 371, 375, 391, 392, 400, 402, 408, 425, 594, 616

Page, Florence Lathrop (1858–1921) was married to Thomas Nelson Page, US Ambassador to Rome 1913–1919. Her first marriage was to Henry Field of Chicago, making her the sister-in-law of Marshal Field. 122, 150, 155, 338

Page, Frank Copeland (1887–1951) was an American army Major in the aviation section of the Signal Corps during WWI. He was the 3rd son of Walter Hines Page, US Ambassador to London 1913–1918. 179, 355, 377

Page, George 155

Page, John. 363

Page, Thomas Nelson (1853–1922) was an American lawyer and writer, with eighteen volumes published in 1912. In 1913, President Wilson appointed him as Ambassador to Italy, where he served until 1919. He published *Italy and the World War* in 1920. 72, 117, 119, 120, 123, 126–29, 131, 132, 140, 141, 145, 149, 153–155, 157, 171, 322, 338, 347,

Page, Walter Hines (1853–1922) was the US Ambassador in London, 1913–1918. Gibson had been his First Secretary in

1916. 2, 297–298, 311, 314, 321, 341, 343–344, 369, 377
Page, Willa Alice Wilson (1885–1942) was married to Walter Hines Page, US Ambassador to Britain 1913–1918. She was the mother of Gibson's good friend, Arthur Page. 311, 313, 321–322, 324, 242, 550
Painlevé, Paul (1863–1933) was a French mathematician and statesman. He served his nation as Prime Minister between September 12 and November 13, 1917 – a very short time but full of crises as the Russian state dissolved into Revolution and the Americans entered the war. He served another brief as Prime Minister in 1925. 57, 440
Palmer, Frederick (1873–1958) was an American journalist and experienced war correspondent. Upon the US entry into World War I, Gen. Pershing recruited Palmer to take up the task of accrediting press representatives for the AEF as a Colonel. He was the first war correspondent to be honored with the Distinguished Service Medal and received an honorary doctoral degree from Princeton University. 11, 37, 39, 41, 42, 44, 46–53, 68, 78, 140, 176, 263, 273
Paravincini, Charles Rudolf (1872–1947) was a Swiss diplomat who would later serve as Minister to London 1920–1939. He was married to Elizabeth Cecile von Wattenwyl. 100
Paravincini, Elizabeth Cecile Lillian (von Wattenwyl) (1886–1955) was married to Charles Rudolf Paravincini. 98
Parish, Mrs. 194
Parker, Judge 618
Parsons, Herbert (1869–1925) was an American politician who served in the AEF during the war. He was stationed at Bern as Assistant Military Attaché. 562
Pasha, Bolo aka Paul Bolo (d. 1918) was a French adventurer and financier in the Levant. He became a German agent but the French police and Scotland Yard could not collect enough evidence to convict him. After working from New York to betray France, the American government collected evidence and arrested him in Paris in September 1917. He was charged with treason, convicted and summarily executed on April 17, 1918. 87
Pašić, Nikola (1845–1926) was a Serbian and Yugoslav politician and diplomat who served several times as Prime Minister of Serbia (last being 1912–1918) and Prime Minister of Yugoslavia (1918, 1921–1924, and 1924–1926). In addition, he was the main negotiator for the new state at the Paris Peace Conference. 442–444, 449
Patchin, Ira H. (1883–1926) was an American lawyer who served as secretary for Frank Lyon Polk when he accepted the role as State Department intelligence counselor. Together they founded Secret Intelligence Bureau. He was the brother of Philip and Robert. 16, 22, 23, 296
Patchin, Philip Halsey (1884–1954) was an American diplomat who was Co-Chief of the Bureau of Foreign Intelligence at the Department of State with Gibson, early 1917 to April 1918. By the end of the war, Patchin was assistant to Secretary of State Robert Lansing as well as his Chief of Information. He served as Executive Secretary to the American Commission to Negotiate Peace at the Paris Peace Conference. He went on to lead Standard Oil in California. Philip, the brother of Ira and Robert, was married to Mary "Polly" Wallace Mason. 12, 14, 16, 19, 21–23, 68, 76, 156, 203, 204, 227, 270, 273, 296, 326, 326, 341, 343, 344, 352, 393, 394, 441, 443, 545, 546, 549, 552, 555, 564, 565, 568, 579, 581, 584, 585, 602, 604, 615, 621, 635, 638, 642, 644
Patchin, Robert H. "Bert" (1881–1955) was an American economist and banker who served as secretary of the National Foreign Trade Council in 1914. Later he published two books on the topic. Robert was the brother of Ira and Philip Patchin, and

married to Mary Custis Lee (1876–1922). 23

Patricia of Connaught, Princess (1886–1974) was a granddaughter of Queen Victoria. She married Alexander Ramsey in 1919. 571

Patrick, Mason M. (1863–1942) was an American army officer who Chief of the Air Service under Pershing in France 1918. Later he became the first Chief of the Army Air Corps in 1926–1927. 302

Patterson, Richard C. (1886–1966) was an American mining engineer, army officer and diplomat. In 1918 he was assigned to Paris as an administrator for the American Commission to Negotiate Peace. He remained active in the Army Reserve in the Intelligence division. Later he served as Assistant Secretary of Commerce and Ambassador to both Yugoslavia 1944–1947 and Guatemala 1948–1950 where he was outspoken against communism. 447

Pattison. (YMCA) 300

Pau, Paul (1848–1932) was a French army officer, recalled from retirement to command the army in Alsace 1914. 223

Paulding, Charles Gouverneur (1896–1965) was an American journalist who served as private secretary to Warwick Greene, Chairman of the Rockefeller Foundation in France. They toured waring nations, investigated prison camps, and inspected YMCA work all over Europe. 292

Peaslee, Amos Jenkins II (1887–1969) was an American politician and diplomat serving in the Army during WWI. As of March 1918, he was charged with organizing and running the Silver Greyhounds, the first US diplomatic courier service between Paris and Washington. This service grew to cover more territory as the war wound down and the peace began. Later Peaslee served as a naval commander in WWII and Ambassador to Australia 1953–1956. From 1956–1959, he served as an adviser to President Eisenhower in the area of international law. 469

Pecci, Vincenzo (1810–1903) was Pope Leo XIII from 1878–1903) 62

Peden, Edward Andrew (1868–1934) was an American businessman and president of Peden Iron & Steel Company of Texas. In 1917, he served as Federal Food Administrator for Texas. He was summoned to Europe by Hoover in December 1918 to assist in the distribution of food in Europe. He became a member of Hoover's personal staff, and undertook to organize the "Child Relief Bureau" of the ARA. 634, 648

Peed, George Pullen (1875–1933) was a colonel in the US Army and a surgeon led a team to administer a hospital in Paris. 24

Pell. 391

Peltzer, Fernand (1869–1937) was a Belgian diplomat serving as Ambassador at Bern. He was a brother-in-law to Albert I, King of the Belgians. 98

Peñaranda de Franchimont, Frédéric de (1893–1984) was a Major in the Dutch Military Intelligence Service. 416

Pennoyer, Richard E. (1885–1968) was an American diplomat serving as secretary of the Embassy in London. He was married to Winifred Paget Pennoyer. 227, 403, 572, 610

Percy, Eustace (1887–1958) was a British diplomat 1911–1919. Later he went into public service, presiding over the Board of Education 1924–1918 and as Minister without Portfolio 1935–1936. 313, 549, 604

Perkins, James Handasyd (1876–1940) was the American Commissioner of the Red Cross. Later he served as chairman of National City Bank 1933–1940. 75, 118, 148, 159, 178, 179, 216, 237, 320

Perłowski, Jan (1872–1942) was a Polish diplomat stationed at Laussane who worked with the Central Polish Agency and Committee to Aid Victims of War in Poland.

Later he represented Poland at the League of Nations and was legal adviser to the Polish Legation to the Vatican. He served as Ambassador to Spain and Portugal 1927–1935. 454, 462, 653

Pershing, John J. (1860–1948) was the Commander of the US Army Expeditionary Force in Europe. Pershing retained command of the American forces, for the most part, against British and French wishes. He strongly advocated refusing to allow the Germans an armistice, preferring to push on to a total victory. 3, 4, 12, 34, 41, 42, 46–49, 51, 52, 69, 71, 78, 109, 134, 140, 150, 151, 158, 162, 187–189, 197–200, 211, 219, 224, 231, 237, 250, 252, 260–262, 277, 280, 287–289, 291, 292, 296, 332–334, 339, 340, 370, 376, 384, 401, 421, 437, 440, 626, 630

Pétain, Philippe (1856–1951) was a French military officer who served as Marshal at the end of the war. He became known as "the Lion of Verdun." Later he was Chief of State of Vichy France 1940–1944. 50, 70, 175, 178, 254, 262, 440

Peytral, Paul (1841–1919) was a French politician who served in government positions beginning in 1881, primarily in the realm of finance. 44

Pfeifer, Julius (1864–1934) was an Austrian and then Czech businessman and politician. Beginning in 1906, he served as the chairman of the Union of Industrialists of Rumburk and was on the central committee of the Union of Czechoslovak Industrialists in Prague. 536

Phillips, Ivor (1861–1940) was British army general and liberal politician. He served in the War Office in 1914 and commanded the 38th Welsh Infantry Division as it deployed to France in 1916. 45

Phillips, William "Bill" (1878–1968) was an American diplomat who served as Under Secretary of State 1917–1920, 1922–1924, and 1933–1936. He was Ambassador to Belgium 1924–1927, Canada 1927–1929, and Italy 1936–1941. Later Phillips served as chief of the Office of Strategic Services in London. 19, 47, 68, 71, 76, 203, 216, 258, 339, 342, 343, 347, 351, 372, 374, 385, 514, 572, 597, 625

Picard, François (1855–1961) was a French Army officer, a colonel in 1918 and later a general. 73

Pichon, Stephen (1857–1933) was a French diplomat and politician who served several terms as Minister of Foreign Affairs (1906–1911, 1913, 1917–1920). 42, 72, 166, 200, 222, 356, 440

Pierce, Daniel T. was an American working with the Red Cross in the area of Public Information in Paris. 67, 74, 79, 181, 182, 266, 307

Piłsudski, Józef (1867–1935) was a Polish statesman and military leader. During the First World War, he was the charismatic leader of the Polish Legions, which fought on the ranks of the Austrian Army in order to gain Polish independence. In 1917, he refused to pledge fealty to the German Kaiser and was subsequently arrested. In November 1918, he was escorted from his Magdeburg prison to Warsaw in order to take up affairs as Chief of State and Head of the Polish Army. Under his command, Poland acquired large territories in Ukraine, Lithuania and Germany. After 1922, her took a short break from politics, but had his comeback in his May Coup of 1926, ascertaining him authoritarian power in Poland until his death in 1935. 125, 485

Pionan. 246

Pirelli, Giovianni Basttista (1848–1932) was an Italian rubber industrialist. 212

Pirquet, Clemens von (1874–1929) was an Austrian pediatrician, bacteriologist and immunologist. He was noted for his work to develop a vaccine for small pox and tuberculosis. 470, 477

Pinchot, Gifford (1865–1946) was an American forester and politician. He was appointed as the first head of the US Forest Service in 1905–1912. Pinchot was vocal in criticizing Hoover for ignoring American farmers while catering to "middlemen" during his leadership of the ARA. Later he was Governor of Pennsylvania 1923–1927 and 1931–1935. 594

Pintimalli, Major. 486

Plitz, Erasmus (1851–1929) was a Polish statesman who served on the National Committee in Paris. 348 photo

Plunkett, Horace (1854–1932) was a British agricultural reformer who supported Irish home rule and chaired the Irish Convention 1917–1918. 333

Podmaniczky, Tibor (1884–1960) was a Hungarian nobleman married to an American, Viktoria (or Virginia) Hegeman. 487, 488, 493, 521

Poillon, Arthur, was a Military attaché at the Hague. 625, 643

Poincaré, Henriette Benucci (1858–1943) was married to French Prime Minister Raymond Poincaré. 222, 223, 275

Poincaré, Lucien (1862–1920) was a French Physicist and Rector of the University of Paris. He was Raymond's brother. 76

Poincaré, Raymond (1860–1934) was a French politician who served three terms as Prime Minister of France and President of France from 1913–1920. 44, 70, 76, 214, 221–223, 256, 269, 275, 287, 427, 437, 439, 440

Poland, William B. (d. 1950) was an American civil engineer and railroad expert who worked with Hoover and the ARA. 271, 272, 275, 282, 287, 290, 335, 355, 388, 394, 407, 408, 411, 413, 417, 420, 423, 426, 438, 555, 565

Polignac, Elizabeth Margaret Knight de (1896–1976) was an American who married Marquis Camille Armand Jules Marie de Polignac (1832–1913), a French nobleman who fought with the Confederates in the American Civil War. 180, 211

Polk, Frank Lyon (1871–1943) was an American lawyer and diplomat who served as Counselor of the US State Department (1915–1919), Under Secretary of State (1919–1920), and acting Secretary of State from February to March 1920. He also headed the American Commission to Negotiate Peace in 1919 and represented the United States at the Paris Peace Conference. 14, 17, 42, 60, 63, 67, 68, 76, 82, 104, 123, 140, 155, 164, 203, 216, 248, 251, 270, 271, 275, 279, 297, 347, 365, 374, 385, 394, 572, 640

Pollen, Arthur J.H. (1866–1937) was a British journalist and commentator on navel affairs, writing *for Land and Water* since 1915. 343

Pomeroy. 45, 369

Poncet. 100

"Pooh." 602

Pope Benedict XV – see Giacomo Battista della Chiesa

Pope Leo XIII – See Vincenzo Pecci

Pope Pius IX – See Giovanni Ferretti

Pope Pius XI – See Achille Ratti.

Pope Pius XII - See Eurenio Pacelli.

Porter, Mrs. was the sister of Fred Sterling. 206, 634

Potter, Philip B. was a CRB volunteer from Harvard who saw the invasion of the Germans in 1914 and recorded the US entry into the war, reporting to US Ambassador Whitlock. 282, 318

Preiss, Jaroslav (1870–1946) was a Czech lawyer and economist who worked at Živnostenská Banka from 1904–1938, for many years as general director. From 1918–1920 he sat on the National Assembly and helped direct Czechoslovakian national finances. Later, in 1945, he was arrested for refusing to cooperate with the Nazi occupation and died only two days after his release in 1946. 587

Prince, Morton (1854–1929) was an American neurologist and abnormal psychologist. 212, 244

Q

Quekemeyer, George (1884–1926) was an American Army officer, a graduate of West Point, serving as aide-de-camp to Gen.

Pershing at Chaumont in 1918. Later he served as Commandant of Cadets at the United States Military Academy. 188, 198, 199, 252, 273

R

Radović, Andrija (b. 1872) was a Montenegrin and Yugoslav politician. He served as Prime Minister of Montenegro from 1907–1908, also taking on roles as Foreign Minister and Minister of War and Finance. During the chaos of war, he created a government in exile for the Kingdom of Montenegro in May 1916, located in Bordeaux, France, and acted as Prime Minister May 1916 to January 1917. He served as a delegate to the Paris Peace Conference and founded a democratic party in Montenegro in 1920. 408, 409

Radziwiłł, Elizabeth (1850–1931) was the sister of Felcia Clary und Aldringen. 528, 533

Ragaz, Clara (1874–1957) was a Swiss feminist and pacifist who chaired the Women's International League for Peace and Freedom 1929–1946. She was married to Leonhard Ragaz. 106

Ragaz, Leonhard (1868–1945) was a Swiss Reformed theologian and one of the most extreme pacifist/anti-military radicals in Switzerland. 106, 107, 111, 112

Raikes, Edgar. 352

Rajakavić, Emil 506

Rampolla, Mariano (1843–1913) was an Italian prelate of the Roman Catholic Church who served as Secretary of State for the Vatican 1908–1910. 62

Ramseyer, C. William (1875–1943) was a US Congressman from Iowa. 633

Rappard, William E. (1883–1958) was an American academic and diplomat who assisted the Swiss Mission to the US and lectured at Harvard. He co-founded the Graduate Institute of International Studies in Geneva. He later served as the Rector of the University of Geneva in 1926. 98–100, 102, 108, 110, 364

Ratibor, Prince Maximillian von (1856–1924) was a German diplomat serving as Ambassador to Spain 1910–1918. He was reported to have taken part in biological warfare to prevent neutral Spain's ability to supply livestock to the Allies. 323, 346

Ratti, Achille (1857–1939) was an Italian Monseigneur who was designated to be the first papal nuncio to modern Poland, March 1919-June 1921. When Gibson was posted there, the two men became good friends. In 1922, Ratti was consecrated as Pope Pius XI. 104, 134

Rawlings, Henry Bernard Hughes (1889–1962) was a British naval officer who served as attaché to Poland 1919. He later was second in command of the British fleet in the Pacific. 534

Reading, Lady Alice Edith Isaacs (1866–1930) was married to Rufus Isaacs in 1887, becoming Lady Reading in 1914. Although her health was delicate, she was active in charitable work in India during Lor Reading's term as Viceroy (1921–1926). 16, 343

Reading, Lord, Rufus Daniel Rufus Isaacs, 1st Marquees of Reading (1860–1935) was a British politician who served as Member of Parliament for Reading (1904–1913), Lord Chief Justice of England (1913–1921), British Ambassador to the US (1918–1919), Viceroy of India (1921 to 1926), and Secretary of Foreign Affairs in 1931. 16, 98, 137, 343, 374, 442

Redfield, William C. (1858–1932) was an American politician who served as the first US Secretary of Commerce 1913–1919. 276

Reid, Elisabeth Mills (1858–1931) was the widow of Whitelaw Reid, American publisher of the Herald Tribune. He had served as Ambassador to France in 1889 and Britain in 1905. 375, 378

Reineck, Walter S. (1887–1972) was an American diplomat assigned to Vienna in September 1914. During the war, he took charge of the American archives, then housed at the Spanish Embassy. He went back to work for the American Mission in 1919, and spent the rest of his career in the Foreign Service. 485

Rensselaer, William Stephen van (1886–1930) was an American lawyer and diplomat who served as third secretary in Rome 1915–1917 and in Madrid, from 1917 until his recall in 1918. 323, 351, 383

Reyntiens, Guy (1880–1932) was the brother of Ynès (Gibson's future wife). He worked for Count de Jonghe and then joined the Belgian cavalry. He was wounded badly at the Battle of Yser (October 1914) that he was forced to resign from the military and live in Brussels with his wife, Adrienne Drugman. 589

Reyntiens, Jean-Marie "Jack" (b. 1882) was the brother of Gibson's future wife, Ynés Reyntiens, and married to Myriam Drugman. He was highly placed in Belgian society and volunteered in the 1st Regiment des Guides when the Germans invaded Belgium in 1914. He remained with Albert, King of the Belgians, at the La Havre throughout war. XV, 81, 243, 414, 456, 543, 556–560, 573, 582, 583

Reyntiens, Myriam Drugman (b. 1885) was a Belgian patriot who was a leader of l'Œuvre de l'Assistance Discrète (Discreet Assistance Charity), which helped British and allied soldiers escape from behind enemy lines. She was later inducted into the Most Excellent Order of the British Empire. For reference to her activities, see *New York Times*, October 2, 1915, and *The Obscure Heroes of Liberty* by Kenneth Baker (2018). She was the sister of Adrienne Drugman, who married Guy Reytiens. Myriam was married to Jean "Jack" Reyntiens and a favorite sister-in-law to Ynès Reyntiens, future wife of Hugh Gibson. 81, 243, 414, 416, 417, 456, 543, 554, 556, 573, 574, 581–584, 587, 590, 636, 638, 643, 648

Reyntiens, Ramon (1881–1921) was a Belgian cavalry officer and brother of Ynès Reyntiens, Gibson's future wife. He was gassed during the war and his lungs were badly damaged. After his recovery, he immigrated to Santa Catarina, Mexico, where he was murdered in 1921. XV, 81, 243, 414, 422, 452, 456, 458–460, 543, 556

Reyntiens, Ynès (1888–1950) was a Belgian aristocrat whose father, Robert Reyntiens, had been aide-de-camp to King Leopold I. Her mother, Anita de Errazu, died in 1893, and her father remarried to Lady Alice Portal but died in 1913 leaving Ynès orphaned before the war began. All three of her brothers (Guy, Jean Marie "Jack", and Ramon) were cavalry men, and she was an avid horsewoman. She was quick to become involved in relief work, often collaborating with her sister-in-law Myriam Reyntiens (Jack's wife). For reference to her activities, see *New York Times*, October 2, 1915, and *The Obscure Heroes of Liberty* by Kenneth Baker (2018). She married Hugh Gibson February 1922 in Brussels while he was posted as the US Minister to Poland. VII, XV, 2, 8, 81, 243, 272, 315, 414–416, 422, 426, 433, 435, 439–441, 452, 455–460, 543, 556–560, 573, 582–583, 585, 586, 587, 590

Rhondda, David Alfred (1856–1918) was a Welsh industrialist who served as British Food Controller 1917–1918. 275

Ribot, Alexandre (1842–1923) was a French politician who served four times as Prime Minister, most recently in 1917. 440

Richards, Lewis (1881–1940) was an American volunteer in the CRB and an accomplished pianist. 271, 322, 346, 394, 400, 589, 627, 636,

Richardson, Norval (1877–1940) was an American diplomat who was Secretary of the Embassy in Rome under Thomas Nelson Page 1913–1918. 76, 116, 117, 120, 122–126, 129, 132, 133, 135, 141, 142, 146, 147, 149, 151, 152, 223, 231, 282, 292

Rickey, Harry N. (1868–1926) was an American press magnate who served as ComPub Commissioner in the UK until May 1918. Later he served as the assistant general director of Foreign Section of ComPub. 37

Rickard, Edgar (1874–1951) was a French-born American mining engineer. Beginning around 1900 he edited a mining journal in London. He was a lifelong confidant of Herbert Hoover and friend of Hugh Gibson. 12, 14–16, 21, 22, 164, 181, 545, 552, 645

Rieth, Kurt Heinrich (1881–1969) was a German diplomat who participated in the German occupation administration of Belgium 1915–1918. He was an importer of Russian oil into the region. Later he worked as Counselor in Rome and Paris 1924–1931, then Ambassador to Vienna 1931–1934. In early 1941, Rieth tried to immigrate to the US with the help of Walter Teagle of Standard Oil, but was denied. He spent the rest of his life in the Tangier International Zone. 411

Rietmann, Ernst (1870–1945) was a Swiss journalist and newspaper publisher. In 1918, he was acting editor-in-chief of *Neue Zuricher Zeitung*, and later served as administrative director from 1930–1945. 109, 113

Riggenbach, Samuel Rudolf (1882–1961) was a Swiss art historian from Basel. 109

Riggs, Roland Roger (1884–1970) was an American Naval commander serving as a Naval Attaché to the Embassy in Rome 1917–1919. 123, 133, 142

Robbins, Warren Delano (1885–1935) was an American diplomat and cousin of Franklin D. Roosevelt. From 1909 to 1921, he worked primarily in Latin America. Later he served as Chief of Protocol of the US 1931–1933 and Minister to Canada 1933–1935. 175

Roberts, Elmer (1863–1937) was an American war correspondent with the Associated Press and served as office chief in Paris 1914–1927. Somewhat pro-German, he focused on electrical biochemical inventions. 182, 223, 224, 340

Robilant, Gabrielle "Gaby" was the daughter of Mario and Madame Robilant. 121, 132

Robilant, Mario Nicholis (1855–1943) was an Italian general and representative to the Supreme War Council in Paris. 121

Robinette, Edward B. was an American naval officer assigned as Assistant Naval Attaché at the Stockholm Office of Naval Intelligence during WWI. 43

Robins, Raymond (1873–1954) was an American economist and advocate of organized labor. During the war, he worked with the YMCA and ARC in France. In December 1917, he headed the ARC expedition to Russia, and after that continually advocated for diplomatic relations between the US and Russia. He was influential in Franklin Roosevelt's decision to exchange Ambassadors in 1933. 369

Robinson, Henry Mauris (1868–1937) was an American banker and political advisor. Between 1917 and 1927, he served on the Council of National Defense, the Supreme Economic Council of Peace in Paris, the US Shipping Board, the International Labor Conference, and several other commissions. 587, 590, 612, 627

Rock, Mrs. 133

Rockwood. Navy Surgeon. 310

Rodd, James Rennel (1858–1941) was a British diplomat serving as Ambassador to Italy 1908–1919. 146, 157

Rodd, Lilias Georgina Guthrie (1864–1951) was married to James Rodd. 156–157

Rogers, Walter S. was the Director of the Division of Wireless and Cable Service for the CPI under Creel. From Paris, he arranged for the transmission of Wilson's speeches, coordinating the wireless transmission for correspondents working for three different press associations. 18, 22, 23, 213, 435

Rolland, Romain (1866–1944) was a French writer and mystic who lived in Geneva as a life-long pacifist. 112

Romanones, 1st Count of, Álvaro de Figueroa (1863–1950) was a Spanish politician who served as Prime Minister in 1912–1913 and 1915–1917. He was considered pro-French as opposed to Dato's policy of neutrality. 242

Ronald family. 385

Roosevelt, Eleanor Butler (1880–1960) was an American philanthropist. She was married to Theodore Roosevelt, Jr. 334, 335, 378, 401

Roosevelt, Franklin Delano (1882–1945) was an American politician who served as Assistant Secretary to the Navy (1913–1920), Governor of New York (1929–1932), and President of the United States (1933–1945). 7, 17, 248, 261, 275, 279, 299, 300

Roosevelt, Kermit (1889–1943) was an American businessman, explorer and writer, and the second son of former president, Theodore Roosevelt. Kermit join the British Army in 1917 and fought in the Mesopotamia, earning a British Military Cross. In April 1918, he relinquished his British commission and was transferred to the AEF in France. There he learned that his brother, Quentin, had been shot down over France. Kermit remained on duty until March 1919. Between the wars, he went into the shipping business and continued his explorations. In WWII, he again volunteer in the British Army, but a resurgence of his malaria triggered a medical discharge. He committed suicide in June 1943. 245

Roosevelt, Nicholas (1893–1982) was an American diplomat and journalist who served as an attaché to the Embassy in Paris 1914–1916 and secretary to the US Mission in Spain 1916–1917. He served as a foreign correspondent and editorialist for the *New York Times* and *New York Herald Tribune* 1921–1946, additionally serving in the Office of War Information 1942–1945. Later he served as Minister to Hungary 1930–1933. 615, 618, 620

Roosevelt, Quentin (1897–1918) was the youngest son of Theodore Roosevelt. At age 20, he joined the US Army Air Service. He was shot down while on a mission over France and killed on July 14, 1918. 245, 401

Roosevelt, Theodore "Ted", Jr (1887–1944) was the son of former US President Theodore Roosevelt. He was commissioned into the AEF as a major in April 1917 and wounded at Soissons during July 1918, earning him the Distinguished Service Cross. His younger brother, Kermit, was killed the same month. Later he served as Assistant Secretary of the Navy 1921–1924, Governor of Puerto Rico 1929–1932, and Governor General of the Philippines 1932–1933. He was married to Eleanor Butler Alexander in 1910. 14, 238, 308, 327, 327, 331, 333, 401, 547, 559

Roosevelt Longworth, Alice (1884–1980) was the oldest child of former US President Theodore Roosevelt, only daughter of his marriage to Alice Hathaway Lee Roosevelt. She was a writer, famous social figure and – according to her own account – hedonist. She was married to Nicholas Longworth from 1906 until his death in 1931. 14

Root, Elihu (1845–1937) was an American lawyer and statesman who had served as Secretary of War 1899–1904, Secretary of State 1905–1909, and Senator from New York 1909–1915. He received a Nobel Peace Prize in 1912. In June 1917, President Wilson sent Root to Russia to seek a path of cooperation between the US and the new revolutionary government provided they helped the Allied cause. Later, Root became founding chairman of the Council on Foreign Relations in 1918. 300, 398

Rosanin, Paul. 479

Rose, Lt. 211

Rose, William John (1885–1968) was a Canadian Rhodes scholar at Oxford who went to Prague as a secretary for the YMCA in

1914. During a holiday in Silesia, WWI broke out and he and his wife became prisoners of the Austro-Hungarian authorities throughout the war. When Austro-Hungary collapsed, Rose left his wife in Silesia and undertook a mission to the Western Allies on behalf of the Polish National Council of Teschen. He returned to Poland after the war to help rebuild with the YMCA 1920–1927. Later, Rose became a renowned historian of Slavic Studies. He directed the University of London's School of Slavic and East European Studies 1945–1947. After his retirement, he returned to Canada and helped found the Slavonic Studies program at the University of British Columbia. His story was published by the University of Toronto Press in 1975, *The Polish Memoirs of William John Rose*, edited by Daniel Stone. 396, 397

Rozwadowzki, Jan Emanuel (1872–1935) was a Polish politician and member of the National Committee in Paris. 348 photo

Rublee, George (1868–1957) was an American lawyer and internationalist who represented the US at the Allied Maritime Transport Council in London in 1917. 275

Ruhl, Arthur (1876–1935) was a Harvard-educated American sports journalist who published a war diary from the first year of WWI, *Antwerp to Gallipoli: A Year of the War on Many Fronts* (1916), and was soon to publish *New Masters of the Baltic* (1921). 246, 362

Rumbold, Horace (1869–1941) was a British diplomat who served as Minster in Bern 1916–1919. Later he served as Ambassador to Poland 1919–1920, High Commissioner in Constantinople 1920–1924, Ambassador to Spain 1924–1928, and to Germany 1928–1933. 86, 98, 99, 103

Rupprecht, Crown Prince of Bavaria (1869–1955) commanded the German 6th Army in France from 1914 to 1916, where his troops were facing the British Expeditionary Force. He was one of the first German generals to believe the war could not be won, opposing the scorched earth policy but not able to prevent it. He became head of the House of Wittelsbach when his father died in October 1921. He consistently avoided the German far right movement of Hitler. Rupprecht was forced into exile to Italy in December 1939, where he remained until September 1945, while his wife and kids were interned in German concentration camps. As late as 1954, he had considerable support to become the monarch of Bavaria, possibly all of Germany. 239, 394, 395, 409

Russell, Charles Edward (1860–1941) was an American journalist. 270

Russell, Charles Howland "Charlie" (1891–1965) was an American diplomat who had served in Berlin 1914–1916, The Hague 1917, and Bern 1918. He was also assigned as a delegate on a special mission to Russia in the summer of 1917, and served as a COMPUB speaker. 103, 333, 335, 454

Ryan, John D. was the American Assistant Secretary of War as of September 1918. 383

Ryan, T.R., was a Major in the US Army Engineers who was assigned to Serbia. He later worked in Poland. 514

S

Sage, Margaret Olivia Slocum (1828–1918) was an American philanthropist who inherited a large fortune when her husband, railroad baron Russell Sage, died in 1906. 629

Saint Cermen, Countess, de 74

Salis, John Francis Charles de (1864–1939) was a British diplomat and Minister with a special mission to the Vatican from 1916–1923. He was married to Hélène de Riquet, a Belgian aristocrat. He published a controversial report on the Balkans in 1919. 62, 128, 131, 144

San Martino, Count de. 125

Sanborn, Edwin Luther (1877–1919) was an American army officer who graduated from Harvard in 1898 and served in the AEF in the quartermaster corps in France and special agent in Spain during 1918. 252, 254, 266, 609

Sandow, Billy (1884–1972) was an American professional wrestler and promoter. 458

Sanger, Virginia Sturges (née Osborne) (1882–1955) was the sister of Perry Osborne and friend of Lucy Linn. 34, 41, 57, 174, 230

Sapieha, Adam (1867–1951) was elected Bishop of Krakow in November 1911. He instituted relief efforts for war victims in 1915. When Poland gained its independence in 1918, he insisted that the Polish church should be independent of outside influences, pitting him against Cardinal Archille Ratti, Archbishop of Warsaw and Papal Nuncio. Sapieha was appointed Metropolitan Archbishop in 1925, after Ratti had been elevated to Pope Pius XI. 485

Sapieha, Eustachy (1881–1963) was a Polish statesman who, with Januszajtis-Zegota, attempted a coup d'etat in January 1919. He later served as Prime Minister 1920–1921. 485

Sarrail, Maurice (1856–1929) was a French army general who was dismissed for poor leadership by Joffre in 1915 amidst political uproar. He was active throughout the war, especially in Salonika, but dismissed again in 1917 by Clemenceau. 196

Sawyer, Ernest Edward Sawyer (1850–1937) was a British diplomat posted to Switzerland during WWI. He was married to Ethel Hully. Their daughter was Nesta Sawyer. 98, 103

Sawyer, Nesta (1894–1985), daughter of British diplomat Ernest Sawyer, began writing as a war correspondent at age 17, and went on to become a playwright and philanthropist. She married Seymour Obermer, an American playwright, in 1925. She was a friend of Gibson and of Ynès Reyntiens. It is unclear whether Gibson refers to Ernest or Nesta. 103

Schaix, Major. 182

Schaumex. 194

Schell, Frank R. was an American army officer in the AEF, a major in the infantry at G-4. 568

Schelling, Ernest H. H. (1876–1939] was an American pianist, composer and conductor. Between 1896 and 1899, he was the only pupil of Ignacy Paderewski. During WWI, he served in the US army and military attaché in Bern where he gathered information about conditions in Poland. He was married to Lucie Howe Draper. After Lucy's death in 1938, Ernest married the 21 year old Helen "Peggy" Marshall. Their wedding in April was followed closely by his death in 1939. 98, 102, 105, 453, 535, 541, 542, 545, 546, 548, 562

Schiller, Louise S. was married to Ferdinand C. S. Schiller (1864–1935), a German philosopher who immigrated and taught at the University of Southern California. 279

Scholle, Gustave (b. 1863) was an American diplomat who served from 1909–1919. He was chargé d'affaires in Spain 1912 and later served in Cuba. 323, 592

Schroeder, Kurt von (1889–1969) was a German aristocrat, financier and army officer who served as a reserve officer and merchant banker during WWI. His dissatisfaction with the Versailles peace later led to his support of Hitler and the Nazi party. After WWII, he was convicted of crimes against humanity and imprisoned for three months. 589, 601, 613

Schule, Lt. 81

Schutzenhoffer. 653

Schwab, Charles M. (1862–1939) was an American steel magnate, running Bethlehem Steel 1903–1932. He became Director General of the Emergency Fleet Corporation, with authority over all shipbuilding in the US in April 1918. He was known for his innovative methods. 282

Schwarz-Hiller, Rudolf (1876–1932) was a Viennese lawyer and local politician serving on City Council from 1910–1923. He also headed the Central Office of Care for War Refugees, a member of the nutrition council, and a board member of the Jewish Community in Vienna. 523, 524

Scott, Hugh L. (1853–1934) was an American army general who served as Chief of Staff 1914–1917, then Commander of Camp Bix in 1918. 166

Scott, James Brown (1866–1943) was an American authority on international law who served as Special Adviser to the State Department 1914–1917, technical advisor to the American Commission to Negotiate Peace, and delegate to the Paris Peace Conference in 1919. 79, 229, 398

Scott, Joseph (1867–1958) was an American lawyer and an international commissioner for the Knights of Columbus. He served as chairman of the Los Angeles draft exemption board 1917–1918. 227, 233, 250–252

Scranton, Jack, was a young American who helped Gibson in the Legation in Belgium in November 1914. 346

Scriven, George P. (1854–1940) was an American Army officer who commanded the Aviation Section of the US Signal Corps 1913–1917. He was involved with the National Advisory Committee of Aeronautics and various military assignment until the early 1930's when he retired. 120, 134, 149

Sczrinski. 652

Sebastian. 92, 103

Seippel, Paul (1858–1926) was a Swiss professor from Geneva who taught at the University of Zurich. 107, 112

Seel. 267, 301

Semyonov, Grigory Mikhaylovich (1890–1946) was a leader of the White Russian movement in Trans Baikal 1917–1920 and supported by the Japanese. He was later accused of violence against American soldier of the Expeditionary Corps, but acquitted and returned to China. He was captured by Soviet troop in 1945 and executed as a counterrevolutionary in 1946. 171

Seracolt. 313

Serruys, Daniel (1875–1950) was a Belgian-French economist appointed to negotiate measures of peace during WWI. 277

Seyda, Marian (1879–1967) was a Polish lawyer and member of the National Committee in Paris, for which he ran the press office. 348 photo

Shaler, Millard King (1880–1942) was an American mining engineer and friend of Hoover's who had volunteered in the CRB during the war. He later went into making films. 273, 346, 407, 553, 555

Sharp, George Clough (1897–1972) was the son of US Ambassador William G. Sharp. During the summer of 1918, he worked as his father's private secretary in Paris. He graduated from Ecole libre des Sciences Politiques in 1918 and Columbia School of Law in 1922. He practiced law as a partner in the Sullivan & Cromwell firm in New York 1929–1971. During WWII, he served in the US Army and OSS. 90, 237, 333

Sharp, William Graves (1859–1922) was an American politician and industrialist. He served in the US Congress as the representative from Ohio 1909–1914, and was appointed as Ambassador to France by President Wilson in 1914, where he served until 1919. He was married to Hallie M. Cough. 3, 18, 34, 39, 40, 57, 59, 67, 72, 82, 90, 161, 176, 201, 213, 222, 224, 232, 234, 247, 255, 259, 292, 339, 340, 344, 347, 351–354, 356, 358, 362–364, 368, 370–372, 374, 378, 385, 387, 390, 402, 440, 548, 625

Sheehy-Skeffington, Johanna "Hanna" (1877–1946) was an Irish nationalist and suffragette. Her husband, Francis Skeffington, was shot and killed during the Easter Rising in 1916. Hanna became an executive in Sinn Féin in 1917. She lectured throughout the US during 1917 and 1918, raising money for the Irish cause. 251

Sheldon. 438, 440

Sheridan, Philip Henry, Jr. (1880–1918) was an American cavalry officer who served as aide to President Theodore Roosevelt 1905–1907 but resigned that post to return to active duty in 1917. 15

Sherman. 200

Shiverick, Fritz (1896–1936) was an American football star at Cornell University serving in the army during WWI. 352

Shoecraft, Eugene "Shoe" (1892–1973) was an American diplomat serving as secretary at the Embassy in London. Later he served in Prague and Vienna. 311, 324, 341, 393, 404, 405, 407, 428, 430

Simonds, Frank H. (1878–1936) was a journalist from Massachusetts who worked for numerous New York newspapers such as *The Evening Sun* and *The Tribune* and published a five-volume history of the First World War. Between 1919 and 1932, he attended all major international peace conferences in Paris. 616

Simons, Algie Martin (1870–1950) was an American socialist journalist and political activist who edited the *International Socialist Review* 1900–1910. He changed from being anti-war to an advocate of military preparedness in 1917. In July 1918, Simons served as a member of American Socialist and Labor Mission to Europe to fight the dispirited workers during the war. Later, he served as an economist for the American Medical Association 1931–1950. 257, 270

Simpson, John Lowery "Pink" (1891–1981) was an American banker and financial consultant who served in the Commission for Relief in Belgium (CRB) 1915–1917, and then the American Relief Administration (ARA) in 1918–1919. He went on to lead J. Henry Schroder Banking Corporation, Schroder Trust Company and Bechtel Corporation between 1925 and 1961. 39, 132, 164, 228, 270, 271, 273, 282, 283, 402, 410, 493, 512, 514, 515

Sims, William Snowden (1858–1936) was a US Navy Admiral who commanded US forces in Britain. He worked effectively with his British counter-part Admiral Sir Lewis Bayly, but complained that the Navy Department in Washington, then under the direction of Franklin D. Roosevelt, was failing to provide him with necessary information, authority and forces. 86, 153, 324, 331, 346, 359, 378

Sisson, Edgar (1875–1948) was an American journalist serving with the Committee on Public Information in Petrograd, Russia, in 1918. He obtained and published *The German-Bolshevik Conspiracy*, a collection of 68 Russian documents designed to discredit the Russian Revolution. Even at that time, their veracity was debated and George Kennan deemed them to be forgeries in 1956. 266, 351, 395, 435, 526

Skinner, Robert Peet (1866–1960) was an American newspaper publisher and consular agent in Berlin 1914 and London 1914–1924. Later he served at several other posts including Ambassador to Turkey 1933–1936. 343

Skirmunt, Konstanty (1866–1949) was a Polish diplomat and politician who represented the Polish National Committee in Rome. He later served as Ambassador to Rome 1919–1921, Polish Minister of Foreign Affairs 1921–1922 and Minister/Ambassador to London 1922–1934. 125–127, 130, 146, 348, 393

Slade, George T. (1871–1941) was an American army officer serving as director-general of the US Army Transportation Corps in Europe 1918–1919. He had managed the Northern Pacific Railroad from 1907 to 1918, and returned to that post after the war, serving until 1940. 215, 221

Slocum, Stephen L'Hommedieu (1859–1933) was an American army officer serving as Military Attaché in London 1917–1918. He

was awarded a Distinguished Service Medal in July 1918 for his exceptionally meritorious service during WWI. 166, 630
Smith, Capt. 43, 48
Smith, Lieutenant 245
Smith [London-Berlin courier] 46, 233
Smith, Addison T. (1862–1956) was a US Congressman from Idaho. 633
Smith, Albert Gilbert was the Federal Fuel Administrator in Cuba in July 1918. In 1921, he was president of Ward Line Shipping Co. 1921 and in 1923 he became president of the American Steamship Owners Association. 211
Smith, H. Alexander (1880–1966) was an American volunteer with the Food Administration. He later served as a Republican Senator from New Jersey (1944–1959). He volunteers with Hoover's Finnish Relief Fund in World War II. 212, 216, 413
Smith, Harry, was the brother of Albert of the Ward Line Shipping Co. 211
Smith, Sydney Yost (b. 1857) was an American diplomat who served as a drafting expert to the American Commission to Negotiate Peace in Paris 1918. 441
Smithers. 269
Smulski, John F. (1867–1928) was a Polish-American publisher and banker from Chicago. He was President of the Polish National Council. 652
Sobánski, Wladyslaw (1877–1943) was Polish diplomat and member of the National Committee in Paris. He was a leader in the Red Cross in Russia during the war, and served as Minister to Belgium 1919–1924. 348 photo
Solf, Wilhelm H. (1862–1936) was a German diplomat and statesman serving as Secretary for Foreign Affairs October 3-December 13 1918. He has previously served as Secretary for the Colonies 1911–1918. 361, 374
Sonnenschein, Adolph (1862–1939) was an Austrian-Czech industrialist who was the Central Director of the Witkowice Mining and Ironworks Union in Moravia 1916–1920. 538
Sonnino, Sidney (1847–1922) was an Italian politician who served as the Foreign Minister 1914–1919. Of Jewish and Protestant heritage in predominantly Roman Catholic Italy, he had been Prime Minister 1906 and 1909–1910 and held several other cabinet positions. 76, 145, 150, 176, 178, 222, 376, 644
Sophia of Prussia (1870–1932) was a member of the House of Hohenzollern who married Diadochos Constantine, Crown Prince of Greece in 1889. When he ascended to the throne in 1913, she became Queen consort of the Hellenes. She was active in charity work and led initiatives in education, hospitals, orphanages and food kitchens. She served as nurse during the Balkan Wars in 1912–1913. After the assassination of King George I in 1913, she was crowned Queen (rather than consort). Her German family became a liability as WWI neared its finale, Constantine was dethroned in June 1917. Constantine and Sophia were returned to the throne in December 1920, and reigned until his abdication in September 1922. 373
Southgate, Richard Brigham (b. 1863) was an American diplomat serving at both the War Trade Board and the Embassy in Paris 1918–1919. He continued his career in both Europe and Latin America. 194, 237, 292
Spargo, John (1878–1966) was a Britain-born American politician and biographer of Karl Marx. After WWI, he turned away from socialism and became a member of the Republican Party in the mid 1920's and supported Coolidge and Hoover. 257
Speares, General Sir Edward Louis (1886–1974) was a British general who headed the Military Mission in Paris 1917–1920. He was newly married to Mary "May" Borden-Turner in 1918. 85

Sperry, William H. "Will" (1885–1963) was an American army veteran who had served in the CRB and fought in WWI. 183, 219, 282, 413, 557

Speranza, Gino (1872–1927) was an American lawyer and journalist. In 1912, he gave up his legal practice to write about Italy as a featured correspondent for the *New York Evening Post* and the *Outlook*. After the war, he became an Attaché on Political Intelligence for the Embassy in Rome until 1919 when he returned to the US. He was married to Florence Speranza. 124, 131, 141, 146. 152

Spring-Rice, Cecil (1859–1918) was a British diplomat serving as the Ambassador to the United States 1912–1918. 91

Squier, George Owen (1865–1934) was an American soldier and scientist. He was Chief of the Aviation Section of the US Signal Corps from May 1916 to February 1917, and then Chief Signal Corps officer during the war. 281

St. Cyres, Henry Stafford Northcote, Viscount St. Cyres (1869- 1926) was a British diplomat serving as secretary and counselor of the British Legation in Bern. He married Dorothy Morrison in 1912. 98, 102

St. Paul. 215

St. Paul, Marquise, Marie Charlotte Diane Feydeau de Brou (1848–1943) was a French philanthropist and musician married to Charles de Chaumont, Marquis St. Paul. 124

Stabler, Jordon Herbert (1885–1938) was an American diplomat serving as Chief of the Division of Latin American Affairs. He was in Paris handling affairs of Latin American, Spain, Portugal and Liberia with the American Commission to Negotiate Peace. He served in various posts in Latin America and at disarmament conferences both before and after the Paris Peace Conference. He married to Elizabeth "Bessie" Wells in 1915. 572, 630

Staněk, František (1867–1936) was a politician and leader of the Czech National Movement in Paris. He served as the Minister of Public Works and Labor 1918–1919, Minister of Post and Telegraph 1919–1920, and Minister of Agriculture 1921–1922. 379, 478, 539

Stanton, Miss. 121, 124, 125, 172, 338

Stanwood, Capt. 503

Steed, Henry Wickam (1871–1956) was a British journalist who wrote for the *London Times* from Rome 1897–1902 and Vienna, 1903–1913. From 1914 to 1919, he served as the foreign editor of *The Times*, becoming general editor from 1919–1922. 130, 551, 619

Sefton, Pennington (1895–1987). 431

Stephens, Judge. 478

Stephens, Frederick Dorsey (b. 1891) was an American who volunteered in the CRB 1914–1916 and served in the US Army during WWI. Later, he worked with the ARA 1921–1922 and then for the relief of Finland and Poland during WWII. 54, 573

Sterling, Frederick Augustine (1876–1957) was an American diplomat serving as secretary of the Embassy in Paris. Later he would be the first US representative in the Irish Free State 1927–1934, Envoy to Bulgaria 1934–1936, and Sweden 1938–1941. 32, 59, 61, 82, 85, 151, 206, 216, 223, 237, 252, 266, 331, 340, 351, 356, 358, 364, 370, 423, 443

Stetson, John B., Jr. (1884–1952) was an American businessman and diplomat. He volunteered early for service during WWI and was an instructor at the military aviation school in Tours, France, 1917–1920. Later he served as Ambassador to Poland 1925–1930. 230, 235, 237, 248, 250, 269, 270, 272, 292, 296, 301, 303, 305, 318, 325, 326, 329, 340, 347, 348, 350, 351, 353, 355, 357, 368, 370, 372, 433, 436, 450, 545, 573, 616

Stettinius, Edward Reily, Sr. (1865–1925) was an American business executive who worked for J.P. Morgan as the chief buyer of war supplies for the Allies. When the

US entered the war, he was in charge of procurement of supplies for the US Army. He served as Assistant Secretary of War in April 1918. 214, 216, 248, 252, 264, 328, 331, 383, 390, 422, 423, 432, 550, 593

Stevenson, Robert Louis (1850–1894) was a Scottish writer famed for *Treasure Island*, *Kidnapped*, and *The Strange Case of Dr. Jekyll and Mr. Hyde*. 124

Stickney. 212, 302

Stockton, Gilchrist B. "Gil" (1890–1973) was an American businessman, a Naval Reserve officer 1917–1950 and aide to Admiral Sims 1917–1919. He served as the business executive for the CRB 1915–1916 and for the ARA 1919–1920. He was Chief of Mission to Austria 1919–1920, and later as Minister 1930–1933. He earned the rank of Rear Admiral in 1945. 267, 312, 324, 331, 653

Stone, Donald Leroy was an American professor at Harvard University and later the chief press censor for the AEF in Paris July 1917 to October 1918, remaining on Pershing's staff until June 1919. 219, 282, 367

Stone, Melville Elijah (1848–1929) was an American publisher and founder of the Chicago Daily News. He managed the Associated Press. 223–225, 340, 575

Storey, Charles M. (1889–1980) was an American serving at the Department of Justice who worked in political intelligence and with the commission related to prisoners of war. He joined a small sub-committee to the American Mission to Negotiate Peace 1918–1919 along with Lawrence Martin, Nicholas Roosevelt, F.E. Parker, Jr. 331, 517, 519

Stovall, Pleasant (1857–1935) was an American journalist and legislator who served as Ambassador to Switzerland 1913 to 1919. 61, 93, 95, 98, 99, 104, 105, 301, 334

Straight, Willard D. (1880–1918) was an American investment banker, diplomat and journalist who ran *New Republic* 1914–1918. 47, 382, 393, 395, 408, 420, 423

Stratton. 279

Strauss, Albert (1864–1929) was an American businessman and investment banker with J&W Seligman & Co since 1901. He served as vice governor of the Federal Reserve Board 1918–1920. 584, 595

Strauss, Lewis (1896–1975) was an America businessman, naval officer, and key figure in the development of nuclear power in the US. In 1917, he volunteered to serve as Hoover's assistant at the US Food Administration and later ARA, without pay. He performed so well that he became a trusted partner and secretary during the Paris Peace Conference in 1919. At the same time, Strauss worked with the American Jewish Joint Distribution Committee (JDC). Strauss became a partner in Kuhn, Loeb & Co, 1929–1941. He joined the US Naval Reserve, commission as an intelligence officer, in 1925. During WWII he was on active duty with the Bureau of Ordnance. President Truman elevated Strauss to Rear Admiral in 1945. In 1947, he went to work for the Atomic Energy Commission as one of the five commissioners. By 1953, President Eisenhower appoint Strauss as Chairman of the AEC, and awarded him the Presidential Medal of Freedom in 1959. 271, 274, 278, 282, 419, 447, 545

Strauss, Oscar (1850–1926) was an American politician who served as Secretary of Commerce under Theodore Roosevelt (1906–1909) and Ambassador to the Ottoman Empire under William Taft (1909–1910). 647–648

Strimpl, Ludvík (1880–1937) was a Czech artist and legionnaire working with the provisional government in Paris. He worked closely with Edvard Beneš. 374, 577, 578

Strother, French (1883–1933) was an American author and editor who worked with Doubleday, Page & Co. which produced Henry

Morgenthau's *All in a Life-time* (1922). He also wrote *Fighting Germany's Spies*, published by Doubleday in 1918. 18, 19

Stuart, Arthur Campbell (1881–1972) was a Canadian newspaper magnate who ran propaganda operations for the British. After raising a regiment in Canada, he became Military Secretary to Lord Northcliff's mission to the US. Then, from London, he served as the deputy director of Propaganda in Enemy Countries. He played a similar role in WWII. 344

Stuart, John McHugh was an American news reporter in Paris for the International News Service. 241

Sullivan, Mark L. (1874–1952) was an American journalist who edited *Collier's Weekly* 1914–1917. In late 1918 and 1919, he was in Paris to manage press issues for the Peace Conference, during which time he filed several articles. 443, 552

Summerall, Charles Pelot (1867–1955) was a senior officer in the US Army, serving in France. Some of commands, especially in November 1918, were controversial. 54, 55, 79

Summers, Leland L. (d. 1927) was an American engineer and head of the Chemical Division of the American War Industries Board. He was one of the first to recognize the military/industrial uses of fertilizers and synthetic chemical industrial products. He was aware that the Germans were amassing these products before 1914 and predicted their wide-spread use. He served as on the Economic Section of the American Commission to Negotiate Peace in Paris 1919. 297

Suydam, Henry West (1891–1955) was an American war correspondent with the *Brooklyn Daily* Eagle 1915–1918. In 1918, he took on confidential work for the US Justice Department and later served as press secretary to Secretary of State John Foster Dulles, 1953–1959. 214, 217

Swan, John Mumford (1870–1949) was an American physician who served in the US Army Medical Corps 1915–1919 at Base Hospital 19 in France. Then he was sent by the Red Cross to investigate health problems in Haiti. Later he was in private practice in Rochester, New York. 83

Sweeney, Walter C. (1875–1963) was an American Army officer serving on Gen. Pershing's staff, replacing Palmer as head of press relations and military censorship. 47, 52, 187

Swift, Eben (1854–1938) was an American army major general who headed the US Military Mission to Italy and was commander of US troops in Italy 1917–1918. 159

Swift, Welsey Merrit was the 3rd secretary at the American Legation in Belgium. 417

Swing, Raymond Gram (1887–1968) was an American journalist both in print and on the radio. He was the leading American voice from Britain during WWI. 91, 129, 162

Swope, Herbert Bayard (1882–1958) was an American journalist. 572

Sychrava, Lev (1887–1958) was a Czech lawyer, journalist and politician. He went to Switzerland in 1914 to publish propaganda for the Czech state. In 1916, he moved to Paris as publisher of the *Czechoslovak Independence*. After completing several diplomatic missions, he was appointed as the first ambassador of Czechoslovakia to France 1918–1924. Between the world wars, ran the National Liberation newspaper. He spent 1939–1945 in the Buchenwald concentration camp. He immigrated to the United Kingdom in 1948. 383

Széchenyi de Sárvár-felsővidék, Count László (1879–1938) was an Austro-Hungarian officer and diplomat who married Gladys Vanderbilt. During WWI they placed their Budapest palace at the disposal of the army, which quartered 600 reservists there. László later became the first Hungarian Minister to the US 1922–1933, and then to the UK. 485

Szende, Pál (1879–1934) was a Hungarian politician who served as Minister of Finance November 1918 to March 1919. 490

Szilassy, Julius von (1870–1935) was a Hungarian diplomat in the Austro-Hungarian Empire. He married American Louise-May Hecker in 1905. He served in various locations before and during WWI, and was one of the few Austrian diplomats to continue in service. He was the first Hungarian envoy to Switzerland from February to April 1919. Later he published books on diplomacy as well as his memoirs. 493

T

Taft, Charles Phelps II "Charley" (1897–1983) was the son of former US President William Taft and younger brother of Bob. He was a lawyer, involved with the YMCA, and later served as Mayor of Cincinnati, Ohio, 1955–1957. 432

Taft, Robert "Bob" (1889–1953) was an American lawyer and politician, and son of former US President William Taft. During 1918 and 1918, he was the legal adviser to Hoover and the ARA. Later he served as Senator from Ohio 1939–1953. 145, 406, 420, 423, 426, 430, 432, 436–4387, 447, 449, 545, 551, 573, 592, 605, 607, 611, 613, 626, 632, 634, 638

Tardieu, André (1876–1945) was a French diplomat who served in the Chamber of Deputies 1914–1924. After enlisting in the army, he was wounded in 1916. He acted as French Prime Minister Clemenceau's lieutenant during the 1919 Paris Peace Conference. Tardieu himself served as Prime Minister of France under several governments between November 1929 and June 1932. 16, 163, 222, 245, 246, 269, 278, 340, 437, 440, 449

Taylor, Captain 227

Taylor, Alonzo Englebert (1871–1949) was an American professor of physiological chemistry at the University of Pennsylvania 1910–1921. He served as the representative secretary of the War Trade Board 1917–1919. Later he became director of the Food Research Institute at Stanford University. He published *The Food Problem* with Vernon Kellogg (1917) and *The New Deal and Foreign Trade* (1935). 211–216, 227, 275, 293, 297, 298, 406–408, 411, 421, 423, 426, 436, 438, 449, 451, 452, 454, 460, 461, 464, 467–470, 474, 476, 477, 481, 486, 487, 495, 497, 498, 543, 564, 565, 568, 570–572, 579, 584, 600, 615, 639, 641, 647, 649–651

Terlinden, Paul (1858–1935) was a Belgian aristocrat serving as Mayor of Rixensart 1884–1921. During the war he was active in alleviating suffering and was arrested and imprisoned by the Germans for his activities in 1917. His wife, Valentine Bosquet, worked as a nurse to the Belgian troops at the front. 560, 561

Thackara, Alexander M. (1848–1937) was an American diplomat serving as Consul General in Paris 1913–1924. 78, 90, 363, 386

Thaw, Benjamin "Ben", Jr. (1888–1937) was an American diplomat serving as secretary of the Embassy in Paris. 1915–1920. He became First Secretary of the Legation in Warsaw under Gibson in 1920. Later he served in London 1930–1933. 219, 293

Thomas, Albert (1878–1932) was a French socialist politician serving as Minister of Armaments 1916–1917. 356, 556

Thomas, James Henry (1874–1949) was a British trade unionist and Labor politician who championed railway workers. He later scandalized the nation with budget leaks in 1936, prompting his exit from politics. 45

Thompson, William Oxley (1855–1933) was an American Presbyterian minister who served as President of Ohio State University 1899–1924. 357

Thompson, William Preston (1895–1961) was an American army officer serving as aide de camp to Gen. Frank McCoy July 1918 to September 1919. 369

Thomson, Basil Home (1861–1939) was a British intelligence and police officer as well as a prison and colonial administrator. In his role as Chief of Criminal Investigation, he interviewed Dutch dancer "Mata Hari" in 1916 and discovered her work with French intelligence. He wrote about this and other experiences in *Queer People* (1922). In 1919, Thomson was appointed Director Intelligence and placed in overall charge of every intelligence agency in the United Kingdom. He served in this capacity until 1921. 425, 426

Thompson, Mlle. 57, 65, 67, 79, 85, 87

Thorpe, Harvey "Harry" (d. November 1918) was an American surgeon from Los Angeles who joined the army to serve as a captain in the medical corps. On his way to Europe, he developed pneumonia after a case of the flu, and passed away at sea. 497

Timmins. 233

Tinant, Major J. Th. was a Belgian Army officer serving in the *Sureté Militaire Belge*. 319

Tisza, István (1861–1918) was the Hungarian Prime Minister twice, 1903–1905 and 1913–1917. Although economically forward-looking, he was a social reactionary who refused even modest land reforms or allowing more than ten percent of the population to vote. He was assassinated on October 31, 1918. 378

Tobey. 324

Tobin, Richard M. "Dick" (1866–1952) was an American banker and diplomat who served in the Naval Reserve in France during WWI. He was the officer in charge of cable traffic between the US and Europe, housed at the Embassy. He also acted as a censor to make certain no secrets were unintentionally revealed. From 1923 to 1929, he served as Minister to the Netherlands. 268

Thomas, Albert (1878–1932) was a French socialist serving as Minister of Armaments during WWI. 184

Tonnelat, Ernest (1877–1948) was a French journalist who was charged with sending propaganda to enemy countries regarding airplanes and their military use. 78–81, 91

Topping, Thomas T. (b. 1884) was an American journalist who served as private secretary to Brand Whitlock, US Minister to Belgium. Topping penned "The Long Vigil" for the *Red Cross Magazine*, January 1918, citing German atrocities. 41, 44, 66, 67, 89, 184, 222, 227, 266, 308, 339, 370

Torrey, Clare Morse (1879–1954) was an American soldier and diplomat. He had volunteered with the CRB and then joined the First Army at Chateau Thierry. Later he worked at the US Embassy in Paris and directed the Finnish Relief Fund in WWII. 234, 235, 273, 283, 545, 566, 635, 638, 648

Tower, Gertrude, was a friend of Cornelia Armsby. 185, 194

Towers, John Henry "Jack" (1885–1955) was an American Naval officer and pioneer aviator. During the war, he supervised the Naval Reserve Flying Corp and became Assistant Director of Naval Aviation. His distinguished naval career was capped with the role of Pacific Commander in 1947. 17

Townsend, Reginald (1890–1977) served as the associate editor of *The World's Work*, published by Doubleday, Page and Co. Extreme myopia prevented him from active military service in 1917, so Townsend became the editor of the *Red Cross Magazine* and went to France in early 1918. After the war, he returned to Doubleday. In retirement, Townsend helped establish Radio Liberty which beamed information to the Soviet Union at the height of the Cold War, along with Radio Free Europe. 24, 34, 326, 354

Train, Harold Cecil (1875–1945) was an American lawyer and Naval Attaché in Rome. He also wrote legal thriller novels. He was

Biographical Index — 733

married to May Philipps (1889–1980). 120, 126

Trainor, Joseph H. (b. 1881) was an American diplomat serving as vice-Consul in Paris 1918–1919. 401

Trotsky, Leon (1879–1940) was a Soviet revolutionary who opposed Stalin's bureaucracy in Russia. Exiled in 1929, Trotsky was assassinated in Mexico City by Soviet agents in 1940. 231, 246, 247, 298

Trubnikoff. 258

Tuck, William Hallam "Friar" (1890–1966) was an American chemical engineer who volunteered for the CRB in 1915. He joined the British Army in 1916, before transferring to the US Army in 1918 where he was a major in the 314th Field Artillery of the 80th division. He married a Belgian woman, Hilda Bunge, in April 1920. After the war, he resumed work with the CRB until 1922. Having developed a friendship with Hoover, Tuck worked with various relief organizations during WWII. In 1946–1947, Tuck accompanied Hoover and Gibson on the Food Survey Missions. He was the recipient of many honors. 282, 283, 395, 549, 553, 555, 573

Tumulty, Joseph P. (1879–1954) was an American attorney and politician who served as the private secretary of President Wilson from 1911 to 1921. 17, 35, 236, 571

Tusar, Vlastimil (1880–1924) was a Czech journalist and politician serving as the Czech representative in Vienna. He had been elected to the Austria Reichsrat in 1911, but played a vital role in the formation of the new Czech state. He remained in Vienna until July 1919 when he became Prime Minister of Czechoslovakia. He then served as ambassador to Berlin 1921–1924. 467, 472, 525

Tweedmouth, see Marjoribanks.

Tyler, Royall (1884–1953) was an American historian who served in the AEF as Chief of American Section, Interallied Bureau, Paris. He was proficient in French, German and Spanish. After the Armistice, he was a Field Observer for the American Commission to Negotiate Peace, 1918–1919. Later he was Financial Adviser to Hungary in 1924. He spent most of WWII in Switzerland doing intelligence work under Allen Dulles. 86, 200, 233, 301, 401, 548

Tyrrell, William "Willy" (1866–1947) was a British diplomat 1889 to 1928, serving as private secretary to Sir Edward Grey 1907–1915. From 1916 to 1919 he was the head of the Political Intelligence Department. Later, he was Ambassador to France 1928–1934 and a member of the Commission on Polish Affairs. 251, 311, 313, 331, 644

U

Umberto II of Italy (1904–1983) was the Crown Prince of Italy and son of Victor Emmanuel III. Upon his father's abdication in 1946 he took the throne but only ruled for only 34 days. 153, 155, 448

Ursel, Louis Marie Alexandre d' (1886–1980) was a Belgian aristocrat and cavalry officer. He was part of the Belgian Mission to the US in August 1917, to which Gibson was attached from the State Department. Later he served as Military Attaché in Paris and later he headed the Belgian embassy in Bern, 1940–1942. 15, 18, 65, 223, 522

V

Van Arsdale. 267

Van Bree, Firmin "Peter" (1880–1960) was a Belgian Chevalier and businessman who served on the General Council of the Catholic University of Louvain and the Board of Directors of the Hoover Foundation. He was a central figure in the Commission for Relief in Belgium, providing both organizational skills and imaginative solutions. 553

Van Deman, Ralph (1865–1952) was an American Army officer and surgeon. In May

1917, the US created the Military Intelligence Section with Van Deman as the head, providing operational intelligence for the AEF in France 1917–1918. After the war, serving under Nolan, Van Deman oversaw security for the Paris Peace Conference and was responsible for 'Negative Intelligence' for the American Commission to Negotiate Peace. Between the world wars, he had several more tours of duty and retired in 1929. During WWII, he was consulted by the War Department on matters of intelligence and received the Legion of Merit award. 189, 232, 233, 236, 301, 308, 343, 352, 353, 366, 402, 438, 617, 645

Van den Branden, Adrien, of Reeth (1899–1980) was a Belgian lawyer, magistrate and politician serving as a public prosecutor in Brussels. For much of WWI, he was a political prisoner and again in WWII. After the war he served briefly from August 1945 to March 1946 as Minister for War Victims. 229, 236, 240, 241

Vanderbilt, Gladys (1886–1965) was the youngest daughter of Cornelius Vanderbilt and first cousin of Consuelo Vanderbilt who became Duchess of Malborough. She married Hungarian Count László Széchenyi (1879–1938) in 1908 who was a military officer, diplomat and venture capitalist. During WWI, they placed their Budapest palace at the disposal of the army, which quartered 600 reservists there. László served as the first Hungarian Minister to the US 1922–1933 and then to Britain. 23, 485

Vandervelde, Emile (1866–1938) was a Belgian politician and socialist. As Minister of State in 1914, he supported the concept of resistance to the German invasion. He was a delegate for Belgium to the Paris Peace Conference and Treaty of Versailles, and later the League of Nations. 394

Van Dyke, Paul (1859–1933) was an American historian and brother of Henry van Dyke. He taught history and political science at Princeton after 1898. 90, 152

Van Rensselaer Berry, Walter (1859–1927) was an American lawyer and diplomat serving as President of the American Chamber of Commerce in Paris 1916–1923. 222, 258

Van Rensselaer, Mariana (1851–1934) was an American author on architectural criticism, fiction and children's literature. She was married to Schuyler Van Rensselaer. 383

Van Rensselaer, Stephen (1764–1839) was one of the founding fathers of the United States and politician in New York. 323

Venizelos, Eleftherios (1864–1932) was the Greek Prime Minister 1910–1920 and again 1928–1930. 197

Vermeren, Mme. 67

Victor Emmanuel III of Italy (1869–1947) reigned as King of Italy from 1900 until his abdication in 1946. 159, 261, 448, 449

Villeroy, Mr. 378

Vix, Fernand (1876–1941) was a French army officer serving as head of the military mission to Hungary. He arrived in Budapest in November 1918 to oversee the implementation of the armistice terms. He transmitted several reports between December and January, but is most remembered for the one on March 20, 1919 which precipitated the resignation of Karolyi. He left Hungary on March 26, and continued his military career. At the onset of WWII, he was in commander of the French 54th Infantry Division. 519, 520, 523

Viereck, George Sylvester (1884–1962) was a German-American writer and publicist and grandson of German Emperor Wilhelm I. After studying law and political science, he became a journalist for several social democratic newspapers. Between 1907 and 1912, he was known for his Germanophile propaganda. During WWI, he wrote for *The International* and *The Fatherland* to counteract the work of the CPI. Later, he wrote pamphlets for Adolf Hitler and worked with Henry Ford on the America First Committee. He spend from 1942 to 1947 in prison, which he described in *Men and Beasts* (1952). 398

Vilgrain, Ernest (1880–1942) was a French industrialist and wheat mill owner serving as Under-Secretary of State for Food Supply 1917–1920. 419

Villalobar, Rodrigo de Saavedra (1864–1926) was the Spanish Ambassador to Belgium 1913–1926. He and Gibson worked closely together during the early days of the war, and later, Villalobar was the best man at Gibson's 1922 wedding. XV, 64, 65, 394, 395, 404, 410, 553

Villard, Oswald Garrison (1872–1949) was an American journalist who covered stories in Germany, returning to Paris in March 1919. 606

Viviani, René (1863–1925) was a French politician and diplomat who had served as Prime Minister 1914–1915. In 1917, he led a mission to the US to garner military support along with Marshall Joffre. 65, 175, 185, 222, 440

Vollenhoven, Maurits (1882–1976) was the Dutch Minister in Brussels when the war began. He left his legation in Gibson's hands. Later he served as Dutch Minister to Spain where he died. 410

Vopicka, Charles (1857–1935) was a Czech American who served as the US Minister to Romania, Serbia and Bulgaria 1913–1920. 380

Voska, Emanuel Victor (187–1960) was a Czech patriot who collaborated with US intelligence during both WWI and WWII. He worked closely with Tomáš Masaryk, first president of Czechoslovakia. Voska is credited with exposing the Hindu-German conspiracy of 1914–1917 that attempted to ally Indian independence movements with surging national movements in Europe. In 1917, Voska traveled to Petrograd with British agent Somerset Maugham with the objective of propping up the Provisional Government. 232, 274, 396, 397, 401, 526, 535, 540

Vrbenský, Bohuslav (1882–1944) was a Czech dentist, journalist, politician and was a founder of the Federation of Czech Anarchists. He spent much of the war years in Austrian custody. After joining the Czech Socialist Party in 1918. He served as Czechoslovakia Minister of Nutrition November 1918-July 1919, Minister of Public Works May-September 1920, and Minister of Health September 1921-October 1922. 478, 539

W

Waddington, Mary King (1833–1923) was an American author who wrote primarily about her life as the wife of French diplomat, William Waddington. Throughout WWI she helped to raise funds to help soldiers and refugees. 60

Waddington, William Henry (1826–1894) was a French statesman who served as Prime Minister in 1879 and Ambassador to Britain 1883–1893. He was married to Mary King Waddington. 60

Wadsworth, Eliot W. (1876–1959) was an American diplomat serving in Belgium. Later, in 1922, he was appointed as Chargé d'Affairs of the US Ministry in Belgium. 68, 95, 120

Wadsworth, James W. "Jim", Jr. (1846–1926) was an American politician serving as the US Senator from New York 1915–1927. Later he served in the House of Representatives 1933–1951. 401, 405, 420, 423, 425

Waepenaert, Charles Chevalier de was a Belgian aristocrat who served as Consul General in Cuba 1908–1917. Gibson nicknamed him "Waffleiron." 94, 614

Walcott, Frederic Collin (1869–1949) was an assistant to Hoover in the US Food Administration and ARA during WWI. Later he was elected Senator in Connecticut 1925–1929, and the to the US Senate 1929–1935 During WWII, he was outspoken in his support of Poland and served as co-director of the Commission for Polish Relief 1939–1942. 268–273, 282, 299, 334, 338, 339, 341, 626

Waldo, Captain. 246, 276

Walker, Major 47

Wallace, Hugh Campbell (1864–1931) was an American politician and diplomat who served as Ambassador to France 1919–1922. He was married to Mildred Fuller Wallace. 573

Wallace, Willie. 443, 574, 611

Walrand, Jules Henry (1852–1920) was a French politician serving as mayor of Maubeuge 1888–1919, throughout the German occupation. 419

Walton, E.S., was the US Army quartermaster in Trieste. 500, 501

Waltz, Jean-Jacques (1873–1951), better known as "Hansi", was an Alsatian cartoonist who not only produced idyllic landscapes, but also famous anti-German motives during the First and the Second World War. He was tried by German authorities in 1914 and fled to Switzerland to join the t finally tracked him down in Agen in Southern France and beat him almost to death. He survived and fled again to Switzerland, but died soon after the war. 80, 184

Wanger, Walter (1894–1968) was an American film producer and aviation officer in the Signal Corps in Italy during WWI. He worked on propaganda issues with COMPUB. Wanger's last film was *Cleopatra* (1963). 143, 144, 153–155, 231–233, 249, 250, 370, 371, 375, 393

Warburton, Barclay Harding (1866–1954) was an American diplomat and publisher of the Philadelphia Evening Telegraph. He served as Chargé d'Affairs in London 1914–1917, and then as an aide-de-camp for Pershing in Paris, becoming Military Attaché in March 1918. 180, 235, 258, 260, 350, 386, 387

Ward, Cabot (1876–1936) was an American Army intelligence officer specializing in counter- intelligence. He received a Distinguished Service Award for his contributions. 33, 87, 90, 164–166, 167, 182, 202, 230, 248, 250–252, 254, 260, 288, 291, 302, 327, 337, 347, 382, 383, 393, 394, 399, 400, 636, 640

Ward, John. 557, 572

Ward, Herbert (1863–1919) was a British sculptor, artist and African explorer. During WWI he turned his French home into a field hospital and served in the British Ambulance Committee. He was wounded on duty in 1915, and died in August 1919 from the lingering effects of that injury. He was posthumously awarded the Croix de Guerre. In former US President Theodore Roosevelt's words of 1913, there was "in Paris no more interesting character than Herbert Ward [...] All the mystery and the savagery and the suffering and the ugliness and the harsh beauty of the African forest come out in Mr. Ward's works. Only an artist could have done what he has done, and no artists could have done it had there not lain within him the soul of a great man, a man both strong and pitiful." *The Outlook*, May 17, 1913, p. 100 577, 579, 580

Waroqué, Raoul (1870–1917) was a Belgian industrialist who financed the Brussels World's Fairs of 1897 and 1910. He left his fortune to the Guinotte family. 628

Warren, Whitney (1864–1973) was an American architect of the Beaux-Arts school. During WWI, he was an organizer for Comité des Étudiants Américains de l'École des Beaux-Arts Paris, a student charity in support of the French cause. He also championed the claims of Italy in the Adriatic. 202

Washburn, Stanley (1878–1950) was an American journalist who had served as a special correspondent with *Collier's Weekly* and *The London Times*, traveling to and writing about conditions in Russia and later in Romania and France. He published *Victory in Defeat: The Agony of Warsaw and the Russian Retreat* (1916) and *The Russian Campaign, April to August 1915* (1916). In 1917 he returned to Russia as a military aide on two American diplomatic missions. He was commissioned into the US army in 1918 and did intelligence work in the Toul and Chateau-Thierry sectors. Later Washburn worked in several diplomatic posts. Later he became president of the North Dakota Coal Operators Association 1925–1935. 13, 243, 245, 246, 262, 300

Waterbury, Anne "Nancy" (1903–1959) was the daughter of wealthy stockbroker Lawrence Waterbury II (1877–1943). 630, 631

Watson, Capt., Lt, Major (ranks changed over time) 76, 191, 220

Watson, Edwin Martin "Pa" (1883–1945) was an American Army lieutenant who served as a junior military aide to President Wilson. He arrived in France in spring 1917 and earned both the Silver Star and Croix de Guerre for his distinguished service. He remained in Paris during the Peace Conference, helping draft the Treaty of Versailles. Later he served as a senior military aide to President Franklin Roosevelt. He attended both the Teheran and Yalta Conferences, unfortunately suffering a fatal stroke on the return voyage. 47, 76, 191–193, 220, 245, 352, 367

Watson, Grant. 589

Webb, Electra Havemeyer (1888–1960) was an American art collector who drove ambulances in New York City during the war. Later she established the Shelburne Museum in Vermont. 432

Wedda, John Q. was a Polish-American and secretary of the Polish National Alliance and Polish Immigration League in 1918, as well as US Representative for Polish matters. 369, 393

Weir, William D. (1877–1959) was a Scottish industrialist and politician serving as President of the Air Council in 1918–1919. 264, 293

Weiskirchner, Richard (1861–1926) was an Austrian lawyer and politician who served as mayor of Vienna from January 1913 to May 1919. 452

Wekerle, Sándor (1848–1921) was a Hungarian politician who served three terms as Prime Minister: 1892–1895, 1906–1910, and August 20 to October 23, 1918. 360

Wellington, Laurence C. "Duke" (b. 1891) was an American graduate of Oxford who volunteered for the CRB in 1915. Much of his work on the reconstruction in Belgium was wiped out again during the offensives of 1918. 68, 75, 84, 235, 395, 421, 596

Wellman, Mrs. 235

Wemyss, Rosslyn (1864–1933) was a British Navy Admiral. He represented Britain at the signing of the Armistice. It was his request for the timing to be 11:00 am to compliment the 11th day of the 11th month. He served as British Naval representative at the Paris Peace Conference 1918–1919. He was made 1st Baron Wemyss in 1919. 403, 407, 448, 585, 588, 600, 612

Wetter, Charles H. (1880–1952) was an American army officer serving in France during and after WWI. 544

Weygand, Maxime (1867–1965) was a Belgian-born French army officer who served under Foch in WWI. Later, in 1940. He signed an armistice and collaborated with the Germans as part of Vichy France. 70, 254

Wharton, Edith (1862–1937) was an American novelist and playwright. Throughout WWI she worked for the relief of war refugees and children, and was one of the first foreigner allowed to visit the French front in August 1915. She published several books during the war years and was the first woman to win the Pulitzer Prize for Literature in 1921 for *The Age of Innocence* (1920) 638

Wheeler, John Neville "Jack" (1886–1973) was an American journalist and publishing executive. He founded the Wheeler Syndicate in 1913 and sent Richard H. Davis to Europe as a war correspondent. Gibson was instructed to help him in any way possible. From 1930 to 1966, he managed the North American Newspaper Alliance of over 50 major newspapers. 267, 332

Wheeler, Roy, of the *New York Tribune*. 233

Whipple, A.D was an American who represented Bell Telephone Company and Western Electric Company in Antwerp. He took charge of the house on Vieux Dieu where the head of Western Electric had been located as the Germans invaded Belgium. Whipple was able to leave Antwerp in August 1917, after spending most of the war in German occupied Belgium. He was then reassigned to Paris as of January 1918. 267

White, Francis (1892–1961) was an American diplomat who shared living quarters in Washington with other young diplomats when in town. He served as Minister to Czechoslovakia (1933), Ambassador to Mexico (1953–1957) and to Sweden (1957–1958). 47n

White, John Beaver (1874–1946) was an American volunteer in the CRB serving with Hoover's organization, soon to be the ARA. Later he served on the Fellowship Committee for the Belgian American Educational Foundation. 298, 592, 605, 607

White, Henry (1850–1927) was an American diplomat who served as Ambassador to Italy 1905, where he mediated at the 1906 Algeciras Conference, settling the dispute between France and Germany over economic issues in Morocco. From 1906–1909, he served as Ambassador to France. White's daughter married a German aristocrat, and White found himself sequestered in Berlin for two weeks at the beginning of the war. He was released with his grandchildren. Having strong ties to both Britain and Germany, White remained neutral, which garnered favor with President Wilson. White was appointed as one of the five American Peace Commissioners sent to Paris to develop a peace treaty with Germany in December 1918. He was a signatory to the Treaty of Versailles, and remained until December 1919 to lead the delegation after President Wilson and Secretary of State Lansing returned to the US. He would prove instrumental in obtaining funds for Gibson's future Legation in Warsaw. 132, 440, 547, 563, 595, 643, 649

White, Lawrence Grant "Larry" (1887–1956) was an American architect who served in the Navy during WWI. 132–133, 146–147, 152, 155, 159

White, Sanford B. (1888–1964) was a leading sportsman at Princeton before representing International Harvester Corp in the Midwest. He chaired the Liberty Loan committee at Princeton and enlisted in the Aviation Section Signal Corps in January 1918. 133

White, William Allen (1868–1944) was an American newspaper editor and leader in the Progressive movement. He was a strong supporter of the League of Nations and criticized the isolationism that kept the US out of the League. 552

Whitehouse, Edwin Sheldon (1883–1965) was an American diplomat who served as secretary in Paris, Madrid, Athens, Stockholm, and Saint Petersburg between 1911 and 1919. He participated in the American Commission to Negotiate Peace in Paris 1919, and went on to serve as US Minister to Guatemala 1930–1033 and Colombia 1933–1934. 643

Whitehouse, James Norman de Rapelye (1883–1965) was an American stock broker in New York. He married Vira Boarman Whitehouse in 1898 and they had one daughter, Alice Whitehouse Hjares. 47, 51, 187, 203, 338

Whitehouse, Vira Boarman (1875–1957) was the Director of the Swiss office of ComPub from January to April, and again from July to December 1918. She was an American suffragette, birth control advocate, and owner of the Whitehouse Leather Company. Her controversial work and conflict with US Ambassador to Switzerland, Pleasant Stovall, were some of the issues Gibson was tasked to resolve. She was married to Norman de Rapelye Whitehouse and they had one daughter, Alice Whitehouse Hjares. 37, 49, 63, 68, 71, 76, 91, 94, 97, 99–101, 105, 108, 109, 129, 162, 178, 183, 195, 198, 201, 203, 204, 211, 216, 223, 231, 236, 244, 301, 326, 329, 333, 351, 399

Whiteley, James Gustavus (1866–1947) was an American businessman and financier who promoted the interests of Leopold II, King of the Belgians, in the US. He became an outspoken advocate in the US against the German occupation of Belgium. 20

Whitfield, Paul (1880–1953) was a British naval command who led attacks on German battle cruisers during the Battle of Juttland. His ship, the HMS Nomad, was sunk by enemy fire and he was captured on May 31, 1916. He was held at German prison camps in Mainz, Friedberg, Konstanz and Crefeld. He was expatriated near the end of the war, in time to meet Gibson in Rome on May 31, 1918. 345

Whitlock, Brand (1869–1934) was an American journalist, lawyer and politician who served as Mayor of Toledo, Ohio 1904–1914. He was sent by President Wilson as US Minister to Belgium in 1913, and later upgraded to Ambassador (1919–1921). Gibson served under him during his time in Belgium, 1914–1915. Whitlock published his book on his WWI experience *Belgium under the German occupation: A Personal Narrative* (William Heinemann, 1919) two years after Gibson published *A Journal from Our Legation in Belgium* (Doubleday Page, 1917). 41, 67, 356, 370, 387, 414, 416, 418, 427, 428, 431, 432, 437, 569, 595, 599, 620

Whitlock, Ella Brainerd (1876–1942) was the second wife of Brand Whitlock. She served with him in Belgium 1913–1921. 67, 414, 416

Whitman, Charles S. (1868–1947) was an American politician who served as Governor of New York 1915–1918. He and Mayor John Mitchel were highly competitive, especially over the visit of French Marshal Joffre in May 1917. 153, 154

Whitney, Caspar William (1864–1929) was an American author and war correspondent. He is noted for his coverage of the front in Cuba 1898 and the front in France 1918, and his service in Belgium with the CRB. He was also the President of the American Olympic Committee 1906–1910. 164, 218

Whitney, Courtney (1887–1969) was an American lawyer and army pilot in WWI. Later he served in the Air Force in WWII. 550

Whitridge, Arnold (1892–1989) was an American student at Oxford University who volunteered for the British Royal Field Artillery at the outbreak of WWI, for which he was awarded the British Military Cross for gallantry. He transferred to the US Army as soon as the US entered the war in 1917. Later he taught history at Yale and was president of Calhoun College 1932–1942. In 1942 he served in the Army Air Corps in Europe, Africa and India. 372, 378, 450, 568, 569, 595, 596, 598, 599

Whitridge, Janetta Alexander (1890–1973) was the daughter of New York attorney and financier Charles Beatty Allexander, who maintained a home in Paris. On April 25, 1918, she married Arnold Whitridge. She became a civic leader in New York. 230, 250, 296, 308, 326, 331, 332, 334, 338, 350, 351, 372, 378, 551, 569

Wiborg, May Hoyt "Hoyty" (1888–1964) was an American socialite from New York living in Paris. She was active in the Red Cross and drove ambulances for a French hospital near Meaux. 432

Wickes, Francis (1890–1974) was an American lawyer from Rochester, New York, who served in the CRB. As of spring 1918, he was attached to the press division of the Intelligence Service in Paris. 42, 84, 185, 197, 235, 239, 263, 269, 282, 283, 287, 340, 421

Wielowieyski, Jozef (1879–1951) was the Counselor of the Polish Legation in Paris and a member of the National Committee. 348 photo

Wilber, David Forrest (1859–1928) was an American farmer and vice-president/director of the Wilber National Bank of Oneonta 1883–1896. After serving in Congress as the US Representative from New York 1895–1999, he served as Consul General in Zurich 1913–1915 and Genoa 1915–1921. 117

Wilhelm II, German Kaiser (1859–1941) was the Emperor of Germany from 1888 until his abdication on November 9, 1918. 107, 127, 224, 229–230, 355, 388, 404

Wilhelm, German Crown Prince (1882–1951) was the eldest son and heir of Emperor Wilhelm II. During WWI, he commanded the German 5th Army 1914–1916. He was in command of the German forces during the Verdun Offensive that ended in German failure, and he resigned in November 1916. He was later tried by the Allies as a war criminal and finished his life under house arrest. 111, 389, 391

Willard, Joseph E. (1865–1924) was an American politician and diplomat serving as Ambassador to Spain 1913–1921. 37, 255, 330, 644

Willert, Albert. *Washington Times* correspondent. 550

Williams, Churchill 37

Williams, Commander. 187

Williams, Herbert O. (1887–1967) was an American businessman serving as Commercial Attaché at the Embassy in Paris in 1918. Later he served as Consul in Brussels 1924. 164

Williams, Roger. 263

Wills, Davis B. was an American military and intelligence officer serving as Chief Paymaster for the US Marine Corps in France. He was married to Edith Wills. 41, 75, 84, 164, 220, 229, 233, 244, 258, 259, 263, 296, 306, 332, 340, 362, 373–375, 381, 392, 568, 578

Wills, Edith, was married to Davis Wills. 359, 362, 367, 373, 375, 378, 381, 392, 450, 568, 574

Wilson, Charles S. "Charley" (1873–1947) was an American career diplomat who served as chargé d'affairs in Bulgaria 1919–1921, Minister to Romania 1921–1928 and Yugoslavia 1933–1937. 235, 330

Wilson, F.M. Huntington (1875–1946) was an American diplomat who served as Assistant Secretary of State from 1909 to 1913. Gibson acted as his private secretary (1912–1913). After his diplomatic career, he became a writer, banker and manufacturer. Finally, he served as Director of the Philadelphia Commercial Museum (1928–1932). Wilson married Lucy James (1880–1938) in 1904, but they divorced in 1915. Lucy became god-mother to Gibson's son, Michael Francis upon his birth in 1929. 19, 21

Wilson, Havelock (1859–1929) was a British politician and advocate for the merchant seamen. He avidly supported Britain's involvement in WWI. 341

Wilson, Henry Braid (1861–1954) was a US Naval Commander in the Atlantic during WWI 388, 548

Wilson, Hugh Robert (1885–1946) was an American diplomat who served in Guatemala, Argentina, Germany, Austria, Japan, and Switzerland. He was Minister to Switzerland from 1927 to 1937 when he became Assistant Secretary of State. From March to November 1938, he served as Ambassador to Germany. He was married to Katherine Boyle. 61, 68, 89, 93, 96–103, 106, 108–109, 111, 114, 129, 139, 152, 170, 180, 183–186, 188–190, 194,

195, 197, 198, 203, 220, 231, 235–239, 241, 283, 301, 333, 340, 357, 361, 387, 389–391, 438, 451–455, 560, 562, 564, 568, 571, 574, 653

Wilson, Katherine Boyle was married to Hugh R. Wilson 95, 105, 454, 562, 563

Wilson, Thomas Woodrow (1856–1924) was an American statesman and academic. He served as the 28th President of the United States from 1913 to 1921. He is known for his commitment to democratic principles and the concept of national self-determination and reconstruction in Europe following WWI. Also referred to as 'the President' and 'the Great White Chief.' 1, 2, 5, 20, 52, 61, 71, 73, 82, 86, 92, 93, 97, 104, 105, 107, 125, 143–146, 150, 154, 162, 163, 166, 186–189, 194, 216, 221, 236, 239, 255, 268, 271, 276, 279, 286, 289, 290, 300, 301, 305, 306, 314, 321, 329, 331, 343, 350, 351, 354–362, 365, 368, 369, 371, 372, 374, 376, 377, 379, 386, 391, 393, 395, 398, 400, 401, 419, 420, 437, 438, 440–446, 448, 478, 489, 495, 496, 500, 507, 521, 526, 546–551, 571, 581, 583, 584, 591–593, 595, 596, 599, 607, 608, 619–621, 628, 630, 635–640, 643, 645, 650, 651

Winship, North (1885–1968) was an American Foreign Service Officer acting as Consul in Milan 1917- 1921. Later he served as Minister, then Ambassador to South Africa 1948–1949. 115, 117, 118, 120, 122

Winspeare. 588

Wirth, Frederick, Jr. was an American diplomat serving as vice-consul in Zurich 1918–1919. 106, 108

Wise, Frederick M. was an American Marine officer 1899–1926. 220

Wiseman, William (1885–1962) was a British intelligence officer and banker. From 1914 to 1918, he was the head of the British Military Mission to the US, working closely with Gen. Julius Klein and Col. Edward House. After participating in the Paris Peace Conference he became a partner in the American investment bank, Kuhn, Loeb & Co. from 1929 to 1960. 60, 134, 137, 235, 374

Withers, Miss 194

Witterspach, Lt. 198

Withington, Robert, was a volunteer with the CRB. 282

Wittouck, Albertine Brandies (1872–1957) was born into the Viennese Jewish banking family of Heinrich Brandies. She married Franz Wittouck (1855–1914), who, with Paul Wittouck, bought the Tirlemont sugar refinery in 1894. They owned a house on avenue de la Toison d'Or in Brussels and a country home, Villa Les Bouleaux at Tervuren. She was the mother of Jean, Elisabeth and Marie-Thérèse. 416, 417, 540, 554, 590

Wittouck, Jacques (1882–1987) was a Belgian reserve lieutenant during WWI and an administrator for Sucreire de Pontelongo (sugar refinery) 1910–1948 as well as a silk factory in Tubize. He was commissioner of the Bank of Hainaut 1915–1934, Belgian consul in Monte Carlo and vice-president of Clabecq (steel refinery) 1946–1948. 292

Wittouck, Jean (1891–1984) was a Belgian army officer and son of Albertine and François Wittouck. 417, 418

Wood, Leona P. [1860–1952] was an American nurse who ran a hospital in Belgium. Although Gibson routinely refers to her as "Aunt Leona," it is unclear if she is a relative or if this is an honorary title. There is, however, a strong current of communication and affection between the families. 18, 51, 68, 254, 301, 306, 307, 331, 446, 448–450, 460, 560, 585, 620

Wood, Warren was the son of the woman Gibson refers to as Aunt Leona (Wood). It is not certain if they are related or if "Aunt" is an honorary title. 17, 18, 19, 20, 21, 68, 306, 447, 585, 620

Woodell, Consul General at Athens. 372

Woods, Arthur (1870–1942) was the New York City Police Commissioner from 1914 to

1918. During 1918, he became assistant director of the CPI and a lieutenant colonel in the AEF, Division of Military Aeronautics. In 1920, he received medals from the US, the UK and France for his service. He was married to Helen Morgan Hamilton 14, 15, 17, 271

Woods, Helen Morgan Hamilton (1896–1985) was an American socialite, a descendant of Alexander Hamilton, and granddaughter of J.P Morgan. She was married to Arthur Woods from 1916 until his death in 1942. She served in the Women's Auxiliary Army Corps during WWII, and helped administer the Marshall Plan. Later she married Warren Randolph Burgess. 331

Woodward, Mrs. 132

Woolley, Clarence M. (1863–1956) was an American equipment manufacturer who specialized in gas radiators. He served as a representative on the War Trade Board and as Secretary of the Commerce and War Industries Board in 1918. 331, 372

Woolsey, Lester H. (1877–1961) was an American lawyer serving as Solitictor (legal advisor) of the State Department since June 1917 under Robert Lansing. 363

Worthington-Evans, Laming (1868–1931) was a British politician serving as Minister of Blockade in 1918. Both before and after this post he held many high level positions in the British government including Secretary of State for War 1921–1922. 228

Wouters d'Oplinter, Ferdinand de (1868–1942) was a Belgian politician who served as Minister of Economic Affairs in 1920 and represented Belgium at the League of Nations. 415

Wright, Irene Aloha (1879–1972) was an American historian. After graduating from Stanford University in 1904, she was a writer in Cuba, where she bought and ran the *Cuban Magazine*. She published several books on Cuban history, earning awards from both Cuba and Spain. 614

Wright, Joshua Butler (1877–1939) was an American diplomat serving as Counselor in London. Later he served as Ambassador to Hungary 1927, Uruguay 1930, Czechoslovakia 1934, and Cuba 1937–1939. 372, 641

X – Y – Z

Yarnell, Harry Ervin (1875–1959) was an American Naval officer serving as Aide to Commander Admiral William Sims for US Naval Forces Operating in European Water from December 1917 to September 1918. He was awarded the Navy Cross for his distinguished service. He retired with the rank of Rear Admiral in 1942 but acted as special adviser to the Chinese Military Mission in 1942. 147, 153

Young, Wallace J. (1880–1923) was an American diplomat who served as Consul in Carlsbad 1914–1917, Prague 1919–1920, and Bradford 1922–1923. 592, 611, 621, 627, 638

Zeigler, Captain 233

Zamoyski, Maurycy Klemens (1871–1939) was a Polish aristocrat and leader in the Polish National Council. He and his family had been actively involved in the war efforts: Zamoyski had been decorated by the Russian army, his wife ran a canteen for Polish troops and his son was an aide to Gen. Haller. After the war, Zamoyski would serve as the first Ambassador of Poland to France 1919–1924 and briefly as Foreign Minister in 1924. He was the owner of the Blue Palace in Warsaw which would become the US Legation under Gibson in July 1919. 4, 348, 353, 357, 364, 374

Zichliski, K.Z., was the president of the Polish National Alliance in 1919. 652

Znamięcki, Alexander (1884–1964) was a Polish American who served with Paderewski in Paris and Poland. He worked with the ARA during 1918–1919 461, 463, 466, 467, 638, 653, 654

Place Index

Abbeville 70, 150, 308, 316, 408
Amiens 44, 46, 60, 66, 69–71, 109, 168, 179, 181, 196, 207
Arizona 13
Austria 2, 4–5, 46, 61, 66, 68, 71, 96, 99, 104–106, 120–121, 124–125, 135–136, 139, 142, 144, 146–147, 153, 163, 166, 186, 194, 207, 209–210, 231, 240, 248–250, 278–279, 304, 339, 346, 350, 360, 363, 365, 368, 375–376, 378–381, 383, 386, 389, 392, 417, 419, 436, 452–453, 462–463, 465, 467, 469, 472, 475–476, 482–483, 486–489, 496, 500–501, 511, 519, 523–524, 537, 539, 541, 547, 550, 653
Avesness 418–419

Barcelona 254
Beauvias 308
Belgium 2, 6–7, 12–13, 16, 41, 53, 56–57, 61, 64, 67, 125, 133, 146, 195, 207, 223, 229–230, 233, 240, 244, 269, 274, 342, 370, 373, 380, 383, 390, 394, 400–401, 409, 413–415, 421, 423–424, 472, 475–476, 513, 552–553, 559, 570, 615, 617, 633, 647, 652
Bellegarde 244, 451, 543, 555, 561
Berlin 7, 46, 60, 94, 100, 212, 360, 365, 390, 406, 409, 474, 480, 510, 563–565, 568, 582
Bern 7, 20, 39, 68, 72, 78, 81, 86, 91–92, 95–96, 100, 102–103, 105, 114, 120, 152–153, 169, 181, 184, 209, 233, 236, 241, 299, 305, 331–334, 340, 349, 364, 374, 389, 438, 449, 451–454, 456–457, 459–460, 462, 470, 493, 501, 541–542, 549–550, 556, 559–560, 573, 592, 599, 636
Bordeaux 30, 34, 36, 38, 65, 71, 76, 90, 183, 202, 232, 552
Boulogne 208, 271–272, 298, 309–310, 316, 320, 329, 341, 347, 401–402, 408, 413, 425, 434–435, 438, 584
Brighton 404–406, 580–581

Brussels 2, 6–7, 11, 16, 224, 272, 274, 289, 322, 355, 371, 385, 387, 389, 394–395, 398, 406, 410–411, 413, 418, 422, 426–432, 436–437, 446–447, 450, 466–467, 545, 550–552, 554, 565, 568–569, 575, 580, 584, 586, 589–591, 595, 599–600, 603, 606–607, 610–611, 617, 619, 626–627, 635, 643
Buchs 461–462, 464, 541, 653
Budapest 5, 465, 467–468, 470, 473–474, 485–488, 493, 495, 497, 514–516, 568, 607, 614, 617, 646

Calais 208, 290, 313, 315–316, 320, 337, 568
Cambrai 43, 45, 345, 356, 359, 411, 413
Chaisso 104
Compiègne 38, 41, 66, 73, 75, 195, 207, 411, 418–419, 631
Czechoslovakia 4, 369, 379, 525, 527

Didcot 312–313
Dover 313–314
Dunkirk 208, 235, 306, 313, 315–316, 320

England 4, 45, 70–71, 74, 98, 101, 122, 126, 134, 166, 169, 171, 184, 186, 209, 217, 233, 236–238, 242, 244, 246, 249, 257, 266, 270, 274–276, 302–304, 306, 319, 323, 329, 334, 338–339, 351, 356, 359, 393, 398, 400, 404, 415, 426, 446, 479, 495, 566, 570, 575–576, 582, 618–619, 623, 630, 638, 646
Étaples 316

Feldkirk 462–463
France 2, 4, 7, 11, 24–25, 45, 47, 50, 60, 65–67, 69–71, 73–74, 82, 85, 90, 92, 101, 134, 144, 152, 171, 185–186, 189, 192, 194, 208–209, 212, 214–215, 231, 233, 238, 240, 242, 244, 247–249, 252, 254, 256–258, 260–261, 266, 276–277, 279, 285, 289, 292, 295, 297, 303–304, 306, 308, 313, 330–331, 334, 336, 339, 345–

Place Index

346, 357, 360, 367, 377, 398, 400, 405, 407, 415, 421, 427, 435, 448, 465–466, 472, 475, 477, 479, 495–496, 513, 567, 575–576, 582, 584, 586, 591, 594–595, 602, 620, 623, 626, 647

Geneva 61, 89, 92, 97, 107, 111, 169, 178, 239, 379, 399, 451, 542–543, 556, 561
Germany 1–2, 7, 30, 38, 40, 42, 45, 47, 62, 69, 71, 78, 81, 94, 97, 99, 101–102, 105, 112–113, 119, 135, 143, 169–170, 186–189, 202, 207, 209–210, 213, 224, 228, 234, 236, 239–242, 246–247, 249, 254, 256–257, 273, 276, 287, 299, 304, 327, 329–330, 345–346, 350, 352, 354–355, 359, 363–365, 382–384, 386, 388, 391, 393, 397, 404, 412–414, 417–418, 434, 436, 456, 465, 474–476, 479, 484, 496, 501, 542, 549, 568, 570, 575–576, 584, 587, 595, 597, 600, 606, 618, 622–623
Gouffliers 315–316
Great Britain see England
Guiscard 411–412
Guise 418–419

Hal 411
Ham 38, 411–412
Havre 18, 30, 46, 63, 269, 324–325, 378, 426, 552
Hungary 1–2, 116, 166, 207, 308, 360, 369, 376, 378, 389, 473, 487–490, 492–496, 499, 510, 516, 518–520, 606, 614, 618, 622

Italy 11, 37, 42, 44, 46, 60, 68, 71, 74, 80, 85, 91, 95, 110–111, 115, 117–118, 121–124, 127, 129–130, 134, 137, 140, 142–144, 148–151, 157–159, 179–180, 186, 194, 210, 212, 215, 220, 227, 236, 240, 248–249, 252, 261, 266, 269–270, 279, 288, 290, 297, 299–302, 338–340, 353, 368, 378, 400, 415, 448–449, 474–475, 482, 495–496, 500, 506–507, 564–565, 580, 582, 623

Kansas 13

La Capelle 418–419
Le Catelet 411
Le Hamel 70
Leysin 6, 452–457, 459–460, 542, 550, 554–559, 584, 616
Lille 365–366, 381, 427, 550–554, 589, 635
Lisbon 20, 24, 63, 571, 609
London 2, 7, 11, 16, 20, 34, 37, 39, 42, 46, 48, 54, 60, 63, 70, 86, 98, 134, 136, 138, 151, 157, 170, 179, 195, 211–212, 214–215, 239, 251, 266–268, 270–271, 289, 293, 296–298, 305, 310–313, 320–324, 331–333, 335, 340–344, 346–347, 351, 357, 359, 363, 366–367, 369, 372, 376, 378, 383, 388, 392, 402, 404, 405, 407, 419–420, 422–423, 425–426, 428, 431, 434, 437–438, 450, 459, 488, 550–551, 556–567, 571, 574, 590, 597, 606, 609, 620, 626, 628, 635–637, 639–640, 642

Madrid 20, 132, 211, 235, 252, 255, 258, 323, 346, 360, 377, 608, 613
Maugeuge 418–419
Milan 74, 104, 115, 117, 159
Mons 411, 413, 418–419
Montreuil 316
Montreux 452–453, 455, 559, 561, 613

Noyon 38, 411–412, 418, 631–632

Ostrava 522, 525, 533, 535, 537–538, 607

Paris 1–6, 9, 11–12, 20, 24, 30–34, 36–38, 41, 44–45, 47, 52–53, 56–57, 59, 63, 65–68, 71–79, 84–90, 101–102, 120, 125, 131–133, 135, 139–140, 143, 146–147, 150–153, 159–161, 163, 165–166, 169–176, 178–187, 189–190, 193–198, 200–202, 206–208, 211–221, 223, 226–231, 233, 235–241, 244–245, 248–252, 254, 257–258, 261, 263–266, 268–269, 271–272, 274, 278–279, 281, 283, 287–289, 291, 293, 295–299, 301, 305–307, 313–316, 318–320, 323, 325–329, 331–338, 340–341, 344–345, 347–354, 356–379, 381–383, 385–396, 398, 400–402, 405–408, 410–411, 414, 416, 418–421, 423, 425–429,

432–439, 441–444, 446–447, 449–450, 453, 459, 468, 470, 474, 482–484, 486–487, 491, 493, 497–498, 500, 506–507, 513, 518–519, 521–522, 533–534, 537–540, 542–546, 548–552, 554–555, 557–561, 563–569, 571–574, 576, 578–584, 586, 589–593, 595–596, 598–599, 602–604, 606–611, 614–617, 619–620, 624–629, 631, 633–638, 640–646, 648–651
Poland 4–7, 25, 125, 134, 146, 240, 271–272, 275, 282, 287, 290, 335, 355–356, 364, 374, 376, 388, 392, 394, 396, 399, 407–408, 411, 413, 417, 420, 423, 426, 438, 444, 449, 454–455, 461–462, 467, 484–485, 525, 527, 540, 554, 565, 569, 618, 627, 636, 638–639, 642, 644–645, 648–649, 652–653
Pontarlier 451, 561–562
Portugal 11, 42, 634
Prague 5, 125, 365, 379, 385, 397, 402, 441, 449, 451, 467, 470–471, 473–474, 477–478, 480–482, 484–486, 522–525, 529, 531, 533–535, 537, 539, 545–547, 555–566, 583–586, 590–592, 594–597, 599, 601–603, 606–607, 609–610, 620, 626, 636–641, 645
Provins 198, 200–201, 260

Reigate 342
Rome 20, 61, 63, 72, 76, 78, 82, 86, 93, 103–104, 109, 115–116, 119–120, 122–135, 137, 139–142, 145, 147–149, 152–155, 157–161, 164–167, 171, 179, 182, 186, 203, 223, 231, 279, 296–297, 322, 334, 347, 349, 363, 366, 370, 372, 385, 393, 499–500, 565, 571, 583, 586, 595, 609, 638, 643–644
Russia 2, 7, 25, 96, 100, 112, 124, 134, 136, 146, 170–171, 206, 210, 228, 234, 240, 243, 246–248, 255–258, 268, 276–277, 279, 281, 285, 287, 292, 300, 304–305, 332, 363, 369, 396, 436, 445, 479, 482–483, 491, 504, 515, 522, 529, 540, 560, 574, 618–620, 623–624

Semlin 510, 513–515
Senlis 376, 411, 418, 631, 633

Soignies 411, 413
Southampton 324, 393, 404–406
Spain 7, 11, 37, 39, 42, 48, 93, 104, 186, 233, 236, 242, 248, 254, 268, 329–330, 342, 346, 367, 386, 458, 564, 608
St. Quentin 33, 225, 337, 350, 356–357, 359, 369, 411–412, 418–419
Switzerland 7, 11, 30, 33, 37, 39–40, 42, 45, 48, 61–62, 64, 68, 76, 78, 80–81, 91–95, 97–98, 100, 106–108, 110–114, 123, 129, 136–137, 161–163, 166, 169, 178, 189, 195, 198, 201, 203–204, 211, 216, 236, 239, 241, 249, 260, 268, 270, 292, 299, 302–303, 308, 318, 326–327, 329, 335, 352, 354, 356–357, 365, 381, 383, 386, 391, 414, 422–423, 426, 438–439, 441, 444, 449–451, 456–457, 461, 468, 474–475, 498, 544, 547, 554, 559, 563, 570, 592, 603, 607, 616, 653

Trieste 5, 396, 442, 486, 498–501, 503, 539, 566, 591, 607, 646
Troyes 47, 198, 200, 260, 283, 285, 327

United States 1–2, 4, 7, 32, 37, 43, 62–63, 66, 71, 82, 97, 108, 134, 137–138, 144, 149, 169, 171, 180, 211, 231, 242, 249–251, 257, 305, 348–349, 399, 442, 447, 492, 495–496, 517, 525, 546, 548, 557–558, 573, 576, 582, 591, 622, 626, 635, 639, 647, 652

Valenciennes 411
Vienna 5, 72, 136, 374, 396–397, 399–400, 442, 449, 452, 461–462, 464, 466–470, 473–475, 478–480, 482–484, 486–488, 490–491, 497–499, 508, 512–514, 516–518, 521–525, 531, 533, 537–540, 544, 553, 565, 568, 591, 602, 607, 614, 653

Warsaw 5–7, 95, 364, 453, 460–462, 466–467, 474, 484–486, 533–534, 545–547, 590, 595, 597–598, 601, 603, 609, 614, 636, 638–640, 642, 645–646, 648, 651, 653
Washington 2–3, 11–12, 14–22, 34–35, 39, 41–42, 47, 63, 76, 78, 80, 85, 88, 93, 97–

98, 117–118, 121–122, 127–128, 132, 134, 139–141, 145, 148–150, 158, 164, 170–171, 176, 187–188, 193, 199–200, 203, 212–213, 216, 239, 241, 276, 290, 293, 297, 311, 318, 323, 326, 329, 334–335, 337–338, 341, 345, 348, 352, 363, 380–381, 383, 390, 393, 408, 423, 441, 444, 484, 490, 495, 500, 504, 521, 548, 550, 572, 583, 591–592, 594–595, 610, 634, 648

Yugoslavia 20

Zurich 39, 93–94, 101, 103–107, 111–114, 120, 123, 169, 258, 331–332, 461, 466, 540–541

www.ingramcontent.com/pod-product-compliance
Lightning Source LLC
Chambersburg PA
CBHW031932290426
44108CB00011B/525